This splendid collection invites us to look at the range of perspectives: historical, anthropological ical. The individual essays are invariably insightfu., what they tell us about how people have managed to order their collective lives without turning to political authority. The volume as a whole has as much to offer those familiar with anarchist traditions as others coming to these ideas for the first time.

Chandran Kukathas, Singapore Management University

This *Handbook* surveys the history of anti-authoritarian answers to the basic questions of political philosophy. But the introduction and selections—notable for their clarity, precision, and expertise—also apply various forms of liberatory politics to concrete matters in the contemporary world, including climate change, mass incarceration, military technologies, and even transhumanism. The *Handbook* embodies a coherent, unified account of its subject-matter, demonstrating the continued relevance of a fundamentally challenging tradition. The provocations this potentially controversial volume offers, especially when protesters around the world are chanting 'abolish the police,' could not be more timely.

Crispin Sartwell, Dickinson College

The history and prospects of anarchism are misunderstood—and often misrepresented. There is a renewed interest in questioning the size and function of the coercive state, and mistrust of attempts at reform is growing. Surprisingly, there have been very few attempts to take stock of this broad, and sometimes contradictory, body of thought. The *Handbook* is the right book at the right time. Scholarly enough to be used by philosophers and political theorists, it is also a delightful and intellectually challenging resource for anyone who wants to understand anarchism as a movement.

Michael Munger, Duke University

This *Handbook* is an important and timely contribution to a vitally necessary discussion. New pressures on our inherited political institutions are distorting them in undesirable ways, whether these pressures come from climate change, from the growth of international corporate power, from truly global pandemics, or from globe-spanning terror networks. How can we arrange our political and social affairs such that they enhance human life while simultaneously avoiding or containing the horrific effects of inappropriate modes of organization? This volume offers a wide range of suggestions for our careful consideration.

John T. Sanders, Rochester Institute of Technology

Too much contemporary political philosophy still pays too little attention to anarchist thought. That neglect has always been surprising, not least because no other body of literature so comprehensively explores and challenges the theoretical and empirical foundations of coercive forms of hierarchy and their associated conceptions of justice and authority. Nowhere is the breadth and analytical depth of the anarchist tradition better represented than in the contributions to this *Handbook*.

Hillel Steiner, University of Manchester

THE ROUTLEDGE HANDBOOK OF ANARCHY AND ANARCHIST THOUGHT

This *Handbook* offers an authoritative, up-to-date introduction to the rich scholarly conversation about anarchy—about the possibility, dynamics, and appeal of social order without the state. Drawing on resources from philosophy, economics, law, history, politics, and religious studies, it is designed to deepen understanding of anarchy and the development of anarchist ideas at a time when those ideas have attracted increasing attention.

The popular identification of anarchy with chaos makes sophisticated interpretations—which recognize anarchy as a *kind* of social order rather than an *alternative* to it—especially interesting. Strong, centralized governments have struggled to quell popular frustration even as doubts have continued to percolate about their legitimacy and long-term financial stability. Since the emergence of the modern state, concerns like these have driven scholars to wonder whether societies could flourish while abandoning monopolistic governance entirely.

Standard treatments of political philosophy frequently assume the justifiability and desirability of states, focusing on such questions as *What is the best kind of state?* and *What laws and policies should states adopt?*, without considering whether it is just or prudent for states to do anything at all. This *Handbook* encourages engagement with a provocative alternative that casts more conventional views in stark relief.

Its 30 chapters, written specifically for this volume by an international team of leading scholars, are organized into four main parts:

I. Concept and Significance
II. Figures and Traditions
III. Legitimacy and Order
IV. Critique and Alternatives

In addition, a comprehensive index makes the volume easy to navigate and an annotated bibliography points readers to the most promising avenues of future research.

Gary Chartier is Distinguished Professor of Law and Business Ethics and Associate Dean of the Tom and Vi Zapara School of Business at La Sierra University. He is the author, co-author, editor, or co-editor of seventeen books, including *Anarchy and Legal Order* (2013), *Flourishing Lives: Exploring Natural Law Liberalism* (2019), and *The Logic of Commitment* (2018).

Chad Van Schoelandt is Assistant Professor of Philosophy at Tulane University. His work has been published in *Ethics, Analysis, Philosophical Studies*, the *Philosophical Quarterly*, and *Law and Philosophy*.

THE ROUTLEDGE HANDBOOK OF ANARCHY AND ANARCHIST THOUGHT

Edited by Gary Chartier and Chad Van Schoelandt

NEW YORK AND LONDON

First published 2021
by Routledge
52 Vanderbilt Avenue, New York, NY 10017

and by Routledge
2 Park Square, Milton Park, Abingdon, Oxon, OX14 4RN

Routledge is an imprint of the Taylor & Francis Group, an informa business

Library of Congress Cataloging-in-Publication Data
A catalog record for this title has been requested

ISBN: 978-1-138-73758-7 (hbk)
ISBN: 978-1-315-18525-5 (ebk)

Typeset in Bembo
by River Editorial Ltd, Devon, UK

For
Alicia Homer
and
Wendy Cobb

CONTENTS

PART II
Figures and Traditions 81

PART III
Legitimacy and Order 205

CONTRIBUTORS

Andy Alexis-Baker is Associate Professor of Theology and Religious Studies at Arrupe College of Loyola University Chicago. He has published numerous articles and books on issues of violence and nonviolence and humans' treatment of other animals. As an anarchist and antiwar activist, he has been involved in work for peace and justice, including, for example, antimilitarist work in Vieques, Puerto Rico, where he was placed in a federal prison with many other activists for engaging in nonviolent civil disobedience designed to remove the United States' military from the island.

Ralf M. Bader is Professor of Ethics and Political Philosophy at the Université de Fribourg in Switzerland. His research concerns ethics, metaphysics, Kant, political philosophy, and decision theory. He was formerly a fellow of Merton College and Associate Professor in the Faculty of Philosophy at the University of Oxford, as well as a Bersoff Assistant Professor and faculty fellow in the Department of Philosophy at New York University.

Tom W. Bell is Professor of Law at Chapman University. He is the author of *Your Next Government? From the Nation State to Stateless Nations* (2017) and *Intellectual Privilege: Copyright, Common Law, and the Common Good* (2014). He has appeared on or been quoted in the *Wall Street Journal*, CNN, *The Economist*, the *Los Angeles Times*, and many other news sources.

Peter J. Boettke is University Professor of Economics and Philosophy at George Mason University and Director of the F. A. Hayek Program for Advanced Study in Philosophy, Politics, and Economics at the Mercatus Center at George Mason. Before joining the faculty at George Mason in 1998, he taught at New York University. In addition, Boettke was a national fellow at the Hoover Institution for War, Revolution and Peace at Stanford University during the 1992–1993 academic years and the F. A. Hayek fellow in 2004 and 2006 at the London School of Economics, as well as a visiting professor or scholar at the Russian Academy of Sciences in Moscow; the Max Planck Institute for Research into Economic Systems in Jena, Germany; the Stockholm School of Economics; the Central European University in Prague; and the Charles University in Prague. In March 2011, he was a Fulbright fellow at the University of Economics in Prague, Czech Republic. He served as the President of the Southern Economic Association from 2015–2017, the Mont Pelerin Society from 2016–2018, the Association of Private Enterprise Education from 2013–2014, and the Society for the Development of Austrian Economics from 1999–2001. In 2013, he became Founding Honorary President and Honorary President of the World Interdisciplinary Network for Institutional Research. He currently serves as a co-editor-in-chief of the *Review of Austrian Economics* and associate editor of the *Journal of Economic Behavior & Organization.*

Jason Brennan is Robert J. and Elizabeth Flanagan Family Professor of Strategy, Economics, Ethics, and Public Policy at the McDonough School of Business, Georgetown University. His focus is on politics, philosophy, and economics. As of August 2020, he is the author of thirteen books, including most relevantly to this present volume *Injustice for All* (2019), *When All Else Fails* (2018), and *Why Not Capitalism?* (2014). He specializes in democratic theory, philosophical problems arising from perverse incentives, and the moral foundations of market society.

Jason Lee Byas is a fellow of the Center for a Stateless Society and a PhD student in philosophy at the University of Michigan. His primary interests are in rights theory, punishment, and moral repair.

Rosolino A. Candela is Associate Director of Academic and Student Programs and a senior fellow of the F. A. Hayek Program for Advanced Study in Philosophy, Politics, and Economics at the Mercatus Center at George Mason University. Before coming to George Mason University, Candela taught in the Department of Economics at Brown University, where he was also a Postdoctoral Research Associate in the Political Theory Project. He was also a visiting professor of economics at Universidad Francisco Marroquin, and a visiting fellow in the Department of Political and Social Sciences at the European University Institute.

Kevin A. Carson is Karl Hess Distinguished Research Scholar at the Center for a Stateless Society. He is the author of books including *Studies in Mutualist Political Economy* (2007), *Organization Theory* (2008), and *The Desktop Regulatory State: The Countervailing Power of Individuals and Networks* (2016).

Gary Chartier is Distinguished Professor of Law and Business Ethics and Associate Dean of the Tom and Vi Zapara School of Business at La Sierra University. His scholarship focuses on issues in law and legal theory (particularly natural law theory), political philosophy (especially anarchism), and ethics (for instance, personal formation, personal relationships, and the ethics of production and consumption). He is the author of books including *Flourishing Lives: Exploring Natural Law Liberalism* (2019), *An Ecological Theory of Free Expression* (2018), *The Logic of Commitment* (Routledge 2017), and *Anarchy and Legal Order: Law and Politics for a Stateless Society* (2013).

Billy Christmas is Lecturer in Political Theory and the PPE Programme Director at King's College London, in the Department of Political Economy. He also has affiliations with the Classical Liberal Institute at the New York University School of Law and the Center for a Stateless Society. His primary interests are in political philosophy concern rights, property, and political authority. He is currently completing a book manuscript on property and justice, and he has published articles in journals including *The Journal of Politics*, *Economics and Philosophy*, and the *Philosophical Quarterly*.

Stephen R. L. Clark is Professor of Philosophy Emeritus at the University of Liverpool, and an honorary research fellow in the Department of Theology at the University of Bristol. His books include *The Nature of the Beast* (1982), *Civil Peace and Sacred Order* (1989), *The Political Animal* (Routledge 1999), *Biology and Christian Ethics* (2000), *Understanding Faith: Religious Belief and its Place in Society* (2009), *Philosophical Futures* (2011), *Ancient Mediterranean Philosophy* (2013), and

Plotinus: Myth, Metaphor and Philosophical Practice (2016). His chief current interests are in the philosophy of Plotinus, the understanding and treatment of non-human animals, the philosophy of religion, and science fiction.

Christopher Coyne is Professor of Economics at George Mason University and Associate Director of the F. A. Hayek Program for Advanced Study in Philosophy, Politics, and Economics at the university's Mercatus Center. He is the author of *After War: The Political Economy of Exporting Democracy* (2007); *Doing Bad by Doing Good: Why Humanitarian Action Fails* (2013); *Tyranny Comes Home: The Domestic Fate of U.S. Militarism*, with Abigail R. Hall (2018); and *Defense, Peace, and War Economics* (2020). He is a co-editor of volumes including (with Peter J. Boettke) *The Oxford Handbook of Austrian Economics* (2015) and (with Rachel Mathers) *The Handbook on the Political Economy of War* (2012). He co-edits the *Review of Austrian Economics* and *The Independent Review*. He serves as the book review editor of *Public Choice*.

Jonathan Crowe is Professor of Law at Bond University. His research examines the philosophical relationship between law and ethics. He has also produced significant bodies of work on constitutional law, rape and sexual assault law, international humanitarian law, and dispute resolution. He is the author or editor of nine books and more than ninety peer-reviewed book chapters and journal articles. His work has appeared in periodicals including the *Oxford Journal of Legal Studies*, the *Modern Law Review*, and *Jurisprudence*. His recent books include *Mediation Ethics: From Theory to Practice* (2020), *Natural Law and the Nature of Law* (2019), and the *Research Handbook on Natural Law Theory* (2019). He co-edits the *Journal of Legal Philosophy* with Hillary Nye. He is an Honorary Life Member of the Australasian Society of Legal Philosophy, of which he served as president from 2014 to 2018.

Kevin Currie-Knight is a teaching associate professor in East Carolina University's College of Education. His research focuses on the history and philosophy of (American K–12) education and informal and self-directed learning. He is the author of *Education in the Marketplace: An Intellectual History of Pro-Market Libertarian Visions for Education in Twentieth-Century America* (2019).

David S. D'Amato is a lawyer, businessman, and former legal writing instructor who is currently a columnist for the Cato Institute's Libertarianism.org project and a policy advisor at the Future of Freedom Foundation and the Heartland Institute. He is an opinion contributor at *The Hill*, and his writing has also appeared in *Newsweek*, *Forbes*, *Investor's Business Daily*, the *Washington Examiner*, *RealClearPolicy*, *Townhall*, *The Daily Caller*, *The American Spectator*, *CounterPunch*, and many other publications. He is frequently published by nonprofit, nonpartisan policy research organizations such as the Centre for Policy Studies, the Institute of Economic Affairs, the Foundation for Economic Education, the Ludwig von Mises Institute, and the Institute for Ethics and Emerging Technologies, among others. He earned a JD from the New England School of Law and an LLM in Global Law and Technology from Suffolk University Law School. He lives in Chicago, Illinois.

Daniel J. D'Amico is Associate Director of the Political Theory Project and a Lecturer in Economics at Brown University,. where he teaches and coordinates student programs dedicated to the study of institutions and ideas that make societies free, prosperous, and fair. His current research examines the political economy of punishment and incarceration throughout history and around the world. He has been published in a variety of scholarly outlets, including the *Journal of Economic Behavior and Organization*, the *Journal of Institutional Economics*, *Public Choice*, and the *Journal of Comparative Economics*. He serves as a co-editor of the Advances in Austrian Economics book series. He is a fellow of the Royal Society for the Encouragement of Arts, Manufactures, and Commerce; an affiliated scholar associated with the workshop in Politics, Philosophy, and

Economics at George Mason University; and a co-founder of the Carl Menger Essay Contest sponsored by the Foundation for Economic Education.

Magda Egoumenides studied philosophy in Athens and in London. She has collaborated with the Department of Philosophy at University College London and with the Department of Methodology of History and the Theory of Science at the University of Athens. Since 2009, she has been teaching philosophy at the University of Cyprus. She specializes in moral and political philosophy and has published various articles and two books on philosophical anarchism and political authority, including *Philosophical Anarchism and Political Obligation* (2014). She also writes books for children and has acted non-professionally for more than two decades.

William Gillis is a second-generation anarchist who has been involved in a wide array of activist work since the Battle in Seattle. He holds an undergraduate degree in physics and serves as the Coordinating Director of the Center for a Stateless Society. His writing can be found in a number of compilations, including *Markets Not Capitalism* and *Abolish Work.*

Nathan P. Goodman is a PhD student in the Department of Economics at George Mason University and a PhD fellow at the F. A. Hayek Program for Advanced Study in Philosophy, Politics, and Economics at the Mercatus Center. His research focuses on institutions, defense and peace economics, public choice, and self-governance. He is particularly interested in how alternative institutional arrangements shape the production of security. His research has been published in the *Journal of Institutional Economics*, the *Journal of Private Enterprise*, the Georgetown Journal of International Affairs, and *Peace Economics, Peace Science, and Public Policy*. .

Abigail R. Hall is an Associate Professor in Economics at Bellarmine University in Louisville, Kentucky. She is an affiliated scholar with the Mercatus Center at George Mason University and an affiliated scholar with the Foundation for Economic Education. Her research interests include political economy and public choice, defense and peace economics, and institutions and economic development. She is the co-author, with Christopher Coyne, of *Tyranny Comes Home: The Domestic Fate of U.S. Militarism* (2018).

Michael Huemer is Professor of Philosophy at the University of Colorado at Boulder. He is the author of more than seventy academic articles in ethics, epistemology, political philosophy, and metaphysics, as well as six amazing books that you should immediately buy, including *Ethical Intuitionism* (2005), *The Problem of Political Authority* (2013), and *Dialogues on Ethical Vegetarianism* (2019).

Peter T. Leeson is the Duncan Black Professor of Economics and Law at George Mason University. He is author of the award-winning *The Invisible Hook: The Hidden Economics of Pirates, Anarchy Unbound: Why Self-Governance Works Better than You Think*, and *WTF?! An Economic Tour of the Weird.* Leeson was a visiting professor of Economics at the University of Chicago, visiting fellow in Political Economy and Government at Harvard University, and the F.A. Hayek fellow at the London School of Economics. He is a fellow of the Royal Society of Arts.

Roderick T. Long is Professor of Philosophy at Auburn University. He serves as President of the Molinari Institute and a senior fellow of the Center for a Stateless Society. He is the author of *Reason and Value: Aristotle Versus Rand* (2000), *Rituals of Freedom: Libertarian Themes in Early Confucianism* (2016), and *Wittgenstein, Austrian Economics, and the Logic of Action* (forthcoming). He is editor of the *Molinari Review* and a co-editor of *Anarchism/Minarchism: Is a Government Part of a Free Country?* (2008), *Social Class and State Power: Exploring an Alternative Radical Tradition*

(2018), and the *Journal of Ayn Rand Studies*. He has published articles in journals including *Social Philosophy and Policy*, *Utilitas*, the *Griffith Law Review*, and the *Review of Metaphysics*.

Eric Mack is Professor of Philosophy Emeritus at Tulane University. His primary scholarly project has been the refinement and extension of libertarian-oriented natural rights theory. He has published over 100 scholarly essays on the moral foundations of natural rights, the basis and nature of property rights, economic justice, the nature of law and of spontaneous economic and social order, the scope of legitimate coercive institutions, and the exploration of these topics by seventeenth- and nineteenth-century classical liberal and libertarian theorists. He is the editor of Auberon Herbert's *The Rights and Wrongs of Compulsion by the State and Other Essays* (1978) and Herbert Spencer's *The Man versus the State* (1982). He is also the author of *John Locke* (2013), *Libertarianism* (2018), and *The Essential John Locke* (2019).

Cory Massimino is an independent scholar. He is a fellow of the Center for a Stateless Society. His research focuses on virtue ethics, market process economics, and anarchist political theory. His writings have appeared in publications including *The Guardian*, *The Independent*, and *Playboy*. He lives in Florida with his wife and their four cats.

Paul McLaughlin is Senior Lecturer in Education Studies at Bath Spa University. He previously held positions in philosophy and education at the University of Limerick, Adam Mickiewicz University, and the University of Tartu. He is the author of *Anarchism and Authority: A Philosophical Introduction to Classical Anarchism* (Routledge 2016), *Radicalism: A Philosophical Study* (2012), and *Mikhail Bakunin: The Philosophical Basis of His Anarchism* (2002). His byline has appeared in publications including the *Journal of Moral Philosophy*, the *European Journal of Cultural and Political Sociology*, and *Anarchist Studies*, and in edited books including *Brill's Companion to Anarchism and Philosophy* (2018), the *Encyclopedia of Modern Political Thought* (2013), and *Anarchism and Moral Philosophy* (2012).

Christopher W. Morris is Professor Emeritus of Philosophy at the University of Maryland. His research interests concern political philosophy, political economy, legal theory, and ethics. He is the author of *An Essay on the Modern State* (1998), and is currently working on a new book, tentatively entitled *Social Order, Liberty, and Prosperity*.

Ryan Muldoon is Associate Professor of Philosophy and Director of the Philosophy, Politics and Economics program at the University at Buffalo. Previously, he was a senior research fellow in the Philosophy, Politics and Economics program at the University of Pennsylvania. He was also a core author of the 2015 World Development Report at the World Bank. His primary research investigates how we can turn the challenge of increasing diversity into a resource to be tapped for our mutual benefit. Specifically, he investigates how diversity can lead to more just societies, to an increase in the amount and quality of scientific production, and greater wealth. His scholarship also examines the social and behavioral aspects of development policy. He is the author of *Social Contract Theory for a Diverse World: Beyond Tolerance* (Routledge 2016) and articles in journals including *Philosophical Studies*, *Utilitas*, and *Synthese* and (with Cristina Bicchieri) in the *Stanford Encyclopedia of Philosophy*.

Oliver Sensen is Associate Professor of Philosophy at Tulane University and Vice President of the North American Kant Society. He is the author of *Human Dignity* (forthcoming) and *Kant on Human Dignity* (2011) and the editor of *Kant on Moral Autonomy* (2012) and of four other current or forthcoming essay collections. He has published over sixty articles on Kant's philosophy.

Dan C. Shahar is Assistant Professor of Philosophy (Research) and a member of the Urban Entrepreneurship and Policy Institute at the University of New Orleans. His research focuses on the implications of environmental challenges for liberal societies and their members. With David Schmidtz, he is a co-editor of the latest edition of the popular textbook *Environmental Ethics: What Really Matters, What Really Works* (2018).

Aeon J. Skoble is Professor of Philosophy at Bridgewater State University. He is the author of *Deleting the State: An Argument about Government* (2008) and *The Essential Nozick* (2020); the editor of *Reading Rasmussen and Den Uyl: Critical Essays on* Norms of Liberty (2008); and co-editor of *Political Philosophy: Essential Selections* (1999); *Reality, Reason, and Rights* (2011); the best-selling *The Simpsons and Philosophy* (2000); and three other books on film and television. He has frequently lectured and written for the Institute for Humane Studies, the Cato Institute, and the Foundation for Economic Education, and he is a senior fellow of the Fraser Institute. His principal research foci include theories of rights, the nature and justification of authority, and virtue ethics. He also writes widely on the intersection of philosophy and popular culture.

Jesse Spafford is a research fellow at Trinity College Dublin. He was previously a Mellon/American Council of Learned Societies fellow and a fellow at the Center for Global Ethics and Politics at the City University of New York Graduate Center. His research focuses on assessing debates between libertarians, socialists, and anarchists over the moral status of the market and the state. His work has appeared in the *Journal of Ethics and Social Philosophy*, the *Journal of Value Inquiry*, and *Public Affairs Quarterly*.

Sam Underwood is a doctoral candidate in philosophy at Memorial University of Newfoundland. He is specializing in phenomenology and hermeneutics, with particular interest in the thought of Paul Ricoeur.

Kevin Vallier is Associate Professor of Philosophy at Bowling Green State University. His primary research foci are political philosophy and ethics, with interests in political economy and philosophy of religion. He is the author of *Liberal Politics and Public Faith: Beyond Separation* (Routledge 2014) and *Must Politics Be War? Restoring Our Trust in the Open Society* (2019).

Chad Van Schoelandt is Assistant Professor of Philosophy at Tulane University. His byline has appeared in journals including *Ethics*, *Analysis*, *Philosophical Studies*, the *Philosophical Quarterly*, and *Law and Philosophy*.

J. Martin Vest is an adjunct professor of history at Madonna University in Livonia, Michigan, an historical consultant with Proquest LLC, and a research associate in the University of Michigan Department of History.

ACKNOWLEDGMENTS

We welcome the occasion the publication of this book affords to say "thank you" to many people.

We owe an obvious debt of gratitude to Andrew Beck at Routledge for patiently supporting the publication of the *Handbook* and to Marc Stratton, production editor Christopher Taylor, Andrew Melvin, and Julie Willis at River Editorial for help at various stages of its production.

We thoroughly appreciate the willingness of the *Handbook*'s many authors to contribute, David Gordon's thoughtful and detailed comments on the Introduction, Chandran Kukathas's identification of a footnote error, and John T. Sanders's improvement of the *Handbook*'s bibliography. We are also thankful for the willingness of Hillel Steiner, Chandran Kukathas, Michael Munger, John T. Sanders, and Crispin Sartwell to endorse the book; for the able assistance rendered by Chelsea Jackson and Matthew Reeves when work on the *Handbook* began; and for the opportunity to incorporate in the Annotated Bibliography some entries and annotations that first appeared in Gary Chartier's *The Conscience of an Anarchist* (Apple Valley, CA: Cobden 2011).

In addition to students in his Tulane course on anarchy, Chad Van Schoelandt thanks Trevor Griffith, Jerry Gaus, Kevin Vallier, Nathan P. Goodman, Virgil Storr, and Pete Boettke. Gary Chartier is grateful to the usual suspects—A. Ligia Radoias, Aena Prakash, Alicia Homer, Annette Bryson, Alexander Lian, Andrew Howe, Carole Pateman, Charles Teel, Jr., Christopher C. Reeves, Coco Owen, Craig R. Kinzer, David B. Hoppe, David Gordon, David R. Larson, Deborah K. Dunn, Donna L. Carlson, Elaine Claire von Keudell, Elenor L. Webb, Eva Pascal, Fritz Guy, Gen Mensale, Jeffrey D. Cassidy, Jesse Leamon, John Thomas, Kenneth A. Dickey, Kirsten Rasmussen, Lawrence T. Geraty, Maria Zlateva, Michael Orlando, Nabil Abu-Assal, Nicole Regina, Patricia M. Cabrera, Roderick T. Long, Roger E. Rustad, Jr., Ronel S. Harvey, Sheldon Richman, Stephanie Burns, Trisha Famisaran, Varsha Pravinsih, W. Kent Rogers, Wonil Kim, and Xavier Alasdhair Kenneth Doran—for the usual reasons.

La Sierra University served as the context for Gary Chartier's editorial work on this book. Thanks are thus due to John Thomas, Joy Fehr, Cindy Parkhurst, and Elias Rizkallah, among others, for enabling Chartier to work on this book during his time at La Sierra.

INTRODUCTION

Gary Chartier and Chad Van Schoelandt

I. The Point and Context of the *Handbook*

Anarchy is a social condition free not of *rules* but of *rulers*—and so especially, but not only, of states.[1] *Anarchism* is the project of doing without rulers.[2] And *anarchist thought*, in the broad sense, is concerned with the possibility, desirability, and potential shape of anarchy.[3] The purpose of the *Routledge Handbook of Anarchy and Anarchist Thought* is to introduce you to a broad and diverse range of topics related to the contemporary resurgence of critical reflection on anarchy. It does this by exploring relevant historical figures and movements and by examining contemporary issues in a range of disciplines, including philosophy, economics, and religious studies.

The popular identification of anarchy with chaos makes sophisticated interpretations of the topic—interpretations that see anarchy as kind of social order rather than as an alternative to it—especially interesting. It is increasingly obvious that existing political arrangements confront serious, and perhaps insurmountable, challenges. Strong, centralized governments have struggled to quell popular frustration and resentment, and doubts have continued to percolate about their moral legitimacy and long-term financial stability. Since the emergence of the modern state itself, concerns like these have driven scholars to wonder whether societies could flourish while abandoning monopolistic states entirely. Moreover, many political philosophers have been concerned with understanding problems that individuals within anarchic arrangements would face in order to understand the role, justification, and appropriate limits of the state. This book is designed to deepen understanding of anarchy—among both scholars and thoughtful non-academic readers—at a time when anarchist ideas have attracted considerable attention.

Discussions of anarchy as an analytical model in economics, political science, and international relations theory and as a normative model in legal and political philosophy have been matched by growing interest in anarchist ideas in the political sphere. In the United States, for instance, the Ron Paul movement propelled many of those who originally embraced it beyond electoral politics and into support for anarchy. Opposition to corporate-led globalization during the Seattle protests against the World Trade Organization embraced anarchist symbols and values. The Occupy movement embraced a self-consciously anarchist flavor, drawing inspiration from anarchist anthropologist David Graeber and praise, indeed, from Ron Paul. And less dramatic anti-authoritarian attitudes find expression in increasingly vocal challenges to the drug war and to state policing.

Globally, the policies embraced by many governments to the Sars-Cov-2 pandemic have prompted theoretical anarchist critiques and practical anarchist responses—involving the development of alternatives to state service provision and push-backs against restraints on civil and economic liberties.[4] In the United States, the renewed attention to police violence prompted by the murder of George Floyd has also led to on-the-ground activism and critiques of state provision of security services, both with anarchist undertones or explicit anarchist content.

At the same time, libertarian ideas of various sorts are gaining increasing exposure in academe. Where some academics might once have thought only of nineteenth-century Russian anarchists or of Nozick's (anti-anarchist) discussion in *Anarchy, State, and Utopia* when anarchy was mentioned, the work of scholars across a range of disciplines has generated a robust literature concerned with anarchism as a provocative contender among practitioners of social and political philosophy.

The *Handbook* offers students of philosophy at multiple levels an opportunity to engage with serious objections and alternatives to state authority. Standard political philosophy frequently assumes the legitimacy and desirability of states, frequently focusing on such questions as *What is the best kind of state?* and *What laws and policies should states adopt?*, without considering whether it is just or prudent for states to do anything at all. The *Handbook* is designed to enable scholars and students to grapple with a radical and provocative alternative that will cast more familiar views in stark relief.

The *Handbook* features a range of original essays on crucial issues related to the nature, appeal, and viability (or non-viability) of anarchy. It is intended to offer an authoritative, up-to-date introduction that will make it distinctively valuable both in classrooms and in individual and institutional libraries.

II. Background to the *Handbook*

Anarchism is arguably a radical strand within the liberal tradition.[5] But modern political philosophy arguably begins with thinkers, many of them liberals—notably Thomas Hobbes, John Locke, David Hume, Jean-Jacques Rousseau, and Immanuel Kant—who take it as a crucial task to explain and justify the authority of the state in the wake of the demise of theories of divine right.

Writing in a period of profound social upheaval, Hobbes maintains that life without a robust state would be "solitary, poor, nasty, brutish, and short." We need a ruler with potentially absolute power to keep us safe from mutual predation. It is therefore rational—very much in our own interests—to agree with each other to accept the dominance of such a ruler. (We do not, for Hobbes, make any sort of agreement with the ruler, which means that the ruler can't, per se, violate any agreement with us in a way that merits withdrawal of consent and, perhaps, revolution.)

While the social contract seems for Hobbes to be an intellectual device, Locke appears to take it at least perhaps to be genuinely historical. Locke supposes that humans without the state might be able to interact peacefully, but he clearly believes that security of persons and property is substantially enhanced by agreeing to the rule of a limited state. He also believes, however, that consent to such a state can be withdrawn when it is ineffectual or predatory.

Hume is (rightly) skeptical about the idea of any sort of social contract, as either an historical reality or a useful thought experiment. Emphasizing human sociality, Hume sees state authority as rooted in the practical need to maintain order and resolve what we would today characterize as "public goods" problems. We should accept the rule of existing states, for Hume, presuming they're tolerably good at meeting this need.

For Rousseau, state authority emerged from a commitment to collective self-government. Joining together, people form and express the general will through democratic politics, ideally in something like small city-states.

Kant explicitly denies that the idea of a deliberate exit from the state of nature is anything but a thought experiment. But he uses it to make clear why he believes that accepting the authority of a state governed by and enforcing just laws is not merely advisable but morally required. Maintaining justice requires the institutions of the state, he believes, and we act wrongly if we fail to endorse and support these institutions.

Though each of these thinkers defends the state, the approach each takes can be seen as depending on his analysis of what might be expected under anarchic conditions. For instance, the disagreement between Hobbes and Locke regarding the legitimate extent of state power arguably reflects their disagreement about the prospects for life in anarchy. The greater the degree of peaceful cooperation possible without the state, the more restraints on the state are reasonable. An absolute state may thus appear acceptable if violent death is likely for many or most people in a stateless society. A proper analysis of the prospects for and challenges associated with anarchy—at least as a means of discerning (some of) the proper limits of state power—is thus necessary even for many accounts that defend the state.

These thinkers very much represented an increasingly dominant trend in political philosophy in the seventeenth to nineteenth centuries. But the roots of a counter-tradition were also increasingly evident. For instance: Locke had maintained that consent was at the root of state authority, and had recognized that this consent could be withdrawn. But one could easily ask why an individual who did not wish to endorse the state should be understood to be obligated because others had consented. As a result, Locke's consent-based approach could readily be radicalized.

Similarly: Scottish Enlightenment thinkers including Hume, Adam Ferguson, and Adam Smith articulated an essentially evolutionary account of social institutions, of these institutions as produced on a bottom-up basis as products "of human action but not of human design."[6] All of these thinkers assumed that these institutions would function while embedded within societies governed by robust, if limited, states. But one could easily ask whether those institutions needed to ensure social order—notably laws, courts, and police agencies—could not themselves be produced in the same bottom-up fashion as other institutions. Why couldn't the evolutionary account of markets, language, and other institutions be applied to those institutions within which families, markets, and other institutions functioned?

While, as contributions to the *Handbook* make clear, relevant ideas were in circulation much earlier, what we might readily recognize as anarchism emerges in the nineteenth century. In France, the first thinker to *call* himself an anarchist, Pierre-Joseph Proudhon, developed a dialectical approach to thinking about society that included the unequivocal rejection of being governed. In Belgium, Gustave de Molinari elaborated a model for the provision of security without the operation of an entity exercising a monopoly over the use of force in a given geographic area. In England, William Godwin advanced a version of anarchism rooted in something like utilitarianism, Thomas Hodgskin demonstrated the radical potential of anti-statist economics, and the young Herbert Spencer called the authority and necessity of the state into question. In Russia, Peter Kropotkin envisioned a world of peaceful cooperation without dominance, and Mikhail Bakunin highlighted the similarities between authoritarian politics and authoritarian religion: why, he wondered, retain belief in the state after having rejected belief in God? In the United States, Josiah Warren carefully delineated the characteristics of, and sought to model, a society rooted in what he characterized as "individual sovereignty."[7] Warren's successors, including Lysander Spooner and Benjamin Tucker, developed a more elaborate array of normative and analytical social-theoretic ideas about a society without monopolistic rulers.

From the latter part of the nineteenth century through the early part of the twentieth, anarchism's rejection of coercive rule was obscured, replaced in the public mind with an image of anarchists as promoters of revolutionary violence. *Anarchy* came to be treated as synonymous with *chaos*. And while thinkers outside the mainstream, like Albert Jay Nock and Dwight Macdonald, might have thought of themselves as anarchists, anarchist ideas were frequently and reflexively dismissed. The expression of anarchist ideas by some participants in the summer 1968 protests in Europe did little to focus attention on anarchism as a viable socio-political program. Economist Murray Rothbard's elaboration of an account of the economics of law and justice without the state received little attention.

Beginning in the 1970s, the conversation shifted. While the most influential English-language work of political philosophy, John Rawls's *A Theory of Justice*, comfortably endorsed state authority, questions about theoretical and practical alternatives were increasingly evident.[8] In philosophy, Robert Nozick's *Anarchy, State, and Utopia* put the discussion of the viability of anarchy back on the map, and the incisive arguments of John Simmons, Robert Paul Wolff, Joseph Raz, and others raised important critical questions about political obligation. (Nozick himself treated anarchy as a foil, using his critique of anarchism to ground his defense of a minimal state.) In economics, James Buchanan and Gordon Tullock began to explore the viability of anarchy as an analytical device designed to clarify the maintenance of social order. In addition, their development of public choice theory as an approach to the study of politics "without romance" laid the groundwork for a skeptical view of state action rooted in a recognition of the incentives facing state functionaries. Also in economics, Anthony de Jasay highlighted state pathologies and emphasized the possibility that public goods could be provided without the state, and David Friedman sketched out a set of microeconomic arguments designed to show how social organization could be created and maintained without the state. In normative political theory, Carole Pateman, while defending radical democracy, powerfully highlighted problems with conventional defenses of state authority. In formal political theory, Michael Taylor challenged Hobbesian models of social interaction in favor of ones emphasizing genuine cooperation and argued that communities could maintain order without states. Historian James J. Martin sought to revive understanding of the nineteenth-century American anarchists. Religious thinkers like Jacques Ellul and Vernard Eller employed anarchist language to critique what they saw as idolatrous state pretentions. In law, Randy Barnett worked simultaneously to rehabilitate a Lockean version of natural law theory and to put that theory to work grounding a polycentric, stateless legal order, while Henc van Maarseveen and Thom Holterman called attention to a variety of links between primarily European anarchist thought and issues in legal theory. In international relations theory, Hedley Bull underscored the importance of talking about the world's states as existing in a state of anarchy—given the absence of a global Leviathan (a reality to which anarchists have appealed in arguing that no Leviathan is needed at the domestic level). And, in anthropology, James C. Scott and, latterly, David Graeber analyzed anarchic practices and state alternatives on the ground while also reflecting on them theoretically.

Across a range of disciplines, then, anarchy and anarchism became increasingly interesting and, arguably, more respectable as foci of inquiry. Even for those who were disinclined to regard anarchy as viable or desirable, it became increasingly important to examine the *reasons* it wasn't viable or desirable. The resurgence of thought about anarchism meant, at minimum, that the state wasn't complacently taken for granted in philosophy, the social sciences, and elsewhere.

III. The Range and Fruitfulness of Inquiry into Anarchism and Anarchist Thought

Anarchist proposals regarding social organization and anarchist criticisms of existing social institutions directly and indirectly raise a diverse array of normative and positive questions. These questions concern the merits and dynamics of existing institutions; the analysis and evaluation of rationales offered for those institutions; and the potential capacities of alternatives to current institutional arrangements.

We highlight some of these questions in Part III. Some are addressed or implicated by the chapters of this *Handbook*. Others are explored elsewhere (as, for instance, in texts mentioned in the Annotated Bibliography). We include them here for several reasons.

Perhaps most fundamentally, they help to clarify what the study of anarchy and anarchist ideas *looks like*—the range and diversity of the conversation we seek to introduce here. In addition, they help to make evident why something like this *Handbook* is valuable. These questions make the stakes of reflection on state and anarchic alternatives more apparent: attending on them should help you to understand what would be needed for a defense of anarchy or of state authority to succeed. They serve to emphasize the *fruitfulness* of the topic of anarchism and anarchist thought for philosophy, economics, and other disciplines, and so to underscore why the introduction to these topics afforded by the *Handbook* deserves to be followed by focused inquiries in multiple areas. The fact that reflection on anarchy occasions these questions explains why, apart from their individual significance, the *Handbook*'s topics of anarchy and anarchist thought *matter* as spurs to further inquiry.

A. Consent and Related Strategies for State Legitimation

Mediæval political arrangements often featured overlapping jurisdictions, with the existence of each serving to limit the power of the others.[9] And mediæval political theory, frequently rooted in the thought of Aristotle, often treated governmental powers as limited. In subsequent centuries, however, states were frequently assumed to be authoritative because monarchs were assumed to be imbued with divinely delegated rights to rule. The state apparatus was transparently and unapologetically understood as an extension of the monarch's will, so it needed no justification if the monarch's position itself was divinely approved. The assumption of monarchical legitimacy dissolved under critical scrutiny: the doctrine of divine right proved harder to defend on the basis of traditional religious sources than its proponents had supposed, and historical, philosophical, and literary challenges forced a careful rethinking of the nature and status of those sources themselves.

As we noted above, new rationales for state power emerged in the wake of the decline of the doctrine of divine right. Some focused on consent, some on perceived pragmatic necessity. (While many of these were initially understood as new defenses of monarchical power, the putative legitimacy of monarchs' authority came increasingly to be transferred to, broadly speaking, democratic institutions, with parliaments and presidents and premiers stepping into the places of princes and kings.)

Modern theories emphasized the importance of *consent* in grounding state authority—consider, for instance, the assertion in the US Declaration of Independence that states acquire their legitimate authority from "the consent of the governed." Appeals to consent continue to play important roles in validating state claims. But anarchist challenges embody, and prompt consideration of, critical questions including:

- Is consent necessary or sufficient to confer legitimacy on a state?
- If consent *is* necessary or sufficient, must it be *individual* consent or is some sort of *collective* consent sufficient? Must it be explicit, or may it be inferred—and, if so, in what ways?
- Can individual subjects be bound in ways interestingly similar to consent—as, for instance, when they accept certain benefits from states?

B. Public Goods

While consent figured centrally in, for instance, Locke's account of state authority, attention came increasingly to be paid to the potential role of states in producing what today we commonly label *public goods*—goods that are *non-excludable* and *non-rivalrous*. Roughly speaking, in economic terms, a good is *excludable* if it can be offered just to specific people while others can be kept effectively from obtaining it. Thus, if, for instance, the good is offered on the market, it can be provided only to those willing to pay for it. By contrast, delivering a *non-excludable* good to one member of a population ordinarily means unavoidably delivering it to all members of the population, with the resulting temptation to be a free-rider—to take advantage of the good's availability without helping to defray its cost. A good has the property of *non-rivalrous consumption* if adding new consumers of the good (including free-riders) to an array of existing consumers does not significantly detract from the enjoyment of the existing consumers.

A standard argument holds that, given the temptation to be a free-rider, large numbers of people won't contribute to the production of public goods, and these goods will be produced at sub-optimal levels. A state with the ability to force contributions to the production of public goods is therefore necessary. Anarchist objections to the necessity of states as sources of public goods have prompted the consideration of questions including:

- Are there goods that are unavoidably public, or is publicness really just a function of the costs of excluding those unwilling to pay from access to particular goods?
- Are we confident which goods are, in fact, public in the relevant technical sense? Can we tell which goods really are public, and so likely to be (arguably) underproduced, and which goods are genuinely private while conferring spillover benefits on others?
- Given people's heterogeneous preferences, how could state officials accurately determine an efficient level for the production of any public good? When should we expect the inefficiencies of public good production in anarchy to be greater or lesser than those inefficiencies in a state-governed society?
- How might we compare (i) the costs of not obtaining particular public goods against (ii) the costs of maintaining the extractive institutions needed to supply such goods?
- Given the importance of supplying particular public goods, are there reliable non-coercive mechanisms for delivering them? What public goods currently provided by a state could be left to voluntary production?
- What considerations related to class membership and ordinary self-interest might complicate appeals to the state to address dispute-resolution and public-goods problems?

C. Sharing Responsibility

Careful economic scrutiny reveals that very few goods qualify as public in the technical sense. But people often, and understandably, regard it as important that responsibility for the provision of some private goods—education, for instance, and income support for the economically vulnerable—be shared.[10] It is often reflexively supposed that sharing responsibility for delivery of these goods means endorsing (i) their funding by taxation and (ii) the organization of their delivery by the state. Anarchist objections to the assumption that the provision of these goods must be state-delivered and state-funded naturally give rise to questions including:

- What do historical examples of mutual aid teach us about the possibility of sharing responsibility for the delivery of these goods without coercive organization or funding?

- Is it crucial that these goods be delivered in uniform patterns? Or is diversity in this context a useful occasion for discovery and experimentation? If uniformity matters, can non-state institutions offer it?
- Might non-state provision of these goods involve dignitary injuries (say, the encouragement of servility or shame on the part of those receiving assistance)? If so, how might the risk that such harms will occur be minimized?
- Can non-state institutions effectively deliver assistance to children whose parents are unconcerned about or hostile to their welfare? Is state coercion needed to ensure good behavior by such parents? When do states themselves create dangers to child welfare?

D. Security, Dispute Resolution, and Other Aspects of Social Order

Defense of individuals against identifiable predators is a private rather than a public good, though its deterrent effects clearly yield benefits to many others. The same is true of reliable dispute resolution. But these order-maintenance functions are often viewed as among the most crucial tasks of the state. The picture of the state as a source of social order seems quite straightforward and simple at first glance: the state enacts uniform laws, adjudicates conflicts regarding these laws using its court system, and enforces them using its police agencies. States' contributions to order maintenance have often seemed intuitively to be among their most appealing characteristics. Anarchists have, unsurprisingly, challenged the assumption that states are essential guarantors of social order, encouraging reflection on such questions as:

- What role do social norms play in maintaining social order—in restraining predation and unreasonable opportunism, ensuring the performance of agreements, and facilitating cooperation with adjudicatory and law-enforcement institutions? If social norms enable the effective functioning of state order-maintenance institutions, could they not do the same where non-state order-maintenance institutions are concerned?
- While self-regulating spontaneous orders serve many valuable functions, it is often thought that they rely on exogenous legal institutions and would collapse absent such institutions. Is this correct, or can law itself be generated in a manner that is endogenous to spontaneous social orders?
- Real-world legal systems have often been more complex than the simple model of state-based legal uniformity might suggest, with overlapping and sometimes competing mechanisms for making laws, adjudicating conflict, and enforcing laws; we can refer to systems featuring such mechanisms as *polycentric*. Do history or theory suggest that law must be uniform in content or source, or can polycentric legal institutions function effectively? Are there psychic, social, cultural, economic, or normative dynamics in virtue of which legal systems with different sources might be expected to exhibit important overlaps in content?
- Are polycentric legal systems inherently unstable? Can predatory states be expected to emerge inevitably from such systems?
- Are polycentric legal systems inherently unreasonable? Is there something normatively suspect about the operation of multiple legal rules in proximity to each other? Is the idea of deterritorialized law oxymoronic?
- To what extent can state institutions that are at present highly centralized be replaced with decentralized state institutions? To what extent can the competition, decentralization, and experimentation characteristic of anarchy be realized within a state?
- How could a non-state legal system provide satisfactory protection to those—children, the frail, the elderly, the seriously ill, non-human animals—not able to take responsibility for

asserting their own interests? How would the likely performance of non-state legal system compare to the performance of actual or realistically conceivable state legal systems as regards the protection of vulnerable populations?

- Under what circumstances, if any, would the success of an existing state at maintaining social order be a decisive reason to treat it as authoritative?
- Even if ordinarily unwarranted, would the exercise of monopolistic coercive power be justified in an otherwise polycentric legal order when a widespread emergency occurs? If so, how might the relevant emergencies be identified? How might the appropriate limits of emergency powers be limned? How might emergency institutions be constrained in fact? How could it be rendered likely that such institutions would surrender their powers after the emergencies they were designed to address have subsided?

E. Economic Activity

States are deeply enmeshed in economic life. And it is often supposed that they are crucial enablers of economic stability and economic equity. However, anarchists of all stripes have frequently seen the state as the agent and enabler of economic groups on whom it confers unjust privileges and not as a defender against but rather as a source of economic instability. At the same time, anarchists who have agreed about the state's mischief-making role have disagreed radically about the optimal shapes of stateless societies' economic arrangements. Anarchist challenges to the necessity and value of state involvement in the economy and anarchists' own disputes about justice and expediency in economic life encourage reflection on such questions as:

- What rules regarding the acquisition, use, exchange, and abandonment of property are defensible?
- Is individual property in the means of production a creation of the state that would disappear without state support? Or is it a robust source of defense against coercion?
- What is the relationship between private and state hierarchies? To what extent, if at all, are private hierarchies—in businesses, associations, and other institutions—objectionable? Is the resemblance between these hierarchies and state hierarchies largely superficial, or are they subject to similar normative and pragmatic challenges?
- From an anarchist standpoint, should social class be understood as a function of people's relationships with the means of production? Or is class membership better seen as constituted by people's relationships with the state (and perhaps other coercive institutions)?

IV. The Shape of the *Handbook*

In this *Handbook*, scholars from a range of disciplines and with a range of ideological perspectives address questions about the possibility and desirability of anarchy.

We have included contributions in multiple disciplines and standpoints and ones from both academics and independent scholars in the body of the *Handbook* and in the Annotated Bibliography—well aware of the importance of not limiting consideration of vital issues of social organization to those from a single intellectual perspective or from conventional institutional settings.

While the contributors represent and examine a range of perspectives, this *Handbook* devotes what is arguably an unusual amount of attention to the nineteenth-century individualist anarchists. We suspect that these figures have received too little attention in recent discussions of anarchism. But it's also worth noting both that (i) their views are inherently interesting, not least because those views don't map easily onto standard political spectra and (ii) precisely for this reason, they can be seen as offering options capable of building bridges among proponents of diverse anarchist tendencies (as Roderick T. Long stresses in Chapter 2).

Bottom-up social organization obtains on a continuum—or, indeed, on a set of continua. While anarchy lies at one end of that continuum, it's important to think about anarchy on the margins. Between anarchy and totalitarianism lie innumerable possibilities as regards the scope of non-consensual order maintenance and of voluntary activities and institutions. As a number of the *Handbook*'s authors emphasize, various societies and patterns of social organization lie closer to or further from anarchy, featuring wider or narrower scopes for anarchic organization.

Part I, "Concept and Significance," attempts to help readers understand anarchism and anarchist claims and the broad significance of arguments about anarchism.

- Chapter 1, "Anarchism, Anarchists, and Anarchy" (Paul McLaughlin), emphasizes that anarchism itself is an essentially contested concept, considers different accounts of what anarchism amounts to in light of different definitional strategies and foci, and argues for an understanding of anarchism as skepticism about domination and hierarchy.
- Chapter 2, "The Anarchist Landscape" (Roderick T. Long) clarifies distinctions among anarchist tendencies and uses left-wing market anarchism to highlight relationships among these tendencies.
- Chapter 3, "On the Distinction between State and Anarchy" (Christopher W. Morris), makes clear that, just as there is no unambiguous and uncontroversial understanding of anarchism, so, also, the boundaries between anarchy and state are fluid and imprecise.
- Chapter 4, "Methodological Anarchism" (Jason Lee Byas and Billy Christmas), underscores the importance of not assuming the existence or necessity of the state in political philosophy.
- Chapter 5, "What Is the Point of Anarchism?" (Aeon J. Skoble), suggests that arguments about anarchism have immediate practical significance even if articulating them doesn't immediately lead to an anarchic society.

Part II, "Figures and Traditions," examines issues raised by or in relation to individual anarchist thinkers and schools of thought. The focus of this part is on the roots and significance of ideas related to anarchy—positively or critically. While it does not aim to examine every significant figure or tradition significantly related to discussions of anarchy, it is intended to expose you to an intriguing and provocative range of thinkers and ideas.

- Chapter 6, "Anarchism against Anarchy: The Classical Roots of Anarchism" (Stephen R. L. Clark), examines the roots of skepticism about top-down social order in the ancient Mediterranean world.
- Chapter 7, "Kant on Anarchy" (Oliver Sensen), explains why Kant believed it was not only prudent but necessary that we endorse state authority.
- Chapter 8, "Barbarians in the Agora: American Market Anarchism, 1945–2011" (J. Martin Vest), explores the nineteenth-century individualist anarchists and their twentieth- and twenty-first-century heirs.
- Chapter 9, "Rights, Morality, and Egoism in Individualist Anarchism" (Eric Mack) focuses on a vibrant debate among nineteenth-century anarchists over the relationship of morality to anarchism and the relative merits of egoism and alternative moral positions.

- Chapter 10, "Transcending Leftist Politics: Situating Egoism within the Anarchist Project" (David S. D'Amato), provides an alternative perspective on the place of egoism in nineteenth-century anarchism and its successors.
- Chapter 11, "De Facto Monopolies and the Justification of the State" (Ralf M. Bader), makes clear how Robert Nozick can acknowledge the failure of consent-based defenses of state authority while still regarding such authority as legitimate.
- Chapter 12, "Two Cheers for Rothbardianism" (Cory Massimino), offers an appreciative but critical perspective on the work of the twentieth-century anarchist economist and political theorist Murray Rothbard, seeking to show that the positions of Rothbard and those of other anarchists might prove mutually enriching.
- Chapter 13, "Christian Anarchism" (Sam Underwood and Kevin Vallier), calls attention to a long-lived tradition of deep skepticism about state power in Christian thought while questioning the versions of this kind of skepticism voiced by some contemporary Christians.

The chapters that make up Part III, "Legitimacy and Order," consider and develop normative and analytical arguments related to the authority of the state and its value as a source of social order.

- Chapter 14, "Anarchism and Political Obligation: An Introduction" (Magda Egoumenides), explains why conventional accounts of state authority fail to show that such authority is morally binding and how this conclusion sheds light on the indispensable contribution of the anarchist perspective to the debate.
- Chapter 15, "The Positive Political Economy of Analytical Anarchism" (Peter Boettke and Rosolino Candela), engages with a range of economic arguments related to the possibility that social order can be maintained without the involvement of a Weberian monopolist; while not offering a normative argument for anarchism, their insights provide obvious resources for anyone developing such an argument.
- Chapter 16, "Moral Parity between State and Non-State Actors" (Jason Brennan), provides reason to think that state actors' claims to be entitled to do things it would be wrong for others to do are unsustainable.
- Chapter 17, "Economic Pathologies of the State" (Christopher J. Coyne and Nathan Goodman), indicates why states might be expected consistently to distort economic life and to underperform non-state alternatives.
- Chapter 18, "Hunting for Unicorns" (Peter T. Leeson), provides historical evidence that supports the contention that social order can be effectively maintained in the state's absence.
- Chapter 19, "Social Norms and Social Order" (Ryan Muldoon), reflects critically on the potential of social norms to serve as sources of order alternative to state-made laws, highlighting both the difficulties associated with such norms in some social environments and the characteristics of the kind of social setting in which norms might be most appealing as bases of order.
- Chapter 20, "Anarchy and Law" (Jonathan Crowe), explains why law can exist in the absence of the state and what forms it might be expected take.
- Chapter 21, "Anarchy, State, and Violence" (Andy Alexis-Baker), emphasizes that states undermine and attack peaceful social order, offering a critique of state violence as an idolatrous religious phenomenon reflecting a tendency to sacralize brutality and domination.
- Chapter 22, "The Forecast for Anarchy" (Tom W. Bell) examines the social forces that are rendering hope for peaceful anarchy more reasonable.

Part IV, "Critique and Alternatives," focuses on anarchist positions regarding particular socio-political issues, addressing contemporary policy questions and considering the envisioned characteristics of anarchic societies.

- Chapter 23, "Social Anarchism and the Rejection of Private Property" (Jesse Spafford), focuses on a key debate among anarchists: it explores the links between the denial of legitimacy to state power by all anarchists and the denial of legitimacy to private property by some, explaining the worries voiced by these anarchists concerning the potentially oppressive nature of such property.
- Chapter 24, "The Right Anarchy: Capitalist or Socialist?" (Michael Huemer), continues the anarchist debate about property begun in the preceding chapter, arguing that forms of anarchism incorporating respect for markets and robust property rights are strongly preferable to available alternatives.
- Chapter 25, "Anarchist Approaches to Education" (Kevin Currie-Knight), considers historical and normative questions related to educational practice as these might appear from an anarchist perspective.
- Chapter 26, "An Anarchist Critique of Power Relations within Institutions" (Kevin A. Carson), highlights a range of pathologies inherent in hierarchical institutions and links between state power and the occurrence of these pathologies.
- Chapter 27, "Anarchism for an Ecological Crisis?" (Dan C. Shahar), asks how anarchists might respond effectively to large-scale environmental challenges.
- Chapter 28, "States, Incarceration, and Organizational Structure: Towards a General Theory of Imprisonment" (Daniel J. D'Amico), highlights evidence that strongly suggests a link between the predictable incentives faced by state actors and the growth of the carceral state.
- Chapter 29, "The Problems of Central Planning in Military Technology" (Abigail R. Hall), indirectly notes the significance of anarchy by emphasizing the ways in which the inherent liabilities associated with state decision-making renders states more likely than non-state decision-makers to reach poor decisions with respect to military hardware.
- Chapter 30, "Anarchy and Transhumanism" (William Gillis), underscores the inherent links between anarchism and a range of social, cultural, political, and technological proposals designed to help people move beyond the limits currently imposed on human action and interaction by their biological natures.

V. Engaging with the *Handbook*

The chapters of the *Handbook* have been written independently, and you can read them profitably in any order. We hope that the range of disciplines, approaches, and historical foci represented, in whatever fashion you choose to adopt, reflect on, or critically engage with them, will give you a better sense of the richness and diversity of anarchist thought and of the range of important issues anarchist criticisms of existing institutions and practices place on the table. We hope, too, that the Annotated Bibliography will point you toward a range of texts that will enrich your understanding of anarchism from a variety of perspectives. We also hope that you will discover that anarchy need not be a condition of chaotic violence—that its proponents, of all stripes, are advocates of peace and voluntary cooperation and that they see the state as precisely not a source of peace but rather as the preeminent perpetrator and abettor of violence. We hope, in addition, that you will treat the questions we noted in Part III as prompts for reflection—prompts that, along with the *Handbook*'s chapters and the Annotated Bibliography, will lead you to explore the significance of anarchism and anarchist thought for yourself and to extend understanding of these stimulating topics. And we hope, finally, that you will find yourself encouraged, whatever your ultimate response to anarchist proposals, to think more clearly and carefully about the challenges to frequently unquestioned contemporary assumptions that anarchism so pointedly raises.

Notes

1 *Rulers* exert dominance through the use or threat of physical force. Freedom from rulers thus also means (at least) freedom from (i) criminal gangs and others employing large-scale violence to dominate, even if they don't (a) claim legitimacy in the ways in which states do *or* (b) succeed in establishing dominance over particular territories or groups, and (ii) non-state actors *empowered* by states through the receipt of special privileges or statuses dependent on state endorsement and support.

2 When we refer here to anarchism *simpliciter*, we have in mind anarchism understood in this way, as at least endorsement of, and perhaps participation in, a socio-political project. Sometimes, but not always, references to specifically *philosophical* anarchism have in mind simply the rejection of the view that states necessarily or automatically possess any capacity to create moral duties for their subjects.

3 It hardly needs to be said that these definitions are themselves thoroughly contestable, and would not necessarily be endorsed without qualification by all of the contributors to the *Handbook*, much less by all theorists of anarchy and anarchism.

4 Cp. William Gillis, "Anarchism and Pandemics," *Center for a Stateless Society* (Molinari Institute, April 4, 2020), https://c4ss.org/content/52761 (June 10, 2020).

5 Noam Chomsky, for instance, plausibly connects anarchism and liberalism. See Anthony Arnove, "Foreword," *The Essential Chomsky*, by Noam Chomsky, ed. Arnove (New York: New 2008) vii; Matthew Robare, "American Anarchist," *The American Conservative* (American Ideas Institute, Nov. 22, 2013) www.theamericanconservative.com/articles/american-anarchist (June 16, 2020). This is, of course, another issue regarding which anarchists, including contributors to this volume, disagree.

6 Adam Ferguson, *Essay on the History of Civil Society*, 5th ed. (London: Cadell 1782) 205.

7 See, for example, Josiah Warren, "Manifesto," *Libertarian Labyrinth* (Libertarian Labyrinth, Sep. 23, 2016) [1841] www.libertarian-labyrinth.org/anarchist-beginnings/josiah-warren-manifesto-1841/ (Aug. 16, 2020); Rodion Belkovich, *Equitable Commerce: The Mediaeval Origins of American Anarchism*, WP BRP 18/LAW/2013 ([Moscow, Russia:] National Research University, Higher School of Economics) 4, www.hse.ru/data/2013/05/14/1299898751/18LAW2013.pdf (Aug. 16, 2020).

8 For more details regarding the texts to which we allude below, see the Annotated Bibliography.

9 Cp. Harold J. Berman, *Law and Revolution: The Formation of the Western Legal Tradition* (Cambridge, MA: Harvard UP 1983).

10 Both of the goods we offer as examples obviously yield spillover benefits to others, as is true of most goods.

PART I

Concept and Significance

1

ANARCHISM, ANARCHISTS, AND ANARCHY

Paul McLaughlin

I. Introduction

What is the social philosophy of anarchism? What is its relationship to the social action of anarchists? And what is its relationship to the social vision of anarchy? These are the three questions I address conceptually in this chapter. Depending on one's point of view, one might regard it as necessary (or not) to address some of these questions simultaneously. In particular, one might hold that answering the anarchism question requires that we address the anarchists question or the anarchy question. Or, if one is minded as I am, one might regard these questions as independent affairs and the anarchism question as answerable in itself. In this chapter, I will attempt to justify the latter point of view in large part by demonstrating what is wrong with the former. In effect, I will attempt at a conceptual level to divorce "anarchism" from "anarchists" and "anarchy."

What motivates this attempt is original doubt about two prominent conceptions of anarchism. The first is a political conception that conflates "anarchism" with what might more accurately be termed "anarchist-ism." The second is a philosophical conception that conflates "anarchism" with what might more accurately be termed "anarchy-ism." I will analyze and critique both of these conceptions below. But the original doubt here concerns not just possible intellectual error—or misconception of anarchism—but also a certain undesirable practical and theoretical sectarianism that is grounded on the apprehension of, for example, supposedly defining anarchist practices or values. The worry, in other words, is unjustified or even arbitrary exclusion by some ("true anarchists") of others ("false anarchists") from the political and/or philosophical community of anarchism. Needless to say, any account of anarchism will be exclusive. The point here is that exclusion requires justification on non-arbitrary grounds (other than, for example, a particular individual's preferred tactics or personal ethics).

In undertaking such work, one is invariably challenged—at least within this community—over the possibility and/or desirability of conceptual analysis as such, or the conceptual analysis of political terms more particularly, or even the conceptual analysis of anarchism itself. For example, Noam Chomsky maintains:

> The terms of political discourse are hardly models of precision. Considering the way terms are used, it is next to impossible to give meaningful answers to such questions as 'what is socialism?' Or capitalism, or free markets, or others in common usage. That is even truer of the term 'anarchism.' It has been subject to widely varied use, and

> outright abuse both by bitter enemies and those who hold its banner high, so much so that it resists any straightforward characterization.[1]

This is no denial of the possibility or desirability of conceptual analysis as such. Nor is it a denial of the desirability of the conceptual analysis of political terms including "anarchism." But it is a denial of the possibility of the conceptual analysis of anarchism in particular among political terms, of analysis that might yield a "straightforward characterization" or definition of the term.

A stronger claim is made by Benjamin Franks, who insists that "it is misguided to attempt to find ahistorical and universal, decontested concepts [or to fix] the meaning[s] of terms [by identifying] necessary and sufficient conditions" for their application.[2] I take this assertion of misguidedness to be a denial of possibility. In other words, I take Franks to deny the possibility of conceptual analysis of political terms at the very least, if not conceptual analysis as such. Moreover, I also take him to deny the desirability of conceptual analysis—not merely because it is impossible (which may also be Chomsky's position with respect to political terms), but also because "fixing" meaning would be objectionable—or objectionable from an anarchist perspective—even if it were possible. To fix meaning is an act of linguistic authoritarianism, an act whereby one party (the analytic philosopher) imposes "necessary and sufficient conditions" on all others (including anarchist activists).

Let us grant for present purposes the impossibility and undesirability of conceptual analysis understood in Franks's narrow sense. Let us admit that it is impossible to specify necessary and sufficient conditions for the application of (at least political) terms and that it is undesirable to fix and impose (at least political) meaning. However, we may still defend conceptual analysis in quite a different, explicative, sense, borrowing from and going beyond Rudolf Carnap (in a normative direction) in doing so.[3] "Explication" involves the tightening up of "everyday" (say, political) language for "scientific" (say, evaluative) purposes:

> The task of *explication* consists in transforming a given more or less inexact concept into an exact one ... The [inexact concept] may belong to everyday language or to a previous stage in the development of scientific language. The [exact one] must be given by explicit rules for its use, for example, by a definition which incorporates it into a well-constructed system of scientific either logico-mathematical or empirical concepts.[4]

The explicative process of "tightening up" is not intended to reveal essential conceptual truths but to yield more precise and theoretically fruitful concepts that are still familiar from ordinary use within given linguistic communities. These concepts may be specified in terms of seemingly necessary and other more contentious conditions for their use. The former are measures of everyday familiarity; the latter, possible additional requirements for scientific fruitfulness. What result from this explicative process are non-arbitrary stipulative definitions of terms. These definitions are "auditable" as such, to test their non-arbitrariness.

> The task of a concept audit is ... to see to it that the conceptual resources put at a philosopher's disposal by ... pre-established usage have been adequately employed and the prevailing distinctions and connections duly acknowledged.[5]

In other words, anything and everything does not go with conceptual analysis understood in this sense. Ordinary use is to be respected to the greatest possible degree compatible with theoretical employment.

To return to Chomsky's remarks that "terms of political discourse are hardly models of precision" and that "it is next to impossible to give meaningful answers" to questions of political definition: the point of explicative analysis here is to make the imprecisions of ordinary political discourse more precise and ideally (as a regulative ideal) to render them as "models of precision"; and it is possible to provide a meaningful analysis of political discourse by such means, as I hope to demonstrate. That is to say, whatever might be said of conceptual analysis in Franks's narrow sense, I wish to assert: first, the possibility of conceptual analysis qua explication, or the possibility of pinning down political meaning in given linguistic contexts; and, second, the desirability of conceptual analysis qua explication, or the desirability of doing this for particular theoretical (if not other political and practical) purposes. (One might even go further here and assert the necessity of conceptual analysis qua explication for the achievement of such purposes.) A minimal theoretical purpose of conceptual analysis, as I understand it here, is to prevent semantic confusion in the investigation of political phenomena (such that, for example, philosophers may be talking past one another in attempting to evaluate them).

II. On "Anarchist-ism"

Conceptual analysis is not, of course, universally rejected, even by anarchists. There are scholars who have sought to define "anarchism" in very different ways. Michael Schmidt and Lucien van der Walt have argued that conceptual analysis can and should be undertaken for the internal purpose of "identify[ing] the common features of the subject under definition"—thereby "enabling effective analysis and research"—and for the external purpose of "clearly delineat[ing] the category being defined from other categories."[6] Thus, conceptual analysis can disclose the *shared* and *distinguishing* features of anarchism for theoretical purposes. However, they are insistent that the resulting definition should not be too inclusive. Conceptually, their worry is that "a range of quite different and often contradictory ideas and movements [might] get conflated," which would lead to the view that there is "something necessarily incoherent about anarchism." They also worry that anarchism might be regarded as "a movement existing throughout history," rather than "a relatively recent phenomenon" (of a specific communist and revolutionary character).[7] This historical point is central to their analysis, as van der Walt underscores:

> It is a matter of record … that the anarchist movement appeared as something *new* to its contemporaries, rivals, and adherents; with this appearance, anarchism *first* became the topic of scholarly enquiry, police investigation, and media attention. Even writers favouring exceedingly loose definitions of 'anarchism' concede that 'anarchism' did not previously exist as a 'political force' …. The very question of whether there were earlier or 'different schools, currents and tendencies' of anarchism, or an anarchist 'orientation' 'throughout human history' could not even be *posed* before this moment.[8]

Schmidt and van der Walt claim that anarchism only came into existence once it was recognized as a new political force in the 1860s. Curiously, it did not exist when it was first proclaimed and expounded as a social philosophy in the 1840s or when this philosophy was developed under other names prior to the 1840s (by the end of eighteenth century, if not earlier). Thus, anarchism is strictly identifiable with the recognized anarchist movement, or the collective socio-political action of anarchists, from the late nineteenth century onward.

Like Schmidt and van der Walt, Uri Gordon accepts the possibility and desirability of conceptual analysis. He endorses what he calls "Anglo-American … methods and conventions" such that his study of anarchism "chiefly takes the form of analyzing concepts and arguments, making distinctions and giving examples, all with the intention of driving home some point."[9] The account he offers of anarchism is less historically rooted and more contemporary and evolving than that of Schmidt and van der Walt. Nevertheless, like them he identifies anarchism with a "social movement" that is animated by a particular "political culture" and generative of a "collection of ideas."[10] Whatever may be said about anarchism as a theory, it is one that is "grounded in practice."[11] Anarchism is therefore ultimately about what anarchists continue to do collectively as a movement.

Many other scholars have emphasized socio-political action in their analyses of anarchism. For example, David Morland, while skeptical about the conceptual analysis of anarchism (which appears to constitute "an essentially contested concept"[12]), claims that it is possible to say at least one thing about "the very nature of anarchism": as "an ideology it is an active creed" and anarchists "have been, by their very nature, inclined towards activism."[13] What Schmidt and van der Walt and Gordon add to this activist condition is a *collective* condition. Anarchism is not just about the activism of certain *individuals*, but such activism at a *collective* level. This is what yielded an anarchist *movement*, or anarchism in the proper sense, at a given moment in social history.

On this kind of analysis, collective discourse may be added as a seemingly necessary condition to (or included within) collective action. What counts is not just the collective action (narrowly construed) of anarchists, but also the ways in which anarchists talk, theorize, and strategize about such action. David Graeber observes that (*i*) "[a]narchists are distinguished by what they do, and how they organize themselves to go about doing it" and (*ii*) "this has always been what anarchists have spent most of their time thinking and arguing about." As a result, "[a]narchism has tended to be an ethical discourse about revolutionary practice."[14]

It would appear, on the account that emerges above, that anarchism is reducible to the collective socio-political action and discourse of anarchists. Put bluntly, anarchism is what anarchists as a whole do and say (about what they do). So, while one might have supposed that anarchists are defined as such by their anarchism(s), on the contrary, anarchism is properly defined by its anarchists. This anarchist-centered outlook may be termed "anarchist-ism"—the view, again, that anarchism is to be defined in terms of the collective action (perhaps including discursive action) of anarchists; that is, in terms of what anarchist*s* do or have done (perhaps including what they talk about or have talked about). In order to understand anarchism, then, we need to examine what anarchists do (and the way in which this gains theoretical expression), not what they think (and the way in which this gains practical expression).

There are quite obvious problems—both historical and logical—with the "anarchist-ist" conception of anarchism. Historically, it is problematic for this conception that (as I noted above) anarchism was pronounced, elucidated, and defended by individual anarchist intellectuals prior to the existence of anything like a collective anarchist movement. Pierre-Joseph Proudhon is the major case in point.[15] It is also problematic that (at the very least) similar, unnamed views had been expressed by others previously. William Godwin is a noted example;[16] but there are many other strands in the pre-Proudhonian (pre-)history of anarchism.[17] Of course, one may argue against the characterization of such ideas and individuals as anarchist. But it is unjustified to do so on the mere basis that they were not products or parts of a movement that emerged subsequently, inspired by some of these very ideas and individuals (even if the ideas were later modified and the individuals fell out of favour). (Incidentally, the anarchist ideas of Mikhail Bakunin, for example, pre-date and motivate his foundational role in the recognized anarchist movement; and he demonstrably declared himself an anarchist some time before entering the First International.[18]) The anarchist movement is an expression of such ideas—an expression that continues to develop and refine these ideas over time through further reflection (including reflection on associated action). (That said, there is no reason to suppose that anarchist ideas should only continue to develop within this collective and activist context.) At any rate, to deny the complex pre-history of the anarchist movement renders inescapable the question of how or why this movement came into existence in the first place.

Logically, the anarchist-ist conception of anarchism is equally problematic. If anarchism is to be defined in terms of what anarchists collectively do (and perhaps say), we are left with obvious problems pertaining to the identification of relevant actors and actions. How are we to pick out the relevant actors here (without reference to what defines them as such; i.e., their anarchism)? The answer is usually one of self-identification (since other-identification is typically regarded as ignorant and/or oppressive): the relevant actors are those who identify themselves as anarchists or as part of a collective movement of such self-identifying anarchists. Actors are anarchists if they say they are anarchists, and anarchism is what these self-identifying anarchists do (and perhaps say). However, most (if not all) who identify themselves as anarchists deny this identity to (at least some) others who *also* identify themselves as anarchists. So simple self-identification would appear to be inadequate. In any event, even if this problem could be set aside, how are we to pick out the relevant actions of these actors, that is, *anarchist actions* as opposed to *actions of anarchists* (again, without reference to what defines them as such; i.e., their anarchism)? It is the actions of anarchists that are claimed to define anarchism; but presumably not all acts of anarchists are anarchist actions. Arguably, actions are anarchist actions if they are identified as such by people who identify as anarchists. But most (if not all) who identify their actions as anarchist deny this identity to the actions of (at least some) others who do the same. Self-identification would appear to be inadequate once again.

The point I am indirectly attempting to establish here is twofold: first, that anarchism is factually anterior to the anarchist movement; and second, that "anarchism" is logically prior to "anarchist." Anarchist ideas existed before the anarchist movement; and it would be surprising, to put it mildly, if this were not the case. And anarchists (and their anarchist actions) can only be identified with reference to anarchism as a philosophical idea. The nature of this idea will be taken up in the next section. But my bluntly stated response to those who endorse the anarchist-ist conception of anarchism is as follows: anarchism is not what anarchists do any more than liberalism is what liberals do, socialism is what socialists do, conservatism is what conservatives do, and so on. This remains the case even if activism is especially important and informative to anarchists—or, for that matter, proponents of other ostensibly revolutionary outlooks.

If one accepts the above, one may speculate in Adlerian terms about why some anarchists—perhaps uniquely among the politically committed—define their position in such a "back-to-front" way. Two complexes—perhaps independent of one other but more likely connected—may be suggested in this purely speculative explanatory context. One is an intellectual inferiority complex among anarchists: the diminishing sense that they lack the intellectual weaponry of classical Marxists and contemporary liberals, for example.[19] This lack can be and has been dramatically overstated (from Karl Marx himself onward[20]). In any event, there are many legitimate criticisms of this weaponry (some of them introduced by Bakunin in response to Marx[21]). Whatever the causes of this complex, one way of compensating for it may be to develop an activist superiority complex: the flattering sense that anarchists are uniquely and virtuously predisposed towards properly political and even revolutionary action. While classical Marxists and contemporary liberals indulge in ever more complex and arcane theorizing, anarchists set about righting real wrongs (often contrary to the understanding and wishes of the apparently ignorant majority on whose behalf some claim to act). One may respond that there are indeed well-conceived and virtuous forms of activism; but there are mindless and vicious forms, too—some of them arguably evidenced within the anarchist tradition.

The points made in this section about factual anteriority and logical priority may appear obvious and unworthy of protracted analysis. Nevertheless, the anarchist-ist conception of anarchism remains prevalent—if difficult for serious scholars of anarchism to maintain consistently. It is therefore unsurprising that the scholars discussed above all advance alternative conceptions of anarchism which are (issues of origins aside) consistent with the more plausible candidates discussed in the next section. Schmidt and van der Walt define anarchism (quite conventionally from a traditional left-wing perspective) as a revolutionary and libertarian brand of socialism.[22] Gordon defines it most fundamentally (in more contemporary terms) as opposition to domination in all forms.[23] David Morland defines it (in broad and recognizable terms) as opposition to the state.[24] And, finally, David Graeber defines anarchism (in quite complex terms) as "a rejection of all forms of structural violence, inequality, or domination."[25] What, then, are we to make of conceptions of anarchism of this general philosophical kind?

III. On "Anarchy-ism"

If "anarchism" is not to be defined in terms of what anarchists do, it might instead be defined in terms of what anarchists want: an internally shared and externally distinguishing social vision—or imagined form of social alterity—known as "anarchy." This conception is neatly encapsulated by Bob Black:

> Anarchism is an idea about what's the best way to live. Anarchy is the name for that way of living … Anarchists are people who believe in anarchism and desire for us all to live in anarchy.[26]

The social vision of anarchy is characterized by an alternative absence and/or presence—negation and/or realization—of specific social phenomena and values.[27] This vision is traditionally held to be premised upon a certain philosophical ethic and anthropology. Systematically, then, anarchism has been understood to constitute a vision of a good society resting on certain moral principles and understandings of human nature. ("Post-anarchism" I take to represent a sympathetic challenge to anarchism so conceived on anti-foundational, anti-universalist, or anti-essentialist grounds.[28]) Differences over the nuts and bolts of *exactly* what this society might look like—and how we could or should reach it—account for much of the variety in anarchism so understood; but they do not define it as such.

Anarchism, then, is often thought of as the belief in the desirability (if not the possibility) of anarchy, where "anarchy" consists in the alternative negation and/or realization of specific social norms, practices, relations, institutions, and structures. Such a belief may be more or less explicitly stated. And the social vision involved may be more or less elaborate. But holding this belief in itself does not make one a member of a historically recognizable anarchist movement. Nor does it commit one to activism.[29] Of course, there may be compelling additional moral and political reasons to establish or join such a social movement and/or to take action. But these reasons are not built into the definition of anarchism as such.

This anarchy-centered (as opposed to anarchist-centered) conception of anarchism essentially conflates it with what we might term "anarchy-ism." The "anarchy-ist" conception of anarchism is, I think, significantly more common and plausible than the anarchist-ist conception. However, I will argue that it too is ultimately unsustainable. This can be demonstrated by more closely analyzing what is involved in the conception at its bare minimum (underpinning the least elaborate visions of anarchy). Two principal conditions seem to be necessary here: a particular kind of disposition (on the part of the anarchist); and a particular kind of object (to which the anarchist is so disposed). The kind or rather kinds of disposition are relatively clear in the case of anarchism so understood: they are (i) oppositional or (ii) supportive or (iii) both. The object or often objects in question are much more contentious, and I will consider precise examples below; but they include particular kinds of social phenomena (x below) and values (y below). Accordingly, anarchism on this conception can be understood as the belief that society should be arranged (i) without some undesirable x, or (ii) in the name of some desirable y, or (iii) without some undesirable x in the name of some desirable y. This social arrangement constitutes anarchy.

The object of anarchy-ism is often represented in singular terms and I will examine it on this basis. However, it is important to note that, on some accounts, a plurality of objects is either enumerated or subsumed under a single potentially confusing (if not conceptually confused) label. Nathan Jun, for example, catalogues varieties of coercion, domination, oppression, authority, and inequality as objects of anarchist opposition[30] (on libertarian and egalitarian grounds[31]). For Jun, therefore, anarchism is the belief that society should be arranged without specific kinds of coercion, domination, oppression, authority, and inequality for the sake of liberty and equality. Uri Gordon, on the other hand, subsumes varieties of control, coercion, exploitation, humiliation, discrimination, "etc.," under the single object-label "domination"[32] (which appears to be opposed by anarchists on a plurality of moral grounds[33]). For Gordon, therefore, anarchism is the belief that society should be arranged without control, coercion, exploitation, humiliation, discrimination, and other unspecified forms of (what he regards as) domination.

We turn now to some of the recurrent singular objects of anarchist opposition (*x* above) and/or support (*y* above)—or to the most common (anarchy-ist) definitions of anarchism proposed by anarchist theorists and scholars of anarchism. The objects of opposition traditionally include (non-exhaustively) government,[34] state,[35] law,[36] violence,[37] social power,[38] domination,[39] authority,[40] and hierarchy.[41] Traditional objects of support (on which such opposition may rest) include liberty,[42] autonomy,[43] equality,[44] happiness,[45] virtue,[46] flourishing,[47] and other more complex goods.[48] Anarchism (in the anarchy-ist sense) may therefore be defined as the belief that society should be arranged (i) without government/state/law/violence/social power/domination/authority/hierarchy, or (ii) in the name of liberty/autonomy/equality/happiness/virtue/flourishing/some complex good, or (iii) without government/state/law/violence/social power/domination/authority/hierarchy in the name of liberty/autonomy/equality/happiness/virtue/flourishing/some complex good.

In evaluating the anarchy-ist conception in this general form, one may immediately and easily establish that there is no shared anarchist value (distinguishing or otherwise). Whatever it is that anarchists purportedly oppose (or see as desirably absent from anarchy), they oppose for all manner of reasons (deontological, consequentialist, aretaic, etc.) drawn from across the traditional ethical spectrum (and perhaps beyond).[49] This diversity of ethical outlook is sometimes seen as a strength of anarchism, but I will not examine that issue here.[50] (Incidentally, it is likewise easy to establish that there is no shared anarchist conception of human nature.[51]) A similar observation may be made with respect to object *x*: on the face of it, there would appear to be no shared anarchist object of opposition (distinguishing or otherwise), either. If this is all so—if there is no shared object of concern that anarchists envision as absent or present in the ideal social order called anarchy—then anarchism might appear incoherent or even non-existent. However, I believe that it is possible to establish after some further analysis that there is a shared anarchist object of concern. The question remains whether anarchists share an oppositional disposition towards it and therefore whether an anarchy-ist conception of anarchism is ultimately defensible.

Let us return to the individual candidates for (opposed object) *x*. I assume for present purposes that any of these candidates would distinguish anarchism from non-anarchism. That is to say, I accept here (without endorsing the view) that opposition (on whatever moral basis) to government or state or law or violence or social power or domination or authority or hierarchy would distinguish anarchists from non-anarchists. But are any of these candidates shared by anarchists themselves? Do all anarchists oppose (on whatever moral basis) government or state or law or violence or social power or domination or authority or hierarchy? If so, we have arrived at a true definition—or possibly more than one true definition—of "anarchism." But what we ideally wish to arrive at is an *adequate* as well as a true definition: a definition which picks out not only a token or tokens of the type of object that anarchists oppose, but also this very *type* of object. The real definitional question here is therefore the following: is government/state/law/violence/social power/domination/authority/hierarchy the *type* of object that all anarchists oppose (on whatever moral basis)?

In some cases, the answer is negative because the objects in question are unshared. It is simply untrue to say that all anarchists oppose government[52] or law[53] or violence[54] or social power[55] *as such*. Opposition to social power (or any effective capacity in social relations), in particular, would be absurd from almost any perspective. In other cases, the answer is less straightforward. Anarchists do appear to share a concern—indeed a highly critical concern—with the state,[56] domination,[57] authority,[58] and hierarchy.[59] However, it is mistaken in my view to characterize their concern with domination, authority, and hierarchy in simple oppositional terms. There are forms of domination (of the controlling capacity in social relations), of authority (of the capacity to require action or the acceptance of belief in social relations), and of hierarchy (of the structured inequality that emerges from relations of social power, domination, and authority) that at least some anarchists regard as justified in revolutionary if not post-revolutionary circumstances. Violent resistance, expert leadership, and the stratified organization of social forces are morally problematic from an anarchist point of view; but some anarchists have certainly regarded them as consequentially justifiable (in the name of social transformation into anarchy).[60] Some have also foreseen justifiable forms of dominative, authoritative, and hierarchical relations—and even regulation, administration, or government—under anarchy.[61] This demonstrable non-opposition to domination, authority, and hierarchy in fact may seem at odds with stated opposition in principle—or to exemplify a certain inconsistency on the part of some anarchists. However, I believe that it evinces a more nuanced anarchist position with respect to domination, authority, and hierarchy than is generally recognized both inside and outside anarchist circles.[62] I will outline this position in Section IV, but we are not quite ready to move on.

An outstanding candidate for the shared (and distinguishing[63]) oppositional object (x) of anarchism remains, one which may yet support the anarchy-ist conception of anarchism. Anarchism is plausibly the belief in the desirability of anarchy understood as a social order without a state of any kind. Anarchism may fundamentally be about opposition to the state. It is certainly unusual for an anarchist to defend the state in current non-ideal conditions,[64] and unheard of for an anarchist to defend the state in the ideal conditions of anarchy. Indeed, state and anarchy are generally seen by anarchists as revolutionary antitheses. However, an a posteriori anarchist case for the justification of some form of the state—while yet unknown—is arguably conceivable.[65] In any case, this anarchy-ist definition suggests a degree of state-obsessiveness that is difficult to reconcile with the variety of classical and especially contemporary anarchist concerns. The state is not, I contend, the type of object towards which anarchists are somehow disposed, but a notable token of that type; nor is the disposition of anarchists towards this token necessarily oppositional, as I have just suggested, though I concede that it almost always is as a matter of fact.[66]

In summary, the anarchy-ist conception of anarchism identifies anarchism with a belief in the desirability of a society called anarchy in which certain social phenomena (objects of anarchist opposition x) are negated and/or certain social values (objects of anarchist support y) are realized. However, there is no such shared and distinguishing object of anarchist support (y); and if there is a shared and distinguishing object of anarchist opposition (x), it is a token of the relevant type of object of anarchist concern rather than that type itself; all anarchy-ist definitions of anarchism in oppositional terms are therefore inadequate even if true. As I will argue in Section IV, the correct (shared and distinguishing type of) object is picked out by an anarchy-ist definition (and tokens of this type are picked out by other such definitions, too); but the disposition towards this object is misrepresented by the anarchy-ist conception (as oppositional). Before explaining this position in greater detail, however, I want to conclude Section III by noting an important implication of the rejection of the anarchy-ist conception: anarchism is logically independent of anarchy, of the social ideal in terms of which it is so often defined. An anarchist may embrace all manner of social ideals or none at all. This is not to say that an anarchist should not have a social vision or that any social vision is defensible on anarchist grounds. But such matters go well beyond the analysis of "anarchism."

IV. On "Anarchism"

I have defined "anarchism" previously—in relation to "anarchy-ism"—as a distinct disposition towards a familiar object. The disposition as I saw it then was neither oppositional nor supportive, but skeptical. The object was the specific variety of social power known as authority. Hence, I concluded that anarchism was to be defined as skepticism about authority.[67] I now believe that I was right with respect to the disposition but wrong with respect to the (type of) object.

Anarchism is—I still maintain—a form of socio-political skepticism: of authentic doubt rather than blanket opposition. Anarchists of various ethical persuasions share a suspicious and inquiring disposition towards the desirability of all forms and instances of their socio-political object of concern.[68] They are distinguished from non-anarchists in this respect. None of these instances is accepted as self-evidently desirable. Many of them—even those accepted by most people in most places most of the time—are treated as undesirable. And some of them that anarchists are thought to oppose are understood as desirable after all. Anarchists typically seek to undermine undesirable forms in one way or another: by individually or collectively giving voice to their opposition and/or taking counter-actions of various kinds.

It is true to say—as I maintained previously—that anarchists are skeptical about authority. But it is also true to say that anarchists are skeptical about the state, for example. I argued previously that the state—for all the attention it receives in anarchist literature—is merely a token of the type of thing about which anarchists are skeptical, so that it would be mistaken (or inadequate) to *define* anarchism as skepticism about the state.[69] I argued then that the type of thing about which anarchists are skeptical is authority, and defined anarchism accordingly. I now believe this is mistaken and that authority too is a token—albeit a more general token—of the relevant type of thing. This type of thing is domination. I had previously resisted this conclusion on the grounds that it would make anarchism indistinguishable from liberalism.[70] But I now think this was an error—which was inconsistent with my overall analysis—and that I was giving liberalism too much critical credit at the time. Liberalism is not skepticism towards domination or the broad token of this type called authority or the narrow token known as (the political authority of) the state. Liberals exhibit certain skeptical delusions in these regards (as I have witnessed repeatedly in academic discussions of these matters over the years). But these need to be exposed.

Two prominent dispositions—quite at odds with anarchist skepticism—stand out in the history of liberal thought about domination, authority, and the state. One of these is resolutely non-skeptical—indeed dogmatic. The other is only strategically skeptical—or arguably pseudo-skeptical. Liberal dogmatism is most famously expressed by John Stuart Mill:

> All that makes existence valuable to anyone, depends on the enforcement of restraints upon the actions of other people. Some rules of conduct, therefore, must be imposed, by law in the first place, and by opinion on many things which are not fit subjects for the operation of law. What these rules should be is the principal question in human affairs.[71]

This is no argument for "social control" (by various means). It is a simple dogmatic statement of its necessity. And the "principal question" of social theory as anarchists see it is not about the nature and limits of (obviously necessary) social control; rather, it is about its justifiability in its many and varied forms (authoritative and otherwise). The arguably pseudo-skeptical element in liberal thought is represented by the contractarian tradition. Liberal contractarians as I understand them—as effective socio-political counterparts to Descartes—do not doubt the desirability of "social control"; they set out to construct a secure normative foundation for it. "The whole point of the thought-experiment of the social contract is justificatory, namely, to normatively ground the authority of the state [and, I would add, other forms of domination] retrospectively."[72] The defining liberal disposition is not skeptical but supportive; and its defining object is not domination but individual liberty (which it assumes is or tries to establish as compatible with domination of at least some kinds.) Liberalism and anarchism are fundamentally distinct.

Anarchism I now define as skepticism about domination (including authority in general and the authority of the state in particular). Within the history of anarchist thought, particular emphasis has been placed on authority and especially the state for contextual reasons that are easy to explain. These emphases—and especially the apparently universal anarchist rejection of the state—have led many scholars to define anarchism in terms of the wrong disposition and/or the wrong (type of) object. I believe that my definition as it now stands is both true and adequate. It is admittedly thin: stripped of a social vision, ethic, and metaphysic. If it seems so thin as to include ideas and individuals that some anarchists dislike, this is a price I am willing to pay. My view of anarchism is rather ecumenical, which is not to deny that I too dislike certain anarchist ideas and individuals. But definitions should not be matters of taste—a point that many anarchists tend to ignore.[73] In any event, I am satisfied that my definition is not so thin as to render anarchism indistinguishable from liberalism in particular.

There is an alternative perspective on anarchism—already hinted at in the previous section—that gives rise to a related but distinct definition that may also be true and adequate. This perspective appears more prevalent in the social sciences than the humanities: among those inclined and equipped to describe and explain social structures rather than to analyze and evaluate social relations. From this perspective, the (type of) object of skeptical anarchist concern is hierarchy rather than domination. Anarchism, then, may be defined as skepticism about hierarchy. Thus, two conceptions of anarchism emerge: a philosophical conception of *agential anarchism* (defined as skepticism about domination) and a scientific conception of *structural anarchism* (defined as skepticism about hierarchy). As a social philosopher, I tend to focus on the analysis and evaluation of social relations. But I also maintain that social structures are the products of social relations and I argue for the priority (though not the *absolute* priority) of the philosophical over the scientific line of investigation (of domination before hierarchy) here.

V. Conclusion

In this chapter, after defending the possibility and desirability of explicative conceptual analysis of "anarchism," I have argued for (1) the logical priority of "anarchism" to "anarchist"; (2) the logical independence of anarchism and anarchy; and (3) skepticism about domination as a true and adequate definition of (agential) "anarchism." I am conscious that my basic analysis does not constitute an argument for the social philosophy of anarchism or any social vision of anarchy or any roadmap to anarchy or any anarchist ethic or any anarchist conception of human nature or engagement in any form of anarchist activism or membership in any anarchist movement. A comprehensive anarchist philosophy would range over all of this and perhaps more besides. Here, however, I have only attempted to scratch the conceptual surface of anarchism. I hope that this facilitates the ongoing quest for greater understanding.

Notes

1 Noam Chomsky, *What Kind of Creatures Are We?* (New York, NY: Columbia UP 2016) 62–3.

2 Benjamin Franks, "Between Anarchism and Marxism: The Beginnings and Ends of the Schism," *Journal of Political Ideologies* 17.2 (2012): 209, 210, 212.

3 This "going beyond" is clearly explained in the context of experimental philosophy in Joshua Shepherd and James Justus, "X-Phi and Carnapian Explication," *Erkenntnis* 80.2 (2015): 381–402.

4 Rudolf Carnap, *Logical Foundations of Probability*, 2d ed. (Chicago, IL: U of Chicago P) 3. Original emphasis.

5 Nicholas Rescher, *Concept Audits: A Philosophical Method* (Lanham, MD: Lexington 2016) 3.

6 Michael Schmidt and Lucien van der Walt, *Black Flame: The Revolutionary Class Politics of Anarchism and Syndicalism* (Oakland, CA: AK 2009) 41, 43.

7 Schmidt and van der Walt 33, 34, 40.

8 Lucien van der Walt, "(Re)Constructing a Global Anarchist and Syndicalist Canon: A Response to Robert Graham and Nathan Jun on *Black Flame*," *Anarchist Developments in Cultural Studies 2013.1: Blasting the Canon*, ed. Duane Rousselle and Süreyyya Evren (Santa Barbara, CA: Punctum 2013) 195. Original emphasis.

9 Uri Gordon, *Anarchy Alive! Anti-Authoritarian Politics from Practice to Theory* (London: Pluto 2008) 10.

10 Gordon 3–4.

11 Gordon 48.

12 David Morland, *Demanding the Impossible? Human Nature and Politics in Nineteenth-Century Social Anarchism* (London: Cassell 1997) 3.

13 Morland 19.

14 David Graeber, "Anarchism, Academia, and the Avant-garde," *Contemporary Anarchist Studies: An Introductory Anthology of Anarchy in the Academy*, ed. Randall Amster et al. (Abingdon: Routledge 2009) 106.

15 Pierre-Joseph Proudhon, *What is Property?*, ed. Donald R. Kelley and Bonnie G. Smith (Cambridge: CUP 1994) 205: "I am an anarchist …. I have just given you my serious and well-considered profession of faith. Although a firm friend of order, I am, in every sense of the term, an anarchist."

16 William Godwin, *Enquiry Concerning Political Justice*, 2 vols. (London: Robinson 1793) 2: 578–579: "With what delight must every well informed friend of mankind look forward to the auspicious period, the dissolution of political government, of that brute engine, which has been the only perennial cause of the vices of mankind, and which, as has abundantly appeared in the progress of the present work, has mischiefs of various sorts incorporated with its substance, and no otherwise to be removed than by its utter annihilation!"

17 See chapters 1 and 2 of James Joll, *The Anarchists*, 2d ed. (London: Methuen, 1979); and Part Two of Peter Marshall, *Demanding the Impossible: A History of Anarchism* (Oakland, CA: PM 2010).

18 T.R. Ravindranathan, *Bakunin and the Italians* (Kingston: McGill-Queen's UP 1988) 65 and 257n44.

19 Much of the anarchist scholarship encourages this complex. See, for example, April Carter, *The Political Theory of Anarchism* (Abingdon: Routledge 2010) 1: anarchism has "not received much attention from political theorists. There are a number of reasons for this neglect. One is … the lack of any outstanding theoretical exponent of anarchism. There are important, interesting and attractive anarchist writers, but none comparable as social theorists with, for example, Marx. Within the corpus of 'great political thinkers' only Rousseau comes close occasionally to being an anarchist."

20 See Karl Marx's notes on Bakunin's *Statism and Anarchy*: *The Marx-Engels Reader*, 2d ed., ed. Robert C. Tucker (New York, NY: Norton 1978) 542–8.

21 See Mikhail Bakunin's general critique of "scientism": *Michael Bakunin: Selected Writings*, ed. Arthur Lehning (London: Cape 1973) 159–165.

22 Schmidt and van der Walt 33.

23 Gordon 30.

24 Morland 183.

25 Graeber 105.

26 Bob Black, *Defacing the Currency: Selected Writings 1992–2012* (Berkeley, CA: LBC 2012) 37.

27 Ruth Kinna, *Anarchism: A Beginner's Guide* (Oxford: Oneworld, 2005) 5: "Anarchy is the goal of anarchists: the society variously described to be without government or without authority; a condition of statelessness, of free federation, of 'complete' freedom and equality based either on rational self-interest, co-operation or reciprocity."

28 For an anthology that demonstrates the variety evident within post-anarchist thought, see Duane Rousselle and Süreyyya Evren, eds., *Post-Anarchism: A Reader* (London: Pluto 2011).

29 Kinna is therefore wrong to assert in that "[a]narchists are those who work to further the cause of anarchism [or to realise 'anarchy']. [They are] activists [in] a number of categories ranging from educationalists and propagandists to combatants in armed struggle" (4). This is a definition of "anarchist activists" not "anarchists."

30 Nathan Jun, "Rethinking the Anarchist Canon: History, Philosophy, and Interpretation," Rousselle and Evren 88–89.

31 Nathan Jun, *Anarchism and Political Modernity* (London: Continuum 2012) 116.

32 Gordon 32.

33 Gordon 43.

34 Peter Kropotkin, *Kropotkin's Revolutionary Pamphlets: A Collection of Writings by Peter Kropotkin*, ed. Roger N. Baldwin (New York, NY: Dover 1970) 284: "Anarchism [is] the name given to a principle or theory of life and conduct under which society is conceived without government."

35 Kinna 38: "anarchism should be considered as an ideology defined by the rejection of the state."

36 Gerald Runkle, *Anarchism: Old and New* (New York, NY: Delacorte 1972) 118: "In the absence of law and formal punishment, how are men to live together [in an anarchist society]?"

37 Jacques Ellul, *Anarchy and Christianity*, trans. Geoffrey W. Bromiley (Eugene, OR: Wipf 2011) 11: "By anarchy I mean first an absolute rejection of violence."

38 Saul Newman, "Anarchism and the Politics of Ressentiment," *Theory and Event* 4.3 (2000) https://muse.jhu.edu/article/32594: "It is … senseless and indeed impossible to try to construct, as anarchists do, a world outside power."

39 Sal Restivo, *Red, Black, and Objective: Science, Sociology, and Anarchism* (London: Routledge 2016) 203: "The defining focus of anarchism is domination, oppressive power relations."

40 Randall Amster, *Anarchism Today* (Santa Barbara, CA: Praeger 2012) 6: "The rejection of authority is the sine qua non of anarchism."

41 Judith Suissa, *Anarchism and Education: A Philosophical Perspective* (London: Routledge 2006) 62: "the anarchist stance is, above all, not anti-state or anti-authority, but anti-hierarchy."

42 Emma Goldman, *Anarchism and Other Essays* (New York, NY: Dover 1969) 56: "Anarchism [is the] philosophy of a new social order based on liberty unrestricted by man-made law."

43 Robert Paul Wolff, *In Defense of Anarchism* (Berkeley, CA: U of California P 1998) 18: "The primary obligation of man is autonomy [and] it would seem that anarchism is the only political doctrine consistent with the virtue of autonomy."

44 Alan Carter, "Analytical Anarchism: Some Conceptual Foundations," *Political Theory* 28.2 (2000): 231: "Anarchism could be viewed as containing a normative opposition to certain substantive political inequalities, along with the empirical belief that political equality (in the sense of an absence of specific, substantive political inequalities) is inevitably undermined by state power."

45 Derry Novak, "The Place of Anarchism in the History of Political Thought," *Review of Politics* 20.3 (1958): 313: "The search for individual happiness [is] derived from the same intellectual roots from which the anarchists … draw their concept of the aim of life."

46 Benjamin Franks, "Anarchism and the Virtues," *Anarchism and Moral Philosophy*, ed. Franks and Matthew Wilson (Basingstoke: Palgrave 2010) 145: "an account of anarchism based on virtue ethics is … more consistent [than deontological or consequentialist accounts] with the broad stretch of anarchist writings and tactics."

47 Samuel Clark, "Kicking Against the Pricks: Anarchist Perfectionism and the Conditions of Independence," Franks and Wilson 33: "The crude thing I want to say is that a free, non-dominating society [i.e., anarchy] cultivates flourishing, independent individuals; that such individuals in turn support a free, non-dominating society; and that this is the best reason for advocating such a society."

48 See, for example, Alan Ritter, *Anarchism: A Theoretical Analysis* (Cambridge: CUP 1980) 38: "[Anarchists promote freedom], not as a pre-eminent good, but as a concomitant of the communal individuality that is their first concern."

49 I agree here with Suissa: "I believe that … philosophical exercises in establishing the theoretical priority of any one goal or value within anarchist thought are misconceived" (106).

50 See Benjamin Franks, "Anarchism and Moral Philosophy," *Brill's Companion to Anarchism and Philosophy*, ed. Nathan Jun (Leiden: Brill 2018) 189.

51 See Peter Marshall, "Human Nature and Anarchism," *For Anarchism: History, Theory, and Practice*, ed. David Goodway (London: Routledge 1989) 128: "while classic anarchist thinkers, such as William Godwin, Max Stirner, and Peter Kropotkin, share common assumptions about the possibility of a free society, they do not have a common view of human nature." Kropotkin does not even share a view of human nature with fellow "social anarchists" like Proudhon and Bakunin, as I have argued elsewhere. (See Paul McLaughlin, *Anarchism and Authority: A Philosophical Introduction to Classical Anarchism* [London: Routledge 2016] 17–22.) In any case, many contemporary anarchists and post-anarchists (following Marshall [138–44], albeit for different reasons) argue for "the rejection of essentialism about human nature" (Todd May, *The Political Philosophy of Poststructuralist Anarchism* [University Park, PA: Pennsylvania State UP 1994] 118).

52 Terry Eagleton, "[The Rise of Anarchism]," rev. of *The Government of No One: The Theory and Practice of Anarchism*, by Ruth Kinna, *The Guardian* (Guardian Media, Aug. 22, 2019) www.theguardian.com/books/

2019/aug/22/the-government-of-no-one-by-ruth-kinna-review-anarchism (June 16, 2020): "Anarchism isn't opposed to government as such, just to any form of it that isn't self-government."

53 David Osterfeld, "Anarchism and the Public Goods Issue: Law, Courts, and the Police," *Journal of Libertarian Studies* 9.1 (1989): 49: "It is clear from any careful reading of anarchist literature that what anarchists [including Kropotkin] oppose is not law but legislation."

54 April Carter, "Anarchism and Violence," *Nomos* 19 (1978): 320: "The attitudes to violence within the anarchist tradition are complex and contradictory, and the issue remains contentious among anarchists today."

55 Gordon 49: "Anarchists are hardly 'against power.' This common misconception is easily shown untrue by anarchist political language, in which 'empowerment' is mentioned as a positive goal."

56 Mikhail Bakunin, *Statism and Anarchy*, ed. Marshall Shatz (Cambridge: CUP 1990) 135: "We revolutionary anarchists … are enemies of the state and of any form of statehood."

57 Murray Bookchin, *Post-Scarcity Anarchism* (Montreal: Black Rose 1986) 20: "the coming [anarchist] revolution and the utopia it creates [i.e., anarchy] must be conceived of as wholes. They can leave no area of life untouched that has been contaminated by domination."

58 Mikhail Bakunin, *God and the State* (New York, NY: Dover 1970) 35: "[Anarchists] reject all legislation, all authority, and all privileged, licensed, official, and legal influence, even though arising from universal suffrage, convinced that it can turn only to the advantage of a dominant minority of exploiters against the interests of the immense majority in subjection to them."

59 Murray Bookchin, "Anarchism: Past and Present," *Reinventing Anarchy, Again*, ed. Howard J. Ehrlich (Edinburgh: AK 1996) 26: "Whatever else Anarchism meant in the past … contemporary Anarchism must address itself in the most sophisticated and radical terms to … hierarchical society, in its advanced and … terminal forms."

60 See G.P. Maximoff, ed., *The Political Philosophy of Bakunin: Scientific Anarchism* (London: Free 1953) 372ff.

61 Maximoff 253ff.

62 Scholars of anarchism have acknowledged some nuance with respect to authority, at least. See, for example, Samuel Clark, *Living without Domination: The Possibility of an Anarchist Utopia* (London: Routledge 2016) 69–70; Suissa 57–61.

63 I think Samuel Clark is wrong to claim (*Living* 9–10) that the anti-statist definition is non-distinguishing, but right to claim that it is "incomplete." An even more extreme claim for the non-distinguishing nature of this definition is made by Schmidt and van der Walt 42–3. None of the examples cited by Clark or by Schmidt and van der Walt is properly anti-statist.

64 But cp. Roderick T. Long, "Chomsky's Augustinian Anarchism," *Center for a Stateless Society* (Molinari Institute, Jan. 7, 2010) https://c4ss.org/content/1659 (June 16, 2020).

65 A. John Simmons, "The Anarchist Position: A Reply to Klosko and Senor," *Philosophy and Public Affairs* 16.3 (1987): 269–70. Suissa notes this possibility in her critical analysis of the anti-statist definition of anarchism (54–7).

66 The disposition of anarchists towards another, revised candidate for object *x*—authoritarianism as opposed to authority—is indeed oppositional, I think. (See Richard T. DeGeorge, *The Nature and Limits of Authority* [Lawrence, KS: UP of Kansas 1985] 133: "[Anarchists decry] not authority as such, but authoritarianism.") However, authoritarianism (and arguably authority as a whole) is also a token of the relevant type of object, less notable in anarchist thought than the state.

67 McLaughlin ch. 1.

68 Their concern is, I think, founded on a particular kind of intuition that I examine in "Considérations méthodologiques sur la théorie anarchiste," *Philosophie de l'anarchie: Théories libertaires, pratiques quotidiennes et ontologie*, ed. Jean-Christophe Angaut et al. (Lyon: Atelier de création libertaire 2012) 327–53.

69 McLaughlin, *Anarchism* 97.

70 McLaughlin, *Anarchism* 52.

71 John Stuart Mill, *Utilitarianism, On Liberty, and Considerations on Representative Government*, ed. H. B. Acton (London: Dent 1984) 73–4.

72 David Heyd, "Justice and Solidarity: The Contractarian Case against Global Justice," *Journal of Social Philosophy* 38.1 (2007): 113.

73 See Iain McKay et al., *An Anarchist FAQ*, 2 vols. (Chico, CA: AK 2008–12) which, while comprehensive and informative, exhibits a tendency to define anarchism to activist, revolutionary, and socialist taste. I happen to share much of this taste, but I do not try to define "anarchism" accordingly.

2

THE ANARCHIST LANDSCAPE

Roderick T. Long

I. Introduction

The anarchist landscape, like many landscapes, looks different from different vantage points within it. In particular, how one is disposed to draw the boundaries of anarchism often depends on where one is located.

Anarchists agree on rejecting the state, whatever else they disagree about. They do not necessarily agree as to what counts as rejecting the state, however. The federated workers' associations favored by anarcho-syndicalists,[1] the independent democratic communities hailed by libertarian municipalists,[2] and the private security systems advocated by many market anarchists,[3] each strike one anarchist camp or another as states in anarchist guise. My present concern, however, is primarily with anarchist disagreements as to what, if anything, anarchism involves, or should involve, *beyond* opposition to the state.

II. Varieties of Individualism

The terms "social anarchism" and "individualist anarchism" are often used to distinguish two major branches within anarchism. But matters are immediately more complicated. By one accounting, the two groups differ over the role of markets, economic competition, and private ownership in an anarchist society: social anarchists (whether communistic, collectivistic, or syndicalist) tend either to oppose these outright or else to regard their role as properly marginal, seeing them as potential tools of domination and exploitation; for individualist anarchists, by contrast, private ownership is the embodied form that liberty takes, and market competition plays a crucial role in maintaining social cooperation.[4]

But the term "individualist anarchism" is also used quite differently, to refer to forms of anarchism centered on an amoralist egoism based on or in the same vein as the ideas of Max Stirner.[5] While social anarchists, in characterizing their rivals, have often taken Stirnerism and support for markets together as defining features of individualist anarchism, most of the major nineteenth-century thinkers usually identified as individualist anarchists (including Thomas Hodgskin,[6] Josiah Warren,[7] Stephen Pearl Andrews,[8] Ezra and Angela Heywood,[9] Lysander Spooner,[10] William B. Greene,[11] Moses and Lillian Harman,[12] Dyer Lum,[13] and Voltairine de Cleyre[14]) either predated Stirner, ignored him, or explicitly rejected him, and embraced a moralistic orientation Stirner would have found uncongenial.

Even the best-known Stirner enthusiast, Benjamin Tucker,[15] had already become an anarchist before reading a word of Stirner;[16] and after reading him, Tucker seems to have simply picked up his existing system of anarchistic thought and plopped it down onto its new Stirnerist foundations, with only the slightest resulting shifts in the overall structure. Indeed, the contractarian version of Stirnerism that Tucker developed lays such heavy emphasis on Stirner's cooperative dimension (such as the idea of a "Union of Egoists") and so little emphasis on Stirner's moral nihilism (his regarding other people as "food," for example) that Tucker's fellow Stirnerist Dora Marsden, in her debate with Tucker in the pages of her journals *The New Freewoman* and *The Egoist* (1913–1914), could fairly charge him with being a moralist in Stirnerist guise.[17] Tucker often seems to be more an *ethical egoist* after the model of Epicurus[18] or Ayn Rand[19]—one who seeks to ground morality, including a commitment to mutual respect for rights, on egoistic foundations—than the kind of moral nihilist that at least some of Stirner's pages seem to license. (Similar remarks would apply to many thinkers influenced by Tucker, such as Francis Tandy,[20] as well as to more independent anarchist theorists like Anselme Bellegarrigue.[21])

Just as individualism in the market sense need not entail individualism in the Stirnerist sense, so the entailment does not run in the other direction either. There are Stirnerist egoist communists, such as the authors of the 1974 pamphlet *The Right To Be Greedy: Theses On The Practical Necessity Of Demanding Everything*;[22] and there are currents, often labelled "individualist," ranging from the "post-left anarchism" of such thinkers as Bob Black[23] and Wolfi Landstreicher[24] to the views of the eco-terrorist group ITS (Individualists Tending Toward Savagery, aka Individualists Tending toward the Wild),[25] which embrace the moral nihilist strand in Stirner but show no particular affinity for markets. Indeed Stirner himself, while clearly rejecting communism, gives little clear indication as to what economic arrangements he favors; he uses the *language* of private property, but only to say that the true egoist regards everything in the world, including other people, as his own property—which is not the kind of commitment to property that represents a recognition of other people's property rights.

To complicate matters still further, there are thinkers routinely identified as individualist anarchists who *neither* express much enthusiasm for markets *nor* embrace Stirner-style amoralism; examples include Leda Rafanelli, Émile Armand, Han Ryner, and André Lorulot.[26] These thinkers seem to be counted as individualist anarchists simply because they advocated an individualist ethics; but by that standard Emma Goldman, undisputedly a communist anarchist, would have to be reckoned an individualist too, for her ethical views were certainly staunchly individualist.[27] It's not clear that the category is being employed with any great consistency or precision.

Even leaving aside the latter group, it seems safe to say that the label "individualist anarchism" in fact applies to, at the very least, two distinct groups, only barely overlapping—a market-focused one and a Stirner-focused one. Let's leave the Stirner-focused one aside in turn, and consider the market-focused one.

While some anarchists have taken a "let a hundred flowers bloom" approach, seeing market-based and communal forms of anarchism as compatible,[28] for the most part social anarchists and individualist anarchists have regarded each other's positions as misguided. Communist anarchists like Pëtr Kropotkin, for example, argued that individualist anarchism was an unstable combination, and that its proponents would eventually be driven to give up either their anarchism or their individualism.[29] Conversely, individualist anarchists like John Henry Mackay argued that it was communist anarchism that was unstable and that its proponents would eventually be driven to give up either their anarchism or their communism.[30] Nevertheless, with some exceptions, each camp has regarded the adherents of the other as heretics rather than infidels—that is, as deviationists within the anarchist fold rather than as anarchists in name only.

The nineteenth-century thinkers I've mentioned above, in the market-focused individualist anarchist group, while supporting free markets, economic competition, and private ownership, generally opposed what they called "capitalism," meaning the concentration of ownership of the means of production in a small number of hands, thereby requiring most people outside this privileged group to perform wage labour for them on pain of starvation. But, in the twentieth century, a movement arose within the free-market libertarian movement calling itself "anarcho-capitalist," and claiming to be continuing the legacy of individualist anarchism; Murray Rothbard[31] and David Friedman[32] are among the most prominent writers in this group.

III. "Libertarian" Clarifications

Before considering the place, if any, of anarcho-capitalism on the anarchist landscape, let's turn aside briefly to discuss the term "libertarian." Originally this was a generic term for an advocate of freedom of any sort (including not just political freedom but also, for example, metaphysical free will—a meaning it still bears in the free will literature today). Starting around the 1970s, the term came to be generally understood as referring specifically to a radical free-market philosophy (chosen as a replacement for "liberal," which in the twentieth century had lost its earlier free-market associations, especially in the U.S.). But "libertarian" had long been used (and to some degree continues to be used) in the anarchist movement either as a synonym for "anarchist"—and in particular for "social anarchist" (although its use by individualist anarchists is also quite early)[33]—or else for a range of positions only slightly broader than anarchism.[34] The first use of "libertarian"—or rather its French equivalent, *libertaire*—to refer to an adherent of a specific political position rather than to an advocate of freedom more generally, was by the anarcho-communist Joseph Déjacque in 1857.[35] (Nowadays, French has two different equivalents of "libertarian": *libertaire*, meaning an anarchist, and the hideously un-French-looking *libertarien*, meaning a free-market radical.)

In the 1970s, in response to the wider usage of "libertarian" in the free-market sense, many social anarchists started referring to themselves as *left*-libertarians, and categorizing the free-market variety as right-libertarians. However, in the very same period, many free-market libertarians (such as Samuel Konkin[36] and Roy Childs[37]) had independently started using the term "left-libertarian" differently, to refer to the left wing of the free-market libertarian movement (essentially, those who saw the New Left student movement more as allies than as opponents). Thus the very same thinkers might well count as right-libertarians by the first criterion and as left-libertarians by the second. To add to the confusion, in the 1990s and early 2000s, many analytic philosophers, apparently unaware of the two earlier meanings, began using "left-libertarian" with yet a third meaning, to refer to a position that combined individual self-ownership with common ownership of resources, without necessarily endorsing anarchism (though some left-libertarians in this sense are also anarchists).[38]

IV. Anarchists and Markets

In any case, anarcho-capitalists, as I said, are free-market libertarians who identify with the individualist anarchist heritage; but this identification is controversial, as the main line of individualist anarchism has historically rejected capitalism. But anarcho-capitalists (or "ancaps") can point to a number of more-or-less capitalist thinkers in the nineteenth century who are clear precursors of the anarcho-capitalist position, such as Herbert Spencer, Gustave de Molinari, Auberon Herbert, and Wordsworth Donisthorpe; and while these thinkers generally did not apply the anarchist label to themselves, it must be borne in mind that a number of anti-capitalist individualists (such as Warren, Andrews, Greene, and Spooner) did not use the label either.

But social anarchists, for the most part, grant heretic status to anti-capitalists like Tucker and Spooner, regarding them as misguided fellow anarchists, while treating ancaps as outsiders—fake anarchists and fake libertarians. And ancaps have largely returned the favor—not denying social anarchists' status as anarchists (social anarchists are far too well embedded in anarchist history for that to be a plausible move) but denying social anarchists' status as libertarians. For most social anarchists, capitalism is inherently a system of domination and exploitation, opposition to which is an essential part of any libertarian or anarchist project worthy of those names; for ancaps, by contrast, capitalism properly understood is a system of liberty, to which no true libertarian, surely, could be opposed.

Is this dispute over "capitalism" terminological or substantive? As is often the case with these sorts of disputes, it is some of each. By "capitalism," most ancaps mean not the concentration of ownership of the means of production in the hands of an employing class, but simply free markets and private property. By that definition, individualist anarchists like Tucker and Spooner count as pro-capitalist. (Tucker's views on land ownership differ from those that prevail among ancaps, but Spooner's don't, especially.[39] And Spencer is generally treated as a proto-ancap even though his views of land are even more "socialistic" than Tucker's[40] and he also favored replacing wage labour with workers' cooperatives[41]—whereas the "socialistic" Tucker, unlike both Spooner and Spencer, had no objection to wage labour so long as the labour market was properly flat and competitive.)[42] Notably, Voltairine de Cleyre was willing to call her own position, albeit with tongue half in cheek, "capitalistic anarchism" in her 1891 critique of communism.[43] In Thomas Hobbes's words: "Words are wise men's counters, they do but reckon by them; but they are the money of fools."[44]

But the disagreement is more than merely terminological. While ancaps do not make economic concentration and the wage system a *definitional* part of the capitalism they defend, most of them do regard such features as likely, and acceptable, consequences of a free market; whereas the anti-capitalist individualists reject them. Should this disagreement exclude ancaps from being part of the individualist anarchist tradition? Most social anarchists think it should; most ancaps think it shouldn't.

Historically, most individualist anarchists—meaning those recognized by social anarchists as genuine if misguided anarchists—have thought it shouldn't either. Tucker, for example, although he believed and hoped that anarchism would bring about a more economically egalitarian society, took this as an empirical prediction rather than as a matter of definition, and moreover insisted that he would still be committed to anarchism, albeit less enthusiastically so, should the prediction prove mistaken;[45] moreover, proto-ancaps Molinari, Herbert, and Donisthorpe were hailed in the pages of Tucker's journal *Liberty*, the foremost individualist anarchist periodical, as fellow individualist anarchists or nearly so, despite their capitalist tendencies.[46] Indeed, social anarchists undertaking to tell individualist anarchists who counts as a true individualist anarchist can seem a bit presumptuous, like Catholics undertaking to tell Episcopalians whether Mormons count as Protestants.

But since the boundaries of individualist anarchism are in fact disputed, let's substitute the term "market anarchism," meaning any version of anarchism that gives free markets and private property an essential coordinating role in an anarchist society. ("Essential" need not mean "exclusive"; many versions of market anarchism also make room for communal property.)[47] Contemporary continuators of the nineteenth-century individualist anarchist movement (such as Kevin Carson, Charles Johnson, Gary Chartier, William Gillis, and others associated with the Center for a Stateless Society) have made use of the label "left-wing market anarchist" (or "LWMA"), so we can treat the LWMAs as one wing of the market anarchist movement (applying the term retroactively to the Spooner–Tucker group as well), and assign the anarcho-capitalists to the other wing—while reserving debate as to whether all market anarchists, or only the LWMA wing thereof, count as *genuine* anarchists. (LWMAs can also be seen as the anarchist wing of left-libertarianism, in the second of the three senses of "left-libertarian" distinguished above.)

Let me note in passing a further complication: social anarchists and LWMAs share not only an opposition to capitalism but also an opposition to various other forms of oppression, including hierarchies of race, gender, and the like; such opposition is often seen as a crucial part of the "left" in "left-wing market anarchism" (as well as in "left-libertarian").[48] Some anarcho-capitalists share this opposition as well, but others see such issues as irrelevant to their concerns, while still others see hierarchies of race and/or gender as "natural" and worthy of defense; and this has sometimes served as another basis for excluding anarcho-capitalists (all or some) from the anarchist ranks. To be sure, Pierre-Joseph Proudhon, the first thinker to use the "anarchist" label himself, has been claimed for both the social and individualist anarchist traditions (as has the mutualist tradition he inaugurated), despite Proudhon's own intense antisemitism, misogyny, and homophobia. Presumably he is given a pass because he lived in the nineteenth century; but his own anarchist contemporaries were not always so obliging. In fact, the term "libertarian" (or *libertaire*) in its anarchist use was coined by Déjacque as part of a polemic against Proudhon, arguing that Proudhon could be no true libertarian so long as he denied women equal status with men. (Déjacque would go on, in the following year, to use *Le Libertaire* as the title of his journal.)

Returning specifically to the issue of "capitalism," the social anarchist basis for excluding ancaps from the anarchist ranks is not always clear. Precisely what features of ancaps' support for capitalism renders them ineligible for the status of genuine anarchists? It's hard to find any criterion that won't also rule out some LWMAs whom social anarchists want to rule in. For example, social anarchists sometimes point to ancaps' support for private security firms as evidence of crypto-statism; yet LWMAs Tucker, Spooner, and Bellegarrigue, acknowledged by social anarchists to be genuine if misguided anarchists, also supported private security firms. Again, social anarchists will point to ancaps' support for rent and wage labour as incompatible with anarchism. Well, Tucker opposed rent but not wage labour, regarding the latter as no longer exploitative once the wage *system*—the *necessity* to work for others, or starve—had been eliminated; Spooner, by contrast, opposed wage labour but not rent. And not only will these criteria rule out some LWMAs whom social anarchists want to rule in, but they also run the risk of ruling in some ancaps that social anarchists want to rule out; for example, at the time that ancap David Friedman wrote the second edition of his most famous book, *The Machinery of Freedom*, he was also opposed to the wage system;[49] but I'm not aware that any social anarchist has seen this as a reason to welcome *The Machinery of Freedom* into the anarchist canon.

V. Distinguishable Tendencies

But if the criteria for inclusion or exclusion are not completely precise, they are not completely arbitrary either. If we think of political groupings as picked out by family-resemblance concepts rather than by specifications of necessary and sufficient conditions, then it seems reasonable to take social anarchists, LWMAs, and ancaps as forming three camps within which, whatever deviations toward one camp some individuals in another camp may have with respect to this or that specific issue, it will still be the case that members of each camp share a greater ideological resemblance to one another than to those in either of the other two camps.

It will also be the case, though, that LWMAs share more affiliations with each of the other two camps than those two camps share with each other. This is seen, for example, in the fact that while it is rare to find social anarchists favorably citing Rothbard, or ancaps favorably citing Kropotkin, LWMAs are frequently to be found citing both favorably (albeit not uncritically). Social anarchists' greater affinity with LWMAs than with ancaps explains why social anarchists have found it easy to think of themselves and LWMAs as belonging to a common "anarchist" tradition from which ancaps are excluded. And, by the same token, ancaps' greater affinity with LWMAs than with social anarchists explains why ancaps have found it correspondingly easy to think of themselves and LWMAs as belonging to a common "individualist anarchist" tradition from which social anarchists are excluded. And those affinities also explain why LWMAs have historically been friendlier toward both the social anarchist and the ancap camps than those camps have been toward each other.

I don't mean to give the impression that LWMAs can always be counted on to welcome both social anarchists and ancaps as fellow anarchists, or that social anarchists and ancaps can always be counted on to exclude each other while welcoming LWMAs as fellow anarchists. There are always cases of individuals either more or less accepting than this stereotype would suggest. At one point in his career, for example, social anarchist Murray Bookchin was enthusiastic about having right-wing libertarians as allies.[50] (In later and grumpier life he rejected them as fake libertarians;[51] but then again, in later and grumpier life Bookchin rejected most participants in the anarchist movement in general as fake libertarians.[52]) Tucker,[53] while (as noted above) accepting capitalist antistatists as genuine albeit misguided anarchists or near-anarchists, grew increasingly inclined over the course of his career to write anarcho-communists like Kropotkin, Johann Most, and the Haymarket martyrs out of the movement. And neither social anarchist nor ancap acceptance of LWMAs should be exaggerated.

> One thing that (many) social anarchists and (many) ancaps have in common is that they recognise anticapitalist individualist market anarchists as valuable comrades (albeit erring ones) as long as they're dead 19th-century figures like Benjamin Tucker, Lysander Spooner, and Voltairine de Cleyre, and even include them in their favourite anthologies, but as soon as they encounter actual living 21st-century examples of anticapitalist individualist market anarchists, they cringe in horror and shriek either 'capitalist!' or 'commie!' depending on the direction of deviation.[54]

Nevertheless, it remains true *on the whole* that social anarchists and ancaps are readier to recognize LWMAs as deviationists within the fold, while anathematizing each other, and that LWMAs are readier to recognize both social anarchists and ancaps as deviationists within the fold.

If anarchism is concerned with opposition to domination, then social anarchism, which is highly sensitive to ways in which private property relations can enable domination, but relatively insensitive to ways in which *interference* with private property relations can do so—and anarcho-capitalism, which conversely is highly sensitive to ways in which interference with private property a relations can enable domination, but relatively insensitive to ways in which private property relations *themselves* can do so—each seem to be specializing in opposition to one aspect of domination while neglecting another aspect. From that perspective, the LWMA approach seems to represent a more systematic opposition to domination, in virtue of synthesizing the concerns of both of its main rivals without falling prey to the one-sidedness of either.

VI. Left-Wing Market Anarchism as a Mediating Position

There is actually one affiliation that social anarchists and ancaps share with each other and not with LWMAs, and that is the tendency either to identify free markets with capitalism (in the sense of economic concentration and a wage system), or else to assume that the former naturally leads to the latter. The difference is one of evaluation; social anarchists take the case against capitalism (so understood) to constitute a case against free markets, whereas ancaps take the case for free markets to constitute a case for capitalism. For LWMAs, by contrast, free markets and capitalism are incompatible; competition is a natural levelling force, since if one person or group is raking in profits by providing some good or service, then others will imitate them if not prohibited from doing so—and so capitalism is a product of government intervention that could not survive on a free market.[55]

And this is why who counts as an anarchist, or as a libertarian, seems to depend on where on the anarchist landscape one is oneself located. It's natural to take one's own preferred form of anarchism as representing the core of anarchism; slight deviations from that core will still fall within the boundaries, while large deviations from it will fall outside. On economic issues, from the social anarchist perspective, LWMAs are at least half-right (laudably anti-capitalist, mistakenly pro-market) while ancaps are completely wrong (mistakenly pro-capitalist *and* pro-market). Conversely, from the ancap perspective, LWMAs are again at least half-right (laudably pro-market, mistakenly anti-capitalist) while social anarchists are completely wrong (mistakenly anti-market *and* anti-capitalist). But from the LWMA perspective, social anarchists (laudably anti-capitalist, mistakenly anti-market) and ancaps (laudably pro-market, mistakenly pro-capitalist) are each half-right. (Social anarchists like to put the "anarcho" in "anarcho-capitalist" in scare quotes; LWMA Anna Morgenstern has argued that instead it is the "capitalist" in "anarcho-capitalist" that should be put in scare quotes, since implementing ancaps' preferred policies would in fact dismantle capitalism, whether or not ancaps realize this.)[56]

For social anarchists, social anarchism naturally represents the main line of anarchism; LWMAs are deviationists close enough to be within the fold, while ancaps are distant enough to be beyond the pale. For ancaps, it is anarcho-capitalism that represents the main line, if not of anarchism, then at least of libertarianism; LWMAs are deviationists close enough to be within the fold, but social anarchists are beyond the pale. For LWMAs, by contrast, it is the LWMA position that is the main line of anarchism and libertarianism—not in terms of numbers (LWMAs represent a tiny group compared to the other two, a mouse squeezed between the social anarchist elephant and the ancap bear) but in terms of the "objective tendency of the problematic"; and social anarchists and ancaps are both close enough to count as deviationists within the fold rather than outsiders.

Does this mean that one must first decide which purported version of anarchism is most defensible in order to decide which positions are genuinely anarchist, or genuinely libertarian? That would be awkward; in particular, it would leave those who find all purported versions of anarchism or libertarianism equally unappealing with no way of determining any boundaries for the concept. I think we can do a bit better; more precisely, I think there are grounds for accepting the LWMAs' more eclectic drawing of the boundaries even if one is not oneself an LWMA. Fair warning, though: since I am myself an LWMA, my argument might reasonably be taken as a product of LWMA bias. I hope not, but the danger should be kept in mind.

(Note that while I'll be defending an ecumenical view of the anarchist landscape, according to which social anarchists, LWMAs, and ancaps all count as anarchists and libertarians, I do not mean to give the impression that *every* self-described anarchist or libertarian thinker or group should be welcomed in as part of the fold. So-called "national anarchists," for example, while sharing genuine points of affiliation with various forms of anarchism, share far more in common with fascism; and as I take fascism to be point-for-point the polar opposite of anarchism in any of its forms, being more closely affiliated with fascism than with anarchism necessarily means not being a genuine anarchist.)

There are good reasons to regard left-wing market anarchism as standing at the center of the libertarian and anarchist traditions, even if one does not regard it as the most defensible version of anarchism. Nicolas Walter, a social anarchist and historian of anarchism, has stressed anarchism's historical dependence on both (state) socialism and (classical) liberalism.[57] If social anarchism and anarcho-capitalism represent the fullest anarchistic developments of each of these lineages respectively, left-wing market anarchism combines both lineages the most equally.

To be sure, if one focuses solely on the social anarchist and ancap positions (which is easy to do, since they are both more prominent than the LWMA position), the two seem so different that it's easy to come to the conclusion that there's no wider tradition to which both belong. But once the LWMA position is brought clearly into view, its web of affiliation with the other two positions makes it easier to see how all three are part of a common conversation, with LWMAs as the chief mediator. Historically, the conversation can be seen in such phenomena as the mutual influence between Molinari and Proudhon;[58] Tucker's engagement with Herbert and Donisthorpe in the pages of *Liberty*; Sophie Raffalovich's treatment of the Boston Anarchists in Molinari's journal;[59] Dyer Lum's association first with Tucker and later with Albert and Lucy Parsons; de Cleyre's association first with Tucker and then with Goldman and Berkman; the membership of Warren, Andrews, and Greene (and, according to one source,[60] Spooner, though this is doubtful) in the First International; and the influence of proto-ancap class theory on LWMA Hodgskin, and through him on ancaps, LWMAs, and social anarchists alike.

And once one recognizes those affiliations between social anarchists and ancaps that are mediated by LWMAs, it becomes easier to see the significance of those (admittedly fewer) affiliations between social anarchists and ancaps that are *not* so mediated, such as Kropotkin's and Goldman's admiration for proto-ancap Spencer; Spencer's call (even in his more conservative later years) for replacing the wage system with workers' cooperatives; Kropotkin's singing the praises of private enterprise;[61] Rothbard's call for the return of conquistador-stolen land to the peasants[62] and the takeover of government-privileged corporations by their workers;[63] and the enthusiasm for the free mercantile cities of the late mediæval period that unites social anarchists like Kropotkin and Bookchin with proto-ancaps like Augustin Thierry (whom Kropotkin frequently cites) and Charles Dunoyer.[64]

VII. Conclusion

Seen from either the social anarchist or the anarcho-capitalist region of the anarchist landscape, the corresponding region can easily look so distant and so different that it's easy to relegate it to an alien and hostile territory. But, I've argued, once one carefully surveys the intermediate, left-wing market anarchist region, the deep intertwining of root and branch among all three traditions comes more clearly into view.

Social anarchist John Clark offers an apposite observation in his article "Bridging the Unbridgeable Chasm." The purported chasm he has in mind is not the one between social anarchism and anarcho-capitalism, and I have no reason to think he would agree with my use of it here (in fact I have some reason to think he wouldn't).[65] But I do think it applies:

> The idea that there is an 'unbridgeable chasm' between two viewpoints that share certain common presuppositions and goals, and whose practices are in some ways interrelated, is a bit suspect from the outset. It is particularly problematic when proposed by a thinker like Bookchin, who claims to hold a dialectical perspective. Whereas nondialectical thought merely opposes one reality to another in an abstract manner, or else places them inertly beside one another, a dialectical analysis examines the ways in which various realities presuppose one another, constitute one another, challenge the identity of one another, and push one another to the limits of their development. Accordingly, one important quality of such an analysis is that it helps those with divergent viewpoints see the ways in which their positions are not mutually exclusive but can instead be mutually realized in a further development of each.[66]

This passage perfectly describes what I see as the relationship among social anarchism, anarcho-capitalism, and left-wing market anarchism.[67]

Notes

1 See, for example, Rudolf Rocker, *Anarcho-Syndicalism: Theory and Practice* (Oakland, CA: AK 2004).

2 See, for example, Murray Bookchin, *The Next Revolution: Popular Assemblies and the Promise of Direct Democracy*, ed. Debbie Bookchin and Blair Taylor (London: Verso 2015).

3 See, for example, Edward P. Stringham, ed., *Anarchy and the Law: The Political Economy of Choice* (Oakland, CA: Independent 2007).

4 This disagreement is complicated, however, by the fact that the different camps do not all use the term "property" with the same meaning; see Kevin Carson, "Are We All Mutualists?" *Center for a Stateless Society* (Molinari Institute, Nov. 8, 2015) https://c4ss.org/content/40929 (June 15, 2020).

5 Max Stirner, *The Ego and Its Own*, ed. David Leopold, trans. Steven T. Byington and Leopold (Cambridge: CUP 1995).

6 David Stack, *Nature and Artifice: The Life and Thought of Thomas Hodgskin (1787–1869)* (Woodbridge: Boydell 1998).

7 Crispin Sartwell, ed., *The Practical Anarchist: Writings of Josiah Warren* (New York, NY: Fordham UP 2018).

8 Madeleine B. Stern, *The Pantarch: A Biography of Stephen Pearl Andrews* (Austin, TX: U of Texas P 1968).

9 Henry Blatt, *Free Love and Anarchism: The Biography of Ezra Heywood* (Chicago, IL: U Illinois P 1989).

10 Steve J. Shone, *Lysander Spooner: American Anarchist* (Lanham, MD: Lexington 2010).

11 James J. Martin, *Men Against the State: The Expositors of Individualist Anarchism in America, 1827–1908* (Colorado Springs, CO: Myles 1970) 125–38.

12 Hal D. Sears, *The Sex Radicals: Free Love in High Victorian America* (Lawrence, KS: UP of Kansas 1977).

13 Frank H. Brooks, "Anarchism, Revolution, and Labor in the Thought of Dyer D. Lum: 'Events Are the True Schoolmasters'" (PhD diss, Cornell U, 1988).

14 Sharon Presley and Crispin Sartwell, eds., *Exquisite Rebel: The Essays of Voltairine de Cleyre—Anarchist, Feminist, Genius* (Albany, NY: SUNY 2012).

15 Benjamin R. Tucker, *Instead of a Book, by a Man Too Busy to Write One: A Fragmentary Exposition of Individualist Anarchism* (New York, NY: Tucker 1893).

16 Benjamin R. Tucker, "The Life of Benjamin R. Tucker: Disclosed by Himself in the Principality of Monaco at the Age of 74," unpublished ms., New York Public Library archives (Tucker collection) [transcribed by Wendy McElroy] www.wendymcelroy.com/plugins/content/content.php?content.57.

17 Sidney E. Parker, "*The New Freewoman*: Dora Marsden & Benjamin R. Tucker," *Benjamin R. Tucker and the Champions of Liberty: A Centenary Anthology*, ed. Michael E. Coughlin, Charles H. Hamilton, and Mark A. Sullivan (St Paul, MN: Coughlin 1987) 149–57.

18 Phillip Mitsis, *Epicurus' Ethical Theory: The Pleasures of Invulnerability* (Ithaca, NY: Cornell UP 1988).

19 Douglas J. Den Uyl and Douglas B. Rasmussen, eds., *The Philosophic Thought of Ayn Rand* (Urbana, IL: U of Illinois P 1986).

20 Francis Dashwood Tandy, *Voluntary Socialism: A Sketch* (Denver, CO: Tandy 1896).

21 Michel Perraudeau, *Anselme Bellegarrigue: Le Premier des Libertaires* (Saint-Georges-d'Oléron: Libertaires 2012).

22 For Ourselves: The Council for Generalized Self-Management, *The Right to be Greedy: Theses on the Practical Necessity of Demanding Everything* [1974], ed. Bob Black (Port Townsend, WA: Loompanics 1983).

23 Bob Black, *The Abolition of Work and Other Essays* (Port Townsend, WA: Loompanics 1986); Bob Black, *Anarchy After Leftism* (Oakland, CA: CAL 1997).

24 Wolfi Landstreicher, *The Network of Domination: Anarchist Analyses of the Institutions, Structures and Systems of Domination and Exploitation to be Debated, Developed and Acted Upon* (Olympia, WA: Last Word); Wolfi Landstreicher, *Willful Disobedience* (San Francisco: Ardent 2009).

25 Individualists Tending toward the Wild, *The Collected Communiques of Individualists Tending toward the Wild* (n.p.: Plain Words 2012).

26 For the first, see Andrea Pakieser, ed., *I Belong Only to Myself: The Life and Writings of Leda Rafanelli* (Oakland, CA: AK 2014); for the latter three, see *Down with the Law: Anarchist Individualist Writings from Early Twentieth-Century France*, ed. and trans. Mitchell Abidor (Chico, CA: AK 2019).

27 See, for example, Emma Goldman, *The Individual, Society and the State* (Chicago, IL: Free Society 1940).

28 For example, Fred Woodworth explains: "I have no prefix or adjective for my anarchism. I think syndicalism can work, as can free-market anarcho-capitalism, anarcho-communism, even anarcho-hermits, depending on the situation." Qtd. Paul Avrich, ed., *Anarchist Voices: An Oral History of Anarchism in America*, 2d ed. (Edinburgh: AK 2005) 475.

29 Peter Kropotkin, "A Few Thoughts About the Essence of Anarchism," *Direct Struggle against Capital: A Peter Kropotkin Anthology*, ed. Iain McKay (Oakland, CA: AK 2014) 201–4.

30 John Henry Mackay, *The Anarchists: A Picture of Civilization at the Close of the Nineteenth Century*, trans. George Schumm (Boston, MA: Tucker 1894) 145–7.
31 Murray N. Rothbard, *The Ethics of Liberty* (New York, NY: New York UP 1998); Murray N. Rothbard, *For a New Liberty: The Libertarian Manifesto*, 2d ed. (Auburn, AL: Mises 2006).
32 David D. Friedman, *The Machinery of Freedom: Guide to a Radical Capitalism*, 3d ed. (Charleston, SC: CreateSpace 2015).
33 See, for example, Benjamin R. Tucker, "A Want Supplied," *Liberty* 3.13 (Aug. 15, 1885): 4.
34 See, for example, Charles T. Sprading, ed., *Liberty and the Great Libertarians: An Anthology of Liberty, a Hand-book of Freedom* (Los Angeles, CA: Sprading 1913).
35 Joseph Déjacque, *De l'être-humain mâle et femelle: Lettre à P.J. Proudhon* (New Orleans, LA: Lamarre 1857).
36 Samuel Edward Konkin III, "SEK3's History of the Libertarian Movement," *Center for a Stateless Society* (Molinari Institute, Dec. 7, 2012) http://c4ss.org/content/13240 (June 15, 2020).
37 Roy A. Childs, Jr., "How Bad is the U.S. Government?" *The Abolitionist* 2.2 (May 1971): 2–3, www.unz.org/Pub/Abolitionist-1971may-00002.
38 Peter Vallentyne and Hillel Steiner, eds., *Left Libertarianism and Its Critics: The Contemporary Debate* (London: Palgrave 2000); Michael Otsuka, *Libertarianism without Inequality* (Oxford: OUP 2005); Eric Roark, *Removing the Commons: A Lockean Left-Libertarian Approach to the Just Use and Appropriation of Natural Resources* (Lanham, MD: Lexington 2013).
39 Roderick T. Long, "Spooner on Rent," *Austro-Athenian Empire* (n.p., Feb. 21, 2006) http://praxeology.net/unblog02-06.htm#12 (June 15, 2020). For arguments that the difference between Tuckerite occupancy-and-use views and Lockean absentee-ownership views is in large part one of degree more than of kind, see Carson, "Mutualists," and Jason Lee Byas, "How Rothbardians Occupy Part of the Occupancy and Use Spectrum," *Center for a Stateless Society* (Molinari Institute, Nov. 23, 2015) https://c4ss.org/content/41581 (June 15, 2020).
40 Herbert Spencer, *Social Statics: Or, the Conditions Essential to Human Happiness Specified, and the First of Them Developed* (London: Chapman 1851) chs 9–10.
41 Herbert Spencer, *Principles of Sociology*, 3 vols. (New York, NY: Appleton 1896) 3: 535–74 (§§825-39).
42 Benjamin R. Tucker, "Should Labor Be Paid or Not?" *Liberty* 5.19 (April 28, 1888): 4; Benjamin R. Tucker, "Solutions of the Labor Problem," *Liberty* 8.14 (Sep. 12, 1891): 2–3.
43 Rosa Slobodinsky [Rachelle Yarros] and Voltairine de Cleyre, "The Individualist and the Communist: A Dialogue," *Twentieth Century* 6.25 (June 18, 1891): 3–6.
44 Thomas Hobbes, *Leviathan* (London: Crooke 1651) 1.4.
45 Benjamin R. Tucker, "Why I Am an Anarchist," *Twentieth Century* 4.22 (May 29, 1890): 5–6; cp. Benjamin R. Tucker, "Neglected Factors in the Rent Problem," *Liberty* 10.16 (Dec. 15, 1894): 4. And compare, from the other side, social anarchist David Graeber's affirmation that he would still endorse anarchism even if markets turned out to play a more central and crucial role in anarchist society than he predicts: Graeber, *The Democracy Project: A History, a Crisis, a Movement* (New York, NY: Spiegel 2013) 193.
46 Benjamin R. Tucker, "Auberon Herbert and his Work," *Liberty* 3.10 (May 23, 1885): 4–5; Benjamin R. Tucker, "A Prophecy in Course of Fulfillment," Liberty 5.18 (April 14, 1888): 7–8; S. R. [S. H. Randall], "An Economist on the Future Society," *Liberty* 14.23 (Sep. 1904): 2.
47 This is true not only of many anti-capitalist individualists (see, for example, James Tuttle, ed., *The Anatomy of Escape: A Defense of the Commons* [Tulsa, OK: Center for a Stateless Society 2019] but even of some pro-capitalist ones (see, for example, Randall G. Holcombe, "Common Property in Anarcho-Capitalism," *Journal of Libertarian Studies* 19.2 (2005): 3–29, https://cdn.mises.org/19_2_1.pdf.
48 See, for example, Gary Chartier, *Anarchy and Legal Order: Law and Politics for a Stateless Society* (Cambridge: CUP 2012) 378–86; Gary Chartier, "The Distinctiveness of Left-Libertarianism," *Bleeding Heart Libertarians* (n.p., Nov. 5, 2012) http://bleedingheartlibertarians.com/2012/11/the-distinctiveness-of-left-libertarianism/ (June 15, 2020); Kevin A. Carson, "Class vs. 'Identity Politics,' Intersectionality, Etc.: Some General Observations," *Center for a Stateless Society* (Molinari Institute, March 26, 2013) https://c4ss.org/content/17886; Kevin A. Carson, "What is Left-Libertarianism?" *Center for a Stateless Society* (Molinari Institute, June 15, 2014) http://c4ss.org/content/28216 (June 15, 2020); Charles W. Johnson, "Liberty, Equality, Solidarity: Toward a Dialectical Anarchism," *Anarchism/Minarchism: Is a Government Part of a Free Country?* ed. Roderick T. Long and Tibor R. Machan (Aldershot: Ashgate 2008) 155–88, http://radgeek.com/gt/2010/03/02/liberty-equality-solidarity-toward-a-dialectical-anarchism; Charles W. Johnson, "Women and the Invisible Fist: How Violence Against Women Enforces the Unwritten Law of Patriarchy" (unpublished essay 2013): http://charleswjohnson.name/essays/women-and-the-invisible-fist/women-and-the-invisible-fist-2013-0503-max.pdf (June 15, 2020); Roderick T. Long and Charles W. Johnson, "Libertarian Feminism: Can This Marriage Be Saved?" (unpublished essay, May 1, 2005) http://charleswjohnson.name/essays/

libertarian-feminism/; Billy Christmas, "Libertarianism and Privilege," *Molinari Review* 1.1 (Spring 2016): 24–46, http://praxeology.net/MR1-1-S16-CHRISTMAS.pdf.

49 Friedman 144–5 (the text of the third edition is unchanged from that of the second in this regard, though the third edition does include a note in an appendix [334–5] indicating that he's subsequently changed his mind).

50 Jeff Riggenbach, "Interview with Murray Bookchin," *Reason*, Oct. 1979, 34–38, https://reason.com/1979/10/01/interview-with-murray-bookchin/; cp. Jesse Walker, "Murray Bookchin, RIP," *Reason*, July 31, 2006, https://reason.com/2006/07/31/murray-bookchin-rip/.

51 Murray Bookchin, "What is Communalism? The Democratic Dimension of Anarchism," *Democracy and Nature* 3.2 (1995): 1–17, www.democracynature.org/vol3/bookchin_communalism.htm.

52 Murray Bookchin, *Social Anarchism or Lifestyle Anarchism: The Unbridgeable Chasm* (San Francisco, CA: AK 1995); Murray Bookchin, *The Next Revolution: Popular Assemblies and the Promise of Direct Democracy*, ed. Debbie Bookchin and Blair Taylor (London: Verso 2015).

53 Benjamin R. Tucker, "General Walker and the Anarchists," *Liberty* 5.8 (Nov. 19, 1887): 4–5, 8.

54 Roderick T. Long, "They Love Us When We're Dead," *Center for a Stateless Society* (Molinari Institute, Dec. 11, 2016) https://c4ss.org/content/47199 (June 15, 2020).

55 For defense of the LWMA position, see Gary Chartier and Charles W. Johnson, eds., *Markets Not Capitalism: Individualist Anarchism against Bosses, Inequality, Corporate Power, and Structural Poverty* (New York, NY: Minor Compositions-Autonomedia 2011) http://radgeek.com/gt/2011/10/Markets-Not-Capitalism-2011-Chartier-and-Johnson.pdf; Cory Massimino and James Tuttle, eds., *Free Markets and Capitalism? Do Free Markets Always Produce a Corporate Economy?* (Tulsa, OK: Center for a Stateless Society 2016); Kevin A. Carson, *Studies in Mutualist Political Economy* (Charleston, SC: BookSurge 2007) https://kevinacarson.org/pdf/mpe.pdf; Kevin A. Carson, *Organization Theory: A Libertarian Perspective* (Charleston, SC: BookSurge 2008) https://kevinacarson.org/pdf/ot.pdf; Kevin A. Carson, *Labor Struggle: A Free Market Model*, Center for a Stateless Society Paper 10 ([Tulsa, OK: Center for a Stateless Society] 2010) https://c4ss.org/wp-content/uploads/2010/09/C4SS-Labor.pdf; Roderick T. Long, "Left-Libertarianism, Market Anarchism, Class Conflict, and Historical Theories of Distributive Justice," *Griffith Law Review* 21.2 (2012): 413–31.

56 Anna Morgenstern, "Anarcho-'Capitalism' is Impossible," *Center for a Stateless Society* (Molinari Institute, Sep. 19, 2010) https://c4ss.org/content/4043 (June 15, 2020).

57 Nicolas Walter, *The Anarchist Past and Other Essays* (Nottingham: Five Leaves 2009); Nicolas Walter, *About Anarchism* (Oakland, CA: PM 2019).

58 Roderick T. Long, "Molinari and Proudhon: Mutual(ist) Influence?" *Austro Athenian Empire* (n.p., June 15, 2020) https://aaeblog.com/2020/06/15/molinari-and-proudhon-mutualist-influence/ (June 15, 2020).

59 Sophie Raffalovich, "Les Anarchistes de Boston," *Journal des Économistes* 41.3 (March 1888): 375–88.

60 George Woodcock, *Anarchism: A History of Libertarian Ideas and Movements* (Melbourne: Penguin 1962) 460.

61 Kropotkin 122–3.

62 Rothbard, *Ethics* chs 10–11.

63 Murray N. Rothbard, "Confiscation and the Homestead Principle," *Libertarian Forum* I.6 (June 15, 1969): 3–4.

64 For more on the relationships among social anarchism, anarcho-capitalism, and left-wing market anarchism, see Roderick T. Long, "Anarchism and Libertarianism," *Brill's Companion to Anarchism and Philosophy*, ed. Nathan Jun (Leiden: Brill 2018) 285–317; cp. Roderick T. Long, "Anarchism," *The Routledge Companion to Social and Political Philosophy*, ed. Gerald Gaus and Fred D'Agostino (New York, NY: Routledge 2013) 217–230; Roderick T. Long, "Against Anarchist Apartheid," *Austro-Athenian Empire* (n.p., April 1, 2007) https://aaeblog.com/2007/04/01/against-anarchist-apartheid/ (June 15, 2020).

65 John P. Clark, *The Anarchist Moment: Reflections on Culture, Nature and Power* (Montreal: Black Rose 1983) 70, 128.

66 John P. Clark, "Bridging the Unbridgeable Chasm: Personal Transformation and Social Acton in Anarchist Practice," *The Impossible Community: Realizing Communitarian Anarchism* (New York, NY: Bloomsbury 2013) ch. 7. For a similar dialectical orientation in free-market libertarian thought, see Chris Matthew Sciabarra, *Total Freedom: Toward a Dialectical Libertarianism* (University Park, PA: Penn State UP 2000).

67 An earlier version of this chapter benefited from comments at a Molinari Society Symposium held in conjunction with the Eastern Division meeting of the American Philosophical Association in New York, 8 January 2019.

3

ON THE DISTINCTION BETWEEN STATE AND ANARCHY

Christopher W. Morris

I. Introduction

The distinction between the state and anarchy is widely deployed in modern political philosophy. In a number of ways, it is problematic and will be challenged here. Most importantly, the distinction is often thought to be exhaustive, or virtually exhaustive, of the possibilities for political societies or for the political organization of a polity. Quite often the state is defended by arguing that anarchy is awful, and less often anarchy is defended by pointing to the abuse and horrors of states. These arguments tend to assume that state and anarchy exhaust the possibilities. They turn out to be false dilemma arguments. I shall argue that this way of understanding our choices is a mistake, one that blinds us to the variety of alternative forms of political society. The "state of nature" of modern political philosophy is usually thought to be anarchy, and I will suggest a more interesting understanding of our "natural condition". This understanding may reveal some problems with much anarchist thinking.

II. The State/Anarchy Distinction

Some years ago, Robert Nozick challenged the complacency of political philosophers. He wrote:

> The fundamental question of political philosophy, one that precedes questions about how the state should be organized, is whether there should be any state at all. Why not have anarchy? Since anarchist theory, if tenable, undercuts the whole subject of *political* philosophy, it is appropriate to begin with an examination of its major theoretical alternative.[1]

Why then the state, why not anarchy? The question was timely in the early 1970s. Philosophers took for granted that we must live in states, and they focused on the question of how states should be organized and then mainly on questions of the distribution of resources.[2] Many have even understood the history of political thought as focusing primarily on these last questions. To some others, Nozick's suggestion was a breath of fresh air.

In some ways, that suggestion fits quite well with the main tradition of modern political philosophy, which would have us compare the state with the "state of nature" of social contract theory. This natural condition is the real or the hypothetical condition of humans in the absence of a state. The different seventeenth- and eighteenth-century theorists disagreed about the proper description of this "natural" state of affairs, but they took it as the starting point for reflection about the state. In the first part of *Anarchy, State, and Utopia* Nozick takes seriously the proposal that there may be anarchist solutions to the problems that humans encounter in the state of nature. Like most philosophers, he is particularly interested in normative questions about the state's justification and legitimacy.

The suggestion Nozick makes is that we examine anarchist theory, as it is the "major theoretical alternative" to political philosophy, at least in its current or possibly modern form. In his well-known account in Part One of *Anarchy, State, and Utopia*, Nozick argues that something like a state can emerge without violating any of the basic rights of people, which he thinks refutes the claims of anarchists who say that states are necessarily illegitimate or unjust. This argument has been the subject of much commentary, and my interests here lie elsewhere. I wish instead to examine the claim that state and anarchy exhaust or virtually exhaust the alternatives. Nozick's words—the state's "major theoretical alternative"—allow for other alternatives, but he proceeds as most philosophers have in this tradition, by focusing on the disjunctive choice: state? Or anarchy?

Is the distinction between state and anarchy exhaustive or virtually exhaustive? Discussions in the literature as well as the classroom proceed as if it were. There are some reasons for proceeding this way. Doing so simplifies matters, which can be helpful. And an exhaustive distinction between state and anarchy allows one to mount a simple argument for the state (or anarchy): a dilemma argument, in fact. This is, of course, what Hobbes and many others do. His is the most famous dilemma argument for the state: life in the natural condition of humankind is awful; therefore, we must have a state. The argument is very well known, and we need not linger on the omitted details. And many anarchists are also happy to embrace the dilemma structure of the argument and to challenge the picture of the state of nature. The essentially binary structure of the landscape in political philosophy is commonplace.

> The traditional justification of the state—best known to students of political philosophy from the writings of Hobbes and Locke—involved an attempt to demonstrate that the state (or that a certain kind of state) is preferable to that nonpolitical condition called 'the state of nature' (and, thus, that the state is both acceptable and best for us, relative to the state of nature.) The state of nature is often equated with the condition of 'anarchy,' which seems perfectly fair if we are using the word *anarchy* in one only of its familiar senses, where it means 'absence of government.'[3]

> A natural starting-point for thinking about the state is to ask: what would things be life without it? ... We imagine a 'state of nature'; a situation where no state exists and no one possesses political power .... [S]ooner or later, among any fairly sizeable group of people, life in the state of nature will become intolerable. Reason enough, it may be said, to accept that the state is justified without the need for further argument. After all, what real alternative to the state do we have?[4]

This assumption, that the exclusive or virtually exclusive choice we face is "state or anarchy", has had a bad effect on political philosophy. It blinds us to the variety of political alternatives, and it does this by simplifying the actual history of our world beyond recognition. If each political society must be either a state or an instance of anarchy—taking the latter to be a form of political society, if you will—then we lose sight of the many of the historical alternatives: the Roman Empire, late medieval Europe, the German-speaking lands of the Holy Roman Empire, the Islamic caliphates, Christendom, the Hanseatic League. We also fail to understand some of the more contemporary alternatives: British Hong Kong, Singapore, perhaps the European Union. As we shall see, a lot turns on how we think of states.

Philosophers, perhaps especially in the Anglo-American tradition, are raised on a diet of great books from classical Greece and modern Europe and often assume that Hobbes and Locke are engaged in a continuous conversation with Plato and Aristotle about how best to organize political society, the polis and the state being thought of as more or less similar things. But the modern state did not immediately follow Athens and Rome; a millennium of different political institutions and frameworks lies between them and the modern world. The modern state displaced or destroyed a variety of different forms of political organization. The history of our Western polities alone suggests that the binary characterization of the alternatives is mistaken or at least misleading. Our choices are not simple as between "state" and "anarchy"; there is a considerable variety of forms of political organization, and these may be of great interest to us.

Oddly, it shouldn't take much to persuade that the anarchy/state distinction cannot be exhaustive, or even virtually exhaustive. Consider the case of medieval Europe—Europe from roughly the fifth to fifteenth centuries. During this time, Europe was not organized the way it increasingly was in later centuries, as a collection of states. And it was not a state of nature or anarchy. I shall first make a case for this claim and later consider more carefully what we might think of as states. As we shall see later, much turns on how we understand states. The forms of political society in medieval Europe cannot be easily summarized, even for Western Europe. So, let us think first of northern France and England around the eleventh to thirteenth centuries. We find there a complex social and political order quite unlike ours. "Government" consisted of complex hierarchies of lords and vassals. These allegiances were based on *personal* loyalties and land tenure (fiefs). The resulting order was decentralized and fragmented, one in which "public" functions of government were "privatized", and in which rule was indirect, and it was not territorial—very different from what obtains under state rule. Here is Maitland's characterization:

> A state of society in which the main social bond is the relation between lord and man, a relation implying on the lord's part protection and defense; on the man's part protection, service and reverence, the service including service in arms. This personal relation is inseparably involved in a proprietary relation, the tenure of land—the man holds land of the lord, the man's service is a burden on the land, and (we may say) the full ownership of the land is split up between man and lord. The lord has jurisdiction over his men, holds courts for them, to which they owe suit. Jurisdiction is regarded as property, as a private right which the lord has over his land. The national organization is a system of these relationships: at the head there stands the king as lord of all, below him are his immediate vassals, or tenants in chief, who again are lords of tenants, who again may be lords of tenants, and so on, down to the lowest possessor of land. Lastly, as every court consists of the lord's tenants, so the king's court consists of his tenants in chief, and so far as there is any constitutional control over the king it is exercised by the body of these tenants.[5]

The social and political system summarized by Maitland is complex. Governance is largely decentralized, privatized, and indirect, and it is not territorial in the ways it is today. It is *decentralized* and *fragmented*, shared by multiple parties; indeed, there is no "center". Power rests in the hands of distributed networks of lords and their vassals. The Church's power and influence only compound the complexity of medieval governance arrangements. Importantly, political power—what we think of as belonging to the "public" realm—is *privatized*. Power is based on personal relations, "a complex hierarchy of patron–client relationships".[6] A third important contrast with our states is that feudal rule is largely *indirect*. There is no single person or entity, the Church aside, that rules all persons in the realm. Rule is mediated and personal. A lord requests of a vassal that he fulfill his pledge, and that request obligates that vassal; no one else is thereby obligated. The vassal may need to call on *his* vassals, but the latter are not obligated to the (first) lord. In France fidelity was owed only to one's immediate overlord: *vassallus vassalli mei non est meus vassallus* ("my vassal's vassal is not my vassal").[7]

A consequence of the decentralized, privatized, and indirect nature of political power is that it was limited or constrained. The power of any one individual was limited. We have not mentioned the political power of serfs, if only because they had none (or virtually none); independent towns are mentioned below. Our focus is on the rulers, and the power of lords was limited. The foundation for their power was contractual and thus constrained. Duties and rights were conditional; if one of the parties failed in his duties, the other would be released from his. No single person or body possessed complete authority or what the moderns call sovereignty.[8] Moreover, the hierarchy of powers—the hierarchy of lord vassal relationships—was complex in a further way: it need not constitute an ordering. The rule cited above meant that the lord–vassal relationship need not be transitive: if A was B's lord and B was C's lord, it did not follow that A was (also) C's lord. Additionally, a vassal could serve several lords.[9]

Lastly, in this system political authority was largely *personal* and not importantly territorial. Political allegiances were oath-based, referring to persons but not countries or national lands. What we think of as national borders did not exist in any case. The jurisdictions of our states are mostly territorial: laws apply to members (i.e., citizens) of course, but in the first instance they apply to all agents in the state's territory. The obligations of medieval lords and vassals—the individuals who wield power—are mostly contractual. They are thus personal, even when allegiance is exchanged for land.

In late medieval times, in what is now France or England there were monarchs who claimed sweeping powers. Drawing their inspiration from Rome or ancient Israel, these monarchs claimed broad powers to make law and not to be overruled by others. But, at the same time, they were *non sub homine sed sub Deo et lege* ("not under man but under God and the law").[10] And not without reason. Kings were constrained by the Church and its courts. The Church's power was often a significant constraint on the powers of kings and other lords. It was also a center of literacy and wealth, often largely independent of kings and princes. And kings ruled directly only on their own personal lands and indirectly everywhere else. And by comparison to many early modern kings, they were weak, militarily dependent on vassals. Lastly, with the development of commerce (and of money), towns and cities, starting in the eleventh century, became increasingly important economically and politically. Many were independent centers of power, antagonists to much of the feudal order.

What I have described is a period of late medieval European history which could not be characterized as anarchic, but which featured social systems or political societies that were clearly *not* states. Governance was fragmented and decentralized, privatized (not public), indirect and personal, and not essentially territorial. But the important point is that there was *government* in this time. There were controls on people, consisting of systems of law and other effective constraints. There were of course pockets of disorder or "anarchy", either from the collapse of orders or merely in areas in which there were few controls. This is "anarchy" in the sense of disorder. In the classical sense relevant here, *anarchia* refers to social settings without rulers or centralized political authority. In this sense late medieval Europe was not anarchic. We need now to consider more carefully why late medieval Europe does not have *states*. Part of the answer lies in our description of feudal government as decentralized and fragmented, privatized, indirect, and not territorial, and largely personal systems of power. States are systems of centralized, public, direct, and, most importantly, impersonal and territorial rule. Let us then ask: what are states, more precisely?

III. What are States?

There often appears to be considerable agreement about what states are. When in need of a "definition" of the state, political philosophers often cite Max Weber. In the first few paragraphs of a public address that Weber delivered at the University of Munich in 1918 on the subject of "Politics as a Vocation", there is what appears to be a definition of the state.[11] In the third or fourth paragraph of his lecture (the third in the German text), Weber says that "a state is a human community that (successfully) claims the *monopoly of the legitimate use of physical force* within a given territory."[12] This familiar definition is widely used.

The opening paragraph of the Wikipedia entry on "state" says that "[a] state is a compulsory political organization with a centralized government that maintains a monopoly on the legitimate use of force within a certain geographical territory" and later that "[t]he most commonly used definition is Max Weber's."[13] It is noteworthy that no single entity in medieval Europe possessed such a monopoly and that, for the most part, none could be understood as *claiming* one, though this last is less clear.

There are, however, a number of problems with this characterization or, rather, with the standard uses of it. In the lecture Weber qualifies it. And most importantly, elsewhere, in a work less cited for these purposes, Weber expresses a more subtle and complete characterization:

> Since the concept of the state has only in modern times reached its full development, it is best to define it in terms appropriate to the modern type of state, but at the same time, in terms which abstract from the values of the present day, since these are particularly subject to change. The primary formal characteristics of the modern state are as follows: It possesses [1] an administrative and [2] legal order subject to change by legislation, to which the organized corporate activity of the administrative staff, which is also regulated by legislation, is oriented. This system of order [3] claims binding authority, not only over the members of the state, the citizens [...] but also to a very large extent, over all actions taking place in the area of its [4] jurisdiction. It is thus a compulsory association with a [4a] territorial basis. Furthermore, today, the [5] use of force is regarded as legitimate only so far as it is either permitted by the state or prescribed by it.[14]

The fuller characterization is superior to the oft-quoted one from "Politics as a Vocation": "an administrative and legal order", "claims binding authority ... over all actions taking place in the area of its jurisdiction", "a territorial basis". For our purposes note that both characterizations are multi-attributive; the state is defined in terms of *several* attributes. I will make use of this fact. But first let me introduce a third characterization, a much more complex one. In my *Essay on the Modern State*, I said that

> [t]he concept of the modern state, in my sense, then, as it emerges in medieval and early modern history, is that of a new and complex form of political organization. For the purposes of my inquiry, the state is to be characterized in terms of a number of interrelated features.

These features are:

1 *Continuity in time and space.* (a) The modern state is a form of political organization whose institutions endure over time; in particular, they survive changes in leadership or government. (b) It is the form of political organization of a definite and distinct *territory*.
2 *Transcendence.* The modern state is a particular form of political organization that constitutes a unitary public order distinct from and superior to both ruled and rulers, one capable of

agency. The institutions that are associated with modern states—in particular, the government, the judiciary, the bureaucracy, standing armies—do not themselves constitute the state; they are its agents.

3 *Political organization.* The institutions through which the state acts—in particular, the government, the judiciary, the bureaucracy, the police, and the military—are differentiated from other political organizations and associations; they are formally coordinated one with another, and they are relatively centralized. Relations of authority are hierarchical. Rule is *direct*; it is *territorial* (see 1b); and it is relatively pervasive and penetrates society legally and administratively.

4 *Authority.* The state claims to be *sovereign*—that is, the ultimate source of political authority in its territory—and it claims a monopoly on the use of legitimate force within its territory. The jurisdiction of its institutions extends directly to all residents or members of that territory. In its relations to other public orders, the state is autonomous.

5 *Allegiance.* Members of a state are the primary subjects of its laws and have a general obligation to obey by virtue of their membership. The state expects and receives the loyalty of its members and of the permanent inhabitants of its territory. The loyalty that it typically expects and receives assumes precedence over that loyalty formerly owed to family, clan, commune, lord, bishop, pope, or emperor.[15]

This characterization is fuller than the Weberian ones. Item 1a is implicit in the second Weberian characterization, but item 2 needs to be stated explicitly so as to highlight the kind of corporate entity present here. The unitary and corporate nature of modern states is of importance.[16] Item 4 is quite important; states claim not only some kind of monopoly on "legitimate" uses of force and violence but also *authority*. It is not surprising that many social scientists do not want to include normative notions in a characterization of the state, but it is hard to understand what states are without referring to what powers and rights they claim.[17] And other items here—e.g., the allegiance demanded or expected by states (item 5)—are important.

This third characterization was constructed to highlight the distinctive features of modern states and to contrast them with their late medieval alternatives. Modern states resemble Athens and especially Rome only in a few respects, and these latter were long gone when states emerged and replaced late medieval institutions and political systems. Prior to the emergence of modern states there were many alternative forms of political organization, several of which had to be defeated or subsumed for statehood in the modern sense to emerge as the dominant form. Modern states displaced kingdoms, principalities, duchies, independent cities, leagues of cities, empires, the Church (of Rome), and many other alternative political forms, including several of the institutions and practices left over from feudalism. Things might have gone differently, *pace* Hegel. Charles Tilly, arguing against the historian Joseph Strayer, claims that

> In the thirteenth century, then, five outcomes may still have been open: (1) the form of national state which actually emerged; (2) a political federation or empire controlled, if only loosely, from a single center; (3) a theocratic federation—a commonwealth—held together by the structure of the Catholic Church; (4) an intensive trading network without large-scale, central political organization; (5) the persistence of the "feudal" structure which prevailed in the thirteenth century.[18]

That's all history now, so to speak. Today the triumph of the modern state is universal; all but one bit of the landmass of the globe is the territory of a state. Even the European remnants of earlier forms of political organization—the principalities of Monaco, Liechtenstein, and Andorra, the Grand Duchy of Luxembourg, the seat of the Church of Rome (Vatican City)—are dubbed states by political geographers and international lawyers. For us, there are only states (and "failed states"). The historical alternatives have been forgotten, and political philosophers often think that "the state of nature" and "the state" exhaust our options. We note, however, that by *any of these three characterizations there were no states in medieval Europe*, even if there were systems of governance and law; even when and where violence and force were controlled, there were no states.

For some purposes, of course, Weber's first definition may be sufficient. For others, his second or mine may be more useful. Characterizations are largely to be guided by the ends of inquiry and the phenomena that are illuminated thereby. Anarchists and many egalitarians are bound to be suspicious of states and especially of the monopolization of force highlighted by the first Weberian definition.[19] For them the initial centralization of power that occurred ten millennia or so ago gave birth to increasing specialization of functions, with some people or classes coming to monopolize various political functions or roles. They may find the roots of some of our political problems in the ways in which concentrations of power and political specialization make more egalitarian anarchist communities impossible. Michael Taylor is a good example of such a thinker. Other thinkers, including me, want to think about alternatives to our current system of (modern) states but do not think that the kinds of anarchist community that existed several thousand years ago are feasible or attractive alternatives for us. But, as we shall see in Section IV, there is another distinction which may be more useful to political philosophers.

IV. The Structure of the Argument: Many Attributes, Many Possibilities

Note that characterizations of the state, as with any complex entity, are multi-attributive; something is a state insofar as it possesses several attributes. This is certainly the case with Weber's second characterization and with those similar to mine. But it is also true of the simple, widely invoked Weberian definition: "a state is a human community that (successfully) claims the *monopoly of the legitimate use of physical force* within a given territory." This characterization is relatively simple, but note that the kind of human community in question is a *territorial* one. Territoriality is an attribute distinct from the monopolization of force. Further, note that the human community that claims the monopoly is an entity; that is, a single corporate entity. What sort of thing is it? It can't be the king or "the sovereign", understood as a single human being ("the ruler"); no one rules alone. The "ruler" is always a *set* of rulers—in fact, a coalition of coalitions of powerful people. More importantly, "the ruler" is a corporate being of some kind. It may be made of Many, but it is One. In the frontispiece of *Leviathan*, the Sovereign's body is made up of those Many. Something like this may be suggested by Weber's "human community", as it is by many notions of "We, the People". In addition, the important predicate "legitimate" in Weber's simple definition is more complex than it seems to be, but we will leave this aside for now. We should just note that even this simple definition is multi-attributive; there are at least three distinct attributes of states in this oft-invoked definition. Weber's complex definition distinguishes at least five important characteristics of states.

Now why would this be significant? *When political communities satisfy some but not all of the attributes essential to states, they will not be states, or not fully. But they may also not be anarchies.* Unless the defining attributes can only be instantiated together, then polities can exist with some of the attributes but not others. We have mentioned the Principality of Monaco, the Vatican, the Principality of Andorra, and other remnants of medieval Europe. These are considered city-states or countries by some, but this is a bit of a fiction. The co-princes of Andorra, for instance, are the French President and the (Catholic) Bishop of Urgell of Spanish Catalunya. American Indian reservations and Canadian First Nation territories have some state-like features. On the classical view of sovereignty—item 4 in my long characterization of states—member countries of the

European Union have given up their sovereignty or, if this is possible, part of their sovereignty. Classical Athens had some state-like features but not others. Classical empires like that of Rome and the Holy Roman Empire were not modern states and did not claim sovereignty.[20]

Depending on the period of the Middle Ages, Christendom is a political force, sharing some features with empires. And then there are the cluster of contemporary states lumped together as failed or fragile states or characterized using some other term. "Quasi-states", such as many former European colonies, are recognized as states but lack governments with full control of their territories and many other features of developed states.[21] We can find the Democratic Republic of the Congo or the Republic of South Sudan on maps, but they are not full states. Some of these places are anarchic in the sense of disorderly, but they are not anarchies. Coalitions exert control or rival groups seek to extend their control. In the next section we'll call them "limited-access social orders".

One could of course construct an exhaustive anarchy/state distinction, for instance, distinguishing states from non-states (or anarchic from non-anarchic societies). One could stipulate that anything that meets all of the conditions of one of the Weberian definitions would count as a state and that everything else is a non-state. Anarchy would then be the condition of non-states. But, of course, that would be odd. Better would be to stipulate that anarchy is a condition in which people lack rulers and that everything else is a state. Anthropologists do something like that, but they also recognize the variety of "states".[22] Students of the last two millennia of political societies would find either of these exhaustive distinctions useless; they hide the variety of forms of political organization. One cannot understand the modern state except against the background of late medieval Europe. Why did English and French monarchs need to become independent of the Church of Rome and to tame or reach agreements with their aristocrats? Simple definitions are of no use here.

Note as well that the stipulated, exhaustive definitions won't allow for a dilemma argument of the kind favored by some defenders of state or anarchy. These arguments depend on being able to show that one of the two options is just awful or that one is decidedly better than the other. But if the stipulated distinction is such that one of the alternatives groups together a large variety of arrangements—e.g., ancient Egypt, Athens, the Iroquois, Singapore, Andorra, North Korea, Norway—then the choice won't be easy, and the argument won't go through. We shall see this more clearly with the distinction to be introduced in the section that follows.

V. Anarchy and Natural States

Anthropologists are (or were) traditionally concerned with the early, pre-modern societies not studied by historians. Consequently, many have studied acephalous or anarchist societies and have found special significance in the emergence of hierarchical forms of social organizations, sometimes dubbed chiefdoms. These are larger communities than bands or tribes, socially stratified, with chiefs with considerable authority over large areas. The important explanatory notion here may be that of "fissioning":

> All political systems except true states break up into similar units as part of their normal process of political activity. Hunting bands, locally autonomous food producers, and chieftaincies each build up the polity to some critical point and then send off subordinate segments to found new units or split because of conflict over succession, land shortage, failure by one segment to support another in intergroup competition or hostilities, or for some other reason. These new units grow in their turn, then split again. The state is a system specifically designed to restrain such tendencies. And this capacity creates an entirely new society.[23]

The "German tribes" that challenged Rome were large chiefdoms of some complexity. For many anthropologists the transitions from anarchist communities to chiefdoms and then to "states" in something like the first Weberian sense is important. The distinction between anarchist or acephalous communities and chiefdoms and states represents a significant difference in social organization. And the modern and contemporary interest in "the origins of inequality" accentuates this distinction, given that the small acephalous communities are quite egalitarian.[24] There is much interest today in these small communities. Michael Taylor refers to them in his argument that anarchy requires community. It is a mark of acephalous societies that "there is only a minimum concentration of force and scarcely any political specialization of at all. ... The are no leadership positions with formal status."[25]

We have identified the philosopher's "state of nature" with anarchy. Social contract thinkers as well as many anarchists use the anarchist state of nature as the baseline for arguments for or against the state. The state of nature is also a device used by early modern philosophers, as well as classical thinkers like Plato, to lay out their conceptions of human nature, of those aspects of the human untouched or influenced by society or the state. The quarrel between Hobbes and Rousseau in the latter's *Discourse on the Inequality of Man* contrasts two views of human nature; on Rousseau's view, humans uncorrupted by society are quite different from us. However, the notion of the state of nature that's important in this discussion is that of an alternative to the state. It is thus a counter-factual notion, a notion of what would obtain in the absence of a state: "during the time men live without a common Power to keep them all in awe".[26] Hobbes did have the idea of a state with many features of the modern state characterized in Section II. But we may need to rethink the idea of anarchy as being not-a-state; it may be better to think of anarchists as opposed to governments and the resulting concentration of power.

The philosopher's "state of nature", as we have noted, serves as the baseline for many assessments of states. For some social contract thinkers—Rawls would be an important exception—the relevant state of nature is specifically counter-factual, the condition in which we would find ourselves absent the state or, rather, government. Political philosophers, then, might find anarchy less interesting than a particular understanding of the state of nature. This understanding is to be found in the recent work of Douglass North, John Wallis, and Barry Weingast, and I wish to describe their account here. In their *Violence and Social Order*,[27] they distinguish three social orders: the *foraging order, the limited-access order* (or *natural state*), and the more recent *open-access order*. Their focus is on the second and third, as the first occurred ten millennia ago and is not replicated significantly anywhere since. The choice of the label "natural state" may suggest that it should replace the typical interpretations of the "state of nature".[28]

> The natural state is natural because, for most of the last ten thousand years, it has been virtually the only form of society larger than a few hundred people that has been capable of securing physical order and managing violence.[29]

Their theory is explanatory and focuses on the ways in which societies secure order, especially the control of violence. Their distinctions and conceptual framework are meant to help us understand the ways in which different forms of social organization work and how the prosperous and free open-access orders can come about and be maintained.

Societies must secure order and specifically contain and limit violence. North, Wallis, and Weingast focus on the ways this is done:

> In most societies, political, economic, religious, and military powers are created through institutions that structure human organizations and relationships. These institutions

> simultaneously give individuals control over resources and social functions and, by doing so, limit the use of violence by shaping the incentives faced by individuals and groups who have access to violence.[30]

They distinguish "natural" or "limited-access" societies from "open-access" ones. "Natural states use the political system to regulate economic competition and create economic rents; the rents order social relations, control violence, and establish social cooperation."[31] By contrast, beginning in early to mid-nineteenth century, a few open-access societies emerge. These "regulate economic and political competition in a way that uses the entry and competition to order social relations."

> A natural state manages the problem of violence by forming a dominant coalition that limits access to valuable resources—land, labor, and capital—or access to and control of valuable activities—such as trade, worship, and education—to elite groups. The creation of rents[32] through limiting access provides the glue that holds the coalition together, enabling elite groups to make credible commitments to one another to support the regime, perform their functions, and refrain from violence.[33]

Members of the dominant coalition benefit in different ways from these arrangements. They are able more easily to make credible commitments (e.g., agreements, contracts), as these will be enforced (if necessary) by the third-party agency of the coalition, enabling them to set up mutually advantageous organizations (e.g., businesses, associations, schools, churches) more easily. These natural states offer limited access to the capacity (or legal power) to form organizations. So doing creates rents for the members of the dominant coalition, and it also enhances the value of their privileges by making them more productive.[34]

A key idea in the theory advanced by North, Wallis, and Weingast is that "how a social order structures organizations determines the pattern of social interaction with a society."[35] We take for granted that an adult citizen may start a business, form a corporation, start a club or a church, and the like. In our societies, access to these forms of organization is open to all and not controlled by the ruling elites. Access is open in this sense. In natural states, (1) access to organizational form is limited. In addition, (2) trade is controlled ("Natural states always control who trades, and may also control the places they trade and the prices at which they trade.").[36] The authors distinguish between fragile, basic, and mature natural states. Given that social orders of any size larger than a few hundred for the last two millennia have been natural states, there is great variety.

By contrast, open-access social orders allow access to all. And they are much wealthier—by historical standards remarkably wealthy—and much more peaceful and stable. Most readers of this essay will live in such societies. These social orders will have

> open access for organizations of all types, market economies that create a comparative advantage that generate a major portion of the society's wealth, and competitive elections with every citizen enfranchised. Other institutions support rights, such as free press, freedom of expression, freedom of religion and conscience, and the right to assemble. All open access orders have some form of division of powers and multiple veto points. … All open access orders also have judicial and bureaucratic mechanisms for enforcing citizen rights and contracts. And finally, they all have constitutions (whether official documents or small 'c' constitutions) that provide for the limit condition—limiting the stakes of power so that everything is not up for grabs in the next election.[37]

Open-access orders provide unrestrained "entry into economic, political, religious, and educational activities", and they provide support for these organizational form (e.g., contract enforcement). The rule of law is enforced impartially, and exchange is impersonal.[38] The last may be appreciated by contrast with limited-access orders, in which access is limited to some, or is partial and personal; rules are "identity rules", the application and enforcement of which depend on the individual's identity (e.g., membership of a class or of a ruling group).[39] The governments of open-access orders "provide services and benefits to citizens and organizations on an impersonal basis; that is without reference to the social standing of the citizens or the identity and political connections of an organization's principals."[40] Open-access orders also depend on shared beliefs and attitudes of members that emphasize equality of status, inclusion, and sharing.[41] The organizations of civil society help constitute and stabilize the social order.

The account developed by North, Wallis, and Weingast is, as the subtitle indicates, "a conceptual framework for interpreting recorded human history". They wish to understand how the different types of social orders maintain themselves and develop, and how our open-access orders emerge from natural states. I needed to outline major parts of the theory, but our interest here is primarily in the account of natural states incorporated in the theory. North, Wallis, and Weingast characterize these states as "natural", as we noted earlier, because most social orders for the past two millennia have been of this kind.

> Too often, social scientists [and philosophers] in open access societies implicitly rely on the convenient assumption that the societies they live in are the historical norm. In contrast, we argue that the default social outcome is the natural state, not open access. Until two hundred years ago, there were no open access orders; even today, 85 percent of the world's population live in limited access orders. The dominant pattern of social organization in recorded human history is the natural state. We use that appellation rather than the more literal limited access order to remind us that … the natural state emerged at a durable form of larger social organization five to ten millennia ago. The natural state has lasted so long because it aligns the interests of powerful individuals to forge a dominant coalition in such a way that limits violence and makes sustained social interaction possible on a larger scale.[42]

This account of limited-access orders is important for our discussion of the distinction between anarchy and state and of their comparative values. I have identified anarchy, the condition of social life without rulers or concentrated political power, with the philosopher's "state of nature", the condition in which we find ourselves when there is no state. This condition serves as the baseline for evaluation of our current situation, whatever it is, very much as anarchy serves as a baseline for anarchists' condemnation of states. But suppose the real alternative to *our* states, open-access orders, is not anarchy but limited-access orders. In the absence of the kind of state that exists in the US or France or Germany, *that* is the condition we'd find ourselves in absent our current political system. That is, were our state to crumble or vanish, we would find ourselves not in anarchy but in a limited-access society or natural state.[43]

If one thinks of the philosopher's state of nature counter-factually, as the condition we would find ourselves in in the absence of the institutional structures of present society, then it is not anarchy but some kind of limited-access society or natural state. The original anarchy/state distinction is not, we have argued, exhaustive or virtually exhaustive. Equally important, it is not all that useful. There are many alternatives to our kind of state; our modern states were preceded by independent cities (and leagues of cities), feudal social structures, empires, Christendom—"natural states" of various kinds. The distinction between limited- and open-access societies may be more useful for explaining and evaluating our liberal, republican states. The concept of anarchy is of course useful for understanding various forms of "spontaneous order", but these forms depend on social order and the limitation of force and violence, the security of property and of contract, and thus the general frameworks offered by institutions and law.

Perhaps, as I have suggested, it may be more interesting to think of anarchy as the absence of all forms of government or concentration of power. Anarchy in *this* sense may be a utopian ideal, perhaps of a world which may be possible only in the future, when the "state withers away".[44] If anarchy is the absence of all forms of government, then it becomes clear how utopian it is. Anarchist or semi-anarchist communities have existed only in certain contexts. Early human history featured relatively anarchic foraging societies. More recently, a variety of anarchic or semi-anarchic communities have existed, some for multiple generations or even centuries, inside modern states (e.g., kibbutzim in Israel, Amish communities in the US) or religious communities in the Middle Ages (e.g., monasteries), all dependent on protection or other support from larger political frameworks. Anarchist communities are vulnerable to conquest, of course, and need the protection of states or empires. Our world is much more populated than it was at earlier times. Anarchy as a social order does not work on a large scale. The fact that there has never been an anarchist society larger than several thousand is telling. Anarchy is not a serious alternative to our states and social systems; the attempt to build anarchist orders now would almost certainly lead to forms of limited-access social orders.

VI. Conclusion

I have argued against the assumption made by some that anarchy and state exhaust, or virtually exhaust, the alternatives. Defenses of state or anarchy that make this assumption turn out to rely on false assumptions. Exhaustive distinctions can be constructed—e.g., state vs non-state or everything else—but they merely sweep variety under the rug. There is no persuasive dilemma argument for the state or for anarchy. Modern states have many attributes, and there are many "not-a-state" or at least "not-quite-a-state" alternatives to them.

At the end of the quotation in the first section of this chapter, Jonathan Wolff asks, "After all, what real alternative to the state do we have?" We may agree with him here, even if we are quite critical of states. But there are various kinds of states. The ones in which most readers of this essay reside are open-access societies. If the real alternatives to our liberal societies are limited-access orders, then the best states look even better. This is not Hobbes's argument, as he was in effect defending limited-access orders of a special kind, with rulers possessing classical sovereignty. But the argument is similar: limited-access orders are not very attractive, except to the few on top, and even these individuals are not secure—depending on the kind of natural state they inhabit.

Our open-access societies can be improved. Some improvements may involve protecting and strengthening the organizations of civil society where they may be vulnerable or weak. Or they may involve something new. It is hard, of course, to divine the latter. We can say, or at least I would say, that what is feasible depends on path-dependent features of the society in question: on the size of the population, on the history of the people and the culture, on a variety of geopolitical considerations, and on the shifting state of nature or "natural equilibrium". What may work in Norway or Japan may not in the US or the United Kingdom. These path-dependent constraints are themes for another occasion.

Acknowledgements

Talks on this topic were given at the Southern Economic Association meetings, Washington D.C., December 2017; the Philosophy, Politics, and Economics Society Conference, New Orleans,

March 2018; and the Department of Philosophy, University of Maryland. I am grateful to the commentators and audiences, as well as to John Wallis, for helpful comments and discussions.

Notes

1 Robert Nozick, *Anarchy, State, and Utopia* (New York, NY: Basic 1974) 4. Original emphasis.

2 John Rawls is representative of this tradition: "the basic structure of a society conceived for the time being as a closed system isolated from other societies. ... Now I assume that the boundaries of these schemes are given by the notion of a self-contained national community." *A Theory of Justice* (Cambridge, MA: Harvard UP 1971) 8, 457.

3 A. John Simmons, *Political Philosophy* (New York, NY: OUP 2008) 18. In his own work, Simmons himself does not endorse the distinction we are examining here.

4 Jonathan Wolff, *An Introduction to Political Philosophy* (Oxford: OUP 1996) 7, 37.

5 F. W. Maitland, *The Constitutional History of England* (Cambridge: CUP 1909) 143–44. Maitland notes that "If we now speak of the feudal system, it should be with a full understanding that the feudalism of France differs radically from the feudalism of England, that the feudalism of the thirteenth is very different from that of the eleventh century." Many historians today think this an understatement.

6 The phrase is from S. E. Finer's monumental *The History of Government*, 3 vols. (Oxford: OUP 1997) 2: 868.

7 See F. L. Ganshof, *Qu'est-ce que la féodalité?* 5th ed. (Paris: Tallendier 1982) 155; Finer 2: 921.

8 Finer 2: 869, quoting Joseph R. Strayer and Dana Carlton Munro: "The word that sums ups feudal concepts is *dominium* or lordship. Lordship was not sovereignty, though it gave the right to command; it was not ownership, though it gave the right to exploit. It may be best defined as the possession of incomplete and shared rights of government and ownership. No lord had complete control over his subjects or over his lands, his rights overlapped with those of other men. [...] This division of authority was inevitable, since feudal government was based on private relationships. [...] no feudal contract could give a lord a monopoly of political power."

9 See Marc Bloch, *La société féodale*, 2 vols. (Paris: Albert Michel 1939) 1: bk. 2, ch. 1.

10 This principle can be, and was, interpreted in different ways. See Finer 1: 273, Finer 2: 833–88.

11 Max Weber, "Politics as a Vocation", in *From Max Weber: Essays in Sociology*, trans. and ed. H. Gerth and C. Wright Mills (New York, NY: OUP 1946 [1919]) 78. Original emphasis.

12 See Wolff, *Introduction* 39; Michael Taylor, *Community, Anarchy and Liberty* (Cambridge: CUP 1982) 4–5; Robert Paul Wolff, *In Defense of Anarchism* (New York, NY: Harper 1970) 1–3; Crispin Sartwell, *Against the State: An Introduction to Anarchist Political Theory* (Albany, NY: SUNY 2008) 28–33; Roderick T. Long and Tibor R. Machan, eds., *Anarchism/Minarchism: Is Government Part of a Free Country?* (Farnham: Ashgate 2008) vii, 65, 133; Gary Chartier, *Anarchy and Legal Order: Law and Politics for a Stateless Society* (Cambridge: CUP 2013) 1n3.

13 "State," Wikipedia (Wikimedia Foundation, Feb. 15, 2019) https://en.wikipedia.org/wiki/State_(polity) (Feb. 22, 2019).

14 Max Weber, *The Theory of Social and Economic Organization* [Part 1 of *Wirtschaft und Gesellschaft*], trans. A.M. Henderson and Talcott Parsons (New York, NY: OUP 1947) 156 (bracketed section numbers added).

15 Christopher Morris, *An Essay on the Modern State* (Cambridge: CUP 1998) 45–6. Some small changes have been made to the original text.

16 Thomas Hobbes, *Leviathan*, ed. Richard Tuck (Cambridge: CUP 1992 [1651]) chs. 16–17.

17 Christopher Morris, "How (Not) to Define the State" (unpublished ms., nd).

18 Charles Tilly, "Reflections on the History of European State-Making", *The Formation of National States in Western Europe*, ed. Tilly (Princeton, NJ: Princeton UP 1975) 26.

19 I think the importance of coercion, force, and violence is overplayed in contemporary political philosophy, but this is a different topic. See Christopher Morris, "State Coercion and Force", *Social Philosophy and Policy* 29.1 (Jan. 2012): 28–49.

20 "[L]et us think of empires as particular forms of political organization different from classical *poleis* or modern states. They are typically large, composite and diverse, composed of different peoples and previously separate groups or societies, and usually created by conquest. And empires are constituted by a dominant core or center and a subordinate periphery." Christopher Morris, "What's Wrong with Imperialism?", *Social Philosophy and Policy* 23.1 (Win. 2006): 157.

21 Robert H. Jackson, *Quasi-States: Sovereignty, International Relations and the Third World* (Cambridge: CUP 1991).

22 "[E]quating all known political forms by lumping them under one term—'the state'—does nothing to explain the differences among them." Ronald Cohen, "Introduction", *Origins of the State: The Anthropology*

of Political Evolution, ed. Cohen and Elman R. Service (Philadelphia, PA: Institute for the Study of Human Issues 1978) 2.

23 Cohen 4. See also Lucy Mair, "Primitive States", *An Introduction to Social Anthropology* (Oxford: Clarendon-OUP 1965) ch. 8.

24 See, for instance, Kent Flannery and Joyce Marcus, *The Creation of Inequality: How Our Prehistoric Ancestors Set the Stage for Monarchy, Slavery, and Empire* (Cambridge, MA: Harvard UP 2012).

25 Taylor 33. Taylor stresses the phenomenon of "secondary state formation" for the formation of most states: "Societies without a state are subjugated, colonized or absorbed by states" or defensively become state-like (130).

26 *Leviathan*, ch. XIII, para. 8. See also the non-hypothetical examples in para. 11.

27 Douglass North, John Wallis, and Barry Weingast, *Violence and Social Orders: A Conceptual Framework for Interpreting Recorded Human History* (Cambridge: CUP 2009).

28 I must credit Hartmut Kliemt for a remark that made me first think of North–Wallis–Weingast "natural states" as an interpretation of classical states of nature.

29 North, Wallis, and Weingast 31.

30 North, Wallis, and Weingast xi.

31 North, Wallis, and Weingast xii.

32 Footnote added: A *rent* in this technical sense is "a return to an economic asset that exceeds the return the asset can receive in its best alternative use" (19).

33 North, Wallis, and Weingast 30.

34 North, Wallis, and Weingast 30.

35 North, Wallis, and Weingast 35.

36 North, Wallis, and Weingast 38, note 8. In addition, (3) "The origin of legal systems lies in the definition of elite privileges." This interesting claim is difficult to explain quickly and isn't crucial to our concerns. It might help just to think about the Magna Carta, widely cited and invoked to this day and originally an agreement between an unpopular King John and some rebellious barons (1215). This third thesis about natural states is that legal systems develop initially as means to stabilize elite privileges and to pacify conflicts over these privileges (ch. 2).

37 North, Wallis, and Weingast 115.

38 North, Wallis, and Weingast 114.

39 The term is introduced by John Wallis in a new manuscript, tentatively entitled *Leviathan Denied: Rules, Organizations, and Governments.*

40 North, Wallis, and Weingast 113.

41 North, Wallis, and Weingast 111.

42 North, Wallis, and Weingast 13.

43 In his *The Limits of Liberty*, James Buchanan develops the notion of the "natural equilibrium", borrowed from Winston Bush. It is the condition we would be in now were the political order to disappear. This equilibrium in a two-person model is the point where "neither person has an incentive to modify his behavior privately or independently .... [E]ach person may be expending some share of his efforts in defending his stock from the other, another part in taking stocks of the other, and another part in producing goods directly." James Buchanan, *The Limits of Liberty: Between Anarchy and Leviathan* (Chicago, IL: U of Chicago P 1975) 58, also 23–25. Buchanan thinks of this alternative as dynamic, changing at times, and suggests that this feature explains as well as justifies changes in the constitutional order of a society; people's alternatives and bargaining power change along with shifts in the natural equilibrium. The positions of particular individuals or groups may change as their predicted positions in a new natural equilibrium evolve. "Such predictions may be based on imagined shifts in the natural distribution in anarchic equilibrium which always exists 'underneath' the observed social realities" (79).

44 To borrow a phrase from a famous nineteenth-century Marxist, revealing some sympathies to utopian anarchism. "State interference in social relations becomes, in one domain after another, superfluous, and then dies out of itself; the government of persons is replaced by the administration of things, and by the conduct of processes of production. The state is not 'abolished'. *It dies out.*" Friedrich Engels, *Anti-Dühring: Herr Eugen Dühring's Revolution in Science*, trans. Emile Burns (Moscow: Progress 1947 [1894]), www.marxists.org/archive/marx/works/1877/anti-duhring/ch24.htm/. Original emphasis.

4

METHODOLOGICAL ANARCHISM

Jason Lee Byas and Billy Christmas

I. Introduction

Anarchists all share the same basic public policy proposal: abolish public policy. With regard to foreign policy, their position is to abolish the military. With regard to education policy, abolish state schools. With regard to law enforcement policy, abolish the police. And so on and so forth.[1]

Given this total agreement on policy goals, it might seem like anarchists should be free from infighting. As anyone familiar with the anarchist movement knows, they aren't. Each form of anarchism is vigorously opposed by at least one other form, with each often writing the other out of "anarchism" altogether. In anarcho-communist Alexander Berkman's 1929 account of these differences,[2] they are in part disputes about *justice*. For communists like himself, private property and commerce drive domination and injustice, and so must be abolished. For individualists, private property and commerce are fundamental constituents of freedom and justice, and so must be unleashed. Even between market-friendly anarchists, the contents of justice are controversial. For instance, Murray Rothbard puts justice purely in terms of self-ownership, whereas Gary Chartier argues for a much broader conception that includes distributive and relational concerns.[3] These differences are rendered unintelligible within a set of assumptions predominant within academic political philosophy. We refer to this discourse as "the policy framework": it regards prescriptions of justice as little more than prescriptions of public policy.

For instance, in "The Zig-Zag of Politics," where Robert Nozick explained why he had greatly moderated his libertarianism, he wrote that "[t]he libertarian view looked solely at the purpose of government, not at its *meaning*."[4] Taking questions of meaning seriously, he said, means that certain laws and programs must exist to voice "social solidarity and humane concern for others."[5] Beyond that, "[j]oint political action [by which Nozick means state action] does not merely symbolically express our ties of concern, it also *constitutes* a relational tie itself."[6] If true, this presents a considerable problem for anarchists. If the means by which a society not only communicates but *constitutes* certain social relations demanded by justice must involve the state, then justice—or at least part of justice—is conceptually impossible in a stateless society. Moreover, these intra-anarchist disputes look nonsensical, given that there is no institutional organ to institute their different conceptions of justice to begin with.

Anarchists and their critics, then, seem to be speaking different languages. There is a basic methodological difference in the way anarchists and non-anarchists think about politics, often more implicit than explicit. Anarchists see politics and justice as being concerns of social institutions, norms, and relations generally—both inside and outside the state. Much of academic political philosophy talks of politics and justice as if they are definitionally concerns about what states should do, or our relationships with each other through the state. In this chapter, we argue that the anarchists are on the right side of this difference. We call the insight that undergirds the anarchists' understanding of politics and justice "methodological anarchism." We seek to exorcise the policy framework in favor of methodological anarchism. Indeed, we believe it should be embraced by all political philosophers, not only the anarchists among their ranks.

Political philosophers ought to abstain from the policy framework for two reasons. First, it is analytically impoverished inasmuch as, when followed to its logical conclusion, it is unable to engage with enormous areas of analysis that are relevant to what makes a society just or unjust. Second, it instills subtle prejudice against other important approaches to mitigating injustice that are unconcerned with public policy. This also carries the danger of lending ideological support for existing injustices and thereby entrenching them. Accepting our critique of the policy framework and adopting methodological anarchism does not necessarily require the acceptance of any kind of substantive political anarchism. But it does mean thinking a bit more like an anarchist about how to make society more just—thus our characterization of it as "methodological."

II. The Poverty of the Policy Framework

The policy framework is a mode of engagement with principles or theories of justice that treats them as little more than prescriptions for state action. If there is injustice, it is because there is something that the state ought to do but does not (or ought not to do, but does). Once there is justice, it will be because the state has implemented a successful policy (or repealed a policy) associated with this concern. Politics, therefore, is always an exercise in attempting to change states or influencing their actions. Doing so might involve engagement at any number of levels, from directly lobbying legislative officials to acts of civil disobedience, but within the policy framework the end goal is always changing the state's constitution or its laws.

An example of a philosophical argument reflecting the influence of the policy framework is the following:

1. *Theory* entails that every person is entitled to *J*.
2. *J* is constituted by *x*, *y*, and *z*.
3. Therefore, the state ought to provide each citizen with *x*, *y*, and *z*.
4. Therefore, the state ought to enact policy *XYZ*.

We might imagine *J* as some level of material wellbeing such as sufficiency or equality. Correspondingly *x*, *y*, and *z* could be shares of resources with a particular market value or particular goods such as education and health. *XYZ* basically stands in for some modification of the existing welfare state apparatus with the stated objective of giving each person *x*, *y*, and *z*.[7] Arguments often take this form even when they intend to support non-welfare-based conceptions of justice. For example, *J* might be a status of relational, social equality; *x*, *y*, and *z* could be elements of a democratic workplace, sources of equal opportunity for political office, or features of some derivatively valued level of material wellbeing;[8] and *XYZ* could be some extension of existing governmental discretion required for the state to intervene with the stated objective of giving people *x*, *y*, and *z*.[9]

Much of the interesting philosophizing will take place between (1) and (2), but what is conspicuously left out is an argument for why it is the state that should be uniquely concerned or charged with fostering this aspect of justice, and why the proposed policy is the best way to realize this aspect of justice. The kind of argument required could be a conceptual argument that justice entails a state policy of this kind or an empirical argument that such a policy is the best method for achieving justice—but typically we are given neither.

In proposing the methodological anarchist alternative to the analytically and ideologically impoverished policy framework, we join a growing literature that is critical of political philosophy's pre-occupation with, and simultaneous under-analysis of, the state. Tendencies relating to what we refer to as the policy framework have been identified by Jacob Levy, Jason Brennan,[10] Christopher Freiman, and Peter Jaworski, referring to "folk ideal theory," "the Fallacy of Direct Governmentalism," "ideal theories of the state," and "the ought/state gap" respectively.[11] Levy notes that putatively "[p]ure normative theories concern themselves with *what the state should do*," yet states are not mere "machines for dispensing justice, and we are poorly served when our theories imagine them to be."[12] Brennan observes that "[t]heorists and philosophers tend to assume their job is to provide normative grounding for the construction of an ideal nation-state … to determine what counts as a good or bad Leviathan."[13] Freiman argues that injustices identified in the market and civil society are presumed to be soluble only by a state because of the unstated premise that the pathologies of economic and civil society do not affect political institutions.[14] The state is posited as an institution that, by definition, does not suffer the same information and incentive problems that individuals and private associations do. The notion that the state has magical powers that enable it to overcome institutional barriers that cannot be surmounted through any other means is pervasive.

The policy framework is a particular kind of discourse: it is a way of engaging with the theories and arguments of normative political philosophy. It might be instantiated in the inferences drawn from particular theories (as illustrated above), or it might be instantiated in the rhetorical ploys that escort such inferences, designed to make particular theories appear more or less favorable in virtue of their purported implications for policy. It might even play a role in the formulation of a full-blown theory of justice, where particular policy implications are the outcome the theory is constructed to legitimize.

A basic Hobbesianism underlies the policy framework: an assumption that any social order requires an orderer external to the agents being ordered. The problem with such assumptions is that this is not always true, and moreover that the state does not stand outside society in a way that insulates it from the former's general social dynamics. Rather, it just provides a different theatre in which they play out. Thomas Hobbes asserted that each member of society lacks the incentives to comply with rules that reciprocally protect each member, and that only by empowering a monopoly state can each person's security be ensured.[15] Where Hobbes took the state to be the solution to the most basic public goods problem—that of individual security—the policy framework takes it as the solution to other justice-related public goods problems.

In similar respect to Hobbes, the policy framework regards the state as transcending the social problems that call for it. Often this perspective is one where individuals do not have sufficient incentives to voluntarily contribute to various public goods, but without those conversations extending to state action. Little discussion is had about the incentives for those engaging with the state or the incentives of state actors themselves.[16] Unlike the messiness of human society, the state just does what we want it to, and the effects of what it does are what we want them to be. The problem with this view is that the state does not operate any more automatically than does any other social institution.[17] Insisting a priori on state guarantees no more guarantees the desired outcome than insisting on guarantees in the market or civil society.[18] In his Nobel address, James Buchanan echoed the message of Knut Wicksell: "[e]conomists should cease proffering policy advice as if they were employed by a benevolent despot, and they should look to the structure within which political decisions are made."[19] Methodological anarchism involves, inter alia, extending Buchanan and Wicksell's lesson from economics to political philosophy.

A glaringly simple example of the policy framework is, as the title suggests, Ronald Dworkin's book *Sovereign Virtue*.[20] There, he famously defends an abstract, egalitarian ideal, and immediately charges the sovereign with responsibility for implementing this ideal—not in light of any social scientific or normative considerations identifying public policy as the appropriate mechanism for ensuring each citizen receives her equal share of resources, but as if as much was plainly written into the principles themselves. The philosophical arguments for those principles are taken to be philosophical arguments for particular state policies. Similarly, David Miller asserts that normative political enquiry presumes

> that there is some agency capable of changing the institutional structure more or less the way our favored theory demands. It is no use setting out principles for reforming the basic structure if in fact we have no means to implement these reforms. The main agency here is obviously the state: theories of social justice propose legislative and policy changes that a well intentioned state is supposed to introduce.[21]

Beyond the general case, there are a number of more peculiar ways in which this approach to political philosophy can manifest itself. John Rawls, Robert Nozick, and G. A. Cohen have each, at times, operated within the policy framework. We will briefly examine them in turn to see how this pattern of discourse can play out in different ways.

Rawls suggested that the state ought to own (or effectively control) the means of production, and that an allocation branch of government ought to be added to the traditional three branches of executive, judicial, and legislative.[22] Rawls's principles of justice demanded that inequalities should not result from arbitrary socioeconomic factors, and should thus only be permissible when they serve the worst off. He argues that this entails that laissez-faire capitalism and welfare state capitalism are both incompatible with these principles since the goal of these economic systems was not to redistribute socioeconomic advantage in the way demanded by justice.[23] It is the goal, however, of a powerfully interventionist state—so-called property-owning democracy—to do so; therefore, the latter is a priori preferable to the former. Rawls privileged the state with being able to achieve the tasks of justice we give it the necessary power to achieve, but not other kinds of social institutions. He asserted that since it is not the *goal* of capitalism to satisfy the difference people, it cannot be relied upon to do so, and that it *is* the goal of a fiscally powerful democratic state to do so; therefore, it can be relied upon to do so. The actual functions of institutions are ignored, and their teleological justification privileged.[24]

Aside from moralizing the function of the state, the policy framework can also manifest itself in identifying the state as the voice of the people. We have already seen how Nozick makes this claim directly in "The Zig-Zag of Politics." He moves immediately from the fact that we need something which expresses and constitutes our relational ties of concern to the need for particular sorts of state policies. It is worth noting that even before this shift, Nozick also accepted a form of expressive retributivism—the view that in order to socially convey the wrongness of a criminal offender's act, we must punish the offender.[25] Nozick himself does not say that this punishment must be imposed by the state, and his discussion of protective associations in *Anarchy, State, and Utopia* grants the conceptual possibility of punishment carried out by non-state actors.[26] However, we can still see the beginnings of Nozick's embrace of the policy framework on expressive grounds. The identification of public expression with a particular kind of legal act is already evident, and it is not far from this position to his later view that a collective voice must speak through the language of state policies.

In contrast to Nozick and Rawls, G. A. Cohen might seem free of the policy framework. When critiquing Rawls, Cohen argues that "the justice of a society is not exclusively a function of its legislative structure, of its legally imperative rules, but also of the choices people make within those rules."[27] What matters for Cohen is not institutional structures per se, but the distribution of benefits and burdens, however that distribution comes about.[28] Taken at his word, Cohen here is expressing a version of methodological anarchism.[29] All the same, even Cohen slips into the policy framework in his discourse about justice by implicitly privileging the state. Notice that his expansion of justice beyond the state is *to the choices people make within the state's rules*. This framing maintains state primacy, with it as the assumed source of socially operative rules. Our choices *within* those state-given rules *also* matter, but with emphases on the "within" and the "also." This is to say, theorizing about justice is still primarily theorizing about how the state should operate, and then secondarily about how we as individuals should behave.

One can most clearly see the policy framework haunt Cohen in the implicit, rather than explicit, premises of his work. For instance, he famously argues that equal shares of resources are demanded by justice, and that justice therefore demands redistributive taxation.[30] The principle of self-ownership, Cohen believes, is incompatible with the policy of redistributive taxation. He thus rejects self-ownership on those grounds. In this way, Cohen allows institutional prejudices about the necessity and probable success of particular policies shape his theorizing about the abstract content of justice. This same dynamic is present in *Why Not Socialism?*, where he locates justice in the non-state ideal of the camping trip. In asking if this ideal can be applied to society at large, he immediately shifts to statecraft, rather than assessing the feasibility of anarchist communism.[31] With Cohen's subliminal acceptance of the policy framework, legislators, bureaucrats, and police creep back into the picture without argument.[32]

A. What the Policy Framework Is Not

The policy framework ought not be conflated with what some political philosophers call "nationalism": roughly, the idea that relations of justice only exist between compatriots—members of the same nation.[33] This idea, combined with a view that the respective jurisdictions of existing states are sufficiently accurate divisions of nations, might lead one to the view that the state is the only or ultimate vehicle for realizing justice. Indeed, Sen is right to say that

> [t]here is something of a tyranny of ideas in seeing the political divisions of states (primarily, national states) as being, in some way, fundamental, and in seeing them not only as practical constraints to be addressed, but as divisions of basic significance in ethics and political philosophy.[34]

Yet even if this notion were right, it is still not obvious that all justice must be realized in or through the machinery of the state. Relations of justice only between compatriots can still subsist through other institutions which those compatriots participate in and are subject to.

Nor ought the policy framework be confused with "statism" in the particular sense used by some political philosophers[35] to refer to the view that being subject to coercion by one and the same state places such subjects into special justice-relevant relations which do not obtain between themselves and those subject to the coercion of other states.[36] On this view, though the coercive apparatus of the state may engender social relations that are subject to evaluation as to their justice, it need not entail that those relations can only be just via the enactment of particular policies by the state.

The policy framework might or might not be embraced by "nationalists" and "statists" of this kind, since it is a way of framing and articulating normative principles rather than something internal to normative theorizing. Even cosmopolitans—who believe duties of justice are owed to foreigner and compatriot alike—often analyze the nature of global justice and how to achieve it by thinking about what kind of policies ought to be implemented at the state or international level.[37] At the international level as well as the domestic, however, we ought not to presume from the armchair that any particular institution is the one that ought to be charged with realizing justice.[38] No particular set of institutional arrangements for realizing domestic or global justice is entailed by the purely normative content of justice.[39] "Nationalism" and "statism" are normative commitments which do not immediately imply any particular set of institutions.

B. The Analytical Poverty of the Policy Framework

Any analysis of justice that renders it the unique concern of state action is thoroughly impoverished. Looking only, or even chiefly, at the state as a default disables one from analyzing the plethora of other loci of justice and injustice in real societies.

Consider, for a moment, two different societies. Call the first one Iustitia, and the second Iniustitiam. The respective states governing Iustitia and Iniustitiam have virtually identical constitutions and virtually identical laws.[40] Moreover, they are made up of highly similar people—neither absolute saints nor absolute sinners. Iustitia—as its name suggests—is an admirably just society, whereas Iniustitiam is—also as its name suggests—rife with injustice.

In Iniustitiam, large swaths of people starve in the streets, and race is a major factor in determining which members of the society find themselves in that number. Those able to find work are subject to the worst kinds of managerial pressures, with seemingly no reprieve. While women are legally allowed to do as they wish, almost all of them stay at home in rigidly patriarchal relationships. Crime rates are staggering, and the police are often complicit. All the while, a small, select class of people enjoy almost all the wealth, doing their best to blissfully ignore the cries of the proles as they drift from fine dining establishment to fine dining establishment. On sufficientarian, relational egalitarian, luck egalitarian, and libertarian standards, Iniustitiam is Hell.

Iustitia is a bit different. Almost no one goes hungry, aside from those who are fasting on religious grounds. Most businesses are worker cooperatives, and those that are not might as well be, given the respectful nature of the employer–employee relationships. Men and women enter the workforce at almost identical rates and share equally in household labor. Violent crime occurs mostly on television, not in reality. And benefits are widely shared: Iustitians' limited differences in resources result only from robustly voluntary choices. On sufficientarian, relational egalitarian, luck egalitarian, and libertarian standards, Iustitia is Heaven.[41]

As stated previously, the laws and constitutions of Iniustitiam and Iustitia are identical. Yet the differences between these two societies are not accidental. While Iustitia has a powerful labor movement to keep workplace authority in check, this does not exist in Iniustitiam. The Iustitian labor movement is also connected to a robust network of mutual aid societies, with nothing similar in Iniustitiam. While there are, formally-speaking, very serious anti-discrimination laws in both societies, cultural norms make them almost unnecessary in Iustitia, and unenforceable in Iniustitiam. Religious institutions in Iniustitiam spend most of their time reinforcing the low social status of women and racial minorities, whereas religious institutions in Iustitia spend most of their time voluntarily redistributing their wealth downward and holding informal restorative justice seminars.

Iustitia is very obviously more just than Iniustitiam, even if their laws and constitutions are identical. To make the point here even clearer, imagine that they aren't identical. Instead, Iustitia has no state-provided social safety net at all, while Iniustitiam's is quite expensive. Iustitia has no formal anti-discrimination legislation, and Iniustitiam does. And so on and so forth. In that case, while some theorists might think this second version of Iustitia's laws intuitively sound more out of whack with justice than Iniustitiam's, Iustitia is still clearly more just.

That Iustitia can be basically just and Iniustitiam basically unjust counts against the policy framework, but there is still a way of talking about Iustitia and Iniustitiam's differences from within the policy framework. One could say that Iustitia and Iniustitiam are faced with very different circumstances, meaning that the same principles of justice apply themselves very differently in Iustitia and Iniustitiam. Distributive justice could mean that the state does what's necessary to secure that justice, and it may be that this does not require a welfare state for Iustitia, but does for Iniustitiam. Seeing justice as about the state does not mean its demands are not affected by factors beyond the state.

This response overlooks a much simpler solution, however. The circumstances that evoke wonder in Iustitia and horror in Iniustitiam are social circumstances. They are differences not in their public policies but in their social institutions more broadly. One way to bring Iniustitiam closer to Iustitia would be for the state to take over where other institutions have failed. Another option, though, is to simply reform those non-state institutions. An adherent of the policy framework might respond that this would just be a matter of adjusting the background circumstances in a way that makes justice much easier. Either way, the effect is the same—justice can be achieved through any number of ways that bypass public policy. It is more straightforward to say that justice can concern social institutions without any mediation whatsoever through the state's express policies.

A defender of the policy framework might protest that this loses sight of justice as a site of enforceable obligations. There are at least two reasons this reply fails. First, the contrast between Iustitia and Iniustitiam shows that even when claims of justice are equally "legally guaranteed" by those states at some formal level, they are only secure in Iustitia. Another way to put this is that only in Iustitia are they *enforced* in reality. Understanding why this is so requires going beyond the policy framework.

The second and closely related reason is that "enforcement" need not be limited to violent acts of state institutions. When social norms develop and maintain dependable ground-level sanctions, this too is enforcement.[42] Far from stretching our understanding of "justice," this better fits with ordinary language. For instance, consider how much of what is commonly called "social justice" activism is frequently directed at the reform of social norms, not just legal changes.[43]

It is telling that strands of contemporary political philosophy that recognize the importance of social norms as sources of people's compliance with putatively just state demands concern themselves primarily with questions about the state's inculcation of social norms—they treat such norms simply as further targets of public policy.[44] What is strange about such a framing is that state-made laws themselves are just social norms of a particular kind. The ability of states to inculcate compliance with a set of norms is presumed by the possibility of legislation.[45] Where states have trouble obtaining the compliance that is necessary to the success of its policies, the instrumental variable appears to be endogenous. We have just as much reason to see people acting justly as a feature of other norms and institutions besides state-made law. State-made law ought not be regarded "as a largely autonomous tool for securing justice and fair cooperation," but one set of norms among many—with no monopoly on justice.[46]

C. The Ideological Danger of the Policy Framework

There is a danger that in fetishizing state policy as the pinnacle of our concerns about justice, we entrench or legitimize the very real injustices perpetuated by the state. The policy framework invites us to imagine the very best functions the state could perform, and then turn the potential performance of these functions into a kind of justification for the existence of the actual state, and with it, the things it actually does. The direct inference from principles of justice to state policies uncritically presupposes the notion that without a state, there is no justice. Therefore, as a minimal condition of creating a just society, or even mitigating some injustices at the margins, we need a state. The state is the tool and the focus of justice.

The policy framework "overmoralizes" the state, in invoking what it *could* accomplish in accordance with justice, as an explanation for its existence or legitimacy.[47] Its constant invocation of a thoroughly idealized version of a real, historically shaped social institution obscures the very real injustices perpetuated by the state, in large part because of its particular institutional structure, and privileges the potential good functions it could, in principle, perform.[48] For example, by asserting that municipal police forces have the *purpose* of protecting people from crime, and that they *therefore* ought to be given generous leeway when they victimize innocent people in the process, actual police force's actual injustices are entrenched.[49]

If articulating principles or theories of justice in terms of state policies did not represent an implicit endorsement of the actual state, then there would be no reason for political philosophers to pick out this particular institution as their favored justice machine. One rarely if ever hears a political philosopher articulate some principle of justice and then say, "and therefore, the family ought to allocate everyone a sufficiently advantageous share of opportunities for welfare." Or "and therefore, private associations must guarantee each agent her fair share of social and economic capital." Firms, private associations, churches, cities, universities, or international nongovernmental organizations are never charged with being *the* institution that so obviously must be charged with guaranteeing everyone their just entitlements through policy.[50] When these institutions are invoked as vehicles for justice, it is usually government regulation of them that is the locus of the discussion.[51] Or else, it is expected that they provide some evidence that the selected institution is the most appropriately suited to the particular task at hand. The primary function of these institutions is, presumably, readily acknowledged by political philosophers to not be securing justice, yet the same is true of the state. States are not mere "machines for dispensing justice."[52] An entity qualifies as a state if it asserts that it is entitled to serve as the final authority regarding the use of force within a geographical territory and if it exhibits the capacity effectively to maintain its dominance in that territory. It is not clear why we should assume that an institution with these features would necessarily seek to act justly or to foster justice. To expect it to as a matter of course results in the kind of moralization Levy rightly highlights.[53]

It might be argued that the juridical finality of the state makes it the focus of justice. On such an account, when individuals and other social institutions fail to comply with justice, the state can use its coercive power to resolve whatever problem might follow from noncompliance. Once the state settles a matter, there is no further legal remedy, given that any lower-level legal remedies take place within the juridical space of the state's authorization. That is why political philosophers talk about state policy rather than what the family, the firm, etc., should do, because ultimately the state has the legal capability to correct matters when those intermediary institutions fail to comply with justice.

The compliance problem affects the state just as much as any other social institution, however. The monopoly on force being conditionally justified by its effective use of that force to ensure compliance with justice does not entail that that is how its monopoly is in fact used. We must ask: What happens when the entity with juridical finality does not comply with justice? How can that finality be justified when it is not itself operationalized to assure compliance with justice?

The fact is that there is no metaphysically ultimate juridical finality, there is only what society happens to acquiesce to.[54] While the state has the power to intervene in intermediary social institutions, the state's authority itself depends upon an array of other social norms ensuring compliance with the rules that constitute it. "[S]overeignty—where it exists—depends on rules, is constituted by rules, and so cannot intelligibly be regarded as the source of all the rules that make up the legal system."[55] If noncompliance is a problem, then it is also a problem for state action.

The state has ultimate de facto authority over us; we therefore *want* it to use that authority justly. Unfortunately, this does not entail that it *will* do so, nor that we should justify the power on the basis that it *might*. The good intentions theorists have in supporting the state's power for some particular end are not mechanically infused into the state's actual operations. Institutions do not necessarily create the conditions for their own success;[56] they must be judged in accordance with how well they deal with difficult conditions within which they actually operate.[57]

"Concentrated power," as Milton Friedman reminds us, "is not rendered harmless by the good intentions of those who create it."[58] The policy framework promotes support for the state, and hence its power, on the basis that this power could be used for justice. This risks lending legitimacy to the state's many historical and ongoing injustices at the expense of underplaying or even tarnishing non-policy-based alleviations of injustice, particularly those that might simultaneously erode state power.

The rhetoric of justice can sometimes foster injustice. This is particularly true when we use terms with obvious referents in the messy, real world to denote ideal, or idealized, states of affairs. For example, since most people use "capitalism" to refer to the economic system that obtains in the present in many parts of the world, riddled with privileges that render markets anything but free, when some libertarians use "capitalism" to refer to a system featuring genuinely unfettered markets, this can provide ideological cover for those rigged markets.[59] Similarly, when luck egalitarians emphasize that those who are responsible for their disadvantages have no claims of justice on the resources of others, they may be unwittingly supporting invasions of the private lives of the worst off in order to verify that they are "deserving" welfare recipients and not "scroungers."[60] A similar thing is true of the state as it is of capitalism and notions of desert.

While, when many political philosophers say "the state" they have in mind some perfect state that has never existed and may never exist, "the state" in fact refers to a very real thing to most people. The fact that philosophers envision states with all sorts of properties real states do not in fact have does not alter the rhetorical effect. Consider the following analogy, borrowed from Michael Munger, between theorizing about states and how someone might similarly theorize about unicorns.[61] In Munger's hypothetical, there are no unicorns in the real world, yet they are constantly invoked to solve the real world's problems. Through their magic, unicorns can move heavy loads quickly and efficiently around the world, so the unicorn-theorist argues we should use them to solve all our transportation needs. Of course, if you invoke a unicorn as a solution to real social problems, no one would imagine you were offering a serious proposal. But while, as far as we know, "unicorn" has no referent in the real world, "the state" does. Saying that unicorns can solve all our transit problems does not encourage outrageous expectations of, say, real-world horses. But talking about the mythical *state*—the one that exists only in the minds of political philosophers—does lead people to embrace certain attitudes toward real states. As Jacob Levy describes this process,

> Political philosophers are prone to the following fallacy: If we knew precisely what justice demanded and had access to a government that would implement it, we would have a unified system of rights and responsibilities and authority; therefore we know that a disintegrated system is not part of what justice demands; therefore, we know that justice prohibits a disunited system.[62]

Indeed, the policy framework privileges the state in much the same way social contract theory often does: there is a presumption in favor of the state actually doing what we want it to, at least well enough to justify our allegiance. Karl Widerquist and Grant S. McCall spell out this problem:

> Contractarians devote pages and pages of normative argument to support the apparently strong criteria that the state is only justified if it makes everyone better off than they would be in its absence. Yet, with little or no argument, they usually conclude that the

criterion is fulfilled, and they seldom even address the question of what to do when the criterion is unfulfilled.[63]

The policy framework imputes moral purpose to the state even though its actual function tends to go against that purpose. Employing the policy framework thus means providing rhetorical cover for state injustice. To avoid doing this and to undermine the deleterious influence of the policy framework, we should consciously resist use of it. We propose that resistance take the form of adopting methodological anarchism. Methodological anarchism draws a bright line between abstract principles of justice and concrete proposals for specific state policies—or even specific *sorts* of policies. It embodies a thoroughgoing institutional agnosticism about how we ought to enact justice. For example, imagine that we agree on some general sufficientarian principle, in accordance with which everyone is owed the ability to realize some minimal level of welfare. We cannot reason directly from this principle to the claim that the state must provide some sort of a social safety net. We can only reason to the claim that there ought to be a safety net. After comparative institutional analysis, we may conclude that this social safety net should take the form of a state-funded, state-delivered program. However, we might conclude instead that it demands a rebirth of something like pre-welfare state mutual aid societies. In either case, social institutions attempt to provide a safety net. The question is which method is successful, which one can be depended upon.

Importantly, this is not a consequentialist claim that perhaps the goals of justice could be better achieved beyond the state. It is a conceptual decoupling of justice and the state. The state is not a justice machine through which a society speaks and acts, as Nozick claims. It is just one among many institutions that might be thought capable of exhibiting or fostering justice. Its actions have particularly far-reaching effects—hence political anarchists' focus on its abolition—but it is still just one institution among many. Methodological anarchism involves first acknowledging that it is analytically erroneous and morally dangerous to reify society as the state, and then refusing to do so.

III. From Theory to Practice: The Promise of Methodological Anarchism

Not only does methodological anarchism point to a new way of viewing justice, it opens up conceptual space for a different way of seeing political action. Within the policy framework, with concerns of justice tied to state's regulations, laws, and constitutions, political action is naturally aimed at changing these regulations, laws, and constitutions. Political action can take the form of voting, running for office, lobbying for or against legislation, or campaigning for candidates or referenda. It may also come in the form of civil disobedience or educating the public, but the aim of that civil disobedience and education is still always to eventually effect a change in public policy. Political action as understood within the policy framework might even come in the form of revolution, where the aim is to entirely replace one constitution with another. What these forms of political action—which we will refer to broadly as "reform and revolution"—share is that the central, guiding aim is always to change the things states do.

A. Direct Action

It is in contrast to reform and revolution that we understand *direct action*. "Direct action" refers to attempts at directly addressing issues of justice without mediation through state channels.[64] A program of direct action can have as one of its many aims an eventual policy change, but it need not do so, and it is never *limited* to doing so. Within the policy framework, it can be difficult to see how direct action helps achieve justice. We might make do with direct action when putatively appropriate state policies look unlikely, but there is a sense that something is missing in terms of justice. Methodological anarchism makes possible more enthusiastic endorsements of direct action. It thus helps to build an important bridge between political philosophy and the real world, because many concerns of justice typically reified as policy programs have also been pursued through direct action. There is an entire world of human association that political philosophy has ignored in its reliance upon the policy framework.

This is not just the judgement of wild-eyed political anarchists; it is also the verdict of mainstream social science. For instance, the work of Nobel laureate Elinor Ostrom has shown how sophisticated forms of social organization can use social capital to sustainably manage common ecological resources without reliance on the state.[65] Similarly, anthropologist and political scientist James C. Scott shows how many forms of successful socioeconomic organization are illegible to states, and sustaining these forms of organization can often only be achieved through actively resisting attempts by states to force legibility onto a society.[66] Scholars like Ostrom and Scott show that reform and revolution's fundamental assumption, that the state is necessarily the ultimate site of social change, is simply false. To make this general point clearer, we will now discuss its application to various specific domains. The following examples are meant only as a brief glance at what sorts of institutions beyond the state might enter conversations about justice between methodologically anarchist political philosophers.

B. Direct Action: Social Safety Nets

Several theories of distributive justice require the provision of a social safety net. It is often argued that the fact that this is a matter of distributive justice means that this social safety net should not be seen as a form of charity. Rather, it should be understood that those benefitting from this safety net are simply receiving benefits to which they are entitled. It is often further argued that that dependence on charity can place the poor in a position of subordination. If Person A's continued existence depends on Person B's benevolence, Person B is effectively in a position to interfere arbitrarily in Person A's life. We therefore need institutions that dependably provide a social safety net without making those who need it dependent on the good graces of their neighbors. Historically, this has been achieved successfully through direct action.

Before the rise of the welfare state, a robust social safety net existed in the form of mutual aid societies.[67] These private associations were not providers of charity, and they were not viewed as if they were. Their funds came from the pooled resources of members, provided with the expectation that they would receive the societies' benefits once they needed to do so.[68] Among the benefits that these societies provided were access to orphanages and old-age homes, life insurance, and health and accident insurance.[69] They were especially successful in insuring healthcare. At one point, members were able to secure a year's worth of benefits for the price of a day's wage.[70] Thirty percent of Americans over 20 belonged to mutual aid societies in 1920, with even higher numbers among minority ethnic and religious groups.[71]

C. Direct Action: Checks on Private Power

Another concern of justice, especially for neo-republicans and relational egalitarians, is ensuring checks on private power. Elizabeth Anderson makes this especially salient by framing powerful employers as "Communist dictatorships in our midst."[72] Modern workplaces may not have the same powers of repression available to modern states, but they can still be the most sharply felt sites of oppression for many people.

That we need institutional checks on private power does not entail the conclusion that state regulation is required. For there is a ready and obvious case of a private institution meant to combat employer power: that of the labor union. When successful, labor unions provide institutional checks on private power by raising costs for employers who do not accept their demands. There is no conceptual reason to treat this check as any less dependable or real than the checks provided by state regulation.

In fact, political anarchists frequently argue that such private checks are more dependable than state regulation, and act accordingly. The histories of anarchism and radical labor politics are deeply intertwined, as is made most clear by wildcat unions like the Industrial Workers of the World. For a recent example of labor unions engaged in direct action completely unaided by state policy, we can look to the Coalition of Immokalee Workers (CIW), a union not certified by the National Labor Relations Board (NLRB).[73] That union, which represents immigrant farm workers without NLRB certification, has won better wages and work conditions without ever relying on state labor laws. Among the companies it has won victories over are Walmart, Taco Bell, Publix, and other large chains. CIW's successes have not occurred *despite* its lack of NLRB certification, but *because* of it. Its primary tactics, focused on pressuring companies higher up the supply chain, almost entirely fall under the category "secondary action," illegal for NLRB-certified unions. The CIW's successes highlight the capacity of unions to check the private power of employers without any recourse to the state.[74]

D. Direct Action: Protection from Violence

Whatever their disagreements regarding other matters, most theorists of justice share a concern with seeing people protected from violence. Virtually everyone who is not an anarchist, then, assumes that this is a job for the state and its police force. Those functions are often seen as the state's most basic, as is implied by the phrasing in some libertarians' endorsement of the "minimal state." Here too, direct action has worked to supply justice beyond the state.

One such case is Threat Management Center, which has helped defend people in the Detroit area from crime for nearly twenty years. According to its founder, as of 2013 it had served 1,000 homes and 500 businesses, and it uses that money to fund free protection for people in poorer areas that cannot afford it.[75] It is committed to de-escalating violence, embracing a hard rule that its personnel will only shoot second—doubtless in part because, unlike the police, they are legally equal with ordinary people.[76]

E. Direct Action: Remedies for Violence Done

Direct action has also been used in providing moral repair after violence has already occurred. In cases where violence occurs in communities skeptical of or averse to seeking aid from the state's legal system, assorted organizations have engaged in direct action to offer more constructive responses than state institutions. Creative Interventions is one such example, formed in 2004 by organizers with ties to both the anti-violence and prison abolition movements.[77] Its approach emphasizes restorative justice, focusing on those most closely affected by instances of violence, but also putting them in a larger community context.[78] Creative Interventions seeks to discover the full context of the harm done—its causes, impact, and potential for redress—and out of that context, develop goals toward repair.[79] While the founders of Creative Interventions see the project in political terms, they make no assumptions about the politics of those they work with.[80]

F. Direct Action: Routing around Bad State Policies

When injustice is created by bad state policy, one way to fix the problem is to seek to change the relevant policy through reform or revolution. Another option is to route around the state or clean up its mess through direct action. Consider the United States' war on drugs—often considered a paradigmatically unjust policy by many philosophers.[81] One case of direct action responding to the drug war and its consequences is the creation of the Silk Road, a now-defunct online marketplace for illegal drugs.

In an interview with *Forbes* magazine, the Silk Road's founder explicitly framed the project in political terms, emphasizing that it was "about standing up for our rights as human beings and refusing to submit when we've done no wrong."[82] Importantly, the idea was not just civil disobedience against the war on drugs, but protection from it. By providing a platform allowing people to trade illegal drugs more openly, the Silk Road carved out a space in which drug laws had less power to restrict freedom. That space helped mitigate prohibition's negative consequences, since it helped allow for features like a rating system that ensured product quality. The Silk Road itself was shut down in October 2013, and Ross Ulbricht was sentenced to life in prison without possibility of parole for being its alleged mastermind. However, various imitators still exist today.

G. *Beyond Reform and Revolution*

Fully assessing the merits of direct action as an alternative to reform and revolution would take us too far from our present purposes. However, it is worth noting a few considerations that point in direct action's favor.

Compared to revolution, direct action involves much less blood and general chaos. It is also worth remembering that a new government born out of military violence will prove authoritarian. Even in the case of non-violent revolution, there are powerful knowledge problems associated with trying to build a new constitution from scratch and imposing it anew on people who were accustomed to its predecessor. Direct action does not pose the same problems as full-scale revolution because direct action works on a piecemeal basis: we need not change everything to change anything.

Compared to reform, direct action avoids the hurdles inherent to dealing with governments. States are predictably resistant to positive change, and this can be seen from a variety of perspectives. Public choice economics predicts that state actors will tend toward exploitative policies with concentrated benefits and dispersed costs, determined by the differential access to the political process potential beneficiaries have.[83] It also predicts that regulatory agencies won't be particularly helpful in systematically restraining sources of predation and oppression because they will often be created or captured by the very interests they are intended to check.[84] Indeed, there is no a priori reason to think that, given the ends public office can be used for, they will not be sought for those very ends.[85] The regulatory state offers open-ended returns on any costs invested in capture. New Left Marxists[86] as well as radical libertarians[87] essentially agree that the state tends to act as the executive committee of the ruling class. Even when it looks like it is restraining the power of big business, this will usually function to benefit the corporate class as a whole.

Centralized power structures like the state will be used to entrench privilege—because people in society who are already privileged will almost necessarily have better access to the state due to that privilege. This means that when state actors face pressure from the oppressed, they will favor symbolic actions to quell that resistance over substantive changes that would challenge their power.[88] These problems with reform are avoided in direct action, where those with a clear interest in justice may pursue it directly, without having those pursuits frustrated or warped by opposing interests, nor having to convince a legislative coalition before action is taken.

H. *Practicing Safe Politics*

Another benefit of methodological anarchism is that, by turning our attention to direct action, it encourages us to practice safe politics. This point is best understood in light of recent arguments by philosophers Michael Huemer and Jason Brennan for political abstinence.

Huemer's critique of political action is a suggestion that political actors join doctors in ensuring to "first, do no harm."[89] Huemer finds it near-impossible to consistently follow this principle while also engaging in political action. This is because political actors essentially have no idea what they are doing, and are therefore much more likely to do harm than good. The first reason for this is widespread political ignorance—ignorance of the identities of political representatives, their policy positions and voting records, institutional facts about government, the details of particular policies under consideration, the social science and philosophy surrounding those policies, etc.[90] That ignorance is the predictable result of rational (whether or not altogether conscious) assessments of the costs and benefits associated with gaining the relevant information. The instrumental benefits of acquiring knowledge are exceedingly low, given that the average person has almost no chance in personally affecting public policy. The costs of obtaining that information are often very high, requiring extensive research into not only voting records and policy details, but also relevant social science and philosophy. Therefore, people remain ignorant.[91] Since obtaining information needed to determine what actions are just or will foster justice is costly, people pursue the easier goal of presenting themselves as pursuing justice.[92] This leads us to strong, yet ill-informed beliefs, which we treat as precious—since these beliefs are tied up with our self-perception, we resist threatening information.[93] Even experts are overconfident about political questions, with their predictive records only barely exceeding those that might be expected to occur by chance,[94] in part due to inherent difficulties with the predictive capacities of social theory.[95] Taking political action in the face of high levels of ignorance—on one's own part and on the part of those who can be expected to participate in and respond to one's efforts—is highly dangerous, so Huemer advises against it.[96]

Jason Brennan outlines the ways in which democratic politics turns people into "civic enemies." In the United States, strong majorities of both Democrats and Republicans are less likely to hire opposing-party members independent of qualifications.[97] As with political ignorance, political enmity is a predictable product of incentives.[98] First, democratic politics presents us with constrained, suboptimal choices.[99] Second, victory is monopolistic—a victory for one means all others lose.[100] Third, that monopolistic political victory will be imposed using actual or threatened violence.[101] Thus, your political opponents in a democracy are people who wish to prevent the realization of your preferences by forcing you to accept the realization of their contrary preferences. This creates a zero-sum world, where disagreement is always a threat.[102]

The kinds of problems Huemer and Brennan highlight occur when politics is framed in terms of what we have called "reform." Direct action eliminates these problems, and therefore allows us to participate in politics safely. The knowledge necessary for programs of direct action is easier to acquire than the knowledge needed successfully to implement programs of society-wide reform. For example, you don't need to know how to successfully provide stable living arrangements for everyone in poverty; you only need to know how to provide for those in your chapter of a mutual aid society. Furthermore, a political actor implementing a program of direct action has a more intimate connection to and personal stake in the results of the direct action, and thus has an incentive to care more about getting things right. For instance, Creative Interventions participants found themselves continuously interrogating their politically formed assumptions about the dynamics of interpersonal violence, since those beliefs had more concrete and visible effects.[103]

Direct action also heals many of the wounds left by reform's politics of enmity. Our options for political improvement by means of direct action are constrained only by what we can imagine and get away with. Programs of direct action are obviously non-monopolistic—those who believe they can do better are always free to develop their own alternatives. Perhaps most importantly, direct action (unlike reform and revolution) has no necessary connection to violence.[104]

From within the policy framework, we are faced with a troubling dilemma. Humans are indeed political animals, but when politics means policy, acting on our natural political impulses is typically immoral. Methodological anarchism offers a way out, one that enables us to avoid harming and hating our neighbors without retreating into political abstinence.

IV. From Practice to Theory: What Direct Action Reveals

By opening up new paths to political goals, direct action offers escape from the stagnation and animosity of electoral politics. Something similar is true of how methodological anarchism reshapes conceptual territory. The lines between different theories fall differently when the questions our classifications consider go beyond state policy.

For example, consider the claim that as a matter of justice, people ought to stand in relationships of equality, with no person or group of persons dominating any others. This is recognizably a statement of relational egalitarianism, as advocated by philosophers like Elizabeth Anderson and Samuel Scheffler.[105] Consider also the claim that each person is endowed with a set of natural rights acting as side-constraints on others' actions, and that these include rights to appropriate, own, defend, and exchange property. This is recognizably a statement of Lockean libertarianism, as advocated by philosophers like Robert Nozick and Eric Mack.[106] These views are typically taken as obvious and unambiguous enemies. Relational egalitarians often defend redistributive taxation, robust state regulations of employer–employee relationships, and other policies clearly at odds with libertarian rights. If one group is right about which policies justice requires, the other is wrong. Libertarians, then, have reason to deny relational egalitarianism altogether, and relational egalitarians have reason to deny libertarianism altogether. Arguments for and against those total denials are well worn, and unlikely to sway theorists already committed one way or the other.

More interesting permutations can be advanced once we leave the policy framework. Suppose that we grant natural rights libertarianism. It does not follow from the strictures this puts on state policy that relational egalitarian demands must be discarded. Libertarian rights put strictures on the use of force and fraud, but they do not say much about forms of collective social pressure stopping short of violence. It may still be the case, then, that justice demands robust social norms of a kind that develop and maintain relationships of social equality, and that those norms may be enforced through various means of non-violent social coercion. For one such case: suppose that the aforementioned method of direct action against private power, state-independent labor activism, is as effective as its proponents claim. Strikes, boycotts, and other pressure campaigns can then be seen as the social enforcement of relational egalitarian justice. On such a picture, relational egalitarianism would not be eliminated by the success of natural rights libertarianism, it would just be repositioned.[107] Similarly, the bare relational egalitarian requirement of non-domination would not rule out a libertarian conception of rights. It must be further argued that social enforcement is insufficient,[108] and that violence is an acceptable means of shoring up the difference.[109]

While we are sympathetic to this general picture, our point in raising it here is not to defend it. Rather, the foregoing is meant to show the sorts of conceptual space made available by clearing away the policy framework. When theories of justice are uniformly shoved into rough policy approximations, this creates brute incompatibilities not present in more abstract statements. Accordingly, the greater variation in practical implementation offered by methodological anarchism reveals greater variation in theoretical explanation. There is still significant disagreement, but it takes place on a terrain that affords more philosophical mobility. With access to subtler points of partial agreement, this reduces the risk of stalemate. Both practically and theoretically, methodological anarchism helps us break free from political stagnation.

V. Conclusion: The Policy Implications of Rejecting the Policy Framework

Rejecting the policy framework does not make state policy irrelevant, nor do arguments for a politics of direct action conclusively rule out ever participating in efforts designed to foster reform—or, indeed, in extreme cases, in revolution. Methodological anarchism simply puts those efforts in context, offering a greater awareness of alternatives. Seeing the state as just one relevant institution in society among many doesn't mean ignoring the fact that it is, indeed, a relevant institution. That the state's laws cast a backdrop of violence over everything else renders it particularly important, even for the methodological anarchist.

Odd as it might sound, then, there are important *policy implications* of rejecting the policy framework. Though methodological anarchism does not directly entail political anarchism, it does present at least two important reasons to move closer in that direction.

One reason methodological anarchism points toward policy-negativity is that, with direct action on the table, justice will often most forcefully demand that the state to get out of the way. For example, among explanations given for why earlier mutual aid societies fell to the wayside is that licensure laws worked to combat mutual aid societies' model of insurance and delivery of medical care.[110] We can therefore see how a case for liberalizing or even abolishing licensure laws could be made on *distributive justice* grounds, since such laws limit the range of available social safety nets.

Rejecting the policy framework should also lead us to reject particular policies because of the demystification of the state that comes with embracing methodological anarchism. It cautions against the naïve view in which state laws seem to bark from the heavens, "*Fiat iustitia!*" It is essentially this methodologically anarchist point that legal theorist and trans liberationist Dean Spade makes when he argues that LGBTQIA activists should "focus less on what the law says … and more on what impact various legal regimes have on distressed populations."[111] In that spirit, the Sylvia Rivera Law Project, a transgender legal advocacy group founded by Spade in 2002, argues against hate crimes legislation:

> [H]ate crime laws … expand and increase the power of the … criminal punishment system. Evidence demonstrates that hate crime legislation, like other criminal punishment legislation, is used unequally and improperly against communities that are already marginalized in our society. These laws increase the already staggering incarceration rates of people of color, poor people, queer people and transgender people based on a system that is inherently and deeply corrupt.[112]

This point can be generalized. Because states are not justice machines, whose pronouncements can be taken as the pronouncements of society itself, state policies that express recognition for certain individuals are not the be-all-and-end-all of efforts designed to foster the social equality of those individuals. When we need not rely upon a particular state policy to express recognition, we can turn our attention to the concrete costs and benefits of that policy. Given the internal dynamics of state power, even expressively benign policies can work to re-entrench existing social problems and create others. With the state demystified, we can reject those policies and instead seek direct action alternatives.

This brings us back to where we were at the start of this chapter. For part of what makes political anarchism so absurd to its critics is that the policy framework renders government "just another word for the things we do together." In those terms, the abolition of government sounds like the abolition of society and collective action, as shown by questions like "Who will feed the hungry? Who will keep us safe? Who will build the roads?" Because those asking these questions speak a different methodological language, they cannot understand the anarchist reply: "We will."[113]

Anarchism's critics might still find that answer lacking. Entering into a serious conversation about it, though, requires speaking the same language. Justice and politics cannot be definitionally to refer only to concerns of the state. They instead are features of social institutions and social norms broadly. It is implausible that solutions to injustice cannot be found beyond the state, or that the anarchists' "We will" is never the right answer to their critics' questions. Even for those who cannot accept the conclusions of political anarchism, methodological anarchism usefully expands the scope of political philosophy.

The policy framework is thoroughly lacking as a tool of analysis when its implicit premises are pushed to their limit. And employing this framework privileges an institution that has been an enormous source of injustice throughout its history, and thereby risks legitimizing such injustice. Political philosophers, then, should reason, write, teach, and speak within the terms of methodological anarchism. That is, they should come to see the restrictiveness of the policy framework itself, and liberate themselves from its confines.

Acknowledgements

Earlier drafts of this chapter have been presented at the Manchester Centre for Political Theory seminar, February 2016; Association for Private Enterprise Education conference, April 2016; the Philosophy, Politics, and Economics Society inaugural meetings, March 2017; and the Loyola Chicago Graduate Philosophy Conference, October 2017. We are grateful to those audiences for their comments and feedback. We also thank Jason Brennan, Andrew I. Cohen, Alex W. Craig, Nathan Goodman, M. Scott King, Mark Pennington, Karl Widerquist, Liam Shields, Steven Zoeller, and the editors of this volume for useful discussions.

Notes

1 Anarchists do have some differences in policy preferences under the assumption that the state continues to exist, however. For example, see Long, Roderick T. 2010. "Chomsky's Augustinian Anarchism," *Center for a Stateless Society*, January 7, https://c4ss.org/content/1659, accessed 12/28/17; cf. Byas, Jason Lee. 2019. "The Political Is Interpersonal: An Interpretation and Defense of Libertarian Immediatism," in Roger E. Bissell, Chris Matthew Sciabarra, & Edward W. Younkins (eds), *The Dialectics of Liberty: Exploring the Context of Human Freedom*. New York, NY: Lexington; Carson, Kevin A. 2019. "Formal vs. Substantive Statism: A Matter of Context," in Roger E. Bissell, Chris Matthew Sciabarra, & Edward W. Younkins (eds), *The Dialectics of Liberty: Exploring the Context of Human Freedom*. New York, NY: Lexington. The point is just that *even these* anarchists ultimately agree on the ideal policy proposal of abolishing the state altogether.

2 Berkman, Alexander. 1929. *Now and After: The ABC of Communist Anarchism*. New York, NY: Vanguard Press. Ch. 23.

3 Rothbard, Murray N. 1982. *The Ethics of Liberty*. Atlantic Highlands, NJ: Humanities Press; Chartier, Gary. 2009. *Economic Justice and Natural Law*. Cambridge: Cambridge University Press; Chartier, Gary. 2012. *Anarchy and Legal Order: Law and Politics for a Stateless Society*. Cambridge: Cambridge University Press. In addition, the preferred structure of property rights may differ significantly between market anarchists. Rothbard defends familiar Lockean arrangements sans the Lockean proviso, whereas Benjamin Tucker rejects absentee ownership in favor of an occupancy-and-use standard for the validity of an ongoing property right. There may also be a variety of views on the extent to whether the preponderance of property forms ought to be private property or common property. See Rothbard 1982; Tucker, Benjamin. 1897. *Instead of a Book, by a Man Too Busy to Write One*; Christmas, Billy. 2019a. "Ambidextrous Lockeanism," *Economics and Philosophy*, online first.

4 Nozick, Robert. 1989. *The Examined Life: Philosophical Meditations*. New York, NY: Simon & Schuster. Ch. 25; cf. Sanchez, Julian. 2001. "An Interview with Robert Nozick," July 26, www.juliansanchez.com/an-interview-with-robert-nozick-july-26-2001/, accessed 1/30/19.

5 Nozick *Life* 288.

6 Nozick *Life* 288.

7 For example, see Sher, George. 2014. *Equality for Inegalitarians*. Cambridge: Cambridge University Press. 115, 157.

8 Many relational or social egalitarians believe that distributional equality or sufficiency are derivatively valuable from the perspective of justice. For example, see Schemmel, Christian. 2011. "Why Relational Egalitarians Should Care About Distributions," *Social Theory and Practice*, 37: 365–390.

9 As Emily McTernan, Martin O'Neill, Christian Schemmel, and Fabian Schuppert have argued, "[i]f you care about social equality, you want a big state." McTernan, Emily, Martin O'Neill, Christian Schemmel, & Fabian Schuppert. 2016. "If You Care about Social Equality, You Want a Big State: Home, Work, Care and Social Egalitarianism," *Progressive Review*, 23: 138–144.

10 Elsewhere Brennan analyzes this into three biases: the diffidence bias (pessimism about the possibilities of voluntary cooperation), the statism bias (overestimation of how much the state is required to secure social cooperation), and the guarantee bias (overestimation of the need for legal guarantees). Brennan, Jason. 2018. "Private Governance and the Three Biases of Political Philosophy," *Review of Austrian Economics*, 31: 235–243.

11 Levy, Jacob. T. 2015a. "Folk Ideal Theory in Action," *Bleeding Heart Libertarianism* blog, April 28, http://bleedingheartlibertarians.com/2015/04/folk-ideal-theory-in-action/, accessed 2/14/17; Brennan, J. 2016b. *Political Philosophy: An Introduction*. Washington DC: Cato Institute. Ch. 11; Freiman, Chris. 2017. *Unequivocal Justice*. New York, NY: Routledge. 2–4; Jaworski, Peter. 2018. "Privatization and the Ought/State Gap," *Nomos*, 60.

12 Levy *Rationalism* 58. Original emphasis.

13 Brennan *Governance*.

14 Freiman *Justice*.

15 Hobbes, Thomas. 1642 [1983]. *De Cive*, ed. Howard Warrender. Oxford: Clarendon Press; Hobbes, Thomas. 1651 [2012]. *Leviathan*, ed. Noel Malcolm. Oxford: Oxford University Press. This is an empirical commitment that no political philosopher has ever been particularly bothered to prove, as argued in Widerquist, Karl, & Grant McCall. 2015. "Myths about the State of Nature and the Reality of Stateless Societies," *Analyse & Kritik*, 37: 233–257; Widerquist, Karl, & Grant McCall. 2017. *Prehistoric Myths in Modern Political Philosophy*. Edinburgh: Edinburgh University Press. Some contemporary Kantians have, however, framed their arguments for the state as implied by justice a priori—the state as a posit for natural right. For example, see Ripstein, Arthur 2009. *Force and Freedom: Kant's Legal and Political Philosophy*. Cambridge, MA: Harvard University Press. Ch. 9; Stilz, Anna. 2011b. *Liberal Loyalty: Freedom, Obligation, and the State*. Princeton, NJ: Princeton University Press. Ch. 2; Varden, Helga. 2008. "Kant's Non-Voluntarist Conception of Political Obligations: Why Justice Is Impossible in the State of Nature." *Kantian Review*, 13: 1–45; Varden, Helga. 2010. "Kant's Non-Absolutist Conception of Political Legitimacy: How Public Right 'Concludes' Private Right in 'The Doctrine of Right,'" *Kant-Studien*, 3: 331–51; Hodgson, Louise-Philippe. 2010. "Kant on Property Rights and the State," *Kantian Review*, 15: 57–87. For reasons that require much more argument than can be given here, such accounts in fact depend upon practical accounts of the state's ability to be the best provider of assurance of security, determinacy of rights, representing the omnilateral will, none of which conceptually depend upon it being a coercive territorial monopoly—that is, being a state at all. Part of the Kantian republican argument relies on the necessity of laws and a constitutional structure, but the possibility of laws and a constitutional structure without monopoly is precisely the thing posited by many market anarchists. See Long, Roderick T. 2008. "Market Anarchism as Constitutionalism," in Roderick T. Long & Tibor R. Machan (eds) *Anarchism/Minarchism: Is a Government Part of a Free Country*? Aldershot: Ashgate.

16 For example, see Hume, David. 1738 [1826]. *Treatise of Human Nature*, in his *The Philosophical Works of David Hume, vol. 2*. Edinburgh: Black & Tait. III.II.7; Mill, John Stuart. 1848 [1965]. "Principles of Political Economy," in John M. Robson (ed.) *The Collected Works of John Stuart Mill*, 7th ed. Toronto: University of Toronto Press; Gauthier, David. 1986. *Morals by Agreement*. Oxford: Oxford University Press. 342; Kavka, Gregory. 1986. *Hobbesian Moral and Political Theory*. Princeton, NJ: Princeton University Press. 246; Murphy, L., & T. Nagel. 2004. *The Myth of Ownership*. New York, NY: Oxford University Press. 6. A trenchant critique of this assertion is Freiman *Unequivocal* chs 0–1.

17 La Boétie, Étienne de. 1576. *The Politics of Obedience: The Discourse of Voluntary Servitude*, trans. H. Kurz. Montreal: Black Rose; Hume, D. 1758 [1826]. *Essays Moral, Political, and Literary*, in his *The Philosophical Works of David Hume, vol. 3*. Edinburgh: Black & Tait. I. IV.

18 Schmidtz, David. 1997. "Guarantees," *Social Philosophy & Policy*, 14: 1–19.

19 Buchanan, James. M. 1987. "The Constitution of Economic Policy," *American Economic Review*, 77: 243–250.

20 Dworkin, Ronald. 2000. *Sovereign Virtue: The Theory and Practice of Equality*. Cambridge, MA: Harvard University Press.

21 Miller, David. 2001. *Principles of Social Justice*. Cambridge, MA: Harvard University Press. 6.

22 Rawls, John. 2001. *Justice as Fairness: A Restatement*, ed. E Kelley. Cambridge, MA: Belknap Press. 148–150; cf. O'Neill, Martin. 2012. "Free (and Fair) Markets without Capitalism: Political Values,

Principles of Justice, and Property-Owning Democracy," in Martin O'Neill & Thad Williamson (eds) *Property-Owning Democracy: Rawls and Beyond*. New York, NY: Wiley-Blackwell. 83; Rawls, J. 1971 [1999]. *A Theory of Justice*, rev. ed. Cambridge, MA: Belknap Press. 242–251.

23 Rawls *Theory* 244–245.

24 Freiman *Unequivocal* chs 0–1, 3.

25 Nozick, R. 1981. *Philosophical Explanations*. Cambridge, MA: Belknap Press. 363–398.

26 Nozick, R. 1974. *Anarchy, State, and Utopia*. New York, NY: Basic Books.

27 Cohen, G. A. 1997. "Where the Action Is: On the Site of Distributive Justice," *Philosophy & Public Affairs*, 26: 3–33. 9.

28 Cohen *Action* 12.

29 That being said, the methodological anarchist can still see institutions as having a special role beyond that of mere choices without privileging *the state in particular*.

30 Cohen, G. A. 1995. *Self-Ownership, Freedom, and Equality*. Cambridge: Cambridge University Press. Per Cohen's luck egalitarianism, this is of course subject to qualification by the distributive effects of persons' morally culpable choices.

31 Cohen, G. A. 2009. *Why Not Socialism?* Princeton, NJ: Princeton University Press.

32 We thank Jesse Spafford and Chetan Cetty for pressing us on the applicability of the policy framework to Cohen.

33 Miller, David. 1995. *On Nationality*. Oxford: Oxford University Press; Miller, David. 2000. *Citizenship and National Identity*. Oxford: Blackwell; Miller, D. 2013. *Justice for Earthlings: Essays in Political Philosophy*. Ch. 7.

34 Sen, Amartya. 2009. *The Idea of Justice*. Cambridge, MA: Belknap Press. 143.

35 It is often used by anarchists and libertarians to refer to the disposition of those who believe in the justice or necessity of the state very generally.

36 For variations of this view see Waldron, Jeremy. 1993. "Special Ties and Natural Duties," *Philosophy & Public Affairs*, 22: 3–30; Waldron, Jeremy. 2011b. "The Principle of Proximity," *NYU School of Law, Public Law Research Paper*, No. 11–08. https://papers.ssrn.com/sol3/papers.cfm?abstract_id=1742413, accessed 1/31/19; Nagel, Thomas. 2005. "The Problem of Global Justice," *Philosophy & Public Affairs*, 33: 113–147; Ripstein *Force*; Stilz, Anna. 2011a. "Nations, States, and Territory," *Ethics*, 121: 572–601; Stilz, Anna. 2009. "Why Do States Have Territorial Rights?" *International Theory*, 1: 185–213; Stilz *Loyalty*; Risse, Mathias. 2012. *On Global Justice*. Princeton, NJ: Princeton University Press; Blake, Michael. 2013. *Justice and Foreign Policy*. Oxford: Oxford University Press.

37 For example, see Ypi, Lea L. 2008. "Statist Cosmopolitanism," *Journal of Political Philosophy*, 16: 48–71.

38 Pavel, Carmen E. 2015. *Divided Sovereignty: International Institutions and the Limits of State Authority*. Oxford: Oxford University Press. Ch. 5; cf. Pavel, C. 2010. "Alternative Agents for Humanitarian Intervention," *Journal of Global Ethics*, 6: 323–338.

39 See, respectively, Miller *Justice* ch. 1 and Ronzoni, Miriam. 2017. "Republicanism and Global Institutions: Three Desiderata in Tension," *Social Philosophy & Policy*, 34: 186–208.

40 The only differences involve variations that have no obvious bearing on justice, like national symbols, geography, the names of various places, etc.

41 The identification of Iniustitiam as "Hell" and Iustitia as "Heaven" here need not imply that the former is perfectly unjust nor that the latter is perfectly just. The bare fact that Iniustitiami society continues to exist suggests it is not perfectly unjust. One could also find several defects in Iustitia in terms of various theories of justice—for instance, libertarians of a political anarchist stripe will find a grave injustice in the fact that Iustitians still live under a state. Anarchist communists might add to this the fact that Iustitia retains markets and private property. All Iustitia and Iniustitiam are meant to represent is extremes of justice and injustice relative to modern industrialized western nation-states.

42 Cf. Radzik, Linda. 2017. "Boycotts and the Social Enforcement of Justice," *Social Philosophy and Policy*, 34: 102–122; Ostrom, Elinor. 1990. *Governing the Commons: The Evolution of Institutions for Collective Action*. Cambridge: Cambridge University Press.

43 Cf. Long, Roderick T. 2019. "Why Libertarians Should Be Social Justice Warriors," in Roger E. Bissell, Christopher Matthew Sciabarra, & Edward W. Younkins (eds), *The Dialectics of Liberty: Exploring the Context of Human Freedom*. New York, NY: Lexington; Wexler, Lesley, Robbennolt, Jennifer K., & Murphy, Colleen. 2019. "#MeToo, Time's Up, and Theories of Justice," *University of Illinois Law Review*, 2019: 45–111.

44 For example, see McTernan, Emily. 2014. "How to Make Citizens Behave: Social Psychology, Liberal Virtues, and Social Norms," *Journal of Political Philosophy*, 22: 84–104.

45 Cf. Hayek, F.A. 1978. *Law, Legislation and Liberty, Volume 1: Rules and Order*. Chicago, IL: University of Chicago Press; Hasnas, John. 2004. "Hayek, The Common Law, and Fluid Drive," *NYU Journal of Law & Liberty*, 1: 79–110.

46 Barrett, Jacob, & Gerald Gaus. Forthcoming. "Laws, Norms, and Public Justification: The Limits of Law as an Instrument of Reform," in Silje A. Langvatn, Wojciech Sadurski, & Mattias Kumm (eds) *Public Reason and the Courts*. Cambridge: Cambridge University Press. 2.

47 Levy, Jacob T. 2017. "Contra Politanism," *European Journal of Political Theory*, online first. DOI: 10.1177/14748851177183712: 15. For arguments that this has always been intrinsic, in one way or another, to liberal rhetoric, see Losurdo, Domenico. 2011. *Liberalism: A Counter-History*, trans. Gregory Elliot. London: Verso Books; Mulholland, Marc. 2012. *Bourgeois Liberty and the Politics of Fear: From Absolutism to Neo-Conservatism*. Oxford: Oxford University Press.

48 Mills, Charles W. 2005. "'Ideal Theory' as Ideology," *Hypatia*, 20: 165–184.

49 Levy *Folk*.

50 On the tendency to view the moral function of intermediary institutions as strictly subordinate to that of nation states, see Levy, Jacob T. 2015b. *Rationalism, Pluralism, and Freedom*. Oxford: Oxford University Press; Levy *Politanism*.

51 For recent examples, on marriage, the workplace, and religion, see, respectively, Chambers, Clare. 2017. *Against Marriage: An Egalitarian Defense of the Marriage-Free State*. Oxford: Oxford University Press; Anderson, Elizabeth. 2017. *Private Government: How Employers Rule Our Lives (and Why We Don't Talk about It)* Princeton, NJ: Princeton University Press; Laborde, Cécile. 2017. *Liberalism's Religion*. Cambridge, MA: Harvard University Press. We do not mean to claim that these arguments engage in the policy framework in the sense of inferring deductively invalid conclusions about state policy from premises merely regarding abstract principle. Rather, we claim that they do so in the sense of problematizing public policy *itself* and its impact on the family, the workplace, or religion with political philosophy, and elevating the analysis of policy as the most important implications of their sophisticated theories of justice regarding the workings of these institutions.

52 Levy *Rationalism* 58; cf. Levy, Jacob T. 2016. "There is No Such Thing as Ideal Theory," *Social & Political Philosophy*, 33: 312–333. 325.

53 Levy *Politanism*.

54 Long *Anarchism*.

55 Waldron, Jeremy. 2008. "Hart and the Principles of Legality," in Matthew H. Kramer, Claire Grant, Ben Colburn, & Antony Hatzistavrou (eds) *The Legacy of H. L. A. Hart: Legal, Political, and Moral Philosophy*. Oxford: Oxford University Press. 82; cf. Waldron, J. 2011a. "Are Sovereigns Entitled to the Benefit of International Rule of Law?" *European Journal of International Law*, 22: 315–343. 318–319; Hart, H. L. A. 1961 [1994]. *The Concept of Law*, 2nd ed. Oxford: Clarendon Press. 51–61. In so-called non-ideal theory, the feasibility of compliance with a particular principle of justice is explicitly problematized. However, it is always the feasibility of the state compelling the citizenry to comply with justice, rather than the feasibility of the state itself faithfully using its powers only to compel compliance with justice. As Jacob Levy says, "States are … social institutions with organizational dynamics and tendencies of their own … when we introduce the question 'what will states do, when tasked with enacting and enforcing it?' This is a kind of compliance problem, the kind pointed out by the second half of Madison's dictum: 'If angels were to govern men, neither external nor internal controls on government would be necessary.' It seems to me a strange feature of the ideal theory literature that is has focused so completely on the question of whether compliance among the citizenry is a valid modelling assumption, to the neglect of the tacit assumption of compliance by the state." Levy *Thing* 325.

56 Brennan, Jason. 2016a. "Do Markets Corrupt?" in Jennifer A. Baker & Mark D. White (eds) *Economics and the Virtues: Building A New Moral Foundation*. New York, NY: Oxford University Press. 243–247.

57 Pennington, Mark. 2011. *Robust Political Economy: Classical Liberalism and the Future of Public Policy*. Cheltenham: Edward Elgar.

58 Friedman, Milton. 1962 [2002]. *Capitalism and Freedom*, 40th Anniversary Ed. Chicago, IL: University of Chicago Press. 201.

59 Cf. Long, Roderick T. 2006. "Rothbard's 'Left and Right': Forty Years Later," *Mises Daily*, https://mises.org/library/rothbards-left-and-right-forty-years-later, accessed 1/31/19.

60 Axelsen, David V. 2015. "Political Philosophy and Political Change," *Justice Everywhere* blog, Sept 28. http://justice-everywhere.org/education/political-theory-and-political-change/, accessed 2/14/17; Axelsen, David V. 2016. "Aktivistisk Politisk Teori," in R. S. Hansen & S. Midtgaard (eds) *Metoden i Politisk Teori*. Copenhagen: Samfundslitteratur; Axelsen, David V. Unpublished. "Making the World Worse by Saying How It Could Be Better"; cf. Wolff, J. 1998. "Fairness, Respect, and the Egalitarian Ethos," *Philosophy & Public Affairs*, 27: 97–122.

61 Munger, Michael. 2014. "Unicorn Governance," *Foundation for Economic Education* blog, Aug. 11. https://fee.org/articles/unicorn-governance/, accessed 2/16/17.

62 Levy *Politanism* 16.

63 Widerquist *Myths* 224; cf. Widerquist *State*; Pateman, C., & C. W. Mills. 2007. *Contract and Domination*. Cambridge: Polity Press. 54; Pateman, Carole. 1989. *The Disorder of Women: Democracy, Feminism, and Political Theory*. Palo Alto, CA: Stanford University Press. 71; Long, Roderick T. 1995. "Immanent Liberalism: The Politics of Mutual Consent," *Social Philosophy & Policy*, 12: 1–31.

64 De Cleyre, Voltairine 1912. "Direct Action," *Mother Earth*.

65 See Ostrom *Commons*; Ostrom, Elinor 2000. "Social Capital: A Fad or a Fundamental Concept?" in Partha Dasgupta & Ismail Serageldin (eds) *Social Capital: A Multifaceted Perspective*. Washington DC: World Bank Books; Ostrom, Elinor, James Walker, & Roy Gardner. 1992. "Covenants with and Without a Sword: Self-Governance is Possible," *American Political Science Review*, 86: 404–417; Axelrod, Robert. 1984. *The Evolution of Cooperation*. New York, NY: Basic Books; Ellickson, Robert. 1992. *Order without Law: How Neighbors Settle Disputes*. Cambridge, MA: Harvard University Press. Another relevant and important layer to Ostrom's work is that she finds no a priori reason to think that the source of successful cooperation ought to be any one particular level of institutions, but can rather be a function of many interlocking sources of rules and social capital. Cf. Buchanan, James M. 1965. "An Economic Theory of Clubs," *Economica*, 32: 1–14.

66 Scott, James C. 1998. *Seeing Like a State: How Certain Schemes to Improve the Human Condition Have Failed*. New Haven, CT: Yale University Press; Scott, James C. 2014. *The Art of Not Being Governed: An Anarchist History of Upland Southeast Asia*. New Haven, CT: Yale University Press; Scott, James C. 2017. *Against the Grain: A Deep History of the Earliest States*. New Haven, CT: Yale University Press.

67 Cromwell, Lawrence, & David George Green. 1985. *Mutual Aid or Welfare State? Australia's Friendly Societies*. New York, NY: Harper Collins; Beito, David. 1990. "Mutual Aid for Social Welfare: The Case of American Fraternal Societies." *Critical Review* 4: 709–736; Beito, David. 1992. *From Mutual Aid to the Welfare State: Fraternal Societies and Social Services, 1890–1967*. Chapel Hill, NC: University of North Carolina Press; Green, David George. 1993. *Reinventing Civil Society: The Rediscovery of Welfare without Politics*. London: Civitas.

68 Beito *Aid* 723.

69 Beito *Aid* 712–717.

70 Long, Roderick T. 1993/1994. "How Government Solved the Healthcare Crisis: Medical Insurance That Worked—Until Government 'Fixed' It," *Formulations*, 1(2).

71 Beito *Aid* 711–719. Related to this non-state provision of social safety nets: direct action from civil society has also crucially assisted in the wake of disasters. For a variety of cases following Hurricane Katrina, see the stories highlighted in Storr, Nona M., Chamblee-Wright, Emily, & Storr, Virgil H. 2015. *How We Came Back: Voices from Post-Katrina New Orleans*. Arlington, VA: Mercatus Center at George Mason University; Crow, Scott. 2011. *Black Flags and Windmills: Hope, Anarchy, and the Common Ground Collective*. Oakland, CA: PM Press.

72 Anderson *Government* 37

73 Johnson, Charles W. 2014. "Free Market Labor Wins Wage-Boost Victory." *Reason* blog, Jan 28. http://reason.com/archives/2014/01/28/free-market-labor-wins-wage-boost-victor, accessed 12/29/17.

74 On related topics, see Carson, Kevin A. 2008. *Organization Theory: A Libertarian Perspective*. Charleston, SC: BookSurge. On the topic of worker self-management, also see Prychitko, David. 2019. "Context Matters: Finding a Home for Labor-Managed Enterprise," in Roger E. Bissell, Christopher Matthew Sciabarra, & Edward W. Younkins (eds), *The Dialectics of Liberty: Exploring the Context of Human Freedom*. New York, NY: Lexington.

75 Brown, Dale 2013. Interview: "Dale Brown of Detroit-based Threat Management Center is On-Point," video available at www.youtube.com/watch?v=onWC8nNpIco, accessed 1/5/17.

76 Threat Management Center is a case where we can point to a particular organization providing services typically associated with the state, but the point here is much more expansive. No legal system can ever succeed with only the work of those on the state's payroll. The success or failure of the state's provision of deterrence requires "coproduction," which is a series of activities that ordinary persons take to provide for their own security and assist in the security of others. For more on this, see Goodman, Nathan. 2017. "The Coproduction of Justice," in Christopher W. Suprenant (ed.) *Rethinking Punishment in an Era of Mass-Incarceration*. New York, NY: Routledge. Changes at the level of coproduction of security can be just as important as changes in the state's direct production of security in providing assurance that individuals' rights will be respected. For a political anarchist discussion of legal and protective services provided outside the state, see Hasnas, John. 2008. "The Obviousness of Anarchy," in Roderick T. Long and Tibor R. Machan (eds.), *Anarchism/Minarchism: Is Government Part of a Free Country?* Aldershot: Ashgate.

77 The "prison abolition" movement refers to a broad movement seeking to radically change the way we handle crime, often in ways that go beyond just abolishing prisons. The "anti-violence" movement refers to community organizations attempting to address domestic violence and interpersonal violence more generally.

78 Kim, Mimi E. 2011/2012. "Moving Beyond Critique: Creative Interventions and Reconstructions of Community Accountability," *Social Justice*, 37: 14–35. 20–21. For an outline of the community-centric rather than state-centric model of restorative justice animating groups like Creative Interventions, see Christie, Nils. 1977. "Conflicts as Property." *British Journal of Criminology*, 17.1: 1–15.
79 Kim *Critique* 21.
80 Kim *Critique* 22.
81 Husak, Douglas B. 1992. *Drugs and Rights*. Cambridge: Cambridge University Press; Huemer, Michael. 2004. "America's Unjust Drug War," in Bill Masters (ed.) *The New Prohibition*. St Louis, MO: Accurate Press; Cohen, Andrew J., & William Glod. 2017. "Why Paternalists and Social Welfarists Should Oppose Criminal Drug Laws," in Christopher W. Suprenant (ed.) *Rethinking Punishment in an Era of Mass-Incarceration*. London: Routledge.
82 Roberts quoted in Greenberg, Andy. 2013. "An Interview with a Digital Drug Lord: The Silk Road's Dread Pirate Roberts," *Forbes*, Aug 14. www.forbes.com/sites/andygreenberg/2013/08/14/an-interview-with-a-digital-drug-lord-the-silk-roads-dread-pirate-roberts-qa/#5588e2c95732, accessed 12/4/2017.
83 Olsen, Mancur. 1965. *The Logic of Collective Action: Public Goods and the Theory of Groups*. Cambridge, MA: Harvard University Press; Tullock, G. 1980. "Efficient Rent-Seeking," in James Buchanan, Robert Tollison, & Gordon Tullock (eds), *Toward a Theory of the Rent-Seeking Society*. College Station, TX: Texas A&M Press; Holcombe, Randall G. 2018. *Political Capitalism: How Economic and Political Power is Made and Maintained*. Cambridge: Cambridge UP.
84 Stigler, George. 1971. "The Theory of Economic Regulation," *Bell Journal of Economics and Management Science*, 2: 3–21; Winston, Clifford, Robert W. Crandall, William A. Niskanen, & Alvin Klevorick. 1994. "Explaining Regulatory Policy," *Brookings Papers on Economic Activity: Microeconomics*. 1994: 1–49; Lindsey, Brink, & Steven M. Teles. 2017. *The Captured Economy: How the Powerful Enrich Themselves, Slow Down Growth, and Increase Inequality*. Oxford: Oxford University Press.
85 Buchanan, James M., & Gordon Tullock. 1962. *The Calculus of Consent: Logical Foundations of Constitutional Democracy*. Ann Arbor, MI: U of Michigan Press.
86 Kolko, Gabriel. 1963. *The Triumph of Conservatism: A Reinterpretation of American History, 1900–1916*. New York, NY: Free Press of Glencoe; Kolko, Gabriel. 1965. *Railroads and Regulation, 1877–1916*. Princeton, NJ: Princeton University Press; Weinstein, James. 1976. *The Corporate Ideal in the Liberal State, 1900–1918*. New York, NY: Farrar Straus & Giroux.
87 Shaffer, Butler. 1997. *In Restraint of Trade: The Business Campaign Against Competition, 1918–1938*. Lewisburg, PA: Bucknell University Press; Childs, Roy A., Jr. 1971a. "Big Business and the Rise of American Statism, Part One: A Revisionist History," *Reason*, February, https://reason.com/1971/02/01/big-business-and-the-rise-of-a-2/, accessed 2/1/19; Childs, Roy A., Jr. 1971b. "Big Business and the Rise of American Statism, Part Two: A Revisionist History," *Reason*, March, http://reason.com/1971/02/01/big-business-and-the-rise-of-a-2/, accessed 2/1/19; Grinder, Walter E., & John Hagel III. 1977. "Toward a Theory of State Capitalism: Ultimate Decision-Making and Class Structure," *Journal of Libertarian Studies*, 1: 59–79; Radosh, Ralph, & Murray N. Rothbard (eds). 1972. *A New History of Leviathan*. New York, NY: Dutton; Stromberg, Joseph R. 1972. "The Political Economy of Liberal Corporatism," *Individualist*, May; Ruwart, Mary J. 2003. *Healing Our World in an Age of Aggression*. Kalamazoo, MI: SunStar Press; Johnson, Charles W. 2004. "Free the Unions (and All Political Prisoners)," *Rad Geek People's Daily* blog, https://radgeek.com/gt/2004/05/01/free_the/, accessed 2/1/19; Hart, David M., Gary Chartier, Ross M. Kenyon, & Roderick T. Long (eds). 2018. *Social Class and State Power: Exploring an Alternative Radical Tradition*. New York, NY: Palgrave Macmillan; Hart *Capitalism*.
88 These points are also relevant to other dimensions of social domination, not just economic power. For instance, similar reform-skeptical analysis is applied to LGBTQIA issues in Spade, Dean. 2015. *Normal Life: Administrative Violence, Critical Trans Politics, and the Limits of Law*, 2nd ed. Durham, NC: Duke University Press. Also see the essays compiled in Conrad, Ryan. 2014. *Against Equality: Queer Revolution, Not Mere Inclusion*. Edinburgh: AK Press.
89 Huemer, Michael. 2012. "In Praise of Passivity," *Studia Humana*, 1: 12–28. 26.
90 Huemer *Passivity* 13.
91 Huemer *Passivity* 17–18; cf. Somin, Ilya. 2013. *Democracy and Political Ignorance: Why Smaller Government is Smarter*. Stanford, CA: Stanford Law Books; Caplan, Bryan. 2007. *The Myth of the Rational Voter: Why Democracies Choose Bad Policies*. Princeton, NJ: Princeton University Press.
92 Huemer *Passivity* 19.
93 Huemer *Passivity* 19.
94 Huemer *Passivity* 15.
95 Huemer *Passivity* 20–21.

96 Huemer *Passivity* 21–26.
97 Brennan, Jason. 2016. *Against Democracy*. Princeton, NJ: Princeton University Press. 223.
98 Brennan *Democracy* 235–237.
99 Brennan *Democracy* 237–238.
100 Brennan *Democracy* 238–240.
101 Brennan *Democracy* 240–241.
102 Brennan *Democracy* 236.
103 Kim *Critique* 27–31.
104 Admittedly, while it *need not*, direct action can also take the form of violence. Among other problems, direct action in the form of violence typically does not have the benefit of helping us practice safe politics.
105 Anderson, Elizabeth. 1999. "What Is the Point of Equality?" *Ethics*, 109: 287–337; Scheffler, Samuel. 2010. *Equality and Tradition: Questions of Value in Moral and Political Theory*. Oxford: Oxford University Press.
106 Nozick *Anarchy*; Mack, Eric. 2010. "The Natural Right of Property," *Social Philosophy and Policy*, 27: 53–78.
107 Something like this relational egalitarian libertarianism can be seen in Johnson, Charles W. 2008. "Liberty, Equality, Solidarity: Toward a Dialectical Anarchism," in Roderick T. Long and Tibor R. Machan (eds.), *Anarchism/Minarchism: Is Government Part of a Free Country?* Aldershot: Ashgate; Chartier *Anarchy*; Chartier, Gary. 2019. "Radical Liberalism and Social Liberation," in Roger E. Bissell, Christopher Matthew Sciabarra, & Edward W. Younkins (eds), *The Dialectics of Liberty: Exploring the Context of Human Freedom*. New York, NY: Lexington; Christmas, Billy. 2019b. "Social Equality and Liberty," in Roger E. Bissell, Christopher M. Sciabarra, & Edward W. Younkins (eds), *The Dialectics of Liberty: Exploring the Context of Human Freedom*. New York, NY: Lexington; Long *Libertarians*. It can perhaps also be seen many of the nineteenth-century individualist anarchists. It also has clear precedent in the market egalitarian currents of classical liberalism highlighted in the first chapter of Anderson *Government*.
108 The second chapter of Anderson *Government* can be seen as making this sort of argument, by appeal to greater economies of scale following the Industrial Revolution. A libertarian rejoinder might begin by challenging the attribution of workplace authoritarianism to the spontaneous workings of the market. What we mean to emphasize here is a further point: beyond the spontaneous workings of market exchange, we must also consider the merits of non-state actions intentionally taken towards the social enforcement of justice.
109 For instance, the nonlibertarian relational egalitarian could raise worries specific to the idea of natural property rights.
110 Long *Government*.
111 Spade *Life* 17.
112 Sylvia Rivera Law Project. No date. "SRLP On Hate Crimes Laws." *Sylvia Rivera Law Project*. https://srlp.org/action/hate-crimes/, accessed 12/29/17.
113 Cf. Johnson, Charles W. 2009. "We Are Market Forces," in Charles W. Johnson & Gary Chartier (eds) *Markets Not Capitalism: Individualist Anarchism Against Bosses, Inequality, Corporate Power, and Structural Poverty*. New York, NY: Autonomedia.

5
WHAT IS THE POINT OF ANARCHISM?

Aeon J. Skoble

I. Introduction

Anarchism is the position in political philosophy which denies the authority or necessity of political authority. To oppose political authority is not to oppose *authority*. Dentists generally know more about teeth and tooth care than non-dentists; classical historians generally know more about the Peloponnesian War than non-historians. Unlike medical or historical authority, political authority is not a claim about *knowledge*, but a claim about *power*. The ruler does not necessarily claim to know more, but rather claims to be justified in exercising power over others.

The suffix "archon" refers to *rulers*, so, just as *monarchism* recommends a *single* ruler, *anarchism* recommends *no* rulers. But rulers exist, so the word "anarchism" is not a metaphysical claim, but a normative one. "Atheism," by contrast, uses a similar negation-implying prefix, but it is not a normative position. The atheist denies that God exists. Anarchism does not deny that *rulers* exist; rather, it denies claims that rulers are *justified*, that they are entitled to the authority they assert. Rulers are not likely to give up their power just because some philosophical argument says they should. So it's reasonable to ask of the anarchist, *What is the point of the arguments you are making?* In this chapter, I intend to establish that the anarchist's position is worth advancing and has very real consequences even in a world in which political authority is persistent.

II. Some Clarifications

Before proceeding, let me clarify a couple of additional terms. By "states" or "the state," I am not invoking the US-specific distinction between a state government and the federal government, but rather the idea of a "state" as a reasonably well-defined geographical area in which there is a centralized political authority. The authority could be monarchical, democratic, republican, or oligarchical; any kind of government that has authority in the relevant geographic area will qualify. In any kind of state, then, the concept of "ruler," the thing the anarchist wants to do away with, is in play, whether there is one ruler, twelve, 535, or what have you.

The anarchist's claim is not that one form of government is illegitimate and that another would be; it is that no rulers' claims to power over others are legitimate. Sometimes, people who oppose a particular government are accused of being anarchists (indeed, sometimes they even self-describe that way), but, when their goal is to replace the state with a different sort of state, they are actually not anarchists, any more than opponents of one religion qualify as "atheists" for embracing one or more different religions. Hence the slogan "smash the state" might be an anarchist's, but also might not be, depending on whether the sloganeer's goal is to eliminate all centralized political authority, or to replace an existing state with another—to substitute democratic socialism, say, for oligarchy. If we're speaking precisely, it's only anarchism if the goal is no rulers at all.

In addition, to be an anarchist is not to oppose social order generally. "Anarchy" is often used to connote chaos or disorder, yet the anarchist's argument is typically something to the effect that social order is possible without coercive, centralized authority. So the anarchist distinguishes "society" from "state" or "government."

Arguments for anarchism typically include one or more of the following points:

1 Coercion is detrimental to human flourishing and so should be minimized if not eliminated.
2 People have rights, and states necessarily violate rights.
3 The levels of cooperation necessary for social order emerge organically and do not require coercive imposition.
4 Political actors are self-interested and seek their own advantage rather than the common good, so we should favor institutions that deny power to such actors.
5 Political institutions get captured by mechanisms that favor groups who receive concentrated benefits at the expense of the majority over which costs are dispersed.
6 Putative rationales for state authority are unpersuasive, but the burden of proof rests with supporters of such authority.
7 Collective means cannot be morally superior to individual means if the ends are not themselves morally legitimate.
8 Political institutions erode our cooperative natures and make us worse people.
9 The reality of human pluralism makes the existence of alternative arrangements for the maintenance of social order desirable.

This list is not intended to be exhaustive; these are merely some of the more common arguments offered in support of anarchist conclusions.

III. The Limits of Arguments for Anarchism

Suppose for a moment that I have written a philosophical treatise demonstrating with sound reasoning that all arguments justifying state authority are flawed, that society could be expected to function and flourish in the absence of coercive political structures, that social order and dispute resolution would emerge from voluntary arrangements.[1] Would all political philosophers familiar with my devastating arguments likely embrace anarchism? The astute reader will have already noted that philosophy doesn't work that way. There may be plenty of agreement with whatever you have argued, but agreement is virtually always accompanied by dissent. Some of the dissent is rooted in good pedagogical practice—effective teachers present both sides of a dispute and invite students to draw their own conclusions. But a large part of it is due to the very nature of philosophical arguments. Since they're very complex, there are many avenues for disagreement. Any interesting argument will likely contain so many premises and so many inferences that a person looking for a way to disagree will surely have several options to choose from. This may be due to a perverse contrarianism or emotional attachment to a prior belief, or it may be sincere, rational disagreement with some presupposition or implication. In any case, it's not uncommon for people to look at the conclusion of an argument, decide they disagree, and then review the argument looking for ways in which it (must have) gone wrong. After all, if the conclusion is false, some part of the argument must contain a flaw. Since for most people anarchism simply must be false, it wouldn't matter (for them) whether an argument for anarchism were (actually) sound.

But people do sometimes change their minds on the basis of philosophical arguments. Taking the long view of the history of philosophy, we can see many examples—the most relevant for present purposes being arguments for anarchism itself. Every philosophical proponent of anarchism was raised in a society with rulers in which a narrative justifying state authority was widely embraced. So that there are any philosophical anarchists at all is evidence that it's at least possible to make effective, persuasive arguments.[2]

Suppose again for a moment that I have indeed written a philosophical treatise demonstrating with sound reasoning that all arguments justifying state authority are flawed, that society would function and flourish in the absence of coercive political structures, and that social order and dispute resolution would emerge from voluntary arrangements. Suppose, too, that—amazingly—the vast majority of philosophers agreed that I was correct. What would happen? What would likely *not* happen is that the government would disband and all people holding power would renounce it. Broadly speaking, there are two reasons why that is not what would happen.

The first is that people who have power tend to like having power and will be reluctant to give it up. This happens so rarely that when it does, everyone knows about it and finds it remarkable. In general, people with power want to preserve, and if possible, expand their power.

The other reason is that most people think political authority is necessary. Even when they disapprove of some particular ruler or form of government, most people think the occurrence of the flaws to which they object just means they should support a *different* ruler or a *different* form of government. For example, most Democratic voters want to replace a Republican president with one from their own party, not to eliminate the presidency. Opponents of James II wanted to install a different monarch, not to eliminate the monarchy.

As it happens, the second reason is much more important than the first. If people didn't think states were necessary, they would likely wrest power from those seeking to retain it or persuade them to give it up. The robust persistence of the first factor is due to the prevalence of people's belief in the necessity of the state; and indeed, this belief is why the use of violent means to deal with the authorities' grip on power is certain to fail.

IV. Rejecting Anti-state Violence

As long as most people think there should be *some* ruler, any violent action against the ruler will result in the installation of another ruler.[3] The death of the holder of a particular office represents a vacancy to be filled; it does not eliminate the office, or people's perception that the office needs to be occupied. When anarchist Leon Czolgosz assassinated President McKinley, it didn't end the presidency, it just meant that Theodore Roosevelt became president. Removing current members of the government doesn't remove the idea of government. The vacuum would be filled immediately, and no one's beliefs about the ideas of spontaneous order and social rules, or the relationship between liberty and human flourishing, or the coercive nature of government would likely be changed.

Besides that, I suspect the use of violence would be immoral under all but the most extreme circumstances. In dystopian fiction, in which the human spirit is crushed by a totalitarian state, heroic protagonists often use violent means that are portrayed as justified.[4] In the sort of scenario they're confronting, perhaps it would be, but in the actual world *we* live in, the violence wouldn't meet the threshold for legitimacy. Most people think the state is justified, and the state is so intertwined in everyday life that it's hard to argue that every single participant is culpably participatory.

If you go down to city hall, there's a clerk in the water department's office sorting through water meter readings and depositing people's checks for overuse fees. It's just not coherent to claim that this person is the moral equivalent of a concentration camp guard. So when, for example,

Timothy McVeigh bombed the Murrah Federal Building in Oklahoma City, he was mistaken to think it was a morally legitimate target. Most of his victims were more like the water department clerk than the death camp guard, and a number of his victims were children in a day care facility. As McVeigh, and Leon Czolgosz before him, learned the hard way, violent action doesn't change people's minds the way they perhaps hoped it would. The violence is thus immoral in all but the most extreme cases, and largely ineffective in any event.

V. The Significance of Arguments for Anarchism

So, the use of violent means directed against rulers doesn't produce anarchism, and philosophical arguments demonstrating the soundness of anarchism don't produce anarchism. So, the question stands, what is the point of anarchist argument? I think there are two sorts of answers to this, and while I intend to focus on one of them in the remainder of this chapter, I want to at least mention the other: that philosophical arguments need not have practical points—their aim is truth, and as long as an argument is logically pushing towards truth, it need not have any further practical value. However, I think there *is* a practical point to the anarchist's argument, even given the persistence of statist thought amongst most people.

That point is that anarchism is only possible when people's ideas about government and authority change. This is why violent means are not only immoral, but certain to be ineffective. Changing minds requires persuasion, but, even if persuasion is unlikely to lead people to embrace anarchism, reiterating good anarchist arguments can be effective in another way: it can help people rethink the nature and justification of authority generally. A philosophical examination of the justification for government power will necessarily include a consideration of the scope of that power. This can have the salutary effect of getting more people to see that the more we rely on coercion to accomplish social goals, the more we erode civil society. The clearer it becomes that the state's *authority* is limited, the clearer it should become that state *power should be* limited. The more thoroughly it is demonstrated that state power tends to be captured by special interests and used for the private benefit of rulers and their cronies, the more evident it will become that the rulers' rhetoric doesn't match their actions.

Consider another way to think about this point. Some people have said the state is a necessary evil, grudgingly accepting the idea that coercion is bad, state actors are frequently self-interested, and so on. The anarchist's response to this position is typically to argue that the state is *not*, in fact, necessary. But, as is obvious, people resist this conclusion regardless of how cogent the arguments supporting it may be. However, there's also a good deal of complacency in the way contemporary people view the state—many take it as axiomatic that we need the state, and that it's natural for the state to perform this or that function, or even that the state helps to *create* society. Anarchist arguments can help such people think about the parameters of state power. If the state is at best a necessary evil, then we have good reason to limit its power even if anarchism is false; whereas if the state is a positive good, we have far less rationale for limiting its power. The anarchist's ultimate preference is for others to agree that state coercion is unjustified. When they don't, however, it is surely preferable for them to think that the state is a necessary evil than to regard it as an unalloyed good. So, even failing to persuade others of the truth of anarchism, the anarchist is nevertheless working towards creating a freer world by persuading others to see the state's downside.

Anarchist theory can therefore be seen as *both* aspirational and incremental. To say "We will never reach anarchism, so stop wasting your breath!" is to miss the point. Reframing the case for coercive authority structures as warranting skepticism and scrutiny rather than acquiescence and complacency serves a very real purpose even if it's true that, at least for now, most people are likely to reject anarchism.

A person could ultimately reject anarchism while still learning something from the anarchist's critique of the state. For example, rather than automatically assuming that state actors are exclusively or primarily motivated by concern for the common good, a person might come to recognize ways in which rulers' actions preserve their own power and wealth. Coming to see factors like this more clearly has the potential to change someone's default reaction from "This state activity must be good, albeit in some way I don't see" to "I wonder if there is a non-coercive way to accomplish the worthwhile goal this activity is supposed to serve and, if there's not, whether this really is a desirable goal." A person might come to understand that regulations such as occupational licensure are rhetorically defended as serving the common good but they actually represent the use of the state's coercive power to benefit a small group at the expense of the group's competitors and the general public. A person might come to see ways in which state control of dispute resolution incentivizes mass incarceration. The anarchist should welcome such changes in public perception of state power even if the majority of people still do not accept anarchism.

It is thus worthwhile, not pointless, to continue to try to impress upon people the moral deficiencies of coercive authority structures. To make the case against the state is to undermine the idea that coercion is *necessary* for social order, or that it is *beneficial* to human society. It is to point the way towards the continual need to scale back the scope of state power. It is to affirm the priority of liberty and its necessary connection to human flourishing, and to keep us mindful of the ways in which the state, and our often unthinking obedience to it, hinders that flourishing.

Notes

1 I'd like to think I have in fact done this: see my *Deleting the State: An Argument About Government* (Chicago, IL: Open Court 2008). But assume I have not: there are many others, notably Gary Chartier, *Anarchy and Legal Order* (New York, NY: CUP 2013); Michael Huemer, *The Problem of Political Authority* (New York, NY: Palgrave 2013); Gerard Casey, *Libertarian Anarchy* (New York, NY: Continuum 2012); John Hasnas, "The Obviousness of Anarchy," *Anarchism/Minarchism: Is a Government Part of a Free County?*, ed. Roderick T. Long and Tibor Machan (Aldershot: Ashgate 2008) 111–32.

2 Indeed, not just anarchists but minimal-state libertarians are also evidence of this, as none of them was raised in a libertarian society. They would have to have embraced their current positions in virtue of some encounters with philosophical or economic argumentation.

3 In the 2016–19 ABC television series *Designated Survivor*, terrorists kill all of the officers of the legislative, executive, and judicial branches except three. The Constitution makes the title protagonist the new President, and he proceeds to appoint all new cabinet members and supervise the repopulation of Congress. Everyone's first thought is *not* "Yay, anarchy!" It's "Wow, with all the officeholders now murdered, we need to refill the vacant offices right away!" Similar events ensue in Tom Clancy, *Debt of Honor* (New York, NY: Putnam 1995).

4 See, for example, Alan Moore and David Lloyd, *V for Vendetta*, 30th anniv. ed. (New York, NY: Vertigo-DC 2018).

PART II

Figures and Traditions

6

ANARCHISM AGAINST ANARCHY

The Classical Roots of Anarchism

Stephen R. L. Clark

I. Making a Consensual Community

There may somewhere in the multiverse be intelligent creatures who must cope by themselves, like baby turtles, from the moment that they hatch: C. J. Cherryh has perhaps come close to imagining such unashamedly egoistic creatures, "*kif*," in her Chanur sequence.[1] How precisely such creatures would come to treat their conspecifics, how they would learn to communicate or bargain with them for whatever individual advantage, is a matter, so far, for baffled speculation. No readers of this volume are likely to be so alien. We were all born to human parents, taught a mother tongue, and imbued with whatever unexamined attitudes our parents or carers—and their companions—shared. Even in adulthood we are *dependent* animals, requiring the company and services of uncounted others. As Aristotle observed,

> the man who is isolated, who is unable to share in the benefits of political association, or has no need to share because he is already self-sufficient, is no part of the city, and must therefore be either a beast or a god.
>
> *(Aristotle* Politics *1.1253a30: 1995, p.11)*

Even the imagined Cyclopes, "clanless and lawless and hearthless" (1.1253a5, citing Homer *Odyssey* 9.114–5), at least have neighbours who may come running to understand their cries for help. Even they must have households of some sort, in which to beget and bear and rear their offspring. Even they must find their mates from somewhere more or less compatible. "Each of them," said Homer, "rules over his children and wives" (*Politics* 1.1252b20). Such simple households are perhaps replicated amongst the poor even of larger unions: "the poor man, not having slaves, is compelled to use his wife and children as attendants" (*Politics* 6.1322b40: 1995, p.250). Unsurprisingly, being born as wholly dependent creatures, we depend upon our parents or carers, and find ourselves, long before we have any political opinions or rational arguments, bound by affection (mostly) and respect for these larger figures.

> The male parent is in a position of authority both in virtue of the affection to which he is entitled and by right of his seniority [he is typically several years older than his wife]; and his position is thus in the nature of royal authority.
>
> *(*Politics *2.1259b10: 1995, p.33)*

Of course, we also grow up, and grow bigger. Adolescent rebellion against parental authority is likely universal in our species (and in many other mammalian kinds): or rather, rebellion against particular authorities in the hope of ourselves becoming such authorities. The impossible question in Greek rhetoric, it is of some interest to note, was "Have you stopped beating your father yet?" (Diogenes Laertius *Lives* 2.135; see also Aristotle *Nicomachean Ethics* 7.1149b8). The rebel, to modify a remark of Chesterton, does not disrespect authority—he merely wishes to have such authority for himself, so as to respect it more perfectly.[2] As Chesterton concluded, the really dangerous criminal is the modern political philosopher, who genuinely does disrespect the whole notion of "authority" (a point to which I shall return).

Households may turn into clans, retaining the parental hierarchies into which we are born and reared, or else they may find common cause with other households near at hand, partly to demarcate the land that counts as "theirs" and partly to exchange their surplus goods and special crafts. Plato's account of such a development is apostrophized as merely a "city of pigs" by Glaucon (Plato *Republic* 2.372d), but perhaps it is not even, really, a "city" or "township" (polis) at all, but—exactly—a collection of households with no particular common interest in the character and goals of its human agents. "A city cannot be constituted from any chance collection of people, or in any chance period of time" (*Politics* 5.1303a25[3]), though that is the model that social contract theorists have often assumed—as if we were indeed the solitary super-turtles (so to speak) that I imagined earlier!

> Any city (*polis*) which is truly so called, and is not merely one in name, must devote itself to the end of encouraging goodness. Otherwise, a political association sinks into a mere alliance, which only differs in space [i.e. in the contiguity of its members] from other forms of alliance where the members live at a distance from one another.
>
> (*Aristotle* Politics *1.1280b6*[4])

One likely form of authority for a clan or for some other slightly larger social form will indeed be the royal: "just as household government is kingship over a family, so conversely this type of kingship may be regarded as household government exercised over a city, or a tribe, or a collection of tribes" (*Politics* 3.1285b30[5]). One advantage, at least for the stability of the system, of a merely dynastic royalty is that it does not depend on the *merit* of the king that he be king, though his authority may indeed be reduced, and his inheritance rendered illegitimate, if he fails too openly in his quasi-parental duties. But maybe the very claim to be "royal," and to require the sort of affection, respect and proper fear that children may feel for their elders, creates the notion of merit: how is it that this one person, or this one line of descent, "deserves" the office?

> We may imagine one set of circumstances in which it would be obviously better that the one group should once and for all be rulers and one group should be ruled. This would be if there were one class in the city surpassing all others as much as gods and heroes are supposed to surpass mankind—a class so outstanding, physically as well as mentally, that the superiority of the rulers was indisputably clear to those over whom they ruled.
>
> (Politics *7.1332b20*[6])

But once it becomes clear, or widely suspected, that the king and his lineage are not so surpassingly great, his subjects may prefer some more egalitarian system—leaving aside the moments when they replace the king with a sometime-popular despot (one probably unconstrained by family feeling or tradition). After all, even kings—especially kings—depend on others to advise and act for them (*Politics* 3.1287b30); why then might not the king's "friends" and servants do the job without him? Why might they not in their turn solicit support and agents from the common folk? A similar moral may issue from Plato's *Republic*: if the only people we could trust to rule us with intelligence and integrity must be philosopher-kings, and we cannot find such anywhere, perhaps we should be content instead with the "least worst" constitution, in which "every individual can make for himself the kind of life which suits him" (*Republic* 8.557b).

Two further problems arise for royalty which may be answered through a more egalitarian solution. The first is simply that—like parental authority in the household—it may easily become despotic: obedience will then be enforced by threats of violence, as though subjects were no more than slaves. Only those of a "slavish" disposition—in Aristotle's view, barbarians—could put up with this for long: "these barbarian peoples are more servile in character than Greeks (as the peoples of Asia are more servile than those of Europe); and they therefore tolerate despotic rule without any complaint" (*Politics* 3.1285a20; see also 7.1327b25[7]). The better route is a form of community spirit that allows citizens to "live as they like," each taking an equal share in any collective decision-making:

> Such a life, they argue, is the function of the free man, just as the function of slaves is *not* to live as they like. This is the second defining feature of democracy [the first being that all citizens should have equal shares in the making of collective decisions]. It results in the view that ideally one should not be ruled by any one, or, at least, that one should [rule and] be ruled in turns.
>
> (Politics *6.1317b10*[8])

The second problem, by Aristotle's account, is that a city, a polis, is not after all just the same as a household, or even as a clan, and is not best served by too strict a unity. This is Aristotle's chief complaint against Plato's Republic (*Politics* 2.1261a20), that a polis is composed of distinct households and individuals of many kinds and functions. Citizens must have property of their very own, even if there is also some shared property. But how then shall the polis be at peace, if not by affectionate agreement? A merely contractual theory of state-formation, as though some chance collection of lawless persons had come together to swear a pact of mutual defence and forbearance, wholly neglects the need for a common custom underlying all explicit laws and regulations, and presents us with the obvious problem that we cannot now be reasonably bound by any such contracts made by our brigand ancestors (especially if there is no record of any such sensible compact)! It is better to accept that we are all born into communities with their own customs and bonds of affection and respect, and that the question before us is rather how we would prefer to manage our social relations, what simple changes we might wish to make, or realize we have already made. We no more need to make up all the customs by which we live than we need to make up our languages. Fortunately so: "When antient opinions and rules of life are taken away, the loss cannot possibly be estimated. From that moment we have no compass to govern us; nor can we know distinctly to what port we steer."[9]

How far do we need any overt laws and regulations additional to common custom? After all,

> there is no advantage in the best of laws, even when they are sanctioned by general civic consent, if the citizens themselves have not been attuned, by the force of habit and the influence of teaching, to the right constitutional temper—which will be the temper of democracy where the laws are democratic, and where they are oligarchical will be that of oligarchy.
>
> (Politics *5.1310a18)*

And if the citizens are indeed thus attuned, what need is there for further legislation, or any "government" beyond the self-regulation of the whole civic community? Aristotle indeed acknowledges that

> heterogeneity of stocks may lead to faction—at any rate until they have had time to assimilate. A city cannot be constituted from any chance collection of people, or in any chance period of time. Most of the cities which have admitted others as settlers, either at the time of their foundation or later, have been troubled by faction.
>
> (Politics *5.1303a25*[10])

Such factions may lead to war, and be suppressed by violence—so making the members of the subject (that is, the subjugated) population, effectively, into slaves. This is certainly not to advise the outlawing of all immigration, but to acknowledge that native-born and immigrants will need time, and patience, to adjust.

But even if we don't have to make up the customs and communities in which we live, may there not be some profit in imagining how they might, acceptably, be arranged (as political theorists from Democritus to Rawls have done)? What would we reasonably do to rescue ourselves from the imagined "war of each against all"? There is a certain ambiguity in what seems to have been a standard ancient opinion, turning on the imagined "lawlessness" of the days before civil community:

> For the laws are what bind cities together, and as the soul perishes when the body has perished, so the cities are destroyed when the laws are abolished. Hence, the theologian Orpheus hints at their necessity when he says 'There was a time when every man liv'd by devouring his fellow Cannibal-wise, and the stronger man did feast on the weaker … (for when no law was in control each man maintained his right by force of hand, even as it is permitted to fishes and beasts of the wild and the winged ravens and vultures, each to devour the other, for justice exists not among them), until God in his pity for their misery sent to them law-bearing goddesses, and men admired these for the way they stopped the lawless cannibalism more than for the way they civilized life by means of the fruits of the earth.' Hence, too, the shrewd Persians have a law that on the death of their king they must practise lawlessness for the next five days, not in order to be in a state of misery but in order to learn by experience how great an evil lawlessness is, inflicting, as it does, murders and rapine and things which are, if possible, worse, so that they may become more trusty guardians of their kings.
>
> *(Sextus,* Against the Professors *2.31–3;*[11] *see also Hesiod,* Works and Days *274–9)*

Are we to suppose that we need *kings* (that is to say, bullies) or rather a sense of justice, fair play, shame (without which kings and their subjects will certainly degenerate)? Or is this "Orphic" imagining, this thought experiment, merely a projection back into pre-history of the actual Mediterranean experience, in which cities were all, implicitly, at war with each other (Plato *Laws* 1.626a)? What might really bring us a peace that is more than a word? Is anarchy really "lawless"?

Both monarchical and more egalitarian constitutions may issue at last in violence, and despotic control of their subjects. This is not immediately to say that the rulers of such cities will be seeking their own advantage rather than their subjects' (which is the criterion by which both Plato and Aristotle identify degenerate constitutions), but it is clearly very likely that, whatever excuses they may offer, all such violent rule will also be *literally* despotic. Only those (if any) who really should be considered slaves or slavish should be treated *as if* they were slaves, having no conception of their own of a good life for themselves and for their kin, nor any will to achieve it. Whether there are such people as "natural slaves" (who live and behave as slaves whatever the constitution under which they live) is maybe moot. That Aristotle would consider the complaisant subjects of such violent and coercive rule as he observed in eastern empires to be slaves is not. But those who are not thus slavish deserve much better.

> Yet it cannot, perhaps, but appear very strange, to anyone ready to reflect on the matter, that it should be the function of a statesman to be able to lay plans for ruling and dominating neighbouring cities whether or not they give their consent. How can something which is not even lawful be proper for a statesman or lawmaker?
>
> (Politics 7.*1324b25*[12])

Coercion is improper, whether it is of conquered peoples or of the other members of the statesman's polis. And coercion may sometimes be covert, depending on deceit by statesmen and laziness amongst subjects. The twin principles of a democracy are on the one hand that the decisions of the demos, the people, rule, and on the other that all citizens live as they choose (which is not necessarily quite the same as living as they—for the moment—please). Clearly those principles may conflict, if—for example—the poor, being "in the majority," expropriate the property of "the rich," or some majority moral opinion is enforced on those who flatly disagree.

Political community depends on real consensus, founded in the fact that every citizen has a share in collective decision-making—and no decisions are enforced even by stable majority factions on a recognized minority. This can hardly be possible if the supposed polis is the size of Babylon or anything we would now call a "nation-state" (see *Politics* 3.1276a24).

> A city composed of too few members is a city without self-sufficiency (and the city, by its definition, is self-sufficient). One composed of too many will indeed be self-sufficient in the matter of material necessities (as a nation may be) but it will not be a city, since it can hardly have a constitution.
>
> (Politics 7.*1326b*[13])

Of course we may, if we are "free" by temperament and education, accept that not every collective, dialectical decision is as we personally wish, but once it is clear that almost all the collective decisions go against our own and our friends' votes and arguments, the city is on the brink of war: a faction may be as tyrannical as any despot, and must be resisted.

> What if the poor, on the ground of their being a majority, proceed to divide among themselves the possessions of the wealthy—will not this be unjust? 'No, by heaven' (someone may reply); 'it has been justly decreed so by the sovereign body.' But if this is not the extreme of injustice, what is? Whenever a majority takes everything and divides among its members the possessions of a minority, that majority is obviously ruining the city.
>
> (Politics *3.1281a11*[14])

Not all decrees are necessarily just ones, even by local standards. Whether the rich hold their property justly in the first place may also be moot. But the chief moral is that a properly *political* community is both broadly self-sufficient and self-governing, and that all attempts to rule by violence or fraud are improper. David Keyt identified the clearly "anarchist" implications of Aristotle's principles (as also Plato's).

> Aristotle defines a deviant constitution as one under which the rulers rule for their own advantage (*Politics* 3.1279a19–20). He goes on to claim that deviant constitutions are characterized by their use of force (3.1281a23–24; see also 3.1276a12–13), that they are contrary to nature (*para phusin*) (3.1287b37–41), and that they are unjust (3.1282b8–13). Aristotle does not explicitly connect these three claims with each other or with his definition. But the derivation of the anti-coercion principle shows how they can be linked together. That the rulers in a *polis* with a deviant constitution must use force to

maintain themselves in power is a consequence of the nature of their rule. For deviant constitutions are all despotic (3.1279a19–21; 4.1290a25–29; 7.1333a3–6). Under such a constitution the rulers, looking only to their own advantage, treat those outside the constitution, the second-class citizens, as slaves (see 3.1278b32–37 and 4.1295b19–23). Since these outsiders are free men (3.1279a21; see also 4.1292b38–41), there can be no question of their enduring such treatment willingly (see 4.1295a17–23). Thus, under a deviant constitution there is always a group of subjects who obey their rulers only because they are forced to. In a democracy it is the rich; in an oligarchy, the poor; in a tyranny, the free (for tyranny see 3.1285a25–29; 5.1314al0–12). Given the Aristotelian equation of the forced and the unnatural, it follows at once that deviant constitutions are contrary to nature.[15]

II. The Point and Peril of Ethical Concern

So far there is a clear agreement on the part of a wide range of classical writers with one of the staple doctrines of an anarchist philosophy. Political authority cannot rest upon coercion, and the ideal form of human community will be both self-sufficient and self-governing. Everyone who is capable of reaching and acting on a decision about what to do, everyone who has a working conception of what will make a life worth living, must have a say in collective decisions. We cannot avoid the necessity of such collectives, even by wandering away into the wilderness and surviving by our own singular endeavours (a project that only a few exceptional individuals can accomplish, and they only with a lot of luck). Even they will, almost certainly, have to come to some agreement with any neighbouring tribes and cities, even simply to be left alone. But might not simple treaties be enough for us? Might we not agree merely to bring any goods for exchange to some central market, and even conclude a pact of mutual defence against any who would attack that market, or our households? Even the necessity of finding mates from outside our immediate families might be managed by, as it were, the marriage-mart, perhaps with appeals to some recognized "sacred" elements? Such treaties will not be long sustained unless the parties all find an agreeable profit in them, and are all sufficiently alike in what they consider a "fair" trade, or a "just" defence, or a "proper" marriage partner, but there need be no considerable concern for how householders manage their own affairs at home.

A polis, on the other hand, so Aristotle concluded, is dedicated to some particular conception of what a *good* life may be. The end of the city is not mere life; it is, rather, a good quality of life.

> Otherwise, there might be a city of slaves, or even a city of animals; but in the world as we know it any such city is impossible, because slaves and animals do not share in happiness [*eudaimonia*] nor in living according to their own choice. Similarly, it is not the end of the city to provide an alliance for mutual defence against all injury, nor does it exist for the purpose of exchange or [commercial] dealing. If that had been the end, the Etruscans and the Carthaginians would be in the position of belonging to a single city; and the same would be true to all peoples who have commercial treaties with one another. It is true that such peoples have agreements about imports; treaties to ensure just conduct; and written terms of alliance for mutual defence. On the other hand, they have no common offices to deal with these matters: each, on the contrary, has its own offices, confined to itself. Neither party concerns itself to ensure a proper quality of character among the members of the other; neither of them seeks to ensure that all who are included in the scope of the treaties are just and free from any form of vice; and they do not go beyond the aim of preventing their own members from committing injustice against one another. But it is the goodness or badness in the life of the city

> which engages the attention of those who are concerned to secure good government. The conclusion which clearly follows is that any city which is truly so called, and is not merely one in name, must devote itself to the end of encouraging goodness. Otherwise, a political association sinks into a mere alliance, which only differs in space [i.e. in the contiguity of its members] from other forms of alliance where the members live at a distance from one another.
>
> (Politics *3.1280b6*[16])

This latter possibility in turn is the root of another form of anarchist philosophy, less community minded and more in line with what would now be considered "right-wing anarchism" or "libertarianism." The sophist Lycophron, it is said, expressly claimed that the law was only a contract about allowable claims upon one another, without any concern to make the citizens virtuous or just. We know too little of Lycophron to conclude that he therefore promoted the notion of a "minimal state" or "conflict management agencies" concerned only to assess conflicting claims about ownership or injury, still less that he had a working "social contract" theory about our proper obedience to the sort of civil authority that might emerge from what would once have been only a paid service.[17] But that idea, of "justice" as an arrangement between contending parties, saving them from undue harm while requiring them also to forego undue profit (as Glaucon proposes in Plato *Republic* 2.358e), can also be considered an element in the development at least of liberal politics. An element only, and a risky one: Herodotus also noted the possibility that civil authority began with a general agreement to acknowledge the good judgement of a particular man considered "wise."

> As the Medes at that time dwelt in scattered villages without any central authority, and lawlessness in consequence prevailed throughout the land, Deioces, who was already a man of mark in his own village, applied himself with greater zeal and earnestness than ever before to the practice of justice among his fellows. It was his conviction that justice and injustice are engaged in perpetual war with one another. He therefore began his course of conduct, and presently the men of his village, observing his integrity, chose him to be the arbiter of all their disputes. Bent on obtaining the sovereign power, he showed himself an honest and an upright judge, and by these means gained such credit with his fellow-citizens as to attract the attention of those who lived in the surrounding villages. They had long been suffering from unjust and oppressive judgments; so that, when they heard of the singular uprightness of Deioces, and of the equity of his decisions, they joyfully had recourse to him in the various quarrels and suits that arose, until at last they came to put confidence in no one else.
>
> *(Herodotus 1.96–7*[18]*)*

The conclusion of the story has Deioces established as an absolute monarch, with a palace at Ecbatana. The "equity of his decisions," it turns out, was in the end only a gambit, to achieve monarchical power of a sort that Herodotus spends his *Histories* quietly rebuking and contrasting with the willing obedience of (some) Greeks to an impersonal Law. Demaratus, for example, responds to Xerxes' baffled enquiry about how so few Greeks should hope to stand against so many of his army that they are free, but also obedient to Law, "which they fear much more than your subjects fear you" (7.104).[19]

So also Herodotus credits the ascent of the Athenians to their "freedom":

> It is plain enough … that freedom is an excellent thing since even the Athenians, who, while they continued under the rule of tyrants, were not a whit more valiant than any

> of their neighbours, no sooner shook off the yoke than they became decidedly the first of all. These things show that, while undergoing oppression, they let themselves be beaten, since then they worked for a master; but so soon as they got their freedom, each man was eager to do the best he could for himself.
>
> *(Herodotus 5.78)*

This trope, of the "free" Greek or Westerner against the naturally "servile" Easterner, is not one that we should now endorse, but it remains significant for our understanding of what "freedom," *eleutheria,* might mean, and why it is not to be equated with any simple rule of non-interference or even the more difficult attempt at compromise between competing interests. Freedom is a way of living together as equals. A merely "minimal" state, or an alliance, may have no interest in the character of its members, or the way they manage their households, so long as they keep their agreements. But this condition is bound to be unstable: those who keep their agreements *only* from fear of retribution, and esteem their "freedom" *only* so that they can get what they currently desire, may be easily corrupted, and likewise expect their partners to be corrupt. Bargains between desperate brigands, or even complacent burghers, have little force: notoriously, it is hard to ensure cooperation even in the possible partners' ultimate self-interest, when it so often makes selfish sense for either party to defect. The only solutions we seem to have discovered are either to concede sufficient power to Leviathan (monarchical or republican) to suppress rebellion, or else to rear us all in virtuous habits of a proper sort. Anarchists—and Aristotle—reject the option of Leviathan: Aristotle concluded that all *poleis* must be concerned with the virtue of their members, since our goal is not merely *survival,* life on whatever terms, but a recognizably *good* or worthwhile life.

> The city as a whole has a single end. Evidently, therefore, the system of education must also be one and the same for all, and the provision of this system must be a matter of public action. It cannot be left, as it is at present, to private enterprise, with each parent making provision privately for his own children, and having them privately instructed as he himself thinks fit. Training for an end which is common should also itself be common. We must not regard a citizen as belonging just to himself: we must rather regard every citizen as belonging to the city, since each is a part of the city; and the provision made for each part will naturally be adjusted to the provision made for the whole.
>
> (Politics *8.1337a21*[20])

This may be a challenge to a merely "libertarian" philosophy, but not to a more sophisticated anarchism. Anarchists, almost above all others, must have a respect for virtue as this is commonly understood.

But what exactly does Aristotle's virtue require? Much of what he says of virtue, and its importance for any life worth living, should be uncontentious:

> No one would call a man happy who had no particle of courage, temperance, justice, or wisdom; who feared the flies buzzing about his head; who abstained from none of the extremest forms of extravagance whenever he felt hungry or thirsty; who would ruin his dearest friends for the sake of a quarter of an obol; whose mind was as senseless, and as much deceived, as that of a child or a madman.
>
> (Politics *8.1323a25*[21])

But he is also confident that different sorts of virtue, different kinds and levels of goodness, are appropriate for different classes within the polis. How exactly any particular polis orders its affairs or ranks its virtues is a matter for that polis: "self-government" is perhaps a more contentious notion than he allows, if there are always decisions to be made (or customs to be followed) about who counts as a contributing agent. Even when he speaks of such people as are not "naturally" slaves as being themselves "free," as individuals and as members of the polis, he expressly excludes women, children, farmers, mechanics, day labourers, and any other persons incapable, by temperament or occupation, of participating in needful political offices. Nor—as he well knew—were all *actual* slaves also "natural" slaves. Ancient Greek "democracy," by modern liberal standards, was restricted to the freeborn, native, few, even if it allowed more say in the polis than overtly oligarchical regimes. Tyrants and demagogues, he even suggested, were likelier to give support to slaves and women—as both being good informers against their lords!

> Kings are maintained and secured by their friends but it is characteristic of tyrants to distrust them above all others, for whereas everyone wants [to overthrow tyrants], it is their friends who have most power to achieve this. The methods applied in extreme democracies are thus all to be found in tyrannies. They both encourage feminine influence in the family, in the hope that wives will tell tales of their husbands; and for a similar reason they are both indulgent to slaves. Slaves and women are not likely to plot against tyrants: indeed, as they prosper under them, they are bound to look with favour on tyrannies and democracies alike—of course the people likes to act as absolute ruler. This is the reason why, under both these forms of government, honour is paid to flatterers, in democracies to demagogues, who are flatterers of the people, and, in the case of tyrants, to those who associate with them on obsequious terms—which is the function of the flatterer. Tyranny is thus a system dear to the wicked. Tyrants love to be flattered, and nobody with the soul of a freeman can ever stoop to that; a good man may be a friend, but at any rate he will not be a flatterer.[22]
>
> *(*Politics *5.1313b29)*

One further common excuse for the restriction was that only those who could *defend* the city were legitimately its rulers: so Athens allowed poorer folk to play a part because it was more dependent on the oarsmen of its navy than on armed infantry or the still more limited cavalry:

> In Athens the poor and the people generally are right to have more than the highborn and wealthy for the reason that it is the people who man the ships and impart strength to the city; the steersmen, the boatswains, the sub-boatswains, the look-out officers, and the shipwrights—these are the ones who impart strength to the city far more than the hoplites, the high-born, and the good men. This being the case, it seems right for everyone to have a share in the magistracies, both allotted and elective, for anyone to be able to speak his mind if he wants to.
>
> *(Ps-Xenophon,* Constitution *1.2[23])*

Another was that "banausic" occupations limited intelligence and were likely to cripple bodies: a properly "liberal" education, suitable for and supportive of "freedom," would not allow children to take up such occupations (as professional musicians, craftsmen, slave-masters). Some might nowadays add computer nerds, scientists, and bureaucrats to the list of "banausic" persons!

> Occupations are divided into those which are fit for freemen and those which are unfit for them; and clearly children should take part in useful occupations only to the extent that they do not turn those taking part in them into 'mechanical' types. The term

> 'mechanical' [*banausos*] should properly be applied to any occupation, art, or instruction which is calculated to make the body, or soul, or mind of a freeman unfit for the pursuit and practice of goodness.
>
> (Politics *8.1337b*[24])

From which it might follow that Aristotle himself would not approve the Athenian mode of civic defence, as requiring people to have a say in the collective decision-making (as defenders of the city) who could not, by their education and occupation, fulfil that task.

The author we call Ps-Xenophon was yet more explicit in his disdain for "the worse sort of people":

> Everywhere on earth the best element is opposed to democracy. For among the best people there is minimal wantonness and injustice but a maximum of scrupulous care for what is good, whereas among the people there is a maximum of ignorance, disorder, and wickedness; for poverty draws them rather to disgraceful actions, and because of a lack of money some men are uneducated and ignorant.
>
> *(Ps-Xenophon 1.5*[25]*)*

Not only their character but their constitution makes them unreliable:

> For oligarchic cities it is necessary to keep to alliances and oaths. If they do not abide by agreements or if injustice is done, there are the names of the few who made the agreement. But whatever agreements the populace makes can be repudiated by referring the blame to the one who spoke or took the vote, while the others declare that they were absent or did not approve of the agreement made in the full assembly. If it seems advisable for their decisions not to be effective, they invent myriad excuses for not doing what they do not want to do. And if there are any bad results from the people's plans, they charge that a few persons, working against them, ruined their plans; but if there is a good result, they take the credit for themselves.
>
> *(Ps-Xenophon 2.17*[26]*)*

But this must be a corruption of any preferred constitution. If the people ignore the claims of honour and civil friendship, how long can their lordship last? Such chaos will be replaced, sooner or later, by some form of despotic rule, since the people themselves will be shown to be incapable of ruling themselves, or standing by their decisions. And maybe Aristotle was not wholly wrong to think that *some* occupations, *some* educations, unfit us for any share in collective decision-making. Those *wholly* absorbed in, for example, making bridles are not best placed even to train horses, let alone manage the cavalry or the conduct of a war. The same applies—though Aristotle does not explicitly say so—to those absorbed in healing the sick: a doctor does not deliberate about *whether* to heal a patient, but only *how* (*Nicomachean Ethics* 3.1112b12–15). But whether or not time and public effort should be expended, say, on the healing arts is exactly what a civil community may sometimes have to determine, without regard to the fixed options of particular crafts and craftsmen. Should any effort be made to rear disabled or otherwise "defective" children? Should elderly males be encouraged, or even allowed, to procreate?

> The question arises whether children should always be reared or may sometimes be exposed to die. There should certainly be a law to prevent the rearing of deformed children. On the other hand, if the established social customs forbid the exposure of infants simply to keep down the number of children, a limit must be placed on the number

> who are born. If a child is then conceived in excess of the limit so fixed, a miscarriage should be induced before sense and life have begun.... It remains to determine the length of time for which [men and women] should render public service by bringing children into the world. The offspring of elderly men, like that of very young men, tends to be physically and mentally imperfect; and the children of old age are weakly. We may therefore fix the length of time for which procreation lasts by reference to the mental prime. This comes for most men—as some of the poets, who measure life in seven-year periods, have suggested—about the age of 50.
>
> (Politics 7.*1335b19*[27])

The Aristotelian polis, in short, may begin to feel oppressive, even without a distinct organ of government, a distinct class of governors. There must be officers to oversee all manner of implicit regulations (see *Politics* 1321b12–1322b16), but these duties should be shared amongst the citizens. What *sanctions* Aristotle proposes for his imagined (or reported) rules may be unclear: it may be that mere public oversight, and consequent embarrassment, will be enough to do the work (and exile of the offender be a last resort). "To be under the eyes of office-holders will serve, above anything else, to create a true feeling of modesty and the fear of shame which should animate freemen" (*Politics* 7.1331b1[28]). So also with decisions about the extent of "private" property: it may be oppressive to remove excesses of land or money from "the rich," but no civil community will long survive gross inequalities. Either citizens will agree to share or moderate their wealth, or some will find themselves expelled, or the city will descend into war and tyranny. But its continuance will still depend upon the actual, not merely the assumed, agreement of its citizens.

III. Enemies of the Political

One of the strangest comments on anarchistical theory is the suggestion that "anarchists maintain that no questions are political questions."[29] On the contrary, anarchists are bound to be considering politics—that is, the proper management of self-governing communities freed from domination.[30]

> The anarchists conceive a society in which all the mutual relations of its members are regulated, not by laws, nor by authorities, whether self-imposed or elected, but by mutual agreements between members of that society and by a sum of social customs and habits—not petrified by law, routine or superstition, but continually developing and continually re-adjusted in accordance with the ever-growing requirements of a free life stimulated by the progress of science, invention, and the steady growth of higher ideals.[31]

What customs need to be preserved, what modified or adjusted? What practices can be helpfully accepted, and what would be, inevitably, corrosive? Most of these questions are to be answered, precisely, by the citizens of whatever polis, not by theorists, however sensible. Consider an illuminating comment by David Brooks, writing in 2016 about the USA:

> We live in a big, diverse society. There are essentially two ways to maintain order and get things done in such a society—politics or some form of dictatorship. Either through compromise or brute force. Our founding fathers [that is, of the USA] chose politics. Politics is an activity in which you recognize the simultaneous existence of different groups, interests and opinions. You try to find some way to balance or reconcile or compromise those interests, or at least a majority of them. You follow a set of rules,

> enshrined in a constitution or in custom, to help you reach these compromises in a way everybody considers legitimate. The downside of politics is that people never really get everything they want. It's messy, limited and no issue is ever really settled. Politics is a muddled activity in which people have to recognize restraints and settle for less than they want. Disappointment is normal. But that's sort of the beauty of politics, too. It involves an endless conversation in which we learn about other people and see things from their vantage point and try to balance their needs against our own. Plus, it's better than the alternative: rule by some authoritarian tyrant who tries to govern by clobbering everyone in his way.[32]

Better also than the suggestions of an uninvolved political theorist!

But it is still possible to identify some risks and even some opportunities: the most obvious risk is the one described by Herodotus, whereby some agency originally hired to help settle disputes, or facilitate decisions, in a suitably friendly, dialectical way becomes, by degrees, the Master. The temptation to *correct* the obvious errors of an Aristotelian polis leads quickly to a novel despotism: "the way of the Ring to my heart is by pity, pity for weakness and the desire of strength to do good."[33] An associated peril lies in the management of common property: may not such management encroach by careful and seemingly reasonable steps on any remaining "private" property? Even the most "right-wing" or libertarian of political theorists cannot wholly escape the problem, as though everything could be sensibly partitioned as the singular and unquestioned property of single citizens, inherited by steps which may often have been wholly unjust. Conversely, it is all too easy for what should be common property to be appropriated for "private" use and management. In the words of the seventeenth-century protest against enclosures:

> The law locks up the man or woman
> Who steals the goose from off the common,
> But leaves the greater villain loose
> Who steals the common from off the goose.
> The law demands that we atone
> When we take things we do not own,
> But leaves the lords and ladies fine
> Who take things that are yours and mine.[34]

An identical crime is committed by colonialists who seize what they imagine to be "unowned" land or wilderness, without attention to the needs and uses of the "native born." Who owns what, and what such ownership involves, are plainly "political" questions, not merely "legal" ones (to be answered solely by reading documents endorsed or created, exactly, by the thieves). Nor can they be answered "neutrally," by appeal to some universally acknowledged principle, since it is exactly such principles that are in dispute between differing communities and classes. We may, perhaps (as Aristotle hoped), slowly discover at least what practices are likely or certain to be destabilizing failures, ridiculed by all later generations. Amongst those foolish practices, it seems, are both fully collectivist responses and fully idiotic ones (where "idiotic," despite its connotations, means only "individualized"). The super-turtles may perhaps be able to lay claim to their own personal space and property, and bargain by their personal skill and strength with every other turtle. We are born and reared and live within communities we did not build, and share the products of many generations' effort (which were often poorly rewarded).

On the one hand, not all property within the polis should be purely collective, to be used only and entirely as the whole consensus decides. On the other, no particular citizen should ever have so much property as to overwhelm all others. In what Aristotle considers the normal, or "natural," shape of a community there are natural limits on accumulation: no one citizen and no household can plausibly enjoy, own, manage, or maintain more than some definite amount of land or other form of wealth. The creation of *money* to facilitate exchange makes a difference: there is no *natural* limit on how much money could be accumulated by careful management (or sheer luck). And this is made most evident when money itself becomes something to be bartered or rented out, at whatever rate of interest the lender may require. Usury is hateful, and unnatural (*Politics* 1.1258b1).[35] Dante, for that reason, placed usurers (bankers) in the same circle of hell as "sodomites" (*Inferno* 17; see also *Leviticus* 25.36)! The actual sin of Sodom, incidentally, had more to do with the use of wealth than is now commonly remembered, or Dante noted: "Behold, this was the guilt of your sister Sodom: she and her daughters had pride, excess of food, and prosperous ease, but did not aid the poor and needy" (*Ezekiel* 16.49). The duties of free citizens, *eleutheroi*, include—are almost defined by—*generosity*: that is the virtue especially of free men, *eleutheriotes* (*Nicomachean Ethics* 2.1107b9–16). That is why there should be personal, "private" property (*Politics* 2.1263b10). But the unlimited accumulation of such wealth, beyond what any one citizen or household could reasonably use or enjoy or even manage efficiently, is certain to destroy the sort of companionship essential to the polis. This same accumulation may result in a global "unfettered capitalism," of an "anarchic" rather than "anarchistical" kind: mere "lawlessness," allowing those with the power to attempt whatever they please (not necessarily to *achieve* just what they please). That sort of "anarchy" is actually merely oligarchy.

The other chief enemy of the "political" (that is, the careful and companionable sorting out of the problems of collective life) may seem, by contrast, to be ethically high-minded. Even Aristotle, despite his attention to the different morals and manners of differing communities and institutions, was as sure as any other ethical philosopher that virtue and virtuous acts were not dependent on borders. People of one city or nation may *suppose* that different acts are decent, and differing characters of real worth, but what was truly wrong on one side of a border cannot be right on the other, merely by people's saying so (Cicero *Republic* 3.33[36]). Despots may wish us to think otherwise:

> Their first end and aim is to break the spirit of their subjects. They know that a poor-spirited man will never plot against anybody. Their second aim is to breed mutual distrust. Tyranny is never overthrown until people can begin to trust one another; and this is the reason why tyrants are always at war with the good. They feel that good men are dangerous to their authority, not only because they think it shame to be governed despotically but also because of their loyalty to themselves and to others and because of their refusal to betray one another or anybody else. The third and last aim of tyrants is to make their subjects incapable of action. Nobody attempts the impossible. Nobody, therefore, will attempt the overthrow of a tyranny, when all are incapable of action.
>
> (Politics *5.1314a20*[37]*)*

And moral relativism does indeed leave us exposed to threats and bribes.

> The subjectivist in morals, when his moral feelings are at war with the facts about him, is always free to seek harmony by toning down the sensitiveness of the feelings. Being mere data, neither good nor evil in themselves, he may pervert them or lull them to sleep by any means at his command. Truckling, compromise, time-serving, capitulations of conscience, are conventionally opprobrious names for what, if successfully carried out, would be on his principles by far the easiest and most praiseworthy mode of bringing about that harmony between inner and outer relations which is all that he means by good. The absolute moralist, on the other hand, when his interests clash with the

> world, is not free to gain harmony by sacrificing the ideal interests. According to him, these latter should be as they are and not otherwise. Resistance then, poverty, martyrdom if need be, tragedy in a word—such are the solemn feasts of his inward faith. Not that the contradiction between the two men occurs every day; in commonplace matters all moral schools agree. It is only in the lonely emergencies of life that our creed is tested: then routine maxims fail, and we fall back on our gods.[38]

There are, in short, good practical reasons why would-be rebels and revolutionaries should at least hope that most or many of their company are sound objectivists, unlikely to be seduced away by servile fears or fancies. But the very fact of a universal ethic may begin to erode our earlier loyalties, to parents or companions, cities or sacred pledges. And this engenders yet another sort of "anarchistical" outcome: the cosmopolitan. The Cynic philosopher Diogenes of Sinope may seem to be more obviously an "anarchist" than Aristotle, precisely because he did not acknowledge the authority either of particular princes or of ancient custom.[39] Early Stoics were similarly dismissive of many common precepts, urging instead that the better life was to "go along with nature," to accept what usually happens in nature as the proper guide. The dead bodies of our friends, even of our family, were only meat, after all, and sexual desire and fulfilment was not limited to mates socially approved or allowed.[40] The "democratic" nostrum, that each should do as he pleases, was appropriate, at any rate, for those who reckoned themselves "wise": "only the wise man is free, but the inferior are slaves" (Diogenes Laertius *Lives* 7.121).[41] It hardly mattered, in practice, whether such sages were openly atheists or else considered *themselves* the equal of the gods. Rejecting all established ideas of good order in the name of whatever principles they themselves saw reason to accept, they deconstructed notions like property, chastity, or even, in the end, humanity.

This was certainly not what those early Stoics would themselves have wished, as staunch moral realists. Later Stoics were indeed cautious about allowing novices to read the earlier Stoic works[42] and were insistent that we should first of all remember who and what we are (fathers, sons, and citizens) and what our local duties might be (Epictetus *Discourses* 2.10[43]) before seeking to think and act as "citizens of the world," *cosmopolitai*, with no overriding loyalty to household, polis, or imperial dictat (see Diogenes Laertius *Lives* 6.63). We need the background of family life and civil sympathies ever to conceive that there are other transcendent obligations. If those earlier forms are dismissed as only the deceits of despots how shall we ever find any better standard? Must not despotic rule be simply the norm of life, and our best hope be to join the ranks of despots?

> All these, my friends, are views which young people imbibe from men of science [*sophoi*], both prose-writers and poets, who maintain that the height of justice is to succeed by force; whence it comes that the young people are afflicted with a plague of impiety, as though the gods were not such as the law commands us to conceive them; and, because of this, factions also arise, when these teachers attract them towards the life that is right 'according to nature,' which consists in being master over the rest in reality, instead of being a slave to others according to legal convention.
>
> *(Plato* Laws *10.890a)*

It may be a lot more likely, of course, that most such would-be despots will find themselves only the tools of more successful tyrants, having no strength of mind or spirit to resist corruption. An anarchistical philosophy that is only nihilistic, a rejection of the very idea of ethical authority, will usually turn out to serve the interests of another. A better anarchistical philosophy will be the one toward which Aristotle may be seen to gesture: the ideal of a civil community (not necessarily even a single territory) small enough, self-confident enough, to preserve the ties of affection and established custom in a way that allows all those who *can* to share by turns in any important office, to manage their own affairs without overmuch oversight, and slowly to adapt any current customs in the light of changing circumstance and improving knowledge. There are other forms of social life than the master–slave relationship: we can, after all, be friends. Having learnt that truth from our immediate neighbourhood, we may begin to think even aliens and strangers are as human as ourselves (as Hierocles as well as Ezekiel advised.)[44] Without that beginning, thrown upon the world as if we were only turtles, we shall mostly end as slaves.

Notes

1 S. R. L. Clark, "C. J. Cherryh: The Ties that Bind," *Yearbook of English Studies* 37.2, ed. David Seed (London: Maney 2007) 197–214, rptd. *Philosophical Futures* (Frankfurt: Lang 2011) 189–208.
2 G. K. Chesterton, *The Man Who Was Thursday*, ed. Matthew Beaumont (London: Penguin 2011 [1908]) 36.
3 Aristotle, *Politics*, trans. Ernest Barker, ed. Richard Stalley (Oxford: OUP 1995) 185.
4 Aristotle 104–5.
5 Aristotle 122
6 Aristotle 283.
7 See S. R. L. Clark, "Slaves and Citizens," *Philosophy* 60 (1985): 27–46, rptd. *The Political Animal: Biology, Ethics and Politics* (London: Routledge 1999) 23–39.
8 Aristotle 231.
9 Edmund Burke, *Reflections on the Revolution in France*, ed. Conor Cruise O'Brien (Harmondsworth: Penguin 1968 [1790]) 172.
10 Aristotle 195.
11 Sextus Empiricus, *Works*, trans. Robert Bury, Loeb Classical Library (Cambridge, MA: Harvard UP 2014) 205–7.
12 Aristotle 256.
13 Aristotle 262.
14 Aristotle 106–7.
15 David Keyt, "Aristotle, and the Ancient Roots of Anarchism," *Topoi* 15 (1996): 135; see also "Aristotle, and Anarchism," *Reason Papers* 18 (1993): 133–52, rptd. *Aristotle's Politics*, ed. Richard Kraut and Steven Skultety (Oxford: Rowman 2005) 203–22.
16 Aristotle 104–5.
17 See Richard Mulgan, "Lycophron and Greek Theories of Social Contract," *Journal of the History of Ideas* 40.1 (1979): 121–8.
18 Translations of Herodotus are taken from Herodotus, *The Histories*, trans. George Rawlinson (London: Dent 1910).
19 So also Aristotle: "Laws resting on unwritten custom are even more sovereign, and concerned with issues of still more sovereign importance, than written laws; and this suggests that, even if the rule of a man be safer than the rule of written law, it need not therefore be safer than the rule of unwritten law" (3.1287b1; 128).
20 Aristotle 298.
21 Aristotle 252
22 Aristotle 219–20. See also Ps-Xenophon: "Now among the slaves and metics at Athens there is the greatest uncontrolled wantonness; you can't hit them there, and a slave will not stand aside for you. I shall point out why this is their native practice: if it were customary for a slave (or metic or freedman) to be struck by one who is free, you would often hit an Athenian citizen by mistake on the assumption that he was a slave." Ps-Xenophon, "Constitution of Athens," *Works*, by Xenophon, trans. Edgar Marchant, Loeb Classical Library (Cambridge, MA: Harvard UP 1984) 7: 481 (2.10).
23 Ps-Xenophon 7: 474–507.
24 Aristotle 299–300.
25 Ps-Xenophon 7: 497.
26 Ps-Xenophon 7: 495–7.
27 Aristotle 293.
28 Aristotle 279.
29 Jonathan Barnes, "Aristotle, and Political Liberty," *Aristoteles "Politik": Akten des XI. Symposium Aristotelicum. Friedrichshafen/Bodensee 25.8–3.9.1987*, ed. Günther Patzig, (Göttingen: Vandenhoeck 1990) 249–63,

rptd. *Mantissa: Essays in Ancient Philosophy IV*, ed. Maddalena Bonelli (Oxford: Clarendon-OUP 2015) 36–55. The remark is repeated by Andres Rosler, *Political Authority and Obligation in Aristotle* (Oxford: Clarendon-OUP 2005) 151; Rosler also appears to equate the anarchist ideal with a "political vacuum" (153).

30 See S. R. L. Clark, "Townships, Brigands and a Shared Religion," *Griffith Law Review* 21 (2012): 392–412.

31 Peter Kropotkin, *Peter Kropotkin's Revolutionary Pamphlets*, ed. Petr Alekseevich (Whitefish, MT: Kessinger 2010 [1927]). 157, ctd. Brian Morris, *Kropotkin: The Politics of Community* (Oakland, CA: PM 2015) 243.

32 David Brooks, "The Governing Cancer of Our Time," *New York Times*, Feb. 26, 2016, www.nytimes.com/2016/02/26/opinion/the-governing-cancer-of-our-time.html. One reader of the current chapter correctly comments that a principal cause of conflict may be, exactly, a disagreement about what can sensibly or justly be decided by individual persons or smaller collectives, without any need to impose a universal rule. Neither appeals to an imagined "common good" nor to a supposed "right of private property" will be uncontroversial—especially as even the latter will itself constitute a demand to impose a universal rule, as though it is obvious who "owns" what, or what obligations such "ownership" imposes either on the would-be proprietor or on others.

33 J. R. R. Tolkien, *The Lord of the Rings*, 2d ed., 3 vols. (London: Allen 1966) 1:71.

34 Anonymous. See Ian D. Morris, "Who Steals the Common from the Goose?" (17 March 2018) at www.iandavidmorris.com/who-steals-the-common-from-the-goose/ (accessed 17 August 2020).

35 Further on Aristotle's economic theory: Scott Meikle, *Aristotle's Economic Theory*, 2d ed. (New York, NY: OUP 1997).

36 *The Hellenistic Philosophers* 1: *Translations of the Principal Sources with Philosophical Commentary*, ed. A. A. Long and D. N. Sedley (Cambridge: CUP 1987) 432–3 [67S].

37 Aristotle 220–1.

38 William James, "Rationality, Activity and Faith," *Princeton Review* 2 (July–Dec. 1882): 82, rptd. as part of "The Sentiment of Rationality," William James, *The Will to Believe* (New York, NY: Longmans 1896) 63–110. There is also, of course, a downside to such "fanaticism": those willing to compromise their principles may fight more genuinely "civil" wars.

39 See Keyt, "Roots" 130.

40 Long and Sedley 430–1 [67E-G]).

41 Long and Sedley 431–2 [67M]).

42 Long and Sedley 430 [67E]).

43 Long and Sedley 364 [59Q]).

44 Long and Sedley 349–50 [57G]).

7
KANT ON ANARCHY

Oliver Sensen

I. Introduction

Why should one avoid anarchy, according to Immanuel Kant? Kant equates anarchy with "lack of any government,"[1] a condition in which there are no legitimate state powers.[2] He only uses the term "anarchy" eleven times in his published writings, and does not devote a separate chapter or essay to the topic. But he describes a state without a legitimate government as a state of nature, and so Kant's discussion of anarchy then becomes the question why one should leave the state of nature, and submit to a legitimate government. The Kant literature answers this question in different ways.

In this chapter, I first describe how Kant conceives of the state of nature (see Section II). I then present a common interpretation in the Kant literature of why one should leave the state of nature (Section III), and argue for an alternative interpretation (sections IV–VII). Finally, I contrast Kant's views with the influential conceptions of Hobbes and Locke (Section VIII). I argue that Kant conceives of the demand to leave the state of nature as a prescription of reason. However, reason does not prescribe it as a means to something else we want, such as safety, happiness, or a maximum of freedom, but as a categorical command.

II. Kant on the State of Nature

In order to talk about the importance of avoiding anarchy, Kant—like the thinkers of his time—uses a state-of-nature scenario. Unlike Hobbes, however, Kant does not believe that the state of nature would necessarily be a war of all against all, a condition in which life is "solitary, poore, nasty, brutish, and short."[3] According to Kant, it is not necessarily the case that a state of nature would be marked by hostility or violence, or "as Hobbes puts it, a *bellum omnium contra omnes*."[4] Instead, it is always possible that violence might break out, since there is no authority capable of settling disputes: "It should be called only a *status belli omnium contra omnes*, a condition of injustice; a legal condition … in which the determining and deciding of what is to be law can occur no otherwise than by violence."[5] Unlike Hobbes, who believed that even in his time there were areas in the world that were in the state of nature,[6] Kant does not believe that the state of nature ever was an actual situation; he conceives of it merely as a concept of reason: "the *status naturalis* does not exist at all, and never has; it is a mere Idea of reason."[7]

The problem arises in the first place, according to Kant, because human beings have an "*unsociable sociability*."[8] Human beings have a predisposition to seek society, but also a disposition to compare themselves to others, and to try to be superior.[9] If this "crooked wood … [of which] the human being is made"[10] stayed by itself, it would "grow stunted, crooked and awry." So, on the one hand, the development of one's capacities can be achieved "only in society," but, on the other, humans' "own inclinations make it so that they can not long subsist next to another in wild freedom."[11] Thus, even in the state of nature, human beings would not necessarily live in solitude, but might form associations with other human beings.

Kant distinguishes human circumstances of three kinds:[12] a solitary state of nature, a social state of nature, and a state in a civil society under a government and coercive laws. Kant developed this account based on Gottfried Achenwall's work, which he used repeatedly as the textbook for his lectures on natural law. Whereas Achenwall contrasts the state of nature to a social state, for Kant "in the state of nature, too, there can be societies … (e.g., conjugal, paternal, domestic societies in general, as well as many others)."[13] However, there would be no law or enforceable norms of distributive justice in the state of nature: "A condition that is not rightful, that is, a condition in which there is no distributive justice, is called a state of nature (*status naturalis*)." Kant defines "distributive justice" here as "what is the decision of a court in a particular case in accordance with the given law under which it falls, that is, what is *laid down as right*."[14]

What are missing in the state of nature are therefore the three authorities that Kant regards as necessary for a rightful state.[15] A state of nature lacks a universal lawmaker, a judge that can apply the law, and a regent or police force that can enforce the law. In the state of nature "there is need, that is to say, for a universal legislation that establishes right and wrong for everyone, a universal power that protects everyone in his right, and a judicial authority that restores the injured right."[16] The danger of violence in the state of nature arises because, without the three state authorities, everyone is entitled to judge for himself what is right, and there is no way to arbitrate disputes or rule our predation: "Now it is left to the judgement of every individual man, what he will acknowledge to be right or wrong, and he is therefore able to infringe even the freedom of another without hindrance."[17] As a result, human beings "can never be secure against violence from one another, since each has its own right to do *what seems right and good to it*."[18]

The conclusion Kant draws from this analysis is that one should leave the state of nature, and enter a civil condition under the three authorities: "when you cannot avoid living side by side with all others, you ought to leave the state of nature."[19] But why?

III. The Incentive to Leave the State of Nature

There is a sharp divide in the Kant literature surrounding Kant's political philosophy concerned with what is known as the "independence thesis."[20] Some scholars argue that Kant's legal and political philosophy is independent of his moral philosophy in that Kant provides reasons for why one should form a civil society that are independent of his moral philosophy. While Kant argues that the moral philosophy relies completely on a priori grounding,[21] he seems to provide empirical reasons for someone to leave the state of nature.[22]

Kant says, for instance, that human beings "are compelled by need"[23] to leave the state of nature, and this seems to be a very plausible claim in its own right, independently of Kant's arguments. The state of nature as Kant describes it is a condition in which one's life is in danger. Because of the threat of violence, one can also not develop one's capacities fully, and one's freedom to carry out one's plans is severely restricted. So, if one wants the "enhancement of external freedom,"[24] or even basic safety, it is prudent to leave the state of nature and submit to the coercive laws of a civil state.

The strongest textual support for this reading is in Kant's *Toward Perpetual Peace*. There, he says that the "problem of establishing a state … is *soluble* even for a nation of devils."[25] By "devils" here he means beings with purely self-seeking inclinations, and his claim is that, even if one has a multitude of thoroughly selfish beings, "nature comes to the aid … precisely through those self-seeking inclinations … and the human being is constrained to become a good citizen."[26] Kant's argument that even selfish beings should enter a state is that they need laws for their self-preservation.

Kant describes the task of forming a state as follows:

> Given a multitude of rational beings all of whom need universal laws for their preservation but each of whom is inclined covertly to exempt himself from them, so to order this multitude and establish their constitution that, although in their private dispositions they strive against one another, these yet so check one another that in their public conduct the result is the same as if they had no such evil dispositions.[27]

This evidence suggests that Kant bases the claim that one should leave the state of nature not on any distinctive moral considerations, but that the reason to form a state is a "Hobbesian prudential account."[28] Not only would his legal philosophy be independent from his moral philosophy, but more importantly it would not need any further assumptions, such as the Categorical Imperative, or a metaphysically ambitious account of freedom in order to ground political normative claims.

If this is correct, however, then Kant's argument that one should leave the state of nature would depend only on what he would call a "hypothetical imperative."[29] On this view, one should avoid anarchy, and leave the state of nature, *if* one wants to increase one's external freedom (or secure one's self-preservation, etc.). It is then an empirical question[30] whether everyone has this desire, and whether it is the overriding desire for everyone. For instance, if one is faced with a choice of a comfortable life in servitude, or a dangerous journey through the desert that might give one freedom eventually, would everyone choose to enhance her or his external freedom? The argument would also be contingent upon circumstances. There could be situations in which one perceives a weakness in one's enemy, and where it would be advantageous to strike first, rather than subject oneself to laws that protect one's enemy as well. But even if one could assume that all human beings have one particular, highest, and overriding desire (such as for freedom, or self-preservation), the command to avoid anarchy "would still be only contingent"[31] and not an absolute command.

However, even if the empirical evidence can ground a plausible case for the Hobbesian prudential account, there is textual evidence that Kant has something stronger in mind. In the same work in which he seems to advance a prudential justification for leaving the state of nature, *Toward Perpetual Peace*, Kant states explicitly that the injunction to leave the state of nature is "a principle of moral politics," and that "this principle is not based upon prudence but upon duty"[32] and that this principle is characterized by "unconditional necessity."[33] He views a foundation on empirical grounds as "uncertain,"[34] and puts forth "a politics is cognizable a priori,"[35] by which he means that "the human being's own reason makes it a duty for him"[36] to exit the state of nature.

But how exactly does reason do this, and why does the duty to leave the state of nature follow a priori?

IV. The Duty to Leave the State of Nature

Kant holds that it is not just *prudent* to avoid anarchy and form a law-governed state, but that it is a *duty* to do so. A duty is something that one ought to do even if one does not want to do it: "*Duty* is that action to which someone is bound."[37] A duty therefore expresses an obligation, or a necessitation; i.e., an obligation "*makes* necessary an action that is subjectively contingent and thus represents the subject as one that must be *constrained* (necessitated) to conform with the rule."[38] Since an obligation often goes against what one wants to do, it is expressed by an imperative, and since it is not conditioned upon a desire or end one wants to produce, realize, or achieve, it is a *categorical* imperative: "*Obligation* is the necessity of a free action under a categorical imperative of reason."[39] A categorical imperative does not derive from any end that one might seek because of a desire: "A categorical (unconditional) imperative is one that represents an action as objectively necessary and makes it necessary not indirectly, through the representation of some *end* that can be attained by the action."[40] If one abstracts from *all* desires and ends, however, only the *form* of law remains: "The categorical imperative, which as such only affirms what obligation is, is: act upon a maxim that can also hold as a universal law."[41]

Kant argues that these notions of duty, obligation, and categorical imperative "are common to both parts of the *Metaphysics of Morals*,"[42] to ethics as well as the political demand to leave the state of nature. He states the supreme principle of ethics as: "*act only in accordance with that maxim through which you can at the same time will that it become a universal law*."[43] And he states the "principle of right" as: "So act that you can will that your maxim should become a universal law (whatever the end may be)."[44] So, Kant believes that there is one supreme law that expresses the essence of obligation, whether it be such political obligations as the duty to leave anarchy, or moral obligations: "Within this universal law are comprehended both legal and ethical laws."[45]

There is, however, an important difference between ethical and juridical laws, according to Kant, but it does not lie so much in the *content* of the law itself but rather in the way in which one is bound to *follow* the law. Kant distinguishes the law that says what is commanded from one's motive for following this law:

> In all lawgiving ... there are two elements: first, a law, which represents an action that is to be done as *objectively* necessary, that is, which makes the action a duty; and second, an incentive, which connects a ground for determining choice to this action *subjectively* with the representation of the law.[46]

In *ethics*, one should not just *do* the right thing, according to Kant, but also do it *simply because it is right*.[47] But a *legal* rule demands that one engage in some outwardly observable behavior—e.g., stop at a red traffic light—although it does not demand that you do so out of a particular motive:

> All lawgiving can therefore be distinguished with respect to the incentive ... That lawgiving which makes an action a duty and also makes this duty the incentive is *ethical*. But that lawgiving which does not include the incentive of duty in the law and so admits an incentive other than the idea of duty itself is *juridical*."[48]

But for juridical and ethical duties there is the same supreme law that declares that an action is a duty: "a categorical imperative is a law that either commands or prohibits, depending upon whether it represents as a duty the commission or omission of an action."[49]

But how could there be a law that commands independently of what one desires, and why should one think that there really *is* such a law? The first question concerns the source of the supreme laws of duty (cf. Section V), the second question its justification (cf. sections VI and VII). I shall pursue these questions before trying to explain why the law also, on Kant's view, commands one to avoid anarchy and form a law-governed state (cf. Section VIII).

V. The Source of Obligation

Kant rejected desires and inclinations as *sources* of duty because they can only provide prudential and contingent foundations for a command to avoid anarchy. Desires do not ground duties:

"only practical reason ... can do that,"[50] and reason generates duties in a way that its principle "is given a priori by pure reason."[51] What does it mean to say that pure reason gives a principle, and that it does so a priori? How does Kant conceive of the origin or source of the principle of duty? The idea is that a moral command is something "our own ... faculty ... provides out of itself."[52] Independently of what one desires, or how one actually deliberates, one's own reason prescribes "a universal law which we call the *moral law*."[53]

Kant does not conceive of identifying the moral law as a matter of *discovering* any sort of independent reality—of a world of, say, Platonic universals. The moral law thus cannot be discerned by means of "any intuition, either pure or empirical."[54] Rather, "reason ... with complete spontaneity ... *makes* its own order according to ideas ... according to which it even declares actions to be necessary."[55] Reason prescribes duties independently of and prior to experience, "as soon as we draw up maxims of the will for ourselves"[56]—in short, a priori.

Kant calls the source of the law of duty "autonomy," or the "law-giving of human reason."[57] In his theoretical philosophy, Kant argues that reason provides out of itself a priori laws that govern the function of our cognitive faculty, and he argues that practical reasoning about what one is obligated to do incorporates an a priori constitutive principle of reason with respect to our desires: "the understanding is the one that contains the constitutive principles *a priori* for the faculty of cognition ...; for the faculty of desire it is reason, which is practical without the mediation of any sort of pleasure."[58]

Kant's alternative is, therefore, that the law originates directly from one's own reason. This does not mean that the law is innate, in the sense that God, "an implanted sense[,] or who knows what tutelary nature[,] whispers to it."[59] A law that was implanted in us by God or by evolution or some other aspect of nature would not be strictly *necessary*. If moral laws or obligations were based on some contingent feature of our existence, they would, Kant maintains, "lack the necessity that is essential to their concept." They would merely have, at best, a "subjective necessity, arbitrarily implanted in us,"[60] but not an absolute necessity.

If, for instance, our sense of morality were a product of cultural evolution, we would have a very different conception of moral requirements if we had evolved under different circumstances. Imagine two tribes, one of which has developed under conditions of famine for thousands of years, while another has lived in a region that is prone to tsunamis. The first tribe might have survived because its members had adopted a rule calling for them to share food and to assist others more generally. The second tribe might have survived because its members had adopted a rule enjoining: "Run first, then come back for survivors." The rules of each tribe might be deeply ingrained, and psychologically each rule might appear to the members of the tribe accepting it as a necessary command. But, in fact, on the story envisioned here, the commands endorsed by both tribes are historical in origin, and thus contingent. A law can be innate without being strictly necessary.

If Kant's view is not based on empirical, historical, or biological considerations, it is also not based on an ambitious metaphysics. He does not envision obligation as based on a non-natural, supersensible property. The foundation of duty as he understands it is "mixed with no anthropology, theology, physics, or hyperphysics and still less with occult qualities (which could be called hypophysical)."[61] Rather, he argues, moral commands are the spontaneous but necessary products of our reason, a way our reason necessarily functions pre-consciously.

VI. The Conditional Argument

Why should one think that human beings possess a faculty that immediately and spontaneously prescribes necessary duties? Kant gives two arguments in favor of the autonomy of reason. The first one is a conditional argument: only autonomy can yield unconditional obligation. By itself, the argument only shows that "if duty is a concept that is to contain significance and real lawgiving for our actions it can be expressed only in categorical imperatives." But this strategy leaves open the question whether "there really is such an imperative,"[62] and Kant gives a second argument in order to support belief in the reality of the supreme law of duty.

The first argument builds on the idea that we hold duties to be necessary and universal:

> Everyone must grant that a law, if it is to hold … as a ground of obligation, must carry with it absolute necessity; that, for example, the command 'thou shalt not lie' does not hold only for human beings.[63]

At first, this is just an assumption about our ordinary beliefs, but as such it has received backing from empirical science.[64] The second step of the argument is the claim that experience can never yield conclusions marked by strict universality and absolute necessity.[65] Only a priori judgments can feature these qualities—as for instance, the analytic judgment that all bachelors are unmarried. If a statement is necessary and universal, it must be an a priori proposition: "Necessity and strict universality are … secure indications of an *a priori* cognition."[66]

Conversely, Kant argues that "all possible"[67] groundings of duty other than "the fitness of … [the will's] maxims for its own giving of universal laws" would yield "*heteronomy*."[68] And heteronomy cannot ground unconditional obligation: "*heteronomy* of choice, on the other hand, not only does not ground any obligation at all but is instead opposed to the principle of obligation."[69] But why does Kant believe that all alternative theories yield heteronomy, and why does he think that heteronomy cannot ground obligation?

Regarding the first question, Kant argues that any alternative theory ultimately depends upon a desire as the reason a certain rule is prescribed:[70] (i) Suppose one assumes that moral laws come from society, then one still needs a desire to fit into this society and be rewarded in order for those laws to be applicable to oneself. (ii) Or suppose one believes that moral laws are ultimately based on our sentiments. In this case, one has obviously granted that morality is based on feelings and desires.[71] (iii) Kant even argues that a non-natural moral realism, according to which moral requirements are (non-natural) moral properties that are part of the fabric of the world, would ultimately be based on desires. His reason is that all knowledge begins with the senses.[72] This is one of the main results of his *Critique of Pure Reason*. We do not have an intellectual intuition that could intuit non-natural properties:

> we cannot cook up … a single object with any new and not empirically given property … Thus we are not allowed to think up any sort of new original forces, e.g., an understanding that is capable of intuition of its object without sense.[73]

So, in order to detect non-natural value properties, one would need some kind of sensibility. Since one could not discover non-natural properties with one's five senses, the only remaining available way for one to detect them would by means of a feeling.[74] But if a feeling is the foundation of a rule, then "it would, strictly speaking, be nature that gives the law."[75] Since nature rules our feelings and desires, our reason would not give its own law as in the case of autonomy, but would receive the law from outside itself—and this is heteronomy.

Heteronomy cannot yield obligation, according to Kant, because the feelings and desires that are basic, on his view, to heteronomous approaches to moral judgment are constantly in flux: people's feelings and desires vary over time, and one person's feelings and desires differ from those of others. Thus, these feelings and desires "can never be assumed to be universally directed at the same objects";[76] any principles based upon them would "be very different in different people."[77] But even if there were something that everyone wants all of the time, any command based upon a universal desire would still be conditioned and contingent.

> Wherever an object of the will has to be laid down as the basis for prescribing the rule that determines the will, there the rule is none other than heteronomy; the imperative is conditional, namely: *if* or *because* one wills this object, one ought to act in such or such a way; hence it can never command … categorically.[78]

Desires are contingent and relative, and cannot ground a necessarily and universally binding law.

However, so far the argument has only been conditional:

> By explicating the generally received concept of morality we showed only that an autonomy of the will unavoidably … lies at its basis. Thus whoever holds morality to be something and not a chimerical idea without any truth must also admit the principle of morality brought forward.[79]

VII. The Unconditional Argument

Kant recognizes that an additional argument is needed to show "that there really is such an imperative."[80] He does not claim to be able to demonstrate why the human mind prescribes the moral law to human beings: "all human insight is at an end as soon as we have arrived at basic powers or basic faculties."[81] But he believes that he can show that reason really does prescribe this law. If experience cannot yield necessity,[82] but if he can show that the law is necessary, then it must be independent of experience; it must be a priori: "We can become aware of pure practical laws … by attending to the necessity with which reason prescribes them to us and to the setting aside of all empirical conditions to which reason directs us."[83]

Kant presents a thought experiment in order to show that we are aware of the necessity of morality. He envisions a case in which no desire speaks in favor of the morally right action, but in which one's desires favor the immoral alternative. Kant invites us to inquire of someone

> whether, if his prince demanded, on pain of … immediate execution, that he give false testimony against an honorable man whom the prince would like to destroy under a plausible pretext, he would consider it impossible to overcome his love of life, however great it may be.[84]

We can easily structure the example in a way designed to ensure that no desire speaks in favor of refusing to give false testimony. So: the agent has a powerful position at court, and would like to retain this position; he loves his life and family; he does not believe in an afterlife; he does not believe that any good will come from his inaction because someone else will give the false testimony if he does not; and so forth. Even if one construes the thought experiment in this way, the agent still can be envisioned as believing that giving false testimony would be morally wrong, and that he should refuse the prince's request: "he is aware that he ought to do it."[85] Even if no desire speaks for an action, it can still be perceived as necessary.

Kant does not rest his argument on our sense that the moral command is necessary, though. Rather, he uses our sense of what we ought to do to establish that we are justified in believing that we are *free*: "He judges, therefore, that he can do something because he is aware that he ought to do it and cognizes freedom within him, which, without the moral law, would have remained unknown to him."[86] Freedom, here, is the ability to act independently of one's desires, and if no desire inclines one to make a morally required choice but one nonetheless has a sense that one *can* act morally, then one has a sense that one is free, even if he "would perhaps not venture to assert whether he would … [make the moral choice] or not."[87] In this context, freedom is assumed to be in some way causally efficacious—it should be able to move an agent towards the moral action. Kant agrees with Hume that "the concept of causality brings with it that of laws."[88] The content of the moral law cannot be based upon desires, because the thought experiment excludes all desires as motives of the moral action. Therefore, Kant argues, only the *form* of the law remains, and freedom is the metaphysical ground or the "*ratio essendi*"[89] of the Categorical Imperative. Again, this is the same for the moral and the political law:

> Since all obligation also rests on freedom itself, and has its ground therein ... Professor Kant calls all moral laws ... laws of freedom, and includes thereunder the aforementioned *leges justi et honesti* ... inasmuch as they impose on the action the restrictive condition of fitness to be a universal law.[90]

Thus, every moral requirement, every obligation, rests ultimately on a command issued by one's own reason: "The reason is that we know our own freedom (from which all moral laws, and so all rights as well as duties proceed) only through the *moral imperative*."[91] And any duty I have to another being ultimately rests on a duty to follow the moral law enunciated by my own reason:

> For I can recognize that I am under obligation to others only insofar as I at the same time put myself under obligation, since the law by virtue of which I regard myself as being under obligation proceeds in every case from my own practical reason; and in being constrained by my own reason, I am also the one constraining myself.[92]

Moral and juridical laws alike are grounded in the autonomy of reason: the "*ground of obligation* ... rests, as has been sufficiently shown, solely on the autonomy of reason itself."[93] But recall that legal duties only demand the "conformity ... of an action with law, irrespective of the incentive to it" and trace the "*legality* (lawfulness)" of an outward behavior, whereas ethical laws also demand that one act from a certain incentive, and trace the "*morality*" of an action.[94] The difference is relevant in practice to the ways in which a victim can claim a right from another. In both cases, the obligation arises from the agent's own reason. However, in ethics the victim can claim a right by reminding the agent of his duty to follow the law of the agent's own reason:

> the other, having a right to do so, confronts the subject with his duty, i.e., the moral law by which he ought to act. If this confrontation makes an impression on the agent, he determines his will by an Idea of reason, creates through his reason that conception of his duty which already lay previously within him, and is only quickened by the other, and determines himself according to the moral law.[95]

This is different from the legal case. Although the juridical law, "so act externally that the free use of your choice can coexist with the freedom of everyone in accordance with a universal," is "indeed a law that lays an obligation on me,"[96] and is "based on everyone's consciousness of obligation," it "cannot be appealed to as an incentive to determine his choice."[97] One is justified in coercing the other into fulfilling his obligation: "there is connected with right ... an authorization to coerce someone who infringes upon it."[98] This is because what is wrong infringes the political law of freedom, and coercion removes what is hindering that which is commanded by the political law. It is justified by "*hindering a hindrance of freedom*."[99] However, the victim does not claim her right by reminding the agent of his duty, even though the state itself is, on Kant's view, justified in using coercion:

> Thus when it is said that a creditor has a right to require his debtor to pay his debt, this does not mean that he can remind the debtor that his reason itself puts him under obligation to perform this; it means, instead, that coercion which constrains everyone to pay his debts can coexist with the freedom of everyone, including that of debtors, in accordance with a universal external law. Right and authorization to use coercion therefore mean one and the same thing.[100]

In the legal case, too, any obligation is grounded in the autonomy of the agent as a pre-conscious, necessary lawgiving of one's own reason. The difference to the ethical case is merely that the law does not require that one act from a particular motive, only that one do the right thing.

This difference explains Kant's statements about a "nation of devils."[101] Kant's point is not that beings with selfish desires justify the need to found a state on these desires. Rather, he is concerned here with the way in which one can motivate beings who *know* what is right, but are not *motivated* to do the right thing, into following their own reason. The initial problem is that, in order to establish the right constitution of a state, "many assert it would have to be a state of *angels* because human beings, with their self-seeking inclinations, would not be capable of such a sublime form of constitution." The passage addresses a *motivational* problem. The devils already *know* what the right constitution of a state is in virtue of their "understanding." However, they lack the *motivation* to form a state, and it is *this* problem that must be "*soluble* even for a nation of devils." Kant's answer to this problem is to use coercion, in order to "so order this multitude … as if they had no such evil dispositions."[102]

But how does Kant get from the autonomy of reason, and its law, to the command to leave the state of nature? As the "nation of devils" passage makes clear, it is one thing for the supreme law of obligation not to be based upon prudential considerations, but it is another thing to determine why one should be motivated to abide by it, and so to leave the state of nature. How does Kant explain the need to avoid anarchy?

VIII. The Duty to Leave the State of Nature

The grounding and justification of the highest law of obligation means that a human being is under this law even in the state of nature. So, even in a state of nature an agent knows what the principle of obligation declares to be morally right and just. Accordingly, "the state of nature need not, just because it is natural, be a state of *injustice*,"[103] and "in the state of nature, too, there can be societies compatible with rights."[104] Even in terms of property rights, the law that governs obligation is already known in the state of nature: "in terms of their form, laws concerning what is mine or yours in the state of nature contain the same thing that they prescribe in the civil condition."[105] Kant even argues that this *must* be the case, for only autonomy can ground any obligation at all (see above).

There are passages in which Kant seems to put forth a hypothetical reason for leaving the state of nature. Kant says about a subject: "*unless it wants to renounce any concepts of right*, the first thing it has to resolve upon is the principle that it must leave the state of nature,"[106] and that human beings accept the coercive powers of a state "so that they may enjoy what is laid down as right."[107]

These statements can be read as offering a hypothetical reason why one should avoid anarchy: *if* one wants to life in a rightful condition, one should leave the state of nature. But Kant does not, in fact, postulate a desire to live in a rightful state, or a desire (because one fears for one's safety or possession) to avoid anarchy. Rather, the command of duty holds a priori, and this means that there is also an unconditioned command to bring it about: "'You ought to enter this condition,' holds a priori."[108] One should leave the state of nature because only in this way is it possible to fulfill the command of duty. Even if one knows what is in accordance with duty, achieving it "can never be secure"[109] outside a rightful condition, and so, for Kant, outside a state. The reason, again, is that outside of a rightful condition there is no lawmaker, judge, nor police capable of ensuring that justice is achieved:

> It is therefore necessary, as soon as men come close to exercising their reciprocal freedom, that they leave the *status naturalis*, to come under a necessary law, a *status civilis*; there is need, that is to say, for a universal legislation that establishes right and wrong for everyone, a universal power that protects everyone in his right, and a judicial authority that restores the injured right, or dispenses so-called *justitia distributiva* (*suum cuique tribuit*)."[110]

Even in the state of nature, two tribespeople could agree that a just border to their domain is the stream that divides their territories. However, there is no lawmaker, such as a land registry, to lay down who owns the land. Furthermore, if there is a dispute, because the stream dried out in a drought, or it changed its course in a flood, there is no judge to arbitrate what is right in accordance with the law, and there is no police force to see that justice is done. So, the command to leave the state of nature is part of the command of duty. One should abide by laws that one could will to be universal, and, in order to achieve this, one should avoid anarchy.

If this interpretation is correct, then there is a clear difference between Kant's account of why one should leave the state of nature and the accounts of Hobbes and Locke.

In contrast to Hobbes, life in Kant's state of nature is not necessary "solitary, poore, nasty, brutish, and short."[111] One might live in a small community, and not have much interaction with other tribes. There is not automatically a war of all against all.[112] There are important similarities between Kant and Hobbes in that, for Hobbes, too, there are laws in the state of nature, for instance, to seek peace, and to arrange one's liberty in such a way that others grant one the same liberty one grants them.[113] However, there is no need to think that the laws Hobbes envisions as obtaining in the state of nature are more than Kantian "hypothetical imperatives." Hobbes calls the law of reason a precept "by which a man is forbidden to do, that, which is destructive of his life, or taketh away the means of preserving the same; and to omit, that, by which he thinketh it may be best preserved."[114] If one wants self-preservation, and peace, one should give up certain liberties and leave the state of nature. In contrast to Kant's, Hobbes's account is purely prudential.

Kant's account seems close to Locke's. For Locke, too, has argued that in the state of nature there is a law of reason, the "law of nature." Like Kant's, Locke's law of nature prescribes what is needed to protect "life, liberty, and property."[115] However, scholars debate what exactly the foundation and content of this law is.[116] In a voluntarist fashion, it might trace the will of God, and only be binding because it is God's command. Even if it is something that human reason can discern by itself, it seems to track objective moral truths—concerned with, say, what is good for human beings. Kant's account differs importantly from Locke's in this regard. Obligation is not based on the will of God, but is grounded in the autonomy of reason.[117] But it is not only the binding *force* but also the *content* of the moral law that is prescribed by reason alone and does not track any sort of independent truth. Furthermore, Kant's account is not based on *human* reason per se; he argues that his principle is valid for all rational beings, even non-human ones. Finally, Kant and Locke seem to differ on the question whether the state of nature actually existed. Locke believes that it once obtained in the real world,[118] while Kant holds that it is only a thought experiment designed to clarify the justification of coercion.

Kant argues that—whatever our desires, circumstances, or human nature might consist in—there is a direct, unconditional command to avoid anarchy.

Notes

1 Immanuel Kant, *The Conflict of the Faculties* 7:34n. Page numbers in Kant references cite the volume and page of *Kants gesammelte Schriften*, Berlin: de Gruyter 1902ff.; only references to the *Critique of Pure Reason* [KrV] cite the page numbers of the A- and B-editions. All translations of Kant's works are taken from *The Cambridge Edition of the Works of Immanuel Kant*, general editors Paul Guyer and Allen Wood, Cambridge University Press. All the italicized material in the Kant quotes is emphasized in the original texts.
2 Immanuel Kant, *Anthropology from a Pragmatic Point of View* 8:330.
3 Thomas Hobbes, *Leviathan* ch. XIII.
4 Immanuel Kant, *Lectures on the Metaphysics of Morals Vigilantius* ["*Vigil*" in the following] 27:591.
5 Kant, *Vigil* 27:591.
6 Cf. Hobbes ch. XIII.
7 Kant, *Vigil* 27:589.
8 Immanuel Kant, *Idea of a Universal History With a Cosmopolitan Aim* [*IUH*] 8:20.
9 Cf. Immanuel Kant, *Religion Within the Boundaries of Mere Reason* 6:27.
10 Kant, *IUH* 8:23.
11 Kant, *IUH* 8:22.
12 Cf. Sharon Byrd and Joachim Hruschka, *Kant's Doctrine of Right. A Commentary* (CUP 2010) 44–9.
13 Immanuel Kant, *The Metaphysics of Morals* [*MS*] 6:306.
14 Kant, *MS* 6:306.
15 Cf. Kant, *MS* 6:313–6.
16 Kant, *Vigil* 27:590.
17 Kant, *Vigil* 27:589.
18 Kant, *MS* 6:312. This point only refers to determining what is right in a particular situation, not the criterion of rightness itself, as I will argue from Section IV onward.
19 Cf. Kant, *MS* 6:307.
20 Cf. Thomas Pogge, "Is Kant's Rechtslehre a 'Comprehensive Liberalism?'" *Kant's Metaphysics of Morals*, ed. Mark Timmons (OUP 2002) 150–1; Georg Geisman, "Recht und Moral in der Philosophie Kants," *Annual Review of Law and Ethics* 14 (2006): 3–124; and Gerhard Seel, "How Does Kant Justify the Universal Objective Validity of the Law of Right?" *International Journal of Philosophical Studies* 17 (2009): 71–94.
21 Cf. Immanuel Kant, *Groundwork of the Metaphysics of Morals* [*GMS*] 4:389.
22 Cf. Pogge 147.
23 Kant, *IUH* 8:22.
24 Pogge 147.
25 Immanuel Kant, *Toward Perpetual Peace* [*ZeF*] 8:366.
26 Kant, *ZeF* 8:366.
27 Kant, *ZeF* 8:366.
28 Pogge 149.
29 Kant, *GMS* 4:414.
30 Cf. Pogge 147.
31 Immanuel Kant, *Critique of Practical Reason* [*KpV*] 5:26.
32 Kant, *ZeF* 8:378.
33 Kant, *ZeF* 8:377.
34 Kant, *ZeF* 8:378.
35 Kant, *ZeF* 8:378.
36 Kant, *ZeF* 8:365.
37 Kant, *MS* 6:222.
38 Kant, *MS* 6:222.
39 Kant, *MS* 6:222.
40 Kant, *MS* 6:222.
41 Kant, *MS* 6:225; cf. *GMS* 4:402.
42 Kant, *MS* 6:222.
43 Kant, *GMS* 4:421.
44 Kant, *ZeF* 8:377.

45 Kant, *Vigil* 27:526.
46 Kant, *MS* 6:218.
47 Cf. Kant, *GMS* 4:390.
48 Kant, *MS* 6:218–9.
49 Kant, *MS* 6:223.
50 Kant, *ZeF* 8:365.
51 Kant, *ZeF* 8:379.
52 Immanuel Kant, *Critique of Pure Reason* [*KrV*] B2.
53 Kant, *KpV* 5:31.
54 Kant, *KpV* 5:31.
55 Kant, *KrV* A548/B576; italics supplied.
56 Kant, *KpV* 5:29.
57 Kant, *Vigil* 27:499.
58 Kant, *Critique of the Power of Judgment* 5:196–7.
59 Kant, *GMS* 4:425.
60 Kant, *KrV* B168.
61 Kant, *GMS* 4:410.
62 Kant, *GMS* 4:425.
63 Kant, *GMS* 4:389.
64 Cf. Shaun Nichols, *Sentimental Rules* (OUP 2004) 5–7; as well as Chandra Sripada and Stephen Stich, "A Framework for the Psychology of Norms," *Innateness and the Structure of the Mind*, eds. P. Carruthers, S. Laurence and S. Stich, Vol. 2 (OUP 2007) 280–301.
65 Cf. Kant, *KrV* B2-4.
66 Cf. Kant, *KrV* B4.
67 Cf. Kant, *KpV* 5:39.
68 Kant, *GMS* 4:441.
69 Cf. Kant, *KpV* 5:33.
70 Here I will consider three examples. For a discussion of Kant's full argument see my "Kant's Constructisivm" *Moral Constructivism: For and Against*, ed. Carla Bagnoli (CUP 2013) 63–81.
71 Cf. Kant, *GMS* 4:441–5; *KpV* 5:39–41.
72 Cf. Kant, *KrV* B1.
73 Kant, *KrV* B798.
74 Kant, *KpV* 5:58–9.
75 Kant, *GMS* 4:444.
76 Kant, *KpV* 5:26.
77 Kant, *KpV* 5:25.
78 Kant, *GMS* 4:444.
79 Kant, *GMS* 4:445.
80 Kant, *GMS* 4:425.
81 Kant, *KpV* 5:46.
82 Cf. again Kant, *KrV* B3.
83 Kant, *KpV* 5:30.
84 Kant, *KpV* 5:30.
85 Kant, *KpV* 5:30.
86 Kant, *KpV* 5:30.
87 Kant, *KpV* 5:30.
88 Kant, *GMS* 4:446.
89 Kant, *KpV* 5:4n.
90 Kant, *Vigil* 27:523–4.
91 Kant, *MS* 6:239.
92 Kant, *MS* 6:417–8.
93 Kant, *KpV* 5:125–6.
94 Cf. Kant, *MS* 6:219.
95 Kant, *Vigil* 27:521.
96 Kant, *MS* 6:231.
97 Kant, *MS* 6:232.
98 Kant, *MS* 6:231.
99 Kant, *MS* 6:231.

100 Kant, *MS* 6:232.
101 Kant, *ZeF* 8:366.
102 Kant, *ZeF* 8:366.
103 Kant, *MS* 6:312.
104 Kant, *MS* 6:306.
105 Kant, *MS* 6:312.
106 Kant, *MS* 6:312; italics supplied.
107 Kant, *MS* 6:311.
108 Kant, *MS* 6:306.
109 Kant, *MS* 6:313.
110 Kant, *Vigil* 27:590.
111 Hobbes ch. XIV.
112 Cf. Hobbes ch. XIII.
113 Cf. Hobbes chs. XIV-XV.
114 Hobbes ch. XIV.
115 Locke, *Second Treatise* 2.6.
116 Cf. Alex Tuckness, "Locke's Political Philosophy," https://plato.stanford.edu/archives/sum2018/entries/locke-political/ (Summer 2018; last visited September 25, 2019).
117 Cf. again Kant, *KpV* 5:125–6.
118 Cf. Locke 2.14.

8

BARBARIANS IN THE AGORA

American Market Anarchism, 1945–2011

J. Martin Vest

I. Introduction

In the winter of 1949–1950 a handful of friends gathered in the home of Murray Newton Rothbard, a graduate student in economics at Columbia University and a proponent of limited government and laissez-faire. They had convened to indulge a favorite pastime—arguing—and the conversation drifted to the ethical legitimacy of the state when one of those in attendance confronted Rothbard with a particularly trenchant question. If police and courts can be established through majority fiat, he asked, "why not infrastructure or even collectivized industry?" When the gathering broke up in the early hours of the morning, Rothbard found himself still mulling the question, unable to answer it in any way congenial to his existing beliefs. Shortly after, Rothbard decided that the state would, for purposes of moral consistency, have to go.[1] Rothbard's epiphany and the questions it provoked set the course of his activism and scholarship for the rest of his life; and, from then until his death in 1995, he worked tirelessly to spread his vision of a stateless political order, one in which government functions would devolve on freely competing individuals and firms and in which security, courts, and even law would be provided on the open market.

The relationship of Rothbard's vision to the broader terrain of political thought has long caused trouble for the taxonomist of ideas. In this essay, I shift focus away from Rothbard and American libertarianism to detail a longer history of "market anarchism"[2]—a strain of thought of which Rothbard was just one of many brilliant expositors. This lineage, beginning with Pierre-Joseph Proudhon and the American individualist anarchists like Benjamin Tucker, sharply criticized "capitalism" while affirming the rightness and efficacy of private property, trade, competition, and, in some cases, even corporations or "trusts." The entire sweep of anarchist intellectual history, however, cannot be shoehorned into the "market" mold. As we will see, anarchists like Peter Kropotkin had, by the beginning of the twentieth century, jettisoned that framework altogether, insisting on the meaninglessness of private property, scarcity, and competition. Kropotkin and other market-skeptical anarchists profoundly influenced twentieth-century anarchism. As a result, market-oriented anarchism—despite its long history—contrasts sharply in key respects with more recent iterations of anarchist ideology.

While I argue for the historical continuity and distinctness of market anarchism as a strain of political thought, it is not my intention to hypostatize that label or any other, especially given that many of the market anarchists under analysis here recognized no such descriptor. "Market anarchism" functions here as an analytical imposition *on* the historical record rather than an innocent reflection *of* it. My approach is pragmatic. Labels bundle some ideas together and exclude others, simultaneously facilitating and foreclosing on analytical possibilities. This essay employs *market anarchism* as (in the well-worn language of the historian's cliché) an "analytical lens." My intent is not to maintain that only adherents of these ideas qualify as proponents of "real" anarchism, nor to chase any anarchists, living or dead, out of the family circle.

II. Proudhon and the Individualists

Anarchists have claimed as their own such early modern figures as Gerard Winstanley and William Godwin, but the first figure to use "anarchist" self-referentially was a radical book printer from Besançon named Pierre-Joseph Proudhon. Proudhon's thought, contrary to some conceptions, owed much to liberal bourgeois market ideals. First as a youth in the bucolic French Jura in the 1810s and 1820s and then as a wandering journeyman printer, Proudhon evolved a nearly mystical love of the French countryside and its people—a love which was offset by an equally intense suspicion of the centralization and hierarchy of large cities like Paris. Importantly, Pierre-Joseph's work as a printer also led to his engagement with the political and social thought of the prior two centuries and his interaction with the utopian socialist Charles Fourier—experiences which pushed him to ruminate on the political and social problems of the day.[3]

In 1840, Proudhon published his first major work, *What Is Property?* He answered the titular question with a single word—"theft." For Proudhon, the domination of others was no more legitimate an enterprise for agents of the state than it was for proprietors, and he saw scarce difference between the claims of the monarch and those of the landlord. "The proprietor, the robber, the hero, the sovereign—for all these titles are synonymous—imposes his will as law, and suffers neither contradiction nor control; that is, he pretends to be the legislative and the executive power at once." Governments, at their very core, institutionalized domination of man by man, and for that reason were illegitimate. In an epoch-shattering (and often quoted) passage Proudhon imagined a conversation with one of his readers in which he pointed toward a solution.

> What is to be the form of government in the future ? I hear some of my younger readers reply: 'Why, how can you ask such a question? You are a republican.' 'A republican! Yes; but that word specifies nothing. *Res publica*; that is, the public thing. Now, whoever is interested in public affairs—no matter under what form of government—may call himself a republican. Even kings are republicans.'—'Well! you are a democrat?'—'No.'—'What! You would have a monarchy.'—'No.'—'A constitutionalist?'—'God forbid!'—'You are then an aristocrat?'—'Not at all.'—'You want a mixed government?'—'Still less.'—'What are you, then?'—'I am an anarchist.'

If the state could not satisfy the Enlightenment's demand of equality for all, it would have to go.[4]

Proudhon's program, however, did not call for the suppression of the market but for its radical expansion, a process he called the "absorption of government by the economic organism." To begin with, his stance on property was decidedly more nuanced than his flamboyant formula suggested, representing a ratcheting up of Lockean criteria, not their suspension. By "property," he did not mean the individual occupancy, possession, and use of things but the abstract legal title which allowed men, *in absentia*, to exclude others from using them. With *that* type of property, he argued, came the possibility of economic accumulation in the form of ground rent as well as all the attendant social ills of economic inequality. More fundamentally, that kind of property established privileges unsustained by the claims of toil. The person who works an acre of land, whether he has rented it or homesteaded it, has properly mixed his labor with its soil and is the rightful owner of all the resulting benefits, including the improvements to the land. Ground rent represents a usurpation of this right by the landlord. In the case of agricultural production,

Proudhon believed, the answer to present pathologies was simple: the abolition of rent payments and devolution of land titles to those who "mixed their labor" with the soil. With rent payments abolished, the tendency toward accumulation would evaporate, making private property in land a benign institution. Under such circumstances, "you may, without the slightest apprehension, permit the proprietor to sell, transmit, alienate, circulate his property at will." Conversely, Proudhon argued, schemes for nationalization or collectivization of the land were productive of government-grade mischief and, at any rate, would be resisted fiercely by the peasants.[5]

Agricultural property, Proudhon believed, lent itself readily to his individualistic propertarian anarchism. Industry, on the other hand, with its high capital requirements and its dramatic division of labor, presented a thornier set of problems, and here, Proudhon argued, "every industry, operation or enterprise, which by its nature requires the employment of a large number of workmen of different specialties, is destined to become a society or company of workers." Collective ownership of the means of production, however, this was not, and these enterprises would be run on wholly contractual and market oriented bases. In its dealings with the broader society the worker collective must swear off all "combinations" and submit to the "law of competition." Within the company, all positions would be open to all workers, subject to "suitability of sex, age, skill, and length of employment." Importantly, each worker's pay would correspond to the "nature of [his or her] position, the importance of the talents, and the extent of responsibility" and each "shall participate in the gains and in the losses of the company, in proportion to his services." Individual workers would be free to come and go, provided all accounts were settled.[6]

Proudhon exercised a profound, if relatively short-lived, influence over the direction of radical politics in Europe, but in the United States his ideas made a longer-lasting impact. In 1848 an American named Charles A. Dana heard Proudhon speak in the French National Assembly. Impressed with what he heard, Dana returned home to the United States and wrote a series of articles on Proudhon's thought for the *New York Tribune*. Around the same time that Dana was introducing Proudhon to the American public, William B. Greene, son of Massachusetts postmaster Nathaniel Greene, published his own series of articles on Proudhonian banking and credit theory, eventually brought together and published in 1850 as a pamphlet entitled *Mutual Banking*. In subsequent years Greene lobbied the Massachusetts state legislature (unsuccessfully) to throw its weight behind mutual banking, and he also published several translations of Proudhon's work in the radical press, including an excerpt from *What Is Property?*[7]

Greene's Proudhonianism, however, was not the only strain of anti-statist thought vying for the attention of American radicals. For decades, a handful of American intellectuals had pushed the logic of Jeffersonian individualism all the way to its logical, anarchistic, conclusion. Josiah Warren, the father of American individualist anarchism, had participated in Robert Owen's experimental commune at New Harmony, and had come away from the experience convinced of the importance of individual sovereignty in human affairs. Unlike most of the individualist anarchists and libertarians who have followed in his train, Warren not only rejected human relationships built on force, but even looked with suspicion on human "combinations" in general. He argued that "the only ground upon which man can know liberty, is that of disconnection, disunion, individuality." Because of this belief, Warren rejected the institution of government on the grounds that it threw men into combinations which could only cause mischief. Lysander Spooner, a decade Warren's junior, came to similar conclusions regarding the incompatibility of government and individual liberty by extending the natural rights arguments of Jefferson and others. According to this line of reasoning, consent was an ethical prerequisite for all interactions between human beings, including the establishment and maintenance of government. But if the "consent of the governed" meant anything at all, Spooner argued, it must mean the deliberate consent of every single individual subject to the state's authority. No "government" as such could ever meet this requirement, so the state itself was illegal according to the canons of natural law. By the end of his life Greene—and his project of Proudhonian mutualism—had become closely associated with this American individualist milieu.[8]

Greene's importation of Proudhon brought together two great streams of anti-state thought, but it was in the work of another Massachusetts native, Benjamin R. Tucker, that their fusion was fully realized. Born in South Dartmouth in 1854, Tucker developed an interest in individualist anarchism at an early age and met many of the tradition's rainmakers while still in his teens. In 1874, he traveled to Europe to study Proudhon's philosophy, and soon after returning to the United States published a full English translation of *What Is Property?* In 1881, Tucker embarked on the project that would be his most influential, an individualist anarchist newspaper, *Liberty*, which he described as a "journal brought into existence almost as a direct consequence of the teachings of Proudhon, … which lives principally to emphasize and spread them." As if to underscore the centrality of Proudhon to *Liberty*'s mission, the paper's masthead carried a quotation from Proudhon: "Liberty: Not the Daughter but the Mother of Order."[9]

The fusion of Proudhonian mutualism and American individualism effected in the pages of *Liberty* produced an anarchism paradoxically more comfortable with the operations of the market than either of its parent ideologies. American anarchism's individualism—especially in the hands of Warren—had appeared at some points in danger of drifting off into demands for economic autarky, such was its distrust of social entanglements. From the very beginning, however, Proudhon's influence in America tempered this hyper-individualism. In his *Socialistic, Communistic, Mutualistic and Financial Fragments*, for example, William Greene had emphasized the deeply social character of all human enterprises, arguing that "what we possess we owe partly to our own faculties, but mainly to the educational and material aid received by us from our parents, friends, neighbors, and other members of society." Tucker's peculiar amalgam of the two schools moved past this recognition of human interdependence to identify market institutions as the primary site for the reconciliation of individuals' various wants. In defiance of anarchistic common sense, he insisted that wage labor was not slavery, but rather "a form of voluntary exchange," and therefore "a form of liberty." Tucker even stood at the ready to defend that institution most despised by turn-of-the-century progressives and radicals—the trust. Anarchism, he wrote, "discountenances all direct attacks on [trusts], all interference with them, all anti-trust legislation whatsoever." On the contrary, "it regards industrial combinations as very useful whenever they spring into existence in response to demand created in a healthy body."[10]

The differences of opinion between Tucker and his anarchist forebears on these matters owed much to a subtle shift in emphasis in libertarian theory effected by Tucker. For Proudhon, the world's evils stemmed from hierarchies—those embedded in existing property relations as well as in governments. The remedy for hierarchy and its attendant social ills, he believed, was thoroughgoing equality. For Tucker, however, the battleground had shifted onto another set of paired opposites: monopoly and competition. By supporting monopolies in the issuance of money and credit, in access to land, through the levying of tariffs, and through the protection of intellectual property, Tucker argued, the state undermined the salutary effects of competition. A truly free market, he believed, not only would undermine the coercive potential of corporations and wage labor, but would also drive down the revenues to be made through usury, rent, and profit. Competition alone, Tucker argued, would deliver to the worker the full value of his labor, and only through competition could economic justice be achieved.[11]

In 1908, Benjamin Tucker's bookstore and print shop burned to the ground, bringing an end to *Liberty* and to Tucker's participation in anarchist agitation. With his wife and daughter, he relocated to France, where he spent most of the rest of his life before dying in 1939. Tucker's retirement, however, signaled more than the conclusion of a single propagandist's career. *Liberty* had come to serve as the rallying point for an entire movement, bringing together the centrifugal tendencies of American individualist anarchism through Tucker's forceful rhetoric and uncompromising ideological consistency. Other individualist journals existed, but none could fill *Liberty*'s role as the unifying voice of American market anarchism. Had the movement been healthy it might have survived the loss of its flagship journal. But years of infighting over abstruse points of theory and a slow defection of anarchists to the ranks of state socialism had weakened the movement; with the disappearance of *Liberty* the remaining exponents of American market anarchism were scattered to the historical winds.[12]

III. Social Anarchism

Proudhon's rejection of the economic and political status quo, his embrace of "anarchism," and his pyrotechnic written works inspired European radicals, many of whom embraced him as a guiding star of their movement—at least initially. Generally, while these second- and third-generation anarchists retained Proudhon's focus on statelessness as well as his rejection of "capitalism," they quickly moved away from his orientation toward market mechanisms. Market anarchists (like their radical liberal cousins) have often argued for the co-terminousness of market and civil society and have often subsumed within "the market" all voluntary arrangements, but the language and logics of the market have their own historical specificity. The proponents of so-called "social anarchism" embraced conceptualizations of the free society quite at odds with ideas of property, trade, and competition, and their beliefs about the stateless future throw into relief the peculiarities of market anarchism.[13]

The social anarchist tradition has always registered a profound ambivalence about its own relationship with Pierre-Joseph Proudhon. On one hand, its intellectual debt to him has been too substantial to ignore. The incendiary Mikhail Bakunin acknowledged Proudhon as "the master of us all," while Peter Kropotkin, the pacific Russian prince turned libertarian communist, claimed that "Proudhon laid the foundations of anarchism." As late as 1937, the anarcho-syndicalist Rudolph Rocker could describe him as "one of the most intellectually gifted and certainly the most many-sided writer of whom modern socialism can boast." From the very beginning, however, anarchists and scholars of social anarchism harbored doubts about Proudhon's relationship to that tradition. Proudhon, Bakunin wrote, "remained all his life an incorrigible idealist, immersed in the Bible, in Roman law and metaphysics. His great misfortune was that he had never studied the natural sciences or appropriated their method." By the middle of the twentieth century, Proudhon-skepticism had evolved into outright rejection of his relevance. George Woodcock recalled that mid-century anarchists regarded Proudhon with "suspicion and condescension," and in a 1996 essay, activist and author Larry Gambone admitted that he had neglected Proudhon's works for decades because of Proudhon's ill-repute among anarchists. Albert Meltzer's *Anarchism: Arguments For and Against* argued emphatically that Proudhon was a mere *precursor* to anarchism who never "engaged in Anarchist activity or struggle" and who had been sullied by forays into parliamentary participation.[14]

Social anarchism's alienation from its Proudhonian origins, however, had less to do with Proudhon's coolness toward activism or his time as an agent of the state and much more to do with genuine ideological differences with his libertarian descendants. The anarchist thinkers following Proudhon increasingly emphasized the dialectical relationship between self and other, and the inherently "social" nature of individual liberty. Because of this, they moved further and further away from private property and the attendant institutions of contract and exchange. For Mikhail Bakunin, the means of production were to be collectivized. While conceding the necessity of management, he insisted that "the management of production need not be exclusively monopolized by one or several individuals. And the managers are not at all entitled to more pay." Equality of wages aside, Bakunin maintained some of Proudhon's emphasis on individual productivity, believing that the lazy or intransigent are "free to die of hunger or to live in the deserts or the forests among savage beasts." Anyone wishing to partake in the benefits of society, however, "must earn his living by his own labor, or be treated as a parasite who is living on the labor of others."[15]

It was in the hands of the anarcho-communists—and especially those of anarcho-communism's most famous exponent, Peter Kropotkin—that economic calculation and market activity ceased to play any role at all in anarchist theory. In *The Conquest of Bread*, Kropotkin derided as antediluvian the assumption that individual contributions to the social product could be measured and proportionally remunerated.

> No distinction can be drawn between the work of each man. Measuring the work by its results leads us to absurdity; dividing and measuring them by the hours spent on the work also leads us to absurdity. One thing remains: put the *needs* above the *works*, and first of all recognize the right to live, and later on, to the comforts of life, for all those who take their share in production.[16]

In addition to being impossible, Kropotkin believed, the calculation of value was unnecessary. Modern science and technology had finally conquered the age-old problem of economic scarcity and, if relieved from supplying the frivolous and wasteful demands of the middle classes, the fields and workshops of Europe and the United States could easily provide "well-being for all." A few years of such abundance, Kropotkin predicted, would cause the world to exclaim: "Enough! We have enough coal and bread and raiment! Let us rest and consider how best to use our powers, how best to employ our leisure." The problem of incentives, Kropotkin argued, would attenuate with the disappearance of "repugnant and unhealthy drudgery," largely a symptom of the capitalist mode of production. In general, Kropotkin believed, the ostensibly natural human inclination toward self-interest was also an artifact of capitalist society. Rather, within human beings existed a natural predisposition to altruistic behavior, bred into them by eons of evolutionary forces which, he argued, selected for intra-species cooperation rather than competition. Men and women, therefore, generally need not be compelled to contribute to the common good by the threat of starvation, as even Bakunin believed.[17]

Finally, Kropotkin went so far in his rejection of market mechanisms as to cast doubt on the benefits of trade. He cautioned readers that he did not desire "all exchange to be suppressed, nor that each region should strive to produce that which will only grow in its climate by a more or less artificial culture." He did, however, believe that "the theory of exchange, such as is understood to-day, is strangely exaggerated, that exchange is often useless and even harmful." Long-distance trade between communities re-introduced the threat of market calculation with all of its attendant social ills. Far better, he believed, to limit one's dealings to the local commune where need rather than profit dictated the allocation of resources).[18]

The first years of the twentieth century, as we have seen, were hard times for the individualists, but social anarchism was just coming into its own. In the years following 1900, there arose a novel (though not entirely new) emphasis within anarchism on the revolutionary potential of labor unions, an approach which met with greatest success in Spain. There the National Confederation of Labor (CNT) had by the 1930s come firmly under the control of anarchists of the Iberian Anarchist Federation (FAI); when the Spanish Civil War broke out in 1936, the CNT/FAI lent its rifles to the cause of anti-fascism. More than that, it instituted anarchist measures in Republican-controlled territories and by 1937 three million people lived in rural anarchist collectives. In the cities, anarchists seized workshops and factories, with Barcelona's entire industrial plant coming under worker control. The vicissitudes of war, however, buffeted the anarchist experiment. Supply shortages disrupted industry and with it the war effort, while the threat of Franco's looming victory pushed the CNT/FAI into closer and closer collaboration with the Spanish Republican government—itself increasingly a puppet of its only international arms supplier, the Soviet Union.

On December 16, 1939, *Pravda* informed its Soviet readers that in Spain "the purging of the Trotskyists and Anarcho-syndicalists has begun; it will be conducted with the same energy with which it was conducted in the USSR." By the middle of 1937, the Spanish experiment in anarchism was finished. Two years later, Franco's forces defeated the Republicans and ended the Spanish Civil War. The meteoric rise and fall of Spanish syndicalism seemed to exhaust libertarian energies the world over, and, in the postwar period, anarchism's appeal as a mass movement gave way to a global preoccupation with state socialisms of various stripes. Though they had held out a few decades longer, the collectivists found themselves consigned, just like their individualist cousins, to the dustbin of history. The eclipse of libertarian thought, however, was short-lived.[19]

IV. Rothbard and Market Anarchism

The market anarchist tradition in the United States lay dormant from 1908 until the arrival of Rothbard. Born in 1926 to immigrant parents, Rothbard came of age surrounded by communists and communist-sympathizers in New Deal-era New York. Encouraged in part by his father's individualistic tendencies, he drifted into a stubborn opposition to the leftist milieu in which he had been raised, and by his early twenties had cast his lot with the libertarian wing of the Old Right, hungrily consuming the works of Albert Jay Nock, Isabel Patterson, Garet Garrett, and H. L. Mencken. By 1949, his explorations in the libertarian tradition had led him to reject the role of government altogether. The adherents of the postwar libertarian right, however, found themselves in a pitched—and hopeless—battle with the ascendant statist forces in their midst. The "New Right," which coalesced in the 1950s around the intellectual nucleus of William F. Buckley's *National Review*, nominally sought a fusion of three widely diverging strands of right-wing thought and activism: traditionalism, Old Right libertarianism, and anti-communism. In practice, though, the New Right rather swiftly evolved to prioritize anti-communism over all other commitments, with Buckley and others advocating dramatic expansion of government to meet the Soviet threat.[20]

Many erstwhile libertarians made their peace with the new dispensation, but Rothbard was not one of them, and by the early 1960s he found himself sidelined by the gatekeepers of conservative opinion. Just as libertarianism's working relationship with conservatism devolved, Rothbard began casting about for new alliances, and he soon found them in the emergent New Left. Publications and interviews from the sixties feature Rothbard's recurrent appeals for a left–right rapprochement along libertarian lines; and, by the end of the decade, efforts on behalf of such a rapprochement began to bear fruit. In May 1969, Rothbard participated in the formation of the Radical Libertarian Alliance, comprising both disaffected right-wingers like himself and elements of the anti-war left. The Libertarian Party emerged from these efforts three years later. American libertarianism, birthed as a kind of left deviationism from postwar conservatism, had come into its own as a political movement. By the early 1970s, Rothbard had started to distance himself from the "cultural leftism" which pervaded the libertarian movement, and in the 1980s he shifted decisively back to the right, forming alliances with the ascendant "paleoconservative" movement associated with Patrick Buchanan and others.[21]

Despite these shifting alliances, Rothbard's basic program remained remarkably consistent throughout his decades as an expositor of the libertarian creed. At its foundation lay natural law, which he interpreted with Locke to mean that "every man has a *property* in his own *person*," and that "this nobody has any right to but himself."[22] From this, Locke and Rothbard conclude, it follows that the individual's physical efforts, "the labour of his body and the work of his hands," belong to him as well, and that "whatsoever that he removes out of the state that nature hath provided, and left it in, he hath mixed his labour with and joined something to it that is his own, and thereby makes it his *property*."[23] In *Man, Economy and State* Rothbard built on this framework by deducing the economic and political outline of a society which respected in full the natural rights of every individual, concluding that such circumstances would "[lead] to the property structure that is found in free-market capitalism."[24]

Because the concepts of freely competing police agencies and courts are central to his libertarianism, it is worth describing Rothbard's vision of these institutions in detail.[25] In the absence of government, he argued, insurance companies would establish private security services to protect subscribers from crime and to minimize indemnity payouts. While public-option police waste time and resources extracting justice for an abstract "society," Rothbard believed, private police could dedicate themselves to protecting life and limb and restoring stolen property to its rightful owners. If (as would often be the case) the aggressing party had his *own* insurance policy and his *own* police, the altercation could precipitate violence between police forces. But, Rothbard insists, this would be "pointless and economically as well as physically self-destructive." In order to avoid such disruptive and dangerous eventualities (which paying customers would never tolerate, at any rate), each security firm would necessarily "announce as a vital part of its service, the use of private courts or arbitrators to decide who is in the wrong." In practice, each party would plead his case in his own court (which may be associated with his security company). In the not-unlikely event that each court finds in favor of its own client, the case is taken to a third court, agreed on by both firms ahead of time. Its decision would be final and enforceable. At each step in the process, individuals' and firms' cooperation would be impelled by the ancient tactic of ostracism, with intransigent parties risking their access to private courts in the future. Finally, law itself required no centralized planning according to Rothbard. Merchant courts, admiralty law, Anglo-Saxon common law, ancient Roman private law, and ancient Irish law, he points out, were all provided by decentralized "free market" judges who built reputations for expertly applying reason and precedent to concrete legal disputes.[26]

This program's relationship to anarchism is complex, and Rothbard's attitude toward the older tradition reflects some of his ambivalence about this relationship. Predictably enough, he rejected the anarcho-communist project in whole, finding in it not only economic error but also a dangerous commitment to irrationalism. But he also leveled sharp criticisms at the individualists like Spooner and Tucker. He found lacking, for example, Lysander Spooner's faith in juries, insisting on the necessity of rationally derived libertarian law. Even more trenchant were his criticisms of the earlier individualists' understanding of profit, rent, and interest. Both Proudhon and Josiah Warren subscribed to forms of the labor theory of value. To explain the persistence of these features of economic life, then, they turned in varying degree to the notion of monopoly, arguing that the state artificially props up the privileges of landlords, moneylenders, and bosses through force. Rothbard did not deny that state power represented a thumb on the scales of economic distribution, but he did reject the notion that rent, interest, or profit derived exclusively from state-propped privilege. Rather, he pointed toward time preference, and urged the world's individualists to investigate another school of anti-state thought:

> There is, in the body of thought known as 'Austrian economics,' a scientific explanation of the workings of the free market (and of the consequences of government intervention in that market) which individualist anarchists could easily incorporate into their political and social *Weltanschauung*. But to do this, they must throw out the worthless excess baggage of money-crankism and reconsider the nature and justification of the economic categories of interest, rent and profit.[27]

Not surprisingly, the deep disagreements between Rothbard and the anarchists, as well as his affinities with the liberal tradition from Locke to Ludwig von Mises, pushed the economist away from the label "anarchism."[28] Early in his career, he even toyed with the neologism "nonarchist" as a descriptor for his brand of libertarianism. Despite these objections, Rothbard made peace with the term, and by the late 1960s he and his growing cadre of followers had come to call their brand of libertarianism "anarcho-capitalism." This rhetorical gesture has caused consternation ever since, both in the camps of would-be fellow travelers who balk at alliances with "anarchists" as well as among adherents of older forms of anarchism who deny the relevance of Rothbard's vision to their intellectual tradition.[29]

V. Left-Wing Market Anarchism

Like the postwar conservative movement with which it had parted ways, Rothbardian libertarianism proved vulnerable to deviationism, and beginning in the 1970s a number of competing visions sprung up to its left. This strain of thought, like Rothbardianism before it, belongs in large measure to the broad tradition of market anarchisms, but the left libertarians have been promiscuous in their intellectual appropriations. This tendency has made theirs an intellectually dynamic school of political thought, but has also placed some of them in tension with Rothbardian libertarianism and even the broader market anarchist milieu.

One of the earliest and most consistently market-oriented of the left libertarian deviationists was Samuel E. Konkin III. Born in Saskatchewan in 1947 and raised in Edmonton, Konkin first entered political activism as an undergraduate at the University of Alberta. There he served as head of the Young Social Credit League, an organization dedicated to forwarding the bizarre economic theories of the British engineer C. H. Douglas. By 1968, Konkin had discovered libertarianism and had joined the Young Americans for Freedom (YAF) chapter at the University of Wisconsin, where he was enrolled in a graduate program in chemistry. The following year, he traveled to YAF's national convention as a delegate, met Rothbard and other luminaries of the nascent libertarian movement, and—along with all the other libertarians—was expelled from the convention. The episode etched in stone Konkin's commitment to the libertarian cause.[30]

Konkin's passage through the ideological straits of American libertarianism imparted to his thinking a profound affinity for the market. In the institutions of state and economy he located the two opposing dynamics of all human interaction—the coercive and the voluntary. Konkin believed that the negation of the state entailed nothing more nor less than the universalization of the market, and he accepted the broad outlines of Rothbard's free-market account of security, courts, and law. Konkin dissented from Rothbardian orthodoxy, however, with regard to revolutionary praxis. Means, he believed, must be consistent with ends. Since anarchism sought the abolition of political mechanisms in favor of economic ones, it followed that the suitable means to attain that end were economic and not political. Accordingly, he was appalled by the founding of the Libertarian Party, and through the 1970s evolved a body of market anarchist ideas as an alternative to the political approach favored by mainstream libertarians.

In his 1980 *New Libertarian Manifesto*, Konkin limned the details of a program which he called "agorism." In Konkin's hands, un-coerced market activity expanded from the mere end of libertarian activism to its means. The underground economy, he argued, represented the germ of a new stateless society. If freed from the quasi-religious stigmas inculcated by government and its allies, black markets would attract investment, driving profits out of officially-sanctioned activities and depriving the state of revenue. Even more importantly, as the underground economy grew in size and complexity, investors could be expected to commit an increasing amount of resources to addressing security threats, especially those posed by state actors. This, Konkin believed, would give rise to the free-market security-insurance companies of libertarian theory, and would signal the beginning of the end of government.[31]

Another pioneer in market anarchism's leftward shift was former Barry Goldwater speechwriter Karl Hess. Hess's relationship with market anarchism began in 1968, when, after reading an essay by Murray Rothbard entitled "Confessions of a Right Wing Liberal," he publicly cast aside his identity as a conservative and assumed the position of Washington editor of the new *Libertarian Forum*. In a March 1969 article, "The Death of Politics," Hess showcased his embrace of Rothbardian market anarchism. "Laissez-faire capitalism, or anarchocapitalism," he argued, "is simply the economic form of the libertarian ethic" and "encompasses the notion that men should exchange goods and services, without regulation, solely on the basis of value for value .... Economically, this system is anarchy, and proudly so." Already underway, however, was a subtle shift in Hess's thinking away from narrow economism and toward a more open-ended understanding of voluntary action. In a piece published two months later in *Libertarian Forum*, Hess wrote:

> Libertarianism is a people's movement and a liberation movement. It seeks the sort of open, non-coercive society in which the people, the living, free, distinct people may voluntarily associate, dis-associate, and, as they see fit, participate in the decisions affecting their lives ... It means people free collectively to organize the resources of their immediate community or individualistically to organize them ... Liberty means the right to shape your own institutions. It opposes the right of those institutions to shape you simply because of accreted power or gerontological status.

Hess's emphasis on consent rather than any formal political or economic arrangement could prove troublesome to anarchists hoping for an established orthodoxy. "The market," capacious enough to enfold all voluntary interactions, could include such ostensibly anti-market institutions as collective ownership and participatory democracy.[32]

Despite its efflorescence within the libertarian movement of the late 1960s and 1970s, left market anarchism remained a muted tendency until the 1990s, when a resurgent interest in left-wing anarchism occurred in libertarian circles. These latter-day expressions of left market anarchism have included a diverse range of positions and emphases, but a broad consensus of sorts is discernible. No publication has been more influential in highlighting and forging that consensus than a 2011 collection of essays, *Markets Not Capitalism*, edited by Gary Chartier and Charles W. Johnson. In their introduction to the Karl Hess-dedicated volume, the editors argue that the left market anarchists adopt the historical left's criticisms of "persistent poverty, ecological destruction, radical inequalities of wealth, and concentrated power in the hands of corporations, bosses, and landlords." They dissent, however, from the mainstream left's attribution of these problems to private property or market mechanisms. Absent state interference, they argue, markets evidence distinct "centrifugal" tendencies, undermining inequalities of wealth through pervasive and withering competition.[33]

Kevin Carson's essay "Economic Calculation in the Corporate Commonwealth" elaborates one of the most sophisticated of these arguments. Rothbard had earlier pointed out that Mises's response to the "economic calculation problem" demonstrated the limits of central planning when engaged in not only by states but also by corporations. Because corporations internalize transactions and thus insulate themselves from the pricing mechanism, Rothbard argued, they too are subject to all the calculative inefficiencies of governments. Carson builds on Rothbard's argument by expanding the logic of Hayek's slightly different criticism of intervention, which argued that markets capitalize on the dispersed information of individual actors. When applied to the logic of the firm, Carson points out, Hayek's emphasis on dispersed knowledge casts severe doubt on the effectiveness of hierarchical organizations to gather and deploy information. A free market which did not prop up poorly performing corporations, then, would not only whittle down to size the mega-corporations of the "statist quo" but would also select in favor of those organized on less hierarchical lines.[34]

In addition to the leveling and decentralizing effects of stateless economies, Chartier and Johnson's introductory essay emphasizes the politically open-ended potential of free markets and their capacity to create "spaces for social experimentation and hard-driving grassroots activism." Free markets, they argue, foster values that include "not only the pursuit of narrowly financial gain … but also the appeal of solidarity, mutuality and sustainability." In some cases, this broader, more humanitarian set of values might even be necessary for the peaceful and prosperous flourishing of markets themselves. Charles W. Johnson has argued, for example, that the libertarian commitment to non-coercion represents a necessary but insufficient element of a prosperous and peaceful stateless society. In place of a "thin libertarianism" which doggedly refuses discussion of these broader commitments, Johnson encourages a "thick libertarianism" which recognizes the broader matrix of values in which any theory of politics or economics must be situated. While these broader personal commitments *could* be anything, Johnson argues, libertarianism itself supports and embodies a decidedly left-liberal set of values: anti-racism, anti-sexism, and egalitarianism, among others.[35]

VI. Conclusion

Particularly in its more recent manifestations, market anarchism has tended to expand the meaning of "markets" beyond the political-economic concerns of trade and competition to embrace a general emphasis on voluntary action. Karl Hess's thought, for example, continued to evolve through the 1970s, and by the end of the decade he had tamped down much of his earlier emphasis on market activity. In a 1980 essay in *the dandelion* called "Anarchism without Hyphens," he denied the relevance of economic programs to anarchism as such and offered a simple formulation to replace the congeries of anti-state "-isms" then (and now) prevalent: "An anarchist is a voluntarist." More recently, Kevin Carson, whose work has been central in the articulation of twenty-first-century market anarchism, has expressed doubts about "the market" as a general rubric for a non-coercive society.[36]

Market anarchism is at least as old as the social anarchist tradition with which it is often compared. It is in significant ways conceptually distinct from social anarchism, notwithstanding efforts by some within and without the market anarchist tradition to shake "the market" loose from its historical moorings and offer it as a synonym for stateless human interaction. At the same time, the easy conceptual evolution from market anarchisms to non-market anarchisms (particularly on the left) suggests that something more historically complex has happened than the evolution of two hermetically sealed intellectual traditions. Why, we might ask, do market-oriented libertarians often drift off into sympathy with the broader anarchist tradition, even those variants of anarchism which have demonstrated little patience for liberal economics? One answer may be that there has always been an unarticulated relationship between the anarchist project and that realm of ordered chaos the Marxists call the "anarchy of production." Indeed, the authoritarian left has always suspected this. Marx's derisive characterization of Proudhonian mutualism as "bourgeois socialism" is unsurprising in the context of this chapter's claim that Proudhon was a market anarchist. But what to make of Lenin's rejection of the entire anarchist tradition—including its collectivist variants—as "bourgeois individualism in reverse." If "the market" fails to encompass the full complexity of human interactions outside state coercion, it is probably also true that it is one of the closest approximations to hand, and anarchists—even the communists among them—are working from models drawn up in Manchester.[37]

The close relationship between the market and anarchism should not surprise us. Authorities have always recognized the dangers presented by the agora and its inhabitants—often late denizens of the wolf-prowled spaces beyond the city where dangerous men and ideas flourish.

Similarly, anarchists and anarchism have since the middle of the nineteenth century presented another kind of barbarian threat—a vision of what happens if modernity's promises of life, liberty, and property or liberty, equality, and fraternity are taken too seriously. Anarchism's threat to the established order has sometimes taken a more concrete form, as when it guided the hands of terrorists as they prepared daggers, poisons, ropes, and revolvers for the enemies of the people. Market anarchists, though a more pacific lot than the nineteenth-century propagandists of the deed, represent one more barbarian incursion, one that has reached the market and threatens to set loose all of its dangerous forces. But we probably ought not fret. There have, after all, always been barbarians in the agora.

Notes

1 Murray N. Rothbard, "Transcript: How Murray Rothbard Became a Libertarian" [address to 1981 Libertarian Party Convention, Denver, CO], *Mises Wire* (Mises Institute, April 28, 2014) https://mises.org/blog/transcript-how-murray-rothbard-became-libertarian (June 29, 2020).

2 Few will be satisfied with my use of this term. It has generally been employed by left-libertarians to distinguish their more egalitarian and "social" variant of propertarian anarchism from Rothbard's anarcho-capitalism. At least implicitly, then, market anarchism has hitherto been considered exclusive of anarcho-capitalism. I have used the term generically, encompassing not only anarcho-capitalism and its left-libertarian critics, but the entire lineage of market-friendly anarchisms dating back to P.-J. Proudhon.

3 George Woodcock, *Pierre-Joseph Proudhon: A Biography* (Montréal: Black Rose 1987), 1–35. The search for origins has led historians of anarchism to plumb nearly every crevice of modern and pre-modern intellectual history, and figures ranging from Christ and Lao-Tze to Jonathan Swift have been drafted for the cause. See George Woodcock, *Anarchism: A History of Libertarian Ideas and Movements* (New York, NY: World 1971). See also Peter H Marshall, *Demanding the Impossible: A History of Anarchism* (London: Harper 2008), 53–129. On the matter of anarchism's historical specificity I agree with Michael Schmidt and Lucien van der Walt, who "stress [anarchism's] novelty and relatively recent roots" and reject ahistorical presentations of the ideology as a timeless struggle. Lucien van der Walt and Michael Schmidt, *Black Flame: the Revolutionary Class Politics of Anarchism and Syndicalism* (Chico, CA: AK Press 2009), 15. Anarchism, in the modern sense, could not exist before the emergence of the idea of "society," conceived of as a site of human activity independent from the mechanisms of coercive authority. See John R. Ehrenburg, *Civil Society: The Critical History of an Idea* (New York, NY: NYU P 2017); and Larry Sidentop, *Inventing the Individual: The Origins of Western Liberalism* (Cambridge: Belknap Harvard, 2017).

4 Pierre-Joseph Proudhon, *What Is Property? An Inquiry into the Principle of Right and of Government*, trans. Benjamin R. Tucker (Princeton, NJ: Benjamin R. Tucker 1876), 271–272, 279; Woodcock, *Pierre-Joseph Proudhon*, 42–52.

5 Pierre-Joseph Proudhon, *General Idea of the Revolution in the Nineteenth Century*, trans. John Beverly Robinson (New York, NY: Haskell House 1969), 207–215, 240. Woodcock, *Pierre-Joseph Proudhon*, 45.

6 Proudhon, *General Idea of the Revolution*, 216, 222–223.

7 Paul Avrich, *Anarchist Portraits* (Princeton, NJ: Princeton UP 1988), 137–140.

8 William Gary Kline, *The Individualist Anarchists: A Critique of Liberalism* (Lanham, MD: UP of America 1987), 8–21, 35–46.

9 Avrich, *Anarchist Portraits*, 140–143; *Liberty* 1: 12, 3; *Liberty* 1: 1, 1.

10 Kline, *The Individualist Anarchists*, 49, 74–75.

11 Ibid., 74–76.

12 James Joseph Martin, *Men against the State: The Expositors of Individualist Anarchism in America, 1827–1908* (Colorado Springs, CO: Ralph Myles 1970), 271–278.

13 By "social anarchism" I mean the anarchist lineage running from Mikhail Bakunin through Peter Kropotkin to the twentieth-century anarcho-communists and syndicalists. This usage, like "market anarchism," is fraught as all political ideologies are ultimately "social." My employment of the term is merely conventional.

14 First Bakunin quote taken from George Woodcock, "On Proudhon's 'What Is Property?'" *Anarchy*, 106: 353; second Bakunin quote taken from Mikhail Aleksandrovich Bakunin, *Bakunin on Anarchism*, ed. Sam Dolgoff (Montréal: Black Rose Books 2002), 26; Petr Alekseevich Kropotkin, *Evolution and Environment* (Montréal: Black Rose Books 1995), 27; Rudolf Rocker, *Anarcho-Syndicalism: Theory and Practice* (Edinburgh: AK 2004), 4–5. Woodcock, *Pierre-Joseph Proudhon*, xiv; Larry Gambone, *Proudhon and Anarchism: Proudhon's*

Libertarian Thought and the Anarchist Movement (Victoria: Red Lion 2008); Albert Meltzer, *Anarchism, Arguments For and Against* (San Francisco, CA: AK Press 1996), 5.

15 Bakunin, *Bakunin on Anarchism*, 89, 424.

16 Petr Aleksieevich Kropotkin, *The Conquest of Bread* (New York, NY: G. Putnam and Sons 1906), 216. Original emphasis.

17 Kropotkin, *The Conquest of Bread*, 20, 144, 216; Petr Aleksieevich Kropotkin, *Mutual Aid: A Factor of Evolution* (London: William Heinemann 1915).

18 Kropotkin, *The Conquest of Bread*, 255.

19 Marshall, *Demanding the Impossible*, 453–468.

20 Justin Raimondo, *An Enemy of the State: The Life of Murray N. Rothbard* (Amherst, MA: Prometheus Books 2000), 23–58. See also George H. Nash, *The Conservative Intellectual Movement in America, since 1945* (New York, NY: Basic Books 1976); and Paul Gottfried and Thomas Fleming, *The Conservative Movement* (Boston, MA: Twayne Publishers, 1988).

21 Raimondo, *An Enemy of the State*;

Kevin Carson, "The Left-Rothbardians, Part I: Rothbard," The Art of the Possible (blog), 2008. Accessed at the Center for a Stateless Society website, https://c4ss.org/content/12938.

22 John Locke, *Second Treatise of Government and a Letter Concerning Toleration*, ed. Mark Goldie (Oxford: Oxford University Press, 2016), 15.

23 Rothbard believed with Thomas Aquinas that natural law—both in its physical and moral varieties—could be apprehended through observation of unfolding processes and that the potentialities buried in these processes tell us not only what *is* but what *ought* to be. Unfortunately, he argued, the natural-law theorists from Plato to Leo Strauss had incorrectly conflated "society" and "state," transforming man's manifest sociality into a "natural" need for coercive authority. This error, he believed, was not corrected until the early seventeenth century, when John Locke spelled out the individualistic implication of natural rights theory. Locke's understanding of natural right, Rothbard argued, remained "riddled with contradictions and inconsistencies." He believed, however, that the theory was perfected in the writings of Lysander Spooner and Herbert Spencer in the nineteenth century. Murray N. Rothbard, *The Ethics of Liberty* (Atlantic Highlands, NJ: Humanities Press 1982).

24 Rothbard, *The Ethics of Liberty*, 21; Murray N. Rothbard, *Man, Economy, and State: A Treatise on Economic Principles with Power and Market: Government and the Economy* (Auburn, AL: Ludwig von Mises Institute 2009), 1047.

25 One of the first discussions of Rothbard's anarcho-capitalist vision is found in Murray N. Rothbard, "The Real Aggressor," *Faith and Freedom*, April 1954. The classic expression of the free-market defense paradigm is found in Rothbard's *Power and Market*. See Rothbard, *Man, Economy and State and Power and Market*, 1047–1056.

26 Rothbard, *Man, Economy and State and Power and Market*, 1047–1056.

27 Murray N. Rothbard, *Egalitarianism as a Revolt Against Nature and Other Essays*, ed. Roy Childs (Auburn, AL: Ludwig von Mises Institute 2000), 218.

28 The relationship of market anarchism to liberalism is a very important facet of this history. In fact, it was not an anarchist but a nineteenth-century liberal—Gustave de Molinari—who most closely prefigured Rothbard's anarcho-capitalism. For a thorough discussion of Molinari see David M. Hart, "Gustav de Molinari and the Anti-Statist Liberal Tradition, Part I," *Journal of Libertarian Studies*, 5:1, 263–290; David M. Hart, "Gustav de Molinari and the Anti-Statist Liberal Tradition, Part II," *Journal of Libertarian Studies*, 5:4, 263–290; and David M. Hart, "Gustav de Molinari and the Anti-Statist Liberal Tradition, Part III," *Journal of Libertarian Studies*, 6:1, 83–104. For a discussion of the French liberal tradition out of which Molinari emerged, see Mark Weinburg, "The Social Analysis of Three Early Nineteenth Century French Liberals: Say, Comte and Dunoyer," *Journal of Libertarian Studies*, 2:1, 45–63; and Robert Leroux and David M Hart, eds., *French Liberalism in the Nineteenth Century: An Anthology* (London: Routledge 2012). For an explanation of the methodological relationship between the liberal Austrian School of economics and Rothbard's anarcho-capitalism, see Murray N. Rothbard, "Praxeology: The Methodology of Austrian Economics," accessed at the Ludwig von Mises Institute website, https://mises.org/library/praxeology-methodology-austrian-economics.

29 Murray N. Rothbard, "The Death Wish of the Anarcho-Communists," *Libertarian Forum*, January 1, 1970; Murray Rothbard, "Are Libertarians Anarchists?" (Unpublished essay, c. 1955), accessed at the Ludwig von Mises Institute website https://mises.org/library/are-libertarians-anarchists.

30 Jeff Riggenbach, "Samuel Edward Konkin III," accessed at the Ludwig von Mises Institute website https://mises.org/library/samuel-edward-konkin-iii.

31 Samuel Konkin III, *New Libertarian Manifesto* (Los Angeles, CA: Koman Publishing 1983)

32 Raimondo, *Enemy of the State*, 176–189; Karl Hess, "The Death of Politics," *Playboy*, March 1969. See also Carson, "The Left-Rothbardians." Hess's *Libertarian Forum* piece was republished as Karl Hess, "Where Are

the Specifics?" in *Markets Not Capitalism: Individualist Anarchism against Bosses, Inequality, Corporate Power, and Structural Poverty*, ed. Gary Chartier and Charles W Johnson (New York, NY: Autonomedia, 2012), 289–91.

33 Gary Chartier and Charles W. Johnson, "Introduction," in *Markets Not Capitalism: Individualist Anarchism against Bosses, Inequality, Corporate Power, and Structural Poverty*, ed. Gary Chartier and Charles W. Johnson (New York, NY: Autonomedia 2011), 1.

34 Kevin Carson, "Economic Calculation in the Corporate Commonwealth," in *Markets Not Capitalism: Individualist Anarchism against Bosses, Inequality, Corporate Power, and Structural Poverty*, ed. Gary Chartier and Charles W. Johnson (New York, NY: Autonomedia 2011).

35 Chartier and Johnson, "Introduction," 3; Charles W. Johnson, "Libertarianism through Thick and Thin," in *Markets Not Capitalism: Individualist Anarchism against Bosses, Inequality, Corporate Power, and Structural Poverty*, ed. Gary Chartier and Charles W. Johnson (New York, NY: Autonomedia 2011).

36 Karl Hess, "Anarchism without Hyphens," *the dandelion*, 4:13. Kevin Carson, personal communication with author, December 4, 2017.

37 Karl Marx, *The Communist Manifesto* (Chicago, IL: H. Regnery 1950); Vladimir Lenin, "Anarchism and Socialism," in *Lenin's Collected Works* (Volume 5) trans. J. Fineberg and G Hanna and ed. V. Jerome (Moscow: Progress Publishers 1960), 327. For market anarchism's capacious understanding of the market, see Charles W. Johnson, "We Are Market Forces," in *Markets Not Capitalism: Individualist Anarchism against Bosses, Inequality, Corporate Power, and Structural Poverty*, ed. Gary Chartier and Charles W. Johnson (New York, NY: Autonomedia 2011).

9

RIGHTS, MORALITY, AND EGOISM IN INDIVIDUALIST ANARCHISM

Eric Mack

I. Introduction

This chapter begins with a relatively long introduction that sets the context for its primary and fairly narrow focus. That primary focus is a pivotal debate that took place in the pages of *Liberty* (1881–1908), the centerpiece journal of the American individualist anarchist movement that flourished in the last several decades of the nineteenth century. That debate was between contributors to *Liberty* who held that individualist anarchism had to be grounded in explicitly moral principles and contributors who rejected moralism in the name of amoralist Egoism. The Moralists maintained that there were sound moral principles—especially moral principles demanding respect for individual liberty—and that these sound moral principles provided the proper grounding for the individualist form of anarchism to which *Liberty* was devoted. The Egoists argued that the rejection of the authority of morality was the next logical step after the rejection of the authority of religion and of the state, and that anarchism was best grounded upon amoralist Egoism and self-assertion. By 1887, the editor and publisher of *Liberty*, Benjamin Tucker (1854–1939), had explicitly sided with the Egoists and, as a consequence, throughout most of *Liberty*'s history natural morality, natural justice, and natural rights were vigorously *denounced* in the journal that was the primary voice of individualist anarchism.

My primary purpose in focusing on this debate is to show that, while the common supposition is that the Moralists within this debate advocated a natural rights doctrine, the fact of the matter is that natural rights doctrine played no role at all in that debate. The Moralists in that debate were in fact followers of Herbert Spencer (1820–1903), who, like Spencer, often employed the vocabulary of rights but were really quite sophisticated indirect utilitarians. By the time of this debate in 1886–7, Lysander Spooner (1808–87), the great natural rights theorist of the individualist anarchism movement, was nearing the end of his life.[1] And neither Spooner nor anyone who could be described as Spoonerian was to be found among the Moralists. By the time of the Moralist-versus-Egoist debate, moralistic support for anarchist conclusions had already largely shifted from appeals to natural rights to indirect utilitarian arguments that derived from the work of Spencer. In the course of this chapter, I will explain the important difference between the natural rights approach and the indirect utilitarian approach, while documenting the indirect utilitarianism of the principal Moralists.

Robert Nozick brought the term "individualist anarchism" back into the currency of political philosophy when he used this term to designate the Rothbardian free market anarchism that Nozick himself seeks to transcend in Part I of *Anarchy, State, and Utopia.*[2] In a long endnote, Nozick mentions and praises these nineteenth-century American individualist anarchists in a way that suggests that their views closely corresponded to Rothbard's natural-rights-based anarcho-capitalism.[3] Nozick especially recommends the work of the two most powerful thinkers within the group, Lysander Spooner and Benjamin Tucker. "It cannot be overemphasized how lively, stimulating, and interesting are the writings and arguments of Spooner and Tucker."[4] Yet there are significant differences between the standard views of the nineteenth-century individualist anarchists and Rothbardian anarcho-capitalism—both in terms of economic doctrines and in terms of the sort of moral (or amoralist) grounding offered by the proponents of these doctrines.

The individualist anarchists saw themselves as radical critics of capitalism. For capitalism, as they saw it, was a system of state-sponsored monopolies (and other restrictions on free trade) which impoverished the masses and enriched the few primarily by making it extremely difficult for agricultural and mechanical workers to acquire the capital necessary to become self-employed farmers and artisans. And this, in turn, made it extremely difficult for workers fully to capture the fruits of their labor, and enabled those already in command of capital to acquire an illicit share of the fruits of labor's efforts. For this reason, the individualist anarchists tended to reject or at least be highly suspicious of interest and rental income and the profits of employers. In addition, the individualist anarchists tended to subscribe to something close to the labor theory of value, and this tended to lead them to the conclusion that there must be something fishy about any form of income that did not derive solely from the labor of the recipient of that income. Furthermore, most of the individualist anarchists endorsed a current-possession-and-use doctrine of property rights. This doctrine renders legitimate absentee ownership impossible—since absentee owners cannot be current possessors and users. It follows that no charge that a putative owner extracts from another party who is actually occupying and using some resources can be legitimate. So, once again rental income is condemned—along with interest income, which, after all, is merely rental income on money whose putative owner is not currently possessing and using. On the basis of these anti-capitalist conclusions, the individualist anarchists often labeled themselves "socialists"[5] while insisting that their radically anti-statist socialism—grounded in the recognition of genuine private property rights, the sanctity of voluntary contract, and unhindered free trade—placed them in strong opposition to all forms of state socialism.[6] Strikingly, it was precisely because of these characteristic economic features of nineteenth-century individualist anarchism that Rothbard himself explicitly *declined* to label himself an individualist anarchist.[7]

We should note that Spooner, who is almost certainly the nineteenth-century individualist anarchist best known to contemporary free market anarchists and minimal statists, did not conform closely to the trends in economic thought I have just described. Spooner advanced a Lockean labor-mixing theory of private property rights, according to which a labor-mixer's right to the material that he or she had purposively transformed remained in existence as long as the resulting transformation remained in existence.[8] The purposive investor of labor in some (previously unowned) land

> holds the land in order to hold the labor which he has put into it, or upon it. And the land is his, so long as the labor he has expended upon it remains in a condition to be valuable for the uses for which it was expended; because it is not to be supposed that a man has abandoned the fruits of his labor so long as they remain in a state to be practically useful to him.[9]

This entails that the property right persists when the owner, for a charge, steps aside and allows another to make use of the transformed object. Spooner also held that interest income and entrepreneurial profits could be legitimate—although he thought that these would be much decreased when all coercively imposed barriers to trade had been removed. Moreover, unlike most of the individualist anarchists, Spooner never described himself as a socialist.[10]

Spooner was also a strong advocate of the type of natural rights approach to political theorizing that one sees in Rothbard and Nozick and that constitutes the framework within which the debate between the Rothbardian anarchist and the Nozickian minimal statist takes place. Perhaps it was because Rothbard saw the *political* doctrines of the individualist anarchists through the lens of Spooner's natural rights approach that he held that, while he had substantial differences with the individualist anarchists on economic matters, his differences with them on political matters were minor.[11] Perhaps it was because Nozick thought of Spooner—whose most well-known work was a rights-based critique of the consent theory of state legitimacy (Spooner 1870)—as the exemplar of individualist anarchism that Nozick felt comfortable applying to the label "individualist anarchism" to Rothbard's natural rights and pro-capitalist position.

As a result, both Rothbard and Nozick may have contributed to the view that, at least until the Moralist-versus-Egoist debate in *Liberty*, the natural rights approach thoroughly monopolized individualist anarchist political theorizing and that the Moralist opponents of the Egoists must, therefore, have been members of the natural rights camp. I also surmise that to some extent this belief in natural rights dominance among the individualist anarchists has arisen from the mistaken perception of Spencerian indirect utilitarian argumentation as simply being a version of natural rights theorizing. In James J. Martin's *Men versus the State*—the work that remains the best overall account of the individualist anarchist movement—the defeat of the Moralists within this debate is characterized as the defeat of the natural rights view.[12] Spencerian doctrine appears within Martin's discussion of this debate only when *Tucker* is cited as continuing to hold as a supposed complement to his new-found Egoism that social expediency calls for "the greatest amount of liberty compatible with equality of liberty."[13] The identification of the Moralist camp with natural rights advocacy also appears in Wendy McElroy's superb book on a range of important debates that took place in *Liberty*.[14] McElroy entitles her chapter on the Moralist-versus-Egoist debate "Egoism v. Natural Rights." More generally, McElroy mistakenly takes Tucker's belief in natural laws concerning the *causal* conditions of human happiness—a Spencerian element within Tucker's doctrine both before and after his adoption of Egoism—as evidence for his belief in natural rights as *prescriptive* principles.[15] The idea that the Moralists who confronted the Egoists in *Liberty* in 1886–7 were natural rights thinkers appears again in the entry on Benjamin Tucker in *The Encyclopedia of Libertarianism*. In this entry those who opposed Egoism (and who decamped from *Liberty* after Tucker sided with the Egoists) are described as "proponents of natural rights theory."[16] The *Wikipedia* entry on Tucker similarly asserts that, when Tucker converted to "Max Stirner's Egoist anarchism," he abandoned his "natural rights position" and sided with the Egoists against the "Spoonerian Natural Lawyers."[17] Tucker did indeed change his position around the time of this debate. But I hope to show that the debate that occasioned his change was not one between Egoists and Spoonerian natural law advocates.[18]

In Section II of this chapter, I spell out the differences between the sort of natural rights doctrine to which Spooner, Rothbard, and Nozick subscribed and Spencerian indirect utilitarianism. This provides the conceptual background for my claim that the Spencerian indirect utilitarianism which opposed Egoism in the pages of *Liberty* ought not to be conflated with genuine natural rights thinking. In Section III, I describe briefly the actual and waning presence of natural rights thinking within American individualist anarchism and point to some reasons why its presence during those last decades of the nineteenth century has seemed to be greater than it actually was. In Section IV, I will support my core contention that the Moralists who resisted the advance of Egoism in the pages of *Liberty* were, indeed, Spencerian indirect utilitarians. I do so by providing an account of the clash between the chief advocate of Egoism, James L. Walker (1845–1904), and his chief Moralist opponent, the Spencerian indirect utilitarian John F. Kelly (1859–1922). A further reason for recounting this debate is that, to borrow from Nozick's remark about the writings of Spooner and Tucker, the debate between Walker and Kelly is lively, stimulating, and interesting. To my mind, it cannot be over-emphasized how subtle were the arguments of Kelly—who, as Tucker saw it, lost the debate.

II. Natural Rights Doctrine Contrasted with Spencerian Indirect Utilitarianism

Natural rights theories hold that each individual is morally bound to be circumspect in certain ways in her conduct toward all other individuals *out of respect for or out of recognition of certain morally impressive properties that individuals have as persons.* Natural rights theorists invoke such properties as *being self-constituting or autonomous, being project-pursuers, possessing ultimate ends of one's own, existing for one's own purposes and not for one another's purposes,* or *possessing lives of their own to live.* On a natural rights view, the required constraint on one's conduct toward others is a matter of honoring the special moral standing that other persons have in virtue of such properties—or the standing one must in logic extend to others because one has rationally claimed that standing for oneself. The basis for the required constraint in one's conduct for others is a matter of their moral status, not a matter of that constraint's being conducive to desired personal or social outcomes (although it may well also be so conducive).

The doctrine developed by the English philosopher Herbert Spencer—especially in its early and most libertarian form in the first edition of *Social Statics*[19]—is often viewed as a species of natural rights theory. Since *Social Statics* was the work of Spencer's that was most influential on the American individualist anarchist movement, this view of *Social Statics* is one reason for the common belief that this movement as a whole was committed to the natural rights perspective. However, this natural rights reading of *Social Statics* is seriously mistaken. A brief precis of the crucial contentions of *Social Statics* should make this clear.[20] In *Social Statics*, Spencer maintains that the greatest (aggregate) human happiness is the ultimate good. The realization of the greatest human happiness is in accord with the Divine Will.[21] However, Spencer rejects Jeremy Bentham's view that each choice about what particular action one should perform ought to be based upon a calculation of which available action will most advance "the creative purpose." Instead, Spencer maintains that the only feasible route to the achievement of maximum human happiness is "to ascertain the conditions by conforming to which this greatest happiness may be obtained." We must "find out what really is the line of conduct that leads to the desired end. For unquestionably there must be in the nature of things some definite and fixed pre-requisites to success."[22] The crucial thing is to fix upon certain general prescriptions compliance with which necessarily enhances (or tends to enhance) general happiness, rather than to engage on a case-by-case basis in the search for the most expedient action. Spencer explicitly maintains that his dispute with Bentham is a dispute between two variants of utilitarianism—Bentham's "empirical" utilitarianism and Spencer's own "rational" utilitarianism.

Spencer's development of this rational utilitarianism then proceeds by means of a somewhat surprising and underappreciated move. He asserts that the maximization of aggregate human happiness requires that no individual be precluded from achieving his or her own happiness. Hence, Spencer concludes, the maximization of aggregate happiness requires that no individual's maximization of his or her own happiness preclude any other individual's maximization of her own happiness. Since individual happiness is attained through the exercise of one's faculties, the prerequisite for maximizing (aggregate) human happiness is that each individual be allowed to exercise his own faculties subject to the constraint that his exercise not prevent any other individual from exercising her own faculties. Alternatively, each may obtain "complete happiness within his own sphere of activity [as long as he does not diminish] the spheres of activity required for the acquisition of happiness by others."[23] Thus, we arrive at the Law of Equal Freedom, according to which "every man may claim the fullest liberty to exercise his faculties compatible with the possession of like liberty by every other man."[24] This Law of Equal Freedom is further codified in *Social Statics* in terms of various rights; for example, the right to personal liberty, which each individual can enjoy without infringing upon the like rights of others.

Despite this codification in terms of rights, Spencer's doctrine is still *at root* utilitarian. The Law of Equal Freedom is to be followed because following it is the crucial prerequisite for the eventual attainment of "the creative purpose." Punishing individuals for violating this principle lessens the disposition of persons over time to seek to maximize their own happiness in ways that preclude others from maximizing *their* happiness. At the same time, allowing individuals to attain their happiness in ways that may distress others—but do not violate their equal liberty—will lessen the disposition of persons over time to be distressed by others exercising their equal liberty. Both processes, in accordance with "the law of adaptation,"[25] lead to a harmonization of people's interests and, eventually, to a maximization of aggregate happiness that consists in the maximization of each individual's happiness.

III. The Presence and Apparent Presence of Natural Rights Thought in Individualist Anarchism

Appeals to the Sovereignty of the Individual as the fundamental principle governing social relations were central in the writings of Josiah Warren (1798–1874), the acknowledged founder of individualist anarchism. Warren's doctrine was systematically articulated by Stephen Pearl Andrews (1812–86) in *The Science of Society*.[26] Andrews called for "the cordial and universal acceptance of this very principle of the absolute Sovereignty of the Individual—each claiming his own Sovereignty, and each religiously respecting that of all others."[27] And, long after its initial publication, Andrews' *The Science of Society* was serialized in *Liberty* from October 30, 1886 through December 31, 1887; and Tucker eulogized Andrews in "A Light Extinguished."[28] In a later issue of *Liberty*, Tucker honored Warren as "the first man to expound and formulate the doctrine now known as Anarchism; the first man to clearly state the theory of individual sovereignty and equal liberty."[29] We should note, though, that, by this time, if pressed to explain "individual sovereignty," Tucker would likely have described it as an affirmation of self-assertion rather than an affirmation of each individual's *moral rights*.[30]

Many of the works that Lysander Spooner composed in the 1880s were first published in *Liberty*. This included his incendiary "A Letter to Grover Cleveland," which first ran in nineteen installments from June 20, 1885 to May 22, 1886. Tucker's lengthy and moving obituary for Spooner, "Our Nestor Taken From Us," appeared in *Liberty* in May of 1887.[31] One reason one might mistakenly think that Tucker himself was a natural rights advocate—at least during his in his pre-Egoist stage—was his association with and honoring of these three authors—especially Warren and Spooner.

IV. Egoism versus Spencerian Moralism

Now, at last, I turn to the Egoist–Moralist debate. To get to the core of this debate, I focus on the most important and impressive advocate of Egoism and the most important and impressive Moralist opponent of Egoism. Our exemplar of Egoism will be James L. Walker, writing as "Tak Kak," and our exemplar of moralism will be John F. Kelly. As I mentioned above, Tucker ends up siding with Egoism—albeit, while seeking to formulate an amalgam of Egoism and a Spencerian endorsement of equal liberty.[32] Unfortunately, I cannot explore here the complex question of how the components of that amalgam are supposed to fit together to form a worldview that is less wild than Tak Kak's.

Walker, who was strongly influenced by German philosopher Max Stirner (1806–56),[33] initiated the debate with an essay entitled, "What Is Justice?" Walker defines justice as that which is required by a power "to which the individual owes respect and obedience" (Walker 1886a). Justice is what legitimate authority demands. Acting for the sake of justice is, therefore, always a matter of submitting to an external power. According to Walker, for most of human history people believed in justice because they believed in God. When people rejected their superstitious belief in God, they replaced it with superstitious belief in the legitimate authority of the state or society. While anarchists have rejected superstitious belief in state or social authority, they have replaced it with superstitious belief in moral authority. However, the anarchist critique of theological, state, and social authority must be extended to moral authority and, hence, to the conclusion that "there is no moral government of the world." Not even slavery can be said to be unjust because "[t]he idea that slavery is 'unjust' is [merely] the idea that there is a rule or law against it."[34]

Walker continually returns to the theme that, just as God has been overcome, so too must humanity, the substitute for God. In a passage that reminds one of Hegel's description of Spirit transcending the sorrow of infinitude, Walker declares: "The individual who finally becomes conscious of himself is, just as he is, a universe,—humanity itself. He then knows that he has been dreaming about a something which is, after all, himself. He is incomparable."[35] The Egoist "interests himself in any pursuit or neglects any without a thought that he is fulfilling or slighting any calling or mission or duty, or doing right or wrong. All such words are impertinent. Nothing is sacred or above him." It follows that the Egoist has no interest in justifying his conduct; all his thinking concerns how to procure what he desires. "Justification is a piece of superstitious nonsense."[36] "When [a man] comes to full consciousness, he sets up as his own master." He attends to his own impulses and sentiments and is true to them—but not, presumably as a matter of principle. For the fully conscious man possesses ideas but is never governed by them. In "Egoism," Walker says that if a man

> owns himself and is awed by no command, bewitched by no fixed idea or superstition, but does everything with a sense that his acts are his own genuine, personal, sovereign choice … then the man is an Egoist, or one conscious that he is a genuine Ego.[37]

> I simply do my own will. … Those who do their own will we classify as distinct from those who act under awe and obedience to supposed moral obligations—whether conceived as commands or the equivalent impression,—from a source outside the individual telling him to submit himself and forego his own inclinations.[38]

Indeed, Walker equates being governed by "fixed" ideas with *insanity*. "The devotee of the fixed idea is mad." "Egoism is sanity. Non-Egoism is insanity."[39] "[I]deas such as 'right,' 'wrong,' 'justice,' etc. … are merely words with vague, chimerical meanings"—at least when they do not refer to degrees of strength or weakness. If justice in action is understood simply as the strength to perform it, "[i]t is 'just' to enslave those willing to be enslaved." Doing so is at least more just that enslaving a man or a horse that resists enslavement. "There is more virtue in the criminal classes [who resist impediments to their impulses and actions] than in the tame slaves."[40]

Walker illustrates his preference for the resistant criminal over the willing slave in a short piece entitled "Killing Chinese," which was published along with "What Is Justice?" Walker looks with favor upon the prospect of "the willing white slaves of America" resisting the competition of "Chinamen"—who he says are "fitted by nature and heredity to remain slave[s]"—by killing some of them. Walker adds that, when those whites better understand the nature of their own *unwilling* enslavement, "it is very probable that there will be some dead white men." Walker explains that anyone who is shocked by his perspective is "a victim of the fixed idea that all men are brothers—a poetical fragment dissociated from and surviving the idea of the fatherhood of God."[41]

In a later essay, Walker is yet more enthralled by the criminal rebel who knows no bounds. "The egoist, as an irrepressible, conscienceless criminal, is the coming force, who will destroy all existing institutions."[42] When some presently existing Egoists "prey upon the masses, they do so because the masses are exploitable material, easily beguiled filled with spiritual ideas, and entertained with moral doctrines."[43] However, things would be different were *all* or *most* men Egoists. "It will make a great difference when many egoists become fully self-conscious and not ashamed of being conscienceless egoists."[44] Egoists at large "will not act very benevolently toward outsiders." However, according to Walker, if we are both Egoists, "[n]othing that I could do for you (without setting you in power over myself) could fail to be agreeable to me." Walker asks: "Do you not begin to think that by suiting only myself I am really doing far better toward others than by throwing myself away to serve them?"[45] Similarly, Walker asserts that his own will or desires will be aligned against the individual who wrings from others the fruits of their labor. Yet here Walker's reasoning seems to be that he may be the next victim of the wringer. The wringer may become "an obstacle to the realization of my desire."[46] Walker tells us that, *qua* Egoist, he joins the theologian and the Moralist in condemning rape. However, in his case this is not a matter of law or duty but, instead, inclination. Apparently in response to the thought that, as a willful Egoist, he could just as easily have an inclination to rape, Walker asserts: "[W]hen I am well, I shall want to do well."[47]

> There are no Egoists who do not do many acts to help others. Generosity is perfectly Egoistic. There is no quality so distinctively so, in contrast to dutiful moralism. It is a flower of character, without the slightest taint or smut of moral police forces in the forum of consciousness.[48]

Walker also appeals to Stirner's idea of a union of Egoists. Once all or most of us free ourselves from the ideas of duty and obligation, the word "justice" can be used to refer to "the rules of a union of egoists with benefits to at least balance duties; and these duties are simply a matter of contract."[49] Still, all that Walker can mean is that Egoists living among Egoists will each know (and be known to know) that attacks upon others' lives, liberties, and possessions are apt to trigger costly counterattacks. Thus, each will have strategic reasons to avoid such attacks (if they will be detected). As Kelly points out, Walker cannot mean that through contract individuals can place themselves *under obligations* to one another to abide by certain norms. For this would require belief in the "fixed idea" that agreeing to abide by certain rules places one under an obligation to do what one has agreed to do. And Walker himself rejects this idea when he denies that making a promise provides one with a reason to keep it.[50]

Kelly's point about contracts accomplishing little or nothing unless they have a binding effect deserves to be quoted in full.

> [I]t is impossible to base a society upon contract unless we consider a contract as having some binding effect, and that the binding effect of a particular contract can not be due to the contract itself. That is to say, no special obligations could be created for us by a contract unless we were under some general obligations towards each other already, one of these being the keeping of faith.[51]

As we shall see, Kelly also provides arguments for why members of a union of Egoists who do not take themselves to be obligated by their agreements will often *not* abide by rules compliance with which would be beneficial to them.

The last main element in Walker's view is the claim that Egoism—at least when it is sufficiently widespread—provides the firmest basis for anarchism. This is because Egoism undermines all justifications that tyrants may offer for their authority.

> Let us suppose all men Egoists. How would the pope persuade people to support him? How would Bismarck persuade Germans that they have an individual interest in holding Alsace? How would Lord Salisbury persuade Englishmen that they have an interest in holding Ireland? How would Grover Cleveland persuade us to support him and coerce the Mormons?
>
> But for the surrender to fixed ideas and the drilling and teaching which maintains their dominion, the State and the Church would be only so many men, their sacredness gone. How long would their power endure against the surprise, ridicule, indifference, or aversion of a mass of Egoists?

Walker's view seems to be that, in the absence of fixed, superstitious ideas, people will not desire or will to support the pope, support the holding of Alsace or Ireland, or support the coercion of the Mormons. "Egoism, therefore, points to a general letting alone."[52] Indeed,

> Egoism dissolves, not one fixed idea merely, but the habit and faith of fixity, therefore all, and furnishes the condition for the final eradication of all political domination. … We take liberty when we no longer feel bound. The bondage of idea is now the great bondage. … Authority, whether of Egoists or fanatics, can be overthrown only by Egoism.[53]

Yet might not the activities favored by these officials also be genuinely desired or willed by Egoists? Might not such Egoists agree to joint action to more effectively do as they will? Might not these Egoists "take liberty" to join together in such action when they are released from fixed ideas about rights or justice that condemn the activities favored by the pope, Bismarck, et al.? However, Walker denies this. Napoleon was possible only because

> he was taken as an idol, deified and served by the unegoistic devotion of others who did the slaughtering and pillaging. To accomplish all this mischief it was necessary that there be a national spirit and a variety of other hate-breeding superstitions.[54]

Walker holds that, although Egoists will have no natural sympathy with the pope or Bismarck or Napolean, they will by contrast be disposed by natural sympathy to "give all the aid required by any Mormon woman who wanted to leave her husband."[55] This is of a piece with Walker's claim that the fully conscious and, therefore, *conscienceless* Egoist will generally have benevolent and generous feelings at least for other Egoists. "The greatest reason why a particular Ego will not rob his neighbor may be that he does not want to." Although any gratification of taste or appetite exhibits Egoism, Walker holds that, at least in their conduct toward other Egoists, genuine Egoists will not exhibit "repulsive traits of character."[56] Walker's views were brought together in his posthumously published *The Philosophy of Egoism*.[57]

The great opponent of Walker in the 1886–7 Egoist–Moralist debate in *Liberty* was John F. Kelly.[58] Kelly's first response to Walker appears almost in passing within a lengthy critical review of Henry George's book *Protection or Free Trade*.[59] Kelly denounces George's purely instrumental and case-by-case attachment to liberty, and extends this charge to Tak Kak. According to Kelly, for George,

> Liberty is not a good in itself; but is something to be sought after or trodden under foot according as it seems likely to produce immediate material advantages or not. Mr. George does not believe in taking a general principle as a guide; each particular action must be judged by its results,—that is, its direct results. This doctrine, also taught by some ultra-individualists like Stirner and 'Tak Kak,' is really only the revival of the Jesuit maxim that the end justifies the means. As an individual murder may produce beneficial results,—say an increases of wages,—Mr. George, Mr. Stirner, and 'Tak Kak' ought, according to their philosophy approve of it; but the true individualist, the holder of the utilitarian philosophy in its higher form, is bound to condemn the murder, because to generalize murder, as praise of a particular murder tends to do, would disrupt society and ultimately prove injurious to the greater number.[60]

It is very striking here that Kelly invokes the stance of "the true individualist" who Kelly identifies as "the holder of the utilitarian philosophy in its higher [i.e., non-Benthamite, non-direct] form." But what exactly is the argument offered in the final clauses of Kelly's statement? I believe it is a subtle argument that goes as follows:

i. To praise a particular murder on the ground that it yields the outcome that should ultimately be promoted—whether that be individual happiness or the greatest happiness of the greatest number—is to praise anyone's commission of murder if it yields the outcome that should ultimately be promoted. (This is the generalization of which Kelly writes.)
ii. If one's praise is effective, many individuals will endorse their commission of murder when they perceive that their actions will yield optimal outcomes; and they will realize that others also endorse their own commission of such murders.
iii. But it would be profoundly socially disruptive and contrary to the interests of most (if not all) individuals for many people to endorse their commission of murder when they perceive that their actions will yield optimal outcome and to realize that many others also endorse this view. (For this would radically undercut the mutual assurance of peaceful co-existence upon which social order rests.)
iv. Therefore, for the sake of what should ultimately be promoted, one should reject the praise of any particular murder (or the deprivation of liberty involved in murder) on the ground that it yields the outcome that should ultimately be promoted.[61]

Kelly's further conclusion is that, rather than following George in the direct pursuit of the general happiness, one should instead abide strictly by certain general norms—especially the norm against depriving individuals of their equal liberty—that enable each to pursue happiness in ways that do not injure others.

The argument explicated in propositions i–iv targets *instrumental* justifications of infringements upon liberty—justifications of the kind George was proposing. It does not so obviously apply to Walker's apparently *non-instrumental* endorsement (in "What Is Justice?" and "Killing Chinese") of whatever conduct toward others one truly wills to perform. Noting this, however, raises an important question about the nature of Walker's Egoism. Does this Egoism call for one to maximize doing as one wills or desires over one's lifetime—in which case, it will often call for one to engage in actions that one does not will or desire as the necessary means for future willed or desired action—or does it require that, at all times, one acts as one wills or desires? The tone of Walker's proclamations suggests the latter position. The truly free Egoist will not spend much of his time submitting prudentially to the causal necessity of doing *X* in order to be able at some future time to do *Y*, even though he will genuinely will or desire *Y* in the future.

If this is Walker's view, he is unaffected by Kelly's argument that better individual and aggregate *overall* results are attained through common compliance with general norms. He is unaffected because his Egoism does not call for the *overall* maximization of one's willed or desired preferences. On the other hand, if one does as one wills at time t^1 even when one realizes that acting contrary to one's will at t^1 will enable one to act in accord with one's will at t^2 through t^n, doesn't this show one has been captured by a fixed idea—indeed, a superstition—that one must always do as one wills?

Let us return to Kelly's argument for the indirect promotion of outcomes by way of compliance with general principles—even if this argument does not directly rebut Walker's own version of Egoism. In his essay "Intelligent Egotism Anti-Social" Kelly repeats essentially the same argument that I ascribed to him above with the substitution of the norm against breaking promises for the norm against murder.

> I must confess that I have a weakness for keeping a promise because it is a promise, and I fail to see how a civilized society can be maintained when that weakness is not general. For, if one's promising to do a thing does not add to the probability of one's doing it, promises disappear altogether, and contracts and concerted action become impossible except under duress.[62]

Kelly's view is that common compliance—and the expectation of common compliance—with certain general norms is essential for the maintenance and functioning of the social order; and this in turn is essential for the attainment of individual and aggregate happiness.

Therefore, if (as Walker maintains) morality does not genuinely provide us with such norms, rules will have to be enunciated and imposed by force by a political sovereign who himself will stand above the rules which he enacts. According to Kelly, Hobbes rather than Walker grasps the logical implication of the non-existence of natural morality. "[F]rom the necessity of preserving social relations and the non-existence of natural morality … [Hobbes] deduces despotism." A union of conscienceless Egoists would require the mailed fist of a Sovereign Egoist. Hence, rather than providing "the condition for the final eradication of all political domination," Egoism demands political domination.[63]

The initial (Hobbesian) premise of Walker's "What Is Justice?" is that all rule or law is the command of some being with superior power. Compliance with any rule or law is submission to the commanding agent. This is what motivations Walker's revolt against all rule and law—including moral rule and law. Kelly, in contrast, advances a Spencerian conception of moral norms. On this conception, moral norms are the concomitants of social evolution. Hence, they are no one's commands, and compliance with them is not a matter of subordinating oneself to anyone else's will.

Kelly thinks of societal norms as evolving though the selection of rules that are more and more conducive to individual and aggregate happiness. This process, for reasons laid out in *Social Statics*, moves humanity toward principles that ascribe equal rights to all individuals so that "in each generation people [are] less and less inclined to infringe on the rights of their neighbors, until at last, we have, to a great extent, become what Spencer calls organically moral." Indeed, through this process, we will arrive at a state in which each person's achievement of happiness will be compatible with—will even contribute to—the happiness of others. "Then we shall have reached that state which we all desire, that state in which the greatest happiness of each coincides with the good of all."

Further Spencerian themes are present when Kelly considers the individual who is "organized so that his 'good' leads him to commit actions injurious to others." In such a case,

> morality has commands to utter, commands growing more and more positive with the advance of society. Persons so organized must either learn to control their anti-social

> impulses, or they will inevitably be weeded out, until only those are left the pursuit of whose individual 'good' does not interfere with the like pursuit on the part of others.[64]

Evolution selects for persons who are disposed to comply with norms which operate to promote individual and aggregate happiness.

Walker insists that, if everyone is better off acting *in accord with* various norms, including a norm commending the fulfillment of contracts, then everyone will so act even if he or she does not believe that such action is obligatory; i.e., is morally required by those norms. Part of the reason one may be better off acting in accord with one's agreements will be to avoid the hostility or retaliation by one's fellow Egoists.[65] Kelly offers a subtle game-theoretic response. He asks us to envision a society made up of intelligent Egoistic thieves. He then presents the case for simple intelligent Egoism yielding a theft-free world that would be better for everyone.

> [A]ll the time spent in stealing and guarding against theft is wasted. Were all to renounce theft, the total wealth would be as great as before, and the time previously spent in stealing or preventing stealing would be available for the production of more wealth, or the enjoyment of that produced. Here, then, is a splendid opportunity for the display of the powers of intelligent egotism.

Yet, according to Kelly, these individuals will not converge on non-theft.

> It is advantageous to stop stealing; each one is intelligent enough to see this; yet it is out of their power to abstain. For mark that what is really advantageous to the individual is not that he should stop stealing, but that all others should; and while this latter might be such a gain to him as to make it worth his while to quit stealing himself to secure it, yet he can have no certainty his doing so will secure it.[66]

Nor will a contract among these intelligent Egoist thieves yield a stable convergence on non-theft. For such a contract "can be of no binding effect on men who are free from the dominion of 'fixed ideas,' who refuse to keep a promise merely because it is a promise." In the absence of moral principles, convergence on non-theft will only be achieved through political despotism. Hence, contrary to Walker, "[m]orality, instead of being slavery, is the condition of liberty."[67]

Kelly's final objection to Walker is that the normative solipsism of Stirnerite Egoism is incompatible with friendship. "Friendship implies equality, the recognition of others as like one's self, while, according to Stirner, the ego is alone, surrounded only by things which it is for him to use to his best advantage."

Tucker's siding with Tak Kak against the Moralists broke the friendship between Kelly and Tucker, and Kelly's association with *Liberty*. But the most poignant expression of this break was supplied by Kelly's sister Gertrude, who had also been a frequent contributor to *Liberty*.

> My friends, my friends, have you completely lost your heads? Cannot you see that without morality, without the recognition of others' rights, Anarchy, in any other than the vulgar sense, could not last a single day?[68]

V. Conclusion

By the mid 1880s the radical Lockean Lysander Spooner was outside the two mainstreams of individualist anarchist thought—Spencerian indirect utilitarianism and Egoism. This is exemplified in the Moralist-versus-Egoist debate in *Liberty* in which the Moralists were indirect utilitarians, not natural rights advocates. This seems to reflect a more general pattern in nineteenth-century political thought wherein natural rights thinking was crowded out primarily by forms of utilitarianism or amoralist rejections of morality.

Notes

1 For one account of Spooner's doctrine of rights, see Eric Mack, "Lysander Spooner: Nineteenth Century America's Last Natural Rights Theorist," *Social Philosophy and Policy* 29.2 (Sum: 2012): 139–76.
2 Robert Nozick, *Anarchy, State, and Utopia* (New York, NY: Basic 1974).
3 Murray Rothbard, *For a New Liberty* revised edition (New York, NY: Macmillan 1978).
4 Nozick 335n4.
5 Nozick (336n4) notes that the most extensive individualist anarchist discussion of private protection agencies and the possible relationships among them was offered in Francis Tandy, *Voluntary Socialism* (Denver, CO: npu 1896).
6 Benjamin R. Tucker, *State Socialism and Anarchism and Other Essays* (Colorado Springs, CO: Myles 1985 [1886]).
7 Murray Rothbard, "The Spooner–Tucker Doctrine: An Economist's View," *Egalitarianism as a Revolt against Nature*, 2d ed. (Auburn, AL: Mises 2000) 205–18.
8 And, of course, if another party *B* destroys a still-existing feature created by *A*'s labor, *B* is guilty of violating *A*'s property rights.
9 Lysander Spooner, *The Law of Intellectual Property* (1855), *The Collected Works of Lysander Spooner* 3, ed. Charles Shively (Weston, MA: M&S 1971) 22.
10 Rothbard fails to note these economic differences between Spooner and most of the other individualist anarchists in Rothbard, "Doctrine."
11 Rothbard, "Doctrine" 207.
12 James J. Martin, *Men against the State* (Colorado Springs, CO: Myles 1970) 252.
13 Martin 251.
14 Wendy McElroy, *The Debates of* Liberty (New York, NY: Lexington 2003).
15 McElroy 53.
16 Aaron Steelman, "Tucker, Benjamin," *Encyclopedia of Libertarianism*, ed. Ronald Hamowy (Thousand Oaks, CA: Sage 2008) 513–4.
17 "Benjamin Tucker," *Wikipedia* (Wikimedia, Feb. 8, 2020) https://en.wikipedia.org/wiki/Benjamin_Tucker (Mar. 24, 2020).
18 A careful analysis of the path of Tucker's moral and anti-moral ideas does not exist. But it is clear that he was never a Spoonerian natural rights advocate and that he never become as much of an amoralist as he proclaimed. Tucker's view seems always to have been some mixture of endorsing norms because they are advantageous to oneself, because they are advantageous to each person, because they accord with the Law of Equal Freedom, and because one has agreed to them. He continued to appeal to each of these even after and despite his explicit embrace of amoralist Egoism.
19 Herbert Spencer, *Social Statics* (New York, NY: Schalkenbach 1970 [1851]).
20 Spencer's earlier essay "The Proper Sphere of the State" (1843), *The Man versus the State*, ed. Eric Mack (Indianapolis, Liberty Classics 1981), employs the terminology of *natural* rights much more than does *Social Statics*. Yet, even in "The Proper Sphere of the State," the doctrine at work is fundamentally utilitarian. (As far as I know, the American anarchists were unfamiliar with "The Proper Sphere of the State.")
21 In his introduction to the 1864 edition of *Social Statics*, Spencer tells us that he would no longer appeal to the thought that the greatest aggregate happiness was the Divine Idea. He does not tell us to what he would instead appeal.
22 Spencer, *Statics* 61.
23 Spencer, *Statics* 62.
24 Spencer, *Statics* 69.
25 Spencer, *Statics* 76.
26 Stephen Pearl Andrews, *The Science of Society* (New York, NY: Fowler 1852).
27 Andrews.
28 Benjamin Tucker, "A Light Extinguished," *Liberty* 4 (June 19, 1886): 4.
29 Benjamin Tucker, "On the Picket Line," *Liberty* 14 (December 1900): 1.
30 Martin says: "In some ways … [Tucker's] adoption of the newly discussed tenets of egoism was tied up with the understanding of individual sovereignty derived from Warren earlier" (250).

31 Benjamin Tucker, "Our Nestor Taken From Us," *Liberty* 4 (May 28, 1887): 4. In this obituary, Tucker chides Spooner because "[h]e entirely failed to recognize the substantial identity of Herbert Spencer's political teachings with his own simply because Spencer reaches his conclusions by totally different methods." I suspect that Spooner understood better than Tucker the importance of the difference between his own doctrine and that of Spencer.

32 The debate between the Egoists and Moralists re-emerged in *Liberty* in 1895 within a dispute about the rights of children. See McElroy's chapter on "Children's Rights" (69–83).

33 Stirner's core work, *Der Einzige und Sein Eigenthum* (1844), was first published in English as *The Ego and His Own* by Tucker in 1907. On Stirner, see David Leopold, "Max Stirner," *Stanford Encyclopedia of Philosophy* (Stanford, CA: Stanford U, Oct. 22, 2019) https://plato.stanford.edu/entries/max-stirner (Mar. 24, 2020).

34 James L. Walker, "What Is Justice?," *Liberty* 3 (Mar. 6, 1886): 8.

35 James L. Walker, "The Rational Utilitarian Philosophy," *Liberty* 4 (Jan. 22, 1887): 8. Walker's critic, John Kelly, astutely observes that "[t]he unconditioned ego seems nothing else than the absolute—God." John Kelly, "Intelligent Egotism Anti-Social," *Liberty* 4 (May 7, 1887): 7.

36 James L. Walker, "Selfhood Terminates Blind Man's Buff" [*sic*], *Liberty* 4 (July 3, 1886): 8.

37 James. L. Walker, "Egoism," *Liberty* 4 (Apr. 9, 1887): 5.

38 Walker, "Utilitarian" 8.

39 Walker, "Egoism" 5–6.

40 Walker, "Justice" 8.

41 James L. Walker, "Killing Chinese," *Liberty* 3 (March 6, 1886): 8.

42 Walker, "Selfhood" 8.

43 Walker, "Egoism" 6.

44 Walker, "Selfhood" 8.

45 Walker, "Justice" 8.

46 Walker, "Egoism" 5.

47 Yet, on what basis does Walker say that opposition to rape is a component of wellness?

48 Walker, "Egoism" 6. Yet, on what basis does Walker say that generosity is a "flower" of character?

49 Walker, "Justice" 8.

50 Walker, "Egoism" 5.

51 James F. Kelly, "A Final Statement," *Liberty* 4 (July 30, 1887): 7.

52 Walker, "Egoism" 6.

53 Walker, "Egoism" 7.

54 James L. Walker, "Reply to Kelly," *Liberty* 4 (July 2, 1887): 7.

55 Walker, "Egoism" 6.

56 Walker, "Reply" 7.

57 James l. Walker, *The Philosophy of Egoism* (Colorado Springs, CO: Myles 1972 [1905]).

58 McElroy describes Kelly as an advocate of "natural rights," but then observes that he provides "a somewhat utilitarian defense of morality" in his "Morality and Its Origin" (57). See James F. Kelly, "Morality and Its Origin," *Liberty* 4 (Feb. 26, 1887): 7.

59 James F. Kelly, "George's 'Protection or Free Trade,'" *Liberty* 4 (Dec. 11, 1886): 7–8.

60 Kelly, "Protection" 7.

61 I owe this reading of Kelly to Mary Sirridge.

62 James F. Kelly, "Egotism" 7. A more precise statement of this argument would insert "by providing one with a moral reason to do it" between the two main clauses of the second sentence.

63 Kelly, "Egotism" 7.

64 Kelly, "Final" 7.

65 Walker, "Reply" 7. However, Walker cannot explain that hostility or retaliation on the basis of the *wrong* done to these parties.

66 Kelly, "Egotism" 7.

67 Kelly, "Egotism" 7.

68 Gertrude Kelly, "A Letter of Protest," *Liberty* 4 (Aug. 13, 1887): 7.

10

TRANSCENDING LEFTIST POLITICS

Situating Egoism within the Anarchist Project

David S. D'Amato

I. Introduction

Though it is not without its forerunners, egoism as a subset of anarchist thought has its beginnings in *The Ego and Its Own*,[1] Max Stirner's work of unflinching iconoclasm, published in 1844.[2] Stirner's has been variously regarded as the most extreme, revolutionary, radical, and dangerous book ever written,[3] relentless in its attacks on all fixed ideological and philosophical systems. As one of the first truly thoroughgoing critiques of modernity, Stirner's masterwork can be regarded as heralding many of the themes we now recognize in existentialism, poststructuralism, and postmodernism more generally; indeed, his influence on postmodern thought, though woefully underappreciated, is apparent in the works of such notable thinkers as Nobel Laureate Albert Camus, among others. Stirner's unique variety of radical thought is also closely linked to the post-left and post-anarchist literatures; it is clear from these relationships that Stirner's work, if it has not figured prominently in political theory more generally, has at least played an important role in helping anarchism remain self-critical and, therefore, relevant, in allowing us to evaluate, reflect upon, and ultimately move beyond established ideologies and patterns of thought. Though Engels famously named him "the prophet of contemporary anarchism,"[4] Stirner fits only uncomfortably with other anarchists of the first generation. Indeed, there is hardly a definite answer to the question of whether Stirner is an anarchist at all. In his study of Stirner, the Marxist social theorist Max Adler reads him out of anarchism, contending that he cannot be an anarchist because anarchism is a distinct ideological current only insofar as it sits "within [the] socialist labor movement."[5] Post-left anarchists[6] have sought to refocus anarchism outside or beyond traditional preoccupations with class theory, socialism, and labor movement ideology. These anarchists throw a spotlight on an enduring truth: the left's relationship with anarchism has always been fraught with difficulty. For if anarchism is just revolutionary workerism, then it loses its historical character as a *libertarian* critique or interpretation of socialism; yet if anarchism leaves its socialist roots completely in the past—and with it its traditional commitments to, for example, trade unionism and class struggle—then it arguably becomes something else, perhaps the supposedly aimless lifestylism derided famously by Murray Bookchin.

II. The Dynamics of Egoism

For the egoist, all systems of morality—indeed, all claims to objective truth—are superstitions, often positioned precariously on still earlier and more fundamental superstitions, all invented ultimately by human minds. Such superstitions are, therefore, owed nothing—no deference, duty, or devotion. They are projections of human consciousness, to be discarded as easily as they were created.[7] The individual must not allow his creatures, frozen artifacts of his "will of yesterday," to become his commanders.[8] On this view, liberal notions of natural rights are, as Jeremy Bentham said, "rhetorical nonsense";[9] but the egoist goes further, damning every attempt to establish a code of conduct for the individual. If morality is baseless, the egoist says, then whatever the individual wills is permissible; his power—the ability to do the thing—makes it his right.[10] Everything else is so much unfounded religious thinking.

Stirner argued that we give birth to ideas and then project them outward, only to have these ideas—our creations—lord over us and dictate our behaviors and ways of life; these ideas thus become reified, taking on a life of their own. The result is enslavement to moralities, ideologies, and religions, a condition that neuters the experience of life and subordinates the true interests of the individual.[11]

The ideas of Pierre-Joseph Proudhon furnish an apposite contrast to Stirner's. Where Proudhon condemns "the authority of man over man,"[12] Stirner leaves all options available to the unique individual, unmoved by moral claims against authority. Where Stirner celebrates the untrammeled "*own will*" of the individual, recognizing none of the limits with which justice or other aspects of morality might saddle it, Proudhon looks forward to the day when "the sovereignty of the will" and "the right of force" will "retreat before the steady advance of justice," culminating in "scientific socialism." While the classical anarchist is an enemy of the state, careful to distinguish government from society (for example, in Martin Buber's conception, *the political principle* from *the social principle*), the egoist anarchist is no less an enemy of society itself.

The juxtaposition of social power and political power is an important, even central, theme in anarchist history and literature.[13] Much of anarchist thought has been a treatment of this contrast—and, accordingly, of the promise of the eventual and spontaneous emergence of the true social organism from beneath the violence and repression of the state. Since William Godwin (and before), a picture of human perfectibility has, explicitly or otherwise, permeated anarchist (and proto-anarchist) thought.[14] Human beings, sufficiently motivated by reason and guided by experience, will eventually arrive at a free society—harmonious, socially cooperative, and free of domination by the state. Egoists have ridiculed this vision as a naive delusion, oppressive in its own right and dependent for its realization on the emergence of human beings quite unlike any in history.

The tension inherent in the relationship between egoism, which acknowledges no limits on individual thought and behavior, and anarchism, which attempts to moderate individual liberty with the law of equal freedom, is aptly illustrated in the debates of Dora Marsden and Benjamin R. Tucker. Marsden, sparring with Tucker in a 1914 issue of *The Egoist*, writes, "We meant that the kind of people [Proudhon] describes never walked on earth: that they were unreal: figures with no genuine insides, stuffed out with tracts from the Church of Humanity and the Ethical Society."[15]

From the outset, Stirner's ideas put him distinctly at odds with the other classical anarchists, if indeed he can be positioned among them. The question of how to understand him in relation to those anarchists has been the subject of debate and disquiet in anarchist circles; many anarchists see Stirner's egoism as irreconcilable with anarchism.[16]

Anarchists have always rather enjoyed defining one another out of the anarchist movement, complacently satisfied that theirs is the one true anarchism, others' so many heresies. Unsurprisingly, many anarchists have worked themselves into a lather to excommunicate Stirner and those influenced by his thought.

Stirner would not have been troubled by this; indeed, he would likely excommunicate himself from the Church of True Anarchism, as so many egoists have. For the egoist, classical anarchism's opposition and resistance to political and economic authority both does not go far enough and goes too far. It does not go far enough in that it leaves the myriad other potential sources of hierarchical domination and repression unexamined, elevated above the ever-fluctuating desires of the unique, subordinating the ego to various spooks. Yet it goes too far in advancing its own series of constraining concepts and precepts, in instituting "a redemptionist secular religion" founded upon highly tendentious ideas about reason and human nature.

Stirner of course denies the existence of an absolute or universal human essence, seeing in the idea a variety of unsustainable religious faith. In this way, he anticipates Sartre's declaration that "existence precedes essence."[17] Sartre writes similarly that "man is free and there is no human nature in which I can place my trust."[18] The specific individual—ultimately inarticulable, his thoughts, desires, and motives ever in flux—is anterior to proposed essences and universal or absolute truths.

It is generally true of anarchism, even with all of its ideologically uncompromising variations and schools, that it resists being reduced to a static, absolute set of prescriptions or a system. Max Nettlau, the eminent historian of anarchism, exhorts anarchists not to "permit themselves to become fossilized upholders of a given system."[19] Egoist anarchism takes this general concern, the reluctance to embrace a single formula, and extends its application, undertaking the destruction of all fixed ideas. As conceived by Stirner and others in his tradition, egoism is able to liberate anarchism from "universalist limitations," pushing anarchists to interrogate not only capitalism and the state, but other sources of harmful authority.[20] The egoist currents therefore contend that anarchism, "encrusted with leftist clichés," has lost some of its potency. In Stirner's egoism, labor politics loses the traditional place of honor it enjoys in classical anarchism; but rather than filling the void with another collection of sacred idols, egoist and post-left strains of anarchism are satisfied with the void, ready to fill it with their creations. "I am not nothing in the sense of emptiness," Stirner writes,

> but I am the creative nothing [*schöpferische Nichts*], the nothing out of which I myself as creator create everything.
>
> Away, then, with every concern that is not altogether my concern! You think at least the 'good cause' must be my concern? What's good, what's bad? Why, I myself am my concern, and I am neither good nor bad. Neither has meaning for me.[21]

The individual is a creator of value—indeed, the *only* creator of value. Each individual, faced with such bottomless absurdity, ultimately unable to brace himself against false essentials, must decide for himself what is important.

III. Egoism and Contemporary Leftist Ideologies

The obvious facial similarities between such ideas and those associated with existentialism (as found in, for example, Sartre and Camus) led to a second rediscovery of Stirner in the 1960s and 1970s.[22] Stirner's ideas are echoed in Sartre's notion of bad faith, the paradoxical decision to choose (*freely*, for our choices are necessarily free) to renounce our freedom, to deny the inescapable fact of choice and self-authorship and engage instead in self-deception.

Some Stirner scholars have contended that the resemblance is only superficial, that the existentialists, where they have engaged Stirner, have misunderstood him in important ways.[23] Arguing that, as "generalized accommodation[s] to modernity," psychoanalysis and existentialism do not pose a serious threat to the established political order, John F. Welsh rejects proposed rapprochements between Stirner's egoism and existentialism, specifically mentioning Sartre's work in his argument. Welsh argues that Camus and Herbert Read ignore key lessons of Stirner's work and "[denude] *The Ego and Its Own* of its explosive content."[24]

IV. Egoism and Poststructuralism

Saul Newman's vital work approaches Stirner as a precursor to and a lens through which to understand poststructuralism. Certainly Stirner meaningfully anticipates attempts by poststructuralists to stress "difference over sameness and [emphasize] particularity at the expense of universality."[25] Newman notes that Foucault, for example, has thrown into sharp relief the ways in which the universalization of "certain rational discourses"—associated with modernity—has silenced or expelled the voices and lived experiences of homosexuals, criminals, and the mentally ill, among many others.[26] Poststructuralism and anarchism seem to be in conversation, simultaneously informing one another, rather than existing in a relationship of one-way influence.[27]

Leonard Williams introduces Hakim Bey's ontological anarchism within this context, arguing that the anti-essentialism of poststructuralism gives way to a recognition of "the local and contingent nature of political life."[28] Bey's post-left anarchism posits a radical break with politics, an immediate reclamation of areas of autonomy in daily life. Central to this notion is Bey's idea of the temporary autonomous zone; the temporary autonomous zone is presented as the deliberate, immediate creation of an "Outside," a "true space of resistance to the totality" in which the individual rejects the search for order and embraces chaos. Bey sees chaos as lying at the center of his project.

Unlike anarchists who "have been claiming for years that 'anarchy is not chaos'"—who, like all political idealists, seek peace and order—Bey regards order "as death, cessation, crystallization, alien silence."[29] Order here is the triumph of fixed ideas. If classical anarchists see liberty as the mother of order, egoism-tinged anarchisms question the claimed relationship between the two, content to embrace chaos, to disclaim attempts to contrive order from chaotic foundations. Indeed, egoists regard the anarchist project as a creation of those "who desire to dispel the illusory stases of order," who see contrived attempts at order as standing in the way of "the unlimited creative potentials of chaos."[30] Thus, in *Postanarchism*, Newman describes, in terms similar to Bey's, "an anarchism of the here and now," ontologically free and "unencumbered by [the] revolutionary metanarrative" of traditional anarchism, which identifies the eventual disappearance or destruction of state power as its goal.[31]

V. Egoism and Revolution

The idea of revolution is an important point of departure for post-left anarchism. Like other individualists in the anarchist tradition, Stirner has been dismissed by many social anarchists as bourgeois and anti-revolutionary.[32] And indeed egoists have treated the idea of revolution with a level of derision, resisting the notion that, to be free, the individual must wait for a revolution to occur at some remote moment in the future, when workers have become sufficiently class-conscious. For anarchists in the post-left tradition, "the revolution of everyday life" is "the only revolution that matters," rooted firmly in the individual's own wants and purposes, not in political slogans and orthodoxies.[33]

Stirner's idea of insurrection contemplates ongoing, autonomous escapes from the reaches of power instead of active struggles to fight or capture it, motivated by an inward-looking discontent with oneself rather than the "*political* or *social* act" of trying to effect "an overturning of conditions."[34] For Stirner, political or social revolution represents an attempt to put the cart before the horse insofar as it begins by "aim[ing] at new *arrangements*." Stirner says that while insurrection "has indeed for its unavoidable consequence a transformation of circumstances," it does not *start* from this goal, instead contemplating

> a rising of individuals, a getting up, without regard to the arrangements that spring from it. [R]evolution [aims] at new *arrangements*; insurrection leads us no longer to *let* ourselves be arranged, but to arrange ourselves, and sets no glittering hopes on 'institutions.'[35]

Following Stirner, Renzo Novatore regarded anarchists as a "nobility," as "aristocratic outsiders," committed not to revolutionary social change or "the construction of a new and suffocating society," but to the retrieval of self-creation, premised on the idea of the self-consciously "*liberated Human Being*" (emphasis in original and importantly not gendered).[36] This distinction deeply informs the set of projects that make up the various strains of egoist anarchism.

VI. Egoism and Lifestyle Anarchism

Collectivist anarchism bristles at the notion of a liberated individual unwilling to sacrifice herself for the holy cause of revolution. In *Social Anarchism or Lifestyle Anarchism: An Unbridgeable Chasm*, Bookchin bemoans "a latter-day anarcho-individualism"—which he dismissively labels "lifestyle anarchism"—that he sees as "supplanting social action and revolutionary politics in anarchism." In lifestyle anarchism, Bookchin perceives the narcissistic influence of bourgeois culture and "the antirational biases of postmodernism." Concerned to preserve the "socialistic character of the libertarian tradition," Bookchin expects all anarchists in good standing to demonstrate "responsible social commitment" in service to the revolution; they must participate in "organized, collectivistic, programmatic" political action, properly aware of the *true meaning* of freedom.[37] Strictly regimented and imposing all kinds of duties and devoirs, Bookchin's anarchism appears positively authoritarian, reminiscent of Marsden's remark to Tucker about the archism of anarchists. Many of Bookchin's criticisms of "lifestyle anarchism" were anticipated by Marx in his confrontation with Stirner's egoism. So captivated was Marx by Stirner's thought that he dedicated three-fourths of *The German Ideology* to his critique of "Sankt Max."[38] That book decries what Marx and Engels regard as Stirner's "spiritual" and "bourgeois outlook," as well as his supposed confusion about class categories.[39]

Many egoists have agreed with Bookchin's position that their ideas are out of place in the anarchist tradition. Parker, for example, eventually concluded, following Marsden, that anarchism and egoism cannot be reconciled, that the former compels the individual to exalt the abstract ideal of humanity and thus to abstain from acting on his desires. Marsden classes anarchism with Christianity, understanding it as another in a long line of renunciatory systems of self-denial and control. Similarly, Marsden's insight in her exchange with Tucker underscores egoism's unshrinking assault on morality. "Conscience," she writes, "takes the Ego in charge and but rarely fails to throttle the life out of him." Correctly regarding anarchism not as a system without rules, but rather as a most exacting system of behavioral prohibitions, Marsden argues that the archism of "Armies, Courts, Gowns and Wigs, Jailors, [and] Hangmen" is "light and superficial as compared with that of our Clerico-libertarian friends."[40] Here, it seems, Marsden had touched a nerve. Once among her greatest admirers,[41] Tucker soured on Marsden after this exchange, put off by her round rejection of anarchist ideology.

In their keenness to point out problems with treating egoism as leading to, as a form of, or as even compatible with anarchism, egoist thinkers like Marsden and Parker actually affirm Stirner's "centrality and importance to [the anarchist] tradition."[42] In its challenges to anarchism, Stirner's egoism pushes anarchism to remain relevant, to incorporate new discourses and strategies, updating itself for the twenty-first century rather than remaining mired in nineteenth-century categories and ways of thinking about radical struggles.

VII. Egoism and Sexual Liberation

Daniel Guérin identifies important tensions between the egoist approach and the outmoded politics of the labor movement, among them "the endemic homophobia" in the latter and "the exclusive concern with class," while ignoring, for example, what Guérin sees as Stirner's "concern with sexual liberation."[43] Marsden followed Stirner in emphasizing this concern; more recent treatments of her work note her importance as a forerunner of queer theory, her zealous resistance to facile, superficial categories, and her truly avant-garde readiness "to [extend] the status of the autonomous individual to all those who resist categorization."[44]

The journals Marsden edited, including *The Freewoman*, *The New Freewoman*, and *The Egoist*, hosted spirited attacks on "the crass, ostrich-like stupidity of our national attitude on sex matters in general," on "the heavy veil of Decency (so often the bitterest enemy of truth) enshroud[ing] practically all open discussion" of human sexuality and related matters.[45] Neither Stirner nor Marsden let repressive notions of good taste stand in the way of their probing deconstructions of sex and gender ideologies. Over one hundred years ago, Marsden challenged readers with the idea "that there is no definite reality which can be substituted as that to which Woman corresponds," that "in itself feeling is sexless," and that the differences between men and women are "infinitesimally small."[46] She understands gender as a socially-constructed sacred ideal, one that exists apart from "the physical differences which are all which exist of sex."[47] Indeed, Marsden's radical and trailblazing efforts to transcend stale gender norms and stereotypes have drawn the ire of some feminists for allegedly "betraying and undermining [the] political, economic[,] and cultural empowerment of woman."[48] If Marsden's work and ideas prefigure the politics of trans and queer liberation, then such criticisms closely approximate the more general debate between radical feminists and the transgender movement.[49] Others have likewise observed the sex and gender implications of Stirner's work. In discussing his translation of the title of Stirner's only book, David Leopold observes that "Stirner clearly identifies the egoistic subject as prior to gender."[50] Gender is just the kind of dominating abstraction, laden with duties and proscriptions, that Stirner is eager to explode, another (that is, apart from formal political institutions, capitalist relations, etc.) source of authority limiting the unique person.

A proper appreciation of Stirner's ideas allows one to free oneself from both traditional gender roles and guilt or shame associated with one's desires, "to become the owner of his own desires."[51] Indeed, Stirner's egoist ideas were a principal influence on *Der Eigene*, "the world's first homosexual journal," first published in 1896 and "dedicated to unique [*eigenen*] people" "who are proud of their uniqueness [*Eigenheit*] and want to insist on it no matter what the cost!"[52] The individualist anarchist John Henry Mackay, Stirner's biographer, was an important contributor to the journal under the pseudonym Sagitta.

Through Marsden's pioneering efforts, egoism also became a significant influence on modern art and literature. Indeed, her subeditors include influential figures of literary modernism such as Ezra Pound and T.S. Eliot, and no less a literary giant than James Joyce was among her contributors.

VIII. Egoism and Individualism

Assuming that they identify with it at all, egoists prefer to treat anarchism as another way of stating or explaining the importance of individual self-realization, predicated on a certain sensibility perhaps expressed in the idea that "the individual is above all institutions and formulas."[53] And those egoists who do self-identify as anarchists frequently take care to place their individualism in the place of honor, to associate themselves with "anarchist individualism" (as against individualist anarchism).[54]

Yet even the relationship between egoism and individualism is contested, as Stirner's ideas potentially imply a refusal to accept "the constrained and over-regulated forms of individuality on offer to us today."[55] These constrained and over-regulated forms are associated in the literature with liberalism.[56] Stirner's work, as well as that of today's post-left anarchists, is not easily reduced to or understood through the lens of present-day left–right categories; it rejects ideology itself, and so naturally rejects liberalism, which, for Stirner, frees *man*, an abstraction, while subjecting the individual to domination and alienation.[57] Stirner regards liberalism as entailing "the normalization of the individual" through "a whole series of regulatory, judicial, medical and disciplinary procedures," all calculated to erase "difference and individuality."[58]

> Political liberty means that the *polis*, the state, is free; freedom of religion that religion is free, as freedom of conscience signifies that conscience is free; not, therefore, that I am free from the state, from religion, from conscience, or that I am *rid* of them. It does not mean *my* liberty, but the liberty of a power that rules and subjugates me; it means that one of my *despots*, like state, religion, conscience, is free. State, religion, conscience, these despots, make me a slave, and *their* liberty is *my* slavery.[59]

Here, Stirner turns the Enlightenment—and prevailing narratives associated with it—on its head, scornful of the notion that through revolution (Stirner has in mind specifically the French Revolution) the individual had become free. The revolution and the ideas it represented had not defeated authority, had not altered or even reached the underlying structures of domination, but merely ushered in a new host of enslaving abstractions.

Stirner sees "in liberalism only the old Christian depreciation of the I," a rebirth or reinvention of Christianity in the new terms provided by the Enlightenment.[60] Politics is just another incarnation of religion, its projects and plans so many rites and rituals, the state a new god to be propitiated again and again. With affected solemnity and self-seriousness, we line up to vote as we might have assembled to receive the Eucharist, and recognize the moral imperative of paying taxes as we might have understood the duty to tithe.

Still, rather than discarding liberalism as without value or insights, Stirner is catechizing it, eager to expose it to a searching dialectical process that yields new insights and proceeds to a higher level of analysis. His goal is to explode liberalism's boundaries, opening space for a radical, pluralistic "hyper-liberalism," radically accommodative of difference.[61] He offers a route of egress from the left–right political spectrum itself, indeed, from all accepted political categories and existing labels.[62]

Whether or not Stirner was an anarchist, his ideas arguably come to influence the anarchist movement first and most notably through the work of Benjamin R. Tucker, who published Steven T. Byington's celebrated translation of *The Ego and Its Own*, the first in English, in 1907. Tucker encountered Stirner's ideas through his friend and aide, the writer and publisher George Schumm, and James L. Walker, to whom Tucker referred as "the most thorough American student of Stirner."[63]

In his important history of the American individualist anarchists, James J. Martin observes that Josiah Warren's influence on Tucker prepared the ground for Tucker's embrace of egoism. After participating in the utopian socialist communities of Robert Owen, Warren, careful "to preserve the SOVEREIGNTY OF EVERY INDIVIDUAL inviolate" (emphasis in original), "had dismissed altruism and subscribed to enlightened self-interest."[64]

It is nevertheless important not to understate the extent to which Tucker's adoption of egoism was in fact a meaningful break with those who had influenced him rather than an expression of fidelity to them. Tucker's foremost American influences, the immediate predecessors of his explicit "philosophical anarchism,"[65] were deeply committed to fundamentally liberal conceptions of natural and inalienable individual rights. Warren himself positively invoked the Declaration of Independence and extolled "natural liberty." Ezra Heywood, another of Tucker's personal mentors, wrote of "the fundamental right to property." Such earlier American individualists (other important examples include Lysander Spooner, J.K. Ingalls, William B. Greene, and Stephen Pearl Andrews) frequently called upon natural law and "the natural laws of trade" in their arguments against both the capitalist system and the state. Their individualist anarchism was, they believed, the system demanded by the cosmic order, indeed by science itself. (Tucker was, indeed, wont to call his political system "scientific anarchism.") "There are," J.K. Ingalls writes, "certain great laws or first principles which pervade universal Nature, and act with exceptionless uniformity."[66] Indeed, it has been argued that individualist anarchism, particularly its American variant, was more akin to radical liberalism than to other schools of anarchist thought.[67] Much as Stirner's thought pushed the boundaries of traditional liberalism, so did the American individualists radicalize liberalism to create their unique iteration of anarchism.

IX. Stirner and Dialectics

A consideration of the relationship between Stirner's thought and dialectics must entail a consideration of both Hegel and Marx.

Stirner's work emerges within the context of Hegel's philosophy and cannot be fully understood, if understood at all, without a proper appreciation for the basic mechanics of Hegel's dialectical process and his phenomenology.[68] Stirner "had the advantage of being taught his Hegel by Hegel," having attended his lectures on the philosophy of religion, the history of philosophy, and the philosophy of spirit. Whether Stirner's work follows in the dialectical tradition or explodes it is of course the subject of scholarly debate. And indeed it is possible that *The Ego and Its Own*, presenting a trenchant case against many of Hegel's key ideas while employing "the distinctive triadic pattern of Hegel,"[69] does both.

Leopold contends that Stirner exploits the dialectical structure in order to develop his anti-Hegelian arguments, using a "self-conscious parody of Hegelianism."[70] Welsh interprets Stirner's egoism as a method with which to free dialectical social theory "from the Marxian shackles that are used to understand it."[71]

X. Egoist Individualism and Communism

Despite the apparently irreconcilability between Marx's communism and Stirner's egoism—and the history of open hostility I have noted here—some anarchists have seen egoism as implying communism (at least anarchist communism, if not orthodox state communism). Marx and Engels themselves prosecuted "a sterile war against Stirner's book," quite clearly aware of its implications for their communist doctrine. Stirner's book worries deeply about closed, self-contained, and comprehensive systems like their version of communism, which reduce humankind and its apparent classes to "large blob[s] of protoplasmic homogeneity," to borrow the words of anarchist Laurance Labadie.[72] Still, communist anarchists have found in Stirner a radical attack on private property and, paraphrasing Stirner, a revolt against the pressure exerted by the property-owning class.

Emma Goldman, following Stirner, sees private property and capitalism as obstacles to the freedom of the individual—and she opposes these not in spite of her individualism, but because of it. Whereas state communists regard individualism itself as bourgeois and counter-revolutionary, the anarchist communist tradition treats individualism differently, and is thus able to reconcile itself to Stirner. John P. Clark credits Stirner with inspiring Goldman's outlook "on individuality and personal uniqueness,"[73] evident in her claim "that if society is ever to become free, it will be so through liberated individuals." To Goldman, Stirner is misunderstood, seen as "the apostle of the theory 'each for himself, the devil take the hind one,'" when in fact his "individualism contains the greatest social possibilities."[74]

In *The Philosophy of Egoism*, Walker, who frequently contributed to Tucker's *Liberty* under the pseudonym Tak Kak, encapsulates another, decidedly different, possible egoist position on private property: "I have a right to what I can take and openly keep, and another has a right to take it from me if he can."[75] Prudential concerns may encourage one to refrain from a given action, to chart a different course, but not moral considerations in the sense of normative rules outside of and independent of the individual. As a practical matter, the goal of the self-conscious egoist is to "discover where [his] true, most lasting interests lie," "allow[ing] no moral considerations to obscure [his] view."[76] The juxtaposition of Goldman and Walker here demonstrates the general difficulty inherent in claiming Stirner's egoism for *any* political or economic doctrine.

XI. Egoism, Civilization, and Work

If egoism by definition resists all political and economic programs, it also damns society and civilization. Post-left anarchism has thus been closely related also to the primitivist tradition within anarchism, which posits civilization itself as a source—really the primary source—of domination and oppression. Primitivists associate civilization with a process of domestication that has denatured human beings and introduced hierarchical, authoritarian forms of social organization, that has removed people from the condition of wildness.[77] John Zerzan decries the reign of a "techno-scientific hegemony,"[78] a virulent monoculture infecting human beings and the natural world and precluding all other social possibilities. The political left, in Zerzan's thought, is "discredited and dying"; its perspective "surely also needs to go" because it is irrelevant and unable to confront "the steady worldwide movement toward complete dehumanization."[79] In fact, the left—scientific, rationalistic, and industrialist—is responsible in large part for this dehumanization, euphemistically called progress. We are possessed by the mindless desire to consume, captive to the drive for more. Primitivists argue that, prior to civilization, defined roughly as the time before the domestication of plants and animals, human beings enjoyed more gender autonomy and equality and more leisure time, affiliating in less violent societies marked by sharing and equality.[80]

The link back to Stirner and his egoist project is primitivism's focus on denaturing processes, the ways in which modernity, technology, and civilization alienate human beings. Wolfi Landstreicher, however, offers an anarchist egoist critique of civilization that is explicitly non-primitivist, one that inquires, indeed, whether primitivism could be a positive *impediment* to a thoroughgoing anti-civilization project.[81] Landstreicher resists what he sees as primitivists' reification and abstraction of what were actual relationships "between real, living, breathing human beings." The attempt to boil such complex lived relationships down to an essential or idealized quality of *primitiveness*, Landstreicher argues, risks making anarchism another quest for the "eschatological vision" of a perfect future, "a *program* for the future" just like Marxism. It furthermore "dehumanizes and deindividualizes" the actual human beings who become the models of the primitive.

Related to its critiques of society and civilization is post-left anarchism's battle with the labor-movement-left's naive romanticization of work. Rather than stopping at criticizing the exploitation of workers under capitalism, post-left anarchism has been critical of the social institution of work itself, even arguing, "In order to stop suffering, we have to stop working."[82] Post-left anarchists have criticized workerist anarchism for its glorification of work and the factory as a symbol, preferring to call for more radical social interventions. Bob Black, for example, writes: "Work is much easier to glorify than it is to perform." Similarly, Parker, arguing that anarchism will only ever appeal to a small minority, damns "the proletarian mythicists" for saddling anarchists with an "association with the dreary cult of 'the workers.'" Parker quotes John Henry Mackay's contention that anarchism "is not the concern of a single class," emphasizing that it is instead "the concern of every individual who values his individual liberty."[83] For Black, like Stirner, "ideologies like liberalism, humanism, Marxism, syndicalism, and Bookchinism" are much more alike than they are different, linked by the fact that they make demands of the individual, intent on dictating terms and establishing control over her behavior.[84] These ideological systems seek to substitute themselves for the volition of the thinking, feeling, flesh-and-blood unique, living parasitically on it. (Here, again, we have good reason to avoid sexing or gendering the unique.) Black is eager to point out that, when Bookchin "accuses rival anarchists of individualism and liberalism," he is merely repeating the charges that Stalin casts against all anarchists.[85] He further notes that the indictment of post-left anarchists as "decadent" only reveals Bookchin's envy and ressentiment, as the slur lacks any real meaning and serves only to identify "people perceived to be having more fun than you are."[86] Bookchin here appears as a moral scold, bitter at "lifestylists" for rejecting his rigid, burdensome so-called anarchism.

Notwithstanding egoism's aversion to morality, post-left anarchists have at times made conciliatory gestures in the direction of "practice-based virtue approaches" to ethical questions.[87] Newman, for example, acknowledges the desirability of cultivating "certain ethics and virtues for political struggle and autonomous experience," identifying anarchist practices as producing "anti-hierarchical identities and values." Stirner's ideas connecting such values to education were very much ahead of their time; he anticipates later arguments in favor of an active and self-directed process of learning, as opposed to pedagogical approaches that treat the student as the passive recipient of the teacher's knowledge and expertise. For Stirner, education as it exists is fundamentally and irreparably manipulative, "calculated to produce feelings in us, instead of leaving their production to ourselves however they may turn out."[88] Welsh explains that Stirner regards education (and the process of socialization more generally) as inculcating self-renunciation, inverting the relationship between the individual and the object of his studies. Instead of dissecting and digesting the object "as an active subject," the individual is relegated to a position of passivity, of subordination to something external and alien to him.[89]

XII. Conclusion

There is no simple, obvious answer, and quite possibly no right answer at all, to the question of whether Stirner or those he has influenced can accurately be classed as anarchists; his individualism is fundamentally different from the kind usually identified with anarchism: "Human essence, which was seen by the anarchists to be beyond the reach of power, was found by Stirner to be constructed by it."[90] Post-left anarchism has often styled itself as neither left nor right,[91] in an effort to save the anarchist project from the individuality-stifling programs of political visionaries eager to impose their blueprints for the ideal free society. It therefore has no shortage of enemies in an anarchist community with deep historical and ideological ties to the left.

Notwithstanding any commonalities between the thinkers and ideas constituting post-left anarchism, egoist anarchism, or anarchist individualism, it is difficult to justify identifying them as a single school or movement. Indeed, to undertake such school-building would be contrary to the main thrust of Stirner's work, that the irreducible feelings and wants of the unique person are more important and fundamental than the ideas of academics and the movements of activists.[92] These traditions want no part of the political, of its meetings, committees, leaders, or movements, spurning all the varieties of institution-building in favor of "unmediated desire."[93] Stirner's ideas equip anarchists with new analytical tools that discourage us from seeing in anarchism the promise of a final terminus—a post-revolution paradise. Instead, Stirner immerses anarchism in an endless recursive cycle in which power dynamics are repeatedly reconsidered in light of new circumstances and cannot be facilely reduced, for example, "to a mere function of the capitalist economy or class interest."[94]

Notes

1 There are several competing translations of Stirner's title, *Der Einzige und sein Eigentum*. For the first English translation, its publisher Benjamin R. Tucker chose *The Ego and His Own*, an "extremely unfortunate" rendering of the German according to Jason McQuinn, who favors *The Unique and Its Property*. In *T.A.Z.: The Temporary Autonomous Zone* (New York, NY: Autonomedia 1985), Hakim Bey suggests that "*The Unique & His Own-ness* would better reflect [Stirner's] intentions, given that he never defines the ego *in opposition to* libido or id, or in opposition to 'soul' or 'spirit.' The Unique (*der Einzige*) might best be construed simply as the individual self" (67).

2 As David Leopold notes in the introduction to his 1995 Cambridge University Press translation, the book is dated 1845, but was actually published in the latter half of October 1844.

3 Saul Newman writes that Stirner's book "was described as the 'most revolutionary book ever written.' It is certainly the most dangerous." Saul Newman, "Introduction: Re-encountering Stirner's Ghosts," *Max Stirner*, ed. Saul Newman (London: Palgrave 2011) 1.

4 Steve J. Shone, *American Anarchism* (Leiden: Brill 2013) 222.

5 Max Adler quoted in David Osterfeld, "Freedom, Society, and the State: An Investigation Into the Possibility of Society without Government," *Anarchy and the Law*, ed. Edward P. Stringham (London: Transaction 2007) 505.

6 The writings of post-left anarchists have generally referred to their ideas as "post-left anarchy" rather than "post-left anarchism," underscoring the fact that they do not seek to create another -ism, an ideology or system. Here, I refer to "post-left anarchism" to distinguish anarchy as a social condition from anarchism as a movement that aspires toward that condition.

7 As the egoist anarchist writer John Beverley Robinson said, "Whatever gods you worship, you realize that they are *your* gods, the product of your own mind, terrible or amiable, as you may choose to depict them. You hold them in your hand, and play with them, as a child with its paper dolls; for you have learned not to fear them, that they are but the 'imaginations of your heart.'" "Egoism," *Freedom* 38.414 (Jan. 1924): 3.

8 Max Stirner, *The Ego and Its Own* (Cambridge: CUP 1995) 175.

9 Benjamin Gregg, *Human Rights as Social Construction* (Cambridge: CUP 2012) 1.

10 Stirner 92.

11 This paragraph is taken from David S. D'Amato, "Egoism in Rand and Stirner," *Libertarianism.org* (Cato Institute, Mar. 11, 2014) www.libertarianism.org/columns/egoism-rand-stirner.

12 David R. Kelley and Bonnie G. Smith, eds., *Proudhon: What Is Property?* (Cambridge: CUP 1994) 208.

13 Colin Ward, *Anarchism: A Very Short Introduction* (Oxford: OUP 2004), 26–7.

14 In *Political Justice*, Godwin writes "that perfectibility is one of the most unequivocal characteristics of the human species, so that the political, as well as the intellectual state of man, may be presumed to be in a course of progressive improvement." William Godwin, *An Enquiry Concerning Political Justice*, accessed at knarf.english.upenn.edu/Godwin/pj12.html.

15 Dora Marsden, "Views and Comments," *The Egoist* 1.2 (Jan. 15, 1914): 25.

16 Ruth Kinna, "The Mirror of Anarchy: The Egoism of John Henry Mackay and Dora Marsden," Newman, *Stirner* 42.

17 See, for example, Skye Cleary, *Existentialism and Romantic Love* (London: Palgrave 2015), and John Carroll, *Break-Out from the Crystal Palace* (London: Routledge 2010) 17.

18 Sartre, *Existentialism is a Humanism* (New Haven: Yale UP 2007) 36.

19 Joseph A. Labadie remarked similarly, "It is immaterial whether one be a Communist or an Individualist so long as he be an Anarchist. Anarchy, as I see it, admits of any kind of organization, so long as membership is not compulsory." Joseph A. Labadie, "Cranky Notions," *Liberty* 5.18 (April 14, 1888): 16.

20 Giorel Curran, *Twenty-First Century Dissent: Anarchism, Anti-Globalization and Environmentalism* (London: Palgrave 2007) 35.

21 Max Stirner, *The Ego and Its Own* (Cambridge: CUP 1995) 7.

22 The first arguably being the rediscovery of Stirner's book by the individualist anarchists in Benjamin R. Tucker's *Liberty* circle. See Steve J. Shone, *American Anarchism* (Leiden: Brill 2013) 225.

23 John F. Welsh, *Max Stirner's Dialectical Egoism: A New Interpretation* (Lanham, MD: Lexington 2010) 24–28.

24 Welsh 28.

25 Saul Newman, *Power and Politics in Poststructuralist Thought: New Theories of the Political* (Abington, UK: Routledge 2005) 139.

26 Id.

27 Leonard Williams, "Hakim Bey and Ontological Anarchism," *Journal for the Study of Radicalism* 4.2 (Fall 2010): 111.

28 Williams 112.

29 Hakim Bey, *Immediatism* (Edinburgh: AK Press 1994) 2.
30 John Moore, "Lived Poetry: Stirner, Anarchy, Subjectivity and the Art of Living," *Changing Anarchism: Anarchist Theory and Practice in a Global Age*, ed. Jonathan Purkis and James Bowen (Manchester: Manchester UP 2004) 57.
31 Saul Newman, *Postanarchism* (Cambridge, UK: Polity 2015) xii.
32 Kinna 43.
33 Bob Black, "Preface," *The Right to be Greedy* (Loompanics Unlimited, 1983) https://theanarchistlibrary.org/library/bob-black-preface-to-the-right-to-be-greedy-by-for-ourselves (June 2, 2020)
34 Stirner.
35 Stirner 279.
36 Renzo Novatore, "Anarchist Individualism in the Social Revolution," *The Anarchist Library* (Il Libertario, 1919) https://theanarchistlibrary.org/library/renzo-novatore-anarchist-individualism-in-the-social-revolution (June 2, 2020).
37 Janet Biehl, ed., *The Murray Bookchin Reader* (London: Black Rose Books 1999) 164.
38 Paul Thomas, "Karl Marx and Max Stirner," *Political Theory* 3.2 (1975): 159.
39 Welsh 43n30.
40 Dora Marsden, "Views and Comments," *The Egoist* 1.5 (Mar. 2, 1914): 199.
41 Of Marsden's *The New Freewoman*, Tucker wrote, "I consider your paper the most important publication in existence."
42 Saul Newman, "Introduction: Re-encountering Stirner's Ghosts," Newman, *Stirner* 12.
43 David Berry, "The Search for a Libertarian Communism: Daniel Guérin and the 'Synthesis' of Marxism and Anarchism," *Libertarian Socialism: Politics in Black and Red*, ed. Alex Prichard *et al.* (London: Palgrave 2012) 199.
44 Anne Fernihough, *Freewomen and Supermen: Edwardian Radicals and Literary Modernism* (Oxford: OUP 2013) 180.
45 Dora Marsden, "Intermediate Sexual Types," *The New Freewoman* 8.1 (Oct. 1, 1913): 155.
46 Dora Marsden, "Views and Comments," *The New Freewoman* 2.1 (July 1, 1913): 24.
47 Id.
48 David Ashford, *Autarchies: The Invention of Selfishness* (London: Bloomsbury 2017) 62.
49 I refer here to the long-running debate between "gender critical" radical feminists who have advocated, for example, "womyn-born womyn" positions and policies and the transgender movement generally. For more on this debate and the relationship between feminism and transgender theory generally, see Talia Bettcher, "Feminist Perspectives on Trans Issues," *Stanford Encyclopedia of Philosophy* (Stanford, CA: Stanford U 2009) https://plato.stanford.edu/archives/spr2014/entries/feminism/trans/ (June 2, 2020).
50 Leopold xl.
51 Yvonne Ivory, *The Homosexual Revival of Renaissance Style, 1850–1930* (London: Palgrave 2009) 79.
52 Ivory 59.
53 John Beverley Robinson, "Egoism," *Slaves to Duty*, by John Badcock, Jr. (Colorado Springs, CO: Myles 1972) 32.
54 See, for example, the works of E. Armand and Renzo Novatore, among others.
55 Newman, *Postanarchism* 20.
56 Id.
57 See generally Saul Newman, "Politics of the Ego," Newman, *Power* 13–30.
58 Newman, "Politics" 28.
59 Stirner 97.
60 Newman, *Power* 14.
61 Kinna 44–45.
62 Newman, "Introduction: Re-encountering Stirner's Ghosts," *Stirner* 13.
63 Max Stirner, *The Ego and His Own* (New York, NY: Benj. R. Tucker 1907) ix.
64 James J. Martin, *Men Against the State* 251, 14.
65 We must take care not to confuse Tucker's use of "philosophical anarchism" with the technical meaning often assigned to the term by contemporary scholars. Tucker explicitly supports the elimination of the state, whereas, as a technical term today, "philosophical anarchism" may describe the view that *even if* the state is desirable in a certain sense, there are reasons that we are not obligated to obey its rules.
66 Joshua King Ingalls, "Uprightness the Only Path to Safety: A Sermon," Libertarian Labyrinth, http://wiki.libertarian-labyrinth.org/index.php?title=Uprightness_the_only_Path_to_Safety (August 17, 2020).
67 See William Gary Kline, *The Individualist Anarchists: A Critique of Liberalism* (Lanham, MD: University Press of America 1987), in which Kline argues that individualist anarchism was, rather than a truly radical critique

of American society, merely a peculiar example of liberalism. Albert Weisbord similarly contends that individualist anarchists like Josiah Warren, Lysander Spooner, and Benjamin R. Tucker represent a "bourgeois Liberal-Anarchism" fundamentally unlike other more radical anarchisms. Weisbord, *The Conquest of Power* (New York, NY: Covici-Friede 1937): 225.

68 See, for example, Welsh 36; Jason McQuinn, "John Clark's Stirner: A Critical Review of *Max Stirner's Egoism*," https://theanarchistlibrary.org/library/jason-mcquinn-john-clark-s-stirner-a-critical-review-of-max-stirner-s-egoism (June 2, 2020).

69 Lawrence S. Stepelevich, "Hegel and Stirner: Thesis and Antithesis," *Idealistic Studies* 6.3 (September 1976) www.unionofegoists.com/authors/stirner/max-stirner-criticism/hegel-and-stirner-thesis-and-antithesis-by-lawrence-stepelevich/ (June 2, 2020).

70 David Leopold, "Max Stirner," *Stanford Encyclopedia of Philosophy* (Stanford, CA: Stanford U, 2019) https://plato.stanford.edu/entries/max-stirner/ (June 2, 2020).

71 Welsh 269.

72 M. George van der Meer, "Examining Exploitation: One Mutualist Perspective," Center for a Stateless Society, https://c4ss.org/content/14777 (August 17, 2020).

73 John P. Clark, qtd. *An Anarchist FAQ* (Oakland, CA: AK Press, 2007) https://theanarchistlibrary.org/library/the-anarchist-faq-editorial-collective-an-anarchist-faq (June 2, 2020).

74 M. George van der Meer, "Examining Exploitation: One Mutualist Perspective," Center for a Stateless Society, https://c4ss.org/content/14777 (August 17, 2020).

75 James L. Walker, *The Philosophy of Egoism* (Denver, CO: Katharine Walker 1905) 34.

76 Badcock 27.

77 Peter Marshall, *Demanding the Impossible* (Oakland, CA: PM Press 2010) 684.

78 John Zerzan, "Why Primitivism?" *Twilight of the Machines* (Port Townsend, WA: Feral 2008) 103.

79 Zerzan 104.

80 Zerzan 107.

81 Wolfi Landstreicher, *A Critique, Not a Program: For a Non-Primitivist Anti-Civilization Critique* (Victoria, BC: Camas 2018).

82 Bob Black, *The Abolition of Work* (Loompanics Unlimited 1986) 17.

83 Bob Black, "Anarchy After Leftism," n.d., https://theanarchistlibrary.org/library/bob-black-anarchy-after-leftism (August 17, 2020).

84 See Black, "Anarchy After Leftism."

85 Id.

86 Id.

87 Benjamin Franks, "Anarchism and Ethics," *The Palgrave Handbook of Anarchism*, ed. Carl Levy and Matthew S. Adams (New York, NY: Palgrave 2019) 563.

88 Stirner 61.

89 David S. D'Amato, "Compulsory Education as Social Control," *Libertarianism.org* (Cato Institute, Sep. 12, 2019) www.libertarianism.org/columns/compulsory-education-social-control (June 2, 2020)

90 Saul Newman, *From Bakunin to Lacan: Anti-Authoritarianism and the Dislocation of Power* (Lanham, MD: Lexington 2001) 75.

91 Jason McQuinn, "Post-Left Anarchy: Leaving the Left Behind," *The Anarchist Library*, https://theanarchistlibrary.org/library/jason-mcquinn-post-left-anarchy-leaving-the-left-behind (June 2, 2020).

92 Welsh 267.

93 Sara C. Motta, "Leyendo el anarchismo a través de ojos latinoamericanos: Reading Anarchism through Latin American Eyes," *The Bloomsbury Companion to Anarchism*, ed. Ruth Kinna (London: Continuum 2012) 261.

94 Newman, *Anti-Authoritarianism* 77.

11
DE FACTO MONOPOLIES AND THE JUSTIFICATION OF THE STATE

Ralf M. Bader

> The fundamental question of political philosophy ... is whether there should be any state at all.
>
> Robert Nozick[1]

I. Introduction

This chapter explains how Nozick's notion of a de facto monopoly makes room for states that are justified in claiming a monopoly on coercion despite lacking authority and despite their citizens lacking political obligation. Along the way, it establishes that political obligation and political authority are fundamentally distinct mechanisms for underwriting content-independent duties, but that neither can plausibly apply in the absence of consent.

II. The Problem of Coercion

States are coercive. They use force as well as the threat of force in order to make citizens commit or omit various actions. It is because of their coercive nature that anarchists consider states to be objectionable. They argue that only consent on the part of all those who are governed by a state can give rise to political obligation or confer the requisite normative powers on the state. The state cannot permissibly claim a monopoly on force within a certain territory unless all the individuals in that territory have consented to its rule. As a result, anarchists consider non-consensual states to be illegitimate. Such states cannot permissibly rule and are morally objectionable.

The crucial question for determining whether the state can be justified is whether it is permissible for the state to use force as well as the threat of force. On what grounds and under what conditions can the state be justified in using coercion? On the face of it, there is a strong presumption against coercion and in favour of liberty.

> Individuals have rights, and there are things no person or group may do to them (without violating their rights). So strong and far-reaching are these rights that they raise the question of what, if anything, the state and its officials may do.[2]

For the state to be justified, it may not engage in rights violations. This means that a justified state can only use coercion on the condition that doing so is permissible and does not violate any rights. The rights of individuals, however, put into doubt the permissibility of state coercion, or at least significantly restrict the scope of permissible coercion, thereby limiting the range of activities in which the state can permissibly engage.

Nozick agrees with the anarchist that states lack authority and that citizens do not have political obligation when consent is absent. In order to address the anarchist's challenge and show that non-consensual states can be justified, Nozick attempts to show that it can be permissible for states to exercise a monopoly of force and coerce their citizens even in the absence of consent.[3] Rather than focusing on the obligations that individual citizens have, Nozick is concerned with the prerogatives that the state has and the actions that it can permissibly perform. In particular, he argues that a non-consensual state can claim a monopoly on coercion without violating the rights of its citizens.[4] States can, accordingly, be justified even though they lack authority and even though citizens lack political obligations.

III. Enforcing Duties

> The moral prohibitions it is permissible to enforce are the source of whatever legitimacy the state's fundamental coercive power has.[5]

Consensual states can have a wide scope of permissible coercion. As long as there are no limits on which rights can voluntarily be surrendered,[6] the scope of coercion that is rendered permissible on the basis of the consent of the governed is, in principle, unlimited. The scope of legitimate coercion on the part of non-consensual states, however, seems to be rather limited. In particular, it appears to be restricted to cases in which the rights of individuals are either removed or overridden.[7]

The non-consensual use of coercion can be justified straightforwardly when it comes to enforcing duties that are enforceable.[8] Coercion is justified if it is used appropriately (i.e., satisfying procedural constraints, proportionality requirements, etc.), both prospectively in order to prevent rights violations and retrospectively in order to punish rights violations and rectify past wrongs. Using force as well as threatening the use of force in order to enforce moral prohibitions that are enforceable does not amount to a rights violation. This is because the relevant rights have been forfeited by the aggressor who has violated or is about to violate someone's rights, thereby rendering the use of coercion permissible.[9] If rights are forfeited as a result of the rights-violating behaviour of individuals, coercion on the part of the state may be permissible.[10]

Whilst the state can be justified in using coercion to enforce moral prohibitions, on the basis that enforceable duties may permissibly be enforced, this justification of coercion does not straightforwardly carry over to the enforcement of compliance with positive laws, in particular laws that—unlike laws against, say, murder—do not simply codify and promulgate natural duties. States standardly make positive laws that go beyond the narrow content of protecting natural rights and use coercion to enforce compliance with these laws. For coercion to be justified in those cases it would either have to be the case that citizens have political obligation or that the state has political authority.

IV. Obligation and Authority

There are two general mechanisms that give rise to content-independent justifications for using coercion to ensure compliance with positive laws: political obligation and political authority.[11] On the one hand, if citizens have an enforceable content-independent obligation to do what the law says precisely because it is the law, then one can use coercion to enforce compliance with positive laws.[12] If citizens have political obligation and owe a duty of compliance, then the state can be justified in using coercion to ensure compliance.[13] On the other hand, coercion can be justified if the state has the requisite moral powers to impose duties on its citizens. If the state has political authority and is able to impose enforceable duties, coercion can be used permissibly to ensure compliance.

These two mechanisms differ in important ways. The former makes law-making into a form of duty-activation, whereas it amounts to duty-creation on the latter.[14] In the first case, citizens have a general duty to do what the law says, which is then triggered by the enactment of particular laws and thereby gives rise to specific duties. These specific duties are derivative. They are derived via factual detachment from a general standing obligation that is naturally understood in terms of a wide-scope requirement: OUGHT(the law requires ϕ-ing $\rightarrow$ ϕ) together with the facts about the specific laws that have been enacted. In the second case, the state exercises a moral power and creates specific duties by enacting laws, so that one acquires a duty to ϕ because it is the law that one should ϕ.[15] Such an exercise of a moral power creates non-derivative duties. This can be understood in terms of a narrow-scope requirement: the law requires ϕ-ing $\rightarrow$ OUGHT(ϕ). In this case, there is no prior standing duty from which the specific duties are derived. Instead, there is a standing liability. Put differently: the contrast is between citizens' being obligated to comply with a law that requires one to ϕ and a law's creating an obligation to ϕ for its citizens. Although one ends up with a duty to ϕ in each case, these duties are generated via different mechanisms. Whilst the political-obligation and political-authority models might seem to be practically equivalent and to generate the same sets of duties, they differ in important respects. Differences emerge, in particular, once one not only focuses on what actions people are required to perform and what the state may enforce but also takes into consideration to whom the duties are owed and who is being wronged in case of non-compliance. Similarly, differences emerge once one ceases to presume a fixed set of citizens but instead considers situations in which the set of citizens varies across time.

First, these mechanisms can differ in terms of the person or group to whom the resulting duty is owed. In the case of political obligation, the obligation is owed by citizens to whomever this general obligation is owed; i.e., the detached duty is owed to the same entity to whom the wide-scope conditional obligation is owed. This is standardly the state, but can also be some other agent or group of agents, such as the other members of a society, as might be thought to be the case, for instance, in the case of a social contract.[16] If x (the state) is owed political obligation by y (the citizen), then compliance with any law that x makes will be owed by y to x, even when the law concerns how y ought to treat z. If one has a standing obligation that is owed to the state, then the derived obligation to treat z in a certain way will not be owed to z (despite its being an obligation that concerns z) but will instead be owed to the state. Although the existence of the law might well give rise to reasonable expectations on the part of z, such that y ends up having (additional) reasons to comply with the law and treat z in a certain way that derive from z's interests, the enforceable obligation that derives from y's political obligation will not be owed by y to z but to x.[17]

In the case of political authority, by contrast, the law creates a duty that can be owed to particular individuals who are identified by the law. If x (the state) has a moral power to change the normative situation of y (the citizen), then it can create a duty for y that y owes to z. This is particularly clear when the state exercises its moral power to create rights and corresponding obligations. The resulting duties will be owed to the particular rights holders, not to the agent exercising the moral power, nor to the community of persons in whose name that agent is acting.[18] The duty created by someone who has authority need not be owed to that agent. If x exercises its authority and creates a (directed) duty for y to treat z in a certain way, then the one who is wronged in case y fails to act accordingly is the person z to whom the duty is owed, not the entity x that exercised authority and created the duty. Although violating a duty that has been created by someone who has the authority to do so conveys disrespect for that authority—i.e., one acts as if no duty had been created, as if the person did not have authority—this phenomenon of disrespect differs from wronging the one to whom the duty is owed.

To whom the duty is owed matters for the question who is being wronged. This, in turn, has various practical consequences such as to whom compensation is owed, to whom one needs to apologise, and which relationships are being impaired. It might be argued that the effects of the two mechanisms can be aligned as long as the state suitably specifies to whom compensation is owed. This, however, requires additional legislation, which means that the two mechanisms are not equivalent in the sense of giving rise to the same duties in the same circumstances. Moreover, whilst this might work when it comes to compensation, it does not work across the board. Problems arise, in particular, when one is concerned with the impairment of relationships. If y owes a duty to the state to the effect that y treat z in a certain way, then the state can make it the case that y needs to compensate z in case of non-compliance and maybe apologise to z, but the state cannot make it the case that y's relationship with z is impaired by non-compliance, and hence cannot make it the case that the apology is an appropriate response to the wronging, since the relationship that is impaired is that in which y stands to the person to whom the duty is owed.

Second, these mechanisms differ in terms of the conditions under which a duty arises for a particular individual.[19] As long as someone has a political obligation to obey the laws of a particular state, this person has a duty to comply with all the laws of that state. If x has political obligation at t, then x is under a duty to ϕ at t if there is a law in existence at t that requires ϕ-ing. In the case of political authority, by contrast, the duty comes into existence at the time of the enactment of the law for all those who at that time have the corresponding liability. If the state exercises its authority at t and creates a law requiring citizens to ϕ, then x is under a duty to ϕ only if x is a citizen and hence is under the authority of the state at the time at which the law is enacted.

This has important implications for those becoming citizens subsequent to the enactment of the law, such as later generations. The case of subsequent generations poses no difficulties for political-obligation approaches.[20] By acquiring a political obligation to obey the laws of a particular state—e.g., by consenting to a state—one is bound to comply with the laws of that state, independently of when they were enacted. Normative powers views, on the contrary, run into difficulties. The enactment of a law gives rise to a duty for those who are subject to the authority at the time of enactment.[21] If a law is enacted at time t, yet x only comes into existence at a later time t' or only becomes a citizen at t' with the liability to have one's normative situation changed by the law-making authority, then x will not be bound by that law. The initial exercise of the power only created obligations for those who had the liability at that time. Since x was not amongst them, the obligation needs to be created for x afresh. Put differently, becoming a citizen, on the political-authority approach, is a matter not of acquiring duties but of acquiring a liability. In order for duties to result from this liability, the authority needs to be exercised afresh; i.e., past exercises do not carry over to those who have only subsequently acquired the liability.[22]

Political obligation and political authority are not two sides of the same coin. They are different mechanisms that generate different duties and operate in different ways. These mechanisms are completely independent of each other. Contra Stephen Perry, it is not the case that we have an entailment in one direction but not the other direction, namely from political authority to the existence of a duty to obey but not vice versa. Instead, we have a forward-entailment problem in addition to the reverse-entailment problem identified by Perry. This is particularly clear when considering cases in which the state has authority but never exercises it, in which case the citizens do not acquire any obligations.[23] In order for political authority to give rise to duties, the relevant moral power must in fact be exercised. When it is exercised, its exercise gives rise to various specific duties, but not to a (general) duty to obey the law. Put differently, whenever there is a law requiring citizens to ϕ, there will be a corresponding duty to ϕ. There will not, however, be a general duty to obey the law. By contrast, a political obligation can be owed without the existence of any laws and without the activation of any duties.

Given a broad construal of the duty to obey the law (one that encompasses specific duties that can be created by law-making alongside the occurrent general duty to obey the law that can be triggered by law-making) as well as of political authority (one that encompasses both duty-creation and duty-activation), there will be entailment in both directions. The specific duties that political authority and political obligation yield (whether activated or created) will be the same when each is considered purely in terms of which actions citizens are required to perform or avoid performing (i.e., when we abstract from the question to whom the duties are owed). Given a narrow construal of each mechanism, by contrast, there will not be any entailment in either direction. As a result, the notion of political authority is not privileged over that of political obligation. Political authority and political obligation are simply two different mechanisms that operate in different ways, give rise to different duties, and can perform different justificatory work.

Whilst both mechanisms succeed in justifying the use of coercion to ensure compliance with positive laws, neither would seem to be applicable in the absence of consent. Political obligation, where this is understood as an enforceable content-independent duty to obey the laws of a particular state, can only be founded on consent. Other proposed mechanisms for explaining political obligation, such as duties of gratitude or fair play, fail to underwrite duties that satisfy the requirements of enforceability, content-independence, and particularity.[24] Although they can give rise to various pro tanto reasons, they do not succeed in generating enforceable content-independent obligations. Similarly, given the moral equality and independence of individuals, there is no natural moral inequality between states and their citizens (of the kind that is, say, suggested by the idea of the divine right of kings). As a result, moral powers have to be acquired. In order to acquire the relevant moral powers, the state would have to be authorised by its citizens: its citizens would need to consensually confer the relevant moral powers on the state.[25]

Since only consent can give rise to political obligation or confer the relevant moral powers on the state, justified non-consensual states are restricted to enforcing natural moral prohibitions and are not allowed to coercively enforce positive laws that go beyond these prohibitions. Laws can only be enforced to the extent that they merely codify and promulgate enforceable natural duties. This means that, in order for non-consensual states to be justified, they must be minimal states, in the sense that they are restricted to enforcing natural duties. If a non-consensual state creates laws and coerces people into doing things that they are not independently obligated to do, then this non-minimal state will be acting impermissibly and will not be justified. It will be coercively enforcing laws that it has created without having the right to do so. By making citizens comply with these laws as well as by punishing them for non-compliance, it will be violating the rights of its citizens.[26]

V. The Monopoly on Coercion

> The state grants that under some circumstances it is legitimate to punish persons who violate the rights of others, for it itself does so. How then does it arrogate to itself the right to forbid private exaction of justice by other nonaggressive individuals whose rights have been violated?[27]

Non-consensual states lack authority and their citizens do not have political obligation. Such states nevertheless have some fundamental coercive power.[28] The justification of coercion on the part of a non-consensual state is based on the right to enforce moral prohibitions. It is permissible for the state to employ (appropriate) force as well as the threat of force to prevent and punish rights violations. However, this is likewise permissible for everyone else. Everyone has the right to use force prospectively to prevent rights violations as well as retrospectively to punish those who have committed rights violations. In short, everyone is at liberty to enforce enforceable moral prohibitions.[29]

The state, however, claims a monopoly on coercion in a given territory.[30] In fact, this is one of the defining features of what it is to be a state (given a Weberian framework).[31] To justify the (minimal) state one must thus establish not only that it is permissible for the state to use coercion to enforce moral prohibitions but also that it is permissible for the state to claim a monopoly on coercion. In short, it has to be permissible for the state to use coercion to stop others from enforcing rights within a given territory.[32]

This means that even an ultraminimal state would seem to go beyond enforcing moral prohibitions by claiming a monopoly on coercion and thereby prohibiting and preventing private enforcement, despite the fact that there would seem to be no duty to refrain from engaging in private enforcement. As a result, it will violate the enforcement rights of those who have not consented to its rule. "If the private exacter of justice violates no one's rights, then punishing him for his actions (actions state officials also perform) violates his rights and hence violates moral side constraints."[33] This suggests that prohibiting private enforcement and claiming a monopoly on coercion itself amounts to a rights violation. This, in turn, implies that coercion on the part of the state in this regard at least will not be permissible. Yet, since the use of coercion needs to be permissible if the state is to be justified, this implies that there cannot be any justified non-consensual state.

Justifying the state's claim to a monopoly on coercion is rather difficult, given that enforcement rights are universal. The state of nature is a situation of moral equality, where no one is inherently subordinate to anyone else. There is no asymmetry as regards fundamental coercive power. Instead, individuals are symmetrically situated with respect to each other. Everyone can use coercion to enforce moral prohibitions and punish wrongdoing. In a civil condition, by contrast, only the state is meant to be justified in doing so. In order for its monopoly to be justified, the state needs to occupy a privileged position.

The state uses force and claims to be justified in doing things that individuals cannot permissibly do. Why is it permissible for the state to prohibit individuals from ϕ-ing (namely enforcing right) when it is fine for the state to ϕ? Explaining this asymmetry is difficult because a protective association derives its rights from its members. As Nozick notes, no new rights emerge at the group level. The rights of a protective association, and likewise of a state, have to be reducible:

> the legitimate powers of a protective association are merely the *sum* of the individual rights that its members or clients transfer to the association. No new rights and powers arise; each right of the association is decomposable without residue into those individual rights held by distinct individuals acting alone in a state of nature.[34]

Accordingly, it would seem that one can establish the requisite moral asymmetry only by means of consent. There are two possibilities. Either individuals voluntarily transfer their enforcement rights to the state and thereby render impermissible their own engagement in private enforcement, insofar as giving up these rights implies that they are no longer at liberty to engage in private enforcement. Or a state that can impose duties (either by exercising political authority or by triggering political obligation) can prohibit private enforcement and can thus make it impermissible for citizens to make use of coercion. Yet, in the absence of consent no such moral asymmetry arises, and it is consequently difficult to explain how the state can be permitted to do things that citizens are not permitted to do.[35]

VI. The De Facto Monopoly

The non-consensual state is not normatively privileged. It does not have some special right that others lack. This means that it does not have a *de jure* monopoly. Only those who have voluntarily transferred some of their rights to the state and over whom the state has some form of authority stand in an asymmetric normative relation to the state. Those who have not consented, by contrast, are the moral equals of the state. The difficulty is thus to reconcile the asymmetry implicated in a monopoly with a commitment to moral equality, without relying on consent.

Nozick's solution to this problem appeals to the notion of a de facto monopoly. Instead of having a *de jure* monopoly, the state merely has a de facto monopoly. The state is not normatively but only empirically privileged. Since there is no *de jure* asymmetry, there is no conflict with moral equality. Yet, the way in which the state is empirically privileged is nevertheless normatively significant. The asymmetry that is involved in a de facto monopoly does not concern the possession of rights but, rather, the exercise of rights. Although the state has the very same rights as everyone else, there is a right that is such that the state is the only one who is able to exercise this right. In virtue of its dominant position, the state is uniquely capable of exercising a right that everyone has.

Nozick points out that the enforcement of rights might well involve procedures which risk being unfair and unreliable and which thereby impose risks on others. He provides two arguments designed to show that this kind of risk imposition can be permissibly prohibited. On the one hand, one can appeal to procedural rights and argue that those who make use of risky enforcement procedures can be prohibited from engaging in enforcement since they would otherwise violate procedural rights. On the other hand, Nozick advances an epistemic principle of border crossing that implies that it is impermissible for x to punish y, even when y is guilty and doing so does not violate y's right, on the grounds that x has not suitably ascertained whether or not y is guilty; i.e., x is not in the requisite epistemic position to permissibly punish y.[36]

Whilst everyone has the right to prohibit enforcement that is based on procedures that they deem to be unfair or unreliable, the dominant protective agency is in a privileged position. It is not privileged because its procedures are somehow guaranteed to be fair and reliable. Nozick does not assume the dominant agency to be epistemically privileged or to have special insight into which procedures are fair and reliable. Instead, it is privileged by virtue of its strength.[37] Its strength puts it into a privileged position because "the right includes the right to stop others from wrongfully exercising the right, and only the dominant power will be able to exercise the right against all others."[38] The dominant agency can, accordingly, permissibly prohibit anyone else, in particular all independents (those individuals who have not consented) from engaging in private enforcement when using procedures that it deems to be unfair or unreliable. What the dominant agency deems to be fair and reliable then becomes the standard that ends up being enforced. Due to its strength, it can permissibly settle the question of what counts as a fair and reliable procedure.[39] Anything that deviates from the standards it adopts and is deemed unfair or unreliable will be prohibited. "The dominant protective agency will act freely on its own understanding of the situation, whereas no one else will be able to do so with impunity."[40] As a result, the dominant agency has a de facto monopoly and thus qualifies as an ultraminimal state.

The notion of a de facto monopoly in this way allows for an asymmetry at the level of the exercise of a right. It thereby justifies the state's claiming a monopoly on coercion in a way that is perfectly compatible with a commitment to moral equality.[41] In particular, it does not require any *de jure* monopoly that could only be established on the basis of unanimous consent on the part of all those governed by the state.[42]

VII. Conclusion

There is room for justified non-consensual states. This space, however, is very narrow and can only be filled by a state that has a de facto but not a *de jure* monopoly. This is the only way in which a state can permissibly claim a monopoly of force without the consent of the governed.[43] Such a state is only justified in enforcing natural rights and prohibiting those who use risky procedures from engaging in private enforcement.[44] As a result, a justified non-consensual state must take the form of a Nozickian minimal state. Non-minimal states, by contrast, can only be justified if their citizens authorise them to perform the additional activities that go beyond those required to enforce enforceable moral prohibitions.

Acknowledgements

For helpful comments on an earlier draft of this chapter, I am grateful to Roger Crisp and Johann Frick.

Notes

1 Robert Nozick, *Anarchy, State, and Utopia* (New York, NY: Basic 1974) 4.
2 Nozick ix.
3 This chapter focuses on the ways in which justification works within the hypothetical scenario that Nozick sketches in part I of *Anarchy, State, and Utopia*; i.e., on what makes a state justified in this idealised hypothetical situation. In Ralf M. Bader, "Counterfactual justifications of the state," *Oxford Studies in Political Philosophy* 3 (2017): 101–131, I explain how this hypothetical account is relevant to the justification of states in the actual world, arguing that historical principles justify the state within the idealised hypothetical scenario, whilst counterfactual principles connect this to the non-ideal circumstances of the actual world.
4 In addition, Nozick claims that justifying the state requires one to show that it is an improvement vis-à-vis the relevant non-state alternative, or that it at least does not constitute a deterioration (cp. Nozick 4–5). How exactly to understand the baseline for comparison is somewhat unclear. Does it have to be an improvement relative to what would happen if the state were to suddenly disappear? Relative to what would have happened had the state never come into existence? Or relative to a non-state situation that could feasibly be brought about? How one is to understand the notion of an improvement is also unclear. Does it have to be a Pareto improvement? Or is it enough that it is an improvement on average? The metric of evaluation is also unclear. Along which dimension does the improvement need to take place? Is the metric specified in terms of well-being, or in terms of the extent to which rights are respected? However one resolves these questions, it will be an empirical question whether a given state classifies as an improvement along the relevant metric vis-à-vis the relevant non-state alternative.
5 Nozick 6.
6 Nozick 58.
7 If one allows for rights to be overridden—i.e., if one does not treat them, at least in some cases, as absolute side constraints—then the state can permissibly infringe rights without violating them (to use Thomson's distinction). "We may (and, indeed, ought to) sometimes act in ways which infringe the rights of others, with no more justification than the great harm that would be done by allowing exercise of those rights. Governments will sometimes have such justifications for coercion (even where they lack the *right* to coerce), particularly where the well-being of many hangs in the balance or where unjust government threatens to replace just" (A. John Simmons, "The Anarchist Position: A Reply to Klosko and Senor," *Philosophy and Public Affairs* 16.3 (1987): 278). At least given a Nozickian view that treats rights as (quasi-absolute) side constraints, this can only be done in emergency situations to avoid moral catastrophes (cp. Nozick 30n). If the infringement of rights needs to meet a less rigorous justificatory burden, then this opens up room for the possibility of a Samaritan approach, in accordance with which the state can permissibly infringe rights in order to protect people from serious harm as long as doing so is not unreasonably costly. "[T]he presumption in favor of each citizen's freedom from coercion is outweighed by the necessity of political coercion to rescue all of us from the perils of the state of nature" (Christopher H. Wellman, "Liberalism, Samaritanism, and Political Legitimacy," *Philosophy and Public Affairs* 25 (1996): 219n13). On this approach, coercion will still be restricted to a limited set of cases.

8 Enforceability is understood in the sense that it is permissible to enforce these duties, not in the weaker sense that it is merely possible to enforce them. The restriction to enforceable moral prohibitions means that we are setting aside non-juridical perfect duties as well as various imperfect duties, such as duties of beneficence, that cannot permissibly be enforced.

9 Cp. Nozick 137–138.

10 In addition to removal by forfeiture, rights can be removed by someone who has the relevant authority to do so; i.e., by someone who has the Hohfeldian moral power to divest individuals of their rights. However, as we will see shortly, the relevant kind of authority can only be established on the basis of consent and hence does not open up any additional room for permissible coercion on the part of non-consensual states. Coercion may also be justified when directed toward innocent threats as well as innocent shields of threats (cp. Nozick 34–5). These difficult cases cannot be accounted for in terms of forfeiture. We can set these cases aside, since they plausibly serve as occasions for the permissible use of coercion not by third parties but only by those actually being threatened.

11 These two mechanisms are general and direct: the making of the law directly gives rise to an obligation. There can be specific indirect cases in which law-making triggers an independent duty; e.g., by solving a coordination problem (cp. Matthias Brinkmann, "A Rationalist Theory of Legitimacy" (DPhil diss., U of Oxford 2016) ch. 1.4.3). Duties that are created in this indirect manner do not satisfy content-independence (although it is arbitrary that a coordination problem is solved in one way rather than another, the reason for complying with the law is not due to its being a law but due to its providing a focal point that can solve the coordination problem) and may well not be sufficiently strong to warrant coercive enforcement.

12 Whilst being content-independent, the obligation can nevertheless be conditional; e.g., an obligation do what the law says because it is the law on condition that it is not unjust. (The same will be true in the case of political authority.)

13 Stephen Perry, "Law and Obligation," *American Journal of Jurisprudence* 50.1 (2005): 263–95, has pointed out that legal systems standardly do much more than attempting to impose obligations and that political obligation is not the relevant notion when it comes to characterising the normative relationship in which a citizen stands to laws that do not impose obligations but, say, attempt to create rights and permissions. (These cases should be characterised in terms of political authority on the part of the state and a liability to have their normative situations changed on the part of citizens.) This point, however, can be set aside for our purposes. When the permissibility of coercion is at issue, we are concerned with the behaviour of citizens. The question, in particular, is whether they are obligated to conform their behaviour in the way required by the law, so that the state can be justified in enforcing compliance. Political obligation will suffice just as well as political authority when it comes to justifying coercion on the part of the state. (Differences only arise if the state has the authority to directly take away the right not to be coerced in a particular way. Coercion could then be justified without having to proceed indirectly via creating a duty that can be coercively enforced.)

14 This terminology is due to Bas van der Vossen, "Imposing Duties and Original Appropriation," *Journal of Political Philosophy* 23.1 (2015): 64–85.

15 This is a narrow account of Hohfeldian powers that is restricted to duty-creation and does not encompass duty-activation. It is a normative view of the moral power that amounts to something more than the mere ability to change the normative landscape. (It is only by working with a normative rather than merely descriptive construal that one can explain why a moral power is a (second-order) right; i.e., one of the specific Hohfeldian incidents of the general notion of a right.) This robust understanding of normative powers goes together with a normative construal of immunities that makes room for immunity-violations; cp. Ralf M. Bader, "Liberty, Threats, and Ineligibility" (unpublished ms.).

16 That political obligation is a case of triggering duties is particularly clear when the duty is owed not to the state but to someone else, as when, for example, citizens promise each other to obey the commands of the state. In that case, the state clearly does not possess a moral power but can merely trigger a pre-existing obligation.

17 This is analogous to the way in which a promise made by y to x to look after z is owed to x. The beneficiary z can come apart from the entity x to whom the duty is owed.

18 Stephen Perry has suggested that the obligation is owed to the community in whose name the state is acting ("Law" 282n36). This, however, is not correct and does not follow from an apt understanding of the ways in which moral powers work in general.

19 Relatedly, they will also differ in terms of the persistence conditions of the duties that are triggered or created.

20 For an account of political obligation across generations, cp. Ela Leshem, "The State as a Moral Person and the Problem of Transgenerational Binding" (DPhil diss., U of Oxford 2018) ch. 3.

21 Cp. Stephen Perry, "Political Authority and Political Obligation," *Oxford Studies in Philosophy of Law* 2 (2013): 34: "[B]oth the power to impose the obligation, and, necessarily, the correlative liability to be subject to the obligation, must exist at the time that the directive is enacted."

22 Whilst one can generate the same sets of duties by means of additional exercises of authority, the fact that additional actions are required to generate these duties implies that the two mechanisms are not equivalent in the sense that they generate the same duties in the same empirical circumstances but at most in the sense that any duty that can be created by one mechanism can also be created by the other.

23 Perry, "Authority" 34, recognises that a moral power can exist without ever having been exercised.

24 Cp. A. John Simmons, *Moral Principles and Political Obligations* (Princeton, NJ: Princeton UP 1979).

25 A further potential mechanism for acquiring authority proceeds via rights forfeiture.

26 This does not mean that all unjustified states are equally bad (cp. A. John Simmons, "Justification and Legitimacy," *Ethics* 109.4 [1999]: 770). Although all unjustified states act impermissibly, they do so to varying degrees. Moreover, they can differ along a number of other dimensions; e.g., the extent to which they promote the welfare of their citizens.

27 Nozick 51.

28 Fundamental coercive power is power that does not rest on the consent of the person to whom it is applied (cp. Nozick 6). Coercive power that is conferred upon the state by those consenting to it is derivative and is only possessed contingently. Nozick is interested in the coercive power that a state does not just happen to possess as a contingent matter of fact but that it possesses fundamentally; i.e., in the conditions under which x (the state) can use force vis-à-vis y (a citizen) in the absence of y's consent. (This is part of the reason why Nozick ignores consent theory. Cp. David Miller, "The Justification of Political Authority," *Robert Nozick*, ed. David Schmidtz (Cambridge: CUP 2002) 16: "It is curious that Nozick gives no explicit attention to a Lockean contract as an alternative, more direct, route from the state of nature to a minimal state."

29 The situation is different when it comes to the right to exact compensation, which only resides with the victim (and which can be waived by the victim); cp. Nozick 135.

30 "A state claims a monopoly on deciding who may use force when; it says that only it may decide who may use force and under what conditions; it reserves to itself the sole right to pass on the legitimacy and permissibility of any use of force within its boundaries; furthermore it claims the right to punish all those who violate its claimed monopoly" (Nozick 23).

31 The monopoly on coercion is the crucial difference between a (dominant) protection agency and a state; more precisely, an ultraminimal state. This chapter only focuses on the monopoly aspect—i.e., on the ultraminimal state—and will set aside the step that results in a minimal state which involves protecting everyone's rights and consequently might be thought to involve an impermissible redistributive element.

32 This has two aspects: on the one hand, the state has to prohibit individuals within its territory from engaging in unapproved private enforcement, and, on the other, it has to prohibit other states, protective agencies, and individuals outside its territory from engaging in unapproved enforcement activities within its territory.

33 Nozick 52.

34 Nozick 89. Original emphasis.

35 The issue of explaining the moral asymmetry that is involved in the monopoly on coercion arises likewise when operating with a less robust conception of individual rights that makes it easier for rights to be infringed without being violated. If rights can be overridden more easily, it is easier for the state to do various things. Yet it is also easier for private individuals as well as other protection agencies and states to do those things, too.

36 Cp. Nozick 106–107. When operating with this epistemic principle, force can permissibly be used not only to enforce rights but also to enforce moral prohibitions that are not rights violations.

37 The fact that it is merely the strength of the agency that accounts for its privileged position suggests that transactional components are inessential for a state to be justified. Although the account of the hypothetical emergence of the state that Nozick advances is a historical account that is partly though not fully transactional, insofar as clients but not independents voluntarily become members of the dominant protective association, this is not essential. If strength is all that is needed to underwrite a de facto monopoly, a protective agency that were to arise *ex nihilo* could permissibly prohibit private enforcement despite not having any (or at any rate not many) clients simply on the basis of being the most powerful protective agency. In chapter 6 of *Anarchy, State, and Utopia*, Nozick tentatively puts forward the suggestion that the right to punish might be possessed jointly rather than individually. "*To the extent* that it is plausible that all who have some claim to a right to punish have to act jointly, then the dominant agency will be viewed as having the greatest entitlement to exact punishment, since almost all authorize it to act in their place. ... Having more entitlements to act, it is more entitled to act" (Nozick 139–40). Unlike the permissibility of prohibiting private enforcement, this greater entitlement is not

based on the strength of the association but on the number of clients that it has and hence can only result from a large number of individuals voluntarily deciding to become clients of that agency.

38 Nozick 109.

39 This is not a crude form of "might makes right." First, the dominant agency does not make it the case that something qualifies as fair. It does not constitute the relevant fairness facts. Instead, it settles, at least to a significant extent, in what way the notion of fairness will be interpreted in its territory and which standard of fairness and reliability will prevail. Second, not just any interpretation will qualify as admissible. It is not the case that anything goes. One can only permissibly prohibit the use of procedures that it is reasonable to deem unfair or unreliable.

40 Nozick 108.

41 There are multiple ways in which the ultraminimal state falls short of the Weberian conception of a monopoly on coercion. First, it does not adjudicate conflicts between non-clients but only prohibits non-clients from private enforcement vis-à-vis the agency's clients (cp. Nozick 109). Second, it does not prohibit independents that are known to use fair and reliable procedures. Third, the Weberian account considers the state to be the sole authoriser of the use of force, yet the dominant protective agency does not claim a *de jure* monopoly but only a de facto monopoly: it prevents and threatens to punish individuals for using unauthorised force, but it does not claim to have a special right to do so. For these reasons, Nozick calls it a "statelike entity" (cp. Nozick 117–118). The argument nevertheless does establish the permissibility of non-consensual rule and succeeds in introducing a normative asymmetry that does not rely on consent.

42 This kind of de facto monopoly can also be found in Kant's justification of the state, according to which the state is uniquely empirically positioned to enforce juridical laws; cp. Ralf M. Bader, "Kant and the Problem of Assurance" (unpublished ms.).

43 Another way to put the point is that the space for states that are justified but lack legitimacy (in the sense in which Simmons, "Justification," uses these terms) is very limited and can only be occupied by Nozickian minimal states that have de facto monopolies.

44 It is possibly also justified in infringing without violating rights in order to address emergency situations if rights are not absolute but can be overridden.

12

TWO CHEERS FOR ROTHBARDIANISM

Cory Massimino

I. Introduction

Murray N. Rothbard (1926–1995) was an economist, historian, political theorist, polemicist, activist, and founder of the variety of market anarchism he dubbed "anarcho-capitalism." Both his supporters and detractors too often remember him for his late-career influence on paleolibertarianism, a movement that sought to synthesize populist conservatism and libertarianism (and, in Rothbard's case, anarchism). After his turn to paleolibertarianism, Rothbard embraced Pat Buchanan and David Duke,[1] and called for the cops to be "unleashed" to "administer instant punishment."[2] My goal here is not to defend Rothbard's paleolibertarianism or reconcile it with anarchism, but to explore aspects and implications of his thought quite apart from paleolibertarianism, of which there is quite a bit. Rothbard had extensive influence on other anarchists, on libertarians, on conservatives, on radical leftists, on Austrian-school economists, and on others. In light of that, I think we should give Rothbard's work another look.

We can embrace important insights offered by Rothbard without endorsing his paleolibertarianism. We can't reasonably regard paleolibertarianism, which he embraced during the last fifteen years of his life, as definitive of his overall position, any more than we can consider Rothbard's prior affiliations with the Old Right[3] or the New Left[4] as somehow reflective of the authentic Rothbard. He enjoyed intra-group politicking and formed and destroyed many political alliances through the course of his life. If we want to understand his ideas, we should focus on the salient themes that can be consistently found across all his work over the course of his entire life and which guided his analytic focus throughout. We can call that bundle of themes "Rothbardianism." My specific interpretations of Rothbard might, at first, confound critics and admirers alike, but I believe they're all backed up by solid textual support. I hope the conversation around Rothbard can move past both cultish admiration and reflexive criticism and instead develop a sense of *critical admiration* for his thought.

"Rothbardianism," I suggest, mainly consists in four broad (and usually disparate) frameworks that he attempted to synthesize and unite into a coherent whole. Rothbard thought all the sciences of human action were interrelated.[5] He was both a *radical* thinker, in the sense of having an integrated, root-and-branch approach to social issues,[6] and a *dialectical* thinker,[7] in the sense of analyzing moral, social, cultural, political, and economic phenomena from different vantage points and levels of generality in order to make apparent different aspects and interrelationships.[8] I will give a broad overview of each of Rothbard's frameworks and the ways in which they fit together and reinforce each other in radical, dialectical fashion: (1) natural law theory in the tradition of Aristotle, (2) individualist anarchism in the tradition of Lysander Spooner, (3) liberal class theory in the tradition of Franz Oppenheimer, and (4) Austrian economics in the tradition of Ludwig von Mises. Then I will consider what other strands of anarchism can learn from Rothbardianism. Finally, I will explore potential lessons Rothbardianism can learn from other strands of thought, particularly classical and contemporary anarchism, and where the future of Rothbardianism might lie.

I want to note that Rothbard was a broad thinker and prolific writer. He was a system-builder with many parts to his system. Boettke notes, "For those who are concerned with not just philosophizing about the world, but changing it, Rothbard provides a vision of a systematic science of liberty."[9] There are surely aspects of Rothbard's lengthy body of work that I won't have time to explore here. But I hope to give a fair account of his overall thought and do justice to his legacy while also building upon it.

II. Natural Law Theory

On Rothbard's view, morality "is a special case of the system of natural law governing all entities of the world, each with its own nature and its own ends." The content of the moral law, then, depends upon the nature of the moral beings it concerns. But what is the essential nature of human beings? Rothbard followed Aristotle in thinking that what distinguishes humans from "inanimate objects and non-human living creatures," who "are compelled to proceed in accordance with the ends dictated by their natures," is the possession of "reason to discover such ends and the free will to choose" among them.[10] Rationality is the faculty that separates humanity from other natural kinds. It's our capacity for reason that enables us to direct our actions towards specific ends of our own choosing.

Not only do humans "always act purposely"; our "ends can also be apprehended by reason as either objectively good or bad for" humans.[11] On Rothbard's view, natural law theory provides a "science of happiness" that "elucidates what is best for man – what ends man should pursue that are most harmonious with, and best tend to fulfill, his nature."[12] Rational deliberation is the essential feature of human beings that we are uniquely suited for and which constitutes our unique flourishing. "The function of a human being is activity of the soul accord with reason."[13]

Central to Rothbard's natural law theory is his individualist ontology: it is only the individual human being "who thinks, feels, chooses, and acts."[14] Humans are metaphysically independent. Only the individual human being can develop the virtues necessary for rational flourishing. Yet the possibility of living a virtuous life presupposes the ability, or the freedom, to act according to virtue, according to one's own moral conscious. Attempts to compel virtue eliminate its very possibility. When people are coerced, they are taken "out of the realm of action into mere motion." Individual autonomy, self-direction, and the freedom to choose are constitutive of virtue. "To be moral, an act must be free."[15] The social conditions of freedom generate and sustain our very ability to act morally. "Force and mind are opposites; morality ends where a gun begins."[16] The centrality of moral agency committed Rothbard to a kind of radical egalitarianism – an egalitarianism not directly committed to economic, social, or legal equality, but rather to equality of *authority*.[17] For Rothbard, liberty is a condition in which no human being exercises authority over another; i.e. exercises physical violence to subject another to one's own ends. "[T]he specific equality of *liberty* … is compatible with the basic nature of man."[18]

But what about external materials, objects which are unlike our body in that we don't possess natural agency over them? A theory of rights that doesn't account for the material world beyond our immediate bodies treats humans as "self-subsistent floating wraiths." Because we are embodied and because we act in the physical world, our existence necessarily requires the ability to transform nature-given resources into usable and consumable objects. Human nature necessitates not only self-ownership, but also ownership of material objects to control and use.[19] Property rights are not tacked-on additions to but specific applications of the right of self-ownership. Long calls this the "incorporation principle," according to which the alteration of external objects such that they become instruments of my ongoing projects transforms them into extensions of myself.[20] Incorporated objects become related to me such that no one can subject them to their purposes without subjecting *me* to their purposes.[21]

Rothbard's natural law theory doesn't reject the Aristotelian insight that human nature is essentially social. On Rothbard's view, self-ownership rights are merely the *application* of our social nature. Humans are *metaphysically* independent, but *socially* interdependent. Rothbard thought our social nature is best expressed by a scheme of self-ownership that enables social cooperation and protects people from being violently subordinated to others' ends. It's our social nature, and the freedom humans require to act on that social nature, that undergirds our obligation to respect the self-ownership rights of others.

Rothbard made a radical, dialectical case for the idea that humans were "not made for one another's uses."[22] He grounded such a theory in the centrality of individual autonomy, self-direction, and freedom to choose for flourishing as rational and social beings. Natural law theory offers a system of compossible rights that are inherent in our humanity and which establishes just physical boundaries between moral agents such that agents can't violently subordinate each other. This view has profoundly "radical and revolutionary"[23] implications for social and political thought.

III. Individualist Anarchism

Rothbard disagreed, not with the view that we're social animals, but with the conventional implications of that view for political theory. Many political theorists see the state as a vehicle of collective decision-making in which the members of a given society come together in the pursuit of common goals. But where many see the state as a bulwark of social cooperation, Rothbard saw it as the epitome of social disintegration.

> A common defense of the State holds that man is a 'social animal,' that he must live in society, and that individualists and libertarians believe in the existence of 'atomistic individuals' uninfluenced by and unrelated to their fellow men. But no libertarians have ever held individuals to be isolated atoms; on the contrary, all libertarians have recognized the necessity and the enormous advantages of living in society, and of participating in the social division of labor. The great non sequitur committed by defenders of the State, including classical Aristotelian and Thomist philosophers, is to leap from the necessity of society to the necessity of the State. On the contrary, as we have indicated, the State is an antisocial instrument, crippling voluntary interchange, individual creativity, and the division of labor. 'Society' is a convenient label for the voluntary interrelations of individuals, in peaceful exchange and on the market.[24]

For Rothbard, the distinction between state and society is of primary importance. The state is merely a subset of society, a single institution among many. What distinguishes the state from other social institutions is its inherently compulsory and predatory nature. "Throughout history, groups of men calling themselves 'the government' or 'the State' have attempted – usually successfully – to gain a compulsory monopoly of the commanding heights of the economy and the society."[25] Such predatory compulsion violates Rothbard's radical egalitarianism of authority and goes against our and rational and social nature.

There are two aspects to the coercive, anti-social nature of the state. First, it's a monopoly. That is, the state has unliterally designated itself as the sole provider of infrastructure, education, arbitration, defense, etc., within its territory. A crucial feature of the state's monopoly status is its "control of the use of violence: of the police and armed services, and of the courts – the locus of ultimate decision-making power in disputes over crimes and contracts." The state necessarily rests on physical coercion that precludes other people or groups of people from providing many of the goods and services it provides. The state's monopoly over the use of violence is directly related to the second aspect of its coercive nature: taxation. "Control of the police and the army is particularly important in enforcing and assuring all of the State's other powers, including the all-important power to extract its revenue by coercion." Non-state entities in society (except criminal enterprises) obtain their income through voluntary trade and/or gifts, whereas states obtain their income by the use of physical coercion. This means that taxation is morally equivalent to theft, "even though it is theft on a grand and colossal scale which no acknowledged criminals could hope to match. It is a compulsory seizure of the property of the State's inhabitants, or subjects."[26] Rothbard is heavily indebted to Spooner, who observed "that the government, like a highwayman, says to a man: 'Your money, or your life.'"[27]

Neither can a majority vote ground a voluntary relationship between any particular person and the state. Even if every state action were endorsed by a majority, this would simply amount to majority tyranny instead of any actual process of voluntary interaction. Popularity does not make the immoral moral. What of the act of voting itself? Has someone who votes in a state election thereby consented to the edicts that result from that election? Rothbard again turned to the work of Spooner, who argued that despite never consenting to the use of the ballot box, citizens are faced with the binary choice of not voting, and becoming a slave, or voting in self-defense, and becoming a master.[28] Any such vote cannot be interpreted as consent.

Rothbard drew heavily on Bastiat, who identified the conflation of state and society as the root problem of state socialism. "Socialism, like the ancient ideas from which it springs, confuses the distinction between government and society ... [E]very time we object to a thing being done by government, the socialists conclude that we object to its being done at all."[29] Hence, opposition to state education, infrastructure, arbitration, defense, etc. is interpreted as opposition to education, infrastructure, arbitration, defense, etc., per se, when in fact there exists a whole array of proposed alternatives to state monopolies such as voluntary trade, entrepreneurship, mutual aid, and decentralized cooperation. On Rothbard's view, these services currently monopolized by the violent, invasive, parasitic, and corrupt state should, could, and would be better provided by unhampered market processes, a view we will consider at more length in the section below on Austrian economics.

Rothbard made a radical, dialectical case that all "external government is tyranny" and that it is necessary we abolish the state because individuals have the right to govern themselves.[30] States inherently depend on violence and prevent their subjects from cultivating virtue, engaging in social cooperation, and leading flourishing lives. Any suppositions of implied consent merely serve to disguise state violence. Yet to fully understand and resist statism, we must also understand the institutions states are intertwined with.

IV. Liberal Class Theory

Rothbard followed Oppenheimer in distinguishing between two fundamental modes of social interaction, two ways of acquiring resources and satisfying one's desires: the economic means, which consists in relying on one's own labor and the equivalent exchange thereof, and the political means, which consists in the physically coercive appropriation of the labor of others, and the organization of which we call the state.[31] Economic means *logically* precede the political means because production *metaphysically* precedes predation. Goods must be produced before they can be appropriated. Social cooperation is prior to states, which only emerge once there exists producers to prey upon; i.e. once conquest and exploitation become viable. Statism causes social disintegration by dividing society into two classes, one that thrives on force and one that thrives on freedom, one that subsists via violent expropriation and one that subsists via voluntary production.

Rothbard argued the "ruling elite" consists in "the full-time apparatus – the kings, politicians, and bureaucrats who man and operate the State; and the groups who have maneuvered to gain privileges, subsidies, and benefices from the State."[32] The ruling class encompasses both the state and the state-adjacent institutions that rely on expropriation for their continued existence. Rothbard lamented the "grave deficiency" of libertarians that "worship Big Business" and fail to realize that under the modern neo-mercantilist, neo-fascist corporate state, "bigness is a priori highly suspect, because Big Business most likely got that way through an intricate and decisive network of subsidies, privileges, and direct and indirect grants of monopoly protection."[33] Rothbard argued the regulations thought to "reign in" big business were actually supported by big business in order to cartelize the economy.[34]

Rothbard consequently took a revisionist approach to the Progressive Era, which he considered a period not in which an altruistic state rescued ordinary people from robber barons, but in which "right-wing collectivism based on war, militarism, protectionism, and the compulsory cartelization of business" reasserted itself disguised in a "proindustrial and pro-general-welfare face." Predatory robber barons were actually propped up at the expense of ordinary people. "The Old Order returned," this time benefitting the army, bureaucracy, and corporations.[35] The dominance of the corporate, neo-mercantilist state heavily depended upon the existence of intellectuals in academia and journalism to foster a socio-cultural atmosphere conducive to statism, militarism, and corporatism.[36]

The Progressive Era reassertion of "right-wing collectivism" was not incidental for Rothbard. He argued that despite conventional categorization, socialism (of the statist variety) is best understood, not as a far left ideology, but a confused, middle-of-the-road ideology, trying to achieve the *ends* of freedom, dignity, peace, and progress (which were historically associated with left-wing liberalism) using the *means* of coercion, hierarchy, exploitation, and militarism (which were historically associated with right-wing conservatism). Socialism is conceptually unstable and doomed to fail because its conservative means are incompatible with its liberal ends.[37] Economic planning is not accidentally but inherently reactionary, modeled on feudalism and consisting in the militarization of economic activity itself.[38] Statism necessitates illiberalism.

In this light, Rothbard's turn to paleoconservatism could be seen as an odd deviation from much of his thought because he previously considered conservatism (excluding the more libertarian Old Right) the polar opposite of libertarianism, going as far as to call conservative-libertarian fusionism "illogical and mythical."[39] After all, if state socialism is an incoherent middle position aiming at liberal ends via conservative means, then the reverse, aiming at conservative ends via liberal means, must also be an incoherent middle position. Only liberal means can achieve liberal ends.

The military-industrial complex was central to Rothbard's liberal class theory. He agreed with Bourne that "war is the health of the state."[40] Rothbard went as far as to say the resources of big businesses bound up in America's "imperialistic foreign policy" ought to be redistributed from the exploiter class back to the exploited class. "Eager lobbyists" and "co-founders of the garrison state" ought to be met with "confiscation and reversion of their property" over to homesteading workers, taxpayers, or both.[41] Rothbard considered capitalists who undertake foreign investments based on land theft against peasants no different than feudal landlords,[42] and argued the descendent of slaves were entitled to reparations[43] – though he rescinded his support for reparations after his turn to paleoconservatism.[44]

Rothbard made a radical, dialectical case against the corporate state, the military-industrial complex, and the class stratification rooted in state violence on behalf of entrenched elites. But to fully understand what undergirded Rothbard's liberal class theory, you must also understand the nature and potential of the market processes exploited by the ruling class.

V. Austrian Economics

Underlying Rothbard's individualist anarchism and liberal class theory was his fundamental belief in the profound benefits of mutually beneficial economic exchange. Rothbard developed his economic theories using the praxeological analysis of his teacher Ludwig von Mises, but replaced Mises's Kantian-rationalist epistemological foundations with Aristotelian-empiricist ones.[45] In the Austrian view, praxeology is the theoretical framework within which we make logical sense of human choices and thereby *interpret* the actions of others.[46] Praxeological analysis has its roots in Socrates's insight that people are motivated by what they believe to be good.[47] Socrates thought actions can be explained in terms of the beliefs and desires of the agents who perform them. "Everyone always wants good things."[48] In this way, Socrates discovered a necessary and conceptual truth about the logical structure of human action by articulating a specific internal relationship between means and ends.

Economic analysis emerges from a distinguishing feature of individual human beings: purposeful action that employs scarce means to attain future ends, "economizing" resources by directing them towards one's most valued desires. The existence of multiple individuals engaged in their own economizing gives rise to the possibility of *interpersonal exchange* as a means to satisfy ends. Mutual exchanges are exchanges in which all parties expect to benefit. The possibility of mutual beneficence is a product of the psychological, physiological, and environmental diversity across human beings, giving rise to situations wherein one party values goods and services they currently possess less than goods and services another party currently possesses, and vice versa. What emerges is a "highly complex, interacting latticework of exchanges" facilitated by specialization under the division of labor.[49] Voluntary trade best embodies individuals' demonstrated preferences, thereby maximizing social utility at any given time.[50]

The possibility for widespread mutual exchange leads to a highly interconnected social order of peaceful cooperation that encourages sympathy, solidarity, benevolence, and friendship.[51] Market processes also incentivize entrepreneurship – the "essence of production" attributable to both producers and consumers – and the efficient allocation of scarce resources through the profit/loss mechanism of the price system. Without price signals that "telegraph" consumers' constantly shifting preferences to producers, it's impossible to narrow the array of *technologically* feasible production projects down to the *economically* feasible ones.[52] Prices emerging from mutual exchange are knowledge surrogates that aid our imperfect cognitive abilities in discovering the most effective way to employ scarce resources.[53]

Where mutual exchange is positive-sum, physical coercion is negative-sum, decreasing social utility[54] and encouraging hostility, violence, and war.[55] Society cannot subsist entirely on physical coercion because exploiters always needs a class of exploited on which to prey. The impossibility of total central planning is seen in the way socialist states, lacking prices that accurately reflect relative scarcities, rely on international and black-market prices to perform internal economic calculation. Rothbard extended Mises's insights into economic calculation from socialist states to capitalist firms. Rational calculability disappears when external markets are absorbed within a single firm, creating increasingly large "sphere[s] of irrationality."[56] Without external market prices, firms have only arbitrary symbols with which to allocate internal factors, implying a "*definite maximum to the relative size of any particular firm on the free market.*"[57] Without the support of the corporate state, these "islands of noncalculable chaos [that] swell to the proportions of masses and continents"[58] would likely suffer competitive losses, undergirding the Rothbardian a priori suspicion of big business.

Crucial to the development of the corporate state was the central bank, which perpetuated the war economy and class stratification by redistributing resources to rent-seeking elites via new money before the emergence of inflation-adjusted prices.[59] Monetary expansion undertaken by central banks also causes business cycles by disconnecting interest rates from genuine savings, inducing widespread entrepreneurial error, and distorting the relative prices of labor, materials, and machines. This "boom" is not a free lunch, but an unsustainable, systematic distortion of the structure of production. During the "bust," economic actors reassert their consumption and investment preferences and liquidate their malinvestments.[60] Fiscal and monetary stimulus designed to prop up prices and induce further investment merely prevents the necessary economic adjustments and prolong the contractionary period.[61] Rothbard envisioned a system of "free banking" and 100 percent gold reserves as the most effective alternative to central banks.[62]

Rothbard made a radical, dialectical case for extended social cooperation in the form of voluntary trade. Praxeological analysis shows that mutual benefit can be realized through mutual exchange and that central planning, whether undertaken by states or firms, is doomed to fail. There are other aspects to natural law theory, individualist anarchism, liberal class theory, and Austrian economics that I don't have the space to touch on here. But I hope to have provided a sketch of Rothbard's thought and shown how he synthesized these four traditions into a harmonious picture that seeks to achieve human flourishing and freedom.

VI. What Other Anarchists Can Learn from Rothbard

Many anarchists have historically exhibited hostility towards natural law theory, liberal class theory, and Austrian economics. They are deeply skeptical of the system of mutual exchange and property rights that Rothbard advocated. Where Rothbard saw the potential for peaceful cooperation and mutual sympathy, many anarchists instead see the potential for anti-social competition and insatiable greed. Chomsky considers Rothbard's vision to be a dysfunctional world of hatred.[63] Rothbard's approach is frequently written out of many understandings of the anarchist tradition. But this robs many anarchists of the insights offered by natural law theory, liberal class theory, and Austrian economics, and how those traditions can prove valuable elements of anarchist thought. Rothbardianism offers compelling alternatives to many aspects of contemporary anarchist theory.

Some anarchists object to natural law theory because they consider it an instance of coercive imposition and external authority. Bakunin maintained that,

> the liberty of man consists solely in this: that he obeys natural laws because he has *himself* recognised them as such, and not because they have been externally imposed upon him by any extrinsic will whatever, divine or human, collective or individual.[64]

Some anarchists, including those that later influenced Rothbard, embraced nihilism and viewed *all* moral claims, not just ones rooted in natural law theory, as unjustifiable impositions. Following Stirner, Tucker acknowledged only those obligations which have been voluntarily assumed.[65] Such a view immediately rules out the existence of natural rights because we are obliged to respect the natural rights of others whether we choose to or not. Moral obligations (including, but not limited to, natural rights) arise from the ongoing project we are all engaged in all the time: living life, pursuing projects, and interacting with others. Annas argues,

> Happiness [in the eudaimonist sense] has the role of being, for each person, *your* happiness, the way *you* achieve living your life well. It is not some plan imposed on you

> from outside, or a demand made by some theory which has not arisen from your own thoughts about your life.[66]

On a eudaimonist view, it isn't sensible to consider moral obligations unjustified external impositions.

Some anarchists accept the existence of moral obligations and rights but ground them in theories other than Aristotelian natural law theory. One option is to ground anarchism in the value of justice; i.e. respecting every individual's inherent autonomy. Such theorists argue the authority of the state is unjust because it violates the autonomy of individuals.[67] Another option is to ground anarchism in the value of benefit; i.e. achieving the greatest consequences for the greatest number. Such theorists argue the authority of the state is harmful because it reaps bad consequences.[68] On the eudaimonist view, this is a false dichotomy. Focusing on justice alone obscures the moral relevance of benefit (and the ways in which the state is harmful), and focusing on benefit alone obscures the moral relevance of justice (and the ways in which the state is unjust). Our conceptions of justice and benefit stand in reciprocal determination, in a way similar to how "master" and "slave" are "relative to themselves."[69] We can't understand one isolated from the other, and vice versa. Long argues, "[J]ustice and benefit are conceptually entangled; their internal conceptual dynamic drives them into alignment with one another." Therefore, "[s]emi-deontological considerations of justice play a role in determining what counts as good consequences; semi-consequentialist considerations of benevolence and prudence play a role in determining what counts as just."[70] We don't have to choose between justice and autonomy on the one hand, and benefit and good consequences on the other. States both violate autonomy and reap harmful consequences. Statism is bad because it's both unjust and harmful.

Bookchin views natural law theory as "basically liberal, grounded in the myth of the fully autonomous individual whose claims to self-sovereignty are validated by axiomatic 'natural rights'."[71] Yet such rights are not "axiomatic" in the sense of being groundless. Natural law theory is grounded in the physical and social requirements for human flourishing. Natural rights constitute our duties to one another as social beings, for social relations gain their worth and meaning from being chosen. They uphold our metaphysical independence so that we have an autonomous space in which to engage in social interdependence. Instead of a static conception of community in which individuals are defined, directed, and determined by predefined roles, Rothbard's natural law theory provides a dynamic conception of community in which different communities can be continually "formed, reformed, and modified."[72] A society that consists in consensual relationships enables people to peacefully progress beyond old, harmful social relations and form new, beneficial ones. By rejecting any "ontological conflict" between "individualism and sociality,"[73] such an account of human nature avoids treating humans in either an "atomistic" manner (which conflates our *metaphysical* independence with *social* independence, reducing the community to a mere collection of individual entities) or an "organicist" manner (which conflates our social *inter*dependence for metaphysical *inter*dependence, dissolving individuals into a mere single communal entity).[74] We are both *in*dependent and *inter*dependent beings.

Natural law theory provides a useful tool for contemporary anarchist theory. For Rothbard, natural rights are the main bulwark against state oppression and reveal state violence for what it truly is. Natural law theory provides a principled justification for anarchist political ideals, whereas other justifications – nihilism, deontology, consequentialism, atomism, and/or organicism – leave anarchism on shaky ground. Not only that, Rothbard's natural law theory spells out the norms to which a society must adhere in order to achieve, and maintain, freedom. It grounds the legal arrangements of a truly free society and a vision of peaceful, voluntary cooperation without the state. Natural rights are integral to any account of human flourishing and freedom.

Rothbard is also written out of many understandings of anarchism because he embraced markets. Anarchism has a long history of opposing markets. Guerin, Bookchin, and other influential anarchist theorists seem unaware of market-process literature and insist that anarchism must be anti-market.[75] On the conventional view, market processes are seen as unfair forces of restraint, authority, and inequality. Rather than facilitating a desirable allocation of scare resources or improving the well-being of the majority, markets are said to disproportionally reward the powerful and harm the marginalized. Many consider exploitation, privilege, power, and hierarchy inherent to markets.[76] Rothbard's vision has been seen as a mere "pretense of statelessness" and "a cleverly designed and worded surrogate for elitist and aristocratic conservatism."[77] Despite their contemporary unpopularity, markets aren't completely foreign to the anarchist tradition. Rothbard's integration of liberal class theory and Austrian economics with individualist anarchism led to a revival of the market anarchism that was pioneered by Molinari in the 1850s.[78] "Liberal anti-statism virtually disappeared" until Rothbard revived it in the late 1950s.[79] But disregarding market-process thought is a central mistake of contemporary anarchist theory.

Traditional interpretations underrate the extent to which Rothbard's market-process thought is deeply egalitarian. The right to exit any social relationship is a powerful check on interpersonal exploitation. Freed markets ultimately permit individuals to make their own decisions, facilitating "symmetrical" social relationships and "equality in the sense that each person has equal power" to make choices. Freed markets promote "self-responsibility, freedom from violence, full power to make one's own decisions (except the decision to institute violence against another), and benefits for all participating individuals."[80] Moreover, unhampered market processes – by taking the logic of separation of powers to its fullest possible extent – check authority, induce accountability, and disperse power far more effectively than arrangements that try to simulate market competition in monopolistic contexts.[81] For these reasons, it's been suggested that Rothbard's *Power and Market* should be renamed *Power or Market*.[82]

The truly exploitative society is one that systematically permits and enables physical coercion. Such a society is defined by asymmetrical power and hegemonic relationships. Unfree markets promote "rule of violence, the surrender of the power to make one's own decisions to a dictator, and exploitation of subjects for the benefit of the masters."[83] For Rothbard, the idea that trade is inherently exploitative and that "one party can benefit only at the expense of the other" (as in traditional Marxist class theories) follows fundamentally mercantilist logic, a view which ignores the consistent propensity for humans to engage in trade for mutual gain.[84]

Rothbard recognized the "natural affinity between wealth and power" and the vicious cycle it creates in which wealth is used to obtain political power, which is then used to obtain more wealth, and so on.[85] But for Rothbard the source of that social power ultimately lies in the state. Rather than preventing exploitation, forceful interference into otherwise free and harmonious exchange is best understood as the *cause* of exploitation. Whenever anyone wielding force (the state, the mafia, democratic federations, etc.) intervenes into market processes, a conflict of interests emerges, creating a "scramble to be a net gainer rather than a net loser – to be part of the intervening team, as it were, rather than one of the victims."[86] For Rothbard, economic exploitation emerges from violent intervention. Dismantling political power would dismantle economic power. It's not so much that economic power is foreign to Rothbard[87] but that he adopted a different causal explanation, and therefore, a different normative analysis of economic power from the ones usually offered by contemporary anarchist theory.

Most anti-capitalist anarchists see decentralized economic planning in the form of democratic federations and the like as the only alternative that avoids the pitfalls of both markets and states. Small-scale, direct deliberation and cooperation is meant to replace the irrationality of impersonal market processes without establishing any sort of tyrannical dictatorship.[88] But abandoning economic freedom in favor of economic planning is counterproductive to many anarchist aims. Economic planning, whether centralized within a state or decentralized within democratic federations, would reap severe calculational chaos without an ounce of egalitarianism.

The knowledge that prices convey about differing technologies, production processes, factor combinations, etc., is generated by a process of *entrepreneurial* rivalry in which tacit judgements about subjective preferences, expectations, and plans are reflected through voluntarily bidding for resources. This is completely different than the *political* rivalry entailed by economic planning. Where entrepreneurial rivalry utilizes dispersed tacit knowledge and conveys information anonymously, political institutions (centralized or decentralized) involve a direct struggle for privilege. Where entrepreneurial rivalry provides useful signals to other market participants through price changes, political rivalry only facilitates new control over the apparatus of planning. Where entrepreneurial rivalry incentivizes satisfying the desires of others better than one's rivals, political rivalry incentivizes intimidation and deception to gain and maintain control.[89] Without the price system, anti-market anarchism would lead to widespread impoverishment and starvation.[90]

Economic planning particularly harms the marginalized by privileging the majority and enabling the domination of sexual, racial, etc., minorities who don't conform to the singular economic plan. Economic planning creates an "aristocracy of pull"[91] by tying the ability to live (and in what fashion) to one's social standing, thereby privileging the popular, persuasive, and charismatic at the expense of the unpopular, awkward, and disliked. Perhaps such an arrangement would yield agreeable results when community printing presses are denied to avowed white supremacists, but when a trans person needs specific medical resources, wouldn't the increased collective decision-making power of transphobes over the "community medical resources" pose a problem in need of a solution? That solution is freed markets, which provide an institutional escape valve for society's most marginalized – a mechanism connecting the ability to live (and how) to one's own independent effort.[92]

Economic planning amounts to an "ambitious aspiration of entirely replacing the competitive market system with a deliberate pre-coordination of all productive activity, incorporating it into a single hierarchical structure."[93] In light of the market-process analysis of economic planning, we must ask if it can really achieve anarchist aims. If state socialism is a confused, unstable position aiming at liberal ends via conservative means, anarcho-communism is its slightly less confused sibling, aiming at liberal ends via some liberal means (voluntary association) but also some conservative means (economic planning). The conventional anti-capitalist anarchist vision of planning shares many of the undesirable features associated with statism; not only planning but also, and despite anarchist intentions, hierarchy, bureaucracy, and domination.

Rothbardianism helps anarchists avoid the misguided temptation to try and leverage the reins of political monopolies for noble ends. Market competition, rooted in and reflective of the right to exit, is the remedy for exploitation because it is a levelling force that disperses socioeconomic power and provides people with more and better options to choose from.[94] Lavoie contends, "The citadels of power are in fact, whether they know it or not, more threatened by the spontaneous forces of the openly competitive market than by any other factor. Power thrives on coercive obstructions to market competition."[95] This points the way towards a model of social change that takes seriously the potential for exit rights, spontaneous order, and economic exchange in helping to liberate marginalized people from institutions of domination.

Anarchists who reject market-process thought are missing out on a rich, robust account of human flourishing and freedom, on which a compelling case for anarchism heavily rests. Market-process thought is so important for contemporary anarchist theory precisely because it best explains how to avoid a society of violence and exploitation and how to create a society of peace and mutual gain. Moreover, market-process thought helps us imagine, and perhaps develop, effective institutional alternatives to statism. Anarchism, to be viable, beneficial, and widespread, must embrace the freedom to trade.

Rothbard's primary contributions to contemporary anarchist theory lie in his integration of anarchism with (1) eudaimonist thought in the tradition of Aristotle, and (2) market-process thought in the tradition of Mises. Such a combination avoids the (1) analytic narrowness of nihilistic, deontological, consequentialist, atomistic, and/or organicist conceptions of anarchism, (2) impoverished models of Marxist class theory and economic planning, including statism now or federations later, and (3) impractical models of social change that discourage entrepreneurial direct action and instead devote resources to the impossible task of leveraging the state and other forms of economic planning for liberatory ends.

VII. Rothbardianism against Domination in All Forms

At the same time, if he were still alive Rothbard would have a lot to learn from other traditions of thought, particularly classical and contemporary anarchism. Rothbard and many of those he's influenced haven't shared the universal hostility to all forms of domination that has been historically characteristic of the anarchist tradition.[96] Rothbardianism provides a useful framework by which to approach moral, political, and economic analysis, but it's also in search of a more comprehensive and holistic account of human flourishing and freedom. Samuels criticizes Rothbard for having an exceedingly narrow conception of interpersonal power and exploitation that blinds him to important injustices.[97] I think Samuels is correct in identifying this deficiency of Rothbardianism. But we need not jettison his core frameworks to save Rothbard from this objection. In fact, the core frameworks of Rothbardianism might prove themselves more complementary to the traditional anarchist opposition to domination in all its forms than both Rothbard and his detractors realize. In my view, Rothbard's concern for equal liberty should extend to a rejection of interpersonal domination; specifically, the domination of women, queer people, racial minorities, children, and/or people with disabilities. A principled opposition to interpersonal domination in all forms could earn Rothbardianism that third cheer.

Rothbard focused his social analysis almost exclusively on *violence*, especially the violence of the state. But what about morally objectionable, yet non-violent, conduct and institutions? Rothbard discussed some institutions in league with the state that he opposed – especially the corporate state, the military-industrial complex, and their intellectual apologists. But he never extended that opposition to institutions that enforce hierarchies reflective of gender, sexuality, race, age, and/or disability. For much of his career, Rothbard denied any inherent relationship between opposition to physical coercion and other considerations; between the domains of politics and culture,[98] a position some Rothbardians still adopt today.[99] Sciabarra considers such a narrow concern for physical coercion insufficiently dialectical and therefore a form of "unanchored utopianism."[100]

Later, Rothbard still considered opposition to physical coercion logically separable from other considerations, but not psychologically, sociologically, or practically separable, a shift that led him to endorse a culturally conservative outlook.[101] Rothbard heavily criticized the Women's Liberation Movement;[102] endorsed "racialist science";[103] dismissed heterosexism, ableism, ageism,[104] and other "victimologies";[105] and looked down upon "free spirits" who didn't want to push others around or be pushed around themselves.[106] Some Rothbardians actively endorse institutions of interpersonal domination. Hoppe contends that societies "dominated by white, heterosexual males … patriarchal family structures … and aristocratic lifestyle[s]" are, in virtue of such domination, more successful, more non-violent, and more prosperous, and that this "Western" model of social organization ought to be "respected and protected."[107]

By focusing almost exclusively on the political structures of physical coercion, Rothbard left a hole in his social theory. He should have been deeply concerned with non-violent domination because "if libertarianism is rooted in the principle of *equality of authority*, then there are good reasons to think that not only political structures of coercion, but also the whole *system* of status and unequal authority deserves libertarian criticism." Such a system includes not just physical coercion, but also ideas, practices, and institutions rooted in submission to authority figures such as superiors in one's personal relationships, family, workplace, and community. Even a stateless society could feature pervasive submission to authority, in which everyone "voluntarily agree[s] to bow and scrape when speaking before the (mutually agreed-on) town Chief." Assuming such behavior is only kept in line through verbal harangues, social ostracism, glorifying the authorities, etc., no one's individual rights would be violated.[108] While not logically incoherent, a culturally conservative outlook is difficult to reconcile with the underlying reasons for libertarian equality: the value of autonomy, self-direction, and the freedom to choose.

If individuals matter so much that none can never be justly subjected to the ends of another via physical coercion, then it seems like they must matter enough that they should just never be subordinated to the ends of another, via physical coercion or otherwise. Non-physical coercion can take the form of subjecting another to one's ends by threatening to deprive them of their human needs such as food, shelter, mental well-being, informed decision-making, social relationships, etc. One has power over another to the extent that one can get them to do something they wouldn't otherwise do *because* of their deprivation.[109] Situations of desperate need and deprivation, where no one has been physically coerced, can give rise to interpersonal domination. Opposition to the hierarchical power imbalances of interpersonal domination can be understood as relational egalitarianism, which aims to abolish all forms of oppression, exploitation, marginalization, and violence such that no one need "bow and scrape" before others as a condition of being afforded dignity. Achieving the goals of relational egalitarianism entails a "social order in which persons stand in relations of equality."[110]

Rothbardians and relational egalitarians alike might be asking if I could really be serious in suggesting that Rothbardianism is complementary with relational egalitarianism. The reason I see such potential in synthesizing the two is because I think, despite their resistance to one another, together they can offer a comprehensive, holistic account of human flourishing and freedom. Anderson rejects such a link on the grounds that the libertarian emphasis on *exit* over *voice* fails to enable people to shape their own social situations through discourse.[111] But Long argues this is a false dichotomy that ignores the way in which exit rights help guarantee voice. After all, a relationship in which all parties are completely free to leave at any time is bound to incentivize mutual listening and concern. Whereas a relationship in which one party has no choice but to acquiesce to the other party is bound to incentivize disregard and disrespect.[112] Physical coercion is best understood as a kind of unequal relationship in which one person denies another's "status as a discursive being," thereby subordinating them to their own ends.[113] Violence is a particular *kind* of domination, though an admittedly unique one.

Coercion can come about through physical force or the leveraging of another's unsatisfied needs. However, physical coercion is an unjust response to non-physical coercion because it's still a kind of coercion; a kind of interpersonal domination. Domination encompasses physical coercion, which always entails one's subordination to the ends of another but is not reducible to physical coercion and can exist without it. Freedom from physical coercion is a necessary, but not sufficient, condition for freedom from domination.[114] Relational egalitarians should consider physical coercion a kind of domination and staunchly oppose both. In virtue of their opposition to interpersonal domination in all its forms, relational egalitarians are ultimately committed to Rothbardian anarchism.

Likewise, libertarians should consider physical coercion a kind of domination and staunchly oppose both. In virtue of his commitment to autonomy, self-direction, and freedom to choose, Rothbard was ultimately committed to relational egalitarianism. The same reasons that led Rothbard to oppose the involuntary authoritarianism of statism should have similarly led him to opposing Johnson's "voluntary authoritarianism" of subservient, hierarchical social relations. Domination leaves no space for reflective deliberation nor the cultivation of virtue through one's own volition. Human flourishing depends on fulfilling certain biological and psychological needs such that we have the "supplies" to actually achieve eudaimonia.[115] Moreover, domination, like physical coercion, undermines the humanity of the one doing the dominating. People who dominate others are not engaged in "reasoned and intelligent cooperation" any more than those being dominated are.

Neither a life of order-taking nor order-giving is fit for rational, social beings. Domination in any form is therefore incompatible with the rational and social requirements of human flourishing. Rothbard was right in seeing the state as a key cause of social power, but he was wrong in thinking it exhausted the existence of social power. The institutions that dominate women, queer people, racial minorities, children, and people with disabilities are not only mutually reinforcing with statism, but deeply unjust in their own right because they rob people of individual autonomy, self-direction, and freedom to choose. Moreover, systematic exclusion and deprivation of marginalized people prevents them from engaging in mutual exchange and improving their abilities through experience and education, thereby lowering prosperity and overall living standards for everyone. It's worth talking specifically about at least some of these avenues of interpersonal domination, how they interact with statism, why they are worth opposing in their own right, and what they have to offer Rothbardianism.

Rothbard fervently opposed feminism and thought the Women's Liberation Movement was characterized by bitter, neurotic, man-hating lesbianism.[116] His positions were not only dreadfully wrong but, to put it lightly, incredibly demeaning to women. I contend that Rothbard should have staunchly opposed patriarchy. Not only has patriarchy been a friend of the state, for "[d]espotism in the state is necessarily associated with despotism in the family,"[117] but it has also historically plagued women with "male entitlement, victim-blaming, and omnipresent gender roles" that enable pervasive violence, coercion, and abuse by men.[118] Patriarchy is an emergent institution consisting in various social practices that subject women to the oppression of men.

It's no coincidence that libertarianism and feminism share common intellectual roots in nineteenth-century radicalism.[119] Both are fundamentally emancipatory doctrines. One is seeking to liberate people from state supremacy; the other, from male supremacy. A feminist anarchism must dismantle the power relations embedded in the gender stratum,[120] teach "women to take care of one another," and work with "self-help clinics, free schools, feminist radio stations, newspapers, and domestic violence shelters."[121] Such an approach is completely compatible with Rothbard's core frameworks. Rothbard should have embraced not just anarchism, but anarcha-feminism.

A consistent feminism must not only oppose patriarchy, but cis-heteropatriarchy, which is the "institutionalization of heterosexuality, cissexual, dyadic, monogamous, and permanent relationships as the only possible and coherent sexuality."[122] Queer people have been historically plagued by controls, rigid definitions, and legal boundaries that constrain diverse expressions of sexual and gender identity,[123] restricting people to narrow "boxes" of sexuality and gender.[124] Furthermore, the state's power to "define, interrogate, restrict, and punish on the basis of gendered expectations" leads to both disproportionate police violence and bureaucracy that forces people, particularly trans people, through economically and psychologically burdensome legal hoops concerning doctors' notes, birth certificates, state identification, passports, social security cards, etc.[125] Opposition to cis-heteropatriarchy is also an emancipatory doctrine. It seeks to emancipate queer people from cis-hetero-supremacy. An anarchism that opposes cis-heteropatriarchy must work to liberate "those who traverse gender and sex" from the "mental and physical constructs that manipulate us into subordination"[126] and use mutual aid to help "queer and trans people facing homelessness, immigration enforcement, criminalization, and other dire circumstances."[127] Such an approach is completely compatible with Rothbard's core frameworks. Rothbard should have embraced not just anarchism, but queer anarchism.

The same reasons that committed Rothbard to feminism and queer liberation also committed him to anti-racism. Rothbard did talk about racist oppression to an extent. He praised the Black Panthers for their ability to "aggravate the white police" and organize black youth,[128] and approved of revolutionary violence targeted at white mobs and police.[129] But he largely seemed concerned with racism only insofar as it was a political problem. Of course, racism is in fact a political problem. Over the course of centuries, state legislation and courts have created a superior class known as "whites" that benefit from "the best access to political power, property ownership, legal protection, social status, and so forth" while "other groups – namely Native Americans and African slaves – were denied access to these resources, as were most incoming immigrant groups."[130] Focusing on the political character of racism helps illuminate the ways in which racism and statism are mutually reinforcing. But focusing solely on the political character of racism reduces the problem of racism entirely to a problem of statism. Racism also consists in various social practices that subject racial minorities to pervasive prejudice and disrespect, systematic discrimination, inferior treatment, and individual and mob violence.

Racial minorities have been historically plagued by displacement, enslavement, colonization, and oppression. Anti-racism, too, is an emancipatory doctrine. It seeks to emancipate racial minorities from racial supremacy. Anarchism can provide anti-racist politics with a lens outside of historically settler colonialist ideologies.[131] The concept of "whiteness" itself emerged as a tool to facilitate widespread land theft, dehumanizing exploitation, and the violent uprooting of entire societies.[132] An anti-racist anarchism must fight for the self-determination of racial minorities,[133] and "challenge white supremacy on a daily basis … refute racist philosophy and propaganda, and … counter racist mobilisation and attacks, with armed self-defence and street fighting, when necessary."[134] Such an approach is completely compatible with Rothbard's core frameworks. Rothbard should have embraced not just anarchism, but black and indigenous anarchism.

The same reasons that committed Rothbard to feminism, queer anarchism, and anti-racism also committed him to anti-ageism. Despite dismissing ageism, Rothbard's analysis often embodied the concept in applying natural law theory to people regardless of age (in fact, Rothbard extended his support for childhood independence to the misguided goal of abolishing child neglect laws[135]). Rothbard considered the compulsory schooling system to be a mass prison in which teachers and administrators functioned as wardens and guards.[136] The state legal system and state education system serve to rob children of fundamental rights and "stunt their free thought, self-expression, individuality, and creativity." The result of state-enabled ageism has been "numbed minds, conditioned for obedience, servitude and, in turn, the perpetuation and magnification of state power."[137] But if the authority of teachers and administrators over children is unjust, so must be the authority of all adults over children – including parents. While Rothbard maintained that children always have an inviolable right to run away from their parents, and even called the parent–child relationship a form of "class struggle," he also considered small children "a kind of property," and granted much latitude to the treatment parents may impose on children while they still live with them.[138]

Children have been historically plagued by "loss of individual autonomy, abridged freedoms, and little participation in decision making." Like feminism and anti-racism, anti-ageism is an emancipatory doctrine. It seeks to emancipate children from adult supremacy. An anti-ageist anarchism must "formulate an anti-authoritarian theory of parenting, education and child-rearing, and to begin the process of liberating children from an oppressive society."[139] Such an approach is completely compatible with Rothbard's core frameworks. Rothbard should have embraced not just anarchism, but youth liberationist anarchism.

The reasons that committed Rothbard to feminism, queer liberation, anti-racism, and anti-ageism also committed Rothbard to anti-ableism. Disability can be understood both in medical terms, as "individual physical or mental characteristic[s] with significant personal and social consequence," and in social terms, as "physical and mental characteristics [that] are limiting only or primarily in virtue of social practices that lead to the exclusion of people with those characteristics."[140] People with disabilities have been historically plagued by contempt, dehumanization, and exclusion. They are regularly "stigmatized, othered, and marginalized" in the form of "society's refusal to include them in the economic, social, familial, and political life of the community" and failure to "acknowledge the diversity of the human experience."[141] Many medical professionals often subject people with disabilities to imprisonment, abuse, and neglect.[142]

Neurodivergent people are significantly disadvantaged by the vast mazes of inscrutable bureaucracy and paperwork of state capitalism,[143] suffer disproportionate amounts of police violence, and are used as political scapegoats in discussions of crime and gun violence (despite being more likely to suffer harm than perpetrate it; one in four suffer sexual, physical, or domestic violence in any given year). Vee notes, "Our society treats those with mental illnesses as freaks at best, and criminals at worst."[144] Like feminism, queer liberation, anti-racism, and anti-ageism, anti-ableism is an emancipatory doctrine. It seeks to liberate people with disabilities from ableist supremacy. An anti-ableist anarchism must "integrate disability justice into our workplace and community engagements" and accommodate the "physical and mental differences of those in social movements."[145] Such an approach is completely compatible with Rothbard's core frameworks. Rothbard should have embraced not just anarchism, but anti-ableist anarchism.

Much of contemporary anarchist theory has integrated Frye's birdcage analogy for understanding how oppressive structures often go unseen because they systemically reduce the choices of marginalized people in interlocking fashion.

> If you look very closely at just one wire in the cage, you cannot see the other wires. If your conception of what is before you is determined by this myopic focus, you could look at that one wire, up and down the length of it, and [be] unable to see why a bird would not just fly around the wire any time it wanted to go somewhere … There is no physical property of any one wire, nothing that the closest scrutiny could discover, that will reveal how a bird could be inhibited or harmed by it except in the most accidental way. It is only when you step back, stop looking at the wires one by one, microscopically, and take a macroscopic view of the whole cage, that you can see why the bird does not go anywhere … [t]he bird is surrounded by a network of systematically related barriers, no one of which would be the least hindrance to its flight, but which, by their relations to each other, are as confining as the solid walls of a dungeon.[146]

Such an analysis is (1) *radical*, a methodological approach that grasps things by their roots and favors systemic change over local fixes;[147] (2) *dialectical*, a methodological approach emphasizing the reciprocal interrelationships among different elements in society;[148] and (3) *intersectional*, a methodological approach emphasizing overlapping, mutually constituting processes that do not exist independently of one another.[149] This "integrated analysis of oppression" suggests that systems of domination "operate with and through each other."[150] Rothbardianism offers an integrated analysis of state domination, but is sorely lacking in its analysis of non-state domination. Intersectional analysis is just the consistent application of the view that humans are metaphysically independent, but socially interdependent. Lord observes, "There is no such thing as a single-issue struggle because we do not live single-issue lives."[151] Intersectionality acknowledges the fundamentally individualistic insight that "no one's experience of oppression is the same."[152]

The intersectional approach pioneered by black feminists[153] is completely compatible with Rothbard's four core frameworks. After all, the state is not some discrete, physical thing. It consists in vast webs of interrelated practices and norms. Every interaction between an agent of the state and a subject of the state is defined by their respective social roles. The identities of politicians, bureaucrats, police officers, etc., are social constructs that emerge from patterns of interaction, creating one group of people privileged with a monopoly on legitimate aggressive violence and another group of people excluded from, and subject to, that monopoly. The state is itself a system of interpersonal domination that violates relational egalitarianism and which operates with and through other systems of interpersonal domination. Statism is another bar in Frye's birdcage.

Most proponents of relational egalitarianism would view Rothbard's ideas as anathema to their project, not just for his late embrace of paleoconservatism (an ideology with little concern for relational egalitarianism and a part of Rothbard's thought I do not intend to integrate with relational egalitarianism), but for his life-long embrace of capitalism. Proponents of relational egalitarianism often consider capitalism to be another system of interpersonal domination. Williams argues, "Capitalism is premised upon having workers under the control of managers and owners," putting them in a "disadvantaged position" and "experiencing a lack of empowerment, efficacy, autonomy, and self-management.[154] Indeed, the situation in which a majority of people spend a third of their time taking orders from authority figures like schoolchildren and prisoners seems directly at odds with the characteristically anarchist opposition to interpersonal domination.[155] Workers have been historically plagued by dehumanization, abuse, and inhumane conditions.

According to Anderson, capitalist firms are analogous to dictatorial governments in which workers acquiesce to their bosses for lack of feasible alternatives.

> This government does not recognize a personal or private sphere of autonomy free from sanction. It may prescribe a dress code and forbid certain hairstyles. Everyone lives under surveillance, to ensure that they are complying with orders. Superiors may snoop into inferiors' email and record their phone conversations. Suspicionless searches to their bodies and personal effects may be routine. They can be ordered to submit to medical testing. The government may dictate the language spoken and forbid communication in any other language. It may forbid certain topics of discussion. People can be sanctioned for their consensual sexual activity or their choice of spouse or life partner. They can be sanctioned for their political activity and required to engage in political activity they do not agree with.[156]

The pervasive domination of workers is a deep injustice that discourages autonomy, self-direction, and freedom to choose. Anti-capitalism is an emancipatory doctrine. It seeks to emancipate workers from capitalist supremacy. Rothbardians and anti-capitalists alike might be asking if I could really be serious in suggesting that Rothbardianism, named for someone who considered "capitalism the fullest expression of anarchism and anarchism the fullest expression of capitalism,"[157] is complementary with anti-capitalism. The reason I see such potential in synthesizing the two is because I think much, though not all, of the disagreement between capitalist anarchists and anti-capitalist anarchists rests on shared mistaken assumptions.

Rothbard defined capitalism as the "right to unrestricted private property and free exchange."[158] Yet private property, for Rothbard, didn't necessarily entail the division between capitalists and workers that the relational egalitarian case against capitalism takes issue with. Rothbard defined private property as an "individual's justified sphere of free action,"[159] which "emanate[s] from an individual's fundamental natural right to own himself" and can take the form of either individual *or* collective ownership.[160] Rothbard didn't consider capitalist hierarchy inherent to capitalism as such. He only considered it a useful organizational means of increasing overall economic efficacy,

Rothbard viewed capitalist hierarchy as justified insofar as it reaps mutually beneficial exchange for all parties involved.[161] But if mutually beneficial exchange could be better facilitated without capitalist hierarchy, Rothbard would've had no substantial objections. In fact, Rothbard once praised experiments in transforming workers into equal, independent entrepreneurs, as well as the participatory democracy practiced by the New Left. He described such projects as "monumental contribution[s] to the age-old problem of reconciling organization with the maximum independence and fulfillment of the individual."[162] However, this affinity for participatory democracy was short-lived,[163] as was most of Rothbard's affinity for the New Left.[164] So, while Rothbard himself dismissed opposition to capitalist hierarchy, his philosophy doesn't completely rule it out. It is possible to jettison the capitalist hierarchy aspect of Rothbard's thought without radically altering the overall frameworks I've discussed.

Rothbard was guilty of what Carson calls "vulgar libertarianism," the tendency to conflate an ideal vision of freed markets for actually existing capitalist hierarchy, treating the latter as somehow automatically built in to the former.[165] In his analysis of the corporate state and big business, Rothbard demonstrated some awareness of that same tendency when invoked by progressives *against* freed markets and capitalist hierarchy (Carson terms their error "vulgar liberalism"[166]), which indicates a comparatively less vulgar outlook than many of his fellow libertarians. Nonetheless, Rothbard never opposed capitalist hierarchy as such. In mistakenly identifying freed markets with capitalism, most capitalist anarchists engage in "vulgar libertarianism" and most anti-capitalist anarchists engage in "vulgar liberalism." This conflation only serves to bolster the power of both the state and capitalism, "rendering genuine libertarianism invisible."[167]

By making the vulgar liberal assumption that freed markets naturally entail capitalism, anti-capitalist anarchists mistakenly endorse economic planning, and by making the vulgar libertarian assumption, libertarians mistakenly endorse capitalist hierarchy. Anarchism needs an alternative to the conventional approaches offered by both capitalist and anti-capitalist anarchists. I believe Rothbardianism, properly modified to integrate a commitment to anti-capitalism, can provide such an alternative: *freed-market anti-capitalism.*

Freed-market anti-capitalism distinguishes between *capitalism* (rule by capitalists and workplace hierarchy) and *markets* (property and free exchange).[168] There is no reason to a priori think that freed markets promote specifically capitalist modes of economic organization, as opposed to, for instance, cooperatives, but also independent contracting, freelancing, micro-enterprises, community workshops, open-source design, desktop manufacturing, household production, mutual aid associations, and unions.[169] Johnson argues that freed-market competition would actually liberate workers from the constraints of capitalist hierarchy, and new, more experimental, autonomous, and horizontal forms of economic organization would emerge.[170]

Rothbard opposed cooperatives because he considered them subject to the same economic irrationality that afflicts economic planning. Worker ownership, according to Rothbard, would abolish external markets and reap calculational chaos.[171] But Prychitko notes that cooperatives can acquire non-labor factors not only by workers' capital contributions, but also through purchasing, renting, or borrowing in external markets. Rothbard was wrong to conflate the cooperative model with economic planning. Worker cooperatives in no way demand the sacrifice of property rights, price signals, or profit/loss mechanisms and are, therefore, completely amenable to institutions of economic freedom. An Austrian market-process approach doesn't rule out anti-*capitalist* anarchism, only anti-*market* anarchism.[172] An anti-capitalist freed market would include horizontal modes of production, but would still have property ownership, contractual exchange, competition, entrepreneurial discovery, and spontaneous orders.[173]

Rothbard argued the efficiency of capitalist hierarchy is demonstrated by the fact that so many workers decline the opportunity to form cooperatives, and instead work for someone who has already saved up productive resources in order to earn income in advance of the sale of their products.[174] On this view, capitalist hierarchy is merely the organic result of differing preferences in saving and consumption. But in this respect, Rothbard ignored the implications of his very own liberal class theory in which modern capitalism is understood as a system of neomercantilism that protects politically entrenched big businesses from the competitive effects of market processes, artificially limits the feasible economic alternatives, and impoverishes those dependent on the corporate state via land-use rules, building codes, zoning restrictions, eminent domain, capitalization requirements, trade protectionism, occupational licensing, excessive permits, price and wage controls, onerous regulations, inscrutable paperwork, irksome inspections, burdensome bureaucracy, and inflation and taxation that favors the politically connected.[175] Capitalist hierarchy reflects not organic variations in saving and consumption preferences, but coercive privilege that "depends at root upon threats of violence that condition socioeconomic relations in wider society."[176] Capitalism is mutually reinforcing with statism.

Indeed, Rothbard's framework is much more congenial to anti-capitalist modes of economic organization than he realized because such arrangements could offer more efficient alternatives to large firms currently benefitting from economic privilege under the corporate state. Rothbard ultimately underrated "the extent to which the large corporation, as an island of incalculability, is insulated from the market penalties for calculational chaos."[177] Rothbard's own insights into economic calculation help show that freed markets would incentivize more worker management of industry in order to overcome the calculational chaos of capitalist firms. As vertical integration increases, firms become more insulated from the price system and their diseconomies of scale grow larger and larger – a process heavily magnified by the state weeding out market competitors and favoring organizational bigness.[178]

Hierarchy, whether of the state or capitalist variety, comes with severe information and incentive problems, subjecting both arrangements to pervasive irrationality. On the Austrian view, calculational chaos is a product of separating *entrepreneurial* from *technical* knowledge. While collective ownership divorces economic decisions from entrepreneurial knowledge (since such knowledge only emerges from market processes), capitalist ownership divorces economic decisions from technical knowledge (since such knowledge only emerges from production processes).[179] In aiming to best utilize technical knowledge and more efficiently allocate scarce resources to better satisfy consumer preferences, firms in a freed market would likely grant more and more autonomy to workers. Competitive pressures would therefore incentivize avoiding "hierarchy as much as possible, and [internalizing] the costs and benefits of organizing production in the same decision-makers."[180] Consistently upholding exit in the *market*place is the best way to secure voice in the *work*place.

Capitalism is a system of domination that lowers living standards through economic irrationality. But economic planning suffers the same problems. The sensible alternative that promotes both relational egalitarianism and shared prosperity is anti-capitalist freed markets. A freed-market anti-capitalist anarchism must entrepreneurially engage in horizontal alternatives to capitalist hierarchies such as cooperatives, independent contracting, freelancing, micro-enterprises, community workshops, open-source design, desktop manufacturing, household production, mutual aid associations, and unions,[181] along with practicing "direct action on the job"[182] to strengthen the bargaining power of workers, such as wildcat strikes up and down the production chain, sit-down strikes, walkouts, slowdowns, boycotts, anonymous whistleblowing, public information campaigns, sick-ins, and "working to rule" (following the rules of bureaucratic corporate mazes to the letter).[183] Such an approach is completely compatible with Rothbard's core frameworks. Rothbard should have embraced not just anarchism, but freed-market anti-capitalist anarchism.

VIII. The Future of Rothbardianism

"Rothbardianism" consists in natural law theory, individualist anarchism, liberal class theory, and Austrian economics. Rothbard synthesized such disparate intellectual traditions into a single, coherent, and fruitful framework of social analysis. Together, the defining frameworks of Rothbardianism can provide contemporary anarchism with (1) a theory of morality that takes our rational and social nature seriously, providing a compelling alternative to the impoverished theories of nihilism, deontology, consequentialism, atomism, and/or organicism; (2) a theory of anarchism rooted in that rich conception of human nature, which lays the groundwork for both liberal class theory and market-process thought; (3) an account of class division that captures the nexus of political–economic–cultural power more accurately than traditional Marxist theories; and (4) an analysis of human action and human interaction that takes mutual exchange seriously, thereby better informing both a critique of the state and a vision for a stateless society. To the extent that they haven't already, other anarchists ought to integrate these core Rothbardian insights into their thought.

Nevertheless, Rothbard's social theory has a gaping hole in its lack of concern for interpersonal domination beyond bare force. A bright future for Rothbardianism depends upon incorporating a more comprehensive and holistic vision of human flourishing and freedom. Just as Rothbard sought to liberate people from unequal authority, he should've sought to liberate people from unequal relationships. Just as Rothbard sought to liberate people from violence, he should've sought to liberate people from domination. Just as Rothbard sought to liberate people from statism, he should've sought to liberate people from cis-heteropatriarchy, racial supremacy, ageism, ableism, and capitalism.

Opposition to interpersonal domination is consistent, and mutually reinforcing, with (1) Rothbard's natural law theory that emphasizes autonomy, self-direction, and free choice; (2) Rothbard's individualist anarchist politics that consistently opposes the state, a primary purveyor and facilitator of interpersonal domination; (3) Rothbard's liberal class theory that provides a robust explanation of social fracturing and corporate statism; and (4) Rothbard's account of extensive social cooperation and mutual respect that occurs within market processes. Rothbardians ought to add relational egalitarianism as the fifth pillar of consistently applied Rothbardian thought. If Rothbardianism incorporates a principled commitment to relational egalitarianism, maybe it can earn that third cheer.

A Rothbardianism that embraces and integrates the value of relational egalitarianism can advocate for social justice, the "branch of justice that evaluates systemic features of society in terms of their impact on social welfare generally, and on that of the least advantaged in particular."[184] Opposition to statism, cis-heteropatriarchy, racial supremacy, adult supremacy, ableist supremacy, and capitalism are all social justice causes Rothbardians should take up in the name of flourishing and freedom. The consistent Rothbardian should completely reject the "illogical and mythical" fusion of conservatism and libertarianism,[185] especially Hoppe's variety, which vainly tries to fuse libertarianism with the alt-right commitment to patriarchal white nationalism.[186] Trying to combine a philosophy of emancipation and progress with a philosophy of hierarchy and traditionalism can only serve to undermine the aims of the former and disguise the aims of the latter. "In any compromise between good and evil, it is only evil that can profit."[187] Rothbardianism needs a consistent means–ends framework, which only relational egalitarianism can provide.

Rothbardianism, by maintaining its core frameworks of natural law theory, individualist anarchism, liberal class theory, and Austrian economics, but working to integrate the framework of relational egalitarianism and, thus, the liberation of women, queer people, racial minorities, children, people with disabilities, and workers, can offer a harmonious, radical, dialectical, and intersectional analysis of human flourishing and freedom. My hope is that Rothbard's approach to anarchism, suitably modified and enriched, can continue to inform and stimulate anarchist research and praxis.

Notes

1 Murray N. Rothbard, "Right-Wing Populism: A Strategy for the Paleo Movement," *Rothbard-Rockwell Report* 3.1 (Jan 1992): 5–14 [5].
2 Rothbard, *Right-Wing* 9.
3 Murray N. Rothbard, "The Transformation of the American Right," *Continuum* (Summer 1964): 220–31 [31].
4 John Payne, "Rothbard's Time on the Left," *Journal of Libertarian Studies* 19.1 (Winter 2005): 7–24.
5 Murray N. Rothbard, *Ethics of Liberty* (AL: Mises Institute 2016) Preface.
6 Murray N. Rothbard, "Do You Hate the State?" *Libertarian Forum* 10.7 (July 1977): 1–8 [1].
7 Murray N. Rothbard, "Strategies for a Libertarian Victory," *Libertarian Review* 7.7 (August 1978): 18–24 [4].
8 Chris Matthew Sciabarra, *Total Freedom: Toward a Dialectical Libertarianism* (PA: Penn State UP 2000) 360.
9 Peter J. Boettke, "Economics and Liberty: Murray N. Rothbard," *Nomos: Series on the Austrian Free-Market Economists* (Fall/Winter 1988): 29–50 [30].
10 Rothbard, *Ethics* 7.
11 Rothbard, *Ethics* 7.
12 Rothbard, *Ethics* 12.
13 Aristotle, *Nicomachean Ethics*, trans. and ed. C.D.C Reeve (IN: Hackett 2014) 1098a1.
14 Rothbard, *Ethics* 21.
15 Murray N. Rothbard, "Frank S. Meyer: Fusionist as Libertarian," *Modern Age* (Fall 1981): 352–63 [53].
16 Ayn Rand, *Atlas Shrugged* (NY: Dutton 1992) 1023.
17 Roderick T. Long, "Equality: The Unknown Ideal" (Mises Oct 2001), https://mises.org/library/equality-unknown-ideal (last visited June 5, 2020).
18 Rothbard, *Economic* 627. Original emphasis.
19 Murray N. Rothbard, *For a New Liberty* (AL: Mises Institute 2006) 36–7.
20 Roderick T. Long, "A Plea for Public Property" (Panarchy 1998), www.panarchy.org/rodericklong/property.html (last visited June 5, 2020).
21 Roderick T. Long, "Land-Locked: A Critique of Carson on Property Rights," *Journal of Libertarian Studies* 20.1 (2006): 87–95 [1].
22 John Locke, *Second Treatise of Government* (NY: Barnes & Noble Books 2004) 4.
23 Rothbard, *Ethics* 18.
24 Rothbard, *Ethics* 187.
25 Rothbard, *Ethics* 161–2.
26 Rothbard, *Ethics* 162.
27 Lysander Spooner, *No Treason: The Constitution of No Authority and a Letter to Thomas F. Bayard* (CA: Pine Tree 1966) 17.
28 Spooner, *No Treason* 26.
29 Frederic Bastiat, *The Law* (NY: Foundation for Economic Education 1998) 29.
30 Benjamin R. Tucker, "State Socialism and Anarchism: How Far They Agree, and Wherein They Differ," *The Individualist Anarchists*, ed. Frank H. Brooks (NJ: Transaction 1994) 77–89 [6].
31 Franz Oppenheimer, The State (NY: Free Life Editions 1975) 24–5.
32 Rothbard, *New Liberty* 64.
33 Murray N. Rothbard, "Unpublished Letter" (Organization and Markets 2008), https://organizationsandmarkets.com/2008/08/06/rothbard-on-big-business/ (last visited June 5, 2020).
34 Murray N. Rothbard, "Confessions of a Right-Wing Liberal," *Ramparts* 6.11 (June 1968): 47–52 [1].
35 Rothbard, *New Liberty* 12.
36 Rothbard, *Confessions* 51.
37 Murray N. Rothbard, "Left and Right: The Prospects for Liberty," *Left & Right: A Journal of Libertarian Thought* 1.1 (Spring 1965): 4–22 [15].
38 Don Lavoie, "National Economic Planning: What is Left?" (Washington, DC: Cato Institute 1985) 230.
39 Rothbard, *Transformation* 31.
40 Randolph Bourne, "Unfinished Fragment on the State," *Untimely Papers* (NY: Huebsch 1919) 145.
41 Murray N. Rothbard, "Confiscation and the Homestead Principle," *Libertarian Forum* (June 1969): 3–4 [3].
42 Rothbard, *Ethics* 70.
43 Rothbard, *Confiscation* 4.
44 Murray N. Rothbard, "Big-Government Libertarians: The Anti-Left-Libertarian Manifesto," *Rothbard-Rockwell Report* 4.12 (Dec 1993): 1–9 [3].
45 Murray N. Rothbard, "In Defense of 'Extreme Apriorism'," *Southern Economic Journal* 23.3 (Jan 1967): 314–20 [18].

46 Murray N. Rothbard, "Man, Economy, and State" (AL: Mises Institute 2004) 1.
47 Roderick T. Long, "Wittgenstein, Austrian Economics, and the Logic of Action: Praxeological Investigations," Work in progress, http://praxeology.net/wiggy-draft.pdf (last visited June 5, 2020) 135.
48 Plato, *Hipparchus* 227d, "Plato: Complete Works," ed. D.S. Hutchinson and John M. Cooper (IN: Hackett 1997).
49 Murray N. Rothbard, "Free Market" (Library of Economics and Liberty), www.econlib.org/library/Enc/FreeMarket.html (last visited June 5, 2020).
50 Murray N. Rothbard, "Toward a Reconstruction of Utility and Welfare Economics," *Freedom and Free Enterprise: Essays in Honor of Ludwig von Mises*, ed. Mary Senholz (NJ: D. Van Nostrand 1956): 224–62 [51].
51 Rothbard, *Man* 101.
52 Rothbard, *Man* 645–7.
53 Ludwig von Mises, *Economic Calculation in the Socialist Commonwealth* (AL: Mises Institute 1990) 15.
54 Rothbard, *Reconstruction* 252.
55 Rothbard, *Man* 101.
56 Rothbard, *Man* 659.
57 Rothbard, *Man* 613. Original emphasis.
58 Rothbard, *Man* 614.
59 Rothbard, *Man* 991.
60 Murray N. Rothbard, *America's Great Depression* (AL: Mises Institute 2000) 11.
61 Rothbard, *Depression* 186.
62 Murray N. Rothbard, *What Has Government Done yo Our Money?* (AL: Mises Institute 2005) 44.
63 Noam Chomsky, "'Anarchism' and 'Libertarianism'," *Understanding Power: The Indispensable Chomsky*, ed. Peter R. Mitchell and John Schoeffel (NY: New Press 2002) 200.
64 Mikhail Bakunin, *God and the State* (NY: Dover 1970) 30. Original emphasis.
65 Benjamin R. Tucker, "The Relation of the State to the Individual," *The Individualist Anarchists*, ed. Frank H. Brooks (NJ: Transaction 1994) 22–7 [5].
66 Julia Annas, *Intelligent Virtue* (Oxford: OUP 2011) 126. Original emphasis.
67 Robert Paul Wolff, *In Defense of Anarchism* (CA: University of California 1998) 18.
68 William Godwin, *An Enquiry Concerning Political Justice, and its Influence on Morals and Happiness* (London: G.G.J. and J. Robinson 1793) 246.
69 Plato, *Parmenides* 133e, "Plato: The Parmenides," trans. Mary Louise Gill and Paul Ryan (IN: Hackett 1996).
70 Roderick T. Long, "Why Does Justice Have Good Consequences?" *Alabama Philosophical Society Presidential Address* (2002).
71 Murray Bookchin, *Social Anarchism or Lifestyle Anarchism: An Unbridgeable Chasm* (CA: AK 1995) 11.
72 Douglas J. Den Uyl and Douglas B. Rasmussen, "The Myth of Atomism," *Review of Metaphysics* 59.4 (June 2006): 841–68 [47].
73 Den Uyl and Rasmussen, *Myth* 45.
74 Chris Matthew Sciabarra, *Ayn Rand: Russian Radical* (PA: Penn State UP 2013) 133.
75 David L. Prychitko, "Expanding the Anarchist Range: A Critical Reappraisal of Rothbard's Contribution to the Contemporary Theory of Anarchism," *Review of Political Economy* 9.4 (1997): 433–455 [50].
76 Peter Marshall, *Demanding the Impossible: A History of Anarchism* (London: HarperCollins 1991) 564.
77 Warren J. Samuels, "Anarchism and the Theory of Power," *Further Explorations in the Theory of Anarchy*, ed. Gordon Tullock (VA: Center for Study of Public Choice 1974): 33–57 [49].
78 David M. Hart, "Gustave de Molinari and the Anti-statist Liberal Tradition: Part 1," *Journal of Libertarian Studies* 5.3 (Summer 1981): 263–290 [85].
79 David M. Hart, "Gustave de Molinari and the Liberal Tradition: Part III," *Journal of Libertarian Studies* 6.1 (Winter 1982): 83–104 [88].
80 Rothbard, *Man* 91.
81 Roderick T. Long, "Market Anarchism as Constitutionalism," *Anarchism/Minarchism*, ed. Tibor R. Machan and Long (VT: Ashgate 2008) 133–154 [41].
82 Milton Shapiro, "Power or Market: Government and the Economy: A Review," *Libertarian Analysis* 1.4 (1971): 22–29.
83 Rothbard, *Man* 91.
84 Rothbard, *Free Market*.
85 David Osterfeld, "Caste and Class: The Rothbardian View of Governments and Markets," *Man, Economy, and Liberty: Essays in Honor of Murray N. Rothbard*, ed. Walter Block and Llewellyn H. Rockwell, Jr. (AL: Mises Institute 1988) 286.

86 Rothbard, *Man* 881.
87 "An Anarchist FAQ," *The Anarchist Library*, https://theanarchistlibrary.org/library/the-anarchist-faq-editorial-collective-an-anarchist-faq (last visited June 5, 2020).
88 Murray Bookchin, "Community Ownership of the Economy," *Green Perspectives* 2 (Feb 1986): 6.
89 Lavoie, *National* 135–6.
90 Murray N. Rothbard, "Anarcho-Communism," *Libertarian Forum* 2.1 (Jan 1970): 1–4 [4].
91 Rand, *Atlas* 379.
92 Jason Lee Byas, "Toward an Anarchy of Production" (Center for a Stateless Society 2014), https://c4ss.org/content/52458 (last visited June 5, 2020).
93 Lavoie, *National* 44.
94 Roderick T. Long, "Free Markets and Private Property: The Road to Social Justice?" (Istanbul Bilgi University 2013).
95 Lavoie, *National* 240.
96 Emma Goldman, "Anarchism: What It Really Stands For" (Panarchy 1910), www.panarchy.org/goldman/anarchism.1910.html (last visited June 5, 2020).
97 Samuels, *Anarchism* 51.
98 Murray N. Rothbard, "Left-Opportunism: The Case of S.L.S, Part One," *Libertarian Vanguard* 2.5 (February 1981): 10–12 [11].
99 Walter E. Block and Ken Williamson, "Is Libertarianism Thick or Thin? Thin!" *Italian Law Journal* 3.1 (2017): 14.
100 Sciabarra, *Total* 200.
101 Rothbard, Big-Government 101.
102 Murray N. Rothbard, "Continue The Struggle," *Libertarian Forum* 1.8 (July 1969): 2–5 [2–3].
103 Murray N. Rothbard, "Race! That Murray Book," *Rothbard-Rockwell Report* 5.12 (Dec 1994): 1–10 [0].
104 Murray N. Rothbard, "The Struggle Over Egalitarianism Continues," [1991] Freedom, Inequality, Primitivism and the Division of Labor (*Modern Age* 1971).
105 Murray N. Rothbard, "Kulturkampf!" *Rothbard-Rockwell Report* 3.10 (Oct. 1993): 1–10 [3].
106 Murray N. Rothbard, "Letter to Bergland," Justin Raimondo, *An Enemy of the State: The Life of Murray N. Rothbard* (NY: Prometheus 2000).
107 Hans-Hermann Hoppe, *Getting Libertarianism Right* (AL: Mises Institute 2018) 55.
108 Charles W. Johnson, "Liberty, Equality, Solidarity: Toward a Dialectical Anarchism," *Anarchism/Minarchism: Is Government Part of a Free Country?* ed. Roderick T. Long and Tibor R. Machan (VT: Ashgate 2008) 155–84 [76]. Original emphasis.
109 Robert Dahl, "The Concept of Power," *Behavioral Science* 2.3 (July 1957): 201–15 [2–3].
110 Elizabeth Anderson, "What is the Point of Equality?" *Ethics* 109 (1999): 287–337 [12–13].
111 Elizabeth Anderson, *Value in Ethics and Economics* (MA: Harvard UP 1993) 160.
112 Roderick T. Long, "Rothbard's 'Left and Right': Forty Years Later" Rothbard Memorial Lecture, Austrian Scholars Conference (2006).
113 Billy Christmas, "Social Equality and Liberty," *The Dialectics of Liberty: Exploring the Context of Human Freedom*, ed. Roger E. Bissell, Chris Matthew Sciabarra, and Edward W. Younkins (MD: Lexington 2019) 275–292 [80].
114 Christmas, Social 83–4.
115 Aristotle, *Nicomachean* 1099b.
116 Murray N. Rothbard, "The Great Women's Liberation Issue: Setting it Straight," *Egalitarianism as a Revolt Against Nature and Other Essays* (AL: Mises Institute 2000): 157–73 [69–70].
117 Herbert Spencer, *Social Statics: or, The Conditions Essential to Human Happiness Specified, and the First of Them Developed* (NY: Robert Schalkenbach Foundation 1954) 161.
118 Kelly Vee, "Sex Slavery Revisited" (Center for a Stateless Society 2015), https://c4ss.org/content/36760 (last visited June 5, 2020).
119 Roderick T. Long and Charles W. Johnson, "Libertarian Feminism: Can This Marriage Be Saved?" (2005), http://charleswjohnson.name/essays/libertarian-feminism/#FN.19 (last visited June 5, 2020).
120 Stacy Aka Sallydarity, "Gender Sabotage," *Queering Anarchism: Addressing and Undressing Power and Desire*, ed. C.B. Daring, J. Rogue, Deric Shannon, and Abbey Volcano (CA: AK 2012): 43–62 [52].
121 Julia Tanenbaum, "Anarcha-Feminism: To Destroy Domination in All Forms," *Perspectives* 29 (Institute for Anarchist Studies 2019).
122 Abbey Volcano, "Police at the Borders," *Queering Anarchism: Addressing and Undressing Power and Desire*, ed. C.B. Daring, J. Rogue, Deric Shannon, and Abbey Volcano (CA: AK 2012): 33–42 [3].

123 Jerimarie Leisegang, "Tyranny of the State and Trans Liberation," *Queering Anarchism: Addressing and Undressing Power and Desire*, ed. C.B. Daring, J. Rogue, Deric Shannon, and Abbey Volcano (CA: AK 2012): 87–100 [88].
124 Sallydarity, Gender 55.
125 Meg Arnold, "The Untenability of Libertarian Transphobia" (Center for a Stateless Society 2015), https://c4ss.org/content/41183 (last visited June 5, 2020).
126 Leisegang, Tyranny 97.
127 Dean Spade, "Their Laws Will Never Make Us Safer," *Against Equality: Prisons Will Not Protect You*, ed. Ryan Conrad (ME: Against Equality 2012): 1–11 [8].
128 Murray N. Rothbard, "The Panthers and Black Liberation," *The Libertarian* 1.4 (1969): 3.
129 Murray N. Rothbard, "The Negro Revolution," *New Individualist Review*, ed. Ralph Raico (IN: Liberty Fund 1961): 467–77 [70].
130 Dana Williams, "From Top To Bottom, A Thoroughly Stratified World: An Anarchist View of Inequality and Domination," *Race, Class & Gender* 19.3–4 (2012): 9–34 [23].
131 "Indigenous Anarchist Convergence: Report Back" (Indigenous Action 2019), www.indigenousaction.org/indigenous-anarchist-convergence-report-back/ (last visited June 5, 2020).
132 "White Supremacy and Anti-Racism" (Black Rose Anarchist Federation n.d.), https://blackrosefed.org/points-of-unity/white-supremacy-anti-racism/ (last visited June 5, 2020).
133 Aragorn! "Locating an Indigenous Anarchism," *Green Anarchy* 19 (Spring 2005).
134 Lorzenzo Kom'boa Ervin, "Anarchism and the Black Revolution," *Black Anarchism: A Reader* (Black Rose Anarchist Federation 2016): 10–71 [12].
135 Rothbard, *Ethics* 101.
136 Rothbard, *New Liberty* 146.
137 Brian Dominick and Sara Zia Ebrahimi, "Young and Oppressed," *NO! Against Adult Supremacy* 3 (Stinney Distro 2019).
138 Murray N. Rothbard, "Kid's Lib," *Egalitarianism as a Revolt Against Nature and Other Essays* (AL: Mises Institute 2000): 145–56 [8].
139 Marc Silverstein, "Anarchism and Youth Liberation," *NO! Against Adult Supremacy* 1 (Stinney Distro 2014).
140 Daniel Putnam, David Wasserman, Jeffrey Blustein, and Adrienne Asch, "Disability and Justice" (Stanford Encyclopedia of Philosophy 2013), https://plato.stanford.edu/entries/disability-justice/ (last visited June 5, 2020).
141 "Disability Justice" (Black Rose Anarchist Federation n.d.), https://blackrosefed.org/points-of-unity/ableism/ (last visited June 5, 2020).
142 Dean Spade, "Afterword to the 2009 Edition," Eli Clare, *Exile and Pride: Disability, Queerness, and Liberation* (NC: Duke UP 2015): 165–171 [69].
143 Vikky Storm, "It's Time For Mad Anarchism" (Center for a Stateless Society 2017), https://c4ss.org/content/48510 (last visited June 5, 2020).
144 Kelly Vee, "Arm the Mentally Ill" (Center for a Stateless Society 2015), https://c4ss.org/content/39669 (last visited June 5, 2020).
145 Disability Justice.
146 Marilyn Frye, "Oppression," *The Politics of Reality: Essays in Feminist Theory* (NY: Crossing 1983) 5.
147 Chris Matthew Sciabarra, "What the Hell Has Happened to the Radical Spirit of Objectivism?" (Rebirth of Reason n.d.), http://rebirthofreason.com/Articles/Sciabarra/What_the_Hell_Has_Happened_to_the_Radical_Spirit_of_Objectivism.shtml (last visited June 5, 2020).
148 Sciabarra, *Total* 136.
149 Jen Rogue and Abbey Volcano, "Insurrection at the Intersection," *Quiet Rumors: An Anarcha-Feminist Reader*, ed. Dark Star (CA: AK 2012): 43–46 [3].
150 Chris Crass, *Towards Collective Liberation: Anti-Racist Organizing, Feminist Praxis, and Movement Building Strategy* (CA: PM 2013) 5.
151 Audre Lorde, "Learning From the 60s," Harvard University (1982).
152 Kelly Vee, "Individualism, Anti-Essentialism and Intersectionality" (Center For a Stateless Society 2015), https://c4ss.org/content/37870 (last visited June 5, 2020).
153 Hillary Lazar, "Until All Are Free: Black Feminism, Anarchism, and Interlocking Oppression" (Institute of Anarchist Studies 2016), https://anarchiststudies.org/until-all-are-free-black-feminism-anarchism-and-interlocking-oppression-by-hillary-lazar/ (last visited June 5, 2020).
154 Williams, From Top to Bottom 20.
155 Kevin Carson, *The Homebrew Industrial Revolution: A Low Overhead Manifesto* (SC: BookSurge 2010) 167–8.

156 Elizabeth Anderson, *Private Government: How Employers Rule Our Lives (And Why We Don't Talk About It)* (NJ: Princeton UP 2017) 38.
157 Murray N. Rothbard, "Exclusive Interview with Murray Rothbard," *New Banner: A Fortnightly Libertarian Journal* (February 1972).
158 Rothbard, *New Liberty* 28.
159 Rothbard, *Ethics* 33.
160 Rothbard, *Ethics* 55.
161 Murray N. Rothbard, "Syndical Syndrome," *Libertarian Forum* 3.5 (June 1975): 2–4 [3].
162 Murray N. Rothbard, "Liberty and the New Left," *Left & Right: A Journal of Libertarian Thought* 1.2 (Autumn 1965): 35–67 [40–1].
163 Murray N. Rothbard, "What Kind of 'Purity'?" *Libertarian Forum* 6.2 (February 1974): 2–3 [2].
164 Murray N. Rothbard, "The New Left, RIP," *Libertarian Forum* 2.6 (March 1970): 1–3 [1].
165 Kevin Carson, "Vulgar Libertarianism Watch, Part 1" (Mutualist Blog 2005), https://mutualist.blogspot.com/2005/01/vulgar-libertarianism-watch-part-1.html (last visited June 5, 2020).
166 Kevin Carson, "Vulgar Liberalism Watch (Yeah, You Read It Right)" (Mutualist Blog 2005), https://mutualist.blogspot.com/2005/12/vulgar-liberalism-watch-yeah-you-read.html (last visited June 5, 2020).
167 Roderick T. Long, "Corporations versus the Market; or, Whip Conflation Now" (Cato Unbound 2008), www.cato-unbound.org/2008/11/10/roderick-t-long/corporations-versus-market-or-whip-conflation-now (last visited June 5, 2020).
168 Kelly Vee, "Anarcho-Capitalism vs. Market Anarchism" (Center for a Stateless Society 2015), https://c4ss.org/content/40654 (last visited June 5, 2020).
169 Carson, *Homebrew* 171–303.
170 Johnson, Liberty 180–1.
171 Rothbard, Man 608.
172 Prychitko, Expanding 448.
173 Gary Chartier, "Introduction," *Markets not Capitalism: Individualist Anarchism Against Bosses, Inequality, Corporate Power, and Structural Poverty*, ed. Charles W. Johnson and Chartier (Autonomedia 2011).
174 Murray N. Rothbard, "The Spooner-Tucker Doctrine: An Economist's View," *Journal of Libertarian Studies* 20.1 (2006): 5–15 [12].
175 Charles W. Johnson, "Scratching By: How Government Creates Poverty as We Know It," *Freeman* 57.10 (December 2007).
176 Billy Christmas, "Libertarianism and Privilege," *Molinari Review* 1.1 (Spring 2016): 24–46 [34].
177 Kevin Carson, *Organization Theory: A Libertarian Perspective* (SC: BookSurge 2008) 219.
178 Roderick T. Long, "History of an Idea; or, How an Argument Against the Workability of Authoritarian Socialism Became an Argument Against the Workability of Authoritarian Capitalism" (Center for a Stateless Society 2008), https://c4ss.org/content/9482 (last visited June 5, 2020).
179 Kevin Carson, "Economic Calculation in the Corporate Commonwealth," *Freeman* 57.1 (June 2007).
180 Carson, *Organization* 222.
181 Carson, *Homebrew* 171–303.
182 "Effective Strikes and Economic Actions" (Industrial Workers of the World n.d.), https://archive.iww.org/about/solidarityunionism/directaction/ (last visited June 5, 2020).
183 Kevin Carson, "Labor Struggle: A Free Market Model" (Center for a Stateless Society 2010), https://c4ss.org/wp-content/uploads/2010/09/C4SS-Labor.pdf (last visited June 5, 2020).
184 Roderick T. Long, "Why Libertarians Should Be Social Justice Warriors," *The Dialectics of Liberty: Exploring the Context of Human Freedom*, ed. Roger E. Bissell, Chris Matthew Sciabarra, and Edward W. Younkins (MD: Lexington Books 2019) 235–54 [37].
185 Grant Babcock, "Fissionism: Why Libertarianism Should Extricate Itself from Conservative Entanglements" (Libertarianism 2014), www.libertarianism.org/columns/fissionism-why-libertarianism-should-extricate-itself-conservative-entanglements (last visited June 5, 2020).
186 Hoppe, *Getting* 82–89.
187 Rand, *Atlas* 965.

13
CHRISTIAN ANARCHISM

Sam Underwood and Kevin Vallier

I. Introduction

Biblical Christian anarchists argue that the teachings of Jesus imply a unique form of anarchism. Christian anarchists believe that followers of Jesus are called to a life of nonviolence, love, and forgiveness. This life stands in stark contrast with the "ways of the world," which are the ways of power, violence, and coercion. Therefore, according to Alexandre Christoyannopoulos,

> the starting point for most Christian anarchists is not so much a critique of the state as an understanding of Jesus's radical teaching on love and forgiveness which, when *then* contrasted with the state, leads them to their anarchist conclusion.[1]

The Sermon on the Mount is the primary biblical inspiration for the positions of many Christian anarchists. Christian anarchists contend that, if we take Jesus at His word in the Sermon on the Mount, and everyone acts as a peacemaker and accepts persecution, the consequence is an anarchist society because the state depends on violence and power for its existence. Tolstoy writes that "Christianity in its true sense puts an end to government. So it was understood at its very commencement; it was for that cause that Christ was crucified."[2]

In what follows, we will explicate the primary claims of the main biblical Christian anarchists, paying particular attention to the expressly biblical arguments they give. In Section II, we consider Christian conceptions of anarchism and Christian anarchists' views about whether anarchic political arrangements are feasible and desirable. In Section III, we explore Christian anarchist perspectives on nonviolence, for nonviolence has historically been a central element of articulations of Christian anarchism. Then, in Section IV, we examine Christian anarchist responses to two potentially problematic biblical passages: Romans 13:1–7 and Jesus's instruction to "render unto Caesar what is Caesar's" in Matthew 22:21.

In Section V, we review an unusual, recent branch of Christian anarchism, Christian *market* anarchism, where rights of private property are the primary structural features of political order and no state exists. Christian anarchists support both free-market capitalism and the abolition of the nation-state. Most biblical Christian anarchists have been sympathetic to socialism, though few had the economics background to give an account of how a socialist anarchist society would operate. The Christian market anarchists combine the anti-statist arguments of the mainstream biblical Christian anarchists with biblical arguments appearing to support private property rights and the value of markets. But they also much more frequently appeal to the language of natural law and natural rights, as well as to economic considerations—especially ones drawn from the Austrian school of economics—in outlining how political order should function. We conclude in Section VI by analyzing how Christian anarchists might resolve their dispute about which economic regime is aligned better to fit with Christian anarchism—capitalism or socialism.

Throughout, we rely upon the work of Christian anarchists such as Leo Tolstoy, Jacques Ellul, and Vernard Eller. We will also draw upon the work of Christian pacifists like John Howard Yoder and Walter Wink. Although these scholars do not identify as anarchists, their writings have exercised considerable influence in the world of Christian anarchism and so it is helpful to consider their arguments insofar as they have informed, and been frequently employed by, Christian anarchist writers. The Christian market anarchists are much less well known, but include Thomas E. Woods, Stephen W. Carson, and James Redford.

II. Biblical Christian Anarchists on the Definition and Feasibility of Anarchism

What do biblical Christian anarchists mean by "anarchism," and do they see "anarchy" as a feasible state of affairs? In this section, we examine the answers to these questions offered by three of the most influential Christian anarchist writers: Leo Tolstoy, Jacques Ellul, and Vernard Eller. We will see that these authors represent distinct, but nevertheless related, perspectives on the nature and feasibility of anarchy.

A. Leo Tolstoy

According to Tolstoy, anarchism is the necessary political outcome of an ethic of radical nonviolence. Tolstoy argues that governments are fundamentally violent insofar as their power rests upon the violent enforcement of laws. Furthermore, he writes, violence is a form of slavery, insofar as to be enslaved is to be "compelled to do what other people wish, against your own will."[3] Tolstoy maintains such slavery must be abolished, which is to say that the state must be abolished. The connection between anarchy and radical nonviolence, however, signals a significant difference between Tolstoy and the other anarchists of his day. Tolstoy explains this difference in the following way:

> The Anarchists are right in everything; in the negation of the existing order and in the assertion that, without Authority there could not be worse violence than that of Authority under existing conditions. They are mistaken only in thinking that anarchy can be instituted by a violent revolution.[4]

Importantly, Tolstoy does not disagree with other anarchists about the *possibility* of anarchy. He does maintain a measured agnosticism regarding exactly what anarchy would look like, though. "To the question, how to be without a State … an answer cannot be given," he writes.[5]

What is of more urgent concern, in Tolstoy's view, is the refusal to resort to violent methods in the pursuit of anarchy. Rather, he argues, only if people nonviolently refuse to support, recognize, or participate in government violence can anarchy begin to take shape. "[I]t is time," he writes,

> for people to understand that Governments not only are unnecessary, but are harmful and highly immoral institutions, in which an honest, self-respecting man cannot and must not take part, and the advantages of which he cannot and should not enjoy …

> And as soon as people clearly understand that, they will naturally cease to take part in such deeds, i.e., cease to give the Governments soldiers and money. And as soon as a majority of people ceases to do this, the fraud which enslaves people will be abolished.[6]

For Tolstoy, then, the way of anarchy is, we might say, the way of *refusal* rather than of *revolt*, and his emphasis on refusal allows him to avoid constructing a blueprint for anarchy. Revolutionaries need some clear notion of anarchy in mind in order to impose it on others. But anarchy will take shape on its own when we cease to call upon, or acknowledge the legitimacy of, the government. As David Stephens explains, "for Tolstoy, the State could only survive with the consent of the governed; a revolution to overthrow it had to take a personal rather than a political form."[7] Since the revolution is personal, it can take shape spontaneously.

It should be noted, though, that Tolstoy does give some indications of what sorts of societies he thinks could take shape. He speaks favorably, for example, of Cossacks of the Urals, "who have lived without acknowledging private property in land. There was such well-being and order in their commune as does not exist in society where landed property is defended by violence."[8] Furthermore, he writes, "I know too of communes that live without acknowledging the right of individuals to private property."[9] In this, we can read the influence of Pierre-Joseph Proudhon, the first thinker to call himself an anarchist, whom Tolstoy had the opportunity to meet. Proudhon famously argues that property is theft,[10] and in a letter from 1865, Tolstoy cites this position favorably, writing:

> the mission of Russia in world history consists in bringing into the world the idea of a socialized organization of land ownership. 'Property is theft' will remain a greater truth than the truth of the English constitution, as long as mankind exists ... This idea has [a] future.[11]

Tolstoy's ideas also remained in many significant ways consistent with some of the main currents of nineteenth-century anarchism. Like many other anarchists, Stephens explains, "Tolstoy's political writings express an uncompromising rejection of Authority and all its trappings, a scathing criticism of Church and State, capitalism and Marxism, militarism and patriotism."[12] It is his uncompromising rejection of violence that makes Tolstoy stand out from the rest of the anarchists of his day.

For Tolstoy, anarchy is the morally necessary negation of the violence of state, church, and capitalism. The exact forms of social organization will vary according to each community's needs, but, in order for each community to be freed from violence and therefore able to achieve such self-determination, Tolstoy is convinced that we must refuse to recognize, support, or participate in government violence. This is the only way to build a new society within the shell of the old.

B. Jacques Ellul

Jacques Ellul's anarchism shares much with Tolstoy's. For both thinkers, anarchism is rooted fundamentally in a rejection of violence. As Ellul writes, "by anarchy I mean first an absolute rejection of violence."[13] Like Tolstoy, then, Ellul consciously departs from any currents of anarchist thought which leave room for violent revolution. What does Ellul's nonviolent anarchism look like? "If I rule out violent anarchism," he explains,

> there remains pacifist, antinationalist, anticapitalist, moral, and antidemocratic anarchism (i.e., that which is hostile to the falsified democracy of bourgeois states). There remains

> the anarchism which acts by means of persuasion, by the creation of small groups and networks, denouncing falsehood and oppression, aiming at a true overturning of authorities of all kinds as people at the bottom speak and organize themselves. All this is very close to Bakunin.[14]

Ellul does indeed come close to Bakunin, for Bakunin was adamantly opposed to any revolution from above—that is, any revolution which would proceed by means of seizing political power—and instead advocated action from below. "The future social organization," according to Bakunin,

> should be carried out from the bottom up, by the free association or federation of workers, starting with the associations, then going on to the communes, the regions, the nations, and, finally, culminating in a great international and universal federation.[15]

It is not only on the question of violence that Ellul departs from the mainstream of anarchist thought. "The true anarchist," he writes, "thinks that an anarchist society is possible .... But I do not." Ellul nevertheless maintains that "the anarchist fight, the struggle for an anarchist society, is essential." This fight involves "the creation of new institutions from the grass-roots level."[16] Through such bottom-up action, meaningful change is indeed possible, but, in Ellul's view, the ideal of anarchy will always remain a pursuit rather than an accomplishment.

What Ellul and Tolstoy share is an uncompromising rejection of violence, as well as a deep suspicion of revolution, if by revolution we mean a violent attack on the existing system of social organization. Such an attack, in their view, can only result in the replacement of one system of violence with another. Christian anarchism is, rather, a call to live differently, to organize our lives anarchically, with no need for the state.

C. Vernard Eller

Vernard Eller's *Christian Anarchy: Jesus' Primacy over the Powers* relies heavily on Ellul's work. Like Ellul, Eller views Christian anarchism as a nonviolent, non-revolutionary way of living according to the kingdom of God rather than the kingdoms of the world. For Eller, too, revolutionary action recognizes—and therefore reinforces—the worldly ways of endless struggles for power, or what he calls "arky politics."[17] Anarchy, therefore, stands fundamentally opposed to revolution. According to Eller:

> 'revolution' is not anarchical in any sense of the word. Revolutionists *are* very strongly opposed to certain arkys that they know to be 'bad' and to be the work of 'bad people.' However, they are just as strongly in favor of what they know to be 'good' arkys that are the work of themselves and other good people like them.[18]

The Christian, according to Eller, has no such faith in the possibility of replacing a bad arky with a good, Christian one. For Eller, anarchy means "the state of being unimpressed with, disinterested in, skeptical of, nonchalant toward, and uninfluenced by the highfalutin claims of any and all arkys."[19] More than anything, then, the Christian anarchist is indifferent to worldly power and neither submits to it nor actively struggles against it.

Furthermore, unlike both Tolstoy—for whom anarchy may indeed be a real possibility—and Ellul—for whom anarchy is not a real possibility—for Eller, the question of possibility is irrelevant. Christian anarchists, he writes, "have no opinion as to whether secular society would be better off with anarchy than it is with all its present hierarchies .... Christian anarchists do not even argue that anarchy is a viable option for secular society."[20] Such anarchy is therefore not rooted in the same kind of antiauthoritarianism of Tolstoy and Ellul. Rather, it simply views human authorities as irrelevant to Christians. Whether these same authorities are necessary or legitimate for the non-Christian world is neither here nor there. The Christian's goal is "the arky of *God*."[21] To be sure, Eller is clear that he does not view God's arky as authoritarian in the same way that human arkys are. "Rather than a heteronomous imposition," he writes, "God's arky spells the discovery of that which is truest to myself and my world."[22] God's arky is a struggle against earthly powers, but not through force, but the cross, self-givingness. Recognizing God's authority therefore has much less to do with recognizing who is in charge, so to speak, and much more to do with recognizing the truth about reality. Anarchy is thus not a universally applicable socio-political vision, but is instead the proper way for the Christian to orient herself towards the worldly sources of power that try to claim her allegiance.

Eller's concerns about whether Christian anarchists should support *any* kind of order at all is a theme expanded upon by some other Christian anarchists. Mark Van Steenwyk addresses the question of authority in his works *That Holy Anarchist* and *The unKingdom of God*. The title of the latter already suggests Van Steenwyk's basic argument: if Jesus's "kingdom" is a kingdom of love, forgiveness, and nonviolence, as opposed to one marked by power and violence, does this not suggest that this "kingdom" is something more like an anti-kingdom or un-kingdom? Van Steenwyk writes that we "need to recognize that Jesus' kingdom isn't the sort that one holds with an iron fist. Rather, it is an unkingdom … Jesus is calling for a loving anarchy. An unkingdom. Of which he is the unking."[23] Jesus's kingdom is in every way the opposite of what a human kingdom would be. To further support the view that Jesus does not claim for himself a traditional, hierarchical, or authoritarian kingship, Christian anarchists often point to the temptation of Jesus by Satan, in which Jesus refuses Satan's offer of political power.[24] Accordingly, Nekeisha Alexis concludes that it is possible for Christian anarchists to "embrace God as Christians and reject masters as anarchists."[25]

III. Nonviolence

The Sermon on the Mount is central to the case for Christian anarchism. Dorothy Day writes, for example, that, for the Catholic Worker Movement, "the Sermon on the Mount is our Christian manifesto."[26] The Sermon is taken as a blueprint for Christian living, and Christian living in accordance with this blueprint is understood to include living the way of peace and making peace with others, along with suffering persecution without resistance.[27] Most Christian anarchists insist that Christians are called to follow these teachings in their plain sense, no matter how difficult or impractical they may seem. Even though power and violence are the ways of the world, Jesus preaches peace and non-resistance, and Christians must take him at His word. As Leo Tolstoy insists, Jesus "meant neither more nor less than what he said."[28] Thus, to follow the teachings of the Sermon on the Mount is to follow the way of radical nonviolence.

Historically, Christian anarchists have therefore been largely pacifists. Indeed, Christian anarchists often appear to have been led to anarchist conclusions precisely by their commitment to nonviolence. The place to begin understanding the biblical Christian anarchists' commitment to nonviolence is with Jesus's overturning of *lex talionis*, the Old Testament law of "an eye for an eye": "You have heard that it was said, 'An eye for an eye and a tooth for a tooth.' But I say to you, Do not resist an evildoer."[29] While some authors read Jesus's instruction here as relevant for *private* or *personal* interactions, Christian anarchists and pacifists insist upon the significant social and political as well as personal implications of His words.

Walter Wink argues that the verb translated as "resist" is best read as referring to "violent rebellion, armed revolt, sharp dissention."[30] Such a reading complements Christian anarchist readings of Jesus's temptation in the wilderness. According to Christoyannopoulos, in Jesus's rejection of Satan's offer to rule the kingdoms of the world,

> Jesus is implicitly distancing himself from the Zealots and their method, a contemporary group of Jewish rebels who wanted to overthrow Roman rule in Palestine by taking power ... His contemporaries expected the messiah to overthrow political oppressors and restore the Jewish monarchy.[31]

In both passages, then, we see Jesus rejecting violence and domination not simply in *personal* situations but in *political* situations as well.

Wink's translation is supported, according to Kurt Willems, when we consider that "*antistēnai* is the word repeatedly used in the Greek version of the Hebrew Bible as 'war-fare' and is also used in Ephesians 6:13 in the context of active military imagery."[32] Neither Wink nor Willems advocates Christian anarchism, but Christian anarchists look to such interpretations—Wink's in particular[33]—to defend their view of Jesus as neither violent nor apolitical, but as an exemplar of revolutionary nonviolence.

Christian anarchists argue that Jesus demonstrates the need to escape the cycle of violence, and the impossibility of doing so by violent means. Ellul, for example, appeals to Jesus's saying that "*All* who take the sword will perish by the sword,"[34] from which Ellul concludes that "The law of the sword is a total law."[35] Accordingly, Ellul writes, "violence begets violence—*nothing else*."[36] For Christian anarchists, the endless cycle of violence can be broken only by nonviolent intervention.

Christian anarchists believe that Jesus points the way beyond the cycle of violence. Immediately after overturning *lex talionis*, Jesus provides His listeners with a pointed example: "But if anyone strikes you on the right cheek, turn the other also."[37] According to Michael Elliott, by the victim's refusal to engage in violence, "the cycle of violence is unexpectedly interrupted."[38] Rather than legitimizing the attacker's use of violence by responding in kind, Jesus challenges His listeners to—perhaps somewhat paradoxically—deny the attacker's power precisely by offering the other cheek. As Ellul cautions, "once we consent to use violence ourselves, we have to consent to our adversary's using it, too."[39] Turning the other cheek is therefore seen by Christian anarchists as a radical refusal to acknowledge the legitimacy of responding to violence with violence. As Tolstoy writes, "all attempts to abolish slavery by violence are like extinguishing fire with fire, stopping water with water, or filling up one hole by digging another."[40] The cycle of violence cannot be escaped through violent means; thus, Jesus challenges His followers to disrupt this mutually accepted employment of violence.

The commitment to nonviolence sets Christian anarchists apart from most of their non-Christian counterparts.[41] However, Christian anarchists and pacifists often appeal to a *prefigurative* argument in support of nonviolence. Prefigurative considerations have long been central to anarchist arguments, so this appeal to prefiguration draws Christian and non-Christian anarchists closer together, even if, ultimately, they often remain separated on the question of violence. According to Nathan Jun, "[t]he 'prefigurative principle' demands coherence between means and ends. That is, if the goal of political action is the promotion of some value, the means and methods employed in acting must reflect or prefigure the desired end."[42] Such coherence between means and ends is precisely what writers such as Tolstoy see as requiring nonviolence. Bart de Ligt—an anarcho-pacifist with a Christian background[43]—writes that "it is impossible to educate people in liberty by force, just as it is impossible to breathe by coal gas."[44] Instead, he insists, "it is the task of the social revolution to go beyond this violence and to emancipate itself from it."[45]

Prefigurative considerations thus play a central role in Christian anarchist defenses of nonviolence. It would be an oversimplification to say that any argument that relies on prefiguration is ultimately an anarchist argument. But Christian anarchists can at least claim that their nonviolence does not violate, but in fact attempts to satisfy, anarchist demands for prefiguration.

Christian anarchists also see in nonviolence possibilities for forgiveness and reconciliation that are foreclosed by violent methods. Shortly after His teachings on nonviolent responses to violence, Jesus says, "You have heard that it was said, 'You shall love your neighbor and hate your enemy.' But I say to you, Love your enemies and pray for those who persecute you."[46] As Christoyannopoulos explains,

> non-resistance, and its concomitant willingness to suffer unjustly, clears the ground for reconciliation because it exposes the destructive violence of the situation and makes a moving plea to overcome it. It lays bare the cycle of violence and it refuses to prolong it.[47]

The nonviolence championed by Christian anarchists is therefore motivated not only by the anarchist desire for consistency between means and ends but also by the Christian desire for forgiveness and reconciliation.

This is not to say that Christian anarchism is simply the combination of otherwise independent Christian and anarchist concerns, however. Rather, Christian anarchists view the desire for reconciliation as deeply consistent with anarchism. For, according to the Christian anarchist perspective, it is precisely this kind of reconciliation that can provide a way out of the cycle of hatred and violence and into a more just and loving society. The state operates according to *lex talionis*—relying on tit-for-tat violence and choosing to identify and fight enemies rather than to forgive them or to seek reconciliation. As Christoyannopoulos concludes, "for Christian anarchists, therefore, on this account as well, the state is an unchristian institution."[48] Christian anarchists see love of enemies as fundamentally anarchic.

Regarding the potentially problematic temple-cleansing episode in the Gospel of John, John Dear and Andy Alexis-Baker argue that the passage in fact does not depict Jesus as acting violently. Dear argues that Jesus's acting violently "would be entirely inconsistent with the Jesus portrayed throughout John's Gospel, as well as the Synoptics."[49] Rather, Dear writes, "most scholars agree that John deliberately paints Jesus as a righteous prophet in the tradition of Jeremiah, who engaged in similar dramatic actions."[50] This suggests that what is important about the scene as depicted by John is not the violence per se, but Jesus's righteous anger. Furthermore, Alexis-Baker argues that a careful translation of the Greek would be the following: "he drove all of them out of the temple, *both* the sheep *and* the cattle."[51] The word "both" is the linchpin here, as it limits "them" to the sheep and the cattle and no one else. Alexis-Baker concludes by also challenging the assumption that the passage shows Jesus violently attacking animals. He writes that "a makeshift whip of rope would hardly do much more than get them moving out the door."[52] Accordingly, in the view of Christian anarchists and pacifists, the passage can be justifiably read in such a way that does not contradict the Christian ethic of nonviolence.

IV. Romans 13 and Rendering unto Caesar

The two most commonly cited biblical passages that present potential problems for the Christian anarchist thesis are Romans 13:1–7 and Jesus's instruction to "render unto Caesar what is Caesar's" in Matthew 22:21, Mark 12:17, and Luke 20:25. Each passage can be read in such a way that it appears that Christians are called to be obedient, tax-paying citizens because God has ordained the governing authorities as instruments of His will. In other words, according to such a reading, a Christian cannot be an anarchist, for anarchists rebel against the legitimate authorities that God has put into power. This section will consider Christian anarchist interpretations of these passages. We will see that, for Christian anarchists, not only do these passages not seriously undercut Christian anarchist claims, but they in fact end up *supporting* the Christian anarchist perspective.[53]

A. Romans 13

Romans 13:1–7 is often presented as quite self-evidently teaching Christians to submit to governing authorities. D.A. Carson and Douglas J. Moo, for example, write: "Serving God does not mean, Paul cautions, that the Christian can ignore the legitimate claims that government makes on us (Romans 13:1–7)."[54] Some Christian anarchists do not dispute this reading, and argue simply that Paul was mistaken. For these thinkers, "*Jesus* is the important teacher, and Paul is just an erring follower who has been given too much kudos by the tradition."[55] Accordingly, these Christian anarchists—Tolstoy among them—are simply not concerned with re-interpreting Paul's teachings when they appear to contradict those of Jesus. If Paul appears to say something contrary to what Jesus said, Jesus's words are to be given precedence. Other Christian anarchists and pacifists, however, seek rather to re-interpret Romans 13:1–7. This desire flows from the conviction that the New Testament exhibits anarchistic and/or pacifistic tendencies, which should not be ignored because of a mere seven verses.[56]

One element of Romans 13 that Christian anarchists and pacifists find especially noteworthy is the fact that it follows immediately upon an apparent near-recitation of the Sermon on the Mount in Romans 12. Stanley Hauerwas emphasizes this fact, noting that the instruction "Let every person be subject to the governing authorities" appears only after Paul exhorts his readers to "love one another," "bless those who persecute you," "live in harmony with one another," "do not repay anyone evil for evil," "live peaceably with all," "never avenge yourselves," and finally, "do not be overcome by evil, but overcome evil with good."[57]

> Seen in that light, Romans 13 is not a betrayal of Jesus' revolutionary Sermon on the Mount … but actually an exegesis of it … In the Sermon, Jesus calls for [H]is followers to love their enemies … In Romans 12–13, Paul is doing the same, and applying Jesus' commandments to the authorities.[58]

From such a perspective, then, Christians are to be "subject" in the same way that they are to turn the other cheek or to give their cloak when asked for their coat: it is a way of frustrating the worldly ways of power and violence and instead overcoming evil with good.

Such "subversive subjection" is further strengthened by Paul's words in Colossians 2:15[59] that Christ "disarmed the rulers and authorities and made a public example of them, triumphing over them in it." What does it mean to be subject to disarmed rulers? Vernard Eller writes that Paul's instruction "is sheerly neutral and anarchical counsel of 'not-doing'—not doing resistance, anger, assault, power play, or anything contrary to the 'loving the enemy' which is, of course, Paul's main theme."[60] From this perspective, the passage teaches *indifference* towards government more than anything else. And this is consistent with Jesus's cautioning against the kind of violent revolution called for by Zealots. Christians are to deny the cycle of violence and power altogether, which means simply refusing to participate in the worldly ways of power, which are the ways of violently displacing one power for another. The Christian anarchist views Christianity as a call to live *otherwise* than fighting for power.

However, Romans 13:1–7 appears to do more than simply present the Christian's role as indifference towards authorities. The passage seems to go so far as acknowledging the legitimacy—indeed, *God-ordained* legitimacy—of the state and its violent enforcement of order. However, Christian anarchists and pacifists think that such a reading is, minimally, an oversimplification. John Howard Yoder, for example, argues that

> God is not said to *create* or *institute* or *ordain* the powers that be, but only to *order* them ... Nor is it that by ordering this realm God specifically, morally approves of what a government does. The sergeant does not produce the soldiers he drills; the librarian does not create or approve of the book she or he catalogues and shelves. Likewise, God does not take responsibility for the existence of the rebellious "powers that be."[61]

1 Samuel 8 appears to affirm such a reading. As Nekeisha Alexis writes, "God makes it clear to Samuel and the Israelites that by choosing a king the Israelites have also rejected God and the freedom God provides from oppression, injustice, war and taxation."[62] Christian anarchists therefore do not read Romans 13 as a statement of God's approval of governing authorities; rather, these rulers "remain living evidence of humanity's rebellion against God."[63]

Furthermore, Yoder writes that "the sword (*machaira*) is the symbol of judicial authority. It was not the instrument of capital punishment," nor was it "the instrument of war."[64] Not only this, but Yoder argues that "verses 3–4 did not include any services that the Christian is asked to render";[65] rather, these verses describe the authorities as carrying out a function "which the Christian was to leave to God,"[66] meaning, in other words, that the role taken up by state authorities is one that can only rightly be claimed by God and therefore state authorities have no claim on the allegiance of Christians. According to such a reading, then, Christians are called to subjection not because of the legitimacy of the rulers but because of Christ's teachings to love one's enemies, to not be conformed to the ways of the world, and to overcome evil with good.

One more curious element of Romans 13:1–7 should be noted: Paul claims that "rulers are not a terror to good conduct, but to bad." Christoyannpoulos points out that Christian anarchists "never really seem to fully make sense of" this passage: "What they do point out, however, is that it cannot mean that these authorities do not persecute good people: they crucified Jesus, Paul himself was beaten by them, and Christians were being persecuted just as Paul was writing these words."[67] What, then, might Paul mean by saying that rulers are a "terror" only to bad conduct? One possibility is that Christians are not to fear rulers, not because rulers will not persecute Christians, but rather because, for the Christian, human rulers are not legitimate sources of authority and so are not to be heeded when their laws conflict with the teachings of Christ. Why fear the authority of those whose authority is not recognized by God? If Christians are members of Christ's kingdom, and His kingdom is "not of this world," then Christians have no reason to concern themselves with human kingdoms.[68]

B. Rendering unto Caesar

Jesus's admonition to "Give to the emperor the things that are the emperor's, and to God the things that are God's"[69] presents another possible problem for Christian anarchism. Despite Jesus's apparently instructing His followers to pay taxes—giving to Caesar what is his, which could be taken further to imply acknowledging the legitimacy of His authority—Christian anarchists read this passage as supporting rather than undermining their anarchist position. Greg Boyd and Paul Rhodes Eddy point out in *The Jesus Legend* that "within Palestine coins were often printed without the customary representation of the emperor on them ... in deference to [Jewish people's] sensitivity to anything that could violate the second commandment."[70] This suggests that Jesus may in fact have been pointing out the Pharisees' potential violation of the

Second Commandment. At issue in this episode, then, would not so much be the question of taxes as the question of to whom allegiance is to be given.

Furthermore, as Jacques Ellul points out, it is with the coins that "the basis and limit of [the emperor's] power" is revealed, for "whatever does not bear Caesar's mark does not belong to him." Most importantly, "Caesar has no right of life and death,"[71] for humans are made in *God's* image, not Caesar's. Dorothy Day, in her oft-quoted response upon being questioned on this passage, similarly says, "[w]hen you give to God what belongs to God, there is nothing left for Caesar."[72] Therefore, Caesar can certainly claim no legitimate dominion over human life.

For many Christian anarchists, therefore, this passage, like Romans 13, displays an attitude of, at best, *indifference* to the governing authorities. It is not a call to *obey*, for the Christian does not owe obedience to human authorities. Neither is it a call to *disobey*. Indeed, in Eller's view, tax evasion is unchristian not because of the legitimacy of taxes, but because "withholding the coin is the 'revolution' that stakes everything upon the contest of human arkys."[73] Instead, the Christian should give Caesar's coins back when asked and get back to the truly important work of pursuing Christ's (un)kingdom.

Thus, once again, we see Christian anarchism as a way of living differently which seeks to operate entirely outside of the political realm, characterized as it is by the endless struggle for power. Christian anarchists attempt to live according to the demands of the (un)kingdom of God.

V. Christian Market Anarchism

As we noted in the introduction, there are two kinds of Christian anarchists—those who defend anarchism primarily on biblical grounds, and those who defend it primarily by appealing to natural law and natural rights commonly associated with Christian theism (there are early figures with no clear commitments on this question, such as David Lipscomb).[74] The biblical anarchists tend to be socialists or friendly to socialism, rejecting property rights as fundamental natural or human rights insofar as they have a theory of property. (Alex Salter argues convincingly that they do not have one.[75]) The natural law anarchists tend to embrace capitalism by embracing natural property rights, arguing that states necessarily violate property rights and so should be abolished. They have rich economic theories, almost always drawn from the Austrian school of economics. They also provide detailed models of how an anarchist economic order would function, again in contrast to the socialists—even those who spoke to the issue briefly, like Tolstoy.[76]

Importantly, though, Christian market anarchists only occasionally argue that Scripture favors their position. They instead offer more modest arguments that their view is compatible with Scripture, dogmatic theology, and in some cases, Catholic social thought. One might be tempted to conclude for this reason that the market anarchists are not true Christian anarchists because, while they are Christian and anarchist, their anarchism is seldom based in a developed understanding of Christian theology, and the arguments for anarchism are rooted in natural law and natural rights can presumably be given apart from revelation.

However, some market anarchists argue that certain biblical and theological commitments tell in favor of anarchism. Since this volume already contains several discussions of market anarchism and the arguments for it, we will not review those arguments here. Instead, we will examine how Christian market anarchists rebuff certain kinds of statist and anti-market commitments and arguments from Scripture, Christian theology, and Catholic social thought. In particular, we will analyze such discussions in the work of James Redford, Stephen W. Carson, Norman Horn, Thomas E. Woods, Jim Fedako, and Alex Salter.

The market anarchists agree with many of the arguments for Christian anarchism adopted by more familiar biblical, socialist anarchists, which we do not need to review. Where they differ is in defending a basis for natural property rights and markets in Scripture and Christian theology, which when combined with anarchist arguments jointly imply anarcho-capitalism. Redford and Carson, for instance, argue that passages like the Parable of the Talents[77] and the Parable of the Tenants[78] (Redford)[79] and the Mosaic Law (Carson)[80] seem to presuppose the legitimacy of private property independently of the state or any nation-state-style government. All three sources (Talents, Tenants, Mosaic Law) treat private property holdings as legitimate and violations as unjust, and they do so independently of any state convention or definition. In this, Carson, Redford, and others follow lines of argument advanced within Christian libertarianism more generally.

Market anarchists also try to show that Jesus's teachings on wealth are not incompatible with capitalism. Market anarchists sometimes argue that Jesus is primarily condemning riches garnered unjustly.[81] Carson advances the fascinating claim that, when God told the Israelites how to govern themselves, no mention is made of large-scale restrictions on property rights and certainly not the abolition of property.[82] Provision is made for the poor, but there is a notable absence of other powers associated with modern states. And commercial relations are treated as ordinary.

On top of this, the yearning for a state in 1 Samuel 8 is condemned as a rejection of God. Thus, if God opposed capitalism and favored the state, He would have said as much in seemingly embracing the private law anarchy found in the Book of Judges. The Israelites plainly have property rights and no state ("In those days there was no king in Israel. Everyone did what was right in his own eyes."),[83] which is rather striking.

There is also something to be said for the idea that the Old Testament *generally* acknowledges rights to property in agrarian, nomadic societies in which there existed no state to create or define or restrict property rights. Examples include interactions between early humans, such as those between different nomadic shepherds, and such as those between Abraham and other small tribes.

Redford focuses primarily on New Testament passages, arguing that Jesus condemned taxation and that Romans 13 should be read in a subversive way as undermining current Roman authority. Carson[84] and Norman Horn[85] argue more plausibly that Romans 13 only specifies when Christians are to obey government, and not the ideal form of government. There is no incompatibility between wanting to abolish or limit the state and having a duty to God to obey the state and its laws in the meanwhile. As Jim Fedako puts it,

> As Christians, we are to obey the legitimate governing authority, but it does not follow that the authority must be the state. Paul's instructions are the same no matter who is in charge. And in a market anarchist world, we would only be forced to obey the governing authorities whose properties we chose to enter.[86]

Carson argues similarly, "Paul's instruction to individual believers to submit to existing authorities does not preclude a people's return to God being our only king under a just Law."[87]

The work of Catholic market anarchists, first and foremost Thomas E. Woods, Jr., argues for the compatibility of Catholic social teaching with capitalism and the right to private property. While many Church teachings seem hostile to the market, Woods interprets those passages as a combination of an authoritative *moral* teaching with a non-authoritative application of the moral teaching to *economic policy*. So, there are authoritative moral teachings about helping the poor, but attempts by popes and other theological authorities to extend these teachings to economic policy to support, say, foreign aid, unions, and a living wage, are not authoritative because these teachings concern moral principles alone, and not their application to the economy based on economic science. The Church has no special expertise in economics, and economic science is in a certain sense value-free, whereas Church teachings are value-laden.

Thus, while Woods does not defend market anarchism in his book on Catholic social teaching, it is not hard to see how a Catholic defense of market anarchism could proceed. Woods and others can acknowledge that moral principles in Catholic social thought are authoritative, and then argue that combining the moral principles with Austrian economics and, indeed, a good deal of basic economics more generally, shows that market anarchism is the best and most just economic regime because it is the best expression of Catholic moral teaching. On this point, Woods often stresses the Catholic teaching regarding subsidiarity, where power should be decentralized to local levels when that is feasible. And since libertarian economics and political science has shown that we can radically decentralize power, the principle of subsidiarity provides a defense of radical political decentralization, which can imply anarchism.

Overall, then, we can generate a formula for justifying Christian market anarchism: (1) adopt Christian anarchist readings of the passages of Scripture that otherwise seem to favor the legitimacy and justice of the nation-state; (2) adopt interpretations of Scripture that favor pacifism and nonviolence, or something near enough; (3) argue that Scripture supports a natural right of private property and that this right is incompatible with socialism; and (4) show that other forms of Christian teaching, like Catholic social thought, the Church fathers, Jewish law, etc., are compatible with market anarchism. Christian market anarchists can then (5) draw on natural reason and natural law to ground a right to private property. Finally, they can (6) take economic insights, especially, perhaps, those embraced by the Austrian school of economics, to show that market anarchism is feasible, stable, and enormously productive in ways that make it superior to the state and anarcho-socialism, especially with regard to the poorest among us. In short, the case for market anarchism synthesizes the classical socialist anarchist critique of the state with the standard arguments offered for political libertarianism, with a dash of biblical exegesis devoted to vindicating property rights.

VI. Resolving the Capitalism–Socialism Disagreement between Christian Anarchists

Christian market anarchists and socialist anarchists seldom engage one another. The most influential Christian socialist anarchists were largely unaware of the market anarchists, in particular since most died before market anarchism was articulated in the late 1970s and the 1980s. And, while market anarchists take on some socialist anarchist arguments against the state, they assume that anarchist socialists' failure to provide a plausible theory of property means that their views on the topic are not authoritative and do not require refutation beyond the standard, non-religious arguments against socialism and anarchist socialism.

But there are some passages in Scripture that might be used to settle the dispute. Salter has argued that the socialist anarchists like Ellul do not have a good explanation of Jesus's use of violence in the temple cleansing.[88] Theorists like Ellul are pacifists, based on a fairly surface-level reading of Jesus's teaching in the Sermon on the Mount.[89] But this raises the question of why Jesus made a whip to force the money-changers out of the temple. As Salter notes, "Christian anarcho-[socialists] are forced to confront the apparent inconsistency between Christ's commandments in the Sermon on the Mount and His actions during the temple cleaning."[90]

There isn't an inherent contradiction here, but Jesus's actions still raise a question for socialist anarchists, since their arguments are so heavily rooted in pacifism, and pacifism seems like it would allow for the formation of property relations, exchange, and so on, leading to anarchist capitalism of some sort. Socialist anarchists also don't seem to have a clear and compelling response. Yoder[91] and Christoyannopoulos[92] think that Christ's actions aren't really violent, which seems mistaken. Ellul[93] argues that the temple cleansing just shows the supremacy of Christ's teachings for us rather than His actions, but it is not clear why Ellul thinks we should prioritize one over the other. Oddly, Ellul doesn't address the temple cleansing in *Anarchy and Christianity*. This might be because he thought that Jesus's actions aren't inconsistent with Ellul's pacifism. But if that is what Ellul thought, he might have explained why, given the apparent tension.

The market anarchist has an easy response: force is permitted to defend private property and avoid violations of property rights in exchange. Jesus's violence is consistent with this. Jesus is defending His own house, the temple, against fraudulent money-changers. His use of defensive violence is thereby justified. Thus, one biblical argument for market anarchism over socialist anarchism is that market anarchism renders the Sermon on the Mount (condemning the initiation of force) consistent with the temple cleansing (permitting defensive force in a very specific case of defending private property). This is roughly the line Redford pursues.[94]

It is unclear, however, why Jesus didn't single out defensive uses of violence as acceptable, so this argument strikes us as far from decisive. If we allow that Jesus's actions were violent, this raises the question of the tenability of both socialist anarchism and market anarchism on the grounds that if Jesus used violence, He might assign some the authority to use violence in His name, which is essentially how Christians who favor the state have defended their position. One might go further than Jesus's express teachings, and draw implications from other teachings. For instance, the Golden Rule[95] might license only defensive violence, since we may want to be able to defend ourselves against others, and so would not endorse the initiation of violence against others.

On the flip side, socialist anarchists can appeal to Jesus's consistent condemnation of wealth-holding and of the rich to show that their position is more consistent with Scripture than market anarchism, insofar as capitalism is associated and even based on the goodness of wealth-holding. Market anarchists see the tension and, as we noted, sometimes argue that the rich of Jesus's day got their riches in ways that violate libertarian justice. The argument, then, is that Jesus is condemning not wealth or riches but *ill-gotten* wealth and riches. And yet, these are not the reasons Jesus cites. It is clear from the discussion with the rich young man[96] that wealth is a grave temptation that can set one against God. One cannot serve God and Mammon,[97] even *legitimately acquired* Mammon. Thus, insofar as market anarchism depends on the legitimacy of allowing large economic inequalities between rich and poor, and socialist anarchism avoids these inequalities, socialist anarchism may be more consistent with Jesus's teachings on wealth, as well as those elsewhere in the New Testament.

A common response is that the Old Testament seems much friendlier to wealth-holding, as people are not required to give up all of their property, but rather to simply alleviate poverty, and in some cases, people seem blessed in virtue of receiving riches, as in Job's compensation.[98] But socialist anarchists can argue that New Testament teachings are more authoritative and direct and so should be decisive.

One way to rectify the tension between Christian market anarchism and Jesus's teachings on wealth is to argue that, while market anarchism allows for economic inequalities, Jesus only condemns large-scale wealth-holding on ethical grounds. Natural justice may permit fairly large inequalities of wealth, but the rich are nonetheless ethically required to be generous, even if no one has the authority to force them to be generous. If this seems odd, just consider that Jesus's teachings might in some ways go beyond natural justice, requiring Christians to do more than what is naturally required of them. This certainly seems to be the case with respect to Jesus's teaching of unilateral forgiveness.[99] Natural justice seems to only require forgiveness when the wrongdoer repents. Along the same lines, Jesus might require His followers to be generous, but think this goes beyond natural justice.

This argument has some force. But market anarchists must still grapple with the force Peter appears to have wielded to kill Ananias and Sapphira,[100] who refused to share their property with the community. The market anarchists will respond that Ananias and Sapphira had voluntarily agreed to become part of the early Church and that one of the conditions of the agreement was wealth-sharing, which does not indicate a rejection of capitalism.

It is also noteworthy that Ludwig von Mises, an Austrian economist held in high esteem by Christian market anarchists (though he himself was an atheist), argued that the apparent socialism in Acts is only a socialism of local people with respect to consumption goods, not capital goods.[101] So even if there should be more sharing among Christians, this does not mean capital should be socially owned, as socialist anarchists demand. While one can doubt Mises's skill at biblical exegesis, the general point stands that the Scriptures seem to speak to a local socialism of consumption goods alone.

Finally, it is an interesting feature of the Epistles that Paul never insists on enforcing a communist mode of economic life and exchange even within churches. Christians are of course required to care for one another, but the idea that everyone in each church must hold so much in common does not seem to be a theme of his writing. It is of course possible that he thought Christian churches simply took this for granted, but of all the problems Paul detects in the early Christian churches, failing to share on the extreme level of the Jerusalem Church does not seem to be among them. Perhaps the communal sharing of the Jerusalem Church had not gone well, and the disciples decided not to encourage it beyond what is required to care for the poor, such as Galatians 2:10, "Only, they asked us to remember the poor, the very thing I was eager to do."

We find these Scriptural arguments complex and inconclusive. But we do think there are at least Scriptural bases for Christian market anarchists and Christian socialist anarchists to settle their dispute one way or another.

Notes

1 Alexandre Christoyannopoulos, *Christian Anarchism: A Political Commentary on the Bible* [Abridged Edition] (Exeter: Imprint, 2011) 31. Emphasis in original.

2 Leo Tolstoy, *The Kingdom of God Is within You*, trans. Constance Garnett (Charleston, SC: CreateSpace, 2014) 123.

3 Leo Tolstoy, "The Slavery of our Time," *Government Is Violence: Essays on Anarchism and Pacifism*, ed. and intro. David Stephens (London: Phoenix, 1990) 145.

4 Leo Tolstoy, "On Anarchy," in *Government Is Violence: Essays on Anarchism and Pacifism*, ed. and intro. David Stephens (London: Phoenix, 1990) 68.

5 Tolstoy, "Anarchy," 68.

6 Tolstoy, "Slavery," 149.

7 David Stephens, "The Non-violent Anarchism of Leo Tolstoy," in *Government Is Violence: Essays on Anarchism and Pacifism*, ed. and intro. Stephens (London: Phoenix, 1990) 18.

8 Tolstoy, "Slavery," 143.

9 Ibid.

10 See Pierre-Joseph Proudhon, *What Is Property? An Inquiry into the Principle of Right and of Government*, trans. Benj. R. Tucker (Mineola, NY: Dover, 1970). Available from http://theanarchistlibrary.org/library/pierre-joseph-proudhon-what-is-property-an-inquiry-into-the-principle-of-right-and-of-governmen.

11 Tolstoy, quoted in Stephens, 9.

12 Stephens, 8.

13 Jacques Ellul, *Anarchy and Christianity*, trans. Geoffrey W. Bromiley (Eugene, OR: Wipf & Stock, 2011) 11.

14 Ellul 13–14.

15 Mikhail Bakunin, "The Paris Commune and the Idea of the State," in *Anarchism: A Documentary History of Libertarian Ideas, Volume One: From Anarchy to Anarchism (300CE to 1939)*, ed. Robert Graham (Montreal/New York/London: Black Rose, 2005) 105.

16 Ellul, 19–20.

17 According to Eller, "The '-archy' root is a common Greek word that means 'priority,' 'primacy,' 'primordial,' 'principle,' 'prince,' and the like" (Eller, *Christian Anarchy*, 1). Furthermore, Eller notes, "in Colassians

1:18 Paul actually identifies Jesus as 'the beginning,' 'the prime,' 'THE ARKY'" (ibid., Eller's capitalization). Thus, for Eller, "Christian anarchy" could also be described as "theonomy—the rule, the ordering, the arky of *God*" (ibid., 3, Eller's emphasis). Nevertheless, Christoyannopoulos concludes that "'Christian anarchism' probably remains the best way to name [Eller's] interpretation of Christianity, because it immediately declares that for its advocates, the rejection of the state and the growth of a stateless society are inevitable political implications of Christianity."

18 Vernard Eller, *Christian Anarchy: Jesus' Primacy over the Powers* (Grand Rapids, MI: William B. Eerdmans, 1987) 3. Emphasis in original.

19 Eller, 2.

20 Ibid., 12.

21 Ibid., 3. Emphasis in original.

22 Ibid., 3.

23 Mark Van Steenwyk, *That Holy Anarchist: Reflections on Christianity & Anarchism* (Minneapolis, MN: Missio Dei, 2012) 14.

24 See Christoyannpoulos, *Christian Anarchism.*

25 Nekeisha Alexis-Baker, "Embracing God and Rejecting Masters: On Christianity, Anarchism, and the State," *The Utopian* 5 (2006): 78.

26 Dorothy Day, "Our Stand," *Catholic Worker* (June 1940, 1, 4): 1.

27 Matt. 5:2–11.

28 Leo Tolstoy, *What I Believe*, trans. Huntington Smith (Guildford: White Crow, 2009) 16.

29 Matt. 5:38–39a.

30 Walter Wink, *Jesus and Nonviolence: A Third Way* (Minneapolis, MN: Fortress, 2003) 13.

31 Christoyannopoulos, 76.

32 Kurt Willems, "Nonviolence 101—Resistance is Futile ... or the Meaning of ἀντιστῆναι (part 2)." The Pangea Blog, Patheos.com (February 7, 2011), www.patheos.com/blogs/thepangeablog/2011/02/07/nonviolence-101-resistance-is-futile-or-the-meaning-of-%E1%BC%80%CE%BD%CF%84%CE%B9%CF%83%CF%84%E1%BF%86%CE%BD%CE%B1%CE%B9-part-2/ (last visited Aug. 21, 2019).

33 See Christoyannopoulos, *Christian Anarchism.*

34 Matt. 26:52. Our emphasis and Ellul's.

35 Ellul, *Violence: Reflections from a Christian Perspective*, trans. Cecilia Gaul Kings (Eugene, OR: Wipf & Stock, 2011) 95.

36 Ibid., 100. Emphasis in original.

37 Matt. 5:39.

38 Michael Elliot, *Freedom, Justice and Christian Counter-Culture* (London: SCM, 1990) 33.

39 Ellul, *Violence*, 39.

40 Tolstoy, "Slavery," 145.

41 See, for example, Peter Gelderloos' *How Nonviolence Protects the State.* 2nd ed. (Olympia, WA: Detritus, 2018).

42 Nathan J. Jun, *Anarchism and Political Modernity* (New York, NY: Continuum, 2012) 129.

43 De Ligt served as a pastor in the Reformed Church of the Netherlands before ultimately moving away from Christianity towards universalism. For more on this, see "Bart de Ligt (1883–1938): Non-violent Anarcho-Pacifist," available from www.satyagrahafoundation.org/bart-de-ligt-1883-1938-non-violent-anarcho-pacifist/.

44 Bart de Ligt, *The Conquest of Violence: An Essay on War and Revolution* (Winchester: Pluto, 1989) 72.

45 De Ligt, 168.

46 Matt. 5:43–44.

47 Christoyannpoulos, 41.

48 Ibid., 52.

49 John Dear, "Didn't Jesus Overturn Tables and Chase People Out of the Temple with a Whip?" in Tripp York, Justin Barringer, Shane Claiborne, and Stanley Hauerwas (eds.), *A Faith Not Worth Fighting* For, pp. 184–191 (La Vergne, TN: Wipf and Stock, 2012) 189.

50 Ibid., 188.

51 Andy Alexis-Baker, "Violence, Nonviolence and the Temple Incident in John 2:13–15," in *Biblical Interpretation* 20 (2012): 94. Our emphasis.

52 Ibid. Dear agrees with this assessment, writing, "cattlemen and shepherds used cords and ropes to lead animals up the high stone walkways into the building. Jesus simply took those cords, which the cattle, sheep, and oxen would have recognized, and started to drive them outside" (189).

53 We have not included a discussion of 1 Peter 2:13–25 in this section. This choice was made both in the interest of space and because the passage has received less attention in the Christian anarchist literature than the others. Christoyannopoulos notes that, "for Christian anarchists," 1 Peter 2:13–25 "is actually just repeating the Sermon on the Mount and Romans 13" (156). For a more in-depth discussion of this passage, see Ellul's *Anarchy and Christianity*, and Justin Bronson Barringer, "Subordination and Freedom: Tracing Anarchist Themes in First Peter," in Alexandre Christoyannopoulos and Matthew S. Adams (eds.), *Essays in Anarchism and Religion: Volume II*, pp. 132–172 (Stockholm: Stockholm University Press, 2018). doi: https://doi.org/10.16993/bas.

54 D.A. Carson and Douglas J. Moo, *An Introduction to the New Testament.* 2nd ed. (Grand Rapids, MI: Zondervan, 2005) 392. N.T. Wright appears not to disagree entirely with this approach, but he does offer some important qualifications which bring him closer to the reading of Christian anarchists and pacifists. According to Wright, Paul views it as "vital that he steer Christians away from the assumption that loyalty to Jesus would mean the kind of civil disobedience and revolution that merely reshuffles the political cards into a different order." (*Paul: In Fresh Perspective,* Minneapolis, MN: Fortress, 2005, 78). Such a reading is consistent with the Christian anarchist conviction that the cycles of violence and power cannot be escaped through violent or power-grabbing means. According to Wright's reading, the kingdom of God is so totally other to the kingdoms of the world that the ways that the latter are established and maintained—via, through power and violence—cannot possibly aid the coming of the former. "The church," he concludes, "must live as a sign of the kingdom yet to come, but since that kingdom is characterized by justice, peace and joy in the Spirit (14.17), it cannot be inaugurated in the present by violence and hatred" (79).

55 Christoyannopoulos, 149. Emphasis in original.

56 It is worth noting that some commentators question the legitimacy of Romans 13:1–7. Moo explains that the "argument comes on the scene quite abruptly, with no explicit syntactical connection with what has come before it—and not much evidence of any connection in subject matter either. In fact, vv. 8–10, highlighting the centrality of love for the Christian ethic, seem to relate [to] vv. 9–21, which also focus on love and its outworkings. When we add to these points the allegedly un-Pauline vocabulary of the passage, we can understand why some scholars think that a redactor has added 13:1–7 to Paul's original letter to the Romans" (790–791). Bernard Brandon Scott similarly argues that "Romans 13:1–7 sticks out like a sore thumb" and that "there are three good reasons to doubt that Romans 13:1–7 was part of the original letter." First, "the abruptness with which it interrupts the *pareneses*"; second, "the lack of an eschatological or apocalyptic sense, something essential to Paul"; and third, the passage "does not really fit with Paul's understanding of freedom" ("Romans 13 in Our Time," *Westar Institute*, June 25, 2018. www.westarinstitute.org/blog/romans-13-in-our-time/). It appears, however, that Christian anarchists and pacifists have not exploited this possibility, opting instead either to re-interpret the passage or else simply to read Paul as an imperfect follower of Christ who is therefore capable of being mistaken.

57 Stanley Hauerwas, "God Talk: Religious Speech in Public Discourse." Panel discussion at Duke University. Durham, NC. 5 Mar. 2007.

58 Christoyannopoulos, 151.

59 Many commentators argue that Colossians was not in fact written by Paul, but rather by one of Paul's followers. For example, Carson, Moo, and Morris write: "many recent scholars think that a follower of Paul rather than the apostle himself actually penned the book" (D.A. Carson, Douglas J. Moo, and Leon Morris, *An Introduction to the New Testament*, Grand Rapids, MI: Zondervan, 1992, 332). However, they continue, "It is strongly urged by some that the actual authorship of the letter does not matter. It is agreed that there is a Pauline connection; at the very least the author must have come from the devoted followers of Paul, and he has given a Pauline viewpoint in this letter" (338). Similarly, James D.G. Dunn writes, "I have to confirm the strong likelihood that the letter comes from a hand other than Paul's." However, he writes, "the issue might not be quite so crucial for a full appreciation of the letter's significance" (*The Epistles to the Colossians and to Philemon: A Commentary on the Greek Text*, Grand Rapids, MI: William B. Eerdmans, 1996, 35). It is beyond the scope of the present paper to discuss the matter further; suffice it to say for present purposes that it is reasonable to locate the source of Colossians in Paul's thought even if Paul was not the author of the letter itself.

60 Eller, 199.

61 John Howard Yoder, *The Politics of Jesus*, 2nd ed. (Grand Rapids, MI: William B. Eerdmans, 1994) 201. Emphasis in original.

62 Nekeisha Alexis-Baker, 78.

63 Christoyannopoulos, 153.

64 Yoder, 203.

65 Ibid.

66 Ibid., 198.

67 Christoyannopoulos, 152.

68 Does Paul's behavior in Acts nevertheless suggest that he did, ultimately, view the Empire as worthy of affirmation? N.T. Wright argues that in Paul's writings, "we should expect what we in fact find: that, for Paul, Jesus is Lord and Caesar is not" (*Paul*, 69). Wright thus views Paul's behavior in Acts in the light of this conviction. Paul "is prepared to submit to the courts, but is also more than prepared to remind them of their business and to call them to account when they overstep their duty. He uses his own Roman citizenship when it suits the demands of his mission. But at the same time he is fearless in announcing, and living by, a different allegiance" (*Paul*, 70). This is consistent with the way that many Christian anarchists have read Romans 13—namely, as an admonition to live peaceably with all, including the governing authorities, while nevertheless recognizing that human authorities ultimately have no claim over the allegiance of the Christian.

69 Mk. 12:13–17.

70 Paul Rhodes Eddy and Greg Boyd, *The Jesus Legend* (Grand Rapids, MI: Baker, 2007) 109.

71 Ellul, *Anarchy*, 60–61.

72 Dorothy Day, quoted in Brad Spangler, "Give Nothing unto Caesar," Center for a Stateless Society, 11 October 2010.

73 Eller, 11.

74 David Lipscomb, *Civil Government: Its Origin, Mission, and Destiny, and the Christian's Relation to It* (Nashville, TN: McQuiddy, 1913); Ed Stringham, "The Radical Libertarian Political Economy of 19th Century Preacher David Lipscomb," in *Independent Institute Working Paper Number 66* (2006).

75 Alexander Salter, "Christian Anarchism: Communitarian or Capitalist?" in *Libertarian Papers* 4 (2012), 151–162.

76 Christian socialist anarchists do occasionally pair their critiques of capitalism with some reflections on what a post-capitalist economy might look like (see, for example, Dorothy Day, "Our Brothers, the Communists," or the "Capitalism" library entry on jesusradicals.com). But engagement in more detailed descriptions of an anarchist economy has not taken center stage in Christian anarchist writings up to this point. Perhaps this is simply because, in calling themselves "anarchists," Christian anarchists are implicitly signalling their agreement with the economic vision of authors such as Proudhon, Bakunin, Kropotkin, etc.—this appears to be the case, for example, with the favorable references to Proudhon and Bakunin by Tolstoy and Ellul, respectively—and so do not see a reason to devote special attention to the question.

77 Matt. 25:14–30.

78 Matt. 21:33–41.

79 James Redford, "Jesus Is an Anarchist" (December 4, 2011). Available at SSRN: https://ssrn.com/abstract=1337761 or http://dx.doi.org/10.2139/ssrn.1337761, 32–33.

80 Stephen W. Carson, "Biblical Anarchism," LewRockwell.com (June 7, 2011), www.lewrockwell.com/2001/06/stephen-w-carson/no-government-but-god/ (last visited Aug. 20, 2019).

81 Redford, 44–45. See also Yoder's discussion of the Jubilee and Jesus' condemnation of unrighteous wealth in *The Politics of Jesus*.

82 Carson.

83 Judges 17:6; Judges 21:25.

84 Carson.

85 Norman Horn, "New Testament Theology of the State," LewRockwell.com (September 29, 2007), www.lewrockwell.com/2007/09/norman-horn/new-testament-theology-of-the-state/ (last visited Aug. 20, 2019).

86 James Fedako, "Romans 13 and Anarcho-Capitalism," (February 25, 2010). www.lewrockwell.com/2010/02/jim-fedako/romans-13-and-anarcho-capitalism/ (last visited Aug. 20, 2019).

87 Carson.

88 Matt 21:12–17; Mark 11:15–19; Luke 19:45–48; John 2:13–16.

89 Matt 5:38–41.

90 Salter, 158.

91 Yoder, 42–43.

92 Christoyannopoulos, 85.

93 Ellul, *Violence*, 17.

94 Redford, 33–34.

95 Matt. 7:12.

96 Matt 19:16–30; Mark 10:17–31; Luke 18:18–30.

97 Matt. 6:24.
98 Job 42:10–17.
99 Matt. 18:22.
100 Acts 5:1–11.
101 Ludwig von Mises, *Socialism: An Economic and Sociological Analysis* (New Haven, CT: Yale UP, 1951) 414.

PART III

Legitimacy and Order

14
ANARCHISM AND POLITICAL OBLIGATION
An Introduction

Magda Egoumenides

I. Introduction

Anarchists believe that relations of domination are immoral. The coercion and exploitation of one individual by another is unjustified, as is the control of the individual by a collective, such as the state. The values of freedom and equality are paramount. A strand of anarchism expresses these positions within the context of philosophical debates about political obligation, and this has a distinct impact on our approach to political institutions.

Anarchism is *skepticism toward authority*.[1] Its unifying position is that not all forms of authority are justified, and we should refrain from any acceptance of them prior to their satisfactory justification. One form of authority that anarchists consider unjustified is the political authority of the state. Although "'anti-statism' does not define anarchism," because anarchists challenge authoritative relations other than those constitutive of the state,[2] the anarchist challenge involves opposition to the authority of *the state*, which focuses on the state's special characteristics as "a specific form of government," namely its being a "*sovereign*," "*compulsory*," "*monopolistic*," and "*distinct*" body.[3] But anarchism's opposition to the state reflects its more general opposition to political authority and institutionalized coercion[4] (see also my discussion of "the political" below), although not necessarily to a looser sense of organized society. So, at its core, anarchism objects to the authority of all political phenomena, institutions, and practices that institutionalize coercion.[5] The features of legal and regulatory enforcement that make it an objectionable form of coercion are also features of the institutionalized coercion of the state.[6] Opposition to the state's *right to rule*, although a non-definitive anarchist concern, is common to all forms of anarchism and its proponents. Opposition to the state's right to rule is a necessary condition of a position's being anarchist, but various anarchist tendencies embrace additional defining characteristics as well. The rejection of the state's right to rule relates to the stronger anarchist challenge to its *right to exist*. This challenge is the upshot of political anarchism, which maintains that the state must be *resisted* as an *evil* and a new social form must emerge that succeeds the state and constitutes an improvement on state-centered patterns of social organization. Thus, in order to pave the way for a complete evaluation of anarchism, including the project of political anarchism, it is helpful to examine the principled rejection of political authority that philosophical anarchism proposes and to detail the positive views, if any, that it expresses. My aim is to analyze this challenge as formulated within the context of the contemporary debate about political obligation.

In this chapter, I describe four basic forms of anarchism in order to clarify the theoretical perspective I defend—that of *critical philosophical anarchism*—and place it in the context of the current debate on anarchism. Then, I explain the problem of political obligation. Finally, I discuss the principal elements of my argument for critical philosophical anarchism. My aim is to prepare the ground for an assessment of the general contribution of philosophical anarchism to the problem of political authority.

II. The Varieties of Anarchism: Defining Critical Philosophical Anarchism within the Context of the Current Debate about Anarchism

I begin with the *different forms of and divisions within anarchism*. One division is that between gradualist and revolutionary anarchism, which refers to the path toward change that anarchists advocate. Another division is between pacifist and terrorist anarchism, drawn according to the methods that anarchists adopt (whether they use peaceful means, like social reconstruction, or violence, like some forms of propaganda by the deed, respectively). (Presumably one might admit the legitimacy of some kinds of force, and so not qualify as a pacifist, while rejecting the use of force against noncombatants, especially as a means of inducing fear, and so not qualify as a terrorist.) These divisions refer mostly to political anarchism, however, and the main logic of any such division remains the same: it primarily concerns the revolutionary methods and the form of economic organization that each school proposes.[7] There is a huge debate around the forms of anarchism, and some favor an "anarchism without adjectives." My focus is on the position that each form of anarchism adopts with regard to the two fundamental problems concerning the state: its right to exist and its right to rule. For the purposes of my argument, I want to distinguish between political anarchism and philosophical anarchism. While the second refers to a very specific debate in philosophy, the one I examine here, the first refers to practically everything else. The first can be further divided into individualist and communal (or social) anarchism and the second into positive (a priori) and negative (a posteriori) anarchism. As a result, we have four main forms of anarchism.

These categorizations serve mostly as clarifications of the main tendencies involved in the anarchist approach to the fundamental issue of political authority. The taxonomy is not exhaustive, and the overlaps are important. Political anarchists can be philosophical and vice versa, and, in the end, outside the specific debate over political obligation, the distinguishing characteristic of political anarchism is that it is also practical. The discussion below consists of a brief description of each form of anarchism in order to arrive at a basic account of the anarchist position that I discuss.

Political anarchism is primarily devoted to the task of demolishing the state. It sees this task as an immediate implication of the rejection of political authority. But this form of anarchism also views the state as a very *bad* form of social organization. The state's badness is a reason for opposing it in addition to the reality that the state's existence and authority remain unjustified. Correspondingly, this critique of the state is premised on a vision of social life without political institutions. *Philosophical anarchism*, on the other hand, concentrates on the critique of political authority and does not necessarily require the abolition of the state. This latter characteristic is reflected in the fact that philosophical anarchism is compatible with "a wide range of alternative political outlooks."[8] Many anarchists are both philosophical and political, but a philosophical anarchist may remain non-political.

Political individualist anarchism is marked by its emphasis on a central aspect of anarchism: the commitment to individual autonomy, or freedom, as a primary value, in the sense that each individual has a capacity and right to be "self-legislating,"[9] to make and act on his or her own decisions—as long as these do "not violate the similar rights of others,"[10] and "avoid causing dramatic social harm."[11] At the basic level, freedom can be conceived as the ability to make uncoerced choices on various issues of one's life under circumstances of adequate knowledge and with an unimpaired capacity for rational deliberation. Anarchists understand freedom in opposition to domination and coercion. In individualist anarchism, absence of coercion is seen primarily as a lack of interference in the private sphere of individual life. The idiosyncratic classical anarchist Max Stirner puts forward a unique individual anarchist view of freedom which replaces freedom with what he calls "ownness."[12] And Crispin Sartwell provides a contemporary example of individualist anarchism.[13] Generally, anarchism is committed to the ideal of self-determination understood as self-development under conditions of proper social relationships, where the subordination of some to others is replaced with mutual respect, equal active participation, and common flourishing. According to this general statement, the absence of subordination and coercion further requires rejecting domination, as well as engaging with aspects more comprehensive than the negative demands of individualist anarchism, which mostly promotes the idea that each individual has an "inviolable sphere of action" with absolute sovereignty.[14] Individualist anarchism views social relationships as interactions among independent beings, able to lead their lives abstracted from their social environment and its impacts. This leads individualist anarchists to emphasize the importance of voluntariness in any relation to and interaction with others and to attack political obligation on the grounds that states are not based on voluntary relations. Thus, they see them as coercive, exploitative, and evil.

Political communal (or *social*) *anarchism* has roots in socialism, but it nonetheless differs from other socialist ideologies, especially in its rejection of politically centralized forms of organization and control (see, for example, the split between Marx and Bakunin).[15] Communal anarchism stresses "the social character of human life": the value of community, mutuality, free cooperation, and, in the general case, social arrangements of a reciprocal character.[16] Its proponents devote themselves to developing visions of society that involve cooperative enterprises in every aspect of social life (economic, cultural, educational, etc.), as alternatives to views of society that include the state as an essential element.[17] These visions are accompanied by the (anarchist) rejection of coercive schemes and are based on reasonably optimistic views of human nature and accounts of morality—like Peter Marshall's approach to the notion of human nature, its use in the anarchist tradition, and its role in anarchist theory.[18] Marshall proposes abandoning the idea of human nature as a "fixed essence,"[19] and viewing the human species in an evolutionary way, taking into account the continual interaction of its many aspects and their capacity for "self-regulation" within open possibilities.[20] This view of human nature is compatible with the position developed here. On similar lines, but even more compatible with our position and more radical, is the view of the self as a "kernel of nothingness" serving as a canvas for constant self-creation, developed in the theory of Stirner and adopted and expanded by poststructuralist thinkers such as Michel Foucault and the anarchist Saul Newman.[21]

Moving to *philosophical anarchism*, I begin with some terminological points in order to arrive at the view I want to defend. Horton distinguishes between *positive* and *negative* philosophical anarchism.[22] Positive anarchism is the stronger, since it provides an explanation for the moral impossibility of the state and thus of political obligation. Negative anarchism is weaker, for it relies merely on "justification by default." That is, for negative anarchism, the failure of all attempts to provide supportive accounts of political obligation is taken to be reason enough for denying the existence of such an obligation, even though no "positive" analysis of why such attempts are bound to fail is provided.[23] These terms correspond to a certain extent to Simmons' notions of "a priori" and "a posteriori" anarchism. A priori anarchism states that the impossibility of legitimacy is inherent in the nature of the state, that some essential feature of the state makes it impossible for it to be legitimate. A priori philosophical anarchists are motivated by prior commitments—e.g., to voluntarism, to egalitarianism, or to communalism—that, on their view, the state fundamentally contradicts.[24] In contrast, the claim of a posteriori anarchism that "all existing states are illegitimate" is based mainly on empirical observations of actual states, rather than on an argument that there is some inconsistency, or incoherence, in the *possibility* of a legitimate state, although this form of anarchism is pessimistic about such a possibility.[25] This is a central reason why a posteriori anarchism does not necessarily lead to political anarchism, why its project is presented as mainly one of theoretical criticism and of enlightenment, and why it leaves room, in many cases, for obedience to particular laws and for the justification of particular obligations on the part of different individuals.

I focus on the negative, or a posteriori, side of philosophical anarchism and intend to evaluate its contribution to the debate on political authority. For this, I adopt an alternative terminology: I define "critical philosophical anarchism" through a combination of the features of the definitions of Horton and Simmons above, which I find the most characteristic of this anarchist position. (Gans coins "critical philosophical anarchism" for the anarchist position that he explains as "the denial of the duty to obey the law which is based on a rejection of its grounds."[26] But the sense in which I use it is more comprehensive, technical, and specific. I give my own definition in the next paragraph.) From negative philosophical anarchism I keep the characteristic that it is a theoretical view grounded on criticisms of accounts of political obligation. Yet I believe that these criticisms are determined by a prior analysis of what is involved in an adequate justification. From a posteriori philosophical anarchism, I take this: Simmons argues that a posteriori anarchism is not based merely on justification by default, but that it is rooted "either in an ideal of legitimacy (which existing states can be shown not to exemplify) or in some account of what an acceptably complete positive attempt [to justify political obligation] would look like."[27] This feature works as a normative horizon for evaluating theoretical defenses of political obligation: a prior standard in reference to which a posteriori anarchism derives its negative conclusions about political obligation and political institutions. These conclusions stem from the failures of the defenses of political obligation and from what these failures reflect about reality.

Given the above two features, I define "critical philosophical anarchism" as the view that examines the best candidates for moral theories of political obligation and derives *from their failure*, as a constructive conclusion of its own, the result that there is no general political obligation and that in this respect political institutions remain unjustified. Operative in this approach is a prior standard of theoretical criticism merged with *some idea of what an ideal legitimate society should be like*. The main input of this standard is to stress what political societies must *not* be like in order to be considered legitimate. Critical philosophical anarchism considers all existing states to be illegitimate insofar as they fail to meet this ideal, especially the demand for non-domination. In this, it is in line with political anarchism. Ultimately, the position of critical philosophical anarchism is a mix of philosophical and political anarchism.

My aim is to examine this anarchist position as it figures within the debate about political obligation, in order to determine its contribution regarding our approach and relation to political institutions. I stress both its critical perspective and its ideal of legitimacy as the defining features of this position, incorporating elements of essential value in the arguments against political authority.

These parameters are compatible with certain valuable features of social anarchism. In fact, this compatibility is not limited to social, or communal, anarchism. It is, to my mind, necessary in any anarchist vision that displays two features of communal anarchism, namely, on the one hand, its recognition of the social dimension of human beings and, on the other, its idea of free social relationships and decentralized, cooperative forms of social order along with an attention to matters of economic equality and distribution. Such perspectives are found in many contemporary anarchist writings. The essentially social character of human life is reflected both in anarchist proposals for free social relationships and in the claims regarding the defects of relations of domination. These claims have important implications for defenses of the state in light of its coercive character and its underlying corruption, as well as for considering the independence of "state actors."[28] Communal anarchism contains a positive project, namely the establishment of human cooperative relations free of both domination and exploitation. But its relation to coercion appears unclear and problematic, because it seems to re-introduce coercive structures, tactics, and attitudes in its visions of social reconstruction.[29] The most demanding project of anarchist theory would consist of a combination of the communal anarchist ideal with the attack on coercion reflected in the exacting perspective and standard of legitimacy that critical philosophical anarchism defines. This chapter attempts to prepare the way for this combination.

Anarchism enters the debate on political obligation with a concern about freedom, which is immediately related to an attack on dominative authority. Anarchism concentrates on the importance of self-governance. But how can self-governance be compatible with external constraints? The respect for self-government and the rejection of constraints are characteristic anarchist tenets, each of which might take, and at times has taken, priority over the other within the anarchist tradition. Still, an anarchist can insist on the priority of freedom and criticize political institutions without any prior rejection of constraints in general. The anarchist is sensitive to the fact that most *political* constraints create problems for self-determination. It is with this realization that the critical philosophical anarchist criticizes the way traditional defenses of political institutions work. What he wants to point out is that, if these defenses start with a different perspective on political institutions, one that centrally involves a positive relation between institutions and self-determination, such defenses will more successfully address the difficulties they face in the effort to justify political reality. The debate, and with it our relation to the state, can then develop in a different light, which will provide more fruitful ways of assessing political authority.

At this point, I would like to refer briefly to certain categories of anarchist thought that continue to form the debate within the anarchist arena today and to which critical philosophical anarchism might be related in some significant way. This will help situate this latter form of anarchism within the current debate, preparing the way for more general current anarchist concerns.

The first category is *new anarchism*, which is rooted in Errico Malatesta's thought[30] and appears today in the work of Noam Chomsky.[31] Based on Bakuninian ideas and Kropotkinian orthodoxy, Malatesta's critique of mainstream anarchism marked the transition from classical to new anarchism. Although greatly influenced by those major anarchist thinkers, Malatesta moved from their preoccupation with big ideas, their intellectual reverence for Marx, and their excessive revolutionary optimism (and the dogmatism related to it) to a more practical outlook that was pragmatically engaged with the realization of a just society.[32] Despite criticisms that this activism encouraged intellectual incoherence and simplicity, new anarchists made theoretical advances and their thought prefigured the New Left and its reorientation toward social analysis and cultural critique. Emma Goldman's anarchic-feminism is a characteristic example.[33] At present, Noam Chomsky is the most representative contemporary new anarchist. He has not developed a general theory of anarchism, and he sees anarchism more as a historically developed trend, sharing Malatesta's suspicion of the creation of big theoretical systems. Yet he has contributed a sharp social and political criticism to anarchism with his analysis of the role of propaganda in determining the opinions of people regarding economic issues, international relations, and war affairs. Above all, Chomsky has developed a profound critique of the propaganda of the media as a method of social control in "open" societies.[34]

Chomsky offers a parallel at the practical level to the thorough criticism that, as argued here, critical philosophical anarchism offers at the theoretical level. The latter can also be compatible with the concerns of individualist anarchism, such as those of Marx Stirner[35] and of our contemporary Herbert Read,[36] who refers to the priority of the aesthetic development of the individual, of a creative individuality free of all forms of social oppression. Furthermore, critical philosophical anarchism can be inspired by postmodern anarchism, as it appears in the work of Todd May and Saul Newman, with a focus on social critique and change rather than just political or economic change.[37]

In my opinion, however, critical philosophical anarchism's compatibility with social anarchism, and its concerns with the social and political implications of its criticism of obligation, can be seen better in its connection with another category of contemporary anarchist thought: the *neo-classical eco-anarchism* as it appears in the works of Murray Bookchin and Alan Carter. Critical philosophical anarchists can develop their own micropolitics of power. It is nevertheless important to examine the relation of critical philosophical anarchism to the most promising contemporary implementations of anarchist visions and practices rooted in the social anarchist concern with free and equal social relationships, to carry its principles even further to meet present demands and correct past prejudices. Bookchin's theory is promising to this end. Since this theory also has its shortcomings, however, my proposal is that it should be evaluated with reference to the perspective of critical philosophical anarchism. One can apply the critical philosophical anarchist test of legitimacy to Bookchin's account. During this project, it is also helpful to build on the ideas of Samuel Clark,[38] Benjamin Franks,[39] and Uri Gordon[40] regarding existing anarchist practices that widen the contemporary anarchist utopian picture.

III. The Problem of Political Obligation

A. *The Correlativity Thesis*

The problem of the existence and justification of political obligation is usually taken to be identical to the problem of the justification of political authority, which involves the establishment of the state's (claim to the) right to rule. This right is most often seen as the logical correlate of an obligation to obey: when we assert the state's right to rule, we *automatically* recognize that citizens have a political obligation to the state (the "doctrine of 'logical correlativity'").[41] Alternatively, this correlativity of right and obligation can be conceived as a normative doctrine: if we have one, we *should* have the other. On this view, political obligation is understood as either a normative condition for or a normative consequence of political authority, although not identical to it. This means that either authority or obligation is already independently justified and becomes the ground of the other. Theorists are divided concerning whether to accept correlativity in any of the above senses. Defenders of political obligation and philosophical anarchists usually adopt correlativity.[42] This perspective might be explained to a significant extent by the fact that these theorists conceive political authority, or the right to rule, as something more than mere permission to coerce. For example:

> What we really have in mind is a right to make laws and regulations, to judge and to punish for failing to conform to certain standards, or to order some redress for the victims of such violations, as well as a right to command.[43]

Also, "Authority on the part of those who give orders and make regulations is: a right to be obeyed. We may say, more amply: authority is a regular right to be obeyed in a domain of decision."[44] Characteristically, defenders of non-correlativity conceive authority as mere liability or permission to coerce, which is justifiably distinct from, and does not necessarily entail, a duty to obey; that is, political obligation.[45] Green has a useful discussion of objections to logical and to normative correlativity.[46] To the extent that political authority is understood as a complex right to exclusively and coercively make regulations, impose duties, and demand compliance (i.e., command and be obeyed, or, more inclusively, *issue directives*—"directives" is a wider term, more suitable than "command," and covers all cases of authoritative utterance[47]—and have them followed), then it is properly taken as correlative to a complex set of obligations constituting a general obligation to comply, i.e., political obligation. I take this correlativity as one central sense of legitimacy, whether in its logical or in its normative form. Since normative correlativity already involves substantive considerations about the nature of political authority and our relation to it, however, it is sufficient to focus on this form of correlativity for us to keep in mind that it is in the nature of the state's claim-right to rule to generate obligations to it.

B. The Two Main Aspects of the Problem of Political Obligation

Thus, the problem of political obligation is primarily the problem of finding a special justification for the various obligations imposed on citizens by their political institutions, which are correlative to a complex right of those institutions to rule those citizens. As Horton rightly points out, the *question of justification* is presupposed by the issues of the *author* and of the *scope* of political obligations, which are also central, and in general "has been taken to be the kernel of the philosophical problem of political obligation."[48] It is with regard to the question "Why should we obey political authority?" that I evaluate the anarchist position. The traditional philosophical discussion of political authority concerns attempts to account for *de jure* political authority, that is, authority that *has* the right to rule—or is exercised in accordance with a certain set of principles or rules—rather than for de facto political authority, namely one that *claims* to have this right and has this claim *acknowledged* by its subjects.[49] Because no state has the right to rule, the anarchist demands the moral justification or, in other words, the legitimacy of de facto authority. This problem has also been identified as that of *state legitimacy* morally understood. I use "state legitimacy" interchangeably with "state authority" and "political obligation."

Political obligation has traditionally been regarded as that notion through which we must understand a *special relationship* between individuals and the political institutions of their country of residence. There are two main features of the nature of the problem of political obligation:

(a) *The state, the law, and political institutions in general have a special character and status.* This is described by four theses:[50]

- The *sources thesis*: political institutions take their own validity from within the political/legal structure, from legally defined criteria and standards.
- The *particularity thesis*: citizens are taken to have a special relationship with their own government as it determines by itself the conditions of membership within its territory. This means that political institutions have a particular constituency to which they apply and any justification of political obligation should provide a basis for obeying one's own particular government with its own criteria for membership: "the particularity requirement."[51]
- The *coercion thesis*: institutional requirements may be backed by coercion. The state is sovereign and monopolistic in the sense that it determines the rights and duties of its citizens in an authoritarian, permanent, and exclusionary way. With respect to this function, legal sanction, or coercion, is its primary means.
- The *independence premise*: an account of political obligation should include criteria that show the independent nature of the "political" (as this nature is reflected in the elements of the three previous theses), and it is by appeal to this essentially political nature of

institutions that political obligation should be justified. That is, the special commitment that such an obligation is supposed to express needs to be shown to be necessarily connected to its *political nature.* I call these four premises "the theses on the political."

(b) *The commands of political authorities are directed at the behavior of individuals in the public domain.* This means that such commands have a direct effect not only on the beliefs of individuals, but also on their actions (such directives guide their practical reasoning and behavior). In this way they are reasons for action—*normative requirements* with the power to direct action. More importantly, political obligations are understood to be *moral* in character.[52] They are the defining terms of a special moral relationship between citizens and their polity, a concomitant of the latter's status as a normative power; that is, of its claim to a moral right to impose directives on its citizens. Yet the most convincing reason for requiring a moral ground is that it provides the most appropriate way of *filtering* political requirements in order to decide which of them can properly be attributed the status of obligation. Thus, it works as a criterion for distinguishing requirements that can be accepted as valid laws from unacceptable requirements. When, for example, individuals are presented with laws against bodily harm and laws discriminating against a specific group of people (such as immigrants), they need to be able to assert the acceptability of the former and exclude the latter by reference to a stable testing ground. Since institutions have a considerable effect on our lives, such filtering is necessary and valuable, because it demands that institutions need to be sufficiently motivated in doing so; there have to be convincing reasons in favor of their interference. A moral ground provides the strongest basis for normative requirements, creating a distance from our institutions that is beneficial to a critical assessment of their function and quality. These points express the second important aspect of the issue of political obligation as traditionally understood: a justification of political obligation must involve the provision of *moral grounds* for supporting political institutions.

Together (a) and (b) say that an adequate justification of political obligation involves the *recognition of the legitimacy of political authority qua political, on the basis of moral reasons.* Following philosophical anarchists, I see the need to defend the existence of special obligations in the political domain with *moral* principles and arguments as inevitable. This is mainly because of the direct and dominant role that political institutions, with their requirements and present practices, play in our social lives and because they claim the right to do so. The demands of political institutions primarily affect individual self-determination and social equality, which gives rise to a constant requirement to put limits on these institutions rooted in individual life and morality. As the anarchist reminds us, domination and coercion can never be desirable in themselves. They are always a defect, needing to be counterbalanced by merits that are sufficiently strong to legitimate the agencies that incorporate them. The very fact that obligations are requirements, which involve a "pressure to perform," makes explicit the tie between obligation, domination, and coercion, thus pressing the demand for proper justification.[53] These points relate to the other central feature in the traditional understanding of the debate over political obligation: the attempt to ground the political *qua political.* To appeal occasionally (or even frequently) to moral reasons as justifications for compliance with particular laws does not constitute a moral recognition of the authority of the law.

C. Quality- and Interaction-Based Evaluations of Political Institutions

Two central elements of the evaluation of states that are found in discussions of political obligation are *quality* and *specific interaction.* The former involves general positive qualities or accomplishments of institutions (such as justice and the supply of important goods), and it is a commonplace in moral arguments for their existence. The latter refers to "morally significant features of the specific histories of interaction between individual persons and their polities" (components such as actually giving one's consent).[54] These elements ground Simmons' distinction between "*generic*" and "*transactional* evaluations."[55] I also apply, in relation to the first kind of evaluation, the term "institutional morality," which is drawn from an analogous distinction between "theories of institutional morality" and "theories of emergence."[56] Judgments about the *nature* of political institutions, the qualities that might make them morally acceptable, provide a basic condition that institutions must satisfy, and in this respect they affect judgments about political obligation. (The basic idea here is that we cannot morally bind ourselves to immoral institutions.) Some of the theories of political obligation employ them more centrally, as grounds of that question. But the general moral relationship based on the nature of a state overall differs from the particular moral relationship that is the focus of the problem of political obligation. It is important to see whether the one can ground the other and, in general, to assess the role of institutional qualities in justifying political obligation. I see the problem of political obligation as concerned with grounding a special bond between individual and government through understanding "the *relationship* or *transaction* which could create" such a bond.[57] In this paper, I stress the fact that political obligation is a special bond between a *particular* government and each *particular* citizen. Having such a particularized character, political obligation seems more likely to derive from very specific relationships, characterized by the actual and particular features of direct transaction, and it is doubtful that these can be captured by more generally described connections between states and subjects.[58] Thus, political obligation appears more relevant to the category of *transactional evaluation*.

Whether or not justification and legitimacy are separate dimensions of institutional evaluation and whether or not justification in terms of institutional qualities is directed primarily at the existence of the state, anarchism challenges political institutions with regard to both existence and obligation. This paper concentrates on its position with regard to the particular relationship of political obligation. Nevertheless, I believe that the critical philosophical anarchist perspective makes the problem of political obligation central for a broader evaluation of political institutions, and thus ultimately a challenge to their very existence.

D. The Conditions of Political Obligation

The four theses that define the political nature of obligation and the demand for a moral ground are accompanied by certain formal conditions that have traditionally been used to determine theories of political obligation and that are pressed by anarchists. In the next few pages I will clarify which of these conditions remain operative, and introduce their role within the debate on political obligation.

Theories of political obligation, which attempt to morally justify a political kind of requirement, are constrained by four formal conditions: *particularity*, *generality*, *bindingness*, and *content-independence*. I call them "the conditions of political obligation." These conditions appear as merely formal requirements, which a theorist of political obligation might find reasons to dispense with, against the anarchist standpoint. But their role is indispensable in the debate about political obligation, as is the way these conditions characterize the anarchist perspective, ultimately helping decide the anarchist contribution to this debate. They are justifiably offered as determinants of the link required between the political nature of obligation and its moral justification.

The particularity thesis, which defines a central part of the nature of the political, itself provides a first condition on how to attempt to assign moral weight to the bond of political obligation, namely that we show the moral significance of citizens being bound to *their own* states.

Being coherently in the nature of political institutions to address their requirements to a specific constituency, *particularity* is a natural and inevitable condition within the debate.

Two other general assumptions of a justification of political obligation involve the demand of "universality," namely that moral justification applies to all subjects with regard to all laws, and the demand of "singularity in ground," namely that all obligations are based on one and the same moral reason.[59] Both of these assumptions have been questioned and rejected.[60] For arguments against "universality" in particular, see Green.[61]

Nevertheless, in order to justify political obligation, a sufficient amount of *generality* is necessary. I insist on generality and on the other three conditions of political obligation proposed by philosophical anarchists because they provide an appropriate (and perhaps the most suitable) way of ascribing to the traditional understanding of the problem of political obligation the significance that it has. Generality corresponds to the centralized and monopolistic character of political institutions. Also, it captures a central characteristic of the anarchist approach to accounts of political obligation, namely that we should be interested "in describing all moral requirements which bind citizens to their political communities."[62] Klosko[63] and other defenders of the state recognize the necessity of generality, and it is in fact this aspect that has created the most difficulties for them. All accounts of political obligation proposed so far fail to justify political obligation for *most* of the people. Thus, the justification of a general political obligation has not yet been given.

The other two conditions that work as proper formal constraints on accounts of political obligation become very explicit in the last facet of the problem to which I want to draw attention, namely our understanding of the character of the notion of political obligation. A good example is Raz's proposal. Political obligation "is a general obligation applying to … all the laws on all occasions to which they apply."[64] It is not an "incidental reason."[65] It is a reason to obey the law *because it is the law*; that is, "to obey the law *as it requires to be obeyed.*"[66] As stressed above, political obligation is not only the obligation to obey the law but involves much more, such as the duties of citizenship, which involve supporting political institutions in other ways; for example, by participating in the defense of one's country. Yet here I use Raz's discussion to make a different point about the character of political obligation and I adopt his terminology only as part of that discussion. The point here is that political obligation involves the acceptance of the directives of the law not only with regard to their content, but also as far as the conditions or criteria by which they may be overridden are concerned. The law is not absolute, but the considerations under which it is defeated should be recognized by the law itself. Such considerations might be strong moral reasons that override the obligation to obey the law, but one's acting according to them irrespectively of any recognition of their application by the law itself constitutes a violation of the law. Thus, although the application of the law does not imply that reasons other than those recognized by the law are less important, the law is "exclusionary" and "its rules and rulings are authoritative."[67] It is in the very nature of the law and it is its *raison d'être* that it functions as a conclusion of practical reason, already excluding certain considerations; this is what the law is. Given this understanding of political obligation, it is possible to recognize that what anarchists deny is a *general obligation to obey political institutions as they require to be obeyed.*[68] These considerations are represented by the terms "content-independence" and "bindingness," which designate the last two conditions of political obligation.

The upshot of the above discussion is that the four conditions of political obligation already provide defining features of the political nature of such obligations, which is a central aspect of the debate.

In sum, the problem of political obligation concerns fundamentally: (a) an *ethical* relationship between people and the political community of which they are members; that is, one involving *moral grounds* for a special relationship to our polities. These grounds are strong, but neither absolute nor exhaustive. This issue is also (b) *political* in the sense that membership in a polity is characterized by the special features of its political nature as defined by the theses on the political and as reflected in the conditions of political obligation. The arguments introduced in the final part of this chapter are approached on the basis of accepting the debate over political obligation in these terms.

IV. The Main Aspects of an Argument for Critical Philosophical Anarchism

In this section, I present the main parts of my argument for critical philosophical anarchism in relation to the problem of political obligation. My argument is that *the main perspective and ideas of critical philosophical anarchism can be appealing to anybody*, whether they are anarchists or not. I myself am not a self-proclaimed anarchist. Nevertheless, my opinion is that the critical philosophical anarchist position on political obligation is correct and that the virtues of this view make an examination and acknowledgment of its contribution worthwhile.

Critical philosophical anarchism has been criticized as a purely negative view, one that works as a denial of positive defenses of political institutions without offering an alternative positive proposition of its own.[69] This criticism is anticipated by the usual understanding of philosophical anarchism as a view relying merely on justification by default (see the presentation of negative anarchism above). Without denying its theoretical function (which I retain and stress in my definition of it), I argue that this anarchist view involves something more positive than it first appears to do: the arguments of critical philosophical anarchism express *a prior perspective*. This perspective is characteristically anarchist in its motivating concerns and its proposals, one that is also indispensable for theorists of political obligation and necessary for the evaluation of institutions more generally. A closer analysis of anarchist arguments against defenses of political obligation is the first step toward this objective. The four conditions of political obligation that anarchists employ play a central role within the analysis and understanding of the anarchist perspective. These formal requirements define characteristic features of the political nature of the obligations in question: taken *together* "the conditions of political obligation" *express* this political nature itself, that is, the particularistic, coercive, centralist, permanent, and exclusive character of the institutions to which these obligations relate. They become useful vehicles for very valuable yet neglected elements of the anarchist position as their formality leads to wide-ranging moral conclusions. In part, the examination of anarchist criticisms of political obligation serves to establish (the role of) these conditions as definitive of the link between the political and the moral features of the problem of political obligation. This point can be employed to demonstrate the value of the philosophical anarchist perspective. The crux of my argument is that the anarchist perspective involves an insight that everyone needs to share. It indicates that the lack of a special relationship that characterizes political institutions (which exists when the conditions of political obligation are satisfied) raises a fundamental question as to whether they can exist and function at all.

The anarchist *ideal of legitimacy*, as part of the definition of critical philosophical anarchism, is another aspect of this anarchist view which plays a central role in its positive contribution. Philosophical anarchists defend voluntarist, communitarian, egalitarian, and ecological visions of the ideal society. Because they are not dominating models of society, they serve as indications of the proper relations that institutions must have in order to be legitimate and justified in the eyes of human beings. Characteristically, these ideals are also in constant interaction with the social visions of political anarchism. The fact that such ideals underlie the arguments of critical philosophical anarchism provides another factor explaining the positive character of this form of anarchism. Both the anarchist social visions and the anarchist attacks on the state aspire to a better understanding of human nature and society and to an assessment of human actions, relations, and achievements compatible with the most commonly shared moral values. I endorse the claim that anarchists are concerned with "*the quality of relations between people*," namely with defending and realizing within society direct and many-sided relations, characterized by reciprocity and equal authority and participation.[70] This is a ground that can be shared by many anti- and non-authoritarian theorists (McLaughlin is right to stress that anarchism is *non-authoritarianism* rather than an anti-authoritarian view, since it does not reject every form of authority as such)[71] with or without anarchist convictions. Furthermore, the arguments that bring the defenders of the state and anarchists into conflict refer to issues of an explicitly social character. (A good example is provided by the argument from public goods. This argument focuses on the importance of coordinating activities in order to secure the production and distribution of goods vital for a decent life, and it reveals conflicting intuitions—those of anarchists on the one hand, and those of their opponents on the other.) The positive horizon defined by political social anarchism provides a suitable background for addressing these concerns. I want to argue that this horizon is compatible with and in fact already incorporated within the challenge of critical philosophical anarchism. Political social anarchists oppose the state not only because of its illegitimacy, but also because of its essentially dominative, coercive, corruptive, and therefore *evil* character. But this characterization of the state as evil is not an essential element of philosophical anarchism, although it may play a part in certain philosophical anarchist views. It is necessary to combine a diagnostic of what goes wrong in domination and coercion, as expressed in philosophical anarchist views, with an explicit prescriptive horizon of harmonious social relations. The required link might be found in a theoretical account that includes a properly articulated ideal of legitimacy that will set a standard, elements of which must be met by any vision of society.

On reflection, we would all probably agree with the anarchist on the question of the values needed to defend obligation and institutions. In examining different theories of political obligation in their dialogue with the anarchist perspective, we should approach them with respect to different instances of the anarchist ideal of legitimacy. A related central aim is to carry the role of the ideal of legitimacy further: to examine how, more generally, it can make the task of the justification of political institutions harder. One can consider how the debate as defined by the anarchist and its results for political obligation might affect further defenses of constraints even within a background presupposing that we need, and remain with, political institutions. The extension of the role of the anarchist ideal of legitimacy is an analysis of the anarchist perspective's effect on any justification of constraints. More precisely, the ideal standards, in the light of the failure to justify political obligation, help further evaluations of institutions by imposing the relevant moral criteria as principled conditions on existing and newly arising forms of domination. Thus, the anarchist contribution should be estimated both with regard to what it offers to the debate on political obligation itself and with respect to the implications of the results of this debate for more general evaluations of political institutions. In these functions, the ideal of legitimacy and the anarchist criticisms become two expressions of one comprehensive view.

This view states primarily that legitimacy is *exigent* because it is difficult to see how political institutions can meet the requirements of the moral forms of the standard of legitimacy. If the anarchist conclusions about political obligation are correct, both the four conditions that constrain accounts of political obligation and the ideals reflecting proper social relations that states fail to meet indicate something about the political that every theorist must attend to—and they provide the way for doing so. The defenders of political institutions assume what they should seek to prove: they focus on the merits of political institutions and attempt to derive political obligation from them. Instead, they should address the prior question about what institutions demand of us and whether these demands are justified. Political institutions cease to be viewed as lovable, and they need to be tested *continually* on the basis of *the problems* they create. This is a shift in our conception of our political relationships that will not, however, entail widespread disobedience and chaos. The reason for this is that we have to work with existing institutions and build the new in the shell of the old. Yet such a shift can *radically* affect our political relationships and lives. In my opinion, philosophical anarchism both requires drastic revision in our thinking about political relations and entails radical change in our political lives. I see this as a positive effect of the anarchist perspective.

This claim leads to a conclusive point. The anarchist criticisms and ideal of legitimacy explain *the link between philosophical and political anarchism*: they remind us that the enduring deficiency of the state is a position that is initially shared by both forms of anarchism, and the moral criteria of philosophical anarchism are intended to be inherent in the society that political anarchism seeks to create. A demonstration of the compatibility of political anarchist social visions with the perspective and ideals of legitimacy of critical philosophical anarchism establishes continuity within the anarchist ideology. Such a demonstration is necessary as a test on both sides of anarchism. It would provide the required combination of a diagnostic of what goes wrong with political coercion and an explicit positive horizon of non-dominative harmonious social relations.

Notes

1 Paul McLaughlin, *Anarchism and Authority: A Philosophical Introduction to Classical Anarchism* (Aldershot: Ashgate 2007) 29–36.
2 McLaughlin 97.
3 David Miller, *Anarchism* (London: Dent 1984) 5, original emphasis.
4 Miller 5.
5 Cp. McLaughlin 74–80. Compare April Carter's discussion of the state in relation to its "specific organs" and especially of the five factors of governmental action in modern states; see April Carter, *The Political Theory of Anarchism* (London: Routledge 1971) ch. 2.
6 See Uri Gordon, *Anarchy Alive! Anti-Authoritarian Politics from Practice to Theory* (London: Pluto 2008) 67–9.
7 George Woodcock, *Anarchism: A History of Libertarian Ideas and Movements* (Harmondsworth: Penguin 1975) 19; McLaughlin 2.
8 John Horton, *Political Obligation*, 2d ed. (London: Macmillan 2010) 132.
9 Robert Paul Wolff, *In Defense of Anarchism* (New York: Harper 1970) 14.
10 Horton 115.
11 A. John. Simmons, *On the Edge of Anarchy* (Princeton: Princeton UP 1993) 267.
12 Max Stirner, *The Ego and Its Own*, ed. David Leopold (Cambridge: CUP 1995) 145–6, 154.
13 Crispin Sartwell, *Against the State: An Introduction to Anarchist Political Theory* (Albany: SUNY P 2008) ch. 5.
14 Miller 30.
15 James Joll, *The Anarchists*, 2d ed. (London: Methuen 1980) ch. 4; McLaughlin 158.
16 Miller chs. 4, 12; Horton 119-20.
17 Petr Al. Kropotkin, *The Conquest of Bread and Other Writings*, ed. Shatz Marshall (Cambridge: CUP 1995); Petr Al. Kropotkin, *Fields, Factories and Workshops Tomorrow* (London: Allen 1974); Petr Al. Kropotkin, *Mutual Aid: A Factor of Evolution* (Boston: Extending Horizons 1955); Murray Bookchin, *Toward an Ecological Society* (Montreal: Black Rose 1980); Murray Bookchin, "Libertarian Municipalism," *The Murray Bookchin Reader*, ed. Janet Biehl (London: Cassell 1997) 172–96.
18 Peter Marshall, "Human Nature and Anarchism," *For Anarchism: History, Theory, and Practice*, ed. David Goodway (London: Routledge 1989) 127–49.
19 Marshall 138.
20 Marshall 139–44.
21 Stirner; Michel Foucault, *Discipline and Punish: The Birth of the Prison*, trans. Alan Sheridan (London: Penguin 1991); Saul Newman, *The Politics of Postanarchism* (Edinburgh: Edinburgh UP 2011).
22 Horton 124.
23 Horton 124.
24 Wolff, *Defense*; A. John Simmons, "Philosophical Anarchism," *For and Against the State: New Philosophical Readings*, ed. John T. Sanders and Jan Narveson (Lanham: Rowman 1996) 20–1.
25 Simmons, "Anarchism" 19–39.
26 Chaim Gans, *Philosophical Anarchism and Political Disobedience* (Cambridge: CUP 1992) 2.

27 Simmons, "Philosophical," 36, n. 9.
28 Alan Carter, "Outline of an Anarchist Theory of History," *For Anarchism. History, Theory, and Practice*, ed. David Goodway (London and New York: Routledge 1989); Alan Carter, "The Nation-State and Underdevelopment," *Third World Quarterly* 16.4 (1995): 595–618.
29 Horton 122–3.
30 Errico Malatesta, *Anarchy*, trans. Vernon Richards (London: Freedom 1984); Errico Malatesta and Vernon Richards, eds., *Errico Malatesta: His Life and Ideas. Compiled and edited by Vernon Richards* (London: Freedom 1965).
31 Noam Chomsky, *For Reasons of State* (New York: Vintage Books 1973); Edward S. Hermanand Noam Chomsky, eds., *Manufacturing Consent: The Political Economy of the Mass Media* (New York: Pantheon Books 1988); Robert F. Barsky, *Noam Chomsky: A Life of Dissent* (Cambridge, MA: MIT 1997); Peter Wilkin, *Noam Chomsky: On Power, Knowledge and Human Nature* (New York: Saint Martin's 1997); Noam Chomsky, *The New Military Humanism: Lessons from Kosovo* (London: Pluto 1999); James A. McGilvray, *The Cambridge Companion to Chomsky* (Cambridge: CUP 2005).
32 McLaughlin 160–1.
33 Emma Goldman, *Anarchism and Other Essays* (New York: Dover 1969).
34 Herman and Chomsky, "Propaganda Problem."
35 Stirner.
36 Herbert Read, *The Philosophy of Anarchism* (London: Freedom 1940); Herbert Read, *Anarchy and Order: Essays in Politics* (London: Souvenir 1974).
37 Todd May, *The Political Philosophy of Poststructuralist Anarchism* (University Park: PSU 1994); Newman.
38 Samuel J. A. Clark, *Living Without Domination: The Possibility of an Anarchist Utopia* (Aldershot: Ashgate 2007).
39 Benjamin Franks, *Rebel Alliances: The Means and Ends of Contemporary British Anarchisms* (Edinburgh: AK/ Dark Star 2006).
40 Gordon.
41 A John Simmons, *Moral Principles and Political Obligations* (Princeton: PUP 1979) 58, 195–7; Simmons, "Philosophical," 21, 36, n. 11.
42 Simmons, *Principles*; Alan J. Simmons, "Justification and Legitimacy," *Ethics* 109(4) (1999): 739–71; Leslie Green, *The Authority of the State* (Oxford: Clarendon 2008); Joseph Raz, *The Authority of Law: Essays on Law and Morality* (Oxford: Clarendon 1979); Joseph Raz, "Introduction," *Authority*, ed. Joseph Raz (Oxford: Basil Blackwell 1990); Joseph Raz, "Authority and Justification," *Authority*, ed. Joseph Raz (Oxford: Basil Blackwell 1990) 115–41; Gertrude E. M. Anscombe, "On the Source of the Authority of the State," *Authority*, ed. Joseph Raz (Oxford: Basil Blackwell, 1990), 142–73; Horton; McLaughlin.
43 Raz, "Introduction," 2.
44 Anscombe 144
45 David D. Raphael, *Problems of Political Philosophy* (London: Macmillan 1976); Robert Ladenson, "In Defense of a Hobbesian Conception of Law," *Authority*, ed. John Raz (Oxford: Basil Blackwell 1990) 32–55.
46 Green 234–40.
47 McLaughlin 54.
48 Horton 12–3.
49 Wolff, *Defense* 2; Simmons, *Moral* 41–2, 196, 206; Simmons, "Justification" 746–51; Joseph Raz, *The Morality of Freedom* (Oxford: Clarendon; New York: OUP 1986) 18–19; Raz, "Introduction," 3; McLaughlin 59.
50 Saladin Meckled-Garcia, "Membership, Obligation and Legitimacy: An Expressivist Account" (Unpublished PhD diss., U College London 1998) 14–8.
51 Simmons, *Moral* 31–5; Green 227–8.
52 Raz, *Authority* 244; Horton 13–5.
53 Simmons, *Moral* 7.
54 Simmons, "Justification," 764.
55 Simmons, "Justification," 764, original emphasis.
56 Meckled-Garcia ch. 2.
57 Simmons, *Moral* 4, emphasis mine.
58 Simmons, *Moral* 31–5.
59 Jonathan Wolff, "Pluralistic Models of Political Obligation," *Philosophica* 56 (2, 1995): 10.
60 Simmons, *Moral* 35–7.
61 Green 240–7.
62 Simmons, *Moral* 37, 55–6.

63 George Klosko, "The Principle of Fairness and Political Obligation," *Ethics* 97. 2 (Jan., 1987) 353–62.
64 Raz, *Morality* 234.
65 Raz, *Morality* 234.
66 Raz, *Morality* 236, emphasis mine.
67 Raz, *Morality* 236–7.
68 Green 225–6.
69 Jonathan Wolff, "Anarchism and Skepticism," *For and Against the State*, ed. John T. Sanders and Jan Narveson (Lanham: Rowman and Littlefield 1996) 99–118.
70 Michael Taylor, *Community, Anarchy and Liberty* (Cambridge: CUP 1982) 3, emphasis mine.
71 McLaughlin 28–9, 33–6.

15

THE POSITIVE POLITICAL ECONOMY OF ANALYTICAL ANARCHISM

Peter J. Boettke and Rosolino A. Candela

> How can it be that institutions which serve the common welfare and are extremely significant for its development come into being without a *common will* directed toward establishing them?
>
> *Carl Menger*[1]

I. Introduction

Both the study of political economy and the study of anarchy are motivated by the same fundamental question: what are the institutional conditions under which it is possible to pursue the extensive gains from productive specialization and realize peaceful social cooperation without command? Understood this way, the study of anarchy is simply a subset of political economy; the two are distinct, though not mutually exclusive. Political economy as a positive and analytic study of governance employs two basic starting points as it seeks to explain why certain societies have grown rich while others have remained relatively poor. In the first, and standard, approach, a set of institutional arrangements is treated as exogenously given *and* a governing entity is assumed to have acquired a monopoly on legitimate force. The relevant institutional arrangements include well-defined and exchangeable private property rights and freedom of contract under the rule of law. Given such preconditions, the threat of force is utilized as a means to enforce private property rights, thereby establishing the framework that facilitates large-scale trade and capital accumulation, which are the prerequisites for economic development. If these preconditions are not in place, the presumption is that a society will be hopelessly caught in a violence trap,[2] one in which violence remains the predominant means of accumulating wealth, either directly through private predation or indirectly through state predation. The implication of this approach is that the absence of government will generate a negative-sum societal outcome.

A second approach to political economy—and the focus of this chapter—neither takes rules as given nor assumes that monopoly enforcement of such rules occurs. We refer to this approach as *analytical anarchism*. This approach is concerned with a positive study of *endogenous rule formation* by individuals within a particular society.[3] Such rules emerge out of the self-interest of these individuals, though not necessarily from any deliberate design. Grounded in economic reasoning, analytical anarchism requires neither an abandonment of the notion of scarcity (and hence of competition), nor does it require the benevolent transformation of human nature. Moreover, analytical anarchism is not a *normative* study[4] of a world in which the threat of force is absent. Given the ubiquity of scarcity, competition will inevitably emerge as a way of resolving conflicts among ends, and, therefore, force will always remain as one among many forms of competition over resources. Analytical anarchism is thus not an assessment of whether or not coercion should or should not take place. Rather, it is an analysis of how rules emerge and under what conditions *the discretionary use of force can be minimized* in the enforcement of such rules.

The purpose of this chapter is to provide a critical overview of the burgeoning literature concerning analytical anarchism. We begin, in Section II, by clarifying the presumption of social disorder that prevails among economists and other social scientists skeptical about the ability of anarchy to facilitate social order. In Section III, we outline some ambiguities and misconceptions in the analytical study of anarchy and discuss its importance for political economy overall. In Section IV, we outline and analyze two theoretical approaches that have been used to illustrate various historical cases of anarchism across time and place. We distinguish between an *exclusionary approach* to analytical anarchism and an *inclusionary approach* to analytical anarchism. Though these two approaches are not mutually exclusive, they are distinct from each other, in that they illustrate alternative mechanisms under which the conditions of anarchy can be relatively peaceful and productive. Section V concludes with implications for future research in political economy.

II. The Presumption of Social Disorder without the State

From a political economy perspective, it is impossible to understand the emergence of analytical anarchism in the second half of the twentieth century without first placing it in its appropriate intellectual context. By the mid-twentieth century, a presumption of market failure[5] had come to dominate neoclassical economic theory, particularly in the field of public economics. Advocates of this presumption hold that market processes are exacerbated by inefficiencies—judged in relation to an ideal of perfection competition—associated with asymmetric information, externalities, monopoly power, public goods, and macroeconomic instability. Government intervention is treated as a necessary corrective for such market failures. Our purpose here is not to address the presumption of market failure, or the corresponding government failures associated with government intervention as a corrective to market failure, per se.[6] Rather, we will focus on the principal critique of analytical anarchism in political economy—the presumption that a state monopoly on the use of coercion is necessary for social order to prevail. We will thus be concerned with the *predominant* economic justification for the role of the state, namely the provision of public goods, including the establishment of secure property rights and the enforcement of contracts. Our work reflects the recognition that challenges to public goods theory have provided the theoretical building blocks that analytical anarchists can use to illustrate anarchy across time and place.

Beginning in the latter half of the twentieth century, economists such as Armen Alchian, James Buchanan, and Ronald Coase[7] began to critique the theory of public goods that served as the principal economic justification for belief in the state's essential role. According to Paul Samuelson's articulation of this theory, a public good, a good that is non-excludable and non-rivalrous, will unavoidably be suboptimally provided by the market for two reasons: (i) if private entrepreneurs are unable to exclude non-payers from the benefits of a good, large numbers of people will free-ride, declining to pay for their shares of the good, which will thus be underprovided; and (ii) the inability to establish property rights in public goods will keep entrepreneurs from using the price mechanism required to allocate these goods to their most valued uses.[8]

If a good is non-rivalrous, as public goods are said to be, the marginal cost of providing an additional unit of the good is zero. If a good is non-rivalrous, then, even if the price mechanism could be utilized to allocate the good, it would be suboptimal to charge a positive price for the good. This is because pricing the marginal consumption of an additional unit of a non-rivalrous good will result in suboptimal consumption of the good.

Among the examples of public goods provided by Samuelson were lighthouses.[9] Since ships passing in the night could simultaneously benefit from the light provided by a lighthouse without being stopped for payment, free-riding would result in the inefficient provision of lighthouses.

James Buchanan provided one of the earliest critiques of Samuelson by developing a theory of *club goods*.[10] According to Buchanan, the fact that a good is non-rivalrous doesn't mean that it must also be non-excludable. For example, access to a swimming pool at a private country club may readily be restricted to members of the club. If a good is excludable, consumption of the good can be restricted; free-riding can thus be ruled out, and with it a Samuelson-style case for government provision of the good.[11] For example, Coase challenged the notion that government financing and production of lighthouses,[12] which had been "simply plucked out of the air to serve as an illustration,"[13] was actually necessary. An empirical analysis of the operation of lighthouses in England and Wales prior to their nationalization in 1836 made clear that lighthouses could be privately constructed and financed and that non-payers of lighthouse services could be excluded from zero-price access to these services through the collection of fees, known as "light dues," at ports.[14] Therefore, lighthouses could qualify as club goods.

Armen Alchian and William Allen posed one of the earliest challenges to the notion that national defense was a public good by challenging the assumption of non-rivalry. As they frame it, the standard treatment of national defense as a non-rivalrous public good assumes that this good "is shared by everyone. More of it for one person does not mean less for someone else."[15] As a result, on a common view, it qualifies as "a public good and should be provided via government taxes and operation." In response, they ask the following question: "Does greater anti-missile defense for New York City mean greater defense for Houston, Texas?"[16] Both Tyler Cowen and Chris Coyne use a similar illustration to point out that, when the *marginal* unit of analysis is properly defined, what might be regarded as a public good is in fact rivalrous (as when the good in question is defense and the unit of analysis is defense from individual missiles).[17] As a result, additional resources allocated toward the defense of New York from missile attack come with *rising* opportunity costs of foregone defense against missiles targeted at Houston.

To be sure, Alchian, Buchanan, and Coase weren't anarchists. None of them intended to contribute directly to the study of analytical anarchism. They simply sought to challenge the notion that certain goods were *inherently* non-rivalrous and non-excludable without empirical study, and thus to reject the idea that the market provision of such goods could be known a priori to be subject to market failure.[18] However, their critique of the public goods justification for state action obviously raises questions about which goods, if any, must be provided by the government; it thus contributes important building blocks for analytical anarchism.

The most direct origins of the explicit study of analytical anarchism can be traced back to the Center for Study of Public Choice at Virginia Polytechnic Institute and State University.[19] Beginning in the 1970s, public-choice economists began to analyze the capabilities of individuals to engage in peaceful social cooperation without government. Although the idea that this might be possible no doubt seemed new and radical, rigorous economic inquiry into the potential dynamics of social order without the state dated back to at least the work of economist Carl Menger. Due to the civil unrest that emerged during the Vietnam War and the Civil Rights movement, James Buchanan, Gordon Tullock, and Winston Bush undertook a radical re-examination of alternative institutional arrangements for governing society. This analytical inquiry into the prospects for anarchism resulted in publications such as *Explorations in the Theory of Anarchy* and *Further Explorations in the Theory of Anarchy*.[20] As Bush observed,

> It is not surprising that 'anarchy' and 'anarchism' have reemerged as topics for discussion in the 1960s and the 1970s, as tentacles of government progressively invade private lives and as the alleged objectives of such invasions receded yet further from attainment.[21]

Given the historical context in which they were writing, Buchanan, Bush, and most of the other contributors regarded anarchism with skepticism.[22] They understood anarchy as a social condition characterized by the absence of law, involving banditry, violence, and general social disorder. These scholars uncritically identified *government* with *governance*. "The anarchists of the 1960s," Buchanan supposed, "were enemies of order, rather than proponents of any alternative organizational structure."[23]

Scholars studying the possibility of social cooperation without the state have continued to raise questions about the prospects for anarchy. For example, using economic analysis to understand the Sicilian Mafia, Diego Gambetta has argued that organized crime can facilitate trust and third-party contract enforcement where other means of enforcing property rights and contracts are deficient or absent.[24] However, on the basis of his empirical analysis, he concludes that the case of Sicily suggests that third-party enforcement of property rights and contracts under anarchy will ultimately be extortionary:

> Anarchists have argued that the state ought to disappear altogether for there is no need for its services. But this view is entirely different from advocating the privatization of justice and protection services. Among the few authors who argue in favor of the latter is Murray Rothbard .... He seems oblivious to the fact that the society he is proposing exists already in Sicily and can hardly be described as a success.[25]

However misplaced Gambetta's reference to Sicily as an example of anarchy may be, since it didn't meet the conditions of anarchy in the first place,[26] his criticism prompts two important observations not only about the positive *and* empirical study of anarchy but also about political economy in general. First, the historical *observation* of cases of anarchy is not synonymous with the *analysis* of anarchy itself. As Avinash Dixit notes, "case study [analysis] or empirical research should not treat each case as a mere narrative or description of an isolated situation; it should attempt to place it in an overall framework of other cases and theories."[27] The historical success or failure of anarchy, as compared with government, in facilitating social cooperation under the division of labor requires an *explanation* of facts, not merely a *description*. And an explanation requires the use of *theory*, the purpose of which is to understand *why* particular historical case studies illustrate the viability of social order without the state.

Whether or not anarchy features peaceful social cooperation and exchange or whether it will degenerate into social disorder and violence is dependent upon to the viability and likelihood of *voluntary* institutional mechanisms that *filter out* individuals who promote social disorder and *filter in* individuals who are expected to contribute to social order. We will discuss these sorts of exclusionary and inclusionary mechanisms in Section IV. For now, we simply want to emphasize that analytical anarchism is fundamentally an empirical study of the endogenous formation of rules that facilitate cooperation without command. It is therefore a radical inquiry into the *sources* of the formation of such rules. As we argue in the next section, *any* inquiry into the nature and causes of the wealth and poverty of nations requires, as an analytical starting point, the assumption of anarchy. Anarchy-focused inquiry is especially relevant if the social scientist is addressing the causes of relative success or failure of governments to secure property rights and facilitate contractual exchange as compared with anarchy.

III. Why Assume Anarchy in Political Economy?

The political economy of governance proceeds on two levels of analysis. A "higher" level of analysis focuses on *the rules of the game* and is concerned with both formal and informal institutions, *as well as their enforcement.* A "lower level" focuses on individuals' interactions in pursuit of their goals. Understanding this dual level of analysis provides a useful framework for unpacking and clarifying particular misperceptions with regard to the study of anarchy.

The very mention of the word "anarchy" provokes an image of a world that is, at best, disorderly and chaotic, or, even worse, a Hobbesian jungle in which people are solitary and poor and life is nasty, brutish, and short. From this perspective, an anarchic society is one that is deeply deficient because, lacking *government,* it also lacks *governance.* But the absence of *rulers* need not mean the absence of *rules.* Anarchy can be understood as simply the absence of *government*—of the state, of a territorial monopoly on putatively legitimized force—rather than of *governance.* Misperceptions of or ambiguities inherent in anarchism as an analytical or normative project rest on the unwarranted conflation of anarchy understood as *a particular set of outcomes* and anarchy understood as an *institutional form of governance.* These two senses of *anarchy* are related but are nonetheless distinct from each other. The popular association of anarchy with chaos and disorder rests on the assumption that these are necessary features of social interaction in the absence of government, without which no rules for governance could exist. There are at least three reasons to doubt this assumption, implying that anarchy can be more peaceful and prosperous than the conventional wisdom suggests.

First, international commerce operates in a condition of anarchy. According to the World Trade Organization, the ratio of international trade in goods and commercial services to world gross domestic product (GDP) increased from just over 20 percent in 1995 to roughly 30 percent in 2014.[28] This figure represents a tremendous amount of wealth that is generated outside the shadow of the state, roughly equivalent to the GDP of the United States. The institutional basis for international commerce can be traced back to the emergence of what is known as the Law Merchant, or the *lex mercatoria.* The Law Merchant was a set of customary laws that began to emerge during the eleventh century, at a time when international trade was beginning to increase in Europe.[29] It emerged from independent sets of localized customs within particular jurisdictions that proved to be common across jurisdictions. Not only did the norms constituting the Law Merchant emerge voluntarily, though unintendedly, from the commercial interactions of merchants, but disputes regarding the application of these norms were adjudicated by private merchant courts to which the parties had voluntary recourse and non-violently enforced by threat of ostracism. The discipline of repeated dealing and the fear of the potential loss of future income because of boycotts by other merchants incentivized merchants to comply with merchant court rulings. Given that the politically fragmented nature of medieval Europe raised the transaction costs of enforcing property rights and adjudicating contractual disputes across jurisdictions, a commonly accepted set of legal institutions emerged to reduce transaction costs, at least where state enforcement of international commerce was lacking.[30] By the fourteenth century, many European governments had codified or begun to codify and enforce commercial laws that had initially formed elements of the Law Merchant. International commerce operates within an institutional framework that resembles the one that obtained in medieval Europe. Today, cross-border disputes among merchants are resolved under the umbrellas of arbitration associations similar to medieval merchant courts. According to the International Chamber of Commerce, among the largest of these associations, merchants voluntarily comply with its private arbitral decisions 90 percent of the time under threat of reputational pressures.[31]

Second, the evident deficiencies of and the clear limits facing actually existing governments highlight the importance of treating anarchy as a baseline point of comparison, as argued by economist Raghuram Rajan. Without "assuming anarchy" as an analytic starting point, as well as building positive transaction costs into our analysis, "economic theory offers us little guidance on how strong institutions are created and nurtured."[32] The "blame for this neglect should be attached to the canonical model in economics: the complete markets model."[33] Though Rajan admits that "some abstraction is important, gross abstraction can make a model irrelevant. And for many situations, at least in the developing world, the complete markets model is too far distanced from reality to be useful."[34] The evidence provided by the *Fragile States Index* (FSI), an annual report compiled by the Fund for Peace, best illustrates Rajan's point. Of the 178 countries measured in the FSI, roughly 31 countries are indicated under "alert," implying that such countries have governments that are dysfunctional, predatory, and on the verge of collapse.[35]

Though a theoretical case can be made that a territorial monopoly on coercion can facilitate economic development, empirically it does not necessarily imply that (a) governments are able to effectively to monopolize coercion and/or that (b) such preconditions are necessary for relatively greater prosperity.[36] Whether such claims hold will depend on empirical comparative institutional studies of a comparative institutional nature. Analytical anarchism, like political economy itself, is a study of comparative institutional arrangements, not a comparison between ideal statelessness and imperfect actually existing, imperfect states, and/or vice versa. Recent experience in Somalia nicely illustrates this point. Since the collapse of the predatory regime of Mohamed Siad Barre in 1991, Somalia has effectively been in a condition of anarchy. Perhaps unexpectedly, key elements of human welfare and economic development have improved during Somalia's period of statelessness.[37] To be sure, Somalia is still desperately poor. Thus, a critic might say, statelessness in Somalia does not illustrate the superiority of anarchy over the operation of a territorial monopoly on coercion. The critic's claim implies that, if a monopoly government in Somalia were to credibly establish political constraints on predation, economic and social outcomes would prove superior to those that obtain under anarchy. This might indeed be the case *if* such a government were a live option in contemporary Somalia. "If 'good government' is not one of the options in Somalia's institutional opportunity set, anarchy may be a constrained optimum. Among the options that are available, ultra-predatory government and statelessness, statelessness may be preferable."[38] The problems with the exogenous imposition of formal, Western liberal democratic institutions—without the rule of law—is particularly noted by Dutch legal scholar Michael van Notten, who married into and lived within the ambit of the Samaron Clan in Somalia. As he observes:

> A complicating factor in understanding Somali society is that, in the past 30 years, a million or more Somalis have emigrated to Europe and North America. From there, they have become a highly vocal political lobby in their country of origin. These Somalis are enjoying every advantage of the clan system while being spared most of its disadvantages. The advantages they enjoy are mutual support and comradeship. *The main disadvantage they are spared is the clans' destructive involvement in politics.* While these Somalis of the diaspora see that the clan structure has become a system pitting all clans and even sub-clans against one another, they generally fail to detect the cause. They don't see that the clan system only became such a monster with the introduction of democracy. They also overlook the fact that the essence of Somali society consists not in the clans, but in the customary law. Finally, they don't understand that the 'West' owes its wealth not to democracy, but rather to the protection of property rights, and that democracy [without the rule of law] is undermining and destroying those rights.[39]

This raises what we regard as the more relevant question of analytical anarchism, and for a political economy in general: what is the endogenous process by which a society expands its institutional opportunity set to include governance that places credible constraints on coercion? The long process of economic development turns on the institutional transition "from subsistence to exchange,"[40] a movement from small-scale trading and small-scale capital accumulation to medium-scale trading and medium-scale capital accumulation and, finally, to large-scale trading and large-scale capital accumulation. The trigger for the transition at each stage is the development of institutions that increasingly secure protection for people and their property from predation. Exogenous changes can undermine this endogenous, cumulative process of rule formation. In Somalia, this "transition is not easy and is far from complete."[41] This is because

> the expectation, actively promoted by the United Nations, that a central government would be reestablished in the near future led clan militias and remnants of the former government into armed conflict, often in disregard of customary law and their elders. Each group manoeuvered to be in the most favorable position to capture the formidable array of powers of the future government.[42]

Third, perhaps the most important reason to assume anarchy as an analytical starting point in political economy is that collective action problems likely evident in a dysfunctionally anarchic society might prove worse in a society under the rule of a dysfunctional state. Since the 1990s, multiple events—including the collapse of communism in Eastern and Central Europe, ethnic and religious fractionalization in the Balkans and the Middle East, and the exportation of liberal democracy to failed and weak states in the developing world—have demonstrated that effective governance depends on the endogenous formation of rules rather than their exogenous imposition. "Any proposal for change," as Buchanan argued, "involves the status quo as the necessary starting point. 'We start from here,' and not from someplace else."[43] Buchanan's point is not only more pressing with regard to failed and weak states today; it is also reinforced by Raghuram Rajan's rationale for assuming anarchy:

> a better starting point for analysis than a world with only minor blemishes may be a world where nothing is enforceable, property and individual rights are totally insecure, and the enforcement apparatus for every contract must be derived from first principle[44]

so that, from this analytic starting point, we can then understand how enforcement mechanisms emerge even in the most unlikely of cases.

IV. Theoretical Approaches to Analytical Anarchism

From the perspective of analytical anarchism, problems of collective action affect not only anarchy, but also government. The market and the state are alternative institutional embodiments of governance. The market and the state in a given society emerge from the social interactions of the individuals constituting the society.[45] When markets or states function well, they can harness the productive and creative abilities of heterogeneous individuals across time, place, race, creed, and gender.

Social cooperation without the state is clearly possible among small numbers of homogeneous agents with low discount rates.[46] But analysts skeptical about the viability of anarchy maintain that social disorder will emerge under anarchy whenever groups are large, agents are heterogeneous, and agents' discount rates are high. On the skeptics' view, in the latter situation, the provision of public goods will be undermined by non-cooperation in the form of free-riding or predation. Simply put, there are high costs to "filtering in" or including "patient" and cooperative individuals and "filtering out" or excluding "impatient" and non-cooperative individuals. And both kinds of filtering are necessary if property rights are to be protected, contracts enforced, and public goods provided.

The problem of heterogeneity, not just in ethnicity, religion, sex, or wealth but also in the capacity and willingness to use force, poses a serious problem not only for anarchic governance but, indeed, for any sort of governance. Buchanan and Tullock acknowledge that their

> analysis of the constitution-making process has little relevance for a society that is distinguished by a sharp cleavage of the population into distinguishable social classes or separate racial, religious, or ethnic groups sufficient to encourage the formation of predictable political coalitions and in which one of these coalitions has a clearly advantageous position at the constitutional stage.[47]

Focusing specifically on anarchy, Daniel Sutter emphasizes that there is a distinction between securing initial possession of goods and services and providing enforceable agreements, and that the former must proceed the latter. The emergence of secure property rights, however, will depend on the distribution of force in society.[48] Because of the asymmetric distribution of force relationship between the protection agencies and individuals under a condition of anarcho-capitalism "the resulting distribution of rights may be highly skewed, with no effective freedom of choice between agenc[ies]."[49] Even scholars who have otherwise demonstrated the possibility of social cooperation without the state do not necessarily reject the necessity of government. While Robert Ellickson acknowledged that residents of Shasta County, California, were able to develop informal norms that served as preferable alternatives to legal rules and enforcement mechanisms,[50] he maintains that individuals needed government to provide them with "the Brooklyn Bridge, lighthouses, relatively clean air, and welfare programs suited to a geographically mobile society."[51] Ellickson's examples are typical of those commonly advanced in the course of economic arguments for monopoly governments.

In reality, however, the provision of public goods is a challenge not only for non-monopolistic social institutions but also for the state. To argue that the marginal cost of securing property rights by the state to an additional individual is zero, and therefore non-rivalrous, implicitly assumes homogeneity among individuals, and therefore assumes away the very problem of governance upon which the economic argument for the necessity of the state is characteristically premised. Recall that the state is supposed to be necessary, and anarchy to be non-viable, when, among other things, individuals are heterogeneous. But, when they are, scarce resources will be required to identify if in fact a given individual is "homogenous" with respect to her or his ability to cooperate with other individuals. The opportunity cost of each heterogeneous individual's membership in a given society is the cost of the foregone resources needed (a) to secure the property rights of others in the society if that individual turns out to threaten them and (b) to secure that individual's own property rights against others. Because of this foregone cost, the protection of such rights isn't a public good: it's rivalrous. Thus, institutional mechanisms for excluding non-cooperative individuals are *endogenous* and arise to reduce the transaction cost of acquiring information required to sort cooperative individuals from non-cooperative individuals.

To rule out the possibility of anarchy on the basis of the existence of large groups of heterogeneous and uncooperative (i.e. high-discount-rate) individuals puts the cart before the horse. Analytical anarchism approaches the issue of whether or not social cooperation in anonymity is possible, absent the state, by (a) beginning, from an analytic starting point, with the challenges posed by the need for social order in a society that is *already* large, heterogeneous, and inhabited by potentially uncooperative people; and (b) focusing on mechanisms of *inclusion* and *exclusion* available to such people.[52] On the margin, the size and degree of homogeneity and the level of cooperation are not *preconditions* of peaceful and productive social interaction under anarchy, but *by-products* of institutional mechanisms of inclusion and exclusion. "[I]t is far more likely that feelings of friendship and communion are the *effects* of a regime of (contractual) social co-operation rather than the cause."[53] Such institutional mechanisms emerge precisely because of their effectiveness in reducing the costs of identifying potential gains from trade, specifically by incentivizing the discovery of margins on which individuals are able to communicate about their willingness to engage in cooperative behavior.[54]

Among political economists working in the intellectual tradition of analytical anarchism, there are two distinct, though not mutually exclusive, approaches to illustrating how social cooperation can be facilitated without the state.

The first is the *exclusionary* approach, which stresses the role of *ex ante* mechanisms useful for "filtering out" untrustworthy and non-cooperative individuals from those who are trustworthy and cooperative. This approach emphasizes private provision of public goods, particularly the security of property rights, through mechanisms that make the exclusion of non-cooperators possible, in effect turning what is otherwise a public good into a club good.

The work of Edward Stringham exemplifies this approach. Stringham has illustrated the emergence and enforcement of rules governing stock exchanges in Holland and England in the seventeenth and eighteenth centuries, respectively, in the absence of state enforcement of contractual obligations.[55] Stockbrokers benefited from devising clear and predictable rules governing stock trading, but enforcing such rules posed a collective action problem for them. The potential loss of income suffered from fraudulent stockbrokers' free-riding on the reputations of other stockbrokers incentivized the joint provision of governance as a club good, one that utilized ostracism as a key enforcement tool. For example, in the coffeehouses of London, where English stock exchanges had had originally emerged, acts of deliberate fraud, or even unintentional default, by particular brokers resulted in their names being written on a blackboard. This form of boycott encouragement helped to protect other brokers from the risks of dealing with untrustworthy peers. At the same time, it incentivized other brokers to behave honestly and reliably in order to safeguard their access to potential future income.[56] The self-policing club arrangements Stringham has studied reveal the amazing creativity used by brokers, among others, to reduce the cost of excluding uncooperative individuals through *ex ante* sorting. The strategies Stringham describes exemplify the capacity of exclusionary mechanisms to transform large-group settings into more manageable small group settings, with the result that, even when a population pool is initially heterogeneous, those who are accepted into membership are more or less homogeneous on the margin that matters for the group—in this case, as in many others, with respect to honesty and trustworthiness.

The second, *inclusionary*, approach focuses on *ex post* mechanisms of "filtering in" potentially cooperative individuals. In effect, the non-rivalrous feature of public goods, according to this approach, is a *by-product* of inclusionary mechanisms that create margins of homogeneity among otherwise heterogeneous individuals. The result of the use of such inclusionary mechanisms is the evolution of generally applicable norms and rules from which all individuals can simultaneously benefit.

The work of Peter Leeson illustrates the exploration of this approach in various historical and cultural settings. For example, the extension of credit by producers of goods increased the costs of theft and the benefits of trade among middlemen in late precolonial Africa.[57] Given that middlemen during this period were the sole suppliers of firearms to interior communities, the distribution of force favored their ability to plunder, rather than trade.[58] However, credit served as a pre-contractual mechanism of inclusion that reduced the likelihood of predation. Credit allowed producers to trade with goods that did not yet exist, thus increasing the cost of theft for middlemen. In addition, by increasing the cost of theft for middlemen, who could not steal what had not yet been produced, this mechanism "filtered in" those individuals with lower discount rates, therefore incentivizing future repeated dealings, and "filtering out" those middlemen inclined to engage in violent theft. Thus, the extension of credit was a pre-contractual inclusionary mechanism capable of producing a public good—in this case self-governance—privately by eliciting a demand for trade among those middlemen patient enough to value the prospect of a future stream of income derived from trade rather than theft.

Leeson's work on pirate communities also defies the conventional wisdom with respect to the viability of anarchy.[59] On pirate ships, large groups of heterogeneous agents,[60] presumably with high discount rates, organized themselves under democratically elected captains and quartermasters constrained by constitutional rules (including ones, predating the formulation of the US Constitution, that mandated the separation of powers) and provided economic safety nets for the disabled.

Other inclusionary mechanisms facilitating peaceful social interaction between heterogeneous groups under anarchy include intermarriage between warring clans on the border between England and Scotland prior to their union[61] and the adoption of customs, practices, and languages to signal credibility and trustworthiness among strangers attempting to trade.[62] Such inclusionary mechanisms can enable people to overcome geographic and social distance in order to realize the gains from social cooperation under the division of labor.

V. Conclusion

Analytical anarchism is a research program exploring the possibility of endogenous rule formation, governance in accordance with emergent rules, and thus of collective action emerging from the bottom up rather than dependent on top-down management. There *are* goods that are to one degree or another non-excludable or non-rivalrous or both, and that may thus not be produced, or not be produced at appealing levels, absent some sort of collective action. However, rules making possible the needed kinds of collective action can be created and sustained endogenously. Social-evolutionary processes must be cultivated in order to ensure that people can realize the benefits of social cooperation without command.

This outcome can be achieved in the course of peaceful social cooperation featuring exclusionary and inclusionary mechanisms. Though the inclusionary and exclusionary approaches are analytically distinct, they are intertwined empirically in multiple settings. The availability of each helps to enable social cooperation among heterogeneous individuals by, among other things, reducing the payoffs to violent and uncooperative behavior.[63] Thus, they provide convergent support for the occurrence of catallaxy.[64] By calling attention to social mechanisms that create and sustain bottom-up social order, analytical anarchism helps in perhaps unexpected ways to teach the *fundamental* lesson of political economy. Political economy in general, and analytical anarchism in particular, help to show us how it is possible to convert potentially violent situations into ones in which people can and do engage in mutually beneficial exchanges. They also show how people can set in motion, as an unintended by-product, the evolution of rules facilitating the occurrence of such exchanges among anonymous traders without the use of force.

Notes

1 Carl Menger, *Investigations into the Methods of the Social Sciences with Special Reference to Economics* (New York, NY: New York UP 1985) 146.

2 Gary W. Cox, Douglass C. North, and Barry R. Weingast, "The Violence Trap: A Political Economic Approach to the Problems of Development," *Journal of Public Finance and Public Choice* 34.1 (2019): 3–19.

3 See Peter J. Boettke, "Anarchism as a Progressive Research Program in Political Economy," *Anarchy, State and Public Choice*, ed. Edward Stringham (Northampton, MA: Elgar 2005) 206–19; Peter J. Boettke, "Anarchism and Austrian Economics," *New Perspectives on Political Economy* 7.1 (2011): 125–40.

4 Our empirical and analytical focus is not intended to reflect a dismissive attitude regarding important normative and theoretical contributions to the study of anarchy. An overview of analytical anarchism must acknowledge its precursors, including the works of Murray Rothbard, Walter Block, and David Friedman. Their contributions have influenced and inspired scholars engaged in the analytical anarchist project today. See Murray N. Rothbard, *Power and Market: Government and the Economy* (Menlo Park, CA: Institute for Humane Studies 1970); Murray N. Rothbard, *For a New Liberty: The Libertarian Manifesto* (New York, NY: Macmillan 1973); Murray N. Rothbard, *The Ethics of Liberty* (Atlantic Highlands, NJ: Humanities 1982); Walter Block, *Defending the Undefendable*, 2d ed. (Auburn, AL: Mises 2011); David D. Friedman, *The Machinery of Freedom*, 3d ed. (Charleston, SC: CreateSpace 2015).

5 The term "market failure" was coined by economist Francis Bator, "The Anatomy of Market Failure," *Quarterly Journal of Economics* 72.3 (1958): 351–79.

6 For a more complete discussion of this point, see Peter J. Boettke and Peter T. Leeson, "Introduction," *The Economic Role of the State*, ed. Boettke and Leeson (Northampton, MA: Elgar 2015) xi–xxv.

7 We draw attention to the work of Alchian, Buchanan, and Coase because, by pioneering the development of property rights economics, public choice economics, and law and economics, respectively, each of them redirected the analytical focus of economic analysis to questions related to choice *over* institutional arrangements rather than *within* institutional arrangements and the role of institutional entrepreneurship in devising institutional arrangements capable of providing public goods. See Peter J. Boettke and Rosolino A. Candela, "Alchian, Buchanan, and Coase: A Neglected Branch of Chicago Price Theory," *Man and the Economy: The Journal of the Coase Society* 1.2 (2014): 189–208; and Peter J. Boettke and Rosolino A. Candela, "Rivalry, Polycentricism, and Institutional Evolution," *Advances in Austrian Economics* 19 (2015): 1–19.

8 Paul A. Samuelson, "The Pure Theory of Public Expenditure," *Review of Economics and Statistics* 36.4 (1954): 387–9.

9 See Paul A. Samuelson, *Economics: An Introductory Analysis*, 5th ed. (New York, NY: McGraw-Hill 1961) 192–3; Paul A. Samuelson and William D. Nordhaus, *Economics,* 19th ed. (New York, NY: McGraw-Hill 2009) 37. Samuelson was not the first economist to justify government intervention in the financing of lighthouses on the grounds of non-excludability. John Ramsey McCulloch and, more notably, John Stuart Mill were among the earliest economists to assume that the potential of free-riding justified government involvement in the provision of lighthouses. See John Ramsey McCulloch, "On the Frequency of Shipwrecks," *Edinburgh Review* 60 (1835): 338–53; John Stuart Mill, *Principles of Political Economy* (Amherst, NY: Prometheus 2004).

10 See James M. Buchanan, "An Economic Theory of Clubs," *Economica* 32 (1965): 1–14.

11 Harold Demsetz has also noted that there is a further distinction, obscured by Samuelson, between *public* goods and *collective* goods. Both are non-rivalrous. But only in the case of collective goods is it "*impossible* to exclude nonpurchasers" (emphasis original). See Harold Demsetz, "The Private Production of Public Goods," *Journal of Law and Economics* 13.2 (1970): 254.

12 Ronald H. Coase, "The Lighthouse in Economics," *Journal of Law and Economics* 17.2 (1974): 357–76.

13 Coase 375.

14 For an extension of Coase's analysis to the case of lightships, see Rosolino Candela and Vincent Geloso, "The Lightship in Economics," *Public Choice* 176.3–4 (2018): 479–506; Rosolino Candela and Vincent Geloso, "Coase and Transaction Costs Reconsidered: The Case of the English Lighthouse System," *European Journal of Law and Economics* 48.3 (2019): 331–49.

15 Armen A. Alchian and William R. Allen, *University Economics: Elements of Inquiry,* 3d ed. (Belmont, CA: Wadsworth 1972) 250.

16 Alchian and Allen 250.

17 Tyler Cowen, "Public Goods Definitions and their Institutional Context: a Critique of Public Goods Theory," *Review of Social Economy* 43.1 (1985): 53–63; Christopher J. Coyne, "Lobotomizing the Defense Brain," *Review of Austrian Economics* 28.4 (2015): 371–96.

18 In "Public Goods Definitions," Cowen builds on this point by arguing that the degree to which any good is non-rivalrous or non-excludable depends on its institutional context.

19 For a more comprehensive overview of the relationship between the study of public choice and the study of anarchy, see Benjamin Powell and Edward P. Stringham, "Public Choice and the Economic Analysis of Anarchy: A Survey," *Public Choice* 140.3–4 (2009): 503–38.

20 Gordon Tullock, ed., *Explorations in the Theory of Anarchy* (Blacksburg, VA: Center for the Study of Public Choice 1972); Gordon Tullock, ed., *Further Explorations in the Theory of Anarchy* (Blacksburg, VA: University 1974).

21 Winston Bush, "Individual Welfare in Anarchy," Tullock, *Explorations* 5.

22 An important exception was David Friedman, Assistant Professor of Economics at Virginia Tech between 1976 and 1980.

23 James M. Buchanan, "Reflections after Three Decades," Stringham, *Anarchy* 192.

24 See Diego Gambetta, ed., *Trust: Making and Breaking Cooperative Relations* (Oxford: Blackwell 1988); Diego Gambetta, *The Sicilian Mafia: The Business of Private Protection* (Cambridge, MA: Harvard UP 1993).

25 Gambettta, *Mafia* 275n3.

26 Though the Sicilian Mafia emerged because of the state's failure to secure and enforce private property rights, this does not imply the complete absence of the state itself. It would be more precise to argue that the predatory nature of the state in Sicily created the conditions for its emergence of the Sicilian Mafia as a substitute mechanism of property rights enforcement in the early nineteenth century. See Peter J. Boettke and Rosolino A. Candela, "Productive Specialization, Peaceful Cooperation, and the Problem of the Predatory State: Lessons From Comparative Historical Political Economy," *Public Choice*, forthcoming; Rosolino A. Candela, "The Political Economy of Insecure Property Rights: Insights from the Kingdom of Sicily," *Journal of Institutional Economics*, forthcoming.

27 Avinash K. Dixit, *Lawlessness and Economics: Alternative Modes of Governance* (Princeton, NJ: Princeton UP 2004) 22.

28 World Trade Organization, *International Trade Statistics 2015* (Geneva: WTO 2015) 17.

29 Bruce L. Benson, "The Spontaneous Evolution of Commercial Law," *Southern Economic Journal* 55.3 (1989): 644–61.

30 Benson provides several reasons why the Law Merchant emerged during this period. The first reason is that state law did not recognize or enforce what merchant law acknowledged. For example, government courts typically would not consider disputes that included (i) contracts made in another nation, (ii) contractual agreements which involved the payment of interest, or (iii) books of account as evidence despite the fact that merchants held them in high regard. Second, merchant courts were chaired by judges from the relevant merchant community, who had specialized and particular knowledge of technical issues involved in merchant disputes. Therefore, merchant courts could generally adjudicate disputes in a more expeditious manner. See Benson 649–50.

31 Peter T. Leeson, "One More Time with Feeling: The Law Merchant, Arbitration, and International Trade," *Indian Journal of Economics and Business* 29 (2007): 29–34; Peter T. Leeson, "Anarchy Unbound: How Much Order Can Spontaneous Order Create?" *Handbook on Contemporary Austrian Economics*, ed. Peter J. Boettke. (Northampton, MA: Edward Elgar 2010) 136–153; Peter T. Leeson, *Anarchy Unbound: Why Self-Governance Works Better Than You Think* (New York, NY: CUP 2014).

32 Rajan Raghuram, "Assume Anarchy?" *Finance and Development*, Sep. 2004: 56.

33 Raghuram 56. Raghuram goes further to describe the complete markets model as one in which "everyone is fully informed; every eventuality is anticipated in contracts; all contracts are enforced by omniscient, incorruptible courts; and governments automatically take care of all the public goods and interfere in none of the private ones."

34 Raghuram 56.

35 See J.J. Messner, ed., *Fragile States Index Annual Report 2019* (Washington, DC: Fund for Peace 2019).

36 Though not an anarchist, economics Nobel Laureate Douglass North has observed: "The existence of a state is essential for economic growth; the state, however, is the source of man-made economic decline." See Douglass C. North, *Structure and Change in Economic History* (New York, NY: Norton 1981) 20.

37 Peter T. Leeson, "Better Off Stateless: Somalia before and after Government Collapse," *Journal of Comparative Economics* 35.4 (2007): 698–710; Benjamin Powell, Ryan Ford, and Alex Nowrasteh, "Somalia after State Collapse: Chaos or Improvement?" *Journal of Economic Behavior and Organization* 67.3–4 (2008): 657–70.

38 Leeson, "Stateless" 707; see also Peter T. Leeson and Claudia Williamson, "Anarchy and Development: An Application of the Theory of Second Best," *Law and Development Review* 2.1 (2009): 77–96.

39 Michael van Notten. *The Law of the Somalis: A Stable Foundation for Economic Development in the Horn of Africa*, ed. Spencer Heath MacCallum (Trenton, NJ: Red Sea 2005) 9. Emphasis added.

40 P.T. Bauer, *From Subsistence to Exchange* (Princeton, NJ: Princeton UP 2000).

41 Van Notten 8.

42 Van Notten 8.

43 James M. Buchanan, *Collected Works of James M. Buchanan 7: The Limits of Liberty* (Indianapolis, IN: Liberty Fund 2000) 101.

44 Rajan 57.

45 See Richard E. Wagner, *Politics as a Peculiar Business: Insights from a Theory of Entangled Political Economy* (Northampton, MA: Elgar 2016); Paul Dragos Aligica, Peter J. Boettke, and Vlad Tarko, *Public Governance and the Classical-Liberal Perspective: Political Economy Foundations* (New York, NY: OUP 2019).

46 Janet T. Landa, "A Theory of the Ethnically Homogenous Middleman Group: An Institutional Alternative to Contract Law," *Journal of Legal Studies* 10.2 (1981): 349–62; Avner Greif, "Reputation and Coalitions in Medieval Trade: Evidence on the Maghribi Traders," *Journal of Economic History* 49.4 (1989): 857–82; Avner Greif, "Contract Enforceability and Economic Institutions in Early Trade: The Maghribi Traders' Coalition," *American Economic Review* 8.3 (1993): 525–48; Lisa Berstein, "Opting Out of the Legal System: Extralegal Contractual Relations in the Diamond Industry," *Journal of Legal Studies* 21.1 (1992): 115–57; Barak Richman, *Stateless Commerce: The Diamond Network and the Persistence of Relational Exchange* (Cambridge, MA: Harvard UP 2017).

47 James M. Buchanan and Gordon Tullock, *The Calculus of Consent: Logical foundations of Constitutional Democracy* (Ann Arbor, MI: U of Michigan P 1962) 80.

48 Daniel Sutter, "Asymmetric Power Relations and Cooperation in Anarchy," *Southern Economic Journal* 61.3 (1995): 602–13

49 Sutter 604. On the issues discussed in the text relating to impact of the distribution of rights and the returns to violence on the viability of anarchy, see John Umbeck, "Might Makes Rights: A Theory of the Formation and Initial Distribution of Property Rights," *Economic Inquiry* 19.1 (1981): 38–59; Jack Hirshleifer, "Anarchy and Its Breakdown," *Journal of Political Economy* 103.1 (2005): 26–52; Rosolino A. Candela and Vincent Geloso, "Statelessness and the Endogeneity of Generalized Increasing Returns: Acadian Settlers and Native Americans Before 1755," *SSRN Working Paper*, https://papers.ssrn.com/sol3/papers.cfm?abstract_id=3028206 (2019; last visited January 15, 2020).

50 Robert C. Ellickson, "Of Coase and Cattle: Dispute Resolution Among Neighbors in Shasta County," *Stanford Law Review* 38.3 (1986): 623–87; Robert C. Ellickson, *Order without Law: How Neighbors Settle Disputes* (Cambridge, MA: Harvard UP 1991).

51 Robert C. Ellickson, "A Hayekian Case Against Anarcho-Capitalism: Of Street Grids, Lighthouses, and Aid to the Destitute," *New York University Journal of Law and Liberty* 11.1 (2017): 372.

52 See Boettke, "Anarchism" 125–40. Emphasis original.

53 Murray N. Rothbard, *Man, Economy, and State: A Treatise on Economic Principles* (Princeton, NJ: Van Nostrand 1962) 85.

54 See Peter J. Boettke and Rosolino A. Candela, "Rivalry, Polycentricism, and Institutional Evolution," *Advances in Austrian Economics* 19 (2015): 1–19.

55 Edward Stringham, "The Emergence of the London Stock Exchange as a Self-Policing Club," *Journal of Private Enterprise* 17.2 (2002): 1–19; Edward P. Stringham, "The Extralegal Development of Securities Trading in Seventeenth Century Amsterdam," *Quarterly Review of Economics and Finance* 43.2 (2003): 321–344; Edward P. Stringham, *Private Governance: Creating Order in Economic and Social Life* (New York, NY: OUP 2015).

56 Stringham, "Emergence" 6–7.

57 Peter T. Leeson, "Trading With Bandits," *Journal of Law and Economics* 50.2 (2007): 303–21;

58 Leeson, "Trading" 306.

59 Peter T. Leeson, "An-arrgh-chy: The Law and Economics of Pirate Organization," *Journal of Political Economy* 115.6 (2007): 1049–94; Peter T. Leeson, *The Invisible Hook: The Hidden Economics of Pirates* (Princeton, NJ: Princeton UP 2009).

60 Black and white sailors served together on pirate ships, and the proportion of black sailors was generally *higher* on pirate ships than on conventional merchant ships (see Leeson, *Hook* 157).

61 Peter T. Leeson, "The Laws of Lawlessness," *Journal of Legal Studies* 38.2 (2009): 471–503.

62 See Peter T. Leeson, "Endogenizing Fractionalization," *Journal of Institutional Economics* 1.1 (2005): 75–98; Peter T. Leeson, "Social Distance and Self-Enforcing Exchange," *Journal of Legal Studies* 37.1 (2008): 161–88.

63 See, for example, John Umbeck, "The California Gold Rush: A Study of Emerging Property Rights," *Explorations in Economic History*, 14.3 (1977): 197–226; Terry L. Anderson and P.J. Hill, *The Not So Wild, Wild West: Property Rights on the Frontier* (Stanford, CA: Stanford UP 2004); David Friedman, "Private Creation and Enforcement of Law: A Historical Case," *Journal of Legal Studies* 8.2 (1979): 399–415; and David Skarbek, *The Social Order of the Underworld: How Prison Gangs Govern the American Penal System* (New York, NY: OUP 2014). Though we have used Leeson's work to illustrate the inclusionary approach, he also offers an example of the exclusionary approach similar to Stringham's in "Governments, Clubs, and Constitutions," *Journal of Economic Behavior and Organization* 80.2 (2011): 301–8.

64 For further discussion of the meaning of catallaxy, see F.A. Hayek, *Law, Legislation and Liberty 2: The Mirage of Social Justice* (Chicago, IL: U of Chicago P 1976) 108.

16

MORAL PARITY BETWEEN STATE AND NON-STATE ACTORS

Jason Brennan

I. Introduction

Suppose I believe that people are too fat, so I storm 7-Eleven with a gun and declare, "From now one, no one may purchase Big Gulps!" Suppose I believe Americans should not live high while people die, so I hack into upper-middle-class and rich people's bank accounts and redistribute their wealth to poor people. Suppose I believe Americans should support one another and prioritize each other's welfare over the welfare of foreigners. So, I arrive at a BMW dealership while brandishing a gun and tell customers, "You may buy German, but only if you give $1,500 to Detroit autoworkers." Suppose I believe space exploration is a vital project. So, I build elaborate and expensive space-research equipment, which I pay for by hacking into Americans' bank accounts.

If I did any of these things, you would probably call the police and demand I be arrested. The police would indeed show up and arrest me, or perhaps even kill me.

Yet, while you would think my actions are criminal, our own governments do these same things. Governments regularly issue commands, backed with threats of violence, about what we may and may not eat, what we may buy, and how much of our income we must redistribute to others or spend on supposed public goods. Many people think there is no problem with that—they believe that governments are permitted to do things ordinary people are forbidden from doing. This leads to a philosophical puzzle: What, if anything, explains why governments and the agents of government have a special moral status in which they are exempt from ordinary moral rules and prohibitions? What, if anything, can explain why government agents may do what I or others may not?

For the purposes of this chapter, let's define a *statist* as a person who advocates installing and maintaining a government. (I'm not using the word "statist" as a pejorative here.) Following the philosopher Gregory Kavka, I understand a *government* to be the subset of a society which claims a monopoly on the legitimate use of coercion, and which has coercive power (more or less) sufficient to maintain that monopoly.[1] An *anarchist* is a person who rejects government so defined; i.e., a person who believes that social order and peace can be properly maintained without relying on a monopoly of coercive violence. Anarchists often believe that governments are unjust. Or, more weakly, many anarchists simply believe non-governmental mechanisms for protecting rights and property, or for maintaining public goods, are all things considered superior to governmental mechanisms.

One way to illustrate the difference between statists and anarchists concerns their view of government and non-governmental actors. Statists generally believe that government actors have at least four special moral powers and privileges:

1 *Legitimacy/Special Enforcement Powers*: The special moral permission to create and enforce rules over certain people within a geographic area. For example, a government may forbid adults from smoking marijuana and may send police to violently apprehend marijuana users.
2 *Authority*: A special moral power to create, in others, a *moral obligation* to obey the rules and commands certain government agents issue. For example, when a government issues a law forbidding you from using marijuana, you thereby acquire a moral obligation to refrain from smoking pot *because* the government said so.
3 *Special Immunity*: When government agents act unjustly, we are not permitted to defend ourselves or others from their unjust actions. For example, even if marijuana criminalization is unjust, you may not fight back against a police officer who arrests you for pot possession. You must instead submit to arrest and accept punishment.
4 *Punishment*: The government has the legitimacy and authority to punish people who ignore its commands or violate its rules. For example, if the cops catch you smoking pot, the government can throw you in jail, take some of your money, and issue a public proclamation that you are a criminal.

To be more precise, statists believe that government agents, in virtue of being government agents, possess these moral powers and privileges *more extensively* than ordinary civilians do. For instance, if I order you to stop smoking pot, the statist would say my "order" confers upon you no duty to stop. But if the Drug Enforcement Agency issues that exact same order, the statist holds that you thereby acquire a duty to comply.

Now, most statists, except for totalitarians, believe there are limits on what the state may do and on how expansive these four moral powers and privileges are. Most people believe that the state has limits on what rules it may issue and how it may enforce those rules, that you might not have a duty to obey certain highly unjust commands or laws, and that you might have some right to resist government injustices. Nevertheless, statists generally hold that you owe greater respect, deference, and subservience to government agents than you do to private actors.

In contrast, anarchists generally hold that government agents and private civilians are *on par* morally speaking. Call this the *Moral Parity Thesis*: government agents and private civilians are fundamentally morally equal; government bodies and civilians are fundamentally morally equal. Anarchists tend to hold that government agents, despite their legal offices, do not have any special right to create and enforce rules, do not have any special right to punish, do not have any special right to be obeyed, and do not have any special immunity against being resisted when they act unjustly.

The anarchist issues the statist a challenge: identify some property or set of properties which (some) governments (tend to) possess and which civilians lack, which plausibly explain why governments would have some extra degree of legitimacy, authority, special immunity, or right to punish. First, I discuss anarchist responses to various arguments which purport to show states have legitimacy and authority. Second, I discuss general responses to the issue of whether state agents enjoy special immunity. Third, I cover the question of whether the state, and only the state, can punish. My goal here is not to settle these issues—indeed, each topic is itself a subject of hundreds of books—but rather to illustrate precisely what it means for anarchists to hold that governmental and non-governmental agents are morally on par.

II. The Huemer Test

In *The Problem of Political Authority*, anarchist philosopher Michael Huemer examines a wide range of arguments which purport to establish that some governments have legitimacy and authority.[2] The statist has to identify some special feature or set of features F that at least some governments tend to have and which civilians tend to lack, which explains why governments and their agents acting ex officio would possess these two special moral powers and privileges.

When the statist offers a candidate for F, Huemer then asks two questions:

1 Is F plausible in its own right?
2 Is it possible for a civilian or private agent also to possess F? If a civilian, private agent, or group of private agents possessed F, would we also conclude that the civilian/private agent had legitimacy, authority, or whatever other special status the statist attributes to government?

We might call questions 1 and 2, taken together, the *Huemer Test*. When the statist offers an account of why the government or its agents possess some privileged moral status, we should accept that account only if it passes the Huemer Test; that is, only if the statist has satisfactory answers to both of these questions.

In a sense, part 2 of the Huemer Test is a test of moral parity. It is meant to examine whether the statist believes that government and civilians are in principle on par, or whether the statist instead believes that government is somehow special. Many times, after the statist has offered some account of F, Huemer constructs a parallel case in which civilians also possess F. Yet in almost all of these cases, we would conclude the civilians do not have legitimacy and authority, despite possessing the special features that supposedly explain why governments have legitimacy and authority. This shows that the statist's purported theory of legitimacy and authority is mistaken, or perhaps that the statist inadvertently believes (for unknown reasons) that government and civilian agents are not morally on par.

Let's illustrate this with a cartoon case. Suppose someone said that the reason US government agents have legitimacy and authority is because they work in or near Washington, DC. First, we would ask, is that even a plausible explanation for why the US federal government would have authority? Obviously not—that's why I'm using it as a cartoon illustration here. (I'll examine a more plausible case below.) Second, we can then ask whether it's possible for non-governmental agents (such as I, Jason Brennan) to possess or instantiate the feature of "working in or near DC." Of course, they can. So we might draw a parallel: Jason Brennan and Drug Enforcement Agency (DEA) bureaucrats both work in DC; thus, they both can and do possess the special feature meant to explain why government agents have legitimacy and authority. However, if Jason Brennan ordered you not to smoke pot and threatened to throw you in jail for doing so, you would conclude both (a) that you had no duty to obey his commands and (b) that he had no permission to enforce his command.[3] Accordingly, "working in or near DC" cannot be the special property or feature that explains why the DEA is authoritative and legitimate. Both I, Jason Brennan, and the DEA instantiate that property, but no one would think that makes the DEA authoritative.

Again, that is a silly example meant to illustrate the general principle. Let's now examine how a popular and far more plausible theory fails the Huemer Test.

III. Fair Play and the Huemer Test

To review, governments generally claim to possess two special moral powers:

1 *Legitimacy*: The permission to create and enforce rules over certain people within a geographic area.
2 *Authority*: The ability to create in others a *moral obligation* to obey those rules.

Legitimacy is the power that could make it permissible for the government to tax you. Authority is the power that could make it impermissible for you to refuse to pay your taxes. Legitimacy makes it okay for the police to arrest you.

Let's briefly examine how one prominent theory of legitimacy and authority fails the Huemer Test. I do not have space to cover all such theories here (and other chapters in this volume may provide more depth). My goal in doing so is to illustrate how morality parity appears to exist between state and non-state actors.

One major theory of legitimacy and authority, devised by H. L. A. Hart, holds that legitimacy and authority arises out of a duty of fair play:

The Fair Play Theory

> When a number of persons conduct any joint enterprise according to rules and thus restrict their liberty, those who have submitted to those restrictions when required have a right to a similar submission from those who have benefited by their submission.[4] Further, in such cases, it is permissible to *coerce* others to comply with this duty.

The idea here is that when some people incur a sacrifice in order to produce public goods that benefit all, the other people who benefit have a duty to contribute to the production of those goods as well. It would be unfair of them to free-ride on the provision of these goods when others are sacrificing to provide them.

The philosopher Robert Nozick notes that at least in some cases, this line of argument seems implausible. He illustrates at least one case with his "public address system" thought experiment. He asks you to imagine that your neighbors create a public entertainment system, with loudspeakers throughout your neighborhood. Each neighbor takes turns playing songs, reciting poetry, conducting interviews, or whatnot. You enjoy the system. One day, let's say Day 138, they come to you and say that it's *your* turn to spend the day entertaining people. Must you do so? Most people conclude no—even though you benefited from the system, you aren't duty-bound to participate in it and it would be wrong to force you do to so. Part of the reason for this judgment seems to be that you had no good way of *avoiding* receiving the benefits—you couldn't opt out without great expense to yourself. But this seems to hold for most of the benefits the state provides as well.

However, perhaps there are other fair play cases where it's plausible there *is* a duty to contribute to some common good. Here is one such case from Huemer:

> You are in a lifeboat with several other people. You are caught in a storm, and the boat is taking on water, which needs to be bailed out. Other passengers take up containers and start bailing. The other passengers' efforts are clearly sufficient to keep the boat afloat; thus, no large negative consequences will result if you refuse to bail. Nevertheless, it seems obvious that you should help bail water. Intuitively, it would be unfair to let the others do all the work.[5]

The public-address-system and lifeboat cases are both instances where the fair play principle applies, but it only the latter seems obligatory. This shows at the very least that Hart's Fair Play Theory is incomplete, since it does not distinguish between the two cases. The difference, Huemer says, is that in the lifeboat case the others are genuinely doing something useful, the costs they assume are necessary to produce the common good, you do indeed receive a fair share of the benefit being produced, your participation would indeed help produce the good, the costs to you of participating are reasonable and fair, and, finally, your participation does not stop you from doing something more important.[6] In the public-address-system case, your participation comes at the expense of other important things you could do with your life.

Now, Hart intends the Fair Play Theory to explain both why government may coerce us into "doing our fair share" and why we would have a duty to obey the government's commands, edicts, and laws. Hart and others who endorse the Fair Play Theory claim that *obedience to the law* is morally analogous to helping to bail water out of the lifeboat.

Huemer subjects the theory to part 2 of the Huemer Test. He notes that governments do not simply demand that we, say, pay a small amount of taxes to maintain peace and public order. They instead impose and enforce a wide range of other rules, such as laws requiring you to go through thousands of hours of training before you can braid others' hair for money, laws forbidding you from smoking pot, or laws requiring you to turn in escaped slaves. Huemer then asks us to imagine that a private person did something similar in the lifeboat case:

> Obedience to the law, according to advocates of the Fair Play [Theory], is analogous to helping bail water out of a lifeboat. But in view of the aforementioned laws, a closer analogy would be as follows. The lifeboat is taking on water. The passengers gather and discuss what to do about the problem. A majority (not including you) want [fellow passenger] Bob to devise a solution. Bob thinks for a minute, then announces the following plan:
>
> i) All passengers shall start bailing water out of the boat;
> ii) They shall pray to Poseidon to ask for his mercy;
> iii) They shall flagellate themselves with belts to prove their seriousness; and
> iv) They shall each pay $50 to Sally, who helped Bob get elected.
>
> You know that item (i) is useful, item (ii) useless, and items (iii) and (iv) harmful to most passengers. Nonetheless, most other passengers participate in all four parts of Bob's plan. If you refuse to pray, self-flagellate, or pay Sally, do you thereby act wrongly? Do you treat the other passengers unfairly?[7]

Here, Huemer asks us to imagine that Bob is playing the role the state does. Bob, like actually existing states, is in a position to coordinate other people's behavior. He has some enforcement power. Like real states, he does not merely prescribe that we abide by rules necessary to protect our lives and welfare, but also issues a number of other seemingly irrelevant, useless, harmful, counterproductive, or unjust rules. Huemer then notes that it seems implausible that Bob has the legitimacy to enforce rules (ii)–(iv) and it is further implausible that the passengers would have any duty to abide by (ii)–(iv). If so, the Fair Play Theory does not explain why a state would have the legitimacy or authority to create and enforce rules such as prohibitions on prostitution, marijuana use, and so on.

Now, Huemer might well concede that if a state were *necessary* to ensure peace and sufficient level of rights protection, then we should instantiate a state. But, again, he argues this is compatible with moral parity between state and non-state actors. Consider: in the lifeboat case above, Huemer would agree that Bob may coerce others to bail out the water. Similarly, if the state may coerce us to pay taxes to fund the police (assuming, generously, that this is the only and best way to maintain the peace), it is not because the state has some special property individual agents necessarily lack.

IV. Self-Defense and Defense of Others against Government Injustice

Consider the following sets of cases:

A. A masked man starts firing at people in the park.
B. John sincerely believes marijuana is bad for us. He captures anyone he sees who possesses marijuana and, after holding a public trial for them in his living room, locks them in his basement for thirty days.
C. A hacker takes control of American drone bombers and uses one to kill a known terrorist, in the process knowingly killing hundreds of innocent civilians nearby.

Most people would judge that in cases like A–C, you would be permitted to use violence, even deadly violence, to stop the perpetrators of these acts. You have a right of self-defense and a right to defend others from injustice. English common law holds that people have a right to protect themselves and others against threats such as assault, battery, rape, and murder.[8] According to the common law doctrine of self-defense, one person (the "killer") may justifiably kill another (the "adversary") when:

1 The killer is not the aggressor, and
2 He *reasonably believes* he (or someone else) is in *imminent danger* of severe bodily *harm* from his adversary, and
3 He reasonably believes that killing is *necessary* to avoid this danger.[9]

Note that the common law regards meeting these conditions as *justifications*, not merely excuses, for homicide. The distinction is that, when one has an excuse, the law considers the homicide wrongful, but one's liability may be reduced. When one is justified in killing another, the act of killing is not *wrong* at all.

Now consider a different set of cases:

D. A police officer pulls over a minivan full of kids. Inexplicably, even though there is no sign the mother driving the van is armed, he immediately begins shooting at the van's windows as soon as he emerges from his car.[10]
E. State leaders decide to criminalize marijuana, despite the overwhelming evidence it is far less dangerous than alcohol.[11] They order cops to capture anyone who possesses marijuana, and, after holding a trial for them in a fancy courthouse, lock those people in the courthouse's basement for thirty days.
F. The US President orders American drone bombers to kill a terrorist, in the process knowingly killing hundreds of innocent civilians nearby.

On their face, cases D–F seem roughly analogous to cases A–C, except that in D–F the wrongdoers are government officials acting ex officio rather than private civilians. (If you wish, to make the cases more analogous, imagine the actors in both sets of cases have the same motives and information.) Yet most people, especially the most strongly statist, would judge it impermissible to use violence in self-defense or defense of others in cases D–F, even though they would judge it permissible in the analogous cases A–C.

The standard or prevailing statist view is that government agents enjoy a special or privileged status when they commit unjust actions. The standard view holds both that government agents have a special permission to perform unjust actions—actions that we would judge evil and impermissible were a non-government agent to perform them—and also that these agents enjoy a special right against being *stopped* when they commit injustice. Government agents somehow *may* perform unjust acts, and we're supposed to stand by and *let them*. We may later *complain* when government agents act badly. We may demand that *other* government agents punish their colleagues for their colleagues' bad behavior. We might protest, write letters to newspaper editors and senators, and vote for better candidates.[12] But, statists generally think, we're not supposed to *stop* injustice ourselves.

Thus, many people subscribe to what I call the *Special Immunity Thesis*.[13] The Special Immunity Thesis holds that there is a special burden to justify interfering with, trying to stop, or fighting back against government agents who, acting ex officio, commit injustice:

The Special Immunity Thesis

> Government agents—or at least the agents of democratic governments—enjoy a special immunity against being deceived, lied to, sabotaged, attacked, or killed in self-defense or defense of others. Government property enjoys a special immunity against being damaged, sabotaged, or destroyed. The set of conditions under which it is permissible, in self-defense or defense of others, to deceive, lie to, sabotage, attack or kill a government agent (acting ex officio), or to destroy government property, is much more stringent and tightly constrained than the set of conditions under which it is permissible to deceive, lie to, sabotage, attack or kill a private civilian, or destroy private property.

In contrast, one might reject the Special Immunity Thesis in favor of the *Moral Parity Thesis*:

The Moral Parity Thesis

> The conditions under which a person may, in self-defense or defense of others, deceive, lie to, sabotage, attack, or kill a fellow civilian, or destroy private property, are also conditions under which a civilian may do the same to a government agent (acting ex officio) or government property.

The Moral Parity Thesis holds that justifying self-defense or the defense of others against government agents is on par with justifying self-defense or the defense of others against civilians. Or, strictly speaking, the Moral Parity Thesis, as stated, allows that it could be *easier* to justify self-defense against government agents than against private civilians.

If the Moral Parity Thesis is true, this would have radical implications. It would allow that you could use violence to resist arrest for a wrongful or mistaken law, or to break out of jail after a mistaken or wrongful conviction. You could kill a cop who uses excessive violence. You could assassinate a president or general who starts or leads an unjust war. You could destroy government property being used to violate civil or economic rights. You could lie to wrong-doing government agents.

Defenders of the Special Immunity Thesis thus need to identify some morally significant feature that governments possess, which civilians lack, which might explain why we would lack a right of self-defense against government wrongdoing though we would have a right to defend against civilians acting the same way.

One might think there is an easy argument here. Governments, the statist might claim, have legitimacy and authority, while civilians do not. Governments have permission to create and enforce rules and have a right to be obeyed when they do so. Civilians lack such moral powers.

But there are two major problems with this kind of reasoning. First, as the discussion above illustrated, there are serious flaws with all the theories of government authority and legitimacy; we seem to have excellent grounds for being skeptical that governments have authority at all. But even if one thinks that governments have some authority—e.g., that you have a duty to pay your fair share of taxes and obey the speed limit—that will not be enough to justify the Special Immunity Thesis. Defenders of this thesis must argue that governments specifically have the authority to commit severe injustices and evils, the very injustices and evils we would be permitted to resist (using deception, sabotage, or violence) if private civilians perpetrated them. It's one thing to argue that the government has a right to be obeyed when it creates and tries to enforce a socially beneficial rule that promotes justice. It's far from clear anyone has shown that. But it takes even more work to show that a government has a right to be obeyed when it creates and enforces bad rules that promote injustice, or when its agents act in horrible ways.

One might instead argue that government agents enjoy special immunity for these other reasons:

1 *The anti-vigilante principle*: We are not supposed to take justice into our own hands when a fair and reliable public system of justice is in place.
2 *The good-faith objection*: Government agents often act in good faith and are following orders, doing what they believe to be right.
3 *The fall-out objection*: If citizens resist government officials, other government officials might respond by ramping up their degree of injustice. For instance, if you were to shoot police officers who are in the process of killing a subdued, unarmed, prostrate man, a SWAT team would come and start shooting people.

But these other purported reasons to believe government officials enjoy special immunity are also problematic for two major sets of reasons.

First, these reasons do not really distinguish between government and civilian cases. We can illustrate that by employing the Huemer Test: imagine an analogous case involving civilians, and then see whether the case seems plausible or different there. For instance, if the anti-vigilante principle supposedly forbids us from acting in self-defense against government wrongdoing, why would it not also forbid us from acting in self-defense against civilian wrongdoing? The objection offers no principled difference. Similarly, suppose a civilian, through a bizarre set of circumstances, comes to rationally but mistakenly believe that I am a terrorist en route to destroy the new World Trade Center. He tries to apprehend me with deadly violence. Though he acts in good faith, I am still allowed to defend myself against him. So, we can ask the person who offers the good-faith objection, what makes government agents who act wrongly but in good faith any different? Finally, if I resist the Mafia or a local criminal gang's injustice, they might also retaliate. The fall-out objection, if successful, implies not only that government agents have special immunity, but also that criminals with the power to retaliate also enjoy special immunity. It offers us no principled account of why governments are different.

Of course, the believer in special immunity could bite the bullet and say that governments are not in principle different. He could say that, yes, in some cases, civilian wrongdoers also enjoy special immunity; the difference is that government agents are statistically more likely to enjoy special immunity than, say, Mafia hitmen or muggers. But this brings us to the second problem: none of these objections seems particularly plausible as a reason to refrain from self-defense or defense of others.

For instance, the anti-vigilante principle is usually invoked to argue that you should not unilaterally punish wrongdoers or police crime yourself, but instead allow impartial courts and professional police or well-trained private security forces to do so. It does not mean that, if a would-be rapist tries to assault you, you are not allowed to resist or defend yourself. Accordingly, since the plausible version of the principle allows self-defense against civilian wrongdoers, it is unclear why it would not also allow self-defense against governmental wrongdoers.

Similarly, the fall-out objection seems to hold that you lose your right to defend yourself or others provided the wrongdoer credibly threatens (implicitly or explicitly) to commit further wrongs in response to your otherwise justifiable self-defense. Suppose a would-be rapist tries to assault you, and you start to defend yourself. Suppose he responds, credibly threatening, "If you don't allow me to rape you, I hereby promise I will retreat and then rape *four* other women instead." It seems implausible, or at least very controversial, to hold that this would remove your right of self-defense. Why, then, would it be any different if the government issued a similar threat?

There are of course other arguments for special immunity, and I cannot review them all here. However, this section has illustrated the problem with the Special Immunity Thesis and summarized some of the major issues anarchists and others of a broadly liberal mindset might have with it. Many of the major arguments for the Special Immunity Thesis seem, on further consideration, implausible in their own right, and they further fail to give us a principled distinction between government and civilian actors.

V. The Question of Punishment

In day-to-day parlance, we say that private agents might "punish" one another for their transgressions. For example, perhaps your angry spouse "punishes" you for forgetting your anniversary by demanding you sleep on the couch. But states claim for themselves the right to inflict far more than social sanctions. The law forbids your spouse from punishing you by imprisoning you, forcibly taking away your money or property, inflicting physical pain upon you, or depriving you of life and liberty. In contrast, most states claim the legal power to punish you in these ways. What, if anything, explains the difference?

Contractarian philosopher John Locke famously argued that the state's right to punish ultimately is an extension of a private right to punish held by all civilians. He argues that, in the state of nature (i.e., anarchy), people are still bound by various moral laws and extra-legal conventions. Every individual has the right to punish any other person who violates others' rights or breaks certain moral rules. However, Locke claims, the problem with private punishment is that we individuals tend to be biased judges, too lenient on ourselves and too harsh on those who harm us. Private punishment thus creates various "inconveniences," and our disagreements over private punishment could lead to violent conflict. Locke argues we should resolve this problem by instituting (as best we can) an impartial, public system of justice, which will correct those inconveniences and overcome our biases. Once that system is established, we should defer to it. We alienate our private right to punish.[14]

On Locke's theory, the government possesses no special power or status which individual civilians necessarily lack; rather, it receives its power and status through (what Locke believes is) a voluntary transfer. On Locke's view, at least, government agents and civilians are on morally on par.

In contrast, statist philosopher Alon Harel claims that punishment is a kind of symbolic expression that, as a matter of metaphysical necessity, can only be performed by governmental agents.[15] He does not mean that it *should* only be done by the appropriate agent. Rather, he argues that it is literally impossible, as a metaphysical matter, for private prison wardens and guards to punish prisoners.

Harel rejects private prisons not because they are corrupt or overly violent or because they mistreat prisoners. Rather, he claims they are unjust because such prisons *fail to punish* prisoners.

While private prisons can lock up prisoners, beat them, execute them, feed them, make them perform manual labor, provide them with vocational training, give them moral and religious instruction, and do all of the various daily activities of public prisons, none of this counts as punishment, according to Harel. Only when state employees perform these activities do they qualify as aspects of punishment. Harel argues that imprisonment counts as punishment only when the prison guards and wardens are direct employees of a state. Since justly convicted criminals ought to be punished, he claims, then such criminals ought to be sent to public rather than private prisons.

Harel thus needs to identify some special feature (or set of special features) F that public prisons can have that private prisons necessarily lack, where F is some property one might plausibly believe is a necessary condition for being able to administer punishment. He needs to explain why getting a paycheck directly from the government is so crucial in determining whether a prison guard is *really* punishing a prisoner or just engaging in a sham imitation of punishment.

Harel says he needs to show that the only agent capable of realizing the important value of punishment is the state.[16] Through his book *Why Law Matters*, Harel offers a number of hypotheses about just what F could be, including:

1 To engage in punishment, the agents of punishment must defer to the sovereign and act in accordance with its will independently of what they happen to judge to be in the public interest.[17] They must execute the sovereign's official decisions; they "suppress" their own judgments and pursue the sovereign's judgment instead.
2 The punishing agents must be not inadvertently substitute their own judgment for that of the sovereign; they must engage in a deliberative practice by which they coordinate their understanding of the rules and laws, as well as how to punish others, with other agents engaging in the same practices.[18]
3 The punishing agents must engage in an "*integrative practice*."[19] That is, for agents to act in the name of the public (or of the state or the sovereign), rather than in their own name, the official activities of law-making politicians need to be *integrated* into the agents' processes of decision-making. There needs to be a special connection between the general interest as seen by politicians and the individual agents who execute the judgments.
4 Public prisons, but not private prisons, have a "Hohfeldian liability to the power of public officials to place them under a duty to act in certain ways."[20] The idea here is that public prison workers are duty-bound to accept the sovereign's orders, while private prison workers are not.

But Harel faces two sets of problems with each of these purported differences. First, it seems plausible both that (a) public prisons can and do fail to realize 1–4, while more importantly (b) private prisons can and do sometimes realize 1–4. For instance, a private warden and private prison guards can suppress their own judgments in favor of the sovereign's. They can and often do engage in deliberative practices by which they coordinate their understanding of the rules and laws, as well as how to punish others, with other agents engaging in the same practices. They can and do integrate their decision-making with that of the lawmakers. Further, if you believe that governments have authority, as Harel does, then you must hold by extension that private prison workers have a moral duty to obey the government's orders. Keep in mind Harel is not trying to make the empirical claim that public prisons are more likely to obey the sovereign than private prisons; he's claiming that private prisons as a matter of metaphysical necessity lack some essential property needed to perform genuine punishment. Yet he does not offer a plausible candidate for what that property could be, since every candidate property he identifies can and is sometimes realized by private prisons.

More fundamentally, though, from the anarchist's perspective, Harel's theory seems to beg the fundamental question. Harel presumes (without much argument) that, in order for imprisonment, deprivation of liberty, monetary fines, or the infliction of pain to count as punishment, such punishment must be ordered by a sovereign law-making and law-enforcing agency, which he presumes must be a state or government in the Kavkaian sense. For Harel, punishment is "an expressive or communicative act of condemnation" that must come from a public agent.[21] In his view, in the Lockean state of nature, it is simply *impossible* for anyone to punish anyone else, because there is no *sovereign*. But, an anarchist might wonder, why is it important that there be a sovereign so defined? Why not instead hold that the rules of social life can be suitably public provided that they (a) are widespread and widely recognized social conventions or (b) are widespread and widely recognized moral rules, rather than (c) *laws* in the strictly governmental sense?

In short, Harel presumes anarchism is false from the get-go and then tries to argue that we can't have private prisons. But he does not seem to have a neutral ground for this position that would actually mediate the dispute between statists and anarchists.

VI. Conclusion

Anarchists tend to presume that civilian and governmental actors are morally on par. Government agents do not, in virtue of being government agents, magically acquire special moral privileges, exemptions, or status. If governments tend to have various rights and powers that civilians normally lack, this must in some way be derived from rights and powers that civilians could in principle possess.

The idea of moral parity can be used as a kind of test of various theories of state legitimacy, authority, immunity, or power. The anarchist asks the statist to identify some special feature or set of features F which the state's agents purportedly possess and which explain why state agents enjoy a special moral status. The anarchist then constructs a parallel case in which the civilians also possess F, and then asks the statist if in that parallel case the civilians would possess the special powers the statist attributes to the state. If the statist answers no, this shows the statist's explanation fails—F is *not* why the state has whatever special status it has. If the statist answers yes, this shows that fundamentally civilians and the state are on par. At most, state actors are statistically more likely to possess F than civilians are.

Notes

1 Gregory Kavka, "Why Even Morally Perfect People Would Need Government," *Social Philosophy and Policy* 12 (1995): 2. I insert the qualification "more or less" because no government in history has literally stopped all private violence.
2 Michael Huemer, *The Problem of Political Authority* (New York: Palgrave 2013).
3 You might think you have an independent moral duty not to smoke pot, but you would not think that *my ordering you not to* matters morally speaking.
4 H. L. A. Hart, "Are There Any Natural Rights?" *Philosophical Review* 64 (1995): 185.
5 Huemer 84.
6 Huemer 84–5.
7 Huemer 87.
8 Wayne LaFave, *Criminal Law,* 4th ed. (Washington, DC: Thomson-West 2003) 570.
9 This summarizes and paraphrases LaFave 569–574.
10 David Ferguson, "New Mexico Cop Fired for Shooting at Minivan Full of Kids," *Raw Story* (Raw Story Media, Dec. 7, 2013), www.rawstory.com/rs/2013/12/07/new-mexico-cop-fired-for-shooting-at-minivan-full-of-kids/ (last visited Jan. 13, 2019).
11 Jason Brennan, "Marijuana," *Social Issues in America*, ed. James Ciment (Armonk: Sharpe 2006) 1044–54.
12 See, for example, Eric Beerbohm, *In Our Name* (Princeton: Princeton UP 2012).

13 See Jason Brennan, "When May We Kill Government Agents? In Defense of Moral Parity," *Social Philosophy and Policy* 32 (2016): 40–61; Jason Brennan, *When All Else Fails: The Ethics of Resistance to State Injustice* (Princeton: Princeton UP 2018).
14 John Locke, *Second Treatise of Government,* ed. C. B. MacPherson (Indianapolis: Hackett 1980) 11–4.
15 Alon Harel, *Why Law Matters*. (New York: OUP 2014).
16 Harel 81.
17 Harel 82.
18 Harel 89.
19 Harel 91 (my italics).
20 Harel 93.
21 Harel 96–7.

17
ECONOMIC PATHOLOGIES OF THE STATE

Christopher Coyne and Nathan P. Goodman

I. Introduction

What is the appropriate role of the state? The list of desired activities that many people want the state to perform is potentially endless and includes national defense, policing, dispute resolution, healthcare, humanitarian aid, welfare, environmental regulation, the funding of scientific research, immigration control, financial regulation, monetary policy, park maintenance, health and safety regulation, and drug prohibition, among many others. Proponents of these and other roles for the state tend to assume that the state's taking on a task guarantees that it will achieve the desired end. From this perspective, if the right people are in charge and they have the appropriate resources and "political will" to accomplish a task, they can succeed. Where markets and voluntary association may fail, the state can fill the gap, provided its leaders are good, resolute people with the right ideas and resources to implement their plans.

This *deus ex machina* view of the state, however, ignores crucial insights from economics. It is our contention that, before deciding what the state *should* do, it is imperative to consider what the state *can* do. Determining the limits of what state machinery can and cannot accomplish is crucial if we want to avoid encouraging the wasting of scarce resources and the imposition of harm on the very people the state purports to assist. To understand what tasks states can and cannot accomplish, we seek to answer two general and interrelated questions. First, do political leaders have the relevant knowledge to accomplish the desired task? Second, do they have the right incentives to do so? It is our contention that economics is central to answering these questions and thus to understanding the limits on what state action can achieve.

Economics is the science of human action. Economists study how individuals make decisions about alternative uses of scarce resources. These decisions are shaped by the knowledge individuals can access regarding the alternative uses of resources and by relevant incentives and constraints. Knowledge and incentives, in turn, are shaped by the institutions—the formal and informal rules governing human life—within which individuals operate. Individuals face different institutional constraints when they are competing in the market than when they are competing in the political arena. Different institutional arrangements lead to variations in the knowledge individuals can access and the incentives they face as they act on that knowledge.

Within markets shaped by the institutions of property, contract, and consent, individuals receive feedback in the form of prices, profits, and losses that tells them whether the goods and services they produce are valued more than the inputs they use. This prompts a tendency to use scarce resources in a manner that improves the welfare of other members of society and offers people incentives to produce goods and services that others desire. In the political arena, feedback and incentives capable of playing similar roles are either weak, distorted, or altogether absent. The state is therefore plagued with two persistent and systemic pathologies: (1) political actors often lack the relevant knowledge to accomplish desired goals, and (2) public policy goals are often not compatible with the incentives of those in political power. These problems are systemic features of state institutions and are not dependent on the characteristics of the people wielding power.

In subsequent sections we will discuss these two economic pathologies of the state.[1] The first, the knowledge problem, discussed in the next section, arises from the fact that non-market actors cannot access the economic knowledge that arises from the market process. Attempts by state actors to engage in planning will, therefore, tend to waste resources because planners lack the knowledge and feedback necessary to ensure that scarce resources are used in a manner that maximizes their value. Moreover, economies, and the societies within which they are embedded, are complex systems that political actors lack the knowledge to control. Therefore, state interventions are likely to produce an array of unintended consequences that may harm both the intended beneficiaries of policies and those that fall outside of this target group.

After exploring the knowledge problem, we will discuss the power problem. This problem arises because those with political power often have incentives to act against goals deemed socially desirable. Rather than improving outcomes, the state can instead give powerful people incentives to act in predatory and exploitative ways. Finally, after discussing the power problem and the knowledge problem, we conclude, in Section IV, with a discussion of the significance of these two pathologies of the state for political theory and policy analysis.

II. The Knowledge Problem

Resources are scarce. While humans have potentially unlimited desires, we have only limited resources with which to pursue them. This means that people need to make choices, and that these choices will involve trade-offs, because one use of scarce resources precludes another. Economic actors must decide: should a good or service be produced at all? If the answer is yes, how much of the good or service should be produced? And what is the least costly means of producing that good or service? The answers to these questions are not given. Instead, they must be discovered.

Market prices provide guides that help individuals navigate the dizzying array of choices available. Should you build train tracks with steel or platinum? The use of either material may be technically feasible, but in a society with market prices you know not to use platinum because doing so will be prohibitively expensive. Consider another example: what would happen if a tin mine collapsed?[2] The *supply* of tin would fall, and the *price* of tin would therefore rise. In turn, this would raise the price of goods that involve tin, encouraging consumers to use less of it. Meanwhile, the high price would encourage new producers of tin, and substitutes for tin, to enter the market. The consumers who buy less tin and the producers who enter to provide substitutes might know nothing about the mine collapse. The price change would nonetheless provide them with the economic knowledge needed for them to make decisions about how to allocate scarce resources. The knowledge needed to solve economic problems is context-specific and dispersed across many minds. Prices allow for the communication of this knowledge even though it is not accessible to any single mind.[3]

An entrepreneur purchases, at market prices, the inputs needed to make a given product on the view that the final product will sell for a profit. This is a forecast, however, and not a given. The entrepreneur's conjecture must be subjected to the market test of profit and loss. If the goods a firm produces are valued more highly than the inputs that went into producing them, the revenue generated by the sale of the outputs will exceed the price of the inputs. In other words, a firm that creates value will make a profit. This profit signals to entrepreneurs that consumers value what they are producing relative to alternative uses of the scarce resources used to produce the relevant goods. On the other hand, if consumers value a final good less than the inputs that went into producing the good are valued, the revenue from the outputs will be lower than the price of the inputs. In other words, a firm that destroys value by turning valuable inputs into a less valued output will experience losses. Entrepreneurs will reduce, or altogether cease, the production of the good based on the loss signals they receive. Firms that ignore these signals will ultimately fail. Profit and loss therefore not only provide incentives to produce goods and services that people value, they also provide feedback that indicates whether a business is creating or destroying value.

This communicative role of prices and profit and loss makes them essential for economic calculation—"the decision-making ability to allocate scarce capital resources among competing uses."[4] Many of these insights about the vital role of prices in economic calculation were developed by Ludwig von Mises and F.A. Hayek,[5] who argued that economic calculation was impossible under a system of central planning. Socialists advocated abolishing private property in the means of production in order to rationalize economic activity to overcome the ills of capitalism. Mises and Hayek pointed out that, without private property rights in the means of production, there would be no market in the means of production. Without market exchange, no prices for the means of production would emerge. Without prices as guides, planners would lack the knowledge needed to compare alternative uses of the means of production. In other words, they would be unable to engage in economic calculation and determine the best use of scarce resources. This is the essence of the knowledge problem.

Why does the knowledge problem matter? The main reason is that state planners cannot allocate scarce resources in a manner that maximizes their value from the standpoint of members of society. This raises two key issues associated with the opportunity cost of scarce resources.

The first issue arises in relation to particular goods and services delivered or funded by the government. If the political process determines that a trillion dollars are to be spent on medical care, decisions still need to be made about how the money should be allocated among an array of possible medical care alternatives. Decisions need to be made about who should be eligible for care and for what procedures and other activities payment should be available. Further, in determining for what procedures and other activities payment should be available, planners must determine appropriate quantities and qualities. The goods and services delivered or funded by the government are not homogeneous, and marginal decisions need to be made about the quantities and qualities of these goods and services.

The second issue arises in connection with choices among different categories of goods and services. How do state planners know that a trillion dollars spent on medical care is better, from the perspective of the welfare of private actors, than splitting that money across some mix of medical care, education, roads, environmental protection, or other services? The knowledge problem is multifaceted when it comes to government activities. Absent economic calculation, there is no way for state planners to make such decisions in a manner that takes into account the values of scarce resources to putative beneficiaries.

In the absence of rational economic calculation, planners often rely on output measures to gauge success. For many years, economists widely believed that the economy of the Soviet Union had surpassed the economies of Western capitalist countries in significant ways.[6] But this view was wrong because output statistics can be misleading. There had indeed been increases in output, but these mostly reflected spending on large-scale government projects such as hydroelectric dams, the space program, and military buildups. These large projects exerted impressive impacts on statistics measuring total output in terms of gross domestic product (GDP). But they concealed the reality that people's standards of living were languishing.[7] Aggregate measures, such as GDP, do not differentiate between increased output that is wasteful and increased output that is value-added from consumers' perspectives.

Economists and historians made similar errors in evaluating the effect of World War II on the American economy, widely believing that World War II ended the Great Depression.[8] While unemployment fell substantially, this was mostly a result of military conscription, which forced young men to take on "substantial risks of death, dismemberment, and other physical and psychological injuries."[9] Similarly, GDP rose, but this was a result of producing weapons, not goods or services that consumers valued. In stark contrast, people's consumption of most goods was regulated through state control and rationing. While large-scale government projects increase output, they do not necessarily increase the output of goods and services that people value. Relying on output data alone can tell one what products are being produced. But determining whether increased output creates goods and services consumers value requires rational economic calculation.

The knowledge problem is starkest in socialist economies that attempt to comprehensively, centrally plan their entire economies. However, it is present in all endeavors administered by the state rather than the market. The difference between the comprehensive planning advocated by state socialists and the non-comprehensive planning associated with other state activities is one of degree, not of kind. Genuine socialist states attempt comprehensive central planning, trying to plan almost all economic activity. Most states, on the other hand, attempt to plan particular projects while leaving markets at least relatively free to plan others. This non-comprehensive planning still faces the knowledge problem, because political actors are operating in a non-market context and therefore cannot rely on property, prices, and profits and losses to render their plans rational. "[E]ven the more modest and popular attempts to steer the Market toward particular outcomes are really blind and dangerous obstructions of the very source of that knowledge which is essential to rational economic decision-making."[10]

This applies even to government programs supported by some avowed anti-socialists. State-provided military goods and services, for example, suffer from the knowledge problem because the government selects and delivers goods and services outside of the market context.[11] Absent the ability to rely on economic calculation, there is no rational way for state planners to determine the highest-valued use of scarce resources allocated toward the provision of security, or what resources should be allocated toward the provision of security in the first place.

Even relatively market-oriented economists, who are extremely critical of state planning in other areas of life, typically favor the state provision of military goods and services. This is partially because they see the provision of these goods and services as a public good.[12] A putative good qualifies as a public good when (1) it is hard to exclude people from using the good, and (2) one person's consumption of the good does not reduce the ability of others to consume the good. Because of these characteristics, economists predict that, because of free-riding, public goods will be severely underprovided on the private market relative to the optimal amount that would maximize social welfare. The solution proposed by most economists is for the state to either subsidize the production of public goods or to provide public goods through coercive taxation in order to make up for the underprovision that would otherwise occur.

At first blush, the provision of military goods and services appears to fit the requirements of a traditional public good quite nicely. It is hard to protect my neighbor from a foreign military invasion or a missile strike without also protecting me. Meanwhile, protecting me from foreign aggressors does not make my neighbor any less secure. Because the good has these properties, there is an incentive to free-ride off defensive services paid for by others. Therefore, most economists argue for state coercion to make people pay for military goods and services.[13] It is true that this method can provide more military goods and services than would be provided without the state. However, the free-rider argument for the state provision of these goods and services is that less-than-socially-optimal quantities of these goods and services would be produced if their production were left to the market. The central question is: how can state planners *know* the optimal quantities of military goods and services to produce outside of the market? The answer is that they cannot, for the reasons discussed above.

Planners need to decide both whether to spend money on military goods and services and whether to provide additional units of military-related production. They also need to make choices between different types of military goods and services. For each dollar of military spending, someone must choose whether it should be used to fund a missile defense system, a drone, a tank, body armor, the employment of an additional soldier, or something else entirely. Without market prices as guides, state planners are groping in the dark. They do not know what type of military spending will best use scarce resources to maximize the welfare of private people. For some people, such as pacifists, certain types of military spending may entirely lack value. Yet they too are forced to pay for spending on wars and weapons that they don't value at all and which they would, in fact, strongly prefer were entirely absent.

The economy is a complex system that incorporates dispersed knowledge inaccessible to any single planner or political body. This not only precludes the formulation of rational plans to maximize social welfare; it also means that coercive interventions to achieve the goals of planners are likely to generate an array of undesirable and unforeseen consequences. To understand these "dynamics of intervention," consider the example of state-imposed price controls.[14]

Suppose planners place a price ceiling on milk to make it more affordable for poor consumers.[15] At the artificially lower price, more consumers will want to purchase milk, but fewer producers will want to bring milk to market. This will create a milk shortage, the opposite of what the state planners intended. Not realizing the cause of the shortage, political leaders may respond by subsidizing milk production. Yet these subsidies will divert resources from elsewhere in the economy, creating new unintended hardships. Additional interventions may be introduced to address these hardships. If policies that distort prices are to remain in place, they require ever more regulations and policies to achieve desired outcomes. Each of these subsequent interventions distorts the ability of people to engage in rational economic calculation.

Beyond price distortions, government interventions can also destroy local norms, customs, and patterns of trust that are central to facilitating social harmony.[16] For example, if government welfare programs crowd out mutual aid or alter social norms in poor communities, they may exacerbate poverty rather than alleviating it.[17] The unintended consequences that result as social norms change in communities may then be used as justifications for additional government programs. Further, by changing, and potentially destroying, local norms and customs, government intervention may undermine the ability of private, local actors to engage in self-governance, including experimentation with local solutions to social problems.[18]

In general, state interference in a complex system, whether in the price system or in a broader social system, will yield unintended and unforeseen consequences.[19] These unintended consequences will create rationales for additional interventions, and each intervention will increase the scope of decisions made by political actors who are unable to engage in rational economic calculation or to fully understand the nuances of complex orders in which they intervene.

The nuances of the knowledge problem exist even when well-intentioned, other-regarding state actors are in power. But what happens when we weaken the assumption of benevolence and consider the incentives that political actors face? The next section explores the answer to this question.

III. The Power Problem

Even *if* we assume that political actors have the knowledge they need to improve the welfare of private persons, there is another important question to ask: are the incentives of state actors aligned with those of the people they purportedly intend to benefit? The stated goals of public policies, goals almost always framed in terms of improving the welfare of private people, are often incompatible with the incentives of the politically powerful. If politicians are not benevolent despots, but rather human beings who pursue their own interests, then incentives matter in politics. This basic insight regarding the "symmetry of assumptions" is the core of public choice theory, a subfield of economics that analyzes how incentives operate in non-market settings.[20]

Politicians, like all people, seek to pursue their own goals and interests. Of course people's interests, both in the private and public sectors, are diverse and can be narrowly inward focused, outwardly focused on assisting others, or some mix of both. But the same people inhabit both private spheres of action and public spheres of action. While the people are the same, the institutional environments, and the incentives created by those institutions, vary and therefore produce different outcomes.[21]

One particularly important incentive in democratic politics that shapes political behavior is the desire to be reelected. In order to be reelected, politicians must appeal to voters. Unfortunately, voters have very weak incentives to learn about the details and nuances of political activities. To understand this dynamic, consider the contrast between decision making in democratic politics with decision making in private markets.[22]

In a market, there is a tight link between a consumer's decision about which car to purchase and the outcome. Consumers can customize the cars they choose and internalize the benefits and costs of their choices. Because benefits and costs are internalized, consumers face strong incentives to research and compare cars prior to purchasing them. Incentives in democratic politics are very different. It is very rare that an election is decided by a single vote.[23] Therefore in most elections the outcome will be the same regardless of how an individual votes. So, while it is beneficial to research cars before purchasing, there is practically no benefit to researching politicians before voting.

The problem of political ignorance is made even worse by the fact that voters can never directly compare politicians. It is fairly straightforward to compare cars under similar circumstances, through direct pre-purchase testing or relying on the experiences and evaluations of other experts or consumers who have purchased the vehicle. No such option exists in politics. We will never know what would have happened had a given election turned out differently. Different instances of ignorance might cancel each other out if voters chose their beliefs randomly. But they don't: they are biased, and they are biased toward mistaken beliefs about economics. Voters tend to overstate the harm and understate the benefits of trade, immigration, labor-saving innovations, and markets.[24] Politicians therefore have incentives to pander to rationally ignorant voters with strong prejudices against activities and institutions that drive economic progress. Their willingness to do so sows the seeds of wealth-destroying policies. The ignorance of voters also makes it all too easy for politicians to act opportunistically, using their power to benefit themselves and their friends. After all, what incentives do voters have to carefully research and resist such opportunism?

There are two other issues that weaken the effectiveness of democratic elections as a check on political opportunism. One is the time between elections. The fact that elections are periodic means that voter influence is limited. Consider that each US voter, over each six-year period, casts a maximum of nine votes over four national-level general elections.[25] The minimal feedback provided by each voter leaves significant space for factors unrelated to voters' expressed preferences to influence politics and for political participants to engage in opportunism. This poses a problem because, by the time regularly-timed elections do occur, it may be difficult, if not impossible, to undo the undesirable outcomes brought about by opportunists in the interim.[26]

A second factor which reduces the effectiveness of voting is bundling: each voter casts a single vote for an official who will represent the voter across numerous, complex issues. For example, if a voter agrees with a candidate's position on abortion, but strongly disagrees with the candidate about foreign policy, the voter cannot make choices to separate these two policies from the overall bundle of policies that the candidate represents. These factors further incentivize rational ignorance and limit the ability of voters to provide feedback to political actors regarding specific policies.

The prospects for beneficial state intervention become even more dismal when we look at the incentives faced by bureaucrats. In the private sector, competition selects for firms that maximize profits.[27] Profits, as discussed earlier, reflect whether the goods and services produced are valued more than the resources employed. However, in a state bureaucracy there is no analogous process. So what do bureaucrats maximize?

Public choice economist William Niskanen argued that bureaucrats seek to maximize their discretionary budgets.[28] If an agency's budget is cut, that means fewer resources are available for the bureaucrats and their colleagues to use to accomplish their goals. It also means that the employees are more likely to be fired. This all creates incentives for bureaucrats to spend more. In a private firm, saving money and resources means that profits increase. In a government bureaucracy, a residual budget at the end of a fiscal year sends a signal that the budget is too large and can be cut. Bureaucrats want to be able to credibly tell legislators that they need larger budgets to accomplish policy goals. Budget-maximizing bureaucrats therefore, have an incentive to spend resources even if their spending is wasteful. Even if some amount of government spending is known to optimize social welfare, political incentives will tend to result in spending that exceeds that amount.

In addition, there are significant problems with information transmission in any government bureaucracy. Gordon Tullock illustrates this problem using the "whispering down the lane" game.[29] In this game, information is passed between individuals within a bureaucratic hierarchy, with the message becoming more distorted at every step along the way. The longer the transmission chain becomes, the more noise and errors are introduced. This differs from the knowledge problem, because whispering down the lane involves transmitting known information, while the knowledge problem is about discovering as-yet-unknown knowledge.[30] As bureaucracies become larger—e.g., national rather than local—we should expect issues of communication within bureaus to become increasingly plagued by noise. This noise creates problems for producing goods and services which comport with the desires of the people whose interests bureaucrats are supposed to serve.[31]

State power also generates perverse incentives for private businesses, not just for state actors. Sociologist Franz Oppenheimer identified two means of acquiring wealth: the political means and the economic means.[32] Someone gains wealth using the economic means when she acquires resources through voluntary exchange. Someone gains wealth using the political means, in contrast, when she acquires resources by coercing others. While the economic means are productive or positive-sum, the political means are zero- or negative-sum.

When state power is present, there are incentives for business interests to seek to use it for their own narrow gain. This can take the form of seeking transfers such as subsidies and bailouts, or of lobbying for regulations that suppress competition. Attempting to gain these types of state privileges means expending resources on seeking political favors rather than on developing better products for consumers. Economists refer to this striving for privileges as "rent seeking."[33]

Rent seeking, in turn, breeds cronyism, which involves institutionalized relationships between favored business interests and political elites.[34] This undermines the dynamism of markets by enabling entrenched interests to preserve their established positions and keep out new innovators.[35] It also shifts resources to those with political power at the expense of ordinary people. In a free-market system, positions of economic power are contestable. The dominant firm of one year can find itself displaced by a new competitor the next. Historically, innovations may displace entire industries through "creative destruction."[36] Entrenched firms, when allied with the political elite, can suppress this process by preventing entrepreneurs from entering the market and eroding their market shares. The resulting political capitalism is the product of a proactive, interventionist state which allows businesses to manipulate and distort the unhampered market process.[37]

Can democracy solve the problem of special interests' engagement in rent seeking? At best, the democratic process provides only very weak protection from exploitation by special interests. Rational ignorance is especially relevant here. The harm caused by a regulation or subsidy is typically dispersed across a large population, with the result that each person incurs only a small cost. For example, sugar tariffs increase food prices for American consumers, but only by a few cents per purchase. The time it would take a voter to study sugar tariffs, much less speak with a politician about them, is more valuable to the voter than the cost imposed on the voter by the tariff. Meanwhile, the benefits conferred by the tariff on a domestic sugar farmer are big, which means that the farmer has a strong incentive to pay attention to sugar tariffs, organize an interest group with other farmers, and lobby politicians. Because benefits are concentrated and costs dispersed, organized interest groups use government force at the expense of the public.

Yet another issue is that elections are focused on choosing legislatures while many regulations are designed and implemented by bureaucrats who are not subject to direct elections. In the ideal model of democracy, legislators, who represent voter interests, would select and monitor bureaucrats to ensure that they produced goods and services that improved social welfare. This ideal model does not hold in practice, however, and democratic politics is plagued by principal-agent problems in virtue of which the putative principals (private actors) are unable to effectively monitor and punish their agents (legislators and bureaucrats), who are thus free to engage in relatively unchecked opportunism.[38]

Even if public-spirited voters are paying attention to an issue, they may actively support an intervention that enhances the privileges of private interest groups. To understand this dynamic consider the "Bootleggers and Baptists" model of state regulation.[39] State laws that banned alcohol sales on Sundays were supported by Baptists for moralistic reasons. But bootleggers supported these laws as well, because the laws suppressed their competitors one day each week. Similar coalitions between public-spirited reformers and private interests seeking to profit from state intervention are pervasive.

For example, many people support medical licensing laws to protect patient safety by barring incompetent doctors from the market. But, by restricting the supply of medical providers, licensing laws raise prices. The fact that they do so provides a strong incentive for doctors to support tighter restrictions. Doctors organize through groups like the American Medical Association to secure strict licensing requirements. This raises their wages and increases healthcare costs for everyone else. Similarly, to practice medicine in America, doctors are legally required to complete residencies within the United States. The number of residencies is set by the Accreditation Council for Graduate Medical Education, which is largely run by doctors, who can thus reduce competition by controlling the number of available residency slots.[40]

To economists, an arrangement for producers to control supply is a textbook case of a cartel. Similar licensing cartels are operated by professionals who have even weaker consumer safety rationales for licensing restrictions, including florists and interior designers.[41] As Adam Smith noted long ago, "People of the same trade seldom meet together, even for merriment and diversion, but the conversation ends in a conspiracy against the public, or in some contrivance to raise prices."[42] However, without an enforcement mechanism, a contrivance to raise prices will be unstable because cartel members will have incentives to lower their prices and thereby attract customers away from their higher-priced competitors. Moreover, the high prices the enforcement-free cartel seeks to maintain will provide an incentive for new competitors to enter the market.

The state provides a convenient mechanism for the enforcement of cartel agreements because it can use its coercive powers to exclude competitors and punish existing businesses that deviate from the dictates of the agreements. Business cartels thus support state intervention for self-interested reasons, just like the bootleggers supported Sunday closing laws. They are often joined by public-spirited voters and reformers, akin to the Baptists, who think that regulations that suppress competition will also protect the public interest. The result is often the adoption of regulations that reduce the welfare of private persons.

At the core of public choice theory is the assumption of behavioral symmetry—the same types of actors but operating in different institutions. The problems discussed so far do not depend on agent type and do not assume that politicians, bureaucrats, or politically connected business owners are necessarily any worse than other people in society. Instead, public choice assumes that people have the same motivations in politics as they have in private settings. From this starting point, the focus is on the incentives facing actors in the political arena with an appreciation for how these incentives differ from those within the marketplace. However, it is important to note that political institutions also include selection mechanisms that impact who tends to secure positions wielding political power. The assumption of behavioral symmetry, while a useful analytical tool, may therefore understate the likelihood of bad outcomes in "real world" politics. In practice, who will tend to rise to positions of political power? Economists Frank Knight and F.A. Hayek offered some insight into the answer to this question.

Knight noted that, to centrally plan an economy, authorities would have to "exercise their power ruthlessly to keep the machinery of organized production and distribution running" and that "[t]hey would have to enforce orders ruthlessly and suppress all disputation and argument against policies."[43] He further argued that "the probability of the people in power being individuals who would dislike the possession and exercise of power is on a level with the probability that an extremely tender-hearted person would get the job of whipping-master on a slave plantation."[44] In *The Road to Serfdom*, Hayek made a similar argument, contending that within a regime of central planning the worst people will tend to rise to the top.[45] The reason why is that central planners must be given significant discretionary power to implement plans and deal with unforeseen circumstances. Who will tend to be most attracted to such power and discretion over other human beings? Hayek argued that "the unscrupulous and uninhibited are likely to be more successful" in this system.[46] A system that gives leaders unconstrained discretionary power is likely to attract people who feel comfortable exercising power over others.

While Knight and Hayek were discussing attempts to implement comprehensive planning, their insights are applicable to politics in general.[47] As Robert Higgs notes, "the observation applies to the functionaries of less egregious governments," because "nearly all governments, even those of countries such as the United States, France, or Germany, jokingly described as 'free,' provide numerous opportunities for ruthless and unscrupulous people."[48] As F.G. Bailey argues, political

> [l]eaders are not the virtuous people they claim to be; they put politics before statesmanship; they distort facts and oversimplify issues; they promise what no one could deliver; and they are liars. … [L]eaders, if they are to be effective, have no choice in the matter. They could not be virtuous (in the sense of morally excellent) and be leaders at the same time.[49]

These arguments are grounded in an appreciation of the incentives and selection mechanisms inherent in political institutions. Given the immense power concentrated in such institutions, who is likely to rise to the top? Those who feel comfortable wielding power over others and those with the skill to capture and maintain such power are unlikely to be the most noble and other-regarding people in a society. If virtuous people enter positions of power, they will face numerous perverse pressures.

First, they will face the incentive to bend their principles to maintain their positions of power. If they are unwilling to bend their principles, this will likely lead less squeamish leaders to rise through the ranks and replace them. In a democratic society, for instance, liars and demagogues outperform their principled opponents in elections.[50] Second, once someone is in office, those who desire special privileges will actively seek to suborn her. She will be subject to multiple blandishments; and even if she's relatively principled this may prompt her to favor special interests. Finally, very virtuous, principled office-holders may be tempted, not so much to hand out favors to special interests, but simply to use power in authoritarian fashion to do what they take to be good.

The combination of selection mechanisms and incentives makes centralized political power very dangerous indeed. The relevant dangers reflect not only the potential for waste and dysfunction in politics, but also the risks that follow when a significant amount of power, backed by coercion, is concentrated in the hands of a small number of people. This kind of power can be used to impose significant harm on the very people the state purports to serve. The costs of centralized power are likely to fall on the most marginalized members of society precisely because they lack the voice and ability to avoid abuses of state power.[51]

IV. Conclusion

The state is plagued by two pathologies: the knowledge problem and the power problem. Political leaders persistently and clumsily intervene in the complex system that is the economy. Because they cannot access the knowledge provided by prices, they are blind to the opportunity costs of their actions. Their blindness limits their ability to allocate, and reallocate, resources to their highest-valued uses to ensure that people's preferences are optimally satisfied. Political power also comes with perverse incentives, encouraging a variety of wasteful, destructive, and exploitative behavior. In virtue of these pathologies, states will tend to act in ways that are costly and counterproductive.

If centralized state power is so dangerous, what is the alternative? How can people provide rules, public goods, and other things that people generally want the state to provide? Nobel Laureate economist James Buchanan proposed constraining states using *constitutions*. By establishing rules that bind political leaders and limit their power, Buchanan hoped to empower the "protective state" and "productive state" while limiting the "predatory state."[52] Yet Buchanan's proposal suffers from an obvious difficulty: it's unclear how to enforce the constitution.[53] If political leaders can benefit by violating the constitution, it seems likely that they will do so.[54] How can we deter this type of exploitation?

One solution is polycentricism.[55] According to Vincent Ostrom, Charles Tiebout, and Robert Warren, a system is polycentric if it features "many centers of decision-making that are formally independent of each other."[56] When a system is polycentric, this enables some amount of competition that can check political power.

One key advantage of polycentricity is that it enables exit, which is crucial to a competitive market. A restaurant has an incentive to serve a satisfying meal, because an unsatisfied customer is likely to take her business elsewhere.

Some political scientists suggest that some of the benefits of polycentricity become available when jurisdictions are smaller, even if they continue to control particular geographic territories.

After all, smaller jurisdictions make exit easier. It might be difficult for someone to move away from the United States, but comparatively easy for them to move from one town in Northern Virginia to another. In principle, this means smaller jurisdictions should have stronger incentives to satisfy their customers than larger jurisdictions. Competition among jurisdictions is a mechanism that economists often support as a means of constraining government. James Buchanan favorably terms this "competitive federalism,"[57] while Barry Weingast similarly praises what he calls "market preserving federalism."[58]

The benefits of federalism arise in large part from the ways choices among jurisdictions in a federal state resemble choices in markets, but it is important to remember that federal states are not markets. They are merely *quasimarkets*. Political quasimarkets are highly imperfect, and they are often significantly less competitive than public choice models of federal and similar structures often assume. Quasimarkets suffer from three types of failure which weaken, if not altogether undermine, their theoretically desirable properties: (1) government monopoly failure, (2) political information failure, and (3) unintended consequence failure.[59]

Government monopoly failure occurs when there are barriers to competition among jurisdictions. For example, land-use regulations increase housing prices in some jurisdictions, which increases the cost of moving between jurisdictions. Another example is the fact that quasimarkets for governance are not contestable. It is unlawful for regions to secede, and there is often no easy path for people to establish a startup jurisdiction. The number of firms in a market does not determine whether the market is competitive; contestability does. The fact that political quasimarkets are not contestable implies that they are not competitive.

One alleged benefit of jurisdictional competition, even when jurisdictions are territorial, is that people can compare the service packages offered by different jurisdictions and engage in "yardstick competition."[60] Yet this assumes people know what packages are offered. In practice, they often do not, which creates political information failure. This ignorance should not be surprising to public choice theorists, who emphasize the rational ignorance of voters. This rational ignorance exists at all levels of state operation.

Unintended consequence failures occur when the sorting allowed by polycentricity enables results that policymakers or analysts find undesirable. For example, people who value racial segregation may take advantage of the choice polycentric systems offer in order to sort into racially segregated services. This criticism is often used as an objection to school choice, for example, because one concern is that it will result in racial segregation. "[W]hen the dimensions citizens value most clash with the ones that quasimarket creators—public policy creators—intend citizens to sort along, an important problem from a public policy perspective results."[61]

While many who note these failures encourage state consolidation as a solution, there is another solution: take the "quasi" out of quasimarkets by opting for genuine, nonterritorial polycentricity. In other words, move from a system in which the state provides such services as law and policing to a situation in which these services are provided by private individuals and voluntary associations. This reduces the perverse political incentives that cause quasimarket failures.

Removing governance from state control means that people bear the market costs of their decisions, and therefore have incentives to learn. Rational ignorance, which drives political information failure, is driven by political incentives. Moving toward private governance also makes exit and competition with respect to law and related services genuinely possible. It would therefore eliminate government monopoly failure by ending government monopoly. Governance would become contestable. People could form new voluntary associations to provide governance. They would have the right to secede, all the way down to the individual level. There would also be no state to, for instance, implement zoning laws that raise the cost of moving.

Governance without the state could be provided through a system of clubs, voluntary associations that privately produce goods that have significant public good characteristics.[62] Clubs have stronger incentives to effectively enforce their constitutions than governments do.[63] Clubs are privately owned, and if patrons choose to exit a club, then the club's owners lose revenue. Moreover, the market for clubs is contestable. Because individuals can start new clubs if they wish to do so, "[t]here are [roughly] as many governance organs as individuals demand."[64] Moreover, in a system of clubs, people will tend to join clubs that suit their preferences. This leads to clubs that consist of many like-minded members. Enforcing the constitutions of such clubs is much easier than enforcing the constitutions of monopolistic states, because like-minded members can more easily coordinate threats to leave if constitutions are violated.

Edward Stringham has documented many instances of private governance provided by clubs.[65] Many of these examples relate to contract enforcement and fraud prevention, such as the private governance arrangements used in early stock exchanges and in online payment systems like PayPal. However, he also explains how private police departments operated in San Francisco. Such departments flourished before a governmental police department was established, and even afterward because of the persistent corruption of the governmental police force.[66]

If it is hard to exclude non-payers from receiving a particular good, this creates a free-rider problem. But this problem can be mitigated by tying the good with another good that it is easier to exclude non-payers from.[67] Many people think of policing as necessarily delivered in a way that would ensure that a private police force would be impossible to maintain, because many people would free-ride on police services paid for by others. However, Stringham shows how San Francisco's private police force was able to avoid this problem through bundling.[68] By bundling police services with other products such as real estate, they were able to overcome free-riding.[69] Similar tying and bundling arrangements enable the private production of public goods in a variety of cases.[70]

A system of private governance provides a viable solution to both the knowledge problem and the power problem. When governance is provided by voluntary associations grounded in private property rights, it is embedded within a market. In a market, decision makers can access the knowledge provided by prices. Like other private firms, private providers of governance receive the feedback and discipline associated with profit and loss. Unlike political leaders, they can engage in economic calculation.

Similarly, private governance tames the power problem. It provides private persons with effective exit options to respond to abuse and exploitation by their rulers. By allowing *individuals* to choose which specific governance arrangement they prefer to live under, it weakens their incentives to be ignorant and biased. And by limiting the discretion of rulers, private governance mitigates the tendency for the worst to get on top.

Understanding the economic pathologies of the state may at first seem like a depressing exercise. However, it is crucial for placing constraints on our utopias by delineating what can and cannot be accomplished in the realm of politics. State actors cannot access the knowledge required to maximize social welfare. They also often face perverse incentives, which drive a wedge between their interests and those of private persons. Perhaps most importantly, the awesome powers centralized in the hands of state actors have historically been used to impose significant costs and damage on innocent people.[71]

However, studying these pathologies also helps us understand the possibilities of governance and institutions that do not face such problems. In order to avoid these problems, we should consider governance provided by voluntary associations. That is, we should consider anarchy.

Notes

1 The concepts of the "knowledge problem" and the "power problem" in the context of both comprehensive *and* non-comprehensive state planning were identified by Don Lavoie, *National Economic Planning: What Is Left?* (Arlington, VA: Mercatus 2016).

2 F.A. Hayek, "The Use of Knowledge in Society," *American Economic Review* 35.4 (1945): 519–30.

3 Hayek, "Use"; Esteban F. Thompson, *Prices and Knowledge: A Market-Process Perspective* (London: Routledge 1992).
4 Peter Boettke, "Economic Calculation: The Austrian Contribution to Political Economy," *Advances in Austrian Economics* 5 (1998): 131–58.
5 Ludwig von Mises, *Economic Calculation in the Socialist Commonwealth* (Auburn, AL: Mises 1990 [1920]); Hayek, "Use"; Thompson; Peter J. Boettke, *Calculation and Coordination: Essays on Socialism and Transitional Political Economy* (London: Routledge 2001).
6 David M. Levy and Sandra J. Peart, *Escape from Democracy: The Role of Experts and the Public in Economic Policy* (New York, NY: CUP, 2013): 110–127.
7 Christopher J. Coyne, *Doing Bad by Doing Good: Why Humanitarian Action Fails* (Stanford, CA: Stanford UP 2013): 76.
8 Robert Higgs, "Wartime Prosperity? A Reassessment of the U.S. Economy in the 1940s," *Journal of Economic History* 52.1 (1992): 41–60.
9 Higgs, "Prosperity" 43.
10 Lavoie 56–7.
11 Christopher J. Coyne, "Lobotomizing the Defense Brain," *Review of Austrian Economics* 28.4 (2015): 371–96; Jeffrey Rogers Hummel and Don Lavoie, "National Defense and the Public-Goods Problem," *Journal des Econmistes et des Etudes Humaines: Bilingual Journal of Interdisciplinary Studies* 5.2–3 (1994): 363–77.
12 Christopher J. Coyne and David S. Lucas, "Economists Have No Defense: A Critical Review of National Defense in Economics Textbooks," *Journal of Private Enterprise* 31.4 (2016): 65–83.
13 In reality, many aspects of national defense appear excludable. For example, a missile defense system can defend one metropolitan area and not another. The resources used for that missile defense system can also only be used to defend one city. This means that New York's defense involves the use of resources that could otherwise have been used to defend Los Angeles. Various aspects of defense are therefore not public goods, especially on the national level.
14 See Ludwig von Mises, *A Critique of Interventionism* (New Rochelle, NY: Arlington 1977); Murray N. Rothbard, *Power and Market: Government and the Economy* (Menlo Park, CA: IHS 1977); Sanford Ikeda, *Dynamics of the Mixed Economy: Toward a Theory of Interventionism* (New York, NY: Routledge 1996).
15 Ludwig von Mises, *Planning for Freedom and Twelve Other Essays and Addresses* (South Holland, IL: Libertarian 1974) 22–4.
16 Sanford Ikeda, "Urban Interventionism and Local Knowledge," *Review of Austrian Economics* 17.2–3 (2004): 247–264.
17 Ikeda, "Interventionism."
18 Vincent Ostrom, *The Meaning of Democracy and the Vulnerability of Democracies: A Response to Tocqueville's Challenge* (Ann Arbor, MI: U of Michigan P 1997).
19 James C. Scott, *Seeing Like a State: How Certain Schemes to Improve the Human Condition Have Failed* (New Haven, CT: Yale UP 1999).
20 Previous economists had romanticized the state, treating it as a benevolent despot that can solve market failures. Public choice theorists like James M. Buchanan analyzed "politics without romance." See James M. Buchanan, "The Constitution of Economic Policy," *American Economic Review* 77.3 (1987): 245–50; James M. Buchanan, "Public Choice: Politics Without Romance," *Policy* 19.3 (2003): 13–18.
21 The assumption of symmetry of agent type between private and public sector is just that—an assumption—and not meant to be descriptive. As discussed further below in the text, in practice politicians are not randomly selected members of the population, and this means that their dispositions may be predictably different from those of other people in various ways. They may, for instance, be selected for ambition and lack of principle. Robert Higgs, "Public Choice and Political Leadership," *Independent Review* 1.3 (1997): 466.
22 James M. Buchanan, "Individual Choice in Voting and the Market," *Journal of Political Economy* 62.4 (1954): 334–43; Richard E. Wagner and Deema Yazigi, "Form vs. Substance in Selection through Competition: Elections, Markets, and Political Economy," *Public Choice* 159.3–4 (2014): 503–14.
23 Cecil Bohanan and T. Norman Van Cott, "Now More than Ever, Your Vote Doesn't Matter," *Independent Review* 6.4 (2002): 591–5; Jac C. Heckelman, "Now More than Ever, Your Vote Doesn't Matter: A Reconsideration," *Independent Review* 7.4 (2003): 599–601; Andrew Gelman, Nate Silver, and Aaron Edlin, "What Is the Probability Your Vote Will Make a Difference," *Economic Inquiry* 50.2 (2012): 321–6.
24 Bryan Caplan, *The Myth of the Rational Voter: Why Democracies Choose Bad Policies* (Princeton, NJ: Princeton UP 2007).
25 Donald J. Boudreaux, "Was Your High School Civics Teacher Right After All? Donald Wittman's *The Myth of Democratic Failure*," *Independent Review* 1.1 (1996): 111–28.
26 Robert Higgs, *Delusions of Power: New Explorations of the State, War, and the Economy* (Oakland, CA: Independent 2012) 34–46.

27 Armen A. Alchian, "Uncertainty, Evolution, and Economic Theory," *Journal of Political Economy* 58.3 (1950): 211–21.
28 William A. Niskanen, "Nonmarket Decision Making: The Peculiar Economics of Bureaucracy," *American Economic Review* 58.2 (1968): 293–305; William A. Niskanen, *Bureaucracy and Representative Government.* (Chicago, IL: Aldine-Atherton 1971); William A. Niskanen, "Bureaucrats and Politicians," *Journal of Law and Economics* 18.3 (1975): 617–43; William A. Niskanen, "Bureaucracy," *The Elgar Companion to Public Choice*, ed. William F. Shughart II and Laura Razzolini (Cheltenham: Elgar 2001) 258–70.
29 Gordon Tullock, "The Politics of Bureaucracy," *Selected Works of Gordon Tullock 6: Bureaucracy*, ed. Charles Rowley (Indianapolis, IN: Liberty 2005 [1965]) 241–416.
30 Peter J. Boettke, "Information and Knowledge: Austrian Economics in Search of Its Uniqueness," *Review of Austrian Economics* 15.4 (2002): 263–74.
31 For one application of Tullock's insights to the contemporary issue of postwar nation-building, see Christopher J. Coyne, "*The Politics of Bureaucracy* and the Failure of Post-War Reconstruction," *Public Choice* 135.1–2 (2008): 11–22; Christopher J. Coyne, *After War: The Political Economy of Exporting Democracy* (Stanford, CA: Stanford UP).
32 Franz Oppenheimer, *The State: Its History and Development Viewed Sociologically* (New York, NY: Huebsch 1922).
33 Gordon Tullock, "Welfare Costs of Tariffs, Monopolies, and Theft," *Western Economic Journal* 5.3 (1967): 224–32; James M. Buchanan, Robert D. Tollison, and Gordon Tullock, eds., *Toward a Theory of the Rent-Seeking Society* (College Station, TX: Texas A&M UP 1980); Robert D. Tollison, "Rent Seeking: A Survey," *Kyklos* 35.4 (1982): 575–602.
34 Randall G. Holcombe. *Political Capitalism: How Economic and Political Power Is Made and Maintained.* (New York, NY: Cambridge UP 2018).
35 Mancur Olson, *The Rise and Decline of Nations: Economic Growth, Stagflation, and Social Rigidities* (New Haven, CT: Yale UP 1982); Edmund Phelps, *Mass Flourishing: How Grassroots Innovation Created Jobs, Challenge, and Change* (Princeton, NJ: Princeton UP 2013); Luigi Zingales, *A Capitalism for the People: Recapturing the Lost Genius of American Prosperity* (New York, NY: Basic 2014); Randall Holcombe, "Political Capitalism," *Cato Journal* 35.1 (2015): 41–66.
36 Joseph Schumpeter, *Capitalism, Socialism, and Democracy* (New York, NY: Harper 1942)
37 Randall Holcombe, "Crony Capitalism: By-Product of Big Government," *Independent Review* 17.4 (2013): 541–59; Holcombe, *Political Capitalism.*
38 Robert J. Barro, "The Control of Politicians: An Economic Model," *Public Choice* 14.1 (1973): 19–42; John Ferejohn, "Incumbent Performance and Electoral Control," *Public Choice* 50.1 (1986): 5–25; Timothy Besley, *Principled Agents? The Political Economy of Good Government* (New York, NY: OUP 2006).
39 Bruce Yandle, "Bootleggers and Baptists: The Education of a Regulatory Economist," *Regulation* 7.3 (1983): 12–6; Fred S. McChesney, *Money for Nothing: Politicians, Rent Extraction, and Political Extortion* (Cambridge, MA: Harvard UP 1987); Adam Smith and Bruce Yandle, *Bootleggers and Baptists: How Economic Forces and Moral Persuasion Interact to Shape Regulatory Policy* (Washington, DC: Cato 2014).
40 Dean Baker, "The Problem of Doctors' Salaries," *Politico* (Capitol News, Oct. 25, 2017), www.politico.com/agenda/story/2017/10/25/doctors-salaries-pay-disparities-000557 (Jan. 8, 2018).
41 Megan McArdle, "Licensing Interior Decorators? Let's Nix State-Approved Cartels," *Chicago Tribune*, May 22, 2016, www.chicagotribune.com/news/opinion/commentary/ct-unnecessary-occupational-licensing-20160522-story.html (Jan. 8, 2018).
42 McArdle; Adam Smith, *An Inquiry into the Nature and Causes of the Wealth of Nations* (Edinburgh: Nelson 1827) 54.
43 Frank Knight, "Lippman's *The Good Society*," *Journal of Political Economy* 46.6 (1938): 868–9.
44 Knight 869.
45 F.A. Hayek, *The Road to Serfdom* (Chicago, IL: U of Chicago P 1944).
46 Hayek, *Road* 135.
47 For an application of this logic to foreign policy, see Christopher J. Coyne and Abigail R. Hall, "Empire State of Mind: The Illiberal Foundations of Liberal Hegemony," *Independent Review* 21.2 (2016): 237–250.
48 Robert Higgs, "Public Choice and Political Leadership," *Independent Review* 1.3 (1997): 466.
49 F.G. Bailey, *Humbuggery and Manipulation: The Art of Leadership* (Ithaca, NY: Cornell UP 1988) 174.
50 Bailey.
51 See, for example, Christopher J. Coyne and Abigail R. Hall, "Foreign Intervention, Police Militarization, and the Impact on Minority Groups," *Peace Review* 28.2 (2016): 165–170.
52 James M. Buchanan, *The Limits of Liberty: Between Anarchy and Leviathan* (Chicago, IL: U of Chicago P 1975); Peter J. Boettke, "Economics and Public Administration," *Southern Economic Journal* 84.4 (2018):

938–59; Paul Dragos Aligica, Peter J. Boettke, and Vlad Tarko, *Public Governance and the Classical Liberal Perspective* (New York, NY: Oxford UP 2019).

53 Anthony de Jasay, *The State* (New York, Basil Blackwell 1985).

54 Christopher J. Coyne, "The Protective State: A Grave Threat to Liberty," In, Peter J. Boettke and Solomon Stein, eds. *Buchanan's Tensions: Reexamining the Political Economy and Philosophy of James M. Buchanan* (Arlington, VA: Mercatus 2018).

55 Paul D. Aligica and Vlad Tarko, "Polycentricity: From Polanyi to Ostrom, and Beyond," *Governance: An International Journal of Policy, Administration, and Institutions* 25.2 (2012): 237–262.

56 Vincent Ostrom, Charles Tiebout, and Robert Warren, "The Organization of Government in Metropolitan Areas: A Theoretical Inquiry," *American Political Science Review* 55.4 (1961): 831–42.

57 James M. Buchanan, "Federalism and Individual Sovereignty," *Cato Journal* 15.2–3 (1995/1996): 259–68.

58 Barry Weingast, "The Economic Role of Political Institutions: Market-Preserving Federalism and Economic Development," *Journal of Law, Economics, and Organization* 11.1 (1995): 1–31.

59 Peter J. Boettke, Christopher J. Coyne, and Peter T. Leeson, "Quasimarket Failure," *Public Choice* 149.1–2 (2011): 209–44.

60 Boettke, Coyne, and Leeson 214.

61 Boettke, Coyne, and Leeson 215.

62 James M. Buchanan, "An Economic Theory of Clubs," *Economica* 32 (1965): 1–14.

63 Peter T. Leeson, "Governments, Clubs, and Constitutions," *Journal of Economic Behavior and Organization* 80.2 (2011): 301–8. See also Bruno S. Frey, "Functional, Overlapping, Competing Jurisdictions: Redrawing the Geographic Borders of Administration," *European Journal of Law Reform* 5.3–4 (2005): 543–55.

64 Leeson 304.

65 Edward Peter Stringham, *Private Governance: Creating Order in Economic and Social Life* (New York, NY: OUP 2015)

66 Stringham 117.

67 Harold Demsetz, "The Exchange and Enforcement of Property Rights," *Journal of Law and Economics* 7 (1964): 11–26.

68 Stringham. See also Bruce J. Benson, *To Serve and Protect: Privatization and Community in Criminal Justice* (Oakland, CA: Independent 1998); Edward P. Stringham, ed., *Anarchy and the Law: The Political Economy of Choice* (Oakland, CA: Independent 2007); Bruce J. Benson, *The Enterprise of Law: Justice without the State* (Oakland, CA: Independent 2011).

69 Stringham.

70 Spencer Heath MacCallum, *The Art of Community* (Menlo Park, CA: IHS 1970); Daniel B. Klein "Tie-Ins and the Market Provision of Public Goods," *Harvard Journal of Law and Public Policy* 10 (1987): 451–74; Fred S. Foldvary, *Public Goods and Private Communities: The Market Provision of Social Services* (Cheltenham: Elgar 1994); Robert H. Nelson, *Private Neighborhoods and the Transformation of Local Government* (Washington, DC: Urban 2005); David Beito, Peter Gordon, and Alex Tabarrok, eds., *The Voluntary City: Choice, Community, and Civil Society* (Ann Arbor, MI: U of Michigan P 2002).

71 See R.J. Rummel, *Death by Government: Genocide and Mass Murder Since 1900* (New York, NY: Routledge 1994); Stéphane Courtois, Nicolas Werth, Jean-Louis Panné, Andrzej Paczkowski, Karel Bartošek, and Jean-Louis Margolin, *The Black Book of Communism: Crimes, Terror, Repression* (Cambridge, MA: Harvard UP 1999). For one theoretical framework for understanding these empirical realities, see Higgs, *Delusions* 11–24.

18
HUNTING FOR UNICORNS

Peter T. Leeson

An Unusual Safari

In ancient legend a unicorn is a horse-like creature with a single, spiraled horn sprouting from its forehead. Today this creature is universally regarded as a fantasy, and the term "unicorn" is used to derisively describe phenomena thought equally impossible.

In political economy such phenomena are often anarchic. Conventional wisdom acknowledges the prospect of cooperation without government under ideal social conditions—anarchic cooperation that is fragile. But everyone knows that cooperation without government under worst-case social conditions—robust anarchic cooperation—doesn't exist.

Except, everyone is wrong. This chapter hunts for anarchic unicorns and finds them.[1] There is robust cooperation in anarchic reality.

Conventional wisdom eschews investigating anarchic reality because an important theory, the "logic of continuous dealings"—or rather the stringent assumptions on which that theory is based—seemingly preordains what one will see: the solitary and poor, the nasty and brutish, and the short. In its most effective incarnation the logic of continuous dealings amounts to a society-wide boycott of people who misbehave: cheat someone today and no one will deal with you tomorrow, or indeed ever again. In principle this is a powerful punishment whose threat can induce you to behave without any government at all. But for that threat to be powerful in practice, society must exhibit numerous uncommon features.[2] Here are a few:

- Society must consist of people who are culturally similar. To see why, suppose people speak different languages. In that case, communicating a cheater's identity to others is difficult, so learning about who should be boycotted is too. Cheating is shunned by only a few, so many find it worthwhile to cheat.
- Society must consist of people of similar strengths. If people have different violent capacities, the threat of boycott is meaningless. Weak people can announce their intentions never to deal again with cheaters, but strong people can simply take what they want from the weak and so cheat nonetheless.
- Society must consist of "good apples," people who care enough about the distant future for the distant future to weigh significantly on their current decisions. Consider "bad apples," people who care little about the distant future. If they care little enough, what

they gain by cheating, which is enjoyed now, exceeds what they lose by being boycotted, most of which is sacrificed only down the road. So in a society full of rotten apples, people cheat.

Conventional wisdom is therefore correct that anarchic cooperation reliant *only* on the logic of continuous dealings is fragile. But this does not imply the impossibility of robust anarchic cooperation for a simple reason: the logic of continuous dealings isn't the only mechanism of cooperation without government on which people may rely. Other mechanisms are available that augment or substitute for the logic of continuous dealings, mechanisms that aren't sensitive to the social conditions that pose a problem for that logic.[3]

I present to you three anarchic unicorns observed in the wild:

- *Unicornis diversus*: cooperation without government when society is culturally diverse.
- *Unicornis violentus*: cooperation without government when some people are strong and others are weak.
- *Unicornis criminalis*: cooperation without government when society is populated exclusively by bad apples. In each case the logic of continuous dealings is present but takes a back seat to alternative mechanisms of social order that permit self-governance to flourish where it "should not."

Come, let's go a-hunting.

Unicornis Diversus

Our first anarchic unicorn inhabits precolonial Africa, where a large number of culturally diverse people existed and where government that could oversee their relations often did not.[4] The basic problem these people faced was straightforward. To realize gains from widespread cooperation, they needed to venture outside their own communities. But interacting with people outside their own communities was risky: outsiders were unknown and thus so was how outsiders might behave.

Within communities, where people were culturally similar, information about how individuals behaved flowed freely. But between communities, where people were culturally different, it did not. Thus, while a cheater might be boycotted by the community to which his victim belonged, he probably wouldn't be boycotted by others. The boycott would be limited rather than society-wide.

Limited boycotts limit the punishment with which the logic of continuous dealings threatens cheating. And that limits outsiders' incentive to cooperate. Since the risk of being cheated by outsiders remains high, people don't venture outside their own communities. Gains from widespread cooperation go unrealized.

It's a good thing no one told precolonial Africans that this was their fate. Otherwise, they might not have proved that it wasn't. "[I]ntensive social interaction between various ethnic groupings" and "extensive credit arrangements often between total strangers from different tribes" flourished in precolonial Africa. In other words, there was widespread cooperation without government.[5]

Precolonial Africans achieved this by supplementing the logic of continuous dealings, which is based on punishing cheaters *ex post*, with the logic of signaling, which is based on sorting outsiders *ex ante* according to the likelihood that they'll cheat.[6] The basic strategy followed by the members of a community was simple. Require an outsider who wants to trade with someone in the community to make a costly, specific, upfront investment, the value of which he can recoup only if he behaves. If he misbehaves, boycott him, driving the value of his investment to zero.

The investment needed to be costly—to matter to the outsider—so that its loss would be punishing to him. The investment needed to be specific—have value to the outsider only in facilitating cooperation with the community requiring the investment—so that if that community boycotted him, he would lose his investment. And the investment needed to be upfront—made by the outsider before anyone in the community would trade with him—so that he had an investment he could lose once trade commenced.

For outsiders who intended to behave, making such investments was worthwhile. Since continued cooperation meant continued opportunity to interact with the community, they expected to recover the cost of their investments over time. For outsiders who intended to misbehave, the opposite was true. Since an act of cheating resulted in boycott, they expected to be banned from interacting with the community before they could recover the cost of their investments.

Members of the community requiring the investment could therefore use the fact that an outsider had made the investment, or had not, to discern what kind of trading partner he would make. If the outsider was willing to make the investment, he would make a safe partner, so the community would trade with him. If the outsider was unwilling, partnering with him was risky, so the community stayed away. In other words, costly, specific, upfront investments functioned as signals.

What kinds of investments did precolonial Africans use for this purpose? The kind that reduced cultural diversity—social distance—between them. Outsiders adopted the costly social customs and practices of the communities with whose members they desired to trade.[7]

Some converted to the "religions" of outsiders with whom they wanted to trade, joining their cults and fraternal societies, such as the Ekpe, Okonko, and Ogboni, which performed quasi-religious (and judiciary) functions in precolonial African communities. Sometimes joining a fraternal society required paying an actual "membership fee," imposing a financial cost on newcomers. In other cases "cult membership was open to any who wished to join"—as long as newcomers adopted the society's customs and practices. For example, joining the society might require surrendering one's goods to spirits, behavioral and dietary restrictions, and recurrent participation in society-related activities.[8]

In addition to being costly, these investments were specific, granting a newcomer "membership" in only the religious society he paid to enter or whose customs and practices he followed. They were also upfront. Access to the society first required payment or demonstrated commitment to onerous religious rules and rituals. As a result, religious adoption was an effective signal of an outsider's intention to cooperate.

Other precolonial Africans adopted the property practices of outsiders with whom they wanted to trade. Precolonial communities didn't own the land they used in the sense that they could sell it to others. But they did exercise some control over who could use the land they currently occupied and how it could be used. Often this function fell to "Earth Priests," community leaders representing links to the historical first user of the land.

Earth Priests established ritual customs and taboos relating to this property, which was believed to have mystical properties. To gain access to the community, outsiders had to respect those customs and taboos—to invest significantly in reducing the social distance between themselves and the community's members.

Such investments were costly. For example, an Earth Priest's taboos might prohibit cultivating more fertile land in the area because of its sacred status, requiring newcomers to work less productive soil. An Earth Priest might also require newcomers to make a customary gift to him or to the community "as an expression of goodwill."[9]

These investments were specific to the Earth Priest and hence to the land-using community in question. Because they were required before an outsider was permitted to join that community, they were also upfront. Only by remaining in good standing in the community could an outsider recoup his gift's cost or the cost of cultivating less fertile ground. Thus, only outsiders who intended to behave cooperatively would adopt community members' ritual land customs and taboos, making such adoption an effective signal of credibility.

Precolonial Africans took a feature of their broader society that threatened to prevent anarchic cooperation—cultural diversity—and turned it to their advantage. They leveraged their social differences to supplement the logic of continuous dealings with signaling, facilitating widespread cooperation without government.

Unicornis Violentus

Our second anarchic unicorn also inhabits precolonial Africa. But to find it we need to narrow our sights on the west-central part of the continent where in the nineteenth century a trade flourished in beeswax, ivory, and wild rubber destined for export to Europe.[10] On one side of this trade were African middlemen and the Europeans who hired them to procure goods for export. On the other side were the goods' indigenous producers from whom the middlemen procured wax, ivory, and rubber.

Middlemen operated from European (typically Portuguese) outposts overseen by crown-appointed governors stationed near the coast. Middlemen were highly mobile, usually armed, and traveled in large caravans. Producers inhabited the remote interior of west-central Africa. In contrast to middlemen they were highly immobile, usually unarmed, and lived in small villages. Some villages were parts of African "kingdoms." But from a contemporary perspective at least, these kingdoms were hardly governments. Most important, no government at all—African, European, or otherwise—wielded authority over both sides of the export trade. Thus producer–middleman interactions were anarchic.

For producers in particular, this situation posed a serious problem. They had the goods that middlemen were looking for. And middlemen were strong enough, and producers weak enough, for the middlemen to simply seize what they wanted. Why, then, should middlemen pay for it? Force dominated trade as middlemen's means of procurement.

If communities of producers could refuse to interact with middlemen, they could avoid being plundered. But since most communities were stationary and unarmed, refusal wasn't an option. Who, then, could protect producers from middlemen's plunder?

Not "who," it turns out, but "what"—and a what of the most unexpected kind. To incentivize middlemen to prefer peaceful exchange to violent plunder, producers offered to trade with them on credit.[11] Ordinarily credit is a source of opportunism, not its solution. Separation of payment and provision makes creditors vulnerable to their debtors. In the context of producer–middleman relations, however, this separation supported anarchic cooperation between the strong and the weak. Here's how:

At time t, a community of producers wouldn't produce anything that middlemen sought; the community left wax, ivory, and rubber unharvested. Thus, when a caravan of middlemen came along, there wasn't anything the caravan wanted to take. This was an unhappy situation for middlemen, since traveling from the coast to the interior was arduous and expensive; it took time, and money, and men. Going home empty-handed meant taking a large loss.

Middlemen could avoid that loss, however—indeed, they could profit—if they accepted this proposition from producers: they should pay the producers now—usually offering "immediate consumables," such alcohol, tobacco, and cloth, which were the goods that producers wanted—and the producers would harvest the goods the middlemen sought after the caravan departed. At a specified future date, time $t + 1$, the promised goods would be ready for pick-up; the middlemen could come back and collect what they were owed. This was an ingenious way for the weak to facilitate cooperation with the strong: it's impossible to plunder goods that haven't yet been produced, but credit makes it possible to trade them.

As one nineteenth-century observer described it, "the trader sees himself forced to give credits, and this is indispensable for anyone who takes the risk of trading in such a region, if he wants to do it with any success."[12] In the words of another, "The native would be little inclined to gather the products of his country, were he not given the payment in advance." Middlemen "can buy some products in the interior, these being brought to them by the natives and paid" on the spot.

> In general, however, they cannot purchase very many commodities in this way but instead give the native credit. Where rubber occurs in the forest, and where the elephant occurs, the [middleman] gives payment in advance to the elephant hunter for so and so many tusks, and to the one who wants to bring rubber or beeswax payment for so and so many pounds of rubber or wax. These people then have to wait for months and years until their debtors satisfy them.[13]

Still, debtor-producers *had* to satisfy them eventually, since their creditor-middlemen were stronger and could punish them violently if they did not—the reason credit in this context didn't pose the problem of debtor opportunism.

That's not all. By indebting themselves to their creditor-middlemen, producers created an incentive for those middlemen to abstain from abusing them—and to ensure that other middlemen didn't use violence against them either. To repay what they owed, producers needed to be alive and capable of work. Credit thus linked the financial health of creditor-middlemen to the physical health of their debtor-producers. It transformed the latter from targets of the former's violence into valuable assets the former wanted to protect.

When middlemen returned to a community of producers to collect what they were owed, the only goods available for plunder were their own—the goods owed them. If the middlemen wanted more, they could renew their credit contract. If not, they could go home with their goods for export. What they couldn't do was return in the future and plunder the producers, since if they returned without having renewed their credit agreement they would again find no wax, ivory, or rubber to take. Given the cost of traveling to the interior, middlemen frequently went with the first option, perpetuating a cycle of credit-supported cooperation without government between the strong and the weak.

Unicornis Criminalis

To find our final anarchic unicorn we depart from Africa—in fact, from land entirely. We turn to the eighteenth-century Caribbean pirates. These notorious rogues included men like Blackbeard, whose real name was Edward Teach; "Calico" Jack Rackam, the likely inspiration for Johnny Depp's character in Walt Disney's *Pirates of the Caribbean* movie franchise; and the "pirate philosopher" Sam Bellamy.

Popular pirate fiction makes it easy to forget, but Caribbean pirates were criminals. Thus, they couldn't rely on government to facilitate cooperation between them. This presented a significant problem for pirates because successful piracy required significant cooperation. There was no such thing as a one-man pirate crew; a single person couldn't pirate at all. Maritime marauding necessitated living and working together with many others, packed like sardines into creaky ships for months at sea. Making matters worse, it wasn't the cooperation of just anybody that pirates had to elicit to make their criminal enterprise possible. It was the cooperation of other murderers and thieves—apples as rotten as they come, from the first man to the last.

The necessary ingredients of such cooperation were two. First, if they were to jointly assault and steal from merchant ships—pirates' prey—pirate crewmembers, on average about eighty men, had to abstain from assaulting and stealing from one another. Second, pirate crewmembers needed to empower officers for their ships, such as captains, whose military leadership was required to direct attacks, and simultaneously to restrain those officers from abusing their authority for private gain at the crew's expense.

The logic of continuous dealings by itself offered little help. On the one hand, refusing to interact with a crewmember who, say, stole a fellow seadog's share of the loot wouldn't mean much, since once a pirate ship was away at sea, crewmembers were more-or-less trapped together until the next landfall. Boycotting the cheater after that could be effective, but in the meantime simple shunning wasn't practical.

On the other hand, since pirates were, well, *pirates*, and since the typical pirate's lifespan was rather short, it's probable that the distant future, hence the future losses associated with being boycotted, did not figure prominently in pirates' current decisions. Or at least they did not figure prominently enough for the prospect of being boycotted alone to dissuade all misbehavior.

To address these difficulties pirates developed a system of constitutional democracy.[14] More than half a century before America's Founding Fathers devised a similar system of government for the United States, the Caribbean's most infamous rotten apples did so to secure cooperation among themselves without any government at all. Consider the constitution that governed the pirate crew aboard the *Royal Fortune*:

I. Every Man has a Vote in the Affairs of Moment; has equal Title to the fresh Provisions, or strong Liquors, at any Time seized, and may use them at Pleasure, unless a Scarcity make it necessary, for the Good of all, to vote a Retrenchment.

II. Every Man to be called fairly in Turn, by List, on board of Prizes, because, (over and above their proper Share) they were on these Occasions allowed a Shift of Cloaths: But if they defrauded the Company to the Value of a Dollar, in Plate, Jewels, or Money, Marooning was their Punishment. If the Robbery was only betwixt one another, they contented themselves with slitting the Ears and Nose of him that was Guilty, and set him on Shore, not in an uninhabited Place, but somewhere, where he was sure to encounter Hardships.

III. No person to Game at Cards or Dice for Money.

IV. The Lights and Candles to be put out at eight a-Clock at Night: If any of the Crew, after that Hour, still remained enclined for Drinking, they were to do it on the open Deck.

V. To keep their Piece, Pistols, and Cutlash clean, and fit for Service.

VI. No Boy or Woman to be allowed amongst them. If any Man were found seducing any of the latter Sex, and carry'd her to Sea, disguised, he was to suffer Death.

VII. To Desert the Ship, or their Quarters in Battle, was punished with Death or Marooning.

VIII. No striking one another on board, but every Man's Quarrels to be ended on Shore, at Sword and Pistol.

IX. No Man to talk of breaking up their Way of Living, till each shared a 1000 l. If in order to this, any Man should lose a Limb, or become a Cripple in their Service, he was to have 800 Dollars, out of the publick Stock, and for lesser Hurts, proportionately.

X. The Captain and Quarter-Master to receive two Shares of a Prize; the Master, Boatswain, and Gunner, one Share and a half, and other Officers one and a Quarter.

XI. The Musicians to have Rest on the Sabbath Day, but the other six Days and Nights, none without special Favour.[15]

These pirate "codes," as they're popularly known, or "articles," which is what pirates called them, facilitated cooperation among bad apples in three central ways. First, they instituted laws against behaviors that threatened the collective interest of the crew, such as theft and violence, and stipulated punishments for crewmembers who broke those laws—punishments that were immediate and often corporeal in nature. Aboard the *Royal Fortune*, for instance, Article II of the crew's constitution prohibited theft from a fellow pirate and punished that crime with "slitting the Ears and Nose of him that was Guilty," afterward marooning him.

These features of piratical punishments addressed the problem that pirates' typically short time horizons posed for boycott alone in eliciting cooperation among bad apples. Immediate punishments are felt immediately, not in the distant future, and corporeal punishments are more severe than simple shunning. Piratical punishments thus imposed higher present costs on misbehavior than boycott alone could impose, effectively deterring misbehavior among the kind of people whose cooperation required the threat of especially high present costs.

In a sense, marooning was a boycott: a marooned lawbreaker was a pirate with whom his crew wouldn't interact again. But it was the kind of boycott that permitted pirates to avoid the problem of being trapped on a vessel with a cheater. Marooning was also lethal since the lawbreaker would likely perish of starvation if his circumstance didn't compel him to take his own life first.

Second, pirate constitutions established democracy as a crew's method of collective decision making. "Every Man has a Vote in the Affairs of Moment," as Article I of the *Royal Fortune*'s constitution put it. Most important among such affairs was the selection of the crew's officers. Pirates elected their captains and quartermasters popularly. Whereas the former officers wielded command in times of battle, the latter wielded command in "peacetime"—pirates, like all good constitutionalists, showed prudent concern for the division of power. The quartermaster was in charge of administering constitutionally specified punishments to lawbreakers and distributing victuals and shares of loot.[16]

Just as pirate democracy called for the popular election of pirate officers, it called for their popular deposition—whenever and for whatever reason crewmembers wanted. An officer's deposition could result solely in his removal from office, for instance if he simply proved inept at the task. Or, if an officer abused his authority, for instance by defrauding the crew, deposition could result in his removal from office followed by marooning. Threatened by such punishment, pirate officers—even myopic ones—were incentivized to behave, to use their authority for the benefit of their crews. And if for some reason an officer nevertheless abused his power, his crew wouldn't be stuck with him for its duration at sea; it simply replaced him.

Last but not least, pirate constitutions ensured their own enforcement. Pirate articles were written down and all crewmembers assented to them before going "on the account." It was therefore clear to each crewmember which behaviors were legitimate and which were not, and clear to him that it was also clear to everyone else. This made the threat of being punished for misbehavior credible, as the lawbreaker knew his actions would be seen as law-breaking by the entire crew, which would support his punishment—whether he was an ordinary pirate or an officer.

Thus, an ordinary crewmember who, for instance, stashed a piece of eight from the quartermaster's view knew that his behavior would be seen as theft and punished by the quartermaster, supported—in fact, demanded—by all his colleagues. Likewise, a quartermaster who, say, distributed to a crewmember less than his constitutionally specified share of booty, or a captain who, say, usurped authority granted to the quartermaster by pirate law, knew that the whole crew would see his action as overstepping and thus depose him—potentially worse. The result was anarchic cooperation in floating societies comprised exclusively of rotten apples, facilitated by a system of constitutional democracy designed by rotten apples.

Organizing Your Own Safari

There you have it, three bona fide anarchic unicorns, or at least their silhouettes, observed in the wild. A few tips for arranging your own safari:

- Anarchic unicorns aren't going to just walk up to you and neigh because you'd like them to. To find them you need go out into the wild in search of them. That doesn't mean you have to open a bed-and-breakfast in Mogadishu (though you could).[17] But it does mean you need to engage anarchic reality. Study some historical research. Conduct some fieldwork. Watch a documentary. Do something that exposes to you the incredible variety of ways that real people, past and present, have lived without government.
- You're not that clever, but the people who have to find ways to cooperate without government under less-than-ideal social conditions are. Stated differently, the incentive of such people to find solutions to their particular obstacles to anarchic cooperation is much stronger than yours. This means that successful hunts will almost always start with the empirical, with the facts of the matter: "*What* do/did these people do?" Only after you've established that will it ordinarily be fruitful to move to the theoretical side of things: "*Why* does the thing they do/did work, or not, to facilitate anarchic cooperation in their environment?" Tying to conjure up solutions to problems of anarchic cooperation in a vacuum makes finding anarchic unicorns much harder.
- Don't be discouraged by people who will mock your open-minded engagement with anarchic reality as, well, hunting for unicorns. I've given you at least a little reason to be skeptical of their skepticism. Besides, many of these people are engaged in the most quixotic hunt of all: the hunt for omniscient benevolent government. So why should you listen to them?

Acknowledgement

This chapter is based on, and draws on discussions in, my previously published work, referenced below.

Notes

1 For a more complete discussion of the anarchic realities this chapter considers, as well as others, see Peter T. Leeson, *Anarchy Unbound: Why Self-Governance Works Better than You Think* (Cambridge: CUP 2014).
2 See Peter T. Leeson, "Coordination without Command: Stretching the Scope of Spontaneous Order," *Public Choice* 135.1–2 (2008): 67–78.
3 See Peter T. Leeson, "Pirates, Prisoners, and Preliterates: Anarchic Context and the Private Enforcement of Law," *European Journal of Law and Economics* 37.3 (2014): 365–379.
4 See, for example, Paul Bohannan, "Stateless Societies," *Problems in African History*, ed. Robert Collins (Englewood Cliffs, NJ: Prentice-Hall 1968) 170–2; Philp Curtin, Steven Feierman, Leonard Thompson, and Jan Vansina, *African History: From Earliest Times to Independence* (New York, NY: Longman 1995).
5 Abner Cohen, *Custom and Politics in Urban Africa: A Study of Hausa Migrants in Yoruba Towns* (Berkeley, CA: U of California P 1969) 6.
6 Peter T. Leeson, "Social Distance and Self-Enforcing Exchange," *Journal of Legal Studies* 37.1 (2008): 161–88.
7 Peter T. Leeson, "Endogenizing Fractionalization," *Journal of Institutional Economics* 1.1 (2005): 75–98.
8 Elizabeth Colson, "African Society at the Time of the Scramble," *The History and Politics of Colonialism 1870–1914 1: Colonialism in Africa 1870–1960*, ed. L.H. Gand and Peter Duignan (Cambridge: CUP 1969) 59.
9 Colson, "African Society" 54.
10 Before 1836, this trade also included slaves.

11 Peter T. Leeson, "Trading with Bandits," *Journal of Law and Economics* 50.2 (2007): 303–21.

12 Henrique Augusto Dias de Carvalho, *Expedicao portugueza ao Muatiañvua 5: Ethnographia e historia tradicional dos povos da Lunda* (Lisboa: Imprensa Nacional 1890) 700.

13 Paul Pogge, *Im Reich des Muata-Jamvo* (Berlin: Reimer 1880) 16.

14 Peter T. Leeson, "An-arrgh-chy: The Law and Economics of Pirate Organization," *Journal of Political Economy* 115.6 (2007): 1049–94. See also Peter T. Leeson, "The Calculus of Piratical Consent: The Myth of the Myth of Social Contract," *Public Choice* 139.3–4 (2009): 443–59; Peter T. Leeson, *The Invisible Hook: The Hidden Economics of Pirates* (Princeton, NJ: Princeton UP 2009).

15 Charles Johnson, *A General History of the Pyrates*, ed. Manuel Schonhorn (New York, NY: Dover [1726–1728] 1999) 211–2.

16 Infractions whose punishments were not specified fell to the quartermaster's discretion or to a vote of the crew.

17 On anarchic cooperation in Somalia, see Peter T. Leeson, "Better off Stateless: Somalia before and after Government Collapse," *Journal of Comparative Economics* 35.4 (2007): 689–710.

19

SOCIAL NORMS AND SOCIAL ORDER

Ryan Muldoon

I. Introduction

Once a social group becomes suitably large, it can become difficult to harmonize and coordinate people's behavior. Interests will conflict, disputes will arise, and there is thus a reason to embrace a shared set of rules that can ensure that people, despite moral disagreements, can engage in peaceful social cooperation. Philosophical anarchists argue that one prominent means to solve this coordination problem—formal political institutions that have some coercive power—is illegitimate. Depending on the particular account of anarchism, this can be for different reasons, but generally the failure of legitimacy stems from a lack of proper consent of the governed, or from problems associated with the bare exercise of coercion at all.

Let us suppose that there is no good way to overcome the anarchist's challenge to formal political institutional arrangements. One hope for a way forward in the face of the challenge of harmonizing and coordinating behavior is through the use of *informal institutions* such as social norms. Social norms have the advantage of being driven by communities rather than by rule-making on the part of separate entities like states. But social norms have a number of features that may make them less desirable from the point of view of reducing coercion. In particular, social norms can be arbitrary, overly punitive, and difficult to change. These qualities can make norms an unappealing way to coordinate behavior. However, I argue that norms *can* accomplish much of what we want if we foster communities that are more hostile to easy norm creation. In particular, in more diverse, dynamic settings, we should expect that the norms that can survive are those that can facilitate valuable cooperation and coordination, and encourage tolerance.

II. Social Norms: A Definition

Social norms are informal institutional arrangements that help groups coordinate on particular rules of behavior. A social norm is a behavioral rule R that applies in a particular context C within a given population P.[1] An individual A within this population prefers to follow the rule conditional on their expectation that enough other people in P will follow R in C (empirical expectations), and their expectation that enough other people in P expect A to follow R in C, and may punish A for failing to comply (normative expectations).

This is a reasonably abstract definition, so let's think about its elements and then consider an example. The first element is the fact that the social norm picks out a particular *rule*. This rule can be either permissive—"people can say whatever they want"—or restrictive—"no one can hit anyone else." Permissive rules help make clear what we have some entitlement to do and when an encroachment on that entitlement would be wrong. Restrictive rules concern the boundaries of action—what people are not allowed to do. Sometimes one can just straightforwardly reframe a permissive rule as a restrictive rule or vice versa, but in other instances this becomes difficult. For instance, when there are several possible actions, and the rule aims to coordinate behavior, it will usually be easier to understand the rule as restrictive. An example of this would be "Always drive on the right side of the road." Driving on the left would be equally fine, but the point of the rule is to pick out a behavior to coordinate on: the value of the rule isn't in which behavior is selected but in the fact that *some particular* behavior is selected.

Rules are generally not applicable in all places and times and for all people, and so a social norm picks out when a given rule applies and to whom. That is, it picks a context and a population. Perhaps I think the rule that "people can say whatever they want" is great for the public square, but not so useful in a movie theater, where people might just want to be able to watch movies uninterruptedly. So we can identify either situations in which a given rule does not apply (when it is otherwise generally applicable), or we specify the contexts in which it does in fact apply ("drive on the right side of the road" makes sense for public roads but probably not for your backyard). Likewise, we might think that rules apply to some people and not other people. Members of a club might have rules for themselves that don't apply to non-members. People who hold particular jobs might have rules that govern how they ought to conduct themselves in their various professions. Religious communities might have rules for themselves that don't apply to others. And so on.

So far, we've considered the structural features of norms—they are rules that apply in particular contexts to the members of particular populations. But issues related to individual-level considerations are of particular philosophical interest.

So, let's consider a person who takes herself to be a member of the relevant population, and is trying to determine what to do. Social norms involve a *conditional preference* to follow particular rules—someone will follow a given rule if she believes enough of the other members of the group are following it and expect her to do so, too. So she has *empirical expectations*, beliefs regarding what other people will do. These beliefs are usually formed by looking around and seeing what people *in fact* do; of course, they are sometimes informed by what people *proclaim* that they will do in the future.

Likewise, someone will likely have *normative expectations*, beliefs about what others think she *ought* to do. Normative expectations are second-order beliefs, and so are more prone to error than empirical expectations.

So, for there to be a social norm, a person follows a rule in a particular context because she thinks that most other people are also following the rule, and she believes that they want her to follow the rule as well. Note that this is quite different from a community's adhering to a common set of values in accordance with which all of its members act. For instance, if Alice helps a stranger because she thinks it is the right thing to do, and Bob helps a stranger because he also thinks it is the right thing to do, they are not following a *social norm* at all. They are each taking an individual action that just happens to be the same. That they do so might stem from the fact that they both had common moral upbringings, but in their actions neither Alice nor Bob were relying on social cues regarding what to do.

Social norms are not just common behaviors or common values. Instead, social norms are shared rules that people follow *when they believe others are following them and when they think that others think they should.* The existence of a given social norm is entirely compatible with a situation in which all a community's members personally endorse the norm and think it coheres perfectly with their values—but *also* with a case in which few people endorse the norm and most members of the community regard it as *counter* to their values but in which most members nonetheless feel socially compelled to follow it. This is in part because failures to comply with social norms frequently result in punishments. Some social norms may stay in place simply because people genuinely want to meet others' expectations. Others may stay in place because people fear punishment if they don't comply or because people anticipate social rewards for compliance.

What can we take away from this account of social norms? Social norms in a given community are maintained in place by an epistemic equilibrium within the community: people will continue to follow rules if they think *others* will follow the rules and if they think others want them to follow the rules. Social norms are not merely common sets of behaviors stemming from common values, but are instead fundamentally *social* mechanisms for rule enforcement.

Social norms can be created with intentional collective decision-making, or by a more social evolutionary process.[2] And norms can emerge with no coordination or collective intention.[3] As I will argue later, it can be useful to consider the process by which norms are created when we evaluate their moral status.

III. The Virtues of Social Norms

Social norms have a number of virtues. For our present discussion, norms are most obviously useful as an alternative to formal state institutions. Norms can effectively regulate behavior. They are consistently evident in our normal lives, so each of us has a reasonably good understanding of how they work. They can do this regulatory work quite apart from the kind of social regulation in which the state or other formal institutions do or don't engage. In general, norms emerge from private interactions and collections of individual judgments. Norms come from the communities that are bound by them; in that sense, the authority of the rules is clearer because they are not externally imposed. In this way, norms play clear roles in self-governance. It is quite difficult to impose a norm *externally* on a community if the community does not welcome the norm.

A real appeal of social norms as tools for social regulation is that they can be less aggressive than ones imposed by states. Communities can often solve coordination problems without draconian measures or threats of coercive violence. An eye-roll in response to a disapproved behavior is often sufficient punishment to encourage someone to abide by a community rule. Because the community itself enforces a norm, there is more leeway for context sensitivity as regards whether violations are punished, and if so, how severely. At their best, social norms can slowly ratchet up punishments if doing so is needed, relying as much as possible on markers of social esteem to do the work of maintaining social order.

Social norms can also play important roles in clearly embodying sets of rights or entitlements that people can possess in a given society. Abstract laws or legal commitments are often nicer in theory than in practice. It is easy to find examples of states failing to constrain *themselves* in the way that the law requires. Even minor infractions of the law come with an implicit—and sometimes actual—threat of state-sanctioned violence, but fear of punishment doesn't necessarily motivate positive behaviors by citizens. And the state can frequently fail to uphold the law by leaving protections unenforced, as a result either of a lack of state capacity or of simple apathy.

Social norms, on the other hand, can feature both positive and negative reinforcement mechanisms. Norm adherents can enjoy community esteem, while violators can be punished on sliding scales. Social rules and associated behaviors can more clearly *demonstrate* the commitments of a shared social morality than legalistic state-driven alternatives because the main mechanism enabling a social norm to take root is public norm-following. So a norm of tolerance remains in place when we all see evidence of people's tolerance of others. A rule against littering is maintained when people collect trash, not just when they issue tickets. Social norms are built out of social expectations, and those expectations are most successfully reinforced by visible behaviors that support or comply with relevant rules. Social norms are thus grounded in concrete manifestations of the values that they aim to support. They can serve to exemplify a community's values, rather than just describing them.

Social norms are powerful tools, both because they sometimes emerge as solutions to communities' problems as those problems arise and because a deliberating community can sometimes *choose* a rule for itself and decide how to enforce the rule in a way that is sensitive to the community's particular needs and circumstances. Monitoring conformity to norms and punishing divergence from them can become aspects of those areas of life specifically in need of regulation. Successful informal institutions can, for instance, incorporate social monitoring of the potential misuse of a common pool resource into the activities involved in *using* the resource.[4] There is then no extra action needed by a community, and no need for any extra set of enforcement personnel or agencies. If we are all seen following a given rule, our observable behavior further cements following the rule as the thing to do. If someone breaks a rule that others generally follow, the violation will be noticed by others and quickly rebuked.

Combining the ideas of exemplifying a community's values and responding aptly to specific problems, governance by social norms can at its best be a light-touch means of maintaining social order. Social norms can address those particular practices that actually need regulation, and can do so in a way that's consistent with people's values and sensitive to the contexts in which people live. Ground-level self-governance using social norms can ensure that communities have the rules they need to function—but no more. This is an appealing ideal. The prospect of social norms or other informal institutions playing these kinds of regulatory roles opens up the space of possibilities for minimally coercive communities. Social norms serve regulatory functions and may involve positive or negative sanctions, but they can be lighter-touch and more context-sensitive than state-made and state-enforced laws and regulations. The availability of social norms as means of maintaining social order renders the existence of communities free of formal coercive institutions, even in the predictable absence of perfect or morally pure community members, a live possibility.[5]

IV. Reasons to Worry about Social Norms

While one can straightforwardly envision an ideal community governed by light-touch social norms that enjoy community (and individual) support, the existence and operation of this kind of community are far from *assured.* Indeed, social norms can just as easily be sources of unjust, harsh, and arbitrary coercion. Social norms may not be desirable as our primary means of social coordination, especially if we embrace the concerns of the philosophical anarchist.

In particular, I'd like to focus on four features of norms that make them potentially undesirable for someone worried about ensuring the appropriate grounding of coercive authority. First, social norms can be arbitrary. That is, they may exist not because they provide an important social function, but instead just because they arose accidentally in the course of normal social interaction. A second concern is that norms can be arbitrarily punitive. Even with a fixed, agreed-upon level of punishment, norm enforcement may be the work of a variable number of punishers, so the severity of punishment can depend on factors outside the collective control of a community's members. Third, in the absence of norms that restrain intrusiveness, a community's norms can be far more invasive than state-made laws. Finally, norms can be very hard to change or eliminate. While in a liberal legal system there is a clear mechanism by which laws can be changed or eliminated with immediate effect, no such system can reliably eliminate a norm.

A. *Arbitrariness*

Social norms can be arbitrary. Norms frequently come about in the absence of any individual or collective intention to create a new rule.[6] Indeed, a norm can emerge as a kind of collective mistake: our general desire to coordinate behavior with others when needed can lead us to believe that there are rules that others expect us to follow when in fact we are over-responding to social evidence. Because of this kind of error, some rules come to be *only* because of our mistaken belief in their prior existence. Because norms are epistemic equilibria, we can accidentally lock in new behavioral rules in light of mistaken prior beliefs. Consider the basic dynamic in play: many social rules go unstated, so we scrutinize our environments for rules that we might not know about. If we happen to see a few people doing something similar in a given context, we may treat their behavior as evidence for the possible existence of a rule. As a result, we may begin to follow the rule we believe ourselves to have discovered, and our doing so provides extra evidence for others, and so forth—until there really is a rule in place, even if it came into existence purely because of a cascading series of epistemic errors. Once the rule obtains, it is just as much in force as any other.

This is troubling: the basic dynamic of norm-generation can yield an arbitrarily large number of arbitrary rules, especially in a more-or-less fixed population. If we merely pause and reflect on our social world, especially in smaller, less diverse communities where there is less population "churn," it is easy to see this dynamic play out. We are over-run with social rules, so much so that it is hard even to notice them. Rules specify the color and style of clothing it is appropriate to wear in particular seasons and on particular occasions. Rules govern hair length, facial hair, armpit hair, and leg hair. Rules determine how we use utensils, even identifying the hand in which one should hold a fork—not "merely" the kind of fork appropriate for a given course of food. Rules govern the settings in which and the people for whom wearing hats is appropriate. Rules govern the ways in which we maintain our lawns and the frequency with which we water them. And so on. This is hardly an exhaustive list of arbitrary social rules, of course, but the enumeration I've offered should underscore the utter triviality of many such rules, and the degree to which they regulate areas of life in which there's no particular need for coordination. Nothing is at stake in most of the domains governed by the kinds of rules I've mentioned (except in water-scarce locations, in which watering practices may be significant). None of the kinds of norms to which I've referred likely stems from state action. Indeed, state regulation may simply codify pre-existing social norms. Nonetheless, rules like these—and many other, similarly arbitrary ones—emerge; and people all too frequently feel little compunction about regulating each other's behavior on the basis of such rules. If anything, many people view doing so as fun.

Many social norms come into existence through social evolution. That they do can leave people with the impression that norms probably play valuable functional roles. Perhaps, people suppose, such norms characteristically solve coordination problems, prevent costly outcomes, or facilitate the occurrence of socially beneficial developments in cases in which the pursuit of short-term individual gains might otherwise make these developments less likely. (Consider Hume's argument for the evolution of property rights: despite the fact that at any given moment we might gain from taking someone else's property, we all gain from everyone agreeing to refrain from doing so.[7]) And indeed, it's quite plausible that such explanations are available for some instances of coordination on fixed rules. But the same dynamics can obtain even when there's no genuine coordination problem to be solved. Contingent events, beliefs, and passions can shape social behaviors just as easily as substantial structural challenges. As a result, a social norm can emerge as a solution to a nonexistent problem—a "solution" that is in fact a contingent, arbitrary way of coordinating responses to a set of arbitrarily clustered possible options, none of which actually presents a problem *requiring* coordination. We could likely get by just fine without social norms regarding the wearing of white before or after Memorial Day (or any other day of the year). A whole host of our social rules just don't need to exist at all, even if—because we've lived with them for so long—they've taken on some sort of meaning for us.

All of this is not to say that social norms are useless or bad. Rather, these norms are neutral with respect to most things we might care about normatively. The structure of social norms, and the dynamics by which they come into existence, give us no reason to expect the norms reliably to favor normatively desirable rules over undesirable ones. Social evolution depends on selection pressures, and those pressures need not consistently lead to the emergence of norms that foster liberal emancipation, or any other aspect of flourishing. Instead, the norms that result from selection pressures are likely to encourage the growth of norms that reflect just whatever the people involved happen to favor and the ways in which they happen to understand the social interactions in which they participate. Despite the fact that these norms are incredibly contingent, they can still dramatically shape the agency of the people who follow them.[8] So social norms can be expected to sustain some very good rules, and some fine rules, and, probably, some rather bad rules as well, as judged from whatever normative standpoint you favor. Social norms are, on their own, broadly going to be contingent and arbitrary, and different in different communities.

B. Punitive Character

A second, related worry about arbitrariness concerns punishment. Consider a case in which there is a well-established norm that calls for violations to be punished by the community. Imposing a sanction in response to the violation of a social norm is rarely the responsibility of a specified punisher, as it might be where a violation of state-made law is concerned. While it is possible for a punishment to be collectively administered, it's quite common for punishments to be doled out by individuals. When punishment decisions are individual, there is little ability to coordinate amongst individuals to make sure that the total amount of punishment to which a violator is subjected is proportionate to the offense.

Collectively-delivered punishment might take a variety of forms. Her community might ostracize a violator for some period of time, or deny her access to some local public good or common resource. This sort of punishment can be scaled to the offense and can take past (mis-) behavior into account fairly straightforwardly. But if punishment is carried out by individuals, its *scale* will depend not on some kind of rationalized sense of proportionality but rather on the number of people who happen to pile on.

For instance, imagine a community with a social norm calling for church attendance on Sundays. If an individual fails to attend, many—perhaps most—members of the community may choose independently to impose a punishment. Even if the punishment is mild—the retraction of a party invitation, a scolding, or perhaps even just a pointed eye-roll—those mild punishments add up. There is both the aggregate cost of all of the various punishments *and* the sense of being broadly attacked by one's community. This isn't terribly different from, say, middle school behaviors: a student commits what her peers perceive as a faux pas—and suffers ridicule far out of proportion to the putative transgression. The cost includes not only the totality of the punitive injuries but also the exclusion and subordination effected by the pile-on itself. An obvious variant on this phenomenon is apparent on social media platforms like Twitter. The sheer scale of participation in a popular platform is such that a single disfavored tweet can lead to mountains of vitriol. Even if the tweet merited a rebuke, there is no way to scale the rebuke to match the offense—if anything, as more people pile on, additional would-be punishers find the prospect of joining in attractive. The social media example is extreme, of course, but it highlights the possibility that there can be significant and unrestrained harms that flow from the mechanisms of norms enforcement.

C. Invasiveness

John Stuart Mill notes that there are two kinds of tyranny: the familiar tyranny of the sovereign—when the state uses its monopoly on violence to enforce unjust laws—and the tyranny of the majority—when society itself imposes punishments on those who deviate from prevailing opinion and practice. Mill considered this latter kind of tyranny especially pernicious.

> Society can and does execute its own mandates: and if it issues wrong mandates instead of right, or any mandates at all in things with which it ought not to meddle, it practises a social tyranny more formidable than many kinds of political oppression, since, though not usually upheld by such extreme penalties, it leaves fewer means of escape, penetrating much more deeply into the details of life, and enslaving the soul itself.[9]

The powerful idea here is that (at least absent modern surveillance technologies) it is easy enough to evade monitoring by the state. There simply aren't enough agents of the state, and, at least under liberal regimes, the scope of state activity is limited and reasonably well defined. By contrast, unless one gives up on sociality, there is no escape from one's neighbors. Social monitoring is constant. Social rules are frequently arbitrary, and there is no reason to believe that their content will be subject to limits on scope; the only constraint on the emergence or the substance of new social rules is the existence or content of old social rules.

Social coordination by means of social norms and conventions can be incredibly stifling. A thousand petty tyrants, all relishing the opportunity to impose their wills on others, can belong to any community. And, indeed, petty tyranny is just what we frequently observe in smaller, stable, and more homogeneous communities. The kind of environment that is often described as high in "bonding capital" and thus rich in community solidarity and trust is also the kind of environment likely to feature robust common attitudes, beliefs, and practices. The commonality of these attitudes, beliefs, and practices isn't coincidental. Instead, they are, broadly speaking, socially mandated.

If your values and interests happen to be well aligned with those of the rest of the community, the rich set of norms requiring the behaviors associated with these values and interests will be a source of comfort. Those norms help the dispositions supporting the relevant behaviors to remain stable while quickly suppressing attempts at deviation. But, of course, if you find yourself out of step with these norms, then there really are "fewer means of escape, penetrating much more deeply into the details of life, and enslaving the soul itself." The existence of social connections means the existence of abundant opportunities for careful social monitoring and sanction. Thus, as Mill observes, social norms can be particularly pernicious sources of coercion. Any given social sanction may be quite small; but the overall effect can easily be crushing.

D. Absence of Intentional Control

A last worry with social norms is that there aren't good tools for exercising intentional control over them. A legal system features mechanisms that instantiate Hart's Secondary Rules—the rules of recognition, the rules of change, and the rules of adjudication. The rules of recognition ensure that there's a straightforward way to *identify* the rules. The rules of change outline the mechanism for adding new rules and modifying or eliminating existing ones. And the rules of adjudication outline procedures for determining whether a rule has been violated, and, if so, what sanctions or remedies should follow. These rules help define the formal conditions for a reasonable *system* of rules: you should know what the rules to which you will be subjected *are*, there should be a process to determine whether you've broken the rules, and there should be a way to change the rules. It is easy enough to see how these rules can be satisfied within formal institutions, but each of these secondary rules is harder to satisfy in an environment in which the primary rules are social norms.

The rule of recognition is difficult to satisfy in a norm-governed environment because communities don't ordinarily maintain lists of the norms they enforce—they just enforce these norms. A newcomer will only slowly get a sense of what the relevant rules may be by observing what others do and how people react to particular behaviors. The rule of adjudication doesn't apply cleanly where norm-violations are concerned, since individuals are empowered to judge violations of their communities' rules and punish them as they see fit. That they are means that punishments won't be clearly specified and makes it impossible to ensure that punishments are predictable or proportionate. And it is hard to see how there could be an articulated rule of change in an environment governed by social norms rather than formal laws.

While social norms certainly come and go, and while these norms sometimes are created by collective agreements, there is nothing close to a mechanism for norm change that is comparable to familiar mechanisms legal change. Laws can be difficult to change. But there are clear procedures for altering them. In the United States, for instance, if a bill amending an existing law gets the required number of votes in Congress and is signed by the President, the law has been changed. There is no comparable kind of formal procedure for changing a social norm. The members of a community can deliberate collectively and pledge to eliminate or change a norm, perhaps even agreeing to punish conformity to a now rejected norm, but the community's doing these things does not ensure the old norm's elimination. If people still believe that others expect the behavior for which the old norm called, it will persist.

The same is true where creating a new social norm is concerned. We can all announce our intentions to behave differently and to expect others to behave differently, but our doing so doesn't mean we will all adopt new behaviors. Collective behavior change is remarkably difficult to bring about, even when all of a community's members agree that their behavior should change. Because social norms are epistemic equilibria, people need to be quite confident that past behavior is no longer a guide for future behavior.

V. A Way Forward

Social norms are double-edged. On the one hand, they provide the social tools necessary for achieving non-state social cooperation on a sustainable basis. On the other hand, social norms can be even more coercive than state-maintained laws and regulations. What's more, the kind of coercion they effect is harder to control because of the distributed nature of norm enforcement, and it is very hard to eliminate social norms once they come into being. This tradeoff—less state-driven coercion in exchange for arbitrary and unbounded coercion by one's neighbors—will strike most people as thoroughly unattractive. Maintaining social order using social norms avoids *state* coercion, but it need not yield a reduction in interference or coercion full-stop. Being free of the state does not necessarily mean being free *simpliciter.*

However, there is a way forward. We can make a pattern of social order maintenance rooted in social norms more appealing by finding ways to *weaken* norms, and in particular, to make *arbitrary* norms more difficult to establish. How can we draw on the theory of norms to create environments in which truly *coordinating* norms can take hold, while more contingent norms that merely stifle individual expression lose (or never acquire) vitality? Broadly speaking, the answer is: by fostering an environment hostile to the development of too much *bonding* capital but friendly to the development of *bridging* capital. What we want, in short, is a diverse community, ideally with a reasonable amount of churn in the population and with deep bonds limited to relative intimates.

Homogeneous populations, and ones in which most people are united by cultural, ideological, ethnic, or similar characteristics, are fecund breeding grounds for the emergence of contingent and often irrational social norms. The more a (temporary) behavioral commonality obtains, the easier it is for us to perceive that a social rule is present, and the more likely an arbitrary norm will emerge. By contrast, in a social environment featuring a wide variety of different behaviors, it will be harder for one of these many behaviors to be *perceived* accidentally as a social rule and thus to evolve in to a real (but unreasonable) social rule. Population churn likewise makes social rules more difficult to establish because it is much more difficult to establish stable, mutual social expectations when the population shifts significantly on an ongoing basis. Every new entrant will need to learn relevant rules, and while they are doing so their non-conforming behaviors will weaken norms that aren't already being strictly followed.

While diversity and population churn work to create a relatively hostile environment for *arbitrary* norms, they are less hostile to actually useful *coordinating* norms. The kinds of rules we really *need* if we are to live together—basic agreements on what rights people can claim against each other, mechanisms for dispute resolution, norms of promise-keeping, and so on—possess selection advantages in any community no matter what the makeup of the community's population. No matter who belongs to a community, its members will *always* have reasons to want rules of this sort. It is in everyone's interest for settled rules to exist. The incentives for the adoption of such rules are not sufficient on their own to lead a community's members to select just one particular set of social rules, but they will eliminate a number from contention. The scope of arbitrary restrictions on individual freedom will be much smaller when rules must emerge in an environment in which diverse people want very different things from life. Rules in this kind of environment will more closely resemble the sorts of rules needed to effect an "open society"—rules that foster tolerance.

If rules like these are in effect, a variety of goods may prove harder to achieve—after all, fewer people will robustly embrace the same moral views—but coercion will also be substantially less likely. The characteristics one can expect a society to exhibit, given such rules, are likely to be those evident in, for instance, high-trade locations like port cities: tolerance, respect for robust negative rights, and greater dynamism and experimentation. The occurrence of these characteristics *does* carry costs—notably the absence of the rich set of social interconnections possible in high-bonding-capital communities. Community rules could not be used to pursue communitarian ideals or pressure people to embrace particular perfectionist ideals. A more diverse environment featuring more minimal rules will encourage more individualized values and, plausibly, a greater focus on material cultural, since material culture is more easily shared amongst diverse people.

Homogeneous communities governed by social norms can all too readily adopt arbitrary coercive norms, just as monocultures in farming are vulnerable to pests and disease. Too much similarity allows for harmful norms to take root easily. A more diverse society can respond more robustly to the kinds of harms likely to result from greater ease of coordination—in part because such a society is more inhospitable than a more homogenous one to *any* sort of coordination. The only coordinative rules likely to survive are ones that can be recognized as advantageous from a variety of perspectives. Social norms thrive in parochial environments; in less parochial settings, therefore, far fewer norms can take hold.

VI. Conclusion

Social norms are incredibly powerful social tools. They are viable alternatives to more formal institutional arrangements. But social norms can be even more coercive than formal, state-made laws, and even more arbitrary. Social norms are also more resistant to change. If we are to succeed in moving away from formal institutional arrangements, we need to foster robustly diverse communities, so we can more easily mitigate against the harmful excesses that can occur when a society relies on social norms to maintain order. Social diversity makes social norms far more difficult to entrench, so encouraging diversity in a society can help to ensure that the norms that persist are genuinely valuable.

Notes

1 See Cristina Bicchieri, *The Grammar of Society* (New York: CUP 2006).

2 See Ryan Muldoon, "Understanding Norms and Changing Them," *Social Philosophy and Policy* 35.1 (2018): 128–48.

3 For mechanisms in virtue of which this can take place, see Ryan Muldoon et al., "On the Emergence of Descriptive Norms," *Politics, Philosophy, and Economics* 13.1 (2012): 3–22; and Ryan Muldoon, Chiara Lisciandra, and Stephen Hartmann, "Why Are There Descriptive Norms? Because We Looked for Them," *Synthese* 191 (2014): 4409–29.

4 See Elinor Ostrom, *Governing the Commons: The Evolution of Institutions for Collective Action* (Cambridge: CUP 1990).

5 For one classic argument to this effect, see Michael Taylor, *Community, Anarchy and Liberty* (Cambridge: CUP 1982).

6 Cp. Muldoon et al. and Muldoon, Lisciandra, and Hartmann.

7 David Hume, *A Treatise of Human Nature*, L.A. Selby–Bigge and P.H. Nidditch (eds.) (Oxford: Clarendon Press 1978 [1739]) 490.

8 See Ryan Muldoon, "Perspectives, Norms and Agency," *Social Philosophy and Policy* 34.1 (2017): 260–76 for a more detailed account.

9 John Stuart Mill, *On Liberty* (New York: Scott 2011 [1859]) 8, www.gutenberg.org/files/34901/34901-h/34901-h.htm.

20
ANARCHY AND LAW

Jonathan Crowe

I. Introduction

Can there be law without the state? The notion strikes many people as odd or counterintuitive. Law is so closely associated in the contemporary mindset with the promulgations of government authorities that it is hard to disentangle the two ideas. I begin this chapter by exploring the conception of law that underpins this mindset, as reflected in *legal positivism*, the dominant school of thought in contemporary legal philosophy. The most influential version of legal positivism, I argue, does not necessarily rule out law without the state. However, it favours a centralised or systematic view of legal institutions, due mainly to the link it draws between the notion of legal validity and the normative practices of legal officials. The acceptance of this kind of connection in contemporary social and political discourse partly explains why law under anarchy is hard for people to imagine.

I go on to explore three alternative understandings of law that are more conducive to the idea of legal order without state authority. The first is the idea of *consensual law*, embodied not only in contracts and other voluntary legal and social agreements but also in common forms of dispute resolution, such as arbitration and mediation. The second is the concept of *emergent law*, which conceptualises law as a form of spontaneous order, analogous to the price system or the norms of language. The third is the notion of *natural law*, which focuses on shared normative inclinations attributable to facts about human nature and developed over time in response to the social environment. Each of these conceptions, I argue, represents a form of law-like social ordering that does not depend on recognition by centralised legal authorities. The convergence of these three ideas therefore offers a compelling picture of how law might operate under anarchy.

I conclude by discussing three challenges commonly posed to the notion of law without the state. The first concerns *obedience and enforcement*: why would people obey the law in the absence of state coercion? The second concerns the potential for *gaps in the law*: how would law under anarchy deal with lawbreakers, outlaws, and vulnerable members of the community? And the third concerns the *rule of law*: how would law uphold important constitutional values such as consistency, prospectivity, and coherence without centralised institutions? I suggest that a picture of law under anarchy that draws on the three forms of law discussed previously—consensual law, emergent law, and natural law—offers a credible response to these potential challenges. Law under anarchy would not be perfect, but it is certainly feasible—and offers some advantages over what we have now.

II. Legal Positivism

Legal philosophy today is dominated, for better or worse,[1] by legal positivism—the view that the only necessary factor in determining whether something counts as law is recognition by social sources.[2] Early versions of legal positivism contained a strong bias towards statist conceptions of legal authority. John Austin, widely viewed as the founder of legal positivism,[3] famously defines law as the command of a sovereign, backed up by sanctions.[4] Austin's notion of a sovereign is premised on the notion of a single, dominant source of legal authority within a given jurisdiction. The sovereign is defined as that authority whom everyone habitually obeys and who, in turn, habitually obeys nobody.[5] Austin's theory is therefore unable to accommodate less centralised forms of legal order, including those found in international and customary law. These normative orders, according to Austin, are not law "strictly so called"; rather, they are forms of "positive morality."[6]

The limitations of Austin's definition of law were famously critiqued by H. L. A. Hart, generally acknowledged as the central figure of contemporary analytical jurisprudence. Hart's theory of law deliberately abandons Austin's emphasis on the commands of the sovereign in favour of an analysis of law as a system of social rules.[7] People comply with these rules not primarily because they fear sanctions, but rather because they treat them as conferring obligations.[8] Legal rules are distinguished from other social rules (such as rules of morality and etiquette) by reference to an overarching *rule of recognition* that designates those social sources capable of conferring legal validity. The rule of recognition is itself a social rule stemming from the practices of legal officials.[9] Essentially, something counts as law, for Hart, because legal officials within the jurisdiction recognise it as arising from the kind of source (and being enacted by means the kind of procedure) needed to confer legal status upon it.

Hart's theory of law (unlike Austin's) is not necessarily incompatible with non-state forms of legal order, such as legal regimes rooted in contract or custom. Contractual legal norms can be recognised as stemming from the kinds of processes that enable them to count as legally binding if their status is acknowledged by the secondary rules of the relevant jurisdiction. Indeed, Hart views his theory's ability to accommodate the binding nature of contracts and other legal agreements as one of its main advantages.[10] The legal force of a commercial or marital contract, he points out, does not come directly from the sovereign (as Austin's theory might appear to suggest), but rather from the voluntary agreement of the parties, which is then recognised as binding by legal officials.[11] A similar point applies to laws that arise from social mechanisms other than authority or agreement. An appropriately inclusive rule of recognition, for example, could recognise customary norms as legally valid.

Hart's analysis nonetheless remains less than ideally suited to accommodate the notion of law without the state. This is for four interrelated reasons. None of these reasons, on its own, is fatal to the concept of law under anarchy, but together they show the limitations of Hart's perspective. First, Hart's analysis of law as a species of social rule relies heavily on state-based examples. The paradigm case of law, for Hart, is clearly a law promulgated, recognised, or enforced by a state authority, such as a legislature or judge.[12] His theory of law seems primarily intended to explain these kinds of cases. The problem posed by contract law, for example—a problem that Austin's theory fails adequately to answer—is framed primarily in terms of explaining the nature of the rules applied by state officials in *recognising* certain kinds of contracts as valid and others as unenforceable.[13] The main exception to Hart's focus on traditional state-made law is his discussion of international law (which he sees as the body of law governing relationships *between* states).[14]

Second, Hart's theory tends to emphasise law's centralised or systematic character. The rule of recognition supplies a generic source-based test for legal validity. The legal status of individual norms then depends on whether they have been posited by social sources recognised as authoritative in accordance with this overarching rule. The rule of recognition, to be sure, may be complex and multifaceted,[15] recognising a diversity of authoritative legal sources. It is therefore compatible with a limited form of legal pluralism. Nonetheless, the idea that the validity of all laws within a given jurisdiction can be traced back to a single overarching rule—no matter how complex—fits most neatly with the paradigm of state-made law, in accordance with which all laws enjoy the imprimatur of a single dominant institution. It is less well adapted to deal with genuine cases of legal pluralism, involving multiple independent (and perhaps competing) sets of legal norms operating within the same or overlapping jurisdictions.[16] It therefore sits uneasily with purely consent-based or customary legal orders, which may emerge organically from diverse sources.

Third (and relatedly), Hart's theory struggles fully to accommodate the notion of customary law. The rule of recognition in a given community could accept certain types of customary norms as binding law if they are recognised as such by the practices of legal officials. However, Hart doubts that a *purely* customary set of primary norms is capable of qualifying as law in the full sense of the term.[17] It would, he claims, face serious problems stemming from its lack of an overarching rule of recognition (as well as secondary rules of adjudication and change).[18] Law, for Hart, must be systematised in order to function effectively—at least to the extent required in order for there to be stable and reliable rules governing the exercise of legal powers. Hart seems to assume that resolving this issue requires a significant degree of centralisation of legal authority.[19] This strongly suggests, even if it does not strictly require, a coordinating role for state institutions.

Finally, and perhaps most importantly, Hart's account of the rule of recognition places heavy emphasis on the practices of legal officials. The rule of recognition, for Hart, depends on what would be regarded as authoritative legal sources not by members of the community at large but by the officials tasked with administering and enforcing the rules.[20] Hart seems to doubt whether the normative practices of the community at large would be coherent enough to yield a determinate set of criteria for legal validity,[21] with the result that he focuses instead on the practices of officials. Hart does not say anywhere that the legal officials in question must be *government* officials; they could, in theory, be church officials or other recognised social authorities.[22] Nonetheless, he seems clearly to have state officials in mind. Furthermore, this aspect of his theory seems to rule out radically dispersed forms of legal ordering that do not depend on any centralised source of authority (such as the consensual and emergent forms of law I discuss later in this chapter). Hart's conception of the rule of recognition is therefore less than fully hospitable to law under anarchy.

The general contours of Hart's form of legal positivism are, I think, reflected in popular assumptions about the nature of law and legal validity. The idea of law is closely associated in everyday social and political discussions with the pronouncements of state authorities, such as executive officers, legislators, and judges. People often seem to think about law as something that emanates from the state and its legitimating institutions (such as the constitution from which the state purports to derive its authority); they therefore habitually defer to government agents for authoritative statements of legal sources and contents. This popular view of law is readily explained by political realities. The state's hegemony over political and social power may well lead people to feel that they have little choice but to accept the state's claim to ultimate authority over law's sources and contents. Hartian legal positivism has the merit of explaining how people think about law under these conditions, but it arguably lacks the radical potential other conceptions of law may exhibit for undermining or interrogating the state's hold on power.

III. Decentralising Law

I have argued that Hart's interpretation of the legal positivist outlook tends to encourage the view that recognition by state sources is central—if not essential—to the notion of legal validity.

His emphasis on the role of the rule of recognition and its foundation in the practice of legal officials, while not strictly limited to state institutions, favours a more or less centralised and systematic conception of legal authority. I now want to explore three alternative understandings of law that are more conducive than Hart's theory to the idea of law under anarchy; I will them call *consensual law*, *emergent law*, and *natural law* respectively. Law in a stateless society may not feature centralised legal institutions or a unified rule of recognition, but it could nonetheless be expected to feature stable and reliable legal norms and institutions arising from these three kinds of legal ordering.

A stateless society, in other words, could be ordered by the following non-centralised and non-coercive mechanisms: (1) people's voluntary consent to be bound by contracts and other kinds of agreements, as a way of both forming primary obligations and creating secondary institutions (*consensual law*); (2) the normative, psychological, and sociological pull exerted by evolved legal and social norms, formed and entrenched over time through a process of spontaneous order (*emergent law*); and (3) the normative, psychological, and sociological impetus provided by human normative dispositions, derived from a combination of biological and social causes, and refined through individual and collective decision processes (*natural law*). These three processes would combine to provide a normative framework for social interaction. The following sections examine these ideas in turn.

A. Consensual Law

Hart's account, as we have seen, relies on the idea that law gains its validity from recognition by the normative practices of legal officials. However, the notion of consensual law rejects this assumption. Rather, it views law as a body of norms freely agreed upon by members of the community to order their conduct with respect to one another. This need not involve recognition by any centralised form of legal authority. Consensual law is far from an abstract notion that could only be expected to exist under conditions of anarchy. It plays a central role in most contemporary legal systems. Every time two or more people make a contract or agreement that they accept as legally binding, they create legal norms that order their conduct with respect to one another. Agreements of this sort might involve exchanges of goods and services, interpersonal relationships such as marriages, or settlement of existing disputes.

Hart, as we have seen, emphasised his theory's ability to explain how these kinds of agreements can be recognised as binding by legal officials through the application of the relevant secondary rules.[23] However, as far as the parties to the agreement are concerned, what matters most is not whether legal officials are prepared to recognise their agreement as legally binding, but whether *they themselves* recognise it as binding with respect to *each other*. One reason, to be sure, why parties might see an agreement as binding is because they know (or predict) that it will be enforced by the courts if required. However, most contractual agreements are highly unlikely ever to be litigated. Consider, for example, the agreement I make with the local grocery store when I buy a packet of chewing gum for $2.00. This agreement is an effective mechanism of social ordering in the most direct and obvious sense: namely, it serves to ensure that I end up with the gum and the store ends up with $2.00. The likelihood that this kind of agreement will end up in court is extremely low.[24]

Similarly, two people who marry each other in their local church (or, for that matter, in their backyard) typically make a series of commitments that carry serious weight between them. These commitments are legally binding in the most important sense: they order the conduct of the parties concerned. It may be important to them, for various reasons, that their marriage is recognised by the state, but typically what matters more to them is that it is recognised by each other. The role of the state in each of these cases is a secondary one: if the state ceased to exist tomorrow, there would still be contracts of sale and marriage in much the same way as before. They would still effectively order the conduct of the parties. Why, then, should we think the legal validity of such agreements depends on official acknowledgement?

The notion of consensual law can be extended beyond interpersonal agreements to institutional mechanisms. A number of existing models show how voluntary legal institutions might operate. Most commercial disputes are already resolved by negotiation, mediation, or arbitration rather than by the courts. Family law disputes about matters such as separation and parenting are also often resolved by mediation. Indeed, the proportion of social disputes actually resolved in the formal court system is extremely low. These methods could continue to operate in much the same way without the state. There are also examples of how different sets of legal institutions can resolve potential conflicts. International law is primarily based on the consent of states to be bound by treaties between them (although the role of customary international law complicates this picture somewhat). International courts, tribunals, and other enforcement methods are also traditionally consent-based.[25]

What role does state-made law play in these kinds of dispute resolution mechanisms? It is often said that mediation and other forms of dispute resolution take place in "the shadow of the law,"[26] meaning that parties bargain against the implicit baseline of what they think they would receive in court. However, recent empirical studies caution against placing too much weight on this assumption.[27] Other factors may matter far more to the parties than their perceived legal entitlements, including maintaining business relationships, moving on with their lives, or staying true to their cultural or religious values. Furthermore, even where parties road-test proposals by reference to their legal positions, this may depend less on official state-made law than on the "folk law" they absorb from other members of their communities.[28]

B. Emergent Law

Consensual law represents one way in which recognisably law-like methods of social ordering can emerge without relying on the acknowledgement of any centralised legal authority. A second way in which this might occur is through what I call *emergent law*. Emergent law is a set of customary legal standards that emerges as a form of spontaneous order. The leading contemporary account of emergent law is perhaps that found in the writings of Friedrich Hayek. Hayek argues that many of our most fundamental legal rules, like those against murder or in favour of keeping contracts, cannot be traced back to any originating act by a legislator, a judge, or another official.[29] Rather, legal rules of this kind emerged organically over time as ways for members of a community to coordinate their behaviour and live harmoniously together—coming into existence well before their codification. In this respect, they resemble other customary social norms, like norms of grammar, spelling, and etiquette.

What, then, is the process by which customary social norms arise? A compelling answer to this question can be found in the notion of spontaneous order that is central to evolutionary theories of law and economics. The customs governing a spontaneous order are not planned in advance. As the Scottish philosopher Adam Ferguson puts it, "many human institutions are the result of human action, but not … of any human design."[30] However, this does not mean that the relevant rules are purely random. Rather, they develop over time through processes of trial and error conducted in the course of repeated social interactions. The price system in economics offers an instructive example.[31] Prices aggregate the information available to discrete actors in an economic market and expressed in individual transactions. They enable this information to be communicated between participants in the market, sending signals about the relative supply and demand of various goods and services.

The price system is highly dynamic—it adjusts constantly as players in the market take account of new information and use it to guide their choices. This mechanism cannot be expected to lead to perfect coordination of preferences under actual market conditions, but it arguably plays this role more effectively than any other method available, given the deep challenges presented by economic coordination.[32] The idea that prices play a coordinating function without any deliberate planning is famously expressed in Adam Smith's metaphor of the invisible hand.[33] Prices are not arbitrary, but reflect the flow of information in the market, aggregated through an iterative process involving large numbers of individual transactions. This makes them *look* planned, but in fact it is precisely their unplanned character that makes them effective sources of order. Hayek describes the price system as a tool that humans have "stumbled upon it without understanding it."[34]

The mechanisms of spontaneous order are not confined to economics. Smith argues that *moral* norms can likewise be understood as unintended but desirable consequences of the interactions of members of a community. Our natural desire for mutual sympathy, Smith contends, means we continually imagine ourselves in the positions of others.[35] The consequent realisation that others do not always share our priorities leads us to temper our self-interest so that our motivations attract general approval. This desire to bring our priorities into harmony with the expectations of others leads us to adopt something like the perspective of a disinterested bystander.[36] The system of moral norms arising from this procedure will tend to support social harmony, since it aggregates the preferences of many individuals. Social interaction can therefore produce normative consensus in roughly the same way in which economic markets produce agreements regarding prices.[37]

In a spontaneous order, then, people adopt the practices they think will best enable them to pursue their individual goals and coexist with others in society. If the practices people adopt do not work, they are abandoned in favour of others. In this way, people across a community will come by processes of trial and error to accept common social rules. A trial-and-error process of rule-formation is by no means infallible, but neither is it arbitrary. Law as spontaneous order—or what I am calling emergent law—thus has the potential to serve as a stable, predictable, and adaptive mode of social ordering. It does so, however, without necessarily relying on the imprimatur of the state or any other centralised legal authority. Indeed, Hayek argues that attempts by political authorities to improve customary law are often counter-productive because of the inherent limitations of human knowledge and foresight.[38]

Hayek regards the common law system as another example of spontaneous order.[39] Judges in the common law tradition are bound by the doctrine of *stare decisis* to follow prior decisions. They look at the underlying principles in previous cases to decide what outcome is most consistent with social expectations. The common law method involves making decisions about individual disputes rather than trying to formulate abstract rules intended to apply to diverse future scenarios. Hayek argues that the common law approach brings stability to the law by ensuring that it tracks underlying social norms. The law changes gradually, through the development of precedent, rather than suddenly, through fundamental or radical change.

The common law method thus ensures that law reflects aggregated information about actual disputes rather than being based on simplified models of social interaction. Importantly, however, the common law operates in this way *not* because the judges who develop it happen to be state agents but rather because it is a form of spontaneous order. Voluntary dispute resolution mechanisms of the type discussed in Subsection III.A. could embody this kind of process just as well as state courts, provided only that the adjudicators (or the parties, in the case of non-adjudicative processes) explicitly or implicitly seek coherence with evolved social expectations. It is likely that they would do so—to the same or perhaps a greater extent than state-appointed judges—primarily because the legitimacy in the eyes of the community of the decisions reached by the adjudicators (or parties) would depend upon their doing so. I return to this point later in the chapter.

C. Natural Law

Consensual law and emergent law both order social conduct in stable, reliable, and non-arbitrary ways without necessarily invoking the imprimatur of the state. Natural law plays a similar role. The idea of natural law, as I use it here, is the notion of a set of idealised normative inclinations characteristic of humans by virtue of their shared nature. This definition requires some unpacking.

"Normative inclinations," as I use the term here, involve two components: a disposition to *act* in a specific way and a disposition to *believe* that the action in question is worthwhile or required.[40] Every person possesses a wide range of normative inclinations, so defined. However, there are certain kinds of normative inclinations so widely shared by humans across different cultural contexts as to be aptly described as characteristic of humans as members of a species. The existence of these shared normative inclinations can plausibly be explained by certain facts about human nature.

My use of the term "human nature" is meant to encompass a range of natural facts about humans (roughly, the kinds of facts that can be analysed by the natural and social sciences).[41] I include in this term both facts about human biology and facts about the human social condition. An example might help to illustrate the role these facts play in natural law theorising. Humans across a wide range of different cultural contexts both act in such a way as to preserve familial and neighbourly bonds and believe that such bonds are inherently worthy of preservation. The value of friendship or social connectedness, in other words, is a widely recognised human good (at least at a familial or local level).[42] This normative inclination can plausibly be explained by a combination of facts about human biology (for example, the evolved biological drive to protect one's family and tribe[43]) and facts about the human social condition (for example, the desirability of cooperating with one's immediate familial and social unit to secure food, shelter, and personal safety).

A theory of natural law cannot, however, be simply a description of human normative *inclinations*. This is for two interrelated reasons. First, at an a priori level, a theory of natural law that aims to have moral weight must do more than simply recount empirical facts about human behaviour. Otherwise, it would fall foul of David Hume's famous injunction against deriving moral propositions from factual observations (the "is-ought gap").[44] Second, at an a posteriori level, there are many normative inclinations that are plausibly characteristic of humans that one would not wish to include within a moralised conception of natural law. For example, humans across a wide range of cultural contexts show a disposition to treat out-group members (such as members of other racial or cultural assortments) less favourably than in-group members, and believe they are justified in doing so.[45] This normative inclination can be explained by reference to human biological and social conditions, but it nonetheless sits poorly with many people's considered moral principles.

It is for this reason that I described natural law at the beginning of this section as a set of *idealised* normative inclinations. A theory of natural law, in other words, must provide some method for distinguishing those normative inclinations that serve us well, morally speaking, from those that do not. The suggestion I have made elsewhere is that a theory of natural law is an attempt to capture those normative inclinations that we would hold under ideal conditions of *full imaginative immersion*.[46] Imaginative immersion, in this sense, involves reflecting on the ultimate ends that humans are disposed to value; considering the roles of these goods in one's practical deliberations; extrapolating each deliberation to a range of other contexts; considering what it would be like to both enjoy the good and experience its privation; and considering what it would mean, in diverse circumstances, to treat the good as valuable both for oneself and for others. This process may be expected to yield a fuller understanding of what is truly valuable for humans given their nature *and* what it means to respond *appropriately* to what is valuable.

This conception of natural law, despite the idealisation it involves, is nonetheless salient for human social ordering. This is because something like the full imaginative immersion that forms part of this conception is employed (albeit imperfect) in actual human decision procedures. First, individual humans approximate imaginative immersion when they reflect on the reasons for their practical decisions, considering the implications of these decisions for other cases and situating them in relation to wider explanatory principles and theories, either on their own or (more commonly) in dialogue with others. Second, dispute resolution procedures approximate imaginative immersion when they bring the interests of the parties into dialogue with each other and seek acceptable resolutions. This may occur in an adjudicative process when the decision-maker considers both sides of the story before reaching a decision. It may also occur in a non-adjudicative process, such as a mediation, through direct or mediated communication between the parties.

Third, human *societies* approximate imaginative immersion—on a diachronic, as opposed to a merely synchronic, level—when they draw upon emergent social norms as guides to ethical action and dispute resolution. Emergent social norms, as I observed in the previous section, aggregate the experiences of a wide range of social agents over time. Their dispersed and diachronic character counteracts, to some extent, the idiosyncratic biases of individual agents or social groupings. This is not to deny, of course, that emergent social norms will still reflect the entrenched biases of society as a whole, potentially including discriminatory attitudes of multiple varieties. They therefore remain imperfect. But they are nonetheless important sources of aggregated social knowledge about the kinds of normative inclinations that survive generalisation over a variety of different cases and generations.

Every human community possesses a store of practical knowledge—we might call it a *tradition*[47]—about the forms of life that are best suited to enable members of the community to flourish in their natural and social environment. This body of knowledge typically reflects all three of the mechanisms outlined above: normative reflection and discussion, communal dispute resolution (in both adjudicative and non-adjudicative forms), and normative social evolution. The resulting folk theory of human flourishing approximates, albeit imperfectly, the ideal conditions for natural law theorising. It therefore carries defeasible normative weight. Natural law, in this socially embodied sense, represents an important source of social ordering that supplements and supports the consensual and emergent mechanisms I discussed previously. It guides human conduct in stable and constructive ways without necessarily relying on centralised legal authority.

IV. Law without the State

I began this chapter by asking whether there can be law without the state. I then discussed the bias towards centralised legal authority found in contemporary legal positivism, before examining three alternative conceptions of law: consensual law, emergent law, and natural law. When combined, these three conceptions offer a rich account of varied ways in which law can exist without the state. They show how law-like forms of order can emerge, adapt, and persist in a complex society without relying on the state or any other form of centralised institution. In the remainder of this chapter, I develop this suggestion further, exploring how these three forms of law might combine to address three commonly posed challenges to the notion of law under anarchy.

I will begin by exploring some issues relating to obedience and enforcement. Would people obey the law in a stateless society? How would legal norms be enforced without centralised institutions? Next, I will consider the issue of gaps in legal institutions. How would law under anarchy deal with lawbreakers, outlaws, and vulnerable members of the community? Aren't there risks that people in these categories will fall outside the legal system without some centralised authority to close the gaps? Finally, I will consider some issues posed by the notion of the rule of law. Could law in a stateless society respect the rule of law? Doesn't the rule of law presuppose some level of centralisation that ensures consistency and coherence? I will suggest that, taken together, the three forms of non-state law canvassed previously in this chapter supply a robust foundation for responding to each of these challenges.

A. Obedience and Enforcement

A stateless society might reasonably be expected to feature the three kinds of legal ordering discussed above: consensual law, emergent law, and natural law. Why, though, would people obey the legal norms arising from these sources? Wouldn't they only do so when it suits them? The answer to this question partially depends on the more general issue of why people obey the law. It is tempting to assume that the effectiveness of law depends upon the availability of coercive sanctions. However, we should be wary of overstating the importance of fear in motivating obedience to the law. Empirical evidence suggests that people's most powerful motive for obeying the law is not the fear of being caught but rather the perception that the law is legitimate and therefore *warrants* their allegiance.[48] The vast majority of people in developed Western nations obey the law the vast majority of the time.[49] However, it's hard to explain this by pointing solely to formal enforcement. The total proportion of the population likely ever to subjected to criminal prosecution is fairly low, but most people who have never been in court nonetheless follow the law.

It might be said that it is the *threat* of legal action that keeps people in line rather than actual punishment. However, there are plenty of opportunities to commit crimes in everyday life without much risk of being caught. Petty theft, for example, remains relatively uncommon, despite the frequency with which people leave their belongings unattended in public settings. The vast majority of people simply pass up the repeated opportunities they confront to commit crimes. Hart sought to explain this phenomenon by emphasising the role of social pressure in securing compliance with legal rules. He famously argued that law does not get its force from the threat of punishment but rather from the sense of obligation it imposes.[50] We do not obey the law because we are forced to do so, as suggested by earlier theorists such as Austin. Rather, we obey it mainly because we feel a sense of social obligation. Social pressure to comply with law gives rise to a critical, reflective attitude in relation to our own behaviour.

Hart's analysis (which seems to enjoy empirical support) suggests that people would tend to obey the law even in the absence of centralised or coercive institutions. The most important factor in obedience to law is not the harshness of the sanctions attached to legal rules but rather the stability and perceived legitimacy of the associated social norms. A consensual or customary legal order without formal institutions might still be widely respected if there were consistent social pressure to comply with the relevant rules. The existence of such pressure seems to depend more on whether people see the law as procedurally fair than whether they fear coercive sanctions.[51] Legal obedience, then, does not necessarily depend on formal enforcement mechanisms. It will, however, be bolstered if legal norms and processes are seen as complying with the requirements of procedural justice, such as giving each party to a dispute a fair and equal hearing.[52]

It is important to note, in this respect, that a stateless society is unlikely to totally lack formal legal institutions. It will lack the *centralised* institutions maintained by the state, but a range of consent-based institutions might be expected to arise.[53] This might happen on an ad hoc basis when people engage a security firm to ward off a specific threat, or an arbitrator or mediator to resolve a particular dispute. However, it also seems likely to occur on a more organised and systematic basis. People might, for instance, decide to pay a fee to subscribe to a local security or dispute resolution agency rather than only employing such an agency when they encounter particular problems. A market for security and dispute resolution services would thus be likely to emerge. There might be several options available in a community. Firms that provide efficient, reliable, and procedurally fair dispute resolution options would enjoy market advantages over those that did not. Competing firms would have incentives to make agreements regarding the resolution of disputes between their clients. A firm linked by stable agreements with other leading dispute resolution providers would enjoy additional appeal in the market.

What rules would these dispute resolution providers apply in resolving disputes? Law without the state seems likely to exhibit pluralistic tendencies, as multiple security and dispute resolution service providers are likely to arise in any given community.[54] The infrastructure costs involved in providing such services are not obviously such as to create the likelihood of natural monopolies, although economies of scale might cause the number of providers to decrease over time. Different security agencies and dispute resolution services might choose to recognise different legal rules. People might choose to subscribe to particular agencies based at least partly on the rules different agencies chose to recognise. People might also choose their places of residence based on the rules prevailing in the local community. There are some obvious advantages to this. Legal rules could be responsive to local conditions or community values. People could exit communities with inefficient or unfair rules and move elsewhere, creating a competitive market in legal regimes.

On the other hand, it also seems likely that legal systems under anarchy would converge on a set of common basic rules. Dispute resolution providers would want their processes to be generally accepted and perceived as legitimate. They would therefore have reason to apply existing social norms—arising from consensual, emergent, and natural law sources—rather than inventing their own arbitrary rules.[55] The theories of spontaneous order offered by authors such as Hayek suggest that trial and error tends to lead communities to settle on shared rules of conduct over time. Ineffective and unfair legal rules are likely to be modified or abandoned, especially if they are subject to competition from more effective and equitable approaches. Convergence between different legal regimes would also make interaction between different dispute resolution providers easier (and ease of interaction among providers would surely be attractive to consumers). Providers would therefore have an incentive to standardise their rules and, in particular, to recognise the norms of conduct embraced by wider social institutions.

B. Lawbreakers and the Vulnerable

What if a person refused to join any of the available security or dispute resolution services (even when involved in disputes with others), preferring to rely on her own means of protection and remain outside the reach of the law? A person like this would be a free rider, as she would benefit from the social stability provided by security and dispute resolution services without paying the services' fees. However, the existence of such free riders would not need to present a serious problem so long as they remained uncommon when compared to fee-paying subscribers.[56] Security groups could make their own decisions about how to deal with those who declined their services. This might include choosing not to protect such people from aggression. Services' unwillingness to provide protective services to non-members would create strong incentives for individuals to join available security services. Outlaws would probably be uncommon, since existence as an outlaw would likely be perilous. However, if enough people declined to subscribe to local security services, their unwillingness to do so could encourage providers to be more responsive to local needs.

There might well be some organised groups that would flout community laws and rely on their own means of protection. These outlaw gangs could pose threats to social order. However, there's no obvious reason this problem would be more pronounced in a stateless society than it is under the state. Outlaw gangs present significant social challenges *now*. The state is far from immune to this problem. Indeed, the state arguably exacerbates the problem by aggressively pursuing drug prohibition and other forms of regulation, thereby increasing both the potential gains from illegal conduct and the risks of escalating tensions between organised criminal elements and state law enforcement agencies. People already marginalised by the state, such as undocumented immigrants and unlicensed business operators, are vulnerable in ways that encourage organised criminal activity. The overall incentive structures for outlaws might be significantly different in a stateless environment.

There is another potential concern about law in a stateless society. Even those who are sympathetic to the market provision of legal services often worry about vulnerable people falling through the gaps. What about those who can't afford to pay for protection and dispute resolution? Market incentives offer a partial response to this problem by encouraging service providers to innovate and fill gaps in the market. Services might be expected to be available at a variety of price points in response to local community needs. People might voluntarily subsidise those unable to afford legal services through cooperative and pro bono programs. Subscribers to security and dispute resolution services in a given community would also generate positive externalities for the vulnerable by increasing the general security and orderliness of the community. And it is important to remember that, as I noted above, legal obedience does not depend solely on the availability of formal enforcement. Nonetheless, there would still be gaps and inequalities in access to legal services in a stateless society. But the occurrence of these gaps and inequalities also poses a serious challenge for state-run institutions.[57] No known legal system is immune to this problem.

C. The Rule of Law

Would a legal system of the kind I imagine in this chapter support or undermine the rule of law? Lon L. Fuller's influential theory identifies eight indicia of the rule of law: generality, promulgation, prospectivity, clarity, consistency, observability, constancy, and congruence.[58] The overarching point of these requirements, according to Fuller, is to ensure that law fulfils its purpose of ordering human conduct in accordance with rules.[59] Hayek offers an extended argument to the effect that a decentralised legal system emphasising customary norms is better placed to play this role than one based on the operation of centralised institutions.[60] The top-down character of centralised law, for Hayek, makes it likely to contain prescriptive, detailed rules reflecting the plans and preferences of legislators. Emergent law, by contrast, is likely to emphasise general, end-independent rules compatible with a range of different value preferences and life plans. This kind of law is thus better suited to provide a stable, reliable guide to action for all members of a community.

Hayek doubts that legislators can access the depth and breadth of knowledge needed to solve complex social problems. Centralised law is therefore likely to prove inefficient and in need of constant change. Decentralised law, by contrast, runs less risk of locking in undesirable rules.[61] It allows for innovation and competition in legal norms, leading to more predictable and stable legal rules in the long run. Hayek further contends that a system of law based on spontaneous order tends to advance the value of liberty, understood as freedom from arbitrary coercion.[62] Any legal system restricts liberty by prohibiting people from violating its rules.[63] Hayek acknowledges that "in defining coercion we cannot take for granted the arrangements intended to prevent it."[64] However, a system of general, open-ended rules provides a stable structure within which individuals can live without the need for ongoing, complex discrimination between competing preferences.

Hayek's theory of emergent law, then, rests on the idea that a stable set of general rules outlining the personal sphere of each individual services as the social framework best suited to advance both knowledge and liberty. It helps expand the limits of human knowledge by allowing evolved social norms to direct economic and social action. It also facilitates human flourishing by allowing people to live their lives without the constant threat of arbitrary interference. Hayek contends that this framework is best realised by a classical liberal model of government involving a minimal state constrained by reliable and transparent constitutional rules. Emergent law can evolve and flourish within such a framework.

However, Hayek's position assumes that it is possible to keep state power within reliable constitutional boundaries. There are both historical and conceptual reasons to doubt this assumption. The historical evidence can easily be seen by examining the modes of governance prevailing in modern constitutional democracies. There is not a single case of a modern state in which constitutional government and the rule of law have prevented the imposition of a vast array of administrative regulations.

A compelling explanation for the fact that the creation of the state leads inexorably to an expansion of its power can be found in James Buchanan's influential work with Gordon Tullock on the economics of public choice.[65] Buchanan and Tullock point out that political actors can be expected to respond to incentives in the same ways as other agents. They will be subject, like everyone else, to the human tendency to pursue individual self-interest.[66] They will wish to gain benefits for themselves and people like them while externalising the costs of their choices onto others in the community. The predictable outcome is "overinvestment in the public sector when the investment projects provide differential benefits or are financed from differential taxation."[67] The separation of powers allows judges to check legislatures, but authors like Robert Dahl and Mark Graber have noted that judges themselves are subject to incentives that make them likely to back political elites or strike politically expedient compromises in order to safeguard their own institutional power.[68]

The state, then, poses an inherent challenge to the rule of law, essentially because its activities necessarily involve and encourage the concentration of power. The concentration of power creates incentives for people to try to gain control of the system in order to promote their own interests. The end result is a system of laws at least partly tailored to furthering the values and priorities of particular privileged groups. A system of social order based on consensual law, emergent law, and natural law, on the other hand, disperses power. It is still vulnerable to capture by special interests, insofar as it relies upon security and dispute resolution services to administer and enforce norms. However, the power of these service providers can be expected to be less coercive and monopolistic than that of the state—if only because they do not have the benefit of the state's entrenched monopoly on violence. Law under anarchy would no doubt face its own problems of stability, compliance, and power imbalances. However, it's doubtful whether these would be any worse than the equivalent problems that currently beset state institutions.

V. Conclusion

A stateless society might reasonably be expected to feature the three kinds of legal ordering discussed above: consensual law, emergent law, and natural law. People would make agreements with others in order to trade, cooperate, and resolve disputes; they would then have incentives to keep those agreements in most cases. Their agreements would be supplemented and reinforced by evolved social, legal, and economic norms developed by the relevant communities in order to facilitate social coexistence and cooperation. And these agreements would be further supplemented and reinforced by the normative dispositions exhibited by community members in virtue of their shared human nature, refined through reflection, discussions, and negotiations with one another. These three mechanisms would combine to provide a stable and reliable (albeit imperfect) framework for social interaction.

Law without the state is certainly possible—not only conceptually, but also in reality. Would a stateless society produce a better variety of law than what we currently enjoy under the state? It's hard to be sure. However, the possibility is not as outlandish as most people initially think. Law under anarchy offers ways of dealing with the problems posed by obedience and enforcement, lawbreakers and the vulnerable, and the rule of law—and holds the potential to outperform the state in at least some of these areas. There is value in thinking through the possibilities and challenges presented by law in a stateless society; if nothing else, such an exercise can help us understand the failures of state-made law and think creatively about alternatives. We shouldn't simply assume that our current centralised model of law is the only possible option. There are other forms of law capable of promoting social order—and, in some respects, they could well serve us better than the form we have now.

Notes

1 I say for worse. See, for example, Jonathan Crowe, *Natural Law and the Nature of Law* (Cambridge: CUP 2019); Jonathan Crowe, "Natural Law Theories," *Philosophy Compass* 11.2 (2016): 91–101; Jonathan Crowe, "Law as an Artifact Kind," *Monash University Law Review* 40.3 (2014): 737–57; Jonathan Crowe, "Between Morality and Efficacy: Reclaiming the Natural Law Theory of Lon Fuller," *Jurisprudence* 5.1 (2014): 109–18.
2 Crowe, "Natural Law" 92–3.
3 Cp. H. L. A. Hart, "Introduction," John Austin, *The Province of Jurisprudence Determined* (London: Weidenfeld 1954) xvi.
4 Austin Lecture 1.
5 Austin 193–4.
6 Austin 140–1.
7 H. L. A. Hart, *The Concept of Law* (Oxford: Clarendon Press 1994) 56–7.
8 Hart, *Concept* 82–91.
9 Hart, *Concept* 94–5.
10 Hart, *Concept* 27–8, 33–4.
11 Hart, *Concept* 41, 96.
12 Hart, *Concept* 97–8.
13 Hart, *Concept* 28, 33–4.
14 Hart, *Concept* ch. 10.
15 Hart, *Concept* 263–8.
16 For discussion, see Jonathan Crowe, "The Limits of Legal Pluralism," *Griffith Law Review* 24 (2015): 314, 321–3.
17 Hart, *Concept* 91–9.
18 Hart, *Concept* 76–7.
19 Hart, *Concept* 97–8.
20 Hart, *Concept* 113–5.
21 Hart, *Concept* 114. I believe he was mistaken. Cp. Crowe, "Law."
22 Roger Cotterrell, *Law, Culture and Society* (Aldershot: Ashgate 2006) 37.
23 Hart, *Concept* 27–8, 33–4, 41, 96.
24 Of course, disputes may still arise in such cases: I may get sick from the gum, and sue the store for selling me an unfit product. However, whether or not something like that happens, the transaction itself still involves a legally valid agreement.
25 For discussion, see Jonathan Crowe and Kylie Weston-Scheuber, *Principles of International Humanitarian Law* (Cheltenham: Elgar 2013) 143–63.
26 Robert Mnookin and Lewis Kornhauser, "Bargaining in the Shadow of the Law: The Case of Divorce," *Yale Law Journal* 88 (1979): 950–97.
27 See, for example, Jonathan Crowe et al., "Bargaining in the Shadow of the Folk Law: Expanding the Concept of the Shadow of the Law in Family Dispute Resolution," *Sydney Law Review* 40.3 (2018) 319–38; Becky Batagol and Thea Brown, *Bargaining in the Shadow of the Law: The Case of Family Mediation* (Sydney: Federation 2011).
28 Crowe et al.
29 Friedrich A. Hayek, *Law, Legislation and Liberty*, 3 vols. (Chicago: U of Chicago P 1983) 1:72–144.

30 Adam Ferguson, *An Essay on the History of Civil Society* (London: Cadell 1793) pt III, sect. II.
31 Friedrich A. Hayek, "The Use of Knowledge in Society," *American Economic Review* 35:4 (Sept. 1945): 526.
32 Hayek, "Knowledge" 527.
33 Adam Smith, *An Inquiry into the Nature and Causes of the Wealth of Nations* (London: Strahan 1776) bk IV, ch. 2.
34 Hayek, "Knowledge" 528.
35 Adam Smith, *The Theory of Moral Sentiments* (Oxford: OUP 1976) 9. For helpful discussion, see James R. Otteson, *Adam Smith's Marketplace of Life* (Cambridge: CUP 2002).
36 Smith, *Theory* 69–71.
37 Cp. Otteson, *Marketplace* 114.
38 Hayek, *Law* 1:8–71.
39 Hayek, *Law* 1:72–144.
40 Jonathan Crowe, "Natural Law and Normative Inclinations," *Ratio Juris* 28 (2015): 55–6.
41 Cp. Tyler Burge, "Philosophy of Language and Mind: 1950–1990," *Philosophical Review* 101 (1992): 31–2.
42 For discussion, see Crowe, "Inclinations" 62–3. See also John Finnis, *Natural Law and Natural Rights* (Oxford: OUP 2011) ch. 6.
43 See, for example, Peter J. Richerson and Robert Boyd, "The Evolution of Subjective Commitment to Groups: A Tribal Instincts Hypothesis," *Evolution and the Capacity for Commitment,* ed. Randolph M. Nesse (New York: Russell Sage 2001) 186–220.
44 David Hume, *A Treatise of Human Nature* (Oxford: Clarendon-OUP 1978) 469–70 [bk III, pt I, § I]. For discussion, see Finnis 33–6; Jonathan Crowe, "Existentialism and Natural Law," *Adelaide Law Review* 26 (2005): 55.
45 Marilyn B. Brewer, "In-Group Bias in the Minimal Intergroup Situation," *Psychological Bulletin* 86.2 (1979): 307–24; Donald M. Taylor and Janet R. Doria, "Self-Serving and Group-Serving Bias in Attribution," *Journal of Social Psychology* 113.2 (1981): 201–11.
46 Crowe, "Inclinations" 59–60.
47 Cp. Alasdair MacIntyre, *After Virtue* (Notre Dame: U Notre Dame Press 2007) 222.
48 See, for example, Tom R. Tyler, *Why People Obey the Law* (Princeton: Princeton UP 2006); Tom R. Tyler, "Procedural Justice, Legitimacy and the Effective Rule of Law," *Crime and Justice* 30 (2003): 283–357; Tom R. Tyler, "Psychological Perspectives on Legitimacy and Legitimation," *Annual Review of Psychology* 57.1 (2006): 375–400.
49 Cp. Tyler, *People* ch. 4.
50 Hart, *Concept* 82–91.
51 Tyler, *People* ch. 5.
52 Tyler, *People* 6.
53 For useful discussion, see David Friedman, "Anarchy and Efficient Law," *For and Against the State*, ed. John T. Sanders and Jan Narveson (Lanham: Rowman and Littlefield 1996) 235–54.
54 Cp. Gary Chartier, *Anarchy and Legal Order* (Cambridge: CUP 2013) 244–8.
55 They may also adopt dispute resolution processes, such as mediation, which are interest-based, rather than rule-governed. Cp. Jonathan Crowe, "Two Models of Mediation Ethics," *Sydney Law Review* 39 (2017): 161–5.
56 Cp. James M. Buchanan, "What Should Economists Do?" *Southern Economic Journal* 30 (1964): 220.
57 See, for example, Rebecca L. Sandefur and Aaron C. Smyth, *Access across America: First Report of the Civil Justice Infrastructure Mapping Project* (Chicago: American Bar Foundation 2011).
58 Lon L. Fuller, *The Morality of Law* (Cambridge, MA: Harvard UP 1969) ch. 2.
59 Fuller, *Morality* 96. For discussion, see Crowe, "Morality" 112–3.
60 Hayek, *Law* 1:35–54.
61 Hayek, *Law* 1:35–71.
62 Hayek, *The Constitution of Liberty* (Chicago: U of Chicago P 1960) 134–5.
63 G. A. Cohen, *Self-Ownership, Freedom and Equality* (Cambridge: CUP 1995) 55–6.
64 Hayek, *Constitution* 139.
65 See, for example, James M. Buchanan and Gordon Tullock, *The Calculus of Consent* (Indianapolis: Liberty Fund 2004).
66 Buchanan and Tullock 26.
67 Buchanan and Tullock 162.
68 See, for example, Robert A. Dahl, "Decision-Making in a Democracy: The Supreme Court as a National Policy-Maker," *Journal of Public Law* 6 (1957): 279–95; Mark A. Graber, "The Nonmajoritarian Difficulty: Legislative Deference to the Judiciary," *Studies in American Political Development* 7.1 (1993): 35–73.

21

ANARCHISM, STATE, AND VIOLENCE

Andy Alexis-Baker

I. Introduction

For many people, "anarchy" means "unfettered violence." Media stereotype anarchists as hooligans bent on destroying property and civil society. The authors of a recent *New York Times* story, for instance, note that "some anarchists espouse nonviolence," but they still focus on anarchist violence: sucker-punching fascists, smashing windows, arson, and more. Anarchists are "the left's unwanted revolutionary stepchild"[1] who wear black so they can intimidate people.[2]

But states wage war. Twentieth-century wars caused hundreds of millions of casualties. Fifty to eighty million people died in World War II alone. States are fighting seventeen ongoing wars across the planet—in Syria, Somalia, Darfur, and Myanmar, to name a few locations. More states are acquiring nuclear weapons, with the result that the threat of nuclear annihilation looms over the planet just like climate catastrophe. The Syrian civil war has claimed around a half million lives. The Second Congo War is estimated to have killed three million people. U.S.-led wars in Iraq and Afghanistan, the war in Yemen, and other conflicts contribute to an estimated 300,000 ongoing, war-related deaths per year as of 2014, according to the United Nations.[3]

Rather than condemning state warfare, however, intellectuals and the media habitually *support* state violence. "I am guided by the beauty of our weapons," gushed MSNBC news anchor Brian Williams in 2017 when he saw video of the U.S. Navy launching Tomahawk missiles into Syria because Donald Trump claimed to believe that Syria had used chemical weapons on its civilians. "They are beautiful pictures of fearsome armaments," he continued, "making what is for them a brief flight over to this airfield. What did they hit?"[4] According to Syrian state media, the missiles killed nine civilians, including four children. "I think Donald Trump became president of the United States last night," rhapsodized CNN host Fareed Zakaria.[5] A few months later, *Newsweek* accused Trump of being America's laziest president; at the same time, however, the magazine praised the attack on Syria and urged Trump to build an international war coalition to "remove" Syrian president Bashar al-Assad.[6]

By contrast, anarchists have long denounced the state as a war machine. "The *State* denotes *violence*, rule by disguised, or if necessary open and unceremonious *violence*," declared Mikhail Bakunin. "The State, any State—even when it is dressed up in the most liberal and democratic form—is necessarily based on domination, and upon violence."[7] Peter Kropotkin wrote: "State is synonymous with war."[8] Randolph Bourne declared that "war is the health of the state."[9] Voltairine de Cleyre argued that the state "finally rests on a club, a gun, or a prison, for its power to carry them through."[10] Almost all anarchists would agree with Gustav Landauer that "the struggle against war is a struggle against the state."[11] Anti-war activism has been a hallmark of twentieth-century anarchism. Only some anarchists, however, have been pacifists. Both Bakunin and Kropotkin thought that a revolutionary war would be necessary to stop the military state. Some anarchists fought in armies against the state in Spain and Russia. Because the modern state had disguised its violence under mythologies of consent piety, and democracy, and the state had become sacred as a peacemaker, Bakunin and Kropotkin thought that anarchists should unmask state violence by showing what happens when people challenge state oppression. This meant provoking the state through multiple varieties of dissent.[12] Consequently, a few anarchists embraced "propaganda by the deed," assassinating and terrorizing political leaders and capitalists in the hope of inspiring revolutions, a tactic Bakunin and Kropotkin disavowed. Though only representing only one set of anarchist tendencies, these anarchists fueled the misleading stereotype of anarchism as a whole. Anarchism became synonymous, despite its anti-military and anti-war stances and its desire for a peaceable society, with violence.

Notwithstanding the willingness of a narrow subset of anarchists to engage in violence, the contrast could hardly be starker: "fringe" anarchists are denounced as violent while presidents are actively *encouraged* to wage war. Twenty-first-century black-clad anarchists breaking windows are violent, even though they haven't been responsible for mass killings. Presidents, generals, soldiers, and police personnel, who collectively kill hundreds of thousands of humans annually, defend freedom. Trying to untangle this contradiction requires looking at the process of reasoning that shapes modern thinking about violence.

Part of this thinking is mythological. Myth is a specific type of story that relates to sacred things. Prominent modern myths shroud the state's violence with a sense of sacredness, making critiques of the state a kind of heresy. But the specific modern "technical" way of thinking makes the problem of responding to the state and its violence particularly intractable. Anarchists of various stripes have offered critiques of state violence and the myths that underlie it, and have offered another way.

II. The Myths We Live By

A. *What Is Myth?*

It might seem odd to begin a chapter about anarchism, the state, and violence by writing about myth and the sacred. In modern parlance, "myth" means "spurious history." To put the point bluntly: myths are lies. In the age of science and reason, facts dispel myths, making room for more rational discourse and action. But this superficial view *masks* myth's modern function. Western people think that technological societies are rational in contrast to irrational primitive people. This belief allows a sense of superiority to seep into the mindset of the modern Western person. Westerners have the truth. With truth, the West can liberate others from stupidity and ignorance. For several hundred years, Western people have been conditioned to see their society as unquestionably reasonable, something any rational person would choose.

But the Greeks who coined the term "mythos" originally used it to mean "word" or "speech," a synonym for *logos* (which can generally be translated as "word," "speech," or "reason").[13] Rhetoricians trained students to use both *mythos* and *logos* in arguments: even Plato and Aristotle use myth in their philosophies. Greeks could hold together several kinds of beliefs—beliefs modern people see as contradictory—because they viewed life as developing along many different levels, each requiring its own kind of truth. A myth was true in virtue of the mode in which it was utilized.[14] Myth was a type of speech, but not *false* speech. In viewing myths as tall tales, modern people have ignored how discourses of truth operate subtly to form and shape people's worldviews, possibilities, and actions.

A more nuanced view sees myths as deeply held stories that shape how people see the world—and that, in fact, *construct* worlds. According to Mary Midgley, myths consist in "imaginative patterns, networks of powerful symbols that suggest particular ways of interpreting the world. They shape its meaning."[15] As society's deep-rooted stories, myths structure how people see everything, giving order and meaning to the chaos of everyday life. Jacques Ellul says that myths represent "fundamental image[s] of [the human] condition and the world at large."[16] Through myth, Ellul argues, people orient themselves in a world formed by what they experience as sacred. For example, in the modern world, constant chatter and news overload people with information, making it hard to focus on any one thing for very long. The largely trivial information served up by the mass media helps to obscure crucial, and often troubling, features of the contemporary situation. Myth, by contrast, *unifies* the spatial and temporal fragments of our experience, helping individuals and societies orient themselves with regard to features of reality they take to be sacred. Myth is thus "the veritable spinal column of our whole intellectual system."[17] Myths explain everything and give life coherence and meaning.

Myths do not refer to "facts." Ludwig Wittgenstein notes, for example, that when someone kisses a loved one's photograph, the kisser does not believe the kiss will affect the person in the photograph. The action "aims at nothing at all; we just behave this way and then we feel satisfied."[18] The meaning and action of kissing the photo are the same: love takes the form of kissing the photograph. Humans perform numerous ceremonies and rituals that have no relationship to "right and wrong" because they do not try to describe "facts" as many modern people assume. Myths *do* something. They shape us. They form us. For Ellul, they form a communication network within a sacred topography and orient us within it.

In particular, modern myths about the state form our relationship to the state and its violence. Myth's world-constructing character makes it difficult to dislodge people's trust and faith in the state and its violence. For anarcho-syndicalist Georges Sorel,

> A myth cannot be refuted since it is, at bottom, identical to the convictions of a group, being the expression of these convictions in the language of movement; and it is, in consequence, unanalysable into parts which could be placed on the plane of historical descriptions.[19]

Myths, Sorel explains, express the longings and convictions of a people quite apart from the feasibility of these convictions and the results of attempts to act on them. Because of this, "people who are living in … [a] world … [shaped by] myths are secure from all refutation."[20] Argument using facts to challenge a person's mythological formation is futile because utilitarian and intellectual arguments for action are insufficient since such abstract concepts usually fail to motivate people. The attitudes of people who believe that the state is necessary to make people be civil with one another have been shaped by a myth. More than likely, no facts about state violence will shake their faith. Within the mythological universe that sustains it, the state is immune to fundamental critique in most people's thinking.

B. The State Myth

So, what are the myths that justify state violence?

Myths fuse with the sacred. But Ellul argues that to *see* the sacred requires that we work through myths.[21] In Western states, the most pervasive myth justifying state power and violence is the social contract. Seventeenth- and eighteenth-century philosophers, including Thomas Hobbes, John Locke, Immanuel Kant, and Jean-Jacques Rousseau, established the state by telling a story about humanity's natural condition where isolation as individuals predominates.

For Hobbes, individuals in the original condition covet what others have. Individuals live in fear, therefore, that others will harm them. To end the perpetual warfare of "all against all," individuals agree to exchange their freedom (including the freedom to harm each other) for the protection of the state, a state they fear because it protects but also threatens each individual if they disobey.[22] John Locke tells a related story. In people's natural condition, natural law limits individual violence. However, people quarrel over property and become violent. So, if a person wants to take away another's freedoms and property, Locke says, "it is lawful for me to treat him as one who has put himself into a state of war with me, i.e., kill him if I can."[23] Then vendettas and feuds pervade and "a state of war" ensues since people lack a sovereign to arbitrate conflicts. So, people contract with a state to protect their natural property rights. For Locke and Hobbes, violence impels individuals to exchange their natural condition for the state's protection. "To avoid this state of war … is one great reason of men's putting themselves into society, and quitting the state of nature."[24]

In the eighteenth century, Immanuel Kant also posited a social contract. In a natural condition, "individual human beings, peoples, and states can never be secure against violence from one another, since each has its own right to do *what seems right and good to it* and not to be dependent upon another's opinion about this."[25] Therefore, people must "leave the state of nature" and form a society. So fear of violence from other individuals justifies the state, and once states are formed they act like individuals in the state of nature, so there must be an even larger transnational state to govern them. In addition, even if violence does not pervade our natural condition, the situation would be unjust because justice can only come through a "judge competent to render a verdict having rightful force";[26] that is, through a state with the perceived legitimacy to overwhelm people. Society must compel people to enter the social contract and obey the state: "Hence each may impel the other by force to leave this state and enter into a rightful condition."[27] As with Locke and Hobbes, humanity's original state is disharmonious individuals at war with one another. Only a state based on a contract can end the violence.

Jean-Jacques Rousseau posited an even more radical individualism in the state of nature. On Rousseau's view, in this condition isolation is so complete that persons cannot recognize their own mothers because they have no lasting relationships. Living in isolation means that people do not fight one another. They form a social contract and create a state once they leave their natural isolation because, once they do, violence becomes so endemic that they need to submit to the will of everyone else to have peace. Rousseau claims that individuals form the state to "defend and protect the person and goods of each associate."[28] For every early contract theorists, therefore, rational people agree to a necessary, overarching, violent state that can protect them from each other.

These theories arose as Europeans committed genocide against native people in the "New World" and colonized the land. As the Europeans encountered native people in the Americas, jurists developed property theories based on social contracts that disallowed communal property: individuals who contract hold property; nobody owns common property. Hugo Grotius and Samuel Pufendorf pioneered these legal theories. Locke built upon them. Europeans routinely described native people as irrational and engaged in pointless, endless wars. But the real importance of social contract theory was to describe indigenous people as lacking sovereignty because they did not own land or work it properly. Hobbes drew upon this common view in his description of the natural condition:

> In such a condition, there is no place for industry; because the fruit thereof is uncertain: and consequently no culture of the earth; no navigation, nor use of the commodities

> that may be imported by sea; no commodious building; no instruments of moving, and removing such things as require much force; no knowledge of the face of the earth; no account of time; no arts; no letters; no society; and which is worst of all, continual fear, and danger of violent death; and the live of man, solitary, poor, nasty, brutish, and short.[29]

Hobbes clearly supposes that "the savage people in many places of America"[30] live in what he takes to be humanity's natural condition. When Locke and others took these issues up, they argued that because indigenous people did not "enclose" land and engage in European-style agriculture, the land was actually "vacant."[31] So, social contract mythology warned Europeans that common property ownership would degenerate into the "war of all against all" like "the savages" of the Americas. The myth also justified European aggression. State violence, therefore, lies at the historical heart of social contract myth.

One of the most potent aspects of the social contract myth lies in the way the state takes on a messianic role as the savior of all people from their perpetual warring. The state saves people from endless violence. The state, as the most powerful and fearful entity in a given society, ends the fear of violence and liberates people from the "danger of violent death," as Hobbes puts it.

While the state saves people *from* irrational violence, the state saves people *for* property ownership. For Locke, even though God gave all humanity the earth, private land ownership is the best way to preserve the gift. Human preservation means that there are natural property rights, even if others live on the land. So Locke justified seizing land native people occupied because they kept the land as "an uncultivated waste."[32] The right to pursue possessions coincides with the state's salvation from violence. The power to own property and consume products is the outcome of a state within the social contract mythology. The soteriological justification for the state imagines a transformed state of nature in which individuals pursue their self-interests through accumulation. This transubstantiation happens magically as the state grows.

State violence is rational. Therefore, people call what the state does "force," not violence. Violence lacks legal justification. Force has it. Very few journalists would describe police shooting a suspect as violence. The police used "force." The state has, in Max Weber's famous words, a monopoly on the legitimate use of force.[33] But anarchists reject the distinction political theorists make between state "force" and private "violence." Ellul states,

> I refuse to make the classic distinction between violence and force. The lawyers have invented the idea that when the state applies constraint, even brutal constraint, it is exercising 'force'; that only individuals or nongovernmental groups (syndicates, parties) use violence. This is a totally unjustified distinction. The state is established by violence—the French, American, Communist, Francoist revolutions. Invariably there is violence at the start.[34]

Violence *founds* the state, and states *rule* through everyday practices of violence: "economic relations, class relations, are relations of violence, nothing else."[35] He writes of "administrative violence" and the "violence of the judicial system."[36] There is also "psychological violence," which "is simply violence, whether it takes the form of propaganda, biased reports, meetings of secret societies that inflate the egos of their members, brainwashing or intellectual terrorism."[37] Anarchists have largely agreed with Ellul's analysis.[38]

Yet for most people, deluged with statist propaganda, the state has a legitimate monopoly on force. The social contract myth begins to show why. The state has a monopoly on violence so that its violence can redeem and save people from the fear and threats of violence that engulf them when they lack the protection of Leviathan.

Contract mythology plays its part in "a mythical system"; without this system, the social contract myth cannot function effectively.[39] For many of its defenders, the state is grounded in something like pure Kantian reason. This kind of reason functions automatically: two is always greater than one; three is always greater than two. In war, nuclear weapons must be fought with nuclear weapons; chemical weapons with chemical weapons. The choices people make are technical, contradictions are disallowed, even though they proliferate in the process.

The mythology of the state develops through multiple stages, according to Ellul: rationality, artificiality, automatism, self-augmentation, monism, universalism, and autonomy.[40] Rationality and artificiality emerge through the ways in which the social contract myth subtly pushes the hearer to think of herself as an isolated person apart from the natural or social world. Rather than an unavoidable sacred domain, the natural world is a field of scarce resources over which people compete. It is marked by war. The individual has objectified the natural and social worlds by thinking of herself apart from both and imposing a concept of them as pure threats (stripping them of life-giving power and thus desacralizing them). The myth then bids hearers to eschew ways of thinking about the world (as a living body, for example) and society (as a body unified though and following Christ, for example) as irrational and incapable of ending violence between people who now think of themselves as radical individuals. The rational, secularized state becomes the only way to achieve peace in these circumstances. The choice to view the state as the solution to any conceivable social problem becomes automatic (automatism). All other modes of organizing communal life are eliminated in favor of the state, which because it has a monopoly on legitimate violence is a peacemaker. The state becomes humanity's savior. As Bourne says, "As the Church is the medium for the spiritual salvation of men, so the State is thought of as the medium for his political salvation."[41] The state's violence—and only its violence—is redemptive. Those who enact that violence are its saints and, not infrequently, its martyrs. To decline to "support the troops" or the state's police becomes a kind of modern heresy against "war orthodoxy" within the mythological world of modern statism.[42]

C. The Sacred State

The process of technical reasoning and the mythology Ellul describes lie at the roots of one of the most pervasive reasons for people's uncritical acceptance of state violence in contrast with their denunciation of petty anarchist violence. The state is treated as *sacred*. This does not mean the state has a sacred "essence." Rather, it *functions* as sacred in specific ways. People experience and act in certain ways in relation to sacred entities. Émile Durkheim argued that "anything at all, can be sacred."[43] The term "sacred" does not denote a quality of gods or religious things but rather a feature of "things set apart and forbidden."

Every society, Ellul argues, has sacred *poles*, which elicit intense passions and occasion intense experiences and are subject to rituals and liturgies. These poles are valued not for utilitarian reasons, but because people believe the sacred provides them with meaning and order that are independent of their individual lives. The sacred removes people from quotidian concerns and inducts them into a meaningful existence.[44] Moreover, as an inescapable reality the sacred both threatens and protects life. The sacred imposes order, reimagining time (a cycle of holy days) and space (places of special meaning); and from the vantage-point afforded by the mythology they embrace, people distinguish between the sacred and the profane, the permitted and forbidden. The sacred provides a map for movement through the threat and protection which it itself provides.

For Ellul, "self-augmentation" names the process by which the state has expanded into people's lives to such a degree that people depend on the state and cannot imagine life without it. The state's regulatory agencies, personnel, and programs and its control of the flow of goods entangle it in modern life, making human existence almost unimaginable without its services. The state colonizes people's imaginations. All of its agencies, symbols, and activities form a monolithic whole (monism). The state then expands across the globe to such a degree that to be "stateless" means living in the state of nature in which violence reigns. The mythology that supports the state constrains our thinking about state action in ways that allow the state to reach its full sacred status by becoming unmoored from the "contract" that supposedly grounds it. The state comes to be its own reason for action. Bakunin also notes the state's autonomous morality, mocking those who think Christian morality can tame state violence when the only criterion of good becomes the state itself. When "all that is instrumental in conserving, exalting, and consolidating the power of the State is good, … whatever militates against the interests of the State is bad," the slogan "reason of state" suffices to justify any action, no matter how violently horrific. In social contract mythology, Bakunin notes, "the good" *begins* with the state that saves humanity from its own wickedness,[45] so that no external moral critique of state action is ultimately possible.

People cannot imagine life without the state because it claims to protect, threatens, and gives life order and meaning. It transcends everyday experience yet remains immanent in daily life through symbols and totems, especially flags and police personnel. The state organizes time. The work week and annual holiday cycle mold the citizen's sense of time. The high holy days celebrating the state's salvific violence—President's Day, Memorial Day, Independence Day, Veterans Day, to name a few U.S. holidays—mark time and link people's experiences with American patriotism and memorial blood sacrifice. People narrate history from the state's standpoint: most national or world history courses revolve around the state's wars, which function as mass ritual sacrifices. Globally, states transform the earth into a pattern of bordered territories that recreate the "natural condition" of the mythology: each state does (roughly) whatever it wants and creates an international system marked by war of all against all.[46] Within the United States, land is divided into towns, counties, and states, all represented by state symbols and containing state memorials spaced for pilgrimage or constant reminder. Thus, the state shapes people's everyday lives by controlling time and space. Yet the state transcends the average person's reach, with the capitol buildings of most U.S. states and Washington DC explicitly emulating Roman civic and ecclesiastical structures, for example. One author calls Washington DC "a myth in stone."[47] In virtue of its immanence and transcendence, the state exhibits many of the features of the sacred.[48]

The way in which Americans orient rituals around their government's flag helps clarify the sacred and its violence. Carolyn Marvin and David W. Ingle discuss the rituals, symbols, and emotions that fuel the American state. They argue that American nationalism entails ideas about the sacred: totemic taboos, rituals, and symbols structure the American experience of the sacred. Nationalism, they claim, "is the most powerful religion in the United States, and perhaps in many other countries."[49] The American flag is a transcendent symbol that embodies the nation's ideals and ideologies, unites heterogeneous people into a homogenous nation, combines past and present, and invites the continual willing sacrifice—blood sacrifice that defines the nation-state and keeps the totemic system in place—for the nation's putative benefit.

Congressional debates in 2001 about outlawing flag-burning illuminate the conclusions reached by Marvin and Ingle.

> To fight and die for the flag is to fight and die for the cause in which we believe. … We love and we honor and respect our flag for that which it represents.

> Since the creation of the American flag, it has stood as a symbol of our sacred values and aspirations. Far too many Americans have died in combat to see the symbol of what they were fighting for reduced to just another object of public derision. Simply

put, it is a gross insult to every patriotic American to see the symbol of their country publicly desecrated. They will not tolerate it, and neither will I.

It [the flag] is a solemn and sacred symbol of the many sacrifices made by our Founding Fathers and our Veterans throughout several wars as they fought to establish and protect the founding principles of our great Nation. Most Americans, Veterans in particular, feel deeply insulted when they see our Flag being desecrated. It is in their behalf, in their honor and in their memory that we have championed this effort to protect and honor this symbol.

Human beings do not live by abstract ideas alone. Those ideas are embodied in symbols. And what is a symbol? A symbol is more than a sign. A sign conveys information. A symbol is much more richly textured. A symbol is material reality that makes a spiritual reality present among us. ... Burning the flag is a hate crime, because burning the flag is an expression of contempt for the moral unity of the American people that the flag symbolically makes present to us every day.[50]

The flag, therefore, is a sacred object that needs protection from profanation because it purportedly "makes present" the moral unity of the United States and because people have and will kill and die for it.

The state, Ellul writes, "is the ultimate value which gives everything its meaning."[51] Fused with notions of nationhood in which individuals find purpose and meaning as members of a group, the nation-state becomes "the criterion of good and evil .... It is good to lie, kill, and deceive for the nation."[52] Other anarchists agree. Bakunin argues that the "elastic, at times so convenient and terrible[,] phrase *reason of State*" excuses actions that would otherwise be considered criminal.[53] Here the state reaches the apex of technical reasoning, which excludes all ends outside of itself. The state alone determines life and death and judges right and wrong. Religion's supposedly private "ends" do not constrain state action. The survival, development, and expansion of the state become people's unquestioned and presupposed ends. To refuse to cooperate with the state becomes immoral and heretical. People kill and die for the state; they experience ecstatic frenzy at the national anthem sung just right, and become angry at the slightest insult to the "land of the free."[54] To suggest a life without the state makes about as much sense as suggesting to a stereotypical medieval Catholic that life without Christ would be good.

The state is set apart from the quotidian private conflicts so that those who work as state agents can judge and authorize violence in order to impose order. The state claims to be an arbitrator capable of resolving disputes that would otherwise be settled through violence. The state is, therefore, a peacemaker. But the state requires citizens to kill and die for it as the sacred institution that makes life tolerable. What seems contradictory is necessary for the state as sacred. It gives and takes life. It bestows meaning through blood sacrifice. The state is "the god of war and of order."[55] The state offers people security from conflicts that arise as the "many" compete for resources and dominance. The state, therefore, needs conflicts to justify its existence. It becomes essential for any imaged life within a way of seeing society shaped by the secular/religious and public/private dichotomies.

III. Anarchism and Violence

Anarchists do not see the state as sacred. It has no right to take life or declare that somebody's life is not worth respecting. Anarchists do not believe that individuals are incapable of living peacefully and cooperatively together or that they need the state to keep them safe. Rather, most anarchists—even those who have no problem with defensive violence when attacked—have insisted on the possibility of a peaceable life together organized not through threats of violence from a heavily armed organization that claims moral superiority to do what is forbidden to everyone else, but through practices of mutual aid, compassion, and care for the other that reveal the possibility of a different kind of world, without a sacred god-state to order people around. So, first and foremost, anarchists tell a different story than the one embedded in statist mythology.

To be sure, some anarchists, like iconoclasts of old, have declared their intent to "smash the state." But in doing so they have sometimes only reaffirmed the sacred pretensions that underlie state violence. Undeniably some anarchists have murdered and committed terrorist acts against state and capitalist officials. In 1885, German anarchist Johann Most published his pamphlet *Science of Revolutionary Warfare*, instructing readers on how to make bombs, commit arson, stab, and poison people, and extolled the psychological impact such violence would have on the ruling classes, the "property-monsters," praising the way in which such violence could be expected to "inflict surprise, confusion and panic on the enemy."[56] Under the banner of "propaganda by the deed," anarchists killed numerous public figures, including Czar Alexander II of Russia (1881); Sadi Carnot, the President of France (1894); Spanish Prime Minister Antonio Cánovas del Castillo (1897); Elisabeth of Bavaria, the Empress of Austria and Queen of Hungary (1898); King Umberto I of Italy (1900); U.S. President William McKinley (1901); King Carlos I of Portugal (1908); Russian prime minister Pyotr Stolypin (1911); and King George I of Greece (1913). These killings, along with numerous attempted assassinations and other acts of deadly violence, fueled the popular misconception that anarchists were in principle violent, bomb-throwing miscreants bent on destroying peaceful society.

Most anarchist authors, however, distanced themselves from individual acts of violence. Emma Goldman, de Cleyre, and Landauer denied that anarchist ideas inspired the assassins. Each focused on the wretched conditions capitalist society creates as the primary culprit in creating men willing to murder. Goldman contended that "the tremendous pressure of conditions, making life unbearable to their sensitive natures" and "the wholesale violence of capital and government" impelled some to acts of violence to stop the repressions.[57] "The hells of capitalism create the desperate," wrote de Cleyre, "the desperate act,—desperately!"[58] Landauer argued that anarchist assassins envision a good life, but cannot escape the brutal realities in which "they cannot even feed themselves and their children."[59] Immersion in these realities has disastrous consequences. "Gradually, many elements of their personality die: reflection, consideration, empathy, even their sense of self-preservation," and they become obsessed with revenge until they finally lash out.[60] Many anarchists, therefore, saw assassinations and acts of terrorism as desperate and hopeless actions in which hatred and revenge took hold of the person. In that sense, the assassins were weak, merely lashing out. This type of violence would seem to cede to the state all the power it desires as a sacred, since its action is completely bound up with the state and reinforces the state in a kind of dialectic.

Errico Malatesta suggested that the people carrying out assassinations and engaging in other kinds of propaganda-by-deed serve collectively as a source of warning to all anarchists. These people joined anarchism because they wanted to respect and love others and saw in anarchism the potential for a peaceable world. But they began to justify the opposite of anarchist ideals in order to try to establish anarchism. Having embraced the authoritarian impulses that characterize most political movements, they justify their actions by appealing to the brutality of the regime and minimizing their own violence. In doing so, however, they have entered "on a path which is the most absolute negation of all anarchist ideas and sentiments."[61] These anarchists, Malatesta claims, show all anarchists the kind of abyss into which they can fall if they are not careful about violence and do not purge themselves of hatred and retaliation. Violence, he claims, cannot establish anarchism:

> For us violence is only of use and can only be of use in driving back violence. Otherwise, when it is used to accomplish positive goals, either it fails completely, or it succeeds in establishing the oppression and the exploitation of the ones over the others.[62]

Anarchists' violent actions arise out of a sense of self-righteousness: the state is so evil, and the anarchist cause so transcendent and ideal, that a kind of holy war must be waged to destroy the state and establish anarchism.[63] This type of justification is a secularized form of the justification too often advanced for holy wars, and so of many instances of war carried out by the state. Such a view recreates the hierarchies it opposes, Malatesta argued.

In parallel with Malatesta's denunciation of non-defensive anarchist violence as a kind of authoritarianism, Ellul offers a helpful analysis. Following sociologists who have studied the sacred, Ellul argues that every sacred entails its opposite pole, a sacred of transgression. The sacred of respect and the sacred of transgression function as a kind of dialectic, in which each responds to the other. Revolution is the sacred of transgression for the nation-state. Historically, Ellul notes, revolutions have established states through the execution of the sovereign, which is a kind of founding sacrifice.[64] Revolution thus reintegrates the revolutionary into the sacred, just as festivals functioned to release tensions and reintegrate transgressors into the sacred order of the Middle Ages. Marxist revolutionaries revolt not to *destroy* the state but to reintegrate *themselves* into the state. The goal of transgression against the sacred is to be *reestablish* the sacred. While anarchists seek the state's destruction, far too often the kind of violence some anarchists perpetrate only strengthens state power as the state responds by finding new ways to control people more efficiently. The terrorist is integrated into the state's dominant mythology: the anarcho-terrorist, whether assassinating public figures yesterday or breaking bank windows today, is the irrational perpetrator of violence from whom the state will save people. The state remains sacred as the object of adoration by the masses and hatred by the heretics. Violent transgression against the state only reinforces the state because the state, as a sacred reality, depends on such transgressions and cannot exist without it. The transgression is just another means, ironically, of reinforcing the state's sacredness.

Many anarchists reject violence. Leo Tolstoy taught Christian anarchist pacifism, called for nonviolent resistance to oppression, and urged youth to resist the Russian military draft. Prefiguring the practices and thought of many modern anarchists, Tolstoy extended this nonviolence and non-domination to other animals and advocated vegetarianism as a practice of peaceableness. Ellul espoused an anarchism that entailed "an absolute rejection of violence." He aligned himself with "pacifist, antinationalist, anticapitalist, moral, and antidemocratic anarchism" (since most democracies are shams [and are majoritarian]) and advocated creating "small groups and networks, denouncing falsehood and oppression, aiming at a true overturning of authorities of all kinds as people at the bottom speak and organize themselves."[65] Despite disagreeing with Bakunin about the appropriateness of violence, Ellul thought his position was very close to Bakunin's. Landauer declared that "not war and murder—but rebirth" must be the basis of the anarcho-socialist practices he favored since the most difficult task for anarchists is to abandon their own desires to dominate others.[66] He saw the state as "a social relationship; a certain way of people relating to one another. It can be destroyed by creating new social relationships; i.e., by people relating to one another differently."[67] "Anarchy exists," he wrote, "wherever one finds true anarchists: people who do not engage in violence."[68]

The twentieth century demonstrated that disciplined movements engaged in boycotts, strikes, sit-ins, refusal to cooperate with authorities, sabotage of industry and state machinery, and other creative actions can halt even powerful empires. Mohandas Gandhi, leading massive and successful nonviolent actions intended to end British imperialism in India, dreamed of a world organized into "enlightened anarchy" where people would find more creative ways to live together than violence entails.[69] Gandhian communities were meant to point the way toward this ideal. The ideal of "doing no harm" or "compassion" (*ahimsa*) guides a way of living that focuses not simply on avoiding state domination but also on nourishing the multiple opportunities for equitable and peaceable relationships that obtain outside the sphere of violence. Gandhian thinking fits well with Ellul's and Landauer's understandings of anarchist action and thought—understandings that emphasize the positive value of peaceful, voluntary cooperation rather than reempowering the state by putting (too-often hate-filled) opposition to its violence on center-stage (even as Ellul, Landauer, and the Gandhians recognize that the state must be opposed and resisted).

Ward Churchill, Derrick Jensen, and Peter Gelderloos have argued, by contrast, that Gandhian nonviolence merely strengthens the state. Because violence is part of the political process, any attempt to establish and maintain anarchist institutions will necessarily involve the use of violence. In response, Andrew Fiala has pointed out that these thinkers align themselves with conservative realist political views in accordance with which the state simply is violent because all political action is violent. Violence, for the realists, needs no justification. Violence—or, to boil things down to its most basic, murdering and oppressing others—is just the way of the world.[70] It is hard to see how this thinking could lead to a deeper anarchism that would not be a sacred of transgression as Ellul describes it.

Despite the anti-technology bent of Jensen's reasoning, his approach doesn't really seem to break from the kind of technical reasoning that Ellul argues characterizes modern thinking. The rhetoric seems to move to a high level of abstraction very quickly. And Landauer's critique seems applicable. How, he asks, can anarchists kill other people? He explains:

> When they kill, they do not kill human beings but concepts—that of the exploiter, the oppressor, the representative of the state. This is why those who are often the kindest and most humane in their private lives commit the most inhumane acts in the public sphere.[71]

The process of abstraction is completely bound up with technical reasoning and debases life—treating abstractions as more important than actual people. Landauer suggests that anarchists who are willing to kill

> do not feel; they have switched off their senses. They act as exclusively rational beings ... are the servants of reason; a reason that divides and judges. This cold, spiritually empty, and destructive logic is the rationale for the death sentences handed down by the anarchists. But anarchy is neither as easily achievable, nor as morally harsh, nor as clearly defined as these anarchists would have it. Only when anarchy becomes, for us, a dark, deep dream, not a vision attainable through concepts, can our ethics and our actions become one.[72]

Moreover, violence does not seem to be a very effective tool. Anarchist violence will always be co-opted by the state's myth-makers. Every violent action is simply an example of the chaos, the war of all against all, that threatens the peace that the state is supposed to create and maintain. Because of this ongoing threat, the state must now expand; it must institute new ways of suppressing the irrational, violent offenders, be they unreasonable religious fanatics or anti-social anarchists. The state will then be able not only to use its redemptive violence to reaffirm its sacred power but also to become even more powerful. The surveillance, the violence, the repressive technologies it employs, are necessary; and, the state's advocates suppose, it is irresponsible and reckless not to use every tool at the state's disposal to effect security and therefore peace in the face of threats of irrational violence. The state must survive and expand by any means necessary. Propaganda by the state feeds the state.

To engage in nonviolent direct action, by contrast, is to avoid feeding statist mythology by removing the violent anarchist bogeyman as a rationale for state violence. There is a certain sense in which all nonviolent direct action denies the state its sacred status as the giver and taker of life while liberating revolution from the statist dialectic. Although numerous movements have shown that nonviolent direct action has the potential to damage and overthrow governments, many anarchists maintain that nonviolence is not about efficiency and rationality. To focus just on efficiency and rationality is to underwrite the technical reasoning of the violent state that war is our only source of security. Nonviolent anarchism, Landauer argues, is not about creating the future but about living in this time and place and doing one's best in the present to enact ideals of peaceful, voluntary cooperation. Causing cracks in the wall that surrounds and protects the status quo, he argued, can do far more than a bullet.

Notes

1 See Farah Stockman, "Anarchists Respond to Trump's Inauguration, by Any Means Necessary," *New York Times*, Feb. 2, 2017, www.nytimes.com/2017/02/02/us/anarchists-respond-to-trumps-inauguration-by-any-means-necessary.html (accessed November 27, 2017).

2 Rick Paulas, "What to Wear to Smash the State," *New York Times*, Nov. 29, 2017, www.nytimes.com/2017/11/29/style/black-bloc-fashion.html (Nov. 29, 2017).

3 See Alexandre Marc, "Conflict and Violence in the 21st Century: Current Trends as Observed in Empirical Research and Data," United Nations, www.un.org/pga/70/wp-content/uploads/sites/10/2016/01/Conflict-and-violence-in-the-21st-century-Current-trends-as-observed-in-empirical-research-and-statistics-Mr.-Alexandre-Marc-Chief-Specialist-Fragility-Conflict-and-Violence-World-Bank-Group.pdf (Dec. 12, 2017).

4 Margaret Sullivan, "The Media Loved Trump's Show of Military Might. Are We Really Doing This Again?" *Washington Post*, Apr. 8, 2017, www.washingtonpost.com/lifestyle/style/the-media-loved-trumps-show-of-military-might-are-we-really-doing-this-again/2017/04/07/01348256-1ba2-11e7-9887-1a5314b56a08_story.html?utm_term=.5f9c92d1a193 (Aug. 10, 2017).

5 Kevin Drum, "Donald Trump Is No More Presidential Today Than He Was Yesterday," *Mother Jones*, Apr. 7, 2017, www.motherjones.com/kevin-drum/2017/04/donald-trump-no-more-presidential-today-he-was-yesterday/ (Aug. 10, 2017).

6 Alexander Nazaryan, "Trump, America's Boy King: Gold and Television Won't Make America Great Again," *Newsweek*, Aug. 1, 2017. www.newsweek.com/2017/08/11/donald-trump-hillary-clinton-gop-white-house-potus-bannon-643996.html (Aug. 10, 2017).

7 Mikhail Bakunin, "The Modern State Surveyed," *The Political Philosophy of Bakunin* (London: Free 1953) 211 (italics original).

8 Peter Kropotkin, *The State: Its Historic Role* (London: Freedom 1946) 42.

9 Randolph Bourne, "Unfinished Fragment on the State," *Untimely Papers* (New York: Huebsch 1920) 141, 145.

10 Voltairine de Cleyre, "Direct Action," *Exquisite Rebel: The Essays of Voltairine de Cleyre—Feminist, Anarchist, Genius*, ed. Sharon Presley and Crispin Sartwell (Albany: SUNY 2005) 275.

11 Gustav Landauer, *Rechenschaft* (Berlin: Cassirer 1919) 159. My translation.

12 See Elizabeth Frazer and Kimberly Hutchings, "Anarchist Ambivalence: Politics and Violence in the Thought of Bakunin, Tolstoy and Kropotkin," *European Journal of Political Theory* 18.2 (2019): 3–8.

13 For an etymology of *mythos*, see Pierre Chantraine, *Dictionnaire Étymologique de la Langue Grecque: Histoire Des Mots* (Paris: Klincksieck 1984) 718–19.

14 See Paul Veyne, *Did the Greeks Believe in Their Myths? An Essay on the Constitutive Imagination* (Chicago: U of Chicago P 1988).

15 Mary Midgley, *The Myths We Live By* (New York: Routledge 2003) 1.

16 Jacques Ellul, *Propaganda* (New York: Vintage 1965) 116.

17 See Jacques Ellul, *Presence in the Modern World* (Eugene, OR: Cascade 2016) 67.

18 Ludwig Wittgenstein, "Remarks on Frazer's *Golden Bough*," *Philosophical Occasions: 1912–1951*, ed. James Klagge and Alfred Nordman (Indianapolis: Hackett 1993) 123.

19 Georges Sorel, *Reflections on Violence* (New York: CUP 1999) 29.

20 Sorel 30.
21 See Ellul, *New Demons*, trans. C. Edward Hopkin (New York: Crossroad-Seabury 1975) 121.
22 Thomas Hobbes, *Leviathan* (New York: OUP 1996).
23 John Locke, *Two Treatises of Government* (New Haven: Yale UP 2003) 108 (Second Treatise, ch. 3).
24 Locke 109.
25 Immanuel Kant, *Metaphysics of Morals* (New York: CUP 1996) 90 [6:312] (italics original).
26 Kant 90 [6:312].
27 Kant 90 [6:312]. It is important to clarify, however, that Kant rejected the idea of European colonialism since arguments in its favor "sanction any means to good ends." Kant 53 [6:266].
28 Jean-Jacques Rousseau, *The Social Contract* (New York: CUP 1997) 49.
29 Hobbes 84 (Part 1, ch. 13).
30 Hobbes 85.
31 See James Tully, *An Approach to Political Philosophy: Locke in Contexts* (New York: CUP 1997) 150–1.
32 Locke 116 (Second Treatise, ch. 5).
33 See Max Weber, *The Vocation Lectures* (Indianapolis: Hackett 2004) 38.
34 Jacques Ellul, *Violence: Reflections from a Christian Perspective* (New York: Seabury 1969) 84.
35 Ellul, *Violence* 86.
36 Jacques Ellul, *In Season, Out of Season: An Introduction to the Thought of Jacques Ellul*, trans. Lani K. Niles (New York: Harper 1982) 131.
37 Ellul, *Violence* 97.
38 Of course, calling economics and other such things "violent" can easily lead to justifying physical acts of violence since the two are viewed as equivalent. This is a weakness in Ellul and others who broaden the term "violence" so widely.
39 See Ellul, *Demons* 96–97.
40 See Jacques Ellul, *The Technological Society* (New York: Vintage 1965) 79–147. In the rest of the paragraph, I use David Lovekin's way of describing rationality and artificiality and apply it to social contract myth. For the full technical cycle, see David Lovekin, "Technology as the Sacred Order," *Research in Philosophy and Technology* 3 (1980): 203–22.
41 Bourne 141.
42 See Bourne 143.
43 Durkheim, *The Elementary Forms of the Religious Life* (New York: OUP 2009) 36.
44 See Jacques Ellul, *The Subversion of Christianity* (Grand Rapids: Eerdmans 1986) 52.
45 Bakunin 143.
46 See Bakunin 138.
47 See Jeffrey F. Meyer, *Myths in Stone: Religious Dimensions of Washington D.C.* (Berkeley: U of California P 2001) 50.
48 See Ellul, *Subversion* 52.
49 Carolyn Marvin and David Ingle, "Blood Sacrifice and the Nation: Revisiting Civil Religion," *Journal of the American Academy of Religion* 64.4 (1996): 767.
50 *Congressional Record* 147.99 (United States Government Printing Office), www.gpo.gov/fdsys/pkg/CREC-2001-07-17/pdf/CREC-2001-07-17-pt1-PgH4043.pdf (Aug. 2, 2017).
51 Ellul, *Demons* 80.
52 Ellul 82.
53 See Bakunin 14–2. Original emphasis.
54 Recent outrage and American football players refusing to stand, place their hands on their hearts, and sing the national anthem while facing the American flag illustrates the religious nature of nationalism quite well. It also illustrates the potential violence in this statist nationalism.
55 Ellul, *Demons* 81.
56 Johann Most, *Science of Revolutionary Warfare* (El Dorado: Desert 1978) 11.
57 Emma Goldman, *Anarchism and Other Essays* (New York: Dover 1969) 92, 107.
58 Voltairine de Cleyre, "McKinley's Assassination," *Rebel* 302.
59 Gustav Landauer, *Gustav Landauer: Revolution and Other Writings*, ed. and trans. Gabriel Kuhn (Oakland: PM 2010) 81.
60 Landauer, *Revolution* 81.
61 Errico Malatesta, "Violence as a Social Factor (1895)," *Anarchism: A Documentary History of Libertarian Ideas 1: From Anarchy to Anarchism (300CE to 1939)*1, ed. Robert Graham (Montreal: Black Rose 2005) 161.
62 Errico Malatesta, "Revolution in Practice," *The Method of Freedom: An Enrico Malatesta Reader*, ed. David Turcato (Oakland: AK 2014).

63 The petty violence of those participating in Black Bloc actions might fall into this category of holy violence as well. One cannot help but hear Malatesta denouncing it—hyper-masculine, hyper-righteous, and hyper-despairing—as full of the hate it seeks to abolish.
64 See Ellul, *Demons* 85.
65 Jacques Ellul, *Anarchy and Christianity* (Grand Rapids: Eerdmans 1991) 13–4.
66 Landauer, *Revolution* 89.
67 Landauer, *Revolution* 214.
68 Landauer, *Revolution* 86.
69 See Mohandas K. Gandhi, "Enlightened Anarchy," *The Penguin Gandhi Reader*, ed. Rudrangshu Mukherjee (New York: Penguin 1996) 79.
70 Andrew Fiala, "Anarchism and Pacifism," *Brill's Companion to Anarchism and Philosophy* (Leiden: Brill 2017) 168.
71 Landauer, *Revolution* 91.
72 Landauer, *Revolution* 91.

22
THE FORECAST FOR ANARCHY

Tom W. Bell

I. Introduction: The Future of ... Nothing?

Though defined largely by what it *is not—the state*—anarchism may end up defining what the future of government *is*. A rising chorus claims that political territorialism, as a business model for the governing services industry, has reached the late bubble stage. And when it pops? Some foretell a violent explosion, others a mere catastrophic collapse.

Social disorder always haunts the edges of civilization, and the void left by a dying government might draw forth all sorts of malice. But anarchy does not have to mean chaos. Call them dreamers or visionaries as you see fit, but many current thinkers foresee a softer-than-usual (r)evolution this time around. On this model, written up first in the form of speculative fiction and now written up in computer software, the state not so much explodes as dissolves, its subjects lured away from politics into more distributed and consensual forms of self-governance.

This process less recalls a balloon going *pop!* than soap lather, melting away under a rush of clean water. Popping balloons make toddlers cry, whereas rinsing soap away cleans hands. The parallels thus hold up nicely. For, while *overturning* governments cannot help but cause upset, and often leaves matters much worse off, *outgrowing* governments offers the prospect of a smooth path to a safer, better environment.

After the outline and prefatory comments of this Introduction, the next section reviews some notable past forecasts for anarchy, the sources ranging from scientific socialism to scientific fiction. Section III surveys the ominous signs that statism, in the form and at the scale currently practiced, cannot continue. But will it explode or slowly slump? Section IV explains why some predict that blockchain-based, distributed, crypto-economic networks offer a soft landing, if not for the state itself, then at least for those under its power and protection. Section V concludes by summarizing the findings: the future of government looks less statist than at present, and much more rich in consent. Regardless of what you call it, that represents a form of government worth welcoming.

* * *

Before launching the discussion proper, it bears taking a moment to talk about ... the *A-word*: "anarchy." The word inspires everything from terror to contempt, with a good stretch of ideological ardor and confusion in-between. Defining *anarchy* is not a question of arid semantics but a vital preliminary to the task at hand: predicting the future of the self-same thing.

Anarchy haunts political philosophy with a great and terrible void. It represents not merely a critique of the state, but its negation. Into this ideological vacuum have rushed a great many ideas, from the ridiculous to the brilliant. Yet anarchy itself, as an idea, remains empty, defined not so much by what it *includes* as what it *excludes*: an administrative body that credibly claims the exclusive right to initiate coercion within a particular geographic area—a state.[1] That makes predicting the future of anarchism, the goal here, a bit tricky. How could anyone forecast the future of … nothing?

Methodological individualism at first appears to offer an easy dodge: deny that the state exists in the first place.[2] The most hard-core of those who take this position recognize only the acts of individual persons, dismissing the state as little more than a mass hallucination.[3] If the state does not exist, its negation can hardly have more substance. With no present, it can have no future. QED.

Problem solved? Not quite. To simply deny that the state exists will not satisfy anyone genuinely curious about what sorts of social behaviors humans will exhibit pursuant to their *beliefs* about the state, be it actual or fictional. Methodological individualism, while a useful corrective against reifying political institutions, offers no shortcuts around the task at hand.

Most anarchists recognize the state as something substantial enough to fight against, granting it as much metaphysical heft as the corporations, churches, and other institutions they sometimes also target.[4] Most anti-statists leave what they mean to fight *for*, however, only lightly sketched. Only a few fulfill the popular stereotype of masked bombers raging against all forms of social order.[5] Anarchists proper (supposing such a phrase is not oxymoronic) have no problem with *order*. It is being *ordered* they so dislike. Anarchists, at least as here understood, oppose not *rules* but *rulers*. They desire, create, and support social institutions that govern behavior. *Why? How?* and *What kind?* remain questions open to debate—which anarchists welcome enthusiastically.

Anarchy is not simply a counterweight to the state; it by definition constitutes the space, literal and metaphorical, that surrounds, pervades, and ultimately sustains that peculiar species of social order.[6] States have many other features, but most notably, and in sharp contrast to institutions in anarchist societies, they claim the exclusive power to administer the law coercively within a specified territory. Absent the doctrine of statism, no secular jurisprude would excuse the threats, beatings, and worse doled out by the machinery of the state. Its singular self-exception from the usual rules of social behavior marks the state (as in darker days it also marked the Church) as something unique. It claims a pass on the respect for rights that marks more liberal, humane, and egalitarian societies. The state aspires to greater goods, and toward that end commits greater wrongs, than any merely anarchic society would want or dare.

So goes a positive description of anarchism: the condition of non-statism. Normatively, mileage varies widely. This chapter concludes that, if you favor human freedom, prosperity, and well-being, and if you disfavor institutionalized coercion as compared to mutual consent, you should welcome these trends. To one with those values, at least, the forecast for anarchy looks bright.

II. Some Former Futures of Anarchy

What have others forecast for anarchy? This section does not pretend to offer a comprehensive critique of every theory born of fevered imagination; the limits of time, space, and patience would forbid. Instead, it gives a fair taste of a few of the most popular predictions of what might follow in a world without states.

This sampler offers three flavors of anarchy. First, in Subsection II.A., comes a reminder that Marxism began as avowedly and stridently anarchist doctrine, predicting freedom and plenty in the absence of the state, before taking a fast revolutionary U-turn toward totalitarian socialism.

Subsection II.B. offers a quick survey of anarchist forecasts from a distinctly different school of thought: "market-friendly" libertarianism. Because the most colorful portrayals of the future, and arguably the most accurate, come from speculative fiction, Subsection II.C. looks there to find a whole new collection of predictions about anarchy.

A. Marxist Statism, Anti- and Anti-Anti-

Though now more often associated with totalitarian statism, Marxism pronounced itself at birth and thereafter repeatedly as an avowed anarchist doctrine. "Political power, properly so-called, is merely the organized power of one class for oppressing another," proclaimed *The Communist Manifesto*.[7] With no classes, there can be no class oppression. With no class oppression, there can be no political power. And with no political power, there can be no state. In its place will arise, claimed Marx and Engels, a society organized along emphatically non-oppressive, non-political, *non-statist* principles. And arise it will, like it or not, as a matter of economic determinism. They predicted that, "When, in the course of development, class distinctions have disappeared and all production has been concentrated in the hands of a vast association of the whole nation, the public power will lose its political character."[8]

Exactly how Marx and Engels foresaw a communist anarchist society organizing itself remains unclear. Perhaps the details had to await further technological developments, such as the distributed trustless tokenized crypto-economic blockchain networks that so tantalize present-day anarchists.[9] At all events, the founders of communism had some firm ideas about what their idealized society would *not* be: capitalist. Marx and Engels criticized the alienating division of labor characteristic of capitalist society and offered this oft-quoted description of how their projected communist utopia would abolish labor, or at least the kind.

> [I]n communist society, where nobody has one exclusive sphere of activity but each can become accomplished in any branch he wishes, society regulates the general production and thus makes it possible for me to do one thing today and other tomorrow, to hunt in the morning, fish in the afternoon, rear cattle in the evening, criticize after dinner, just as I have a mind, without ever becoming hunter, fisherman, shepherd, or critic.[10]

Engels returned to the same theme in *Anti-Dühring*, where he claimed (without apparent irony, though also without the benefit of historical hindsight) that after the workers "tak[e] possession of the means of production in the name of society," the state will gently pass into history. The *route* to anarchy that Engels described—abolishing private property—does not seem likely to lead to less statism, but the *destination* that Engels described could easily have come from a crypto-anarchist of recent vintage:

> State interference in social relations becomes, in one domain after another, superfluous, and then dies out of itself; the government of persons is replaced by the administration of things, and by the conduct of processes of production. The state is not 'abolished'. *It dies out.*[11]

After the death of Marx in 1883, Engels continued developing his late comrade's theories. In *The Origin of the Family, Private Property and the State*, Engels observed that the state "has not existed from all eternity" because it arose only with the division of society into classes.[12] The first claim cannot be seriously contested. The second claim can scarcely be taken seriously. Hierarchies pervade not just human societies but even, as a reliable mark of their ubiquity, animal ones.

Nonetheless, having taken a running start at this looming gap between fact and theory, Engels dared to attempt one of the great leaps of Marxist faith:

> We are now rapidly approaching a stage in the development of production at which the existence of these classes not only will have ceased to be a necessity, but will become a positive hindrance to production. They will fall as inevitably as they arose at an earlier stage. Alone with them the state will inevitably fall. The society that will organize production on the basis of a free and equal association of the producers will put the whole machinery of state where it will then belong: into the museum of antiquities, by the side of the spinning wheel and the bronze ax.[13]

It made for lovely rhetoric. In practice, though, and as exemplified in Lenin's later reinterpretation of Engels, the attempted abolition of classes led only to a resurgent state—indeed, a newly all powerful one. In *State and Revolution*, Lenin explained why the political institutions in his grip would by no means wither away soon.

> Engels says that, in taking state power, the proletariat thereby 'abolishes the state as state.' … As a matter of fact, Engels speaks here of the proletarian revolution 'abolishing' the *bourgeois* state, while the words about the state withering away refer to the remnants of the *proletarian* state *after* the socialist revolution.[14]

Notice what he did there? Splitting Engels's "state" into bourgeois and proletarian versions allowed Lenin to insert "socialist revolution" in the gap. Like a wedge hammered into a log, the military order required to overthrow the old ruling elite, driven by the vanguard of the proletariat, with Lenin at its head, would keep splitting a wider and wider gap between the abolition of the bourgeois state and the withering away of proletarian one. And even then Lenin caviled, explaining that, if ever the proletarian state did wither away, it would do so only through "slow, even, gradual change, [in the] absence of leaps and storms, or … of revolution."[15]

With this move, Lenin pulled a revolutionary U-turn, redirecting communism from a cry against politics into a paean to a new, all-powerful, all-consuming state. And he did not hide what sort of government people should expect from Leninist communism. He proclaimed, with brutal candor, "no state is *free* or is a *people's state*."[16]

Whatever future anarchism had in Soviet communism died with Lenin. The totalitarians who followed in his wake did nothing to revive anarchy (except perhaps in the sense of chaos, which they sowed in plenty). It is not the sort of thing to make communist anarchism look very attractive, all told.

Perhaps, though, it is not fair to blame Marx and Engels for the crimes of their nominal followers. Indeed, the two revolutionaries arguably erred only in foreseeing the future too early. Some of the rosier pictures they painted of working for fun in a stateless society find echoes today in the white papers spewed forth by crypto-economic startups seeking token buyers. But, then again, that perhaps says less about the foresight of Marx and Engels than it does about the timeless charms of imagined freedom from want and compulsion.

B. Academic Anarcho-capitalism

Only a fairly hefty tome could reasonably aspire to survey every forecast for anarchy, so this chapter rests content with sampling some wildly varying popular accounts. The prior subsection canvassed Marxism's wending story about what will happen when—or, as it turned out in practice under communism, *if*—statism melts away (which, as it turned out in practice under communism, it did not). This subsection offers a summary of anarchist forecasts from a distinctly different direction: libertarian. It begins with Robert Nozick's critique, albeit one offered from a sympathetic point of view, of the whole idea of libertarian anarchism, and then considers more appreciative takes on the idea from David Friedman and Randy E. Barnett.

Robert Nozick famously used a forecast of sorts to argue against anarchism on the grounds that it could not last, but instead would inevitably lapse into statism. His book *Anarchy, State, and Utopia* lays out his thought experiment.[17] It begins with an idealized system of governance based on respect for personal freedom and property rights so unstinting that it forbids even taxation. Into this anarcho-capitalist Eden, Nozick introduces the problem of conflicting standards for administering justice.

With no state settling the debate, says Nozick, those who interpret and enforce the law, whether individuals or (more likely) the private protection agencies they hire to enforce the law, will disagree on what procedures to apply. Some will disparage alternative procedures as unreliable or unfair, and refuse to allow themselves or those under their protection to suffer mistreatment in accordance with such procedures.

You might think that here as in other markets, albeit with perhaps some sharper jostling, the various protection services would work things out. Violence is not usually a profitable business model.

Instead, Nozick argues that one agency will inevitably come to dominate any given market for protection services.[18] That structural assumption leads Nozick to conclude that a single standard for justice will likewise come to prevail over other contenders. This happens even in what begins as an anarchical society and inevitably ends in the emergence of the functional equivalence of a state. Nozick declares this, so to speak, an immaculate conception—one free of original sin—from the point of view of rights violations, and offers its putative purity as the core of his "invisible-hand" justification of the state.[19]

This is not the place to criticize Nozick's attempt to justify the state; others did that long ago, and well.[20] Here, it suffices to offer his views as a notable account of why anarcho-capitalism might be thought unable to subsist. On that view, the future of anarchism leads to ... statism. Unsurprisingly, other libertarian anarchists offer different views of the future of their preferred social order.

David Friedman's *The Machinery of Freedom* does not offer a comprehensive picture of how a future stateless society might work so much as a mosaic of how people in such a world might solve each of many separate, difficult, crucial problems.[21] Friedman explains, for instance, how voluntary exchange could deal with education,[22] immigration,[23] pollution,[24] law,[25] and national defense.[26] Almost in passing, Friedman also answers a question that libertarians face with eye-rolling frequency: "Who will build the roads?"[27] On Friedman's account (and in sharp contrast to Nozick's), anarchism represents not a transient ideal but the general condition of humankind, historically speaking, and a more practical solution than statism to the greatest challenges of social life.

Though ordinarily limiting himself to the sort of sober academic prose that befits a law professor of some repute, Randy E. Barnett ventures a brief fictional forecast of a stateless legal order in his book, *The Structure of Liberty: Justice and the Rule of Law.*[28] His sketch focuses on legal rather than political, social, or economic features. On Barnett's model, consumers generally arrange to have their legal rights defended not by states but by private RMOs (rights maintenance organizations) modeled on the health maintenance organizations (HMOs) that already provide medical care to so many consumers.[29] Private judges decide cases under terms not much different from those that already apply in arbitrations, and private organizations issue a variety of non-binding codes and commentaries that consumers and service providers adopt or not, as they see fit.[30] Barnett even spins out a disaster scenario—in which private law enforcement agencies battle for dominance in a distinctly state-like way—to show how the system could self-regulate its way back to peaceful competition between non-monopolistic governing services.[31] All told, Barnett makes anarchism sound like a perfectly reasonable framework for suburban subdivisions, corporate parks, big-box stores, and even law firms.

C. Anarchy in Poly-Sci-Fi

Fiction writers have often and famously pictured futures choked with statism. Aldous Huxley's *Brave New World*[32] and George Orwell's *1984*[33] come foremost to mind for many. Contemporary readers might think of the wildly popular *Hunger Games* series, set in a dystopia wherein where whole populations suffer under the whims of a distant ruling elite.[34] The series ends with the emergence of an incipient government, but leaves readers' imaginations to carry on the story.[35]

Writers of fiction have much less frequently attempted actually to portray anarchies, at least in the sense of making them conscious plot devices. J.R.R. Tolkien's Middle-Earth arguably describes an anarchy of sorts, granted. Tolkien himself certainly had a sympathetic view of statelessness, noting in middle age: "My political opinions lean more and more to Anarchy (philosophically understood, meaning the abolition of control not whiskered men with bombs)—or to 'unconstitutional' Monarchy."[36] Despite its deeper lessons about the lust for power, though, a fantasy about hobbits, dragons, and wizards is not likely to reveal much about the future of anarchy in this world, where technology rather than magic works the wonder. For *that* forecasting job, speculative fiction (to use the term its writers typically prefer; *science fiction* or *sci-fi*, in popular parlance) offers a better resource.

The original anarchist world that Robert Heinlein vividly portrayed in *The Moon Is a Harsh Mistress*[37] exerted a large influence on readers and writers. The book describes a lunar society oppressed by the Authority, an Earth-based governing entity that controls and exploits its satellite colony. Heinlein's characters explain the "Rational Anarchist" society of the Loonies; they unspool the whys and hows of their inevitable (and, per the genre, inevitably *successful*) revolution. Heinlein delivers plenty of setbacks, plot twists, and other trappings of stagecraft as only he can, of course. But far more than the style, the *ideas* in *The Moon Is a Harsh Mistress* influenced the political science-flavored science fiction (*poli-sci-fi* as a wag might have it) that followed.

J. Neil Schulman's *Alongside Night* forecasts an America collapsing from the economic effects of an inflated currency and the political effects of a grotesquely overgrown police state.[38] The protagonist, Elliot Vreeland, helps the Revolutionary Agorist Cadre overthrow the state and launch a free-market, individualist-anarchist society in its place. Regardless of its merits as literature or political philosophy, it makes anarchism seem cool, fun, and totally doable, man.

Vernor Vinge's entry in this sampler of notable anarchist sci-fi, *The Ungoverned*,[39] zeroes in on a problem especially salient in anarchist thinking: how to defend a stateless society against statist attack. Set in a post-United States America, the story finds the Republic of New Mexico invading a peaceful anarcho-capitalist society in neighboring (areas making up what was formerly known as the state of) Kansas. Though the clever technological tricks deployed by the prickly defenders play vital roles in driving away the attackers and achieving justice, Vinge takes care to show that good business relations and basic human decency do what mere gadgets cannot: preserve self-governance against enemies within and without.

Neal Stephenson offers a notably well-realized, theoretically robust, and vastly entertaining species of the *poly-sci-fi* genus. Though never set forth explicitly and in full, Stephenson's vision of the future of government appears in the background of several separate and largely unrelated stories, all of which evidently take place in roughly the same fictional universe.[40] In this universe, rising inflation encourages the widespread abandonment of fiat currency in favor of new, untraceable, digital alternatives. States find it impossible to tax online transactions and, starved of revenue from the largest and most vibrant part of the economy, collapse. In the place of states grows a patchwork of voluntary governments, some standalone and built from the bottom-up, some organized as franchise-organized quasi-national entities (FOQNEs), and many assembled into the First Distributed Republic.[41]

Inquiring minds can only wonder whether Stephenson has private notes detailing his forecast and explaining its theoretical foundations—one can only wonder, and hope. In the meantime, he offers an evocative picture of life in his braver, newer world. Consider this scene from his breakout novel, *Snow Crash.* Stephenson presents the scene from the point of view of the novel's heroine, Y.T., a 15-year-old Kourier—a freelance delivery ninja who rides a powered, smart-wheeled skateboard-ish *plank.* Y.T. has been kidnapped and held hostage by L. Bob Rife and his henchman, Tony. They wait within a repurposed Soviet helicopter, its blades powering up for take-off. The gunship sits on the *Enterprise* nuclear aircraft carrier, now a privately owned and operated yacht/warship.

> Another man duck-walks across the flight deck, in mortal fear of the whirling rotor blades, and climbs in. He's about sixty, with a dirigible of white hair that was not ruffled in any way by the downdraft.
>
> "Hello, everyone," he says cheerfully. "I don't think I've met all of you. Just got here this morning and now I'm on my way back again!"
>
> "Who are you?" Tony says.
>
> The new guy looks crestfallen. "Greg Ritchie," he says.
>
> Then, when no one seems to react, he jogs their memory. "President of the United States."[42]

Greg Ritchie disappears from the story a few pages later when a horde of Kouriers, summoned by Y.T., drags the helicopter out of the sky with electromagnetic harpoons before "overwhelming and disarming" the President.[43] You can always count on Stephenson to put on a show. Here, he sends a message, too. The President of the United States, in former times the most powerful man on Earth, falls prey to pacifying children in this future anarchy.

In both *Snow Crash* and his later book, *Diamond Age,*[44] Stephenson describes *distributed republics*—fluid governments that range across the world, occupying many various places at various times and following wherever their citizen-customers go. He presents these as for-profit enterprises, such as Mr. Lee's Greater Hong Kong franchise,[45] or as shattered remnants of former nation-states, such as the leftover bits of the former United States, now known as Fedland. Stephenson portrays the former as tough but fair and, perhaps more important, good value for the crypto-buck. He depicts the latter as a pathetically shrunken relic, psychotically obsessed with false order.

In *Snow Crash*'s future Los Angeles, Fedland occupies an area that "used to be the VA Hospital and a bunch of other Federal buildings; now it has condensed into a kidney-shaped lozenge that wraps around the 405."[46] Over the course of several pages, as if to a soundtrack of kazoos, Stephenson replicates a lengthy memorandum, straight from the administration of Fedland, detailing intra-office policies for bathroom tissue distribution units (i.e., BTDUs, aka "rolls").[47] Lesser authors criticize via numbing bombast; Stephenson kills with mordant humor.

As he describes Fedland, Mr. Lee's Greater Hong Kong, and other FOQNEs, Stephenson offers a veritable bestiary of governing entities. He shows them in their natural environments, jostling for market share against a backdrop of raw, ungoverned, and spectacularly cinematographic lawlessness. Anarchy, at least in these early days of Stephenson's post-state world, is not at all peaceful. But then again, neither is the world—adroitly depicted in Stephenson's superlative *Cryptonomicon*—in which states still run things.[48]

It matters more, once you strip out the engaging characters, gripping incidents, and special effects, that Stephenson depicts a plausible route from here to anarchy-ish (the qualifying suffix added in recognition that states still survive, though much diminished, in his version of the future). Stephenson moreover makes a fair case that life would go on, in many ways better than before, and at all events in a much grander style, in a world with a lot less statism. If anarchy does that well in the real world, we might end up both better off and better entertained.

III. Statism as Speculative Bubble

No less than tulip bulbs or shares in the French Mississippi Company, no less than dot-com initial public offerings (IPOs) or blockchain-based initial coin offerings (ICOs), the state *qua* institution has entered the late stages of an expansion–collapse cycle. Subsection III. A. documents the reality that governments have in recent decades done and promised far beyond what they can afford, resulting in overweening authoritarianism and inevitably unsustainable debt. Subsection III.B. discusses factors that might prick the statist bubble—cryptocurrencies, most likely—and the form of its demise—more of a rapid and largely controllable slump than a violent explosion.

A. *The Expansion of Statism*

More than a few theorists have proclaimed the end days of statism. The most ambitious such forecasts have not been completely borne out, to put it mildly. Marx's prediction of an international communist revolution leading to a classless and therefore stateless utopia provides a case in point.[49] Informed and focused forecasts have done rather better at anticipating government train wrecks, however. And sometimes the signs of a crash loom so large that nobody can miss them.

Ronald Reagan correctly not only predicted the downfall of the most statist empire on Earth but also named the cause, maintaining that "the march of freedom and democracy" would "leave Marxism-Leninism on the ash heap of history as it has left other tyrannies which stifle the freedom and muzzle the self-expression of the people."[50] That was an extreme case, as the subsequent dramatic collapse of the Soviet Union demonstrated. Do the evident tremblings of the global body politic presage another political upheaval?

Statism in general certainly seems to have reached new heights of power. For decades, states have wielded armaments sufficient by most accounts to kill billions and disrupt if not destroy modern civilization.[51] The United States routinely monitors the supposedly private communications of its citizens with little regard for supposedly inalienable constitutional rights.[52]

States abroad show even less regard for their subjects. The government of India has in apparent disregard of its own Supreme Court compelled residents to undergo biometric identification in order to link each to a taxable identity.[53] China's monitoring programs go even farther, including surveillance of public spaces using automated real-time recognition programs and social credit ratings that punish or reward even minor dissent by limiting access to public and private services.[54] The People's Republic also employs mass detention, re-education, and work camps to house tens of thousands of people the government regards not as explicitly guilty of any crime but merely as insufficiently devoted to the state.[55] Other governments doubtless watch with interest, attracted to the prospect of letting machines take over the troublesome business of compelling their subjects' obedience to official edicts.

At the same time that the state grasps for new powers, its financial foundations crumble. To judge from the United States' own cold, hard numbers, the strongest government on Earth will soon go broke. The Governmental Accountability Office (GAO), which serves as something like the financial conscience of the U.S. government, explains why current spending levels are "unsustainable": "Debt held by the public [i.e., federal debt] increased from $15.8 trillion (or 77 percent of gross domestic product (GDP)) at the end of fiscal year 2018 to $16.8 trillion (or 79 percent of GDP) at the end of fiscal year 2019. By comparison, debt has averaged 46 percent of GDP since 1946.The debt-to-GDP ratio is projected to surpass its historical high of 106 percent," racked up by spending on World War II, a bit after the year 2030 on the GAO's accounting.[56]

Around 2030, even if taxes managed to capture 100 percent of all wealth generated in the United States, not enough would come in to pay down the federal debt. From there, the slippery slope leads ever downward to fiscal ruin. The Congressional Budget Office (CBO) concurs, pegging 2028 as the year in which federal debt held by the public will exceed GDP.[57] Among the unhappy consequences:

- Federal spending on interest payments on that debt will increase substantially, especially because interest rates are projected to rise over the next few years.
- Because federal borrowing reduces total saving in the economy over time, the nation's capital stock will ultimately be smaller, pulling down productivity and total wages.
- Lawmakers will have less flexibility to use tax and spending policies to respond to unexpected challenges.
- The likelihood of a fiscal crisis in the United States will increase. Investors will become less willing to finance the government's borrowing unless they are compensated with very high interest rates; if that happens, interest rates on federal debt will rise suddenly and sharply.[58]

Granted, matters have not quite yet reached the point of crisis. But who believes that U.S. politics will change so much between now and 2030 as to inaugurate a new era of long-term, prudent, financially sound planning? Nor is the United States alone in facing a grim fiscal forecast; the National Intelligence Council (NIC) foresees the same sort of economic ruin for governments across the developed world.[59] The private, non-partisan Peterson Institute for International Economics sums up the consensus:

> That government debt will grow to dangerous and unsustainable levels in most advanced and many emerging economies over the next 25 years—if there are not changes in current tax rates or government benefit programs in retirement and health care—is virtually beyond dispute.[60]

That "if" clause offers a way to dodge disaster, of course. But again, internationally as well as domestically, does anyone reasonably expect the current generation of states to swear off buying votes through deficit spending? The recent and enduring riots among *les gilets jaune* in France and elsewhere throughout the European Union suggests only one answer: *Non.*[61] Everybody wants something for nothing. But those who demand more benefits and lower taxes from fiscally failing states stand to get nothing at all—except more trouble, as states lash back at protesters. Thus begin vicious cycles, and thus rise the sorts of social whirlwinds that race before great storms of social change.

B. The Collapse of Statism

Suppose that governments worldwide face severe financial crises in the next few decades. What will finally prick the expanding bubble of public debt? And when it does pop, will statism explode with fatal effect or gently slump into irrelevance?

Most forecasters foresee the next revolution taking place not so much in the streets as on the network; tomorrow's revolutionaries will succeed not by taking over the government but by leaving it behind. Stephenson offers a characteristically entertaining version of how the next revolution might happen—or at least how it might get going—in "The Great Simolean Caper."[62] The caper involves a family in peril, rival brothers, a conspiracy by the U.S. government, a *counter*-conspiracy by the First Distributed Republic, and a scheme to convince the public to abandon fiat money in favor of CryptoCredits, an untaxable virtual currency. The story ends before that great virtual exodus begins, but Stephenson's later books make clear what his version of the Promised Land looks like (hint: not very statist).[63]

Employing a style more functional than entertaining, the NIC offers a remarkably similar forecast in one of several possible scenarios—the one for "Nonstate World"—that it projects as a possibility for 2030.[64] In the NIC's forecast, "[t]he nation-state does not disappear, but countries increasingly organize and orchestrate 'hybrid' coalitions of state and nonstate actors which shift depending on the issue."

Despite the scenario's name, states have not disappeared in "Nonstate World." They remain and, though they face new struggles, only the baddest (because authoritarian) and biggest (because too unwieldy) face existential threats. Smaller jurisdictions do rather nicely in "Nonstate World."[65] The net result, at least compared to the more dire alternatives considered by NIC: "The world is … more stable and socially cohesive."[66]

To judge from trends already well under way, "Nonstate World" (more accurately, "Less-State World") looks rather more likely than a blandly smooth continuation of the present-day world of relatively large and cohesive states. As documented in *Your Next Government? From the Nation State to Stateless Nations*, special jurisdictions have for some decades been turning formerly uniform countries into complicated skeins of overlapping and sometimes mutually exclusive rules.[67] In nearly 75 percent of all countries, and in at least 4,000 locations worldwide (arguably more than 10,000), these special jurisdictions have splintered the authority of the state, creating venues for the express purpose of trying out better methods of governance.[68] Prompted by economic migrants seeking asylum as refugees, moreover, states have increasingly begun splitting their borders, and now also their interiors, into special international zones, creating areas within their territories geographically, but outside the scope of many of their laws.[69] The result: an environment ripe for rapid change.

What will trigger the most rapid and turbulent, if not violent, phase in the collapse of the state? The late Timothy C. May, Intel scientist and industry sage, long ago (in Internet years) foretold that technological developments—advances in computer networks and specifically encryption—would inevitably doom the state:

> A specter is haunting the modern world, the specter of crypto anarchy. Computer technology is on the verge of providing the ability for individuals and groups to communicate and interact with each other in a totally anonymous manner …. Interactions over networks will be untraceable, via extensive rerouting of encrypted packets and tamper-proof boxes which implement cryptographic protocols with nearly perfect assurance against any tampering …. These developments will alter completely the nature of government regulation, the ability to tax and control economic interactions, the ability to keep information secret, and will even alter the nature of trust and reputation.[70]

Though May did not exactly rue these developments, he viewed his preferences as irrelevant to their inevitability.

> The State will of course try to slow or halt the spread of this technology, citing national security concerns, use of the technology by drug dealers and tax evaders, and fears of societal disintegration .... But this will not halt the spread of crypto anarchy.[71]

May hedged his bets on *when* the events he projected would take place[72] and said little more about the mechanism than that cryptography would hide virtual lawbreakers from local law enforcement so that "a kind of 'regulatory arbitrage' ... [could] be used to avoid legal roadblocks."[73] More recent analysts offer up-to-date and fuller versions of the story, but the overall narrative remains the same: high-tech will outcompete old statism in the market to serve citizen-customers, initiating an exodus from centralized coercive governments to distributed and consent-rich ones.[74]

At one time, it seemed that Bitcoin might offer a fast escape from fiat currency and statist rule.[75] The bloom has faded on that particular rose, but new and potentially better crypto-governance services continue to appear. The next section sketches the sort of world these might create.

IV. Anarchism from the Bits Up

How would a world with less and less statism work? Locally, the same human nature that works now to keep families, peer groups, and private institutions going would continue to do so. But at larger scales the crypto-anarchist world promises to outgrow—one might say *transcend*—statism. How? To summarize the views of a various commentators in their own favored terminology: *What central planners do in the state using coercive force, open-source protocols will do in permissionless networks using distributed ledger databases and public key cryptography.*

That packs a lot of technical assumptions into a few obscure words. In practical effect, it would most likely mean using digital telecommunications devices to buy governing services such as vehicle registration, business formation, and (crucially) banking from an open network of providers, instead of having those services provided in real space by a provider that monopolizes services within a defined geographic territory. That kind of crypto-anarchist utopia would not differ much from the present world in outward appearance. Functionally, though, it would run on entirely different code, computer and legal.

Bitcoin and other cryptocurrencies already challenge the state's monopoly on money. Newer blockchain-based services offer private alternatives to other state functions, including dispute resolution,[76] registration of property interests,[77] and even citizenship of a sort.[78] Computer code has begun entering terrain formerly reached only by legislative code. How far will the process go?

Edan Yago predicts "semi-independent alternatives to the nation-state itself."[79] And he is hardly alone. Max Borders foresees "an upgrade to our social operating system" and calls on us "to imagine jurisdictions as being pulled away from terra firma and standing armies. It's cloud governance and thus also cloud community."[80] Melanie Swan sums up the emerging (virtual-) world view: "Blockchain-based governance systems could offer a range of services traditionally provided by governments, all of which could be completely voluntary, with user-citizens opting in and out at will."[81]

This revolution eschews violence, and does not even directly challenge existing institutions. It instead aims to grow alongside state structures, interfacing only when and if necessary and then on terms that serve the network. Vitalik Buterin, creator of Ethereum, says he aims to build a "completely parallel kind of world that's totally separate from the existing one ... . [T]he goal is definitely to help improve the mainstream world, but we're on a different track."[82] Toward that end, the Ethereum network offers the prospect of a governance system in the cloud with payments made in the local cryptocurrency, Ether, and services including identification, banking, and even health care. States hardly enter the picture—very much by design.

Bitnation claims to offer a software package that would-be "Citizens" can download and use to join the "Decentralized Opt-In Jurisdiction" of a purely online "nation" (or to create an entirely new one from scratch).[83] As the capitalization and quote marks suggest, Bitnation gives these terms special (and much diluted) meanings. There is little reason to think that a Bitnation "Passport" would get a "Citizen" of any virtual "Nation" through any traditional port of entry. Bitnation also claims to offer services such as party identification and reputation scoring, peer-to-peer arbitration, and notarization of legal documents.[84] These services do not seem to have seen significant use, leaving Bitnation's generous promises and bold predictions largely untested. Despite those caveats, the project offers a vision of how distributed governance might actually work and has begun crawling toward making it a reality (inasmuch as *reality* properly applies to an entirely virtual community). Whatever the first real distributed non-state government looks like, it probably will include parts not radically different from those painted in Bitnation's pretend version.

All that assumes, of course, that distributed governments in the cloud do not, like clouds themselves in the physical world, melt into thin air. That seems the likely fate of many crypto-challengers to the state. Consider, for instance, the first digital autonomous organization (Genesis DAO). A coding bug threw Genesis DAO into a governance crisis so severe that the protocol's founders had to split the community into two separate and irreconcilable parts by implementing a "hard fork" in the underlying protocol.[85]

Recall, too, that all the many glowing predictions of governments sustained solely by bits assume these new polities will not fall prey to the same sorts of problems that have long troubled more solid ones. It may turn out, to the surprise of people who have grown more accustomed to staring at screens than into eyes, that computer code cannot do all the things necessary for human governance. Perhaps working communities need more than telecommunication to create friendships, defy orders, detect treason, show mercy, and do all the other things, good and bad, that shape human governance.[86]

Another caveat: visions of crypto-anarcho-capitalist utopias tend to downplay the efficacy of nation-states in combating competitors. States of one form or another have been around for millennia; modern ones for about 500 years. Statists count the world's richest and wisest among their number. They have powerful incentives to resist challenges to their rule. The People's Republic of China has only begun to explore the potential of technologies designed to control whole populations. Technology can serve crypto-anarchists or uber-statists. Who will control the future of governance remains uncertain.

V. Conclusion: The Government of the Future?

Brazil's bright but seemingly elusive potential earned it a label at once both uplifting and wistful: "The country of the future."[87] Unwilling to let irony speak for itself, some wags feel compelled to add "and it always will be."[88] The same label might well describe anarchy: "The government of the future." Must anarchy always remain, like Brazil in the eyes of the wags, nothing more than an imaginary ideal? No; anarchy exists here and now.

Anarchy is not an ideal form of government too good for our imperfect world. Quite the contrary. When understood as the absence of statism, anarchy *pervades* social life. It appears in the countless voluntary acts of courtesy, kindness, and grace, from the trifling to the heroic, that fill the better part of human relations.[89] The food that parents place before their children; the gifts that friends exchange on special (or even ordinary) occasions; the tidings shared between neighbors, co-workers, and strangers—these kinds of connections, far more than regulation, taxation, or conscription, make social life *sociable*. These alone give social life ... *life*.

Humans once lived in anarchy only—*anarchy* both in the sense of *statelessness* and of *chaos*. They left both conditions in one move, entering the servitude of statism to escape the chaos of human and natural violence. Those who formed the first states instituted governments powerful enough to kill or to save. Some doubtless meant well; many likely meant ill. Regardless, states rose and persisted. But recent thinking suggests that statism is not the only way to mitigate human wickedness and natural disaster. It may well turn out, despite the seeming paradox, that anarchy offers a more harmonious, peaceful, and *orderly* way of life.

The interesting question is not whether humans can live together without the threat of institutionalized coercion looming in the background. They did so long before the state arose, have continued doing so since, and will keep at it if ever statism disappears. Anarchy is not the government of the future only, but of the past and present, too.

* * *

This chapter addressed the question "What is the future of anarchy?" As the discussion revealed, the forecast for anarchy is not a question of *if* but of *how much*; not a question of *when* but *how quickly*; and not a question of *why* in any sense at all. In answer to those questions, the chapter concludes with this prediction:

> Anarchy in the sense of stateless governance will increase gradually in scale and scope until around 2030, at which time many and major states will fail financially. They will consequently abandon many former powers and services, some of which consent-rich distributed economic systems will adopt. Despite political turbulence and scattered local outbreaks of chaos, this process will generate significant and widely distributed improvements in human freedom, prosperity, and well-being.

Even beyond the usual caveats that should accompany *any* prediction—including the limits of human cognition, an uncaring and capricious nature, and the vagaries of fate—two wild cards bear particular note. First, because simple math foretells that the great statist bubble must pop around 2030, the moment of crisis will tend to work its way backwards, from the future to the present. Panic will arise when pressure to avoid the looming disaster overwhelms the exits, so to speak. This will cause its own disaster, like those crushed in a crowd fleeing a burning assembly, sometime before 2030.

Second, given that many of the fiscal woes of nation-states can be traced back to states' promises to support increasingly elderly populations, the advent of age-reversing therapies might alter extant political bargains enough to throw guesses about future trends to the wind.[90] Saving humans, the greatest resource,[91] from senescence, the universal scourge of humankind, would generate wealth, financial and cultural, beyond measure. In that happy event, statism would not have to crash in financial ruin. It might crash or wither just the same, of course, but for other reasons and by means of other, presumably less violent, means.

Finally, to answer the question "What is the future of anarchy?" in less clinical terms: "Most likely, and with any luck, *more*." In other words, we might reasonably hope that the future will bring less institutionalized coercion and more mutual consent, less hate, and more love.

Acknowledgements

Thanks go to Gary Chartier, Alec Isaac, Sarah Skwire, Eric Hennigan, Boris Karpa, Fred Curtis Moulton, Jr., James Stacey Taylor, Anselm Hook, Matt Gilliland, Tennyson McCalla, Zoe

Miller, Monty Cosma, and Rob Nielsen. The views expressed here do not represent those of any principal, associate, or agent of the author.

Notes

1 See Max Weber, *The Theory of Social and Economic Organization*, ed. Talcott Parsons, trans. A. M. Henderson and Parsons (Oxford: OUP 1947 [1922]) 154 (offering the standard definition of the state).

2 See Joseph Heath, "Methodological Individualism," *The Stanford Encyclopedia of Philosophy*, ed. Edward N. Zalta (Stanford: Center for the Study of Language and Information 2015), https://plato.stanford.edu/archives/spr2015/entries/methodological-individualism/.

3 See, for example, John Hasnas, "The Obviousness of Anarchy," *Anarchism/Minarchism: Is a Government Part of a Free Country?*, ed. Roderick T. Long and Tibor R. Machan (Farnham: Ashgate 2008) 111–32.

4 See, for example, Michael Bakunin, "Critique of the Marxist Theory of the State," *Michael Bakunin on Anarchy*, ed. Sam Dolgoff (New York: Vintage 1971) 327, available at https://libcom.org/files/Bakunin%20on%20Anarchy%20(1971).pdf ("We, the revolutionary anarchists … . are the enemies of the State and all forms of the statist principle.")

5 Those qualify more as *philokaosists* (lovers of chaos) than *anarchists* (opposers of rulers).

6 See James C. Scott, *The Art of Not Being Governed: An Anarchist History of Upland Southeast Asia* (New Haven: Yale UP 2010); James C. Scott, *Against the Grain: A Deep History of the Earliest States* (New Haven: Yale UP 2018).

7 Karl Marx and Friedrich Engels, "Manifesto of the Communist Party," *Marx and Engels: Basic Writings on Politics and Philosophy*, ed. Lewis S. Feuer (Garden City: Anchor-Doubleday 1959) 29.

8 Marx and Engels 29.

9 See Section IV, below.

10 Karl Marx and Friedrich Engels, "Excerpts from *The German Ideology*," Feuer 254.

11 Frederick Engels, "Socialism Utopian and Scientific," trans. Edward Aveling, Feuer 106. Original emphasis.

12 Friedrich Engels, "Excerpt from *The Origin of the Family, Private Property and the State*," Feuer 394.

13 Engels, "Excerpt from *The Origin*."

14 Vladimir Lenin, "State and Revolution," *Essential Works of Marxism*, ed. Arthur P. Mendel (New York: Bantam 1961) 113 (quoting Engels, *The Origin of the Family, Private Property and the State*). Original emphasis.

15 Lenin 112–3.

16 Lenin 115. Original emphasis.

17 Robert Nozick, *Anarchy, State, and Utopia* (New York: Basic 1974).

18 Nozick 15–7.

19 Nozick 119.

20 See, for example, several articles collected in the special issue of *Journal of Libertarian Studies* 1 (Winter 1977) by Randy E. Barnett, Roy A. Childs, John T. Sanders, and Murray Rothbard. See also George H. Smith, "Justice Entrepreneurship In A Free Market," *Journal of Libertarian Studies* 3 (Winter 1979): 405–26.

21 David Friedman, *The Machinery of Freedom*, 3d ed. (Charleston: CreateSpace 2015).

22 Friedman 53–60.

23 Friedman 67–9.

24 Friedman 99–100.

25 Friedman 110–6.

26 Friedman 131–9.

27 Friedman 70–2.

28 Randy E. Barnett, *The Structure of Liberty: Justice and the Rule of Law*, 2d ed. (Oxford: OUP 2014).

29 Barnett 284–5.

30 Barnett 286–90

31 Barnett 294–7.

32 Aldous Huxley, *Brave New World* (New York: Harper 1998 [1932]).

33 George Orwell, *1984* (New York: Signet 2008 [1949]).

34 Suzanne Collins, *The Hunger Games* (New York: Scholastic 2008); Suzanne Collins, *Catching Fire* (New York: Scholastic 2009); Suzanne Collins, *Mockingjay* (New York: Scholastic 2010).

35 See Marlon Lieber and Daniel Zamora, "Rebel Without a Cause," *Jacobin*, Jan. 16, 2016, www.jacobinmag.com/2016/01/hunger-games-review-capitalism-revolution-mockingjay-suzanne-collins (arguing that the heroism of the lead character, Katniss, "ultimately rests not on her bow and arrow skills or her role in the rebellion, but in her total rejection of politics").
36 J.R.R. Tolkien, letter to Christopher Tolkien, Nov. 29, 1943 [no. 52], *Letters of J.R.R. Tolkien*, ed. Humphrey Carpenter (New York: Houghton 1995) 63.
37 Robert Heinlein, *The Moon Is a Harsh Mistress* (New York: Putnam 1966).
38 J. Neil Shulman, *Alongside Night* (New York: Crown 1979).
39 Vernor Vinge, *The Ungoverned* (Wake Forest: Baen 1985), www.baen.com/Chapters/1416520724/1416520724___4.htm.
40 Neal Stephenson, "The Great Simolean Caper," *Time*, March 1, 1995, web.archive.org/web/20071226061705/www.time.com:80/time/magazine/article/0,9171,982610-1,00.html; Neal Stephenson, *The Diamond Age* (New York: Bantam 1995); Neal Stephenson, *Snow Crash* (New York: Del Rey 1992).
41 "*The Diamond Age*," Wikipedia, https://en.wikipedia.org/wiki/The_Diamond_Age (May 24, 2020).
42 Stephenson, *Crash* 506.
43 Stephenson, *Crash* 541.
44 Stephenson, *Crash*.
45 Mr. Lee's Greater Hong Kong franchise is the "grandaddy" of the FOQNEs. Stephenson, *Crash* 54.
46 Stephenson, *Crash* 208.
47 Stephenson, *Crash* 335–40.
48 Neal Stephenson, *Cryptonomicon* (New York: Avon 1999).
49 See Subsection II.B., above.
50 Ronald Reagan, "Ronald Reagan Address to British Parliament" (June 8. 1982), The History Place, www.historyplace.com/speeches/reagan-parliament.htm.
51 For a survey of the estimates of the effects of an all-out nuclear war, see "Nuclear Holocaust," Wikipedia, https://en.wikipedia.org/wiki/Nuclear_holocaust.
52 Patrick Toomey, "The NSA Continues to Violate Americans' Internet Privacy Rights," ACLU National Security Project, August 22, 2018, www.aclu.org/blog/national-security/privacy-and-surveillance/nsa-continues-violate-americans-internet-privacy.
53 Vindu Goel, "'Big Brother' in India Requires Fingerprint Scans for Food, Phones and Finances," *New York Times*, April 7, 2018, www.nytimes.com/2018/04/07/technology/india-id-aadhaar.html; "India's Biometric Identity Scheme Should Not Be Compulsory," *The Economist*, April 15, 2017, www.economist.com/leaders/2017/04/15/indias-biometric-identity-scheme-should-not-be-compulsory.
54 "China Has Turned Xinjiang into a Police State Like No Other," *The Economist*, May 31, 2018, www.economist.com/briefing/2018/05/31/china-has-turned-xinjiang-into-a-police-state-like-no-other.
55 Maya Kosoff, "China's Terrifying Surveillance State Looks a Lot Like America's Future," *Vanity Fair*, July 2018, www.vanityfair.com/news/2018/07/china-surveillance-state-artificial-intelligence.
56 Government Accounting Office, "The Nation's Fiscal Health," www.gao.gov/assets/710/705327.pdf (March 2020).
57 Congressional Budget Office, *The Budget and Economic Outlook: 2018–2028* (April 2018): www.cbo.gov/system/files/2019-03/54918-Outlook-3.pdf.
58 Congressional Budget Office, *Outlook* 6.
59 National Intelligence Council, *Global Trends 2030: Alternative Worlds* (Washington, DC: Office of the Director of National Intelligence 2012) 42, www.dni.gov/files/documents/GlobalTrends_2030.pdf.
60 Joseph E. Gagnon and Marc Hinterschweiger, *The Global Outlook for Government Debt over the Next Twenty-Five Years: Implications for the Economy and Public Policy* (Washington, DC: Peterson Institute 2011) 2, https://piie.com/publications/chapters_preview/6215/iie6215.pdf.
61 See "'Gilets jaunes': le gouvernement face à la mobilisation," *Le Figaro*, www.lefigaro.fr/actualite-france/dossier/hausse-des-carburants-manifestation-des-gilets-jaunes (visited 17 Dec. 2018) (collecting stories relating to the Yellow Vest movement).
62 Stephenson, "Caper."
63 See Subsection II.C., above.
64 National Intelligence Council xiv.
65 Though the NIC does not go quite that far, it foresees "increasing designation of special economic and political zones within countries" (131).
66 National Intelligence Council xiv.

67 Tom W. Bell, *Your Next Government? From the Nation State to Stateless Nations* (Cambridge: CUP 2018) 14–27.
68 Bell, *Government* 23, Figure 1.2–2; Bell, *Government* 24, Figure 1.2–3.
69 Tom W. Bell, "Special International Zones in Practice and Theory," *Chapman Law Review* 21 (2018) 273–302, www.chapman.edu/law/_files/publications/clr-22-1-Bell.pdf.
70 Timothy C. May, "The Crypto Anarchist Manifesto," *Crypto Anarchy, Cyberstates, and Pirate Utopias*, ed. Peter Ludlow (Cambridge, MA: MIT 2001) 62, https://monoskop.org/images/4/42/Ludlow_Peter_Crypto_Anarchy_Cyberstates_and_Pirate_Utopias.pdf.
71 Ibid.
72 Timothy C. May, "Crypto Anarchy and Virtual Communities," Ludlow 75 ("I am making no bold predictions that these changes will sweep the world anytime soon.").
73 May, "Crypto Anarchy" 70.
74 Max Borders, *The Social Singularity* (Austin: Social Evolution 2018) 51–54, 72.
75 See, for example, Vijay Boyapati, "The Bullish Case for Bitcoin," *Medium*, May 2, 2018, https://medium.com/@vijayboyapati/the-bullish-case-for-bitcoin-6ecc8bdecc1 ("[A]s fiat monies continue to follow their historical trend toward eventual worthlessness, Bitcoin will become an increasingly popular choice for global savings to flee to," making it a "generally accepted medium of exchange.").
76 See Kleros, https://kleros.io/(offering blockchain-based dispute resolution services).
77 Andrew Nelson, "De Soto Inc.: Where Eminent Domain Meets the Blockchain," *Blockchain Magazine*, March 5, 2018, https://bitcoinmagazine.com/articles/de-soto-inc-where-eminent-domain-meets-blockchain/
78 See Bitnation, https://tse.bitnation.co/.
79 Edan Yago, "Bit by Antiquated Bit, Democracy is Being Replaced by Crypto," *Wired*, Dec. 19, 2018, www.wired.co.uk/article/crypto-democracy-oligarchs.
80 Borders 117.
81 Melanie Swan, *Blockchain: Blueprint for a New Economy* (Sebastopol, CA: O'Reilly 2015) 48.
82 Nick Paumgarten, "The Prophets of Cryptocurrency Survey the Boom and Bust," *New Yorker*, Oct. 22, 2018, www.newyorker.com/magazine/2018/10/22/the-prophets-of-cryptocurrency-survey-the-boom-and-bust.
83 Susanne Tarkowski Tempelhof et al., *Pangea Jurisdiction and Pangea Arbitration Token (PAT)*, April 2017, https://github.com/Bit-Nation/Pangea-Docs/blob/master/BITNATION%20Pangea%20Whitepaper%202018.pdf.
84 Tempelhof et al. 5.
85 See Samuel Falkon, "The Story of the DAO—Its History and Consequences," *Medium*, Dec. 24, 2017, https://medium.com/swlh/the-story-of-the-dao-its-history-and-consequences-71e6a8a551ee; The Attacker, "An Open Letter," *Pastebin*, June 18, 2016, https://pastebin.com/CcGUBgDG. See also Eliza Mik, "Smart Contracts: Terminology, Technical Limitations and Real World Complexity," *Law, Innovation and Technology* 9.2 (2017): 269–300 (voicing skepticism that networks of smart contracts will avoid the problems that plague typical economic and legal systems).
86 Marcella Atzori, *Blockchain Technology and Decentralized Governance: Is the State Still Necessary?*, Dec. 1, 2015, https://ssrn.com/abstract=2709713.
87 See, for example, Stefan Zweig, *Brazil: Land of the Future* (New York: Viking Press, 1942).
88 "Talk:Brazil," Wikiquote, Feb. 28, 2017, https://en.wikiquote.org/wiki/Talk:Brazil.
89 See Colin Ward, *Anarchism: A Very Short Introduction* (New York: OUP 2004).
90 Bhupendra Singh et al., "Reversing Wrinkled Skin and Hair Loss in Mice by Restoring Mitochondrial Function," *Cell Death & Disease* 9.735 (July 20, 2018), https://doi.org/10.1038/s41419-018-0765-9.
91 See Julian Simon, *The Ultimate Resource* 2 (Princeton: Princeton UP 1998).

PART IV

Critique and Alternatives

23

SOCIAL ANARCHISM AND THE REJECTION OF PRIVATE PROPERTY

Jesse Spafford

Authority dresses itself in two principal forms: the political form, that is the State; and the economic form, that is private property.

Sébastien Faure[1]

I. Introduction

While anarchists stand uniformly opposed to the state, opinions diverge when it comes to what form the economy should take.[2] Within the world of contemporary analytic political philosophy, proponents of anarchism tend to be either *individualist anarchists* or *anarcho-capitalists*, with both varieties of anarchists maintaining that individuals can (a) unilaterally acquire full private property rights over natural resources (though some individualist anarchists exclude land from this category) and (b) exchange goods and services in a market. However, outside of academic philosophy, the majority of self-identified anarchists endorse some variety of *social anarchism* that rejects both markets and the private property rights on which they rest.[3]

This rejection of private property and markets cleanly demarcates social anarchism from its market-friendly counterparts. However, one might wonder whether the position is genuinely distinct from the socialist views to which social anarchism was supposed to serve as a libertarian alternative. After all, Marxists have been heavily influenced by Friedrich Engels' insistence that a communist society would be a stateless one.[4] And, while most socialists do envision the state playing a prominent role in managing the economy, there are several influential exceptions who argue that socialism is best realized via the dissolution of top-down state control in favor of radically expanded, bottom-up democracy—a vision that many social anarchists similarly endorse.[5]

This chapter argues that even when socialists and social anarchists affirm the same conclusions, the latter arrive at those conclusions in a distinctively anarchist way. Specifically, the chapter presents an argument against private property that begins from premises that all varieties of anarchists should be tempted to embrace, namely, those advanced by Michael Huemer in his recent argument for anarchism (or, more precisely, anarcho-capitalism).[6] It then uses these premises—coupled with Huemer's intuition-driven approach to ethical reasoning—to demonstrate that the non-consensual appropriation of unowned resources is theoretically unacceptable. In doing so, it provides a novel path to anti-capitalist conclusions that both expresses and defends the social anarchist philosophical position.

II. Huemer's Anarchism

Huemer's argument against the state begins with the premise that the use of coercion—which Huemer stipulatively defines as the use or threat of physical force—demands special justification.[7] Given that the laws imposed by the state are backed by the threat of force, it then follows that special justification must be given to legitimate these laws. To illustrate this point, Huemer considers the case of the private individual who takes it upon herself to start levying taxes on her neighbors, coercively regulating their behavior, and waging war against other neighborhoods.[8] He argues that the vigilante's behavior is intuitively impermissible, as there is no adequate justification for her coercive behavior. However, most people see there being no moral problem when these same actions are carried out by an agent of the state. Thus, Huemer suggests that most people tacitly assume that there is something special about *the state* (as opposed to its actions) that justifies its use of coercion.[9]

This special property is the state's presumed possession of *political authority*—a moral status that grants its possessor both a right to coercively rule and a right to be obeyed.[10] Specifically, Huemer suggests that these rights are governed by five principles: the rights are *general* in the sense that they apply to (almost) all citizens; the rights are *particular* to the citizens and residents of the governed territory; the rights obtain *independently* of the content of the laws enacted (excluding, perhaps, seriously unjust laws); the rights are *comprehensive* in the sense that the authority has the right to govern a wide array of activities; and the state is *supreme* such that no other agent has these same rights.[11] It is this pair of fairly unrestricted rights that the vigilante lacks and the state purportedly possesses, with this supposed difference explaining why only the state can permissibly use coercion to tax, regulate, and wage war.

But what could ground these supposed rights? In virtue of what fact would the state's use of coercion be permissible given the impermissibility of identical acts by private individuals? As Huemer notes, it is not easy to answer these questions, as many stock justifications for coercion seem, upon reflection, to be insufficient:

> If you have a friend who eats too many potato chips, you may try to convince him to give them up. But if he won't listen, you may not *force* him to stop. If you admire your neighbor's car, you may offer to buy it from him. But if he won't sell, you may not threaten him with violence. If you disagree with your coworker's religious beliefs, you may try to convert him. But if he won't listen, you may not punch him in the nose. And so on. In common sense ethics, the overwhelming majority of reasons for coercion fail as justifications.[12]

However, while these quick justifications for the right to coerce fail, the history of political philosophy features many more sophisticated and elaborate defenses of the state's right to coerce. In the face of this array of purported grounds for political authority, Huemer's argumentative strategy involves identifying the most plausible and influential suggestions and arguing against each of them in turn, typically by presenting counterexamples where the purported ground of political authority obtains but the authority figure in question still seems to act impermissibly in employing coercion. Given the apparent failure of the posited accounts to ground political authority, Huemer concludes that the state thereby has no more right to be obeyed and/or enforce its edicts than a non-state actor has. Finally, he moves from this position of *philosophical anarchism* (i.e., the denial that the state has authority) to a defense of *political anarchism* wherein he argues for the abolition of the state.

Huemer's political anarchism rests on the proposal that all the valuable functions of the state (e.g., the provision of security) can—and should—be taken over by private associations and firms funded by voluntary market exchange rather than taxes. He, thus, expounds a distinctly anarcho-capitalist version of anarchism wherein the rejection of the state's authority is accompanied by an affirmation of private property rights. However, this chapter will argue that the same considerations and argumentative approach that lead Huemer to reject state authority also militate against the conversion of natural resources into private property via purported acts of initial appropriation. Specifically, the following sections will mimic Huemer's argument, beginning with a discussion of the coerciveness of private property before considering—and rejecting—the most plausible posited grounds for the right to coercively enforce property claims. Given the apparent absence of an adequate ground for the right to property, the chapter concludes that those moved by Huemer's argument against political authority ought to be social anarchists, rejecting private property along with the state.

III. Private Property and Coercion

As noted above, Huemer's starting premise is that the activities of the state require special justification because they are coercive, with all laws resting on the threat that physical force will be employed against non-compliers. However, the same is also true of private property claims: to assert that one has the right to some object or land is to maintain that one has the right to exclude others, where that right implies the permissibility of coercive enforcement. Indeed, when the purported owner of some object says, "This is mine, you can't touch it," this expression includes a tacit "or else," where what is threatened almost always includes physical force of the kind that makes her claim coercive in Huemer's sense.

Further, just as the state's use of coercion demands special justification, so, too, does the enforcement of property rights. Recall that Huemer illustrates his claim about the need for special justification by drawing attention to the intuitive unacceptability of coercive state activities when those activities are carried out by a non-state actor. However, one can appropriate this strategy to highlight the troubling aspects of coercive property rights enforcement. Indeed, just as the actions of the state seem impermissible when carried out by a non-authority figure, the enforcement of property rights claims by a non-owner seems similarly unacceptable.

To illustrate this point, consider the case of a cruise ship that docks at a previously undiscovered island. The passengers are excited to spend the day exploring the island, but, before they have a chance to disembark, one passenger runs to the end of the gangplank and declares,

> Sorry, but I have decided that this island is for my personal use only! I forbid any of you from setting foot on it—unless, of course, you pay me $50 and take off your shoes before getting off the boat.

When the first passenger in line ignores this edict and walks onto the island, the declaration–issuer's friends rush over and seize the "trespasser" and begin binding her wrists and ankles. She struggles a bit, but after they spray sunscreen in her eyes, she stops resisting and is carried back onto the ship and locked in one of the cabins until she agrees to stay off the island.

If someone behaved like the declaration-issuer, she would be widely viewed as a menace and kidnapper who wrongfully denies people the freedom to go where they wish. However, when a property owner does the same thing—that is, relies on violence and the infliction of harm to protect some sphere of influence—most people don't see any moral problem. Thus, just as people tolerate coercion when it is employed by purported authorities, they also seem willing to tolerate the coercive acts carried out by purported property owners.

Further, note that the rights popularly ascribed to property owners strongly resemble the rights of authority ascribed to the state: they are *general* in the sense that they apply to all other persons who come into contact with the owner's property (just as an authority claims to govern all those who enter its territory); they are *comprehensive* in the sense that the owner has the right to fully determine what happens with her property; they are *particular* in the sense that the property owner gets to regulate *only* those who come into contact with her property; and the owner is *supreme* in that no other agent has the same rights as she does with respect to her property. Finally, and most importantly for the purposes of this chapter, the rights are *content-independent*: whether or not a person holds a property right does not depend on what she does with the claimed resource (within the bounds of respecting others' rights) or what effect her possession of the resource has on others. This independence doesn't have to be absolute; for example, it may be the case that one has rights over a thing just in case no serious harm will befall others as a result of their exclusion. However, one cannot be said to genuinely own a thing if, for example, one's rights over that thing are contingent on using it in a way that is maximally efficient or furthers some other moral end.[13]

For proponents of property rights, the fact that such rights share both the form and the coercive element of political authority represents something of a problem given that, as Huemer notes, it is difficult to find adequate justifications for coercion beyond consent and self-defense.[14] Indeed, Huemer goes through the prominent proposed justifications for state coercion and argues that each fails, thereby demonstrating just how hard it is to find an adequate ground for permissible coercion. Of course, proponents of property rights have provided their own set of arguments purporting to demonstrate that property owners have the right to coercively exclude others. However, as this chapter will now argue, even the most promising of these accounts fail to adequately justify the coercion associated with private property. Thus, just as Huemer judges the state to be lacking in authority, the chapter will conclude that no one has the right to coercively enforce property claims.[15]

IV. Transformation and Control

While it isn't possible to consider every proposed ground for property rights, there are several popular proposals that have received the endorsement of prominent defenders of private property. If it can be shown that these accounts do not succeed, that will at least be suggestive that no such grounds can be found (though, as with proposed bases for political authority, it is possible that a successful justification might one day be found). Specifically, this chapter will consider three influential accounts of how persons acquire the right to exclude others from previously unowned natural resources, beginning with a Lockean "labor-mixing" view championed by Edward Feser.[16] The chapter will then turn to discussing compensation-based accounts and an alternative labor-mixing account in sections V and VI.

According to Feser, a person gains rights over previously unowned natural resources by either (a) gaining control of or (b) sufficiently modifying those resources.[17] Thus, a homesteader who tills the soil of some unowned patch of land or builds a sizeable fence around its perimeter would thereby come to own that land. However, consideration of other cases casts doubt on Feser's proposal. Consider, for example, the case of a person who deliberately starts a wildfire that scorches an entire forest, blackening thousands of acres of trees and earth. Suppose that a hiker then tries to enter the forest to survey the damage. May the fire-starter have the hiker imprisoned or threaten to shoot her if she does not leave the burned area? Surely not. Thus, the mere modification of land and objects seems insufficient to render coercive exclusion permissible.

Why does Feser think otherwise? To defend his thesis, he considers various cases of resource modification and argues that the more *significant* the modification of the resource, the more plausible an associated ownership claim becomes. For example, he suggests that whittling a piece of driftwood plausibly grants ownership in a way that blowing air on it does not. Similarly, while pouring a can of tomato juice into the sea does not plausibly generate ownership rights, Feser contends that, in the case where one pours a large quantity of nuclear waste into a body of water such that it begins to glow bright green, "it would *not* be implausible in such cases to say that I have come to acquire the sea."[18]

It does not seem charitable to take Feser's contention to be that making the sea glow an irradiated green makes it plausible that one owns the sea, as this judgment would seem to run quite contrary to commonsense intuitive judgments. Rather, he is better understood as claiming that it is *more* plausible that one owns the sea in this case than in the tomato juice case. Indeed, the comparative nature of his claim is more clearly evinced in his description of a third case wherein he suggests that, while it would be "absurd" to think that the United States government owns Pluto (which no person has ever set foot on), it "would not be *absurd* for the United States government … to claim ownership of the area of the moon's surface on which Apollo 11 landed."[19]

The claim, then, seems to be that if modification and/or control increases the plausibility of ownership, then a suitably extensive amount of modification/control is sufficient for ownership. However, an additional problem with this argument—beyond the counterexample discussed above—is that if some fact obtaining enhances the plausibility of a proposition, that might merely show that the fact is a *necessary* condition of that proposition being true rather than a sufficient condition. For example, the claim that someone has memorized Tolstoy's *War and Peace* would be much more plausible if they had read the book at least once than if they had never heard of it. However, it does not follow that having read the book is a sufficient condition for having memorized it. Alternatively, judgments of plausibility might not track anything of moral relevance. For example, it seems much more plausible that the King of Thailand is the legitimate ruler of that country than a pediatrician from Texas. However, it does not follow that the rules of royal succession ground political authority (they are neither a necessary nor sufficient condition of such authority).

The suggestion that control might ground the permissibility of coercive exclusion—where "control" denotes the physical ability to determine what happens to a thing (e.g., via the building of a fence or the deployment of guard dogs)—also seems to run contrary to commonsense morality.[20] Suppose that the pushy passenger in the island case was able to quickly get ashore and repeatedly knock back the gangplank, thereby preventing other passengers from accessing the island. It does not seem that this success entitles her to then deploy violence against anyone who does manage to make it ashore. Indeed, the conclusion that she is so entitled seems to rest on an unacceptable inference from de facto to *de jure* control of resources. Alternatively, one might note that the right to coercively exclude is a right to use force to control a space, with this method of establishing control being what demands justification. Given this, it is unclear how appealing to the fact that control has been established via force—as Feser does when he cites the deployment of guard dogs as one means of establishing control—can ground its own permissibility.[21]

In response to this objection, the defender of Feser might suggest that it is the *non-coercive* control of some resource that grounds the permissibility of coercive control of that resource. In this way, his claim about control could be largely sustained without the problematic assertion that states of affairs can be self-justifying. However, first, the gangplank case casts doubt on the inference from non-coercive control to rightful ownership. And, second, note that the use of force to control some resource is only necessary if non-coercive forms of control prove inadequate—i.e., one *has not established control* of the resource through non-coercive means alone. In other words, even if one grants that the non-coercive control of resources entails the permissibility of coercive control of those resources, any use of coercion entails the absence of such non-coercive control. Thus, there can be no instance of coercive exclusion that is permissible in virtue of there being prior non-coercive control of the resource.

Why think that control—either coercive or non-coercive—grounds property rights? Feser provides two arguments to support this contention. First, he makes the comparative plausibility argument discussed above, citing the moon lander case as evidence that establishing control is a plausible form of initial appropriation. However, as discussed above, such comparative assessments do not establish the desired conclusion. Second, Feser argues that control is what grounds people's *self-ownership*—i.e., the rights they have to use their bodies, exclude others from using their bodies, transfer these rights to their bodies, etc. He posits that what grounds these intuitively plausible rights is that we exercise *control* over our bodies; indeed, a person gains the rights over her body by "just 'showing up' and being the first to 'take possession'" of it, with coercive enforcement of those rights then becoming permissible.[22] Further, if establishing control is how one gains ownership rights of one's body, why wouldn't establishing control of a natural resource also give one rights over that resource?[23]

There are three quick responses that can be made to this argument. First, the argument rests on an equivocation between the kind of control one has of one's body and the kind of control Feser associates with initial appropriation. In the case of the body, the agent exercises direct control over the body in the sense that she can manipulate the body simply by willing it to do certain things; by contrast, the control over resources Feser describes involves physically keeping others from being able to manipulate those resources, e.g., by building a fence or placing armed guards around a patch of land.[24] However, if agential control is what makes the thesis of self-ownership plausible, it is unclear why physical control would make resource ownership plausible.[25]

Second, even if one grants that both forms of control are equally relevant to establishing ownership, Brian McElwee persuasively argues that the plausibility of the self-ownership thesis stems *not only* from the fact that one controls one's own body, *but also* from the facts that one feels pain and pleasure through one's body, one needs one's body, and one's body is irreplaceable when it comes to satisfying this need.[26] If these conditions are individually necessary and jointly sufficient for having ownership of an object, then mere control of a natural resource will not suffice to establish ownership of that resource.

Finally, if one takes seriously Feser's control thesis, then it would seemingly follow that parents own their children. After all, assuming that agency emerges in children sometime after birth, the parents of a child are the first people to "show up and take possession" of its body. Thus, they would seemingly have the right to that body, with the agent who comes to inhabit that body being analogous to the latecomer who arrives at a patch of land that has already been fenced in.[27] This implausible conclusion would seem to be a *reductio* of Feser's argument.[28]

V. Compensation

Rather than ground property rights in modification or control, many defenders of private property contend that some resource can be converted into private property if the exclusion is to the benefit of the excluded—or, at the very least, leaves them no worse off than they would have been in some relevant baseline scenario. Most famously, John Locke suggests that appropriation of natural resources could occur if "enough and as good" is left for others (and certain other conditions are met).[29] Similarly, Robert Nozick argues that an act of appropriation can occur if it leaves others no worse off than they would have been in a world without private property rights.[30] And David Schmidtz argues that appropriation of resources can occur when it prevents the destruction of the commons, as such appropriation leaves the excluded (and latecomers in particular) better off than they would have otherwise been in terms of access to those resources.[31]

Alternatively, many defenders of property rights appeal to the benefits that all persons derive from a *system* of private property, with initial appropriation then sanctioned because it is necessary for bringing about such a system. For example, Loren Lomasky argues that, given that human beings are inclined toward the pursuit of projects—and the pursuit of projects requires de facto control rights over land and resources—the possession of private property rights is a necessary condition of living a rich and meaningful life.[32] He maintains that it is only through sustained control of claimed property that a person can effectively develop her talents, realize her plans, and express herself and her vision. Similarly, Eric Mack argues that the sustained discretionary control of natural resources plays a key role in "individuals' living their own lives in their own chosen ways" via purposive activity.[33] Bas van der Vossen argues that the control of resources is necessary for both "securing the necessities of life" and pursuing projects that are "central to a full and meaningful life."[34] And Jason Brennan, in addition to endorsing Lomasky's proposal, argues that owning property is crucial to feeling "at home" in the world and protecting the owner's sentimental attachments to the particular resources that she has incorporated into her life.[35]

However, the fact that coercion ultimately benefits some other person would not seem to be an adequate justification for that act. As an illustration of this point, consider the case of two castaways stranded on an island with minimal resources. After a few months of bare subsistence, something fortunate happens: a small motorboat washes up onto the beach. However, when the castaways attempt to climb into the boat, they quickly discover that the boat can only carry one of them, as the weight of both causes the bow to submerge. Thinking quickly, one castaway says to the other,

> You have to get out of the boat. There is only room for one of us, and I'm taking it. I can't live my life here; I have goals to achieve and a family back home. I'm sorry, but you need to get back on the beach.

Unwilling to be cowed by her pushy companion, the second castaway refuses to move, crossing her arms defiantly. In response to this refusal to comply, the first castaway declares that the second "has left her no choice" and punches her in the face, physically knocking her off the boat and leaving her bloodied on the beach. Stubbornly, the beaten castaway staggers back to the boat and again tries to climb aboard, but the first pushes her back down and quickly binds her arms and legs, as it is clear this is the only way to keep her from the boat.[36] "I'm sorry it had to come to this," the pushy castaway says, "But, ultimately, this is for your benefit! If I were to stay on the island, there would be many fewer resources to go around; indeed, my departure effectively doubles your wealth! So, you really have no basis for complaint here." She then fires up the engine and motors off toward civilization.

Does the fact that the pushy castaway leaves her companion (significantly) better off in the long run render her use of coercion permissible? Seemingly not. Repeatedly punching and temporarily confining another remains impermissible, even if those actions leave her better off all things considered. It seems clear in this case that the pushy castaway acted impermissibly. However, this assessment would apply equally to the coercion deployed by those property rights claimants: the fact that one person exercising control over some resource would make another's life much better does not make it permissible for the former to threaten, attack, or imprison the latter as a means of controlling that resource.

Note that this conclusion holds even when coercion generates significant benefits for *both* the coercer and the coerced. Indeed, in the island case, both parties benefit significantly from the pushy castaway's employment of coercion, yet the described use of force still seems impermissible. Additionally, consider what Huemer says about mutually beneficial coercion:

> Normally, it is wrong to threaten a person with violence to force compliance with some plan of yours. This is generally true even if your plan is mutually beneficial and otherwise morally acceptable. Thus, suppose you are at a board meeting at which you and the other members are discussing how to improve your company's sales. You know that the best way to do this is to hire the Sneaku Ad Agency. Your plan will be morally unobjectionable and highly beneficial to the company. Nevertheless, the other members are not convinced. So you pull out your handgun and *order* them to vote for your proposal. This behavior would be unacceptable, even though you are acting for everyone's benefit and even though your plan is the right one.[37]

While Huemer intends this case to call into question a purported justification for state authority, it seems to apply equally to the coercive enforcement of property rights: it is wrong to use the threat of violence to force people to act in a certain way with respect to natural resources, even if that plan is otherwise unobjectionable and to everyone's significant benefit.

In addition to the Sneaku case, Huemer's arguments against paternalistic coercion also bear directly on this proposed ground for property rights. Specifically, Huemer considers the case of a person who threatens another with a gun in order to get the latter to stop eating potato chips that were contributing to premature death due to heart disease. In this case, Huemer contends that the use of coercion is "indefensible" despite the fact that it would prevent significant harm from befalling the chip-eater.[38] In other words, he takes coercion to be impermissible even if it provides a very large benefit to the coerced party. Given that the benefits of private property are almost always smaller than those accrued by the chip-eater (namely, being saved from a painful premature death), the fact that the latter cannot justify coercion implies that the former cannot either.

Granted, Huemer also presents a case that seems to elicit the opposite intuition from his paternalism case, namely a case where coercion is used to keep a lifeboat from sinking. In this case, he suggests that the benefit of everyone not drowning justifies a person using coercion to force everyone else to bail water.[39] However, first, one might think that there is an important disanalogy between lifeboat-style cases and the case of private property: while the absence of coercion in the lifeboat case results in everyone suffering severe harm, the absence of private property merely results in foregone material benefit (albeit, potentially significant benefit). Second, even if one thinks there is an analogy between the disaster that comes from not bailing water and the disaster of not having property rights, note that the general principle most plausibly derived from the lifeboat case is that coercion is permissible if (a) it is necessary to avoid severe harm and (b) that harm is much worse than the coercion and its effects. However, very few private property claims meet these jointly sufficient conditions. Thus, the most that the defender of property rights could derive from the lifeboat case is the conclusion that one could use coercion to exclude others from the bare quantity of resources necessary to ensure their survival—and only when such exclusion did not similarly imperil those excluded.

Further, one might reasonably deny that the permissibility of coercion in such cases implies that the coercer has a genuine property right over the resources in question. Recall from Section II that one of the defining features of a property right is that it is *content-independent*—i.e., the right obtains largely irrespective of one's use of the owned resource or others' relations to it. However, if this is a defining feature of a property right, then permissible exclusion grounded in necessity will not qualify as such, as the right to coerce would immediately vanish if either (a) the coercion was no longer necessary to avoid severe harm or (b) the coerced party would suffer comparable harm from being coerced. Given that the principle of severe harm avoidance makes the permissibility of coercive exclusion contingent on a fairly narrow set of circumstances obtaining, it cannot ground any sort of genuine property right.

VI. Expropriation of Labor

The final proposal to be considered here is another neo-Lockean labor-mixing view wherein it is held that coercive exclusion is permitted when persons have labored on some natural resource. Specifically, a popular suggestion is that once a person labors on a resource, any unpermitted use or appropriation of that resource amounts to the expropriation of that person's labor. It is then maintained that the laborer has a prior right against such expropriation, with this right grounding the permissibility of her coercively excluding others from the resource. For example, Mack argues that taking—and, presumably, using without permission—something in which a person has invested her labor is an expropriation of that labor and thereby a violation of her right to self-ownership.[40] Indeed, he argues that taking a created thing is the same kind of expropriation of labor as forcing another to make something for one's own benefit.[41] Similarly, John Simmons argues that when a person works on a resource, she incorporates it into her plans such that any unpermitted use of that resource would be "a violation of [her] right to govern [herself]."[42]

There are two problems with this account. First, some of the same counterexamples that plague the transformation account can be repurposed to raise doubts about invested labor as a grounds for permissible coercion. Consider the forest fire case, but add in the stipulation that the fire-starter expends significant effort to start that fire—e.g., by gathering a large pile of shredded bark and kindling that she finally ignites after hours of intense labor rubbing sticks together. Now, suppose that someone seeks to hike through the scorched territory, only to be stopped by the fire-starter who, with gun drawn, says,

> If you walk through this land, that's equivalent to you having forced me to go through all that effort for your benefit! I refuse to let you enslave me in this way, so I'll shoot you if you set foot on the product of my labor.

In this case, the appeal to invested labor seems inadequate to render exclusionary coercion permissible.

It might be suggested that the fire-starter's demand is unreasonable because the hiker moving through the forest does not preclude the fire-starter from enjoying the fruits of her own labor. Indeed, it seems more like the hiker is free-riding on the efforts of the fire-starter rather than forcing the latter to labor for her benefit. By contrast, if the hiker were to somehow take the forest away from the fire-starter, the latter would have a better claim to having been wronged in a way that warrants the use of coercion to prevent that outcome from obtaining. However, even if one were to affirm this suggestion that the fire-starter *is* wronged by expropriation—though not by mere free-riding—it would still be the case that an appeal to expropriation could ground only a very limited set of property rights, where those rights included a right against expropriation but *not* a full exclusion right (as there would be no right to exclude when others' use of the owned thing does not preclude use by the owner).

Further, it is unclear that invested labor makes it permissible to use coercion to prevent expropriation. Suppose, for example, that the hiker attempted to carry away some of the charcoaled byproducts of the fire. Would the fire-starter's efforts make it permissible for her to threaten the hiker with imprisonment if the latter did not immediately return the blackened wood? Again, the answer seems to be no.

In addition to this apparent counterexample, there is a circularity problem for any account of property rights that appeals to labor investment to ground the permissibility of coercive exclusion.

To see this, consider the case of a vandal who receives permission from a car owner to repaint the latter's rightfully owned car. However, suppose that, upon completing the paint job, the vandal tries to forcibly prevent the owner from driving away in the car, arguing that the owner is taking her labor, where such expropriation amounts to her having been forced to paint the car for the owner's sole benefit. In this case, it seems clear that the vandal's claim lacks merit and her use of coercion is impermissible.

Why does her claim lack merit? The obvious answer is that claims about expropriation are made against a background of property rights, where those rights constrain what counts as expropriation. In this case, the car owner has both the right to exclude the vandal from laboring on her car and the independent right to use her car. Thus, while the owner waives her exclusion right, her use right persists, meaning that she acts fully within her rights when she drives away in the painted car. Given that the action that precludes the vandal from enjoying the fruits of her labor is an action to which the owner has a right, the vandal has no legitimate basis for a complaint of expropriation.[43]

However, if rights-protected action cannot be expropriative (as the vandal case suggests), then the expropriation justification for property rights becomes circular. Note that the proposed account maintains that some person has a right to exclude others from a labored-on resource—i.e., owns the resource in virtue of the fact she has labored on it—(if and) only if their use of that resource would expropriate the labor she has invested in that resource. But, given that property rights constrain what counts as expropriation, the other parties would be expropriating the person's labor only if they have no right to use the resource. Further, presuming that, in the absence of property rights the world is unowned and all are at liberty to use the available natural resources, those others would lack a right to use that resource only if the original person owned the labored-on resource. Thus, on the expropriation account, it follows that some person owns a labored-on resource only if they own that labored-on resource. Given this vicious circularity, the expropriation account ought to be rejected.

To this point, it might be objected that the vandal case involves labor on an *owned* object (the car) while the purported acts of initial appropriation involve labor on *unowned* land and resources. However, note that ownership is not a single unitary right but, rather, a *bundle* of rights including the rights to use, exclude, transfer, etc. Further, note that when some resource is said to be "unowned," this means that all persons may permissibly use that resource—i.e., they have a *right to use* that resource. Thus, the term "unowned" is somewhat misleading, as it implies that all persons have (very) *partial* ownership of the resource, where such ownership involves possessing a use right but none of the other rights that come in the "full ownership" bundle. However, this means that an unowned resource is relevantly analogous to the car in the vandal case, as there the car owner has waived her exclusion right, leaving her with the same kind of partial ownership that all persons have over unowned resources. Granted, the car owner still retains some additional rights beyond the right to use (e.g., a transfer right). However, the intuitive judgment stays the same even if one modifies the case by stipulating that all such rights had been previously waived: the vandal still has no basis for complaint when the (partial) owner of the car drives off with her labor. Given this, the person who labors on some "unowned" natural resource would equally seem to have no basis for complaint when one of its many partial owners walks off with it.

VII. The Anarchist Society

The previous sections of this chapter have attempted to extend Huemer's argument against political authority to indict private property as well, adopting his argumentative strategy and core premises to show that the coercive exclusion associated with private property is impermissible. Specifically, it has considered three of the most influential defenses of private property and argued that none succeeds in grounding the permissibility of its associated coercion. However, if this conclusion is correct, one might wonder about the specific political implications of this normative result. After all, Huemer concludes his book with a lengthy discussion of how a society might function in the absence of a state; thus, one might reasonably ask how a society might function without private property.

In order to answer to this question, one must first determine whether *all* coercive control of resources is impermissible or whether certain instances of coercion are permissible, just not the kind associated with the *content-independent* control posited by defenders of property rights. Some egalitarian-minded social anarchists might be inclined to think that coercive exclusion from resources *is* permissible *if* it is the only way to ensure that all persons live equally good lives (barring, perhaps, inequalities that result from certain sorts of negligent choices). To see what is appealing about this position, consider the case of two castaways stranded on an island lush with peanut plants. One castaway is allergic to peanuts but good at catching fish, whereas the other lacks the arm strength and coordination needed to catch fish. The net result of these differences is that the two are able to live equally good lives, one fishing and sleeping on the beach while the other forages for food inland. However, suppose that one day the allergic castaway begins clearcutting the densest area of peanut plants so that she has a place to play soccer. Further, suppose that the destruction of these plants would impose a great hardship on the uncoordinated castaway, as she would then have to spend many more tedious and difficult hours each day foraging for the scarce peanuts that remain.

Given these stipulations, would it be permissible for the uncoordinated castaway to use coercion to prevent the allergic castaway from destroying the plants on which her quality of life depends? Some egalitarian anarchists might answer in the affirmative, contending that the permissibility of the coercion is grounded in the fact that it is necessary to ensure that the uncoordinated castaway doesn't live a worse life than her companion (due to no fault of her own). In other words, they would endorse a limited and *content-dependent* right to coercively exclude others, where the permissibility of any act of coercion is determined by some egalitarian principle of distributive justice.

If one adopts this view, then the social anarchist political prescription is fairly straightforward: each person should limit her holdings to just the resources assigned to her by the relevant egalitarian principle of distributive justice (e.g., the resources that will allow her to live as good of a life as everyone else). If others are hoarding more than their fair share, she may take the appropriate portion of those resources.[44] And, if others try to take her portion, she may fend them off so long as she operates within the constraints of proportionality. Further, people may band together to form whatever organizations help them to obtain and protect their just shares.[45]

Of course, many empirical questions remain regarding what holdings realize the egalitarian ideal and how those holdings can best be brought about. However, the defender of the normative position can remain agnostic about what kinds of actions and institutional arrangements will best advance this end. While it will eventually be necessary to answer these questions, she can insist that her view simply articulates the moral boundaries that constrain all proposed institutions, namely that such institutions may only make use non-consensual coercion if that coercion is necessary for bringing about or sustaining an egalitarian arrangement.

Alternatively, some social anarchists might reject the intuition that coercion is permissible in the peanut case. Given this rejection, they would insist that the coercive control of resources is *always* impermissible, except when it has been consented to by the victim or, perhaps, when such control is necessary to avoid some sort of moral catastrophe. This position imposes stricter limits on what forms society can permissibly take. Specifically, it would sanction only two forms of resource management, each with its own drawbacks, but both of which avoid the coercion that is omnipresent in regimes of private property (and that persists in a more limited form in the egalitarian anarchist society).

The first form of resource management would be an arrangement of free resource use: all persons could do what they wanted with resources so long as they didn't act on one another's bodies in the process. Of course, absent the right to control these resources, there would be limited incentive for self-interested producers to improve those resources, as others would be free to come and carry off the fruits of their labor. Thus, one might expect the radical anarchist society to be much poorer than its capitalist or egalitarian counterpart (though the ratio of production done for the sake of self-interest vs. community benefit would also be much lower—a result that many social anarchists would find favorable).[46]

To mitigate this incentives problem, a producer in a social anarchist society might opt for an alternative form of resource management wherein she acquires the right to coercively exclude others from her products by obtaining their consent. A low-cost version of this approach would involve getting the consent of just those individuals who are geographically and epistemically positioned to take her products. While this would not give her the right to coercively exclude the people who she did not consult, she might be willing to gamble that these people will not attempt to take her product. For example, she has little need to worry about people living hundreds of miles away coming to take her product, particularly if those people do not know that such production is occurring. Thus, she may reasonably decide the cost of obtaining their consent is greater than the risk of them learning about her product and traveling a long distance to take it.

Alternatively, producers seeking greater security could pursue universal consent via a federated decision-making structure where local councils reach decisions about how society ought to be arranged via consensus—i.e., by getting each of their members to consent to the proposed decision. Each council would then send a representative to a central council to advocate for the arrangement approved by her local council. This central council would then use a consensus procedure to settle on some negotiated position, with representatives then returning to their local councils to get final approval (again, via consensus). Once such approval has been given, the arrangement in question will have received universal consent. Thus, a federated decision-making system would allow coercively enforceable holdings to arise through the granting of consent by all potentially affected parties.[47]

This is only a quick sketch of how universal consent could be achieved, with the subject deserving a more thorough critical discussion than can be given here. However, even absent a careful examination of institutional design, it seems reasonable to conclude that any procedure capable of generating universal consent will be unwieldy and significantly less efficient than a system of non-consensual private property enforcement. This may simply be the price of living in a society that does not tolerate the casual use of coercion to coordinate human affairs. After all, one of the advantages of coercion is that it allows people to carry out their projects without having to go through the trouble of consulting others, as their resistance can be suppressed with violence. However, as Section V has argued, this convenience and efficiency is not sufficient for rendering that coercion permissible.

This conclusion about the form society ought to take is admittedly a radical one. Further, even absent society-wide acceptance of the anarchist normative position, the view still has a radical implication when it comes to one's everyday behavior, namely that it is wrong to use coercion to sustain control of one's holdings (with a possible exception being made if those holdings represent one's "fair share" of the available natural resources). What this chapter has attempted to show is that while these conclusions are radical, they follow from eminently plausible premises about what does and does not justify the use of coercion. Thus, absent an equally radical reconsideration of when coercion is permissible, there is little choice but to follow the argument where it leads, namely to the social anarchist rejection of state and private property.

Notes

1 As quoted by Peter Marshall, *Demanding the Impossible: A History of Anarchism* (London: Harper Perennial, 1992) 43.

2 I am indebted to Jason Lee Byas for his numerous helpful comments on an earlier draft of this chapter.

3 As Roderick Long notes, social anarchists often deny that anarcho-capitalists are genuine anarchists, and vice versa. However, Long rejects this view in favor of a unified conception of anarchism that includes both groups. Roderick Long, "Anarchism and Libertarianism," *Brill's Companion to Anarchism and Philosophy*, ed. Nathan Jun (Boston: Brill, 2018) 286. For a well-known example of the social anarchist rejection of anarcho-capitalism, see Iain McKay et al. "Section F—Is Anarcho-Capitalism a Type of Anarchism?" *An Anarchist FAQ*, 11 November 2008, available at http://anarchism.pageabode.com/afaq/secFint.html.

4 Friedrich Engels, "Socialism: Utopian and Scientific," *The Marx Engels Reader*, 2nd ed., ed, Robert C. Tucker (New York: Norton, 1978) 711–3. Paul Thomas similarly notes that abolishing the state "is a goal anarchists have shared with a good many Marxist and other nonanarchist revolutionaries." Paul Thomas, "Review of *Anarchism: A Theoretical Analysis* by Alan Ritter," *Political Theory* 10.1 (Feb. 1982): 141–4.

5 See Erik Olin Wright, *Envisioning Real Utopias* (New York: Verso 2010). For an example of social anarchist endorsement of this sort of vision, see Murray Bookchin, "Anarchism: Past and Present," *Reinventing Anarchy, Again*, ed. H. J. Erhlich (Edinburgh: AK Press, 1996) 19–30. For a contemporary example in analytic philosophy that suggests anarchism involves the bottom-up democratic management of most resources, see Nicholas Vrousalis, "Libertarian Socialism: A Better Reconciliation between Equality and Self-Ownership," *Social Theory and Practice* 37.2 (Apr. 2011): 211–26, at 221–3. (While Vrousalis refers to such management as "libertarian socialism" rather than "anarchism," his citation of Proudhon and Kropotkin as paradigmatic libertarian socialists suggests he considers the first term to be largely synonymous with the second.)

6 Michael Huemer, *The Problem of Political Authority: An Examination of the Right to Coerce and the Duty to Obey* (London: Palgrave 2013).

7 Huemer 8.

8 Huemer 10–11.

9 Huemer 11.

10 Huemer 5.

11 Huemer 12–3.

12 Huemer 10. Original emphasis.

13 Note that one could attach a similar qualification to the content-independence of authority maintaining that authorities cannot oblige their subjects to inflict serious harm on others.

14 Huemer 10.

15 Kevin Vallier has also noted that Huemer's argument threatens to undermine private property. See Kevin Vallier, "On the Problematic Political Authority of Property Rights: How Huemer Proves Too Much" *Bleeding Heart Libertarians*, 12 August 2013, available at https://bleedingheartlibertarians.com/2013/08/on-the-problematic-political-authority-of-property-rights-how-huemer-proves-too-much/. However, Vallier takes this to be reason to reject Huemer's argument as part of a *modus tollens* inference; by contrast, this chapter affirms Huemer's argument and infers via *modus ponens* that property rights must be rejected.

16 Edward Feser, "There is No Such Thing as an Unjust Initial Acquisition," *Social Philosophy and Policy* 22.1 (2005): 56–80. Feser later moves away from this view and presents a new philosophical foundation for a more limited set of property rights. While many of the proposed grounds might be classified with those accounts discussed below, Feser's effort to ground his argument in the "classical realist" tradition (associated with Aristotle, Augustine, and Aquinas) makes such a grouping a bit tendentious. Unfortunately, addressing his updated view with all of its underpinning metaphysical assumptions goes beyond the scope of this chapter. Those interested in his revised view should see Edward Feser, "Classical Natural Law Theory, Property Rights, and Taxation," *Social Philosophy and Policy* 27.1 (2010): 21–52.

17 An earlier version of this claim is advanced by Murray Rothbard, *The Ethics of Liberty* (New York: NYU Press, 1998) 34. While Rothbard is more influential than Feser, the discussion here will focus on Feser's account, as he provides a more robust defense of his view relative to Rothbard, who seems primarily focused on explicating the position.

18 Feser 65. The tomato juice example is a nod to Nozick's contention that a person who pours a can of owned tomato juice into the sea seems to have lost ownership of her juice rather than gained ownership of the sea. Robert Nozick, *Anarchy, State, and Utopia* (New York: Basic Books, 1974) 175. Original emphasis.

19 Feser 65. Original emphasis.

20 Feser 69.

21 Feser 69.

22 Feser 66.

23 There is another species of argument that argues that the right to self-ownership supports a right to private property because external objects are actually a *part* of the body one owns, even if those objects are both detached from one's "main" body and cannot be manipulated simply via the will. While addressing these arguments is beyond the scope of this chapter, interested readers should see Samuel C. Wheeler, "Natural Property Rights as Body Rights," *Noûs* 14.2 (May 1980): 171–93; Daniel Russell, "Embodiment and Self-Ownership," *Social Philosophy and Policy* 27.1 (2010): 135–67.

24 Feser 65.

25 That agential control is what does the work is reflected in the intuition that it is wrong to act on even unowned objects that an agent is wielding as a direct extension of her body (e.g., an object she is holding or an artificial leg).

26 Brian McElwee, "The Appeal of Self-Ownership," *Social Theory and Practice* 36.2 (Apr. 2010): 213–32.

27 Susan Moller Okin defends this claim at greater length and detail in the context of arguing against Nozick's entitlement theory of justice. See Susan Moller Okin, *Justice, Gender, and the Family* (New York: Basic Books, 1989) 79–85.

28 Feser might reply that when agency emerges within the child, this emergence strips the parents of any property rights they might have over her body. However, it is unclear why this should be so. Is the child's relation to her body not analogous to a latecomer's relation to already-appropriated natural resources? Granted, the child might *need* her body in order to pursue her projects or even survive, but the same might equally be true of the latecomer vis-à-vis appropriated resources. Further, Feser's argument from self-ownership rests upon the claim that self-ownership is established by being the first to show up and take possession of something, with this serving to explain why it is that a person gains ownership of external resources the same way. However, given that it is a person's parents who are actually the first to show up and take possession of the body, Feser faces a dilemma: he must either grant parents continuing ownership of their child's body or admit that there is some basis for latecomers arriving and stripping owners of the property rights they had gained via being the first to transform and control some resource.

29 John Locke, *Second Treatise of Government* (Urbana: Project Gutenberg, 2005) § 27. Retrieved June 18, 2019 from www.gutenberg.org/files/7370/7370-h/7370-h.htm.

30 Nozick 177–81

31 David Schmidtz, "When is Original Appropriation *Required*?" *The Monist* 73.4 (Oct. 1990): 504–18.

32 Loren Lomasky, *Persons, Rights, and the Moral Community* (New York: OUP, 1987).

33 Eric Mack, "The Natural Right of Property," *Social Philosophy and Policy* 27.1 (2010): 53–78, at 62. See also Eric Mack, "Self-Ownership and the Right of Property," *The Monist* 73.4 (1990): 519–43.

34 Bas van der Vossen, "Imposing Duties and Original Appropriation," *Journal of Political Philosophy* 23.1 (2015): 64–85 at 77–8.

35 Jason Brennan, *Why Not Capitalism?* (New York: Routledge, 2014) 75–82.

36 The goal here is to describe the various cases in such a way that the force used is the minimum necessary to prevent a stubborn party from using the claimed resource. Thus, if the use of force in a case is judged to exceed this threshold, it should be re-imagined with less force used. However, the suggestion here is that such modification will do little to diminish the intuition that the use of coercion in the case is impermissible.

37 Huemer 94. Original emphasis.

38 Huemer 97.

39 Huemer 94.

40 Mack, "Natural Right," 72. Mack does not think that laboring on a thing is the only way to establish a property right; however, the expropriation justification for gaining a property right is particular to labor. Mack's other methods of claiming property appeal to property's ability to facilitate a person living her life, as discussed in Section V.

41 Mack, "Natural Right," 72.

42 A. John Simmons, *Justification and Legitimacy: Essays on Rights and Obligations* (Cambridge: CUP, 2001) 262.

43 Herbert Spencer makes a similar argument against the appropriation of land via appeal to the case where a trespasser makes improvements to someone else's owned house. However, his argument differs in two important respects from the argument here. First, he assumes full ownership of the house while, in the vandal case, the ownership of the car is only partial (more on this point at the end of this section). Second, he takes the home-improver to have a claim to the added value to the house, though not the house itself. However, the vandal case casts some doubt upon this conclusion. Does the car owner really owe the vandal compensation for her unsolicited efforts? Perhaps, but much more would need to be said on this

point. See Herbert Spencer, *Social Statistics: Or, the Conditions Essential to Human Happiness Specified, and the First of Them Developed* (London: George Woodfall and Son, 1851) 118–9.

44 This suggestion echoes Peter Kropotkin's claim that people have a "right to possess the wealth of the community—to take the houses to dwell in, according to the needs of each family; to seize the stores of food and learn the meaning of plenty, after having known famine too well," as well as his assertion that the core principle of social anarchism is "take what you need." Peter Kropotkin, *The Conquest of Bread* (Mineola: Dover, 2011) 28, 33.

45 One might wonder about how the production of new goods would occur in the egalitarian anarchist society. Wouldn't it be irrational to produce goods if others have the right to immediately make off with them? Not if one adopts overall quality of life as the "currency" of egalitarian justice as posited immediately above. To see this, suppose a producer is able to make a set of goods that can improve people's lives by a total quantity of Q; however, to produce these goods, she must incur cost C (where C is a reduction in her quality of life). Suppose, then, that the goods—or, more precisely, the benefits generated by these goods—are split up equally between her and all other persons, where the total number of persons is n. Given these stipulations, all other persons would see their lives improve by a quantity of Q/n. However, the producer's life would improve by a quantity of $Q/n - C$, where this "improvement" may actually leave her worse off depending on the size of C. Assuming a baseline of equality, it follows that equal distribution of benefits without any compensation for incurred costs would result in an unequal outcome. Indeed, to reach an equal outcome, the producer would have to be fully compensated for the costs of production with the *remaining* benefits then being distributed equally between everyone—i.e., the producer receives whatever share of her produced goods give her a benefit of $C + ((Q - C)/n)$ while everyone else receives a share yielding a benefit of $(Q - C)/n$. Thus, in a world where people adhere to an egalitarian principle of justice, it will always be rational to produce goods, as one will be receive full compensation for one's efforts plus some additional benefit, albeit not the full benefit produced.

46 That said, if normative views have shifted to the point where social anarchist principles are being widely implemented, it is unclear that either of the following assumptions would still be true: (a) self-interest remains a primary—or even significant—motivation for production and (b) other people will seize a person's products for self-interested reasons. Thus, the worry that an absence of property rights entails stifled production may be unfounded.

47 For a discussion of what pattern of holdings might arise via a process of universal consent, see Alan Gibbard, "Natural Property Rights," *Noûs* 10.1 (1976): 77–86 at 80–2.

24
THE RIGHT ANARCHY
Capitalist or Socialist?

Michael Huemer

I. Introduction: Two Forms of Anarchism

A. Definitions

There are two main varieties of anarchism: the socialist variety (aka "social anarchism" or "anarcho-socialism") and the capitalist variety ("anarcho-capitalism").[1] In this chapter, I argue that anarcho-capitalism is preferable to anarcho-socialism.

First, some definitions. *Anarchists* hold that the ideal form of society would be one lacking any central government, and that we can and should move toward such a system.[2] A *government* is, roughly, an organization that makes laws, imposes them by force on the rest of society, and holds a coercive monopoly (it forcibly prevents anyone else from competing with itself).

Physical capital (aka "capital goods") is a type of good used (repeatably) for producing other valuable goods and services. For example, a clothing factory and the equipment in it qualify as (physical) capital. Dump trucks used to construct buildings are capital. However, raw materials that consumer goods are made of, such as cotton or grain, do not count as capital in the standard sense.

Capitalism is an economic system in which the means of production—physical capital—is owned by private individuals. *Socialism* is a system in which physical capital is collectively controlled, either by the government or by groups of workers.

Socialists are people who endorse socialism. The term "capitalist" (unlike "socialist") has two senses: it is sometimes used to refer to a person who endorses capitalism as a desirable social system, and sometimes used in a quite different sense, to refer to a person who derives income from owning capital. Capitalists in the latter sense are sometimes referred to collectively as "the capitalist class".

Socialist and capitalist anarchists agree in opposing central government. But they disagree about ownership of capital goods: the capitalists want to retain individual ownership of capital goods, whereas socialists want to abolish it.

B. Socialist Anarchism

Socialist anarchists believe that those who work to produce consumable goods and services should also collectively own the capital goods they use for this purpose, rather than these goods being owned by a separate class of people ("the capitalists").[3]

Contrary to what the name might suggest to some, anarchists do not oppose all order, nor do they hold that individuals should act entirely free of social constraints. Socialist anarchists envisage a system in which all businesses are run by the workers, and major decisions are made democratically by worker assemblies. Many variants of this basic scheme are possible. The worker assemblies might include all the workers in some small territory, or be specific to a single business; they might make decisions directly, or elect officials to make most decisions, or rotate decision-making positions among the group; they might seek to make decisions through consensus-building, or through majority vote; they might or might not seek to abolish wages and money.

One might wonder why such a system should be called "anarchy", rather than simply a form of small-scale, democratic government. The system is said to be anarchic because (i) all individuals would have equal power, or as nearly equal as practically possible, and (ii) individuals would voluntarily choose the cooperative or commune that they wished to work in (with the consent of the group) and would be free to leave the group at will. Both of these features allegedly make the system importantly different from all modern states. One might dispute whether this system is truly "anarchic", but it is best to avoid such semantic questions. My interest is in whether the system is good or bad, not what it should be called.

There are three central, closely-related motives for socialist anarchism. First, there is the value of *equality*. In a traditional nation-state, a small minority of society has almost all the political power. Even in a democratic country, there is a class of political elites, along with lobbyists and political donors, who have much more power than the average citizen. The radically decentralized nature of socialist anarchism would make it possible for all to participate in decision-making on a nearly equal basis. Similarly, in a capitalist economy, a small minority of society controls most of the wealth. This is largely due to the ability of individuals to accumulate capital. Anarchist socialists expect income and wealth to be much more nearly equal in their system, with everyone's needs being provided for by the collective.

Second, there is the related value of *freedom*. In a capitalist, government-dominated society, individual workers are not free due to the coercion imposed by the state and the high degree of control that employers exercise over their workers. The inequality in wealth and power inherently inhibits freedom, because the elites with more wealth and power use their advantages to compel those with less wealth and power to obey the will of the elites.

Third, there is the opposition to *exploitation*. Socialists commonly see the capitalist class as exploitative: the capitalists collect a large portion of the value that is produced by businesses, not because the capitalists are doing a great deal of valuable work, but simply because they claim rights over the tools that are needed to produce that value. The capitalists are thus able to live off the productive work of others.

C. Capitalist Anarchism

Anarcho-capitalists, by contrast, have no objection to individual ownership of capital per se. Individuals should be free to organize worker cooperatives if they wish, but traditional, capitalist-owned businesses are equally acceptable. The anarcho-capitalists' central goal is to expand the free market system as much as possible, so that it supplants the state. They believe that all functions of the state should be either privatized or eliminated. The functions of protection and dispute-resolution, currently provided by government police and courts, should be taken over by competing, private businesses. The functions of, for example, business regulation, forcible wealth redistribution, and foreign wars should be eliminated.[4]

Thus, in the anarcho-capitalist society, individuals or organizations would subscribe to security agencies, similar to present-day security guard companies, to provide protection from murderers, thieves, and the like. People would not be *forced* to subscribe; they would merely have the option to purchase services from any of many competing agencies. Businesses would probably hire security to protect their employees and customers, and local homeowners' associations would hire security to protect their residents and guests. This would replace the current system of government-controlled police.

Individuals who had disputes with one another—including disputes in which one person accuses another of a crime—would hire private arbitrators to resolve these disputes. Since no security agency wants to be responsible for protecting a customer who gets in fights and then refuses to have them peacefully resolved, security agencies would require their customers to agree in advance to settle disputes by arbitration. Arbitrators would compete with each other to develop reputations for devising solutions to disputes that appeared to observers to be as fair and generally satisfactory as possible. This system of competing arbitration companies would replace government courts.

Law in an anarcho-capitalist society would be common law. That is, it would rest on precedents set by arbitrators attempting to decide cases in accordance with prevailing moral norms. Arbitrators write down the reasons for their decisions, which are then consulted by other arbitrators in future cases. This would obviate the need for a legislature.

There are two main motivations for anarcho-capitalism. The first is a libertarian conception of *individual rights*. Most anarcho-capitalists hold that all governments violate the rights of individuals. Governments force us to purchase their services (via taxation), whether we want to buy their services or not. More generally, governments make rules and forcibly impose those rules on everyone. This might be acceptable if their rules served simply to enforce the moral rights that all individuals possess. But in fact, governments frequently make unjust, exploitative, or harmful rules.

Governments also coercively prevent competing organizations from offering the same services; for instance, a private business may not set up a competing police force or legal system. This is unjust: either the services the government provides are morally permissible, or they are not. If they are not permissible, then the government must cease providing them. If they are permissible, then it is wrong to forcibly prevent *other* people or groups from providing those same services. Either way, it is wrong to maintain a coercive monopoly. Anarcho-capitalists deem it permissible to provide protection (by force) of individuals' moral rights, and thus hold that private businesses should be able to provide this service.

Second, there is the value of *economic efficiency*, or human wellbeing more broadly. Anarcho-capitalists are impressed by the general ability of competitive markets to provide an adequate supply of relatively high-quality, low-priced goods and services. Goods and services that are provided by coercive monopolies, by contrast, tend to suffer chronic shortages, degenerating quality, and exploding prices. This describes all or most things provided by the government. There are theoretical explanations for this phenomenon that are well-known in economics, and these explanations apply equally to the services of security and dispute-resolution as to other goods and services. Hence, we should expect better, cheaper, and more plentiful security and dispute-resolution services once a free market is introduced.

D. The Right Anarchy

As I have indicated, I aim in what follows to defend anarcho-capitalism as against anarcho-socialism. Here, however, is what I will *not* do: I will not be defending either form of anarchism against *statism*. Arguments in favor of government have been addressed numerous times in other work, by myself and other anarchists.[5] Those other works have also explained how a stateless society might work, and the arguments in its favor, at length.

Suppose, then, that we reject the state. *Given* that, what is the best form of anarchism: socialist or capitalist? I shall contend that anarcho-capitalism is superior for three reasons: (i) anarcho-capitalism has a better response to crime, (ii) anarcho-capitalism embraces the economic contributions of capitalists, (iii) anarcho-capitalism would be more stable than anarcho-socialism.

II. The Crime Problem

When the topic of anarchism arises, the first objection most people think of is that crime would run rampant in an anarchic society. In this discussion, by "crime" I (obviously) do not mean "things prohibited by the state". Rather, I refer to behaviors that wrong others, such that other people have a morally legitimate complaint about them. For example, vandalism, robbery, rape, and murder: these behaviors are wrong whether or not a state prohibits them. A key question for any form of anarchism is what would be done, by whom, to prevent such behaviors, or to address them after the fact.

A. A Capitalist Solution

Anarcho-capitalists have a well-known answer. It is that individuals, businesses, and other organizations hire private security companies to protect people and their property. Where there is a dispute about whether someone committed a crime, a private arbitrator decides on a resolution. The arbitrator can be chosen jointly by the parties to the dispute, e.g., by alternately crossing names off a list of available arbitrators. Anarcho-capitalists expect criminals to be forced to make restitution to their victims (or the victims' families), the amount of required compensation being decided by the arbitrator, with enforcement by the victim's security agency. Criminals who are sufficiently dangerous might be exiled or even executed.

Notice some important features of this answer that mark it as reasonable and non-utopian. First, the theory includes an account of *what motivates* the agents within the system to behave as they are supposed to behave; it does not merely *assume* that they will behave as the theorist desires. The security companies apprehend criminals and enforce judgments against them, because they are paid to do so by the people they are protecting. They attempt to do this well, without too many errors, because otherwise they may lose customers to competing agencies. Individuals submit disputes to arbitration because they are required to do so by the contracts they signed with their security agencies. The agencies require this because arbitration is the least costly way of resolving disputes. The arbitrators attempt to resolve disputes fairly, in accordance with the values of most of society, because they seek to establish reputations for fairness, so that future disputants will not quickly cross their names off the relevant lists.

Second, no changes in human nature are required by this theory. Since the theory relies on ordinary human self-interest, there is no need for speculation about how human behaviors, personalities, or desires will change once anarchy arrives. There is no need to hypothesize that criminal motives will evaporate with the abolition of the state. There is no need for any particularly optimistic account of humans' "true nature".

Third, the theory does not require all or most people in society to adopt some presently-controversial belief system. The agents in the capitalist anarchy do not, for example, need to all adopt a libertarian political ideology. Once the system exists, it is in the interests of each individual to act in the way they are supposed to, regardless of their philosophical ideals—indeed, regardless of whether they *have* any particular philosophical ideals. (This is important because in fact, most human beings have little interest in abstract political or philosophical theories.)

B. Overcoming Crime through Socialism

The social anarchist solution to crime is surprisingly elusive. Many left-wing defenses of anarchism neglect to mention the problem, or address it only very briefly and vaguely.[6] When they do address the problem of crime, socialist anarchists have two main ideas: first, that crime would be greatly reduced under socialist anarchy, because most crime is caused by government and capitalism. Second, that for the few criminals who remain, there would be community-controlled security forces to apprehend them and bring them before popular tribunals to adjudicate their cases.[7]

Begin with the first point, that crime would be much lower under socialist anarchy. This claim is important, because the smaller the crime problem is, the more plausible it is that the problem could be dealt with without a professional, government-like criminal justice system. Why believe that crime would be much lower?

One reason is something that capitalist and socialist anarchists agree on: a good deal of crime is caused by the laws concerning "vice crimes", especially recreational drug use, prostitution, and gambling. Many individuals are directly imprisoned for such victimless crimes. While in prison, they tend to acquire worse criminal tendencies from fellow inmates. In addition, many property crimes are committed by addicts to support their habits, because the drug laws have driven up the prices of drugs to exorbitant levels. The drug laws (and, to a lesser extent, other vice laws) enrich violent, criminal organizations by guaranteeing that criminal organizations will control the industry. The drug trade is fraught with violence because only criminal organizations are available to distribute the product and provide protection for those involved in the trade.

An anarchist society (whether socialist or capitalist) would probably have no vice crime laws, and would thus eliminate a large source of crime. How large? In the United States at present, about 17% of jail and prison inmates are incarcerated for a drug crime, as their most serious offense.[8] So the enormous prison population would be reduced by at least that proportion if drug laws were eliminated. Optimistically, perhaps we might guess that a similar number of people who in fact committed more serious, non-drug crimes would not have done so if not for the drug laws, for the reasons suggested in the previous paragraph. Obviously, we cannot make a reliable quantitative estimate here; I aim only to point toward a vague sense of the magnitude of benefit we might reasonably expect. We should not, for example, wishfully assume that 90% of crime would be eliminated by removing vice crime laws; that would be utopian.

Socialist anarchists suggest several other reasons why crime would be reduced in their society: all individuals would have their needs provided for by the collective, thus reducing the need to commit property crimes; children would be raised in a cooperative, loving community, which would teach them pro-social values; first-time criminals would receive counseling in humane rehabilitation programs; the greater justice of the society would cause members to feel more community spirit.

These last arguments, I believe, are wishful and unrealistic. They might justify us in expecting a slight decrease in crime, but not an enormous decrease. This is because crime has much more robust roots than socialists are willing to recognize: many human beings are selfish and aggressive by nature. Of course, I cannot *prove* this here (nor do socialists attempt to prove their own views about human nature). I can only briefly gesture toward the sort of reasons why I hold a pessimistic view of crime.

Briefly, I believe that human beings are by and large genetically predisposed to selfishness and competition (seeking a higher position within a social hierarchy), and that young males in particular are biologically predisposed toward aggression. This has come about because, in our evolutionary past, those of our ancestors who sacrificed their interests for the good of society were, *by definition*, less successful than those who served their own interests at the expense of others. Therefore, these selfish ancestors left behind more offspring carrying their genes.[9] This is compatible with the fact that humans are also naturally *cooperative*. Social cooperation does not entail selflessness; it only requires the ability to work with others when doing so is to one's own advantage. Selfish people very often find ways to cooperate to *mutual advantage*. Importantly, selfishness is not an artefact of some disordered social structure, nor is it something children are taught by our society. Children become *less* selfish as they are socialized, and human beings have become *much less* prone to violence in modern society than in primitive societies.[10] That is because selfishness and violence are *natural*. It is moral decency that is artificial.

Some people, however, cannot learn moral decency. About 1% of the population are psychopaths, and these individuals make up a large portion of the prison population.[11] (About 3% of people have antisocial personality disorder, of whom about a third are sufficiently antisocial to qualify as full psychopaths. Those with antisocial personality disorder pose problems similar to those posed by psychopaths.) Psychopaths are not people who commit crimes because no one has shown them love, or because they are angry about the injustice of capitalism, or because they are driven to desperation by poverty. They are people who were literally born with *no capacity* for moral reasoning, no capacity to empathize, no capacity to care the slightest bit for anyone else. They tend to be highly skilled manipulators who use their skills to get themselves released from prison early, whereupon they victimize more innocent people. This condition is largely genetic, and treatment is extremely difficult, expensive, and unreliable at best.[12]

Indeed, one might think that anarchists of all stripes should recognize the natural drive of (at least some) humans to dominate or exploit others—after all, humans all over the world have set up governments. It is not as though some domineering alien species landed on a planet full of selfless, egalitarian humans and forced us to set up hierarchies and governments. We human beings created the *status quo* because we wanted to dominate each other.

All of this is to explain why I do not accept the socialists' predictions of a radical reduction in criminal tendencies once socialism arrives. If radical crime reduction were as easy as utopian socialists portray it—if it were as simple as teaching people community spirit, or adopting rehabilitation programs—we would already have done it.

Socialists sometimes point to the well-established correlation between poverty and crime to argue that people are driven to crime by poverty, and therefore that, once poverty is eliminated by socialism, there will be much less crime. This assumes that socialist anarchy would be highly economically productive. Unfortunately, there is no reason to believe this. (See Section III below.) Note also that the crime-poverty correlation may be partly explained by character traits (high time preference, impulsiveness, low respect for social norms) that contribute to both poverty and crime. Eliminating poverty would not eliminate these traits.

Anarcho-capitalists are less prone to wishful thinking about crime: anarcho-capitalists typically assume that crime is caused by selfishness, and they do not claim to be able to educate people into giving up selfishness; they simply seek to make it *not in one's interests* to commit crimes.

Of course, anarcho-socialists accept this to some degree as well: they recognize the need, when they address the problem of crime at all, for *some* use of force on behalf of the community to restrain criminals. As I shall presently argue, however, their unrealistic views of human nature make even this part of their solution to crime problematic.[13]

C. Community Security Forces

Socialist anarchists can generally be prompted to concede that some sort of armed, militia- or police-like force is needed to restrain violent criminals. Indeed, this is common to all serious approaches to the problem of crime, whether anarcho-capitalist, anarcho-socialist, or statist.

Once such a force exists, however, so does the potential for abuse of power—exactly the problem that leads anarchists to reject the state to begin with. Who will prevent the community security force from dominating and abusing the rest of the community? It will not suffice to *stipulate* or *hypothesize* that the security force will serve the community; we must be able to describe a realistic mechanism that would ensure this result, while taking into account natural human selfishness.

Suppose there is some organized group that directs the security force and pays their salaries. Perhaps, for example, there would be a council of officials elected by popular vote of the community. This council could monitor the popular security force and fire anyone found to be behaving improperly. But this just recreates representative government. The problem here is not semantic—the problem is not that the socialist anarchist loses the right to the name "anarchist". The problem is that there were certain central *reasons* for opposing the state—the problems inherent in establishing a group with power over the rest of society—which now apply to the socialist "anarchist's" proposed solution to crime. Whoever controls the security force has power over the rest of the community.

Suppose, on the other hand, that there is no organized group directing the security force. In the event that the force becomes abusive, it is up to the community in general to spontaneously revolt. This is also unsatisfactory. Community members would face a public goods problem: any individual who tries to resist the abusive security force will personally bear the risk of reprisals from a group trained and equipped for capturing violent criminals. This would leave the community in a situation analogous to that of modern-day societies under a government.

It may seem that the problem is insoluble. If we have no armed security force, we are at the mercy of criminals. If we have a security force, we are at the mercy of the security force. If we establish another group to protect us from the security force, then we are at the mercy of *that* group.

The anarcho-capitalist has a solution. It is to have *multiple* security forces, side by side in the same area, offering the same services. If one security agency starts to grow abusive, a customer can switch to a competing agency. The threat of losing clients restrains the agencies from behaving badly. We may call this the *competitive* solution, as contrasted with the *monopolistic* solution (where there is only one security force) proposed by statists and socialist anarchists.

The competitive solution is superior to any monopolistic solution, for three reasons. First, when there is a single security force, it is impossible for community members to know how badly the force is doing, since they have no alternatives to compare it to. They cannot know how much less expensive the service *could* be, how much better at identifying criminals, and so on. The best way to determine these things is to have multiple competing organizations, each attempting to do the best at satisfying clients.

Second, in a competitive system, customers have a greater self-interested motive to form well-informed, rational opinions about their security agency, because they have the ability to switch to another agency if they find one that is better. In a democratic system, individuals have little incentive to seek rational or well-informed opinions, since it is extremely difficult to change election outcomes even if one correctly determines who the best candidate is. If I discover that candidate A is better than B, I cannot simply hire candidate A; I must first convince the majority of other voters to agree with me. The only case in which my vote makes a difference is the case in which the other voters are exactly tied, so that I cast the tie-breaking vote. Since this virtually never happens, voters rationally spend little effort on deciding how to vote.[14] By contrast, in a competitive market, a customer can unilaterally switch to a different provider.

Third, in some cases, an entire organization is problematic—filled with corruption, incompetence, or other problems. In such cases, the democratic mechanism for correcting the situation is extremely cumbersome and unreliable. In a democratic system, one must mount a separate campaign to remove *each* problematic official. Since there are normally multiple unelected bureaucrats working under any public official, one must then hope for the new elected officials to change the bureaucratic staff. If not, one must wait for the next election cycle to elect yet more public officials. By contrast, in a competitive market system, one can immediately drop the entire organization and switch to another one.

These points explain why governments generally fare worse at serving their "customers" than businesses in a competitive industry do. Socialist anarchists recognize the poor performance of governments (even democratic ones) but fail to identify the root causes. The root causes of government failure lie in natural human selfishness, together with the *perverse incentive structure* of democracy. The competitive market turns that selfishness to better purpose by giving people a selfish interest in monitoring their protectors, and giving the protectors a selfish interest in satisfying their customers.

A final word about selfishness. The difference between anarcho-capitalists and anarcho-socialists is not a matter of how much each *values* altruism or community spirit. The difference lies in how much each is willing to *admit the descriptive facts* about human beings. It would of course be wonderful if human beings were naturally altruistic, or if they could be taught to be such. But that doesn't mean we should assume that either of those things is the case. If you don't want it to rain, that doesn't mean you shouldn't bring an umbrella when you go out; you should bring an umbrella if the forecast calls for rain, regardless of how much you may want it to be sunny.[15] Similarly, if you don't want people to be selfish, that doesn't mean that you shouldn't plan for people to behave selfishly; you should plan for humans to behave selfishly if that is what the evidence in fact predicts, regardless of how much you may want people to be selfless. Aligning incentives so that people profit by helping society does not *cause* people to be selfish, any more than umbrellas cause it to rain.

III. The Need for Capitalists

Why do business owners ("capitalists") make more money than their workers? The owner of a factory does not, as such, appear to be doing any productive work, yet he will typically make many times more money than the factory workers who are doing the actual work of producing valuable goods. On the face of it, it might seem that the capitalist must somehow be extracting value produced by the workers—hence the charge of exploitation.

Notice that this charge does not appeal to a specifically left-wing value. Though they rarely use the *word* "exploitation", those on the political right generally agree that individuals ought to be rewarded for their own productive activity, and ought *not* to free ride on the productive work of others. If it is true that capitalists are free-riding, right-wing thinkers should condemn them.

A. Risk Acceptance

In truth, the capitalist serves at least three functions in a modern economy that are crucial to productivity. The first is that of *risk acceptance*. In a modern economy, all business ventures are risky. About half of businesses close down within five years of starting.[16] When a business fails, there will typically be a significant economic loss, which must be borne by someone. Nevertheless, a dynamic, productive economy requires new businesses. Therefore, society needs individuals or groups who are willing and able to risk significant amounts of money. Those who provide the startup funds for a business lose that money if the business fails. Their motive for taking that risk is the promise that, *if* the business succeeds, they will gain large profits. If, when one provides money to start up a business, the business immediately becomes the property of those who work for it (who did not contribute to the startup funds), then few if any people will be willing to start businesses.

So far, this point is compatible with a form of socialism, for the money needed to start a business *could* be provided collectively by the workers who are to work in that business. There is nothing theoretically wrong with this arrangement. In fact, however, relatively few workers wish to take that sort of risk. When one looks for a new job, one does not generally want to have to pay a large amount of money up front to help start the business, and risk losing that money if the business fails. (Notice, by the way, that if employees join a business after it has already started, it would be necessary to charge them money for joining; otherwise, they would gain a benefit that the original workers had to pay for, without themselves paying. This would discourage people from starting a business, or from hiring new workers after doing so.) Only a small minority of society is willing to risk large amounts of money in that way.

It is also true that most workers today cannot *afford* to contribute significant startup funds to a business. This, however, is not the central issue; most people would not start new businesses even if they could. When we dream of winning the lottery, we imagine retiring to Tahiti; we do not imagine taking the money and contributing investment capital to a startup. Thus, even if ownership of all existing businesses were suddenly transferred to the current employees of those businesses, the great majority of employees would swiftly set about selling their shares. The people who would buy those shares would be people with a higher appetite for risk—and they would be providing a valuable service to the sellers, enabling the workers to get hard cash with a known value, which would be safe even if the business should fail, in place of a risky investment.

B. Delayed Gratification

In addition to risk aversion, a second factor that prevents most people from investing in a business is time preference: human beings in general prefer to enjoy benefits in the present or the near future, rather than later. But in order for an economy to grow, there must be savings and investment. This is not a feature of *capitalism*; it is a feature of *human life*. Economic growth requires that someone, rather than consuming whatever resources are available now, uses their resources to attempt to increase the stock of goods that will be available in the future. The motivation for doing this would be the hope of receiving back a larger amount of value than the value one put in.

Individuals vary in their degree of time preference. Some value $100 today about as much as $200 next year. That is a very high time preference, and it means that one would save and invest money only if the expected rate of return on the investment was at least 100% per year. Other individuals, however, have a low time preference; they might, for example, value $100 today about as much as $105 next year. These individuals will save and invest money as long as the expected return is at least 5% per year. In modern society, the majority of people save and invest little, because (in addition to risk aversion) the expected rate of return is not high enough to overcome their time preference. Economic growth depends on unusually low-time-preference individuals.

There is, again, nothing in principle contrary to socialism here. Ordinary workers could in theory provide most savings and investment. In fact, however, few workers have a low enough time preference for this to make sense.

C. Resource Allocation

At any given time, society has finite resources—finite land, savings, natural resources, labor, and so on—and there are indefinitely many ways that these resources *could* be used. Some mechanism must determine how to allocate these limited resources. In the case of labor, for example, the allocation in a free market is decided by employers and employees in a decentralized way: each employer decides how much he is willing to pay for a specific kind of work, each employee decides how much he is willing to accept for each kind of work he is willing and able to do, and the scarce labor winds up being allocated to uses that satisfy these preferences reasonably well.

Of particular interest is the allocation of investment capital. Investment capital (not to be confused with physical capital) is money that people have saved and are prepared to invest. Allocating investment capital in a satisfactory manner is not a simple task. Of all the millions of products present in a modern economy, as well as the indefinitely many more *possible* products, it is far from obvious which products are worth creating a new business, or expanding an existing business, to produce. Most possible uses of investment capital would be failures—the business project would use up resources without ever producing enough value to make up for its costs—and most people are unable to identify which projects would succeed and which would fail. On the other side, some existing uses of wealth are worthy of being curtailed or eliminated. Some mechanism must decide when a business is using up too many resources for the value it is producing, and therefore needs to be downsized or eliminated so as to free up its resources for more valuable uses. If we do not have such mechanisms, then our economy cannot grow and may even shrink as businesses that have, for whatever reason, become inefficient continue to operate.

Capitalists play a key role in the allocation mechanism in market economies. Capitalists, as such, own investment capital and therefore decide to which projects that capital should be given. The capitalists provide this investment capital in exchange for ownership stakes in the businesses or a share of their profits. In an anarcho-socialist society, this would be somehow disallowed—that is the central point of socialism. Thus, the socialists would need some other mechanism for allocating financial resources to businesses. Perhaps the anarcho-socialist community would set aside some portion of the total income of all businesses for investment purposes, and would then vote on how to use this investment capital. Or perhaps the community would elect officials to direct investments and decide when resources should be reallocated.

These socialistic mechanisms of allocating financial resources are inferior to the capitalistic mechanism, for three major reasons. The first reason is the *incentive* structures. In the capitalist system, the individuals allocating capital stand to gain personally if they allocate funds to businesses that turn out to be highly productive, and stand to lose if they allocate funds to failing businesses. They therefore have incentives to devote time and effort to ensuring that they make wise choices. By contrast, the allocation mechanisms acceptable to socialists do not similarly align incentives. If all members of the community must vote on how to allocate investment capital, no individual has the incentive to expend the considerable time and effort to evaluate possible uses of funds, since the individual knows that her own efforts will almost certainly make no difference to what the community decides. If, on the other hand, the community elects an "investment official" to make the decisions, this official will have at most weak incentives to try to make good decisions. In addition, voters will lack adequate incentives to choose the official wisely, if a wise choice requires significant expenditure of time and effort.

The second problem is that most individuals lack the *competence* to make wise investment decisions, even if they were willing to devote time and effort to the task. The capitalist system has a built-in mechanism for dealing with this problem. Those who are bad at making investment decisions lose their money and therefore are forced to stop making investment decisions (or must make fewer and less-consequential ones). On the other hand, those who are good at evaluating business ideas make money, and thereby wind up in a position to make more and larger investment decisions in the future. In the anarcho-socialist system, by contrast, average people are empowered to make decisions about the investment of the community's money. But average people are incompetent at such choices; thus, the community will lose money. Alternately, the average people may elect a presumed expert to invest the community's money. This, however, is more likely to result in the selection of the best *politician* rather than the selection of the best *businessperson*.

A third problem is that, as I have hinted above, there is often a need to *remove* resources from existing businesses, and not merely to allocate new funds to new businesses. If no such mechanism existed, we would still be producing the same number of videotapes, typewriters, and Atari computers as we did in the 1980s. There would still be Blockbuster Video stores in most cities, providing a service that almost no one wants. (Except that perhaps we would never have started producing any of those products, because we would all still be working on farms.) The reallocation of capital can occur because of technological advances, changes in the plans and preferences of consumers, changing trade opportunities with other societies, deterioration of a particular business' ability to satisfy customers, and so on.

In the capitalist system, this reallocation occurs because, when a business becomes inefficient or obsolete, or for any other reason its product becomes less desirable relative to other products, the expected future profits of that business decline, relative to alternatives. When the value of the business' expected profit stream drops below the value of the business' assets (including the money, land, physical capital, and other goods owned by the business), an incentive is created for the capitalists to liquidate the business. The assets are then freed up for more highly valued uses.

In a socialist system, the decision to shrink or liquidate a business must be made democratically, either by a direct majority vote or by elected representatives. Such decisions are almost always unpopular. Even when a business is losing money, most people's instinct is to try to keep the business in operation, so as to "save jobs". The individuals who would be laid off by the business are easily identifiable, and their short-term suffering highly visible. The overall, long-term cost to society of continuing to employ resources in an inefficient manner are less visible, less immediate, less quantifiable. When a business is losing money, this is a signal that the business is *destroying value*—that is, the value of the inputs the business is consuming is greater than the value of the outputs it is producing. But few ordinary people think in these terms. Thus, a socialist society is likely to accumulate inefficient businesses, even businesses that impose net costs on the rest of the community.

Admittedly, this reasoning relies on the market value of goods and services as a measure of their social utility; that is, how much total good they produce for people. For various well-known reasons (diminishing marginal utility of money, unequal initial distribution, mistakes by buyers and sellers), market value is a highly imperfect measure of social utility. Yet even this highly imperfect measure is superior to *no* measure. More precisely, an economic system that systematically tends to approximate to maximizing total market value is superior to a system that has no mechanism for even approximating the maximization of *any* measure of social utility. The socialist system, for reasons just discussed, cannot be expected to approximate to maximizing market value, and there is no reason to think that it would come close to maximizing any other, even very imperfect measure of social utility.

D. Fair Pay

In sum, capitalists serve genuine economically valuable functions. There remains the question of how much capitalists and workers should be paid. You may agree that capitalists deserve *something* for their contributions but still think that, intuitively, they are reaping unfairly large rewards in the capitalist system, compared to average workers.

There is no principled reason, however, to believe that capitalists are systematically overpaid or workers systematically underpaid by the market. In a free market, employees of a business are paid approximately according to their marginal product. That is, a business should be expected to pay a given worker approximately the amount of money that the business itself would lose if that employee were to stop working for the business and not be replaced. The reason for this is that if the market wage of employees in the industry is *less* than the value that a single employee produces for the business, then the business *should* (from the standpoint of self-interest) hire more employees, until this is no longer true. If the market wage is *more* than the value that a single employee produces for the business, then the business should (from the standpoint of self-interest) lay off employees until this is no longer true. So the only stable situation is that in which the market wage is approximately *equal to* the value that the business obtains from a single employee. These are uncontroversial implications of standard price theory, which is the most well established and least controversial part of economics.

Economics, of course, cannot tell us what is *fair*. But, reflecting philosophically, the following seems to be a plausible normative principle:

> *Fair Pay Principle:* Fair compensation for one's contribution to a productive activity is *no greater than* one's marginal product.

An individual cannot reasonably ask to be included in a cooperative endeavor on terms that render the individual's presence a net cost to the group. In particular, if you work for a business, you cannot reasonably expect to be paid so much that the business would be better off without you. If you are, that is unfair to the rest of the people involved in the business.

Because employee compensation in a free market economy approximates to the employee's marginal product, it cannot be said that employees are systematically underpaid. By and large, they are paid the most that could reasonably be asked; if they were paid significantly more, this would in fact be *unfair*.

Similar principles apply to the rewards received by capitalists for the services they provide. Capitalists' expected (time-discounted) rewards are in general approximately equal to the market value of their contributions to business productivity. (Note: this assumes a free market; in actual, modern societies, government policy may unjustly skew the market in favor of larger profits for capitalists.) The main reason for the seemingly "unfairly" high rewards reaped by some capitalists is the very large contribution to productivity that they are able to make. When we see a business owner making fifty times more money than an ordinary worker, this strikes us as maladjusted, since the owner is not, for example, working *fifty times harder* or *fifty times more hours* than the worker. But these are not the correct measures of one's contribution. The correct measure of one's contribution to a business venture is one's marginal product, that is, how much more value is produced by the business because of one's own presence, keeping the other participants fixed. It is entirely plausible that one individual can make a contribution, in that sense, that is fifty times greater than that of an ordinary worker. This is possible because an individual can add something that enables a large number of other people to be more productive—for example, correctly identifying what is or is not a good business plan. Because capitalists contribute to the efficient employment of resources and labor by *many other people*, a capitalist's contribution can be many times more economically valuable than that of a single ordinary employee.

IV. The Stability Problem

Any reasonable proposal concerning the structure of society must address the issue of *stability*: there must be a plausible account of how, once the proposed social structure is in place, it would be able to persist over time in realistic conditions, without changing into some quite different social system. This account should not require the assumption of near-total ideological commitment to the system. In all societies, human beings have conflicting values, conflicting desires, and conflicting beliefs about what is the best way to structure a society. Therefore, a social system must be robust in the face of these kinds of differences among people. The only societies in which large disagreements are not expressed are totalitarian societies.

In the case of socialist anarchism, there must be an account of how a society filled with worker-controlled firms would avoid being taken over by capital-controlled firms, without relying on government-like coercion. There are three reasons why worker-controlled firms would be likely to be replaced by capital-controlled firms.

A. Capitalist Competition

The first major challenge for a worker-controlled business would be competition from capitalist-structured businesses. Even in a society dominated by worker cooperatives, *some* people will attempt to start capitalist-structured businesses. That is, some individuals or groups will attempt to acquire goods that can be used for producing other goods and services, and will offer to pay other people to perform specific tasks leading to the production of useful goods and services (without giving these other people an ownership stake in the physical capital).

State socialists have an answer to this: the government sends police to shut those people down. Anarchist socialists cannot give anything like that answer, since they reject all centralized authority. In the absence of a central authority structure, there is no one to stop capitalist acts between consenting adults. The only coherent, *anarchist* answer the socialist can give is that the market, for some reason, simply will not favor capitalist businesses.

Why might this be? Perhaps socialistic (worker-controlled) businesses will simply be more *economically efficient* than capitalistic businesses; that is, they will produce more valuable goods and services (measured in terms of market prices) per unit of labor and resources used. If so, capitalist businesses would, by and large, be driven out of the market by fair competition.

Convenient as this might be, there is no obvious reason to believe it. Worker-controlled businesses can be, and sometimes are, set up in our current society, but they do not in general out-compete traditional, capitalist businesses. The major reasons are explained in Section III above—capitalists serve economically useful functions. Even in a mostly socialist society, there will be some individuals who are better suited to performing those functions than the average worker. Those individuals would be able to start capitalist businesses that would be, on average, more productive and successful than the socialist businesses. This would create the possibility for personal profit, which would motivate those individuals to make the attempt. Once started, these businesses would tend to expand, while the socialist businesses would shrink, due to normal marketplace competition.

Another answer on behalf of the socialist is that capitalist-structured businesses would have difficulty attracting employees. Why would anyone submit to "wage slavery" (as traditional work is often called), when one has the option to live in a commune, or work for a socialist business, that will provide for all of one's needs?

This question has a simple answer: more money. Most human beings do not merely wish for their needs to be met. Most prefer to have much more than they need. This is a robust feature of human nature that will not change simply because we create worker-controlled businesses. Socialist businesses—if they operate as socialists hope—would have much more egalitarian payment schemes than capitalist businesses; that is, there would be smaller differences (perhaps no differences) between the highest- and lowest-paid workers. By implication, there would be smaller differences in pay between the *most productive* and the *least productive* workers. That is good news for the less productive. But it is bad news for the most productive. And it means that the most productive workers in a socialist business would be the ones most likely to leave in favor of a capitalist business, where highly productive people are capable of earning much greater pay.

Perhaps, one might think, people would remain with socialist businesses for ideological reasons—that is, out of a moral belief in the value of equality, the exploitativeness of wage labor, and so on. This argument, however, is unrealistic. To begin with, it is unrealistic to postulate such ideological uniformity as would prevent there from being *some* capitalist businesses. At a minimum, the committed right-wing libertarians who exist today (this author included) would surely continue to support capitalism, even if a socialist society were created. In addition, there would probably continue to exist a large majority of society who are essentially non-ideological and who prioritize personal interests over political and philosophical ideals.

Once capitalist businesses exist, it is implausible that their expansion will be stopped by a widespread refusal of people to work for them or to patronize them for ideological reasons. Consider that in our society today, it is already possible to join a commune or a worker cooperative. It is not illegal to do so, nor will capitalists send an army to shut down your commune. Yet very few people make any effort to join such groups. Even among the strongest left-wing ideologues, *almost none* attempt to join a commune, and *almost all* continue to work for essentially capitalist businesses and to buy products from other capitalist businesses. Why do they do this? Self-interest. Working for The Man pays better than working on a commune. This suggests that, even if many socialist businesses were available, the overwhelming majority of people, who are less ideological, would be willing to work for capitalist businesses, provided the pay was competitive.

Again, for the most talented, productive people, the pay in the capitalist world would exceed the pay available in socialist communities. Thus, the socialist businesses, already suffering from lower productivity for the reasons cited in Section III, would find themselves systematically losing their best workers, with their least productive workers left behind. This would force them to lower their wages or raise their prices, thus accelerating the problem. Eventually, most would fold under the pressure of competition from capitalist businesses, and we would be left with a world of mostly capitalist firms.

To be clear, the anarcho-capitalist does not favor *prohibitions* on socialistic activity. If a group of people wished to start a commune or a worker-controlled business in an anarcho-capitalist society, they would be welcome to do so. But they would be unable to *force* anyone to join them, and they would face competition from capitalistic businesses and communities. In all probability, only a small number of committed ideologues would join such communes or businesses.[17]

B. Internal Dissolution

The second major threat to the socialist business model would come from within: workers within a socialistic business might decide to *convert* their business to a capitalistic form. To start with, suppose that each worker owns a tradeable stake in the company, saleable to anyone inside or outside the company. In that case, workers with a relatively high time preference or risk aversion (see subsections III.A. and III.B.) would sell their shares to people with lower time preference or higher risk tolerance. Since in fact, most workers have relatively high time preference and are relatively risk averse (compared to capitalists), such sales would be common. This would convert the business to a traditional capitalistic business.

Suppose, on the other hand, that workers do not have tradeable shares. They are entitled to vote on company policy, with no authority higher than the workers, per the socialist ideal. But suppose that the company bylaws specify that one cannot sell one's stake in the company to anyone outside the company, perhaps not to anyone at all. Nevertheless, the workers could vote to change that. Since there is no authority above the workers, there is no one to prevent them from doing so. Furthermore, it would be in the economic self-interest of each worker to vote in favor of allowing workers to sell their ownership stakes in the company, because such a rule would immediately give every worker an economically valuable asset. They could trade that asset for money if they wished, or hold on to it if they valued it more than the money. If the workers initially owned stakes that could only be traded to other workers in the business, it would be in their interests to vote to change that rule so that their stakes could be sold to *anyone*, within or without the business. The reason is that this would increase the value of everyone's shares (an increase in potential buyers, with the same supply, entails an increase in price)—thus, each employee's net worth would immediately grow as soon as the rule was adopted permitting sale to outsiders.

Doubtless some worker-run businesses would resist the temptations to capitalize, out of a philosophical commitment to socialism. But again, it is not realistic to assume that all or most people would place ideological commitment to socialism ahead of their economic self-interest.

Another possibility is that the workers in a socialist business might vote to collectively offer ownership stakes in the company for sale to the public (otherwise known as making an IPO, or initial public offering). The reason for doing this would be that it would generate a large influx of cash into the company, which could be used to increase worker salaries, expand the business, pay off business debt, and so on. If a business did this, it would have a competitive advantage over businesses that refused to sell shares due to a philosophical commitment to socialism. Thus, it is likely that this would occur often.

C. Social Welfare

One more problem would threaten the stability of socialist anarchy. Socialist anarchists envision a system in which a community would provide for the needs of all members, regardless of their ability to pay. The socialists would provide free education for the young, and free housing, food, medical care, and so on for the old and the sick. At the same time, socialist anarchists believe in complete negative freedom of association, meaning that anyone has the right to quit any association at will.

Now suppose that a socialist community is providing free social welfare programs, as described, to its neediest members. These programs must somehow be paid for by the other members—perhaps workers will receive lower pay, or the products they produce will have higher prices, than they would if there were no such social welfare programs. Meanwhile, next to the socialist community is a capitalist community in which there are no free social welfare programs. The socialists shake their heads in disapproval, but since they do not believe in aggressive wars, they must let the benighted capitalists continue in their individualistic ways.

Now, in addition to the reasons cited earlier, there is one more incentive for some people to leave the socialist community. In the socialist community, some people are *net beneficiaries* of the social welfare programs, while others are *net payers*—that is, they pay more to support the programs than the economic value that they receive from the programs. The greatest net payers would be healthy young adults, without children, who possess skills that are highly economically valuable. These individuals would not use the social welfare programs, but their labor would go to support the programs. The net payers will recognize that if they move to the capitalist community, they will be much better off, since they will no longer have to support other people's education, health care, and so on. Some of them decide to do so. This puts a financial strain on the socialist community, which now must support its social welfare programs without the help of some of its formerly most productive members. When the remaining net payers see this, more of them are tempted to follow suit.

Thus, the socialist community finds itself with too many people who need social services and not enough people to support them. The capitalist community finds itself filled with highly economically productive people who have fewer needs, or who are able and willing to pay for their own needs. Capitalist communities will thus grow and prosper under anarchy while socialist communities struggle.

One might suggest that productive individuals would choose to remain in the socialist society because they know that they *might* fall ill one day, in which case the community would support them without charge, whereas the capitalist society would do no such thing. From the standpoint of self-interest, however, it would make more sense for individuals to simply purchase *insurance*, which would be for sale in the capitalist society, against the possibility of such an illness. The cost of insurance for low-risk individuals (those who are young, have healthy lifestyles, and so on) would be lower than the amount required if one must pay an equal share for the support of all the old and infirm.

Alternately, one might hope that highly productive individuals would remain in the socialist society due to charitable impulses. Perhaps they would *enjoy* helping needy members of their community, or perhaps they would simply have a philosophical belief that one *ought* to help.

In fact, even such generous people would have no reason to prefer the socialist community. For once one moves to a capitalist community, one is hardly debarred from helping others. Capitalist societies would host a variety of *voluntary* charities, such as already exist in today's society. One charity might support research on muscular dystrophy, another aid the poor in Bangladesh, and another help protect endangered species. In an anarcho-capitalist community, those with charitable impulses may freely give to whichever charities they choose. Charitably minded individuals should be *better* satisfied with the *capitalist* community, because it leaves them free to choose, individually, which of many causes to support, depending on their own preferences. In the socialist community they would be required to give to whatever the majority of the community voted for, thus leaving them with less to spend either on themselves or on their preferred charities. Thus, *regardless* of whether one is selfish or charitable, the capitalist community is the more rational choice for relatively productive people.

We should not overstate the point. The socialist communities would not necessarily disappear. Some people would remain in them due to inertia, or due to a general philosophical belief in socialism. But over time, capitalist communities would come to comprise most of society, even if we began from a predominantly socialist world.

Of course, the same factors that explain why socialism would be likely to evolve into capitalism also explain why it is unlikely that a country dominated by anarcho-socialist communities would ever come about to begin with. If we ever manage to abolish the state, it is most likely that we would transition directly to anarcho-capitalism, without any detour through socialism.

V. Conclusion

The capitalist version of anarchism is preferable to socialist versions for three main reasons. First, anarcho-capitalism has a superior solution to the problem of crime. The idea of teaching people to be highly selfless is utopian, and there is no evidence that anyone knows how to do this. The idea of creating a community security force, on the other hand, simply reproduces the problems of traditional government. The only solution that genuinely alters the logic that leads to government abuse, while at the same time opposing dangerous criminals with adequate force, is the free market solution of a collection of *competing* protection agencies. The operation of this solution does not depend upon any idealistic assumptions about how altruistic human beings are, about how much human nature can change, or about the prospects for society-wide philosophical agreement.

The second reason for preferring anarcho-capitalism over socialism is that capitalism preserves the valuable functions of capitalists. Socialists mistakenly view capitalists as parasites whose incomes derive from skimming off value produced by workers. In fact, capitalists provide the economically valuable functions of (i) bearing the financial risk inherent in business, (ii) trading short-term consumption for long-term increases in productivity, and (iii) evaluating the promise of businesses and allocating resources accordingly. The high pay of capitalists relative to workers results from the fact that an individual's efficient performance of these functions can make a much greater difference to economic productivity than an ordinary worker's skillful performance of his job. In a market economy, the pay of an individual worker approximates to the worker's marginal product, which is the most that any individual can reasonably ask to be paid.

The final reason for preferring anarcho-capitalism over socialist anarchism is the greater stability of capitalism. In a society with both capitalist and socialist communities or businesses, we should expect capitalist businesses and communities to grow through peaceful marketplace competition until they dominate the landscape. One reason is that capitalist businesses will be more productive on average, due to the valuable functions served by capitalists, as well as the ability to attract the most talented individuals by paying them more than socialist businesses are willing to pay. Another reason is that it would be in the economic self-interest of workers in a socialist community to vote to allow themselves to sell shares of the company (or allow the company to issue stock) to outsiders, thus providing the workers with an immediate financial benefit and reduced financial risk. Finally, socialist communities would be disadvantaged by their policies of providing free social welfare benefits. Those who benefit less from a socialist community's social programs than average would be better off moving to a capitalist community or company, where they would receive greater net pay. Even those with charitable impulses would be best served by moving to anarcho-capitalist communities, where they could choose which causes to direct their charitable dollars to.

The bad news is that socialist anarchy would function poorly. The good news is that it would not last long. In the absence of a state to enforce socialistic constraints, the system would peacefully evolve, by and large, to the more efficient, capitalistic variety of anarchy.

Notes

1 Aside: the common term "social anarchism" is infelicitous, since it suggests that alternative forms of anarchism are *not social.* Of course, anarcho-capitalism is *social* (it involves people living in cooperative groups); it merely fails to be *socialist.*

2 This view is sometimes called "political anarchism", to distinguish it from "philosophical anarchism". Philosophical anarchism holds that individuals do not have an obligation to obey laws merely because they are laws; see A. John Simmons, *Moral Principles and Political Obligations* (Princeton, NJ: Princeton UP, 1979). In this chapter, I focus solely on political anarchism, which is how "anarchism" is usually understood in popular discourse.

3 See, for example, Mikhail Bakunin, *Bakunin on Anarchy*, trans. and ed. Sam Dolgoff (New York, NY: Knopf, 1972); Peter Kropotkin, *The Conquest of Bread* (New York, NY: Vanguard, 1926); Iain McKay et al., *An Anarchist FAQ*, 2 vols. (Chico, CA: AK, 2007), available at www.anarchistfaq.org (accessed April 4, 2019).

4 See Murray Rothbard, *For a New Liberty: The Libertarian Manifesto*, 2d ed. (Auburn, AL: Mises, 2006); David Friedman, *The Machinery of Freedom*, 3d ed. (New York, NY: Chu Hartley, 2014); Michael Huemer, *The Problem of Political Authority* (New York, NY: Palgrave, 2013).

5 See notes 3–4 above. A number of questions and objections are also addressed by Bryan Caplan, *Anarchist Theory FAQ*, version 5.2, http://econfaculty.gmu.edu/bcaplan/anarfaq.htm (1994; accessed April 4, 2019).

6 For example, Bakunin; Kropotkin; Pierre-Joseph Proudhon, *What Is Property?*, trans. Benjamin Tucker (Princeton, NJ: Wilson, 1876).

7 See Scott of the Insurgency Culture Collective, "The Anarchist Response to Crime", https://theanarchistlibrary.org/library/scott-of-the-insurgency-culture-collective-the-anarchist-response-to-crime (2010; accessed March 21, 2019); Emerican Johnson, "How Do Anarchist Police and Military Work?", www.youtube.com/watch?v=Hmy1jjRnl8I (2018; accessed March 21, 2019); McKay, section I.5.8.

8 Wendy Sawyer and Peter Wagner, "Mass Incarceration: The Whole Pie 2019", Prison Policy Initiative, www.prisonpolicy.org/reports/pie2019.html (March 19, 2019; accessed March 26, 2019).

9 See Richard Dawkins, *The Selfish Gene* (Oxford: OUP, 2016). The reason for the greater aggression of males is that in the past, aggressive males killed other males and thereby gained more mating opportunities for themselves. The same did not occur with females, because women are incapable of reproducing more than once in nine months, regardless of how many partners they may have; see Steven Pinker, *How the Mind Works* (New York: Norton, 1997) 494–8, 509–20.

10 See Steven Pinker, *The Better Angels of Our Nature: Why Violence Has Declined* (New York, NY: Viking, 2011).

11 Kent A. Kiehl and Morris B. Hoffman, "The Criminal Psychopath: History, Neuroscience, Treatment, and Economics", *Jurimetrics* 51 (2011): 355–97. Somewhere between 15% and 25% of the prison population are psychopaths; thus, psychopaths are fifteen to twenty-five times more likely to wind up in prison than non-psychopaths.

12 Psychopathy has traditionally been viewed as untreatable. Kiehl and Hoffman, however, discuss recent innovations that appear to produce significant improvements in behavior for psychopaths, albeit at large expense. On the genetic source of psychopathic personality, see Henrik Larsson, Henrik Andershed, and Paul Lichtenstein, "A Genetic Factor Explains Most of the Variation in the Psychopathic Personality", *Journal of Abnormal Psychology* 115 (2006): 221–30.

13 The problem isn't simply an unrealistic view of human nature. More precisely, socialist anarchists tend to recognize the problems of human selfishness and the drive to dominate others *when thinking about the state*, but to forget these tendencies when thinking about the socialist utopia.

14 For some elaboration, see Bryan Caplan, *The Myth of the Rational Voter* (Princeton, NJ: Princeton UP, 2007); Jason Brennan, *Against Democracy*, (Princeton, NJ: Princeton UP, 2016).

15 This analogy is from Friedman (133–4).

16 U.S. Department of Labor, Bureau of Labor Statistics, "Entrepreneurship and the U.S. Economy", Chart 3, www.bls.gov/bdm/entrepreneurship/bdm_chart3.htm (2016; accessed April 4, 2019). But note that not all of these are business failures; 29% of these businesses are viewed by their owners as successes at the time of closure (Brian Headd, "Redefining Business Success: Distinguishing between Closure and Failure", *Small Business Economics* 21 [2003]: 56).

17 I use "ideologue" in a descriptive, non-pejorative sense here: ideologues are simply people who prioritize philosophical and political ideals over more personal concerns.

25
ANARCHIST APPROACHES TO EDUCATION

Kevin Currie-Knight

"'Why do you not say how things will be operated under Anarchism?' is a question I have had to meet thousands of times. Because I believe that Anarchism cannot consistently impose an iron-clad program or method on the future."[1] Emma Goldman wrote this in an essay defending anarchism as a vision for social organization. If anarchism is about allowing people the freedom to organize their affairs as they see fit, as Goldman argues, this understandably makes it difficult for anarchist writers to sketch a substantive vision of how children's education should be organized. This may be, why, in anarchist philosopher Judith Suissa's estimation, "very little has been written, from a systematic philosophical point of view, about the educational ideas arising from anarchist theory."[2]

Indeed, while there exist some book-length treatments of primary and secondary education by anarchist authors,[3] anarchists have tended to treat education as an ancillary issue, to be dealt with in short essays or sections of larger works. From these works, though, we can distill some common themes running through anarchist treatments of education. These themes are of two broad types. Themes of one sort in anarchist writings about education are practical, and concern how education might be provided without the state. The other set of themes is more pedagogical, and concerns what forms of education are most consistent with anarchist principles.

Within this first (practical) set of concerns, anarchists are understandably most united in their opposition to state involvement in education. Insofar as anarchists see the state as a way for the ruling class to subjugate the people, state education is viewed as a way for the state to create willing subjects by means of state propaganda. In William Godwin's words: "[T]he data upon which their [the ruling class's] conduct as statesmen is vindicated, will be the data upon which their instructions are founded."[4] Voltairine de Cleyre similarly cautioned:

> If the believers in liberty wish the principles of liberty taught, let them never intrust [*sic*] that instruction to any government; for the nature of government is to become a thing apart, an institution existing for its own sake, preying upon the people, and teaching whatever will tend to keep it secure in its seat.[5]

Anarchists have tended to see education as a propaganda tool for whatever views the state seeks to inculcate. Anarchists have generally agreed, of course, that the state has a strong interest in educating the young to respect the state. But anti-capitalist anarchists have also tended to see education as indoctrinating the young into support of capitalism. And anarchists with strong commitments to scientific atheism (like Bakunin) have often seen the state as an engine for indoctrinating the young into (state-endorsed) religion.[6]

If anarchists wanted to end the state's control of schools, how would education be provided to the people? Here, many anarchists have been understandably vague: the answer couldn't be much more specific than allowing the people to create and decide on the forms of education they themselves wanted. Proudhon, for instance, suggested that workers' federations would create their own ways (likely, schools) to provide education to the young, while offering parents the option of utilizing some other form of education if they chose.[7] Auberon Herbert articulated his voluntaryist vision of education this way:

> It is plain that the most healthy state of education will exist when the workmen, dividing themselves into natural groups according to their own tastes and feelings, organize the education of their children without help, or need of help, from outside.[8]

Similarly, Leo Tolstoy believed that education wasn't truly free until "the classes which receive the education … have the full power to express their dissatisfaction, or at least, to swerve from the education which instinctively does not satisfy them,—that the criterion of pedagogics is only liberty."[9]

This, of course, leaves wide scope for people to choose diverse forms of education. Some families might choose for their children to attend schools with strict curricular standards. Others might choose more libertarian schools that leave students comparatively free to explore based on their own interests.

On pedagogical matters—questions like what curricula the young should be taught and how teaching should be approached—anarchists were quite diverse. Some, like Proudhon and Herbert, said nothing about these matters, trusting that allowing individuals to choose the approaches that worked best for them and their children would be enough. For these anarchists, we might suppose, there could have been a perceived tension between advancing a philosophy that prizes individual freedom of choice and offering substantive ideas about what educational form is best for people.

Several anarchists, however, *did* offer substantive ideas on what features education should have in an anarchist social order. Perhaps the one that flows most obviously from basic anarchist principles is that education should leave children as free as possible from teacher (and adult) coercion—physical, social, and emotional. To the extent that anarchism is a theory motivated by opposition to unjust hierarchies, it can be argued that teacher/student hierarchies, like adult/child hierarchies more generally, are problematically coercive.

Perhaps the first author to write about the issue of educational hierarchy from an anarchist perspective was William Godwin. Godwin's book *The Enquirer*[10] extended arguments he'd made in his *Enquiry Concerning Political Justice* into the realm of education and child rearing. In *Enquiry*, Godwin argued against political systems based on coercion in light of his belief that individuals should be free to follow their own reasoned human judgments. We can and should attempt to *persuade*, argued Godwin, but we should never *force*. *The Enquirer* was largely an attempt to argue that the same principle should hold true for the education of children. Whenever possible—whenever force wasn't necessary to preserve someone's physical safety—children should be left free to learn through their own experience. Parents and teachers could, of course, attempt to *persuade* children through reason and argument, but should not attempt to force or manipulate by extrinsic threat of punishment or promise of reward.

Other anarchists were similarly sensitive to the importance of children's freedom. In the essay "The Child and its Enemies," Emma Goldman cautioned parents and educators that the existing conventional "ideas of education and training [of children] ... in the school and the family—even the family of the liberal or radical—are such as to stifle the natural growth of the child."[11] Like Godwin, she favored much more freedom for children to develop in their own ways (as opposed to ways demanded by adults).

Other anarchist writers were convinced that conventional methods of teaching too often treated students as passive memorizers, whose duty was to obey teachers' authority. For instance, Leo Tolstoy founded a "school for peasants" in Russia around 1860 (the date is uncertain) near his home at Yasnaya Polyana. The school was organized largely around student freedom: students could, but did not have to, attend formal classes, and teachers were to seduce students into learning by persuasion rather than force.[12]

Voltairine de Cleyre, who taught briefly at a Chicago school founded on anarchist principles, wrote eloquently of her concern for student liberty in schools in which teachers exercised unjust authority. She offered a powerful and mocking comparison between teaching (as it existed in conventional schools) and the less coercive act of gardening.

> Any gardener who should attempt to raise healthy, beautiful, and fruitful plants by outraging all those plants' instinctive wants and searchings, would meet as his reward—sickly plants, ugly plants, sterile plants, dead plants. He will not do it; he will watch very carefully to see whether they like much sunlight, or considerable shade, whether they survive on much water or get drowned in it, whether they like sandy soil, or fat mucky soil; the plant itself will indicate to him when he is doing the right thing. And every gardener will watch for indications with great anxiety. If he finds the plant revolts against his experiments, he will desist at once, and try something else; if he finds it thrives, he will emphasize the particular treatment so long as it seems beneficial. But what he will surely not do, will be to prepare a certain area of ground all just alike, with equal chances of sun and amount of moisture in every part, and then plant everything together without discrimination,—mighty close together!—saying beforehand, 'If plants don't want to thrive on this, they ought to want to; and if they are stubborn about it, they must be made to.'[13]

Because anarchists were most often concerned with the fate of the working classes at the hands of the state, several anarchists made suggestions regarding ways in which education in an anarchist society could best aid and strengthen those classes. One suggestion, made by such anarchists as Pyotr Kropotkin and Francisco Ferrer, was to ensure that everyone be taught thoroughly about science and scientific ways of thinking. Ferrer, who founded the Escola Moderna (Modern School) in Italy on anarchist principles, insisted that the school teach students contemporary science using only the best texts written from a scientific (as opposed to a religious) point of view. Unlike Tolstoy's school, which afforded students a high degree of choice regarding the activities in which they engaged, Ferrer was committed to the conviction that all students needed thorough grounding in science.[14] Kropotkin[15] and Bakunin[16] held similar views about the importance of science education.

The reason for this emphasis was twofold. First, these anarchists viewed science largely in contrast to religion. Religion, they thought, encouraged the teaching of superstition and obedience to a divine authority that could (and often did) foster servile relationships to the state. Science, on the other hand, was rooted in a willingness to *challenge* superstition and authority, a habit of thought that the vulnerable could use to challenge the authority of the more powerful classes.

The second reason these authors stressed science education is that, drawing on scientific work performed by Kropotkin and others, they also believed that a proper understanding of science led to anarchistic conclusions. Building on the biological idea that human nature was naturally cooperative and didn't require government to organize society, and focusing on the apparent ubiquity of non-hierarchical spontaneous orders in the natural world, they supposed that, if students were taught a proper understanding of science and scientific thinking "by means of an extensive system of popular education and instruction, … the question of liberty … [would] be entirely solved."[17]

Another contribution anarchist writers envisioned that education might make to the liberation of the working class was to oppose curricula embodying the conventional split between intellectual and physical work. In conventional schools, these writers observed, some students were taught intellectual curricula and others were educated for manual labor, an educational practice that served to create a caste system. These anarchists argued that, when schools properly fused intellectual and physical labor into instruction for all, not only would an end would be put to this artificial hierarchy, but people would learn to become more independent and to produce things for themselves, hence being less dependent on potentially coercive authority figures. Kropotkin envisioned schools in which

> we shall arrive at teaching everyone the basis of every trade as well as of every machine, by laboring … at the workbench, with the vice, in shaping raw material, in oneself making the fundamental parts of everything, as well of simple machines as of apparatus for the transmission of power, to which all machines are reduced.[18]

Voltairine de Cleyre's vision of an "ideal school" was "a boarding school built in the country, having a farm attached, and workshops where useful crafts might be learned, in daily connection with intellectual training." The ideal school's fusion of physical with intellectual training would enable students to

> learn to use their limbs as nature meant, feel their intimate relationship with the growing life of other sorts, form a profound respect for work and an estimate of the value of it, [and] wish to become real doers in the world, and not mere gatherers in of other men's products.[19]

Notes

1 Emma Goldman, *Anarchism and Other Essays* (New York: Mother Earth 1910) 49.
2 Judith Suissa, *Anarchism and Education: A Philosophical Perspective* (New York: PM Press 2010) 16.
3 Wiliam Godwin, *The Enquirer: Reflections on Education, Manners, and Literature* (London: G. G. J. and J. Robinson 1797); Francisco Ferrer, *The Origins and Ideals of the Modern School,* trans. Joseph McCabe (New York: Watts & Company 1913); Goodman, Paul, *Compulsory Mis-Education, and The Community of Scholars* (New York: Vintage Books, 1964); Murray Rothbard, *Education: Free & Compulsory (*Auburn, AL: Ludwig von Mises Institute 1999).
4 William Godwin, *An Enquiry Concerning Political Justice: And Its Influence on General Virtue and Happiness* (London: G. G. J. and J. Robinson 1793) 304.
5 Voltairine de Cleyre, "Anarchism and American Traditions." *Selected Works of Voltairine de Cleyre*, ed. Alexander Berkman (Mother Earth 1914) 126.
6 Mikhail Bakunin, *God and the State* (Indore: Modern Publishers 1920).
7 Shi Yung Lu, *The Political Theories of P. J. Proudhon* (New York: M. R. Gray 1922) 138–139.
8 Auberon Herbert, "State Education: A Help or Hindrance?" *The Right and Wrong of Compulsion by the State, and Other Essays*, ed. Eric Mack (Indianapolis: Liberty Fund 1978) 58.
9 Leo Tolstoy, "On Popular Education." *The Complete Works of Count Tolstoy: Pedagogical Articles*, trans. Leo Weiner (Boston: Dana Estes and Co. 1904) 29.
10 Godwin, *The Enquirer* 1797.
11 Emma Goldman, "Child and Its Enemies." *Mother Earth* 1:2 *(April 1906)* 7.

12 Leo Tolstoy, "The School at Yasnaya Polyana." *The Complete Works of Count Tolstoy: Pedagogical Articles*, trans. Leo Weiner (London: Dana Estes and Co, 1904) 225–360.
13 Voltairine de Cleyre, "Modern Educational Reform." *Selected Works of Voltairine de Cleyre*, ed. Alexander Berkman (New York: Mother Earth 1914) 324–325.
14 Ferrer, *The Origins and Ideals.*
15 Peter Kropotkin, "The Reformed School." *Mother Earth* 3:1 (1908).
16 Bakunin, *God and the State.*
17 Bakunin.,*God and the State* 32.
18 Kropotkin, "The Reformed School" 261.
19 De Cleyre, "Modern Educational Reform" 339–40.

26

AN ANARCHIST CRITIQUE OF POWER RELATIONS WITHIN INSTITUTIONS

Kevin A. Carson

I. Introduction

Anarchism is a critique of the principle of authority and its negative effects on society. In the popular understanding of anarchism this is most commonly associated with the anarchist critique of the state. But the anarchist critiques of the authority principle as it involves the state are just as applicable to authority relations within institutions.

Just as in society as a whole, authority within hierarchical institutions serves primarily to promote the interests of those who possess it at the expense of those who do not. Authority shifts costs, effort and negative consequences downward, and shifts benefits upward; as such, it is a form of privilege. And like all forms of privilege, it creates fundamental conflicts of interest.

These conflicts of interest, in turn, result in all sorts of related inefficiencies and irrationalities. They take the form, in particular, of distorted information flows and perverse incentives.

II. Distorted Information Flows and Irrationality

When power intrudes into human relationships it creates a zero-sum relationship between superiors and subordinates. In such an environment, it is impossible in principle for those in authority to receive accurate information about the state of affairs within an organization from those subject to their command. According to anarchist writer Robert Anton Wilson,

> A civilization based on authority-and-submission is a civilization without the means of self-correction. *Effective* communication flows only one way: from master-group to servile-group. Any cyberneticist knows that such a one-way communication channel lacks feedback and cannot behave 'intelligently.'
>
> The epitome of authority-and-submission is the Army, and the control-and-communication network of the Army has every defect a cyberneticist's nightmare could conjure. Its typical patterns of behavior are immortalized in folklore as SNAFU (situation normal—all fucked-up). … In less extreme … form these are the typical conditions of any authoritarian group, be it a corporation, a nation, a family, or a whole civilization.[1]

Wilson, writing with Robert Shea, developed the same theme in a fictional format in *The Illuminatus! Trilogy*. "A man with a gun is told only that which people assume will not provoke him to pull the trigger."

> Since all authority and government are based on force, the master class, with its burden of omniscience, faces the servile class, with its burden of nescience, precisely as a highwayman faces his victim. Communication is possible only between equals. The master class never abstracts enough information from the servile class to know what is actually going on in the world where the actual productivity of society occurs. … The result can only be progressive deterioration among the rulers.[2]

This inability of organizational leadership to obtain sufficient or accurate information from below, and the hostile perception of superiors by subordinates, mean that those in the lower echelons of an institution hoard information and use it as a source of rents. The zero-sum relationship resulting from the power differential means that the organizational pyramid will be opaque to those at its top. As organization theorist Kenneth Boulding put it,

> There is a great deal of evidence that almost all organizational structures tend to produce false images in the decision-maker, and that the larger and more authoritarian the organization, the better the chance that its top decision-makers will be operating in purely imaginary worlds.[3]

In *Seeing Like a State* James C. Scott makes the concept of *mētis* (i.e. distributed, situational, job-related knowledge) do much the same work as distributed or situational knowledge did in Friedrich Hayek's "The Uses of Knowledge in Society." And like Wilson, he associates it with mutuality—"as opposed to imperative, hierarchical coordination."[4] Although Scott's primary focus is on the state's attempts to render society legible and subject to its control, the same principles apply to organizational leadership ("seeing like a boss"). Scott's follow-up to *Seeing Like a State* was *The Art of Not Being Governed*, on the reciprocal effort by lower orders to render themselves illegible to governing authorities, and hence ungovernable. This is equally true of subordinates within an organization who attempt to render themselves illegible to their superiors in order to evade control and exploitation. The information-hoarding evoked by authority is directly at odds with the effective use of knowledge. For *mētis* to be effectively brought to bear within an organization, there must be two-way communication between equals, where those in contact with the situation—the people actually doing the work—are in a position of equality with those making the decisions, or actually make the decisions themselves.

Not only had Wilson previously noted this connection between mutuality and accurate information in "Thirteen Choruses," but (like Scott) he alluded to Proudhon:

> [Proudhon's] system of voluntary association (anarchy) is based on the simple communication principles that an authoritarian system means one-way communication, or stupidity, and a libertarian system means two-way communication, or rationality.
>
> The essence of authority, as he saw, was Law—that is … effective communication running one way only. The essence of a libertarian system, as he also saw, was Contract—that is, mutual agreement—that is, effective communication running both ways.

An institutional hierarchy interferes with the judgment of Hayek's "people-on-the-spot," and with the aggregation of dispersed knowledge of circumstances, in exactly the same way a state does in society at large.

Hierarchical organizations are, to use the phrase of Martha Feldman and James March, *systematically* stupid.[5] They are incapable of making effective use of the knowledge of their members, so that they are less than the sum of their parts. Because a hierarchical institution is unable to aggregate the intelligence of its members and bring it to bear effectively on the policy-making process, policies have unintended consequences. Once policies have been made, organizational leadership cannot obtain accurate feedback as to its effects. It's not that the top echelons of a hierarchy are made up of people who are especially dumb; it's that hierarchy, by its very nature, makes *anyone* in those positions dumb. The members of a hierarchy are smarter as individuals than they are collectively. Nobody—not Bill Gates, not Jeff Bezos, not even the Randian superman John Galt—is "smart" enough to manage a large, hierarchical organization or make it function rationally. As Matt Yglesias put it,

> the business class, as a set, has a curious and somewhat incoherent view of capitalism and why it's a good thing. Indeed, it's in most respects a backwards view that strongly contrasts with the economic or political science take on why markets work.
>
> The basic business outlook is very focused on the key role of the *executive*. Good, profitable, growing firms are run by brilliant executives. And the ability of the firm to grow and be profitable is evidence of its executives' brilliance. This is part of the reason that CEO salaries need to keep escalating—recruiting the best is integral to success. The leaders of large firms become revered figures. … Their success stems from overall brilliance. …
>
> The thing about this is that if this were generally true—if the CEOs of the Fortune 500 were brilliant economic seers—then it would really make a lot of sense to implement socialism. Real socialism. Not progressive taxation to finance a mildly redistributive welfare state. But 'let's let Vikram Pandit and Jeff Immelt centrally plan the economy—after all, they're really brilliant!'
>
> But in the real world, the point of markets isn't that executives are clever and bureaucrats are dimwitted. The point is that *nobody* is all that brilliant.[6]

No matter how intelligent managers are *as individuals*, a bureaucratic hierarchy insulates those at the top from the reality of what's going on below, and makes their intelligence less *usable*.

III. Irrational Incentives and Conflicts of Interest

Because the senior management of large institutions don't live under the effects of their policy, and they are insulated from negative feedback from those who do suffer, the CEO of one organization will happily inform their counterparts at other organizations of how wonderfully their organization's new "best practice" worked out. One of the central functions of a hierarchy is to tell naked emperors how great their new clothes look.

When someone operates on the assumption that they will internalize the consequences of their own actions, they have an incentive to anticipate what could go wrong. And they continually revise their decisions in response to subsequent experience. Normally functioning human beings—that is, those of us who are in contact with our environment and not insulated from it by our own authority—are constantly correcting our courses of action.

Authority short-circuits this feedback process. Because it shifts the negative consequences of decisions downward and the benefits upward, decision-makers operate based on a distorted cost–benefit calculus so that it benefits them to adopt policies whose net social effects are negative. And because it blocks negative feedback, the leadership of an institution is subject to the functional equivalent of a psychotic break with reality.

This is a principle that operates fractally. If institutional leadership is able to adopt policies and practices beyond the point of net negative returns, on a societal level entire industries, or institutional complexes, are able to follow organizational models centered on such counter-productive practices.

Ivan Illich, in *Tools for Conviviality*, used the term "second watershed" to refer to the adoption of technologies, organizational approaches, policies, etc., beyond the point of "net social disutility" or "counter-productivity." The first threshold of a technology or tool results in net social benefit. But beyond a certain point, increasing reliance on that technology results in net social costs and increased disempowerment and dependency to those who rely on it. Rather than being a service to the individual, the technology reduces them to an accessory to a machine or to a bureaucracy.[7]

The classic example is the automobile. The cheap motorcar originally served those in areas of low population density, like farmers, who were underserved by in-town transit systems or intercity rail. But as towns and cities were redesigned around "car culture" (i.e. monoculture residential suburbs and big-box stores or strip malls linked by freeways replaced mixed-use communities where work and shopping were within foot, bike or public transit range of home), the automobile became a necessity for everyone. And most towns and cities continue to follow the urban design approach of the mid-twentieth century which created that state of affairs, even when that approach is clearly counter-productive and exacerbates social pathologies. The orthodox prescription for traffic congestion is to build new subsidized freeways, which only generate even more traffic as new subdivisions and strip malls spring up around the newly-built cloverleafs.

What Illich failed to recognize was the role of authority relations in going beyond the second watershed and creating counter-productivity. Indeed, he framed such results as the inevitable trajectory in adoption of a technology if society did not actually resort to the authority principle to *prevent* it. But in fact the social pathologies of the second watershed are possible only when some are in a position of privilege from which they can use power to force the negative externalities of a given decision on others while appropriating the benefits of it for themselves. Privilege—coercive authority—is a mechanism for separating the good and ill effects of a policy or practice from each other, and diverting them to different persons or classes. Because of such authority, the privileged individual does not fully internalize all the positive and negative consequences of their behavior on a single balance sheet. When people deal with one another as equals, on the other hand, no one is able to adopt a technology beyond its net negative effects because no one is in a position to externalize the negative effects on others.

Where authority exists, dominant institutions are able to flourish well past the point at which they're a net drain on society. Although they are failures from the standpoint of the majority of people in society, their performance is entirely a success from the standpoint of those who collect the CEO salaries and bonuses. Large institutions are "successful" at achieving goals that are largely artificial—goals defined primarily by the interests of their governing hierarchies, rather than by their ostensible customers or those directly responsible for serving customer needs.[8]

Hierarchical institutions treat not only front-line production workers, but also customers or clients, as means to management's ends. Edgar Z. Friedenberg coined the term "conscript clienteles" to describe this phenomenon.

> A large proportion of the gross national product of every industrialized nation consists of activities which provide no satisfaction to, and may be intended to humiliate, coerce, or destroy, those who are most affected by them; and of public services in which the taxpayer pays to have something very expensive done to other persons who have no opportunity to reject the service. This process is a large-scale economic development which I call the *reification of clienteles*. …

> Although they are called 'clients,' members of conscript clienteles are not regarded as customers by the bureaucracies that service them, since they are not free to withdraw or withhold their custom or to look elsewhere for service. They are treated as raw material that the service organization needs to perform its social function and continue in existence.[9]
>
> Taken together, a large proportion of the labor force [he estimated about a third] employed in modern society is engaged in processing people according to other people's regulations and instructions. They are not accountable to the people they operate on, and ignore or overlook any feedback they may receive from them.[10]

Friedenberg limited his use of the term largely to bureaucracies directly funded with taxpayer money, and those like schools and prisons whose "clients" were literally unable to refuse service. The public schools, for example.

> It does not take many hours of observation—or attendance—in a public school to learn, from the way the place is actually run, that the pupils are there for the sake of the school, not the other way round.[11]
>
> This, too, is money spent providing goods and services to people who have no voice in determining what those goods and services shall be or how they shall be administered; and who have no lawful power to withhold their custom by refusing to attend even if they and their parents feel that what the schools provide is distasteful or injurious. They are provided with textbooks that, unlike any other work, from the Bible to the sleaziest pornography, no man would buy for his personal satisfaction. They are, precisely, not 'trade books'; rather, they are adopted for the compulsory use of hundreds of thousands of other people by committees, no member of which would have bought a single copy for his own library.[12]
>
> School children certainly fulfill the principal criterion for membership in a reified clientele: being there by compulsion. It is less immediately obvious that they serve as raw material to be processed for the purposes of others, since this processing has come to be defined by the society as preparing the pupil for advancement within it. ... Whatever the needs of young people might have been, no public school system developed in response to them until an industrial society arose to demand the creation of holding pens from which a steady and carefully monitored supply of people trained to be punctual, literate, orderly and compliant and graded according to qualities determining employability from the employer's point of view could be released into the economy as needed.[13]

In so doing he significantly underestimated the prevalence of institutions managing conscript clienteles. He neglected, for one thing, those in the private sector whose clients are nominally free to refuse their services, but likely won't because competition is restricted by cartels or oligopoly markets of one kind or another. Consider, for example, the number of goods that are designed by one stovepiped R&D bureaucracy for sale to the stovepiped procurement bureaucracy of another institution, to be used by people to whom neither bureaucracy is remotely accountable; this is the reason the enterprise "productivity" software foisted on employees by corporate IT departments is so godawful, and why patient care equipment sold to hospitals is so poorly designed. Likewise when intellectual property restrictions prevent competition in design quality, or worse yet poor design is permanently institutionalized via path dependency even after patents expire.

The zero-sum relationship between superiors and subordinates within a hierarchy also results in irrationalities because, given the fundamental conflict of interest, those in direct contact with a situation cannot be trusted to act on their own judgment and initiative. Because the institution does not exist as a vehicle for the goals of its members, there is no intrinsic connection between their personal motivation and their roles in the organization. Institutions must therefore resort to standardized work rules, job descriptions, and all the rest of the Weberian–Taylorist model of bureaucratic rationality. Those who know most about a situation and are the best judges of alternative courses of action have no interest in common with the leadership of the organization. Because someone might use her initiative in ways detrimental to the interests of the organization, a set of rules must be set in place to prevent anyone from doing anything at all. Unlike self-managed organizations and horizontal networks, which treat the human brain as an asset, hierarchical rules systems treat it as a risk to be mitigated.

But this is entirely rational, from the perspective of those involved. Because of the fundamental conflict of interest built into the authority relations of a hierarchy, workers have absolutely no incentive to contribute their judgment to improving work processes, and every incentive to sabotage efficiency. They know that any contribution they make to increased productivity will be expropriated by management in the form of downsizings, speed-ups and increased management compensation. Hence workers commonly engage in "satisficing," or doing the minimum necessary to keep their jobs, and management must spend enormous amounts of money on front-line supervisors or monitoring and surveillance technologies to protect themselves from a workforce whose interests are fundamentally at odds with their own.

Job descriptions and union work rules are the other side of the coin to Taylorist work rules. Management cannot be trusted with the discretion to make the most efficient use of labor because it will inevitably abuse that discretion to its own benefit. Work rules, whether imposed by management or by labor, result from mutual distrust within a hierarchy. Power, to repeat, creates zero-sum relationships by definition. Superiors attempt to externalize effort on subordinates and skim off the benefits of increased productivity for themselves. Because subordinates know their contributions to organizational productivity will be expropriated by management, subordinates rationally minimize their expenditure of effort and do the minimum necessary to avoid getting fired. Both superiors and subordinates filter or hoard information of benefit to the other party, and attempt to maximize the rents from keeping each other ignorant. In this zero-sum relation, where each side can only benefit at the expense of the other, each party seeks mechanisms for limiting abuses by the other.

Paul Goodman illustrated the need for such constraints on individual initiative, in directly adopting the most common-sense and lowest-cost solutions to immediate problems, with a seemingly minor example from the New York City public school system:

> To remove a door catch that hampers the use of a lavatory requires a long appeal through headquarters, because it is 'city property.' …
>
> An old-fashioned type of hardware is specified for all new buildings, that is kept in production only for the New York school system.[14]

> When the social means are tied up in such complicated organizations, it becomes extraordinarily difficult and sometimes impossible to do a simple thing directly, even though the doing is common sense and would meet with universal approval, as when neither the child, nor the parent, nor the janitor, nor the principal of the school can remove the offending door catch.[15]

The problem with authority relations in a hierarchy is that, given the conflict of interest created by the presence of power, those in authority cannot *afford* to allow discretion to those in direct contact with the situation. Systematic stupidity results, of necessity, from a situation in which a bureaucratic hierarchy must develop arbitrary metrics for assessing the skills or work quality of a labor force whose actual work they know nothing about, and whose material interests militate against remedying management's ignorance.

Most of the constantly rising burden of paperwork exists to give an illusion of transparency and control to a bureaucracy that is out of touch with the actual production process. Every new layer of paperwork is added to address the perceived problem that stuff still isn't getting done the way management wants, despite the proliferation of paperwork saying everything has being done exactly according to orders. In a hierarchy, managers are forced to regulate a process which is necessarily opaque to them because they are not directly engaged in it. They're forced to carry out the impossible task of developing accurate metrics to evaluate the behavior of subordinates, based on the self-reporting of people with whom they have a fundamental conflict of interest. The paperwork burden that management imposes on workers reflects an attempt to render legible a set of social relationships that by its nature must be opaque and closed to them, because they are outside of it.

Each new form is intended to remedy the heretofore imperfect self-reporting of subordinates. The need for new paperwork is predicated on the assumption that compliance must be verified because those being monitored have a fundamental conflict of interest with those making the policy, and hence cannot be trusted; but at the same time, the paperwork itself relies on their self-reporting as the main source of information. Every time new evidence is presented that this or that task isn't being performed to management's satisfaction, or this or that policy isn't being followed, despite the existing reams of paperwork, management's response is to design yet another—and equally useless—form.

Arbitrary work rules result of necessity when performance and quality metrics are not tied to direct feedback from the work process itself. They're a metric *of* work *for* someone who is neither a creator/provider nor an end user. A bureaucracy can't afford to allow its subordinates discretion to use their common sense, because in a zero-sum relationship any discretion can be abused.

IV. How Can This Irrational System Survive?

So why is this state of affairs able to continue? With all this dysfunction, how are authoritarian institutions able to survive at all, let alone function in even the most minimal manner? The answer is that, while the authority principle results in irrationality, it also shields those in authority from the negative consequences and instead forces their subordinates to bear the brunt of dealing with them. In addition, the organization itself is part of a larger, interlocking macro-system of authority that protects it from many of the negative external consequences of its authority.

Such institutions are able to survive only under special circumstances. First, they must exist in an artificially simple and stable environment. As an institution becomes larger and experiences increased overhead and bureaucratic ossification, it simultaneously becomes more and more vulnerable to fluctuating conditions in its surrounding environment, and less able to react to them. To survive, therefore, the large institution must control its surrounding environment.

In regard to the large mass-production corporation, John Kenneth Galbraith wrote, the long-time horizons for product development and the enormous up-front commitment of capital meant that a firm required a reasonable degree of predictability regarding things like wages and prices. And the outlay of capital required some reassurance—some *guarantee*—that the product would be bought in sufficient quantity to amortize the investment when it came off the assembly line.

> [Machines and sophisticated technology] require … heavy investment of capital. They are designed and guided by technically sophisticated men. They involve, also, a greatly increased lapse of time between any decision to produce and the emergence of a salable product …
>
> The large commitment of capital and organization well in advance of result requires that there be foresight and also that all feasible steps be taken to insure that what is foreseen will transpire.[16]

> [I]n addition to deciding what the consumer will want and will pay, the firm must make every feasible step to see that what it decides to produce is wanted by the consumer at a remunerative price. … It must exercise control over what is sold. … It must replace the market with planning.[17]

Barry Stein, a heterodox economist specializing in decentralism and economies of scale, characterized Galbraith's solution as "suppressing turbulence": "to control the changes, in kind and extent, that the society will undergo."[18]

In concrete terms, this means coordinated action at a societal level by giant corporations and the state to provide the stable environment required for the survival of the large organization. Each industry must be dominated by few enough oligopoly firms to engage in administered pricing to pass on the costs of R&D and capital investment to the consumer, without any disruption by significant competition in price. And those firms must coordinate the introduction of major technological improvements so that earlier investments can be phased out in an orderly manner without competitive disadvantage to any of the leading firms. As Paul Goodman characterized it, a handful of firms "competing with fixed prices and slowly spooned-out improvements."[19] To achieve this the state introduced regulations to create stable oligopoly markets and restrict the level of competition, pursued fiscal and monetary policies to maintain sufficient levels of aggregate demand (up to and including the creation of a permanent war economy), and even created entire new industries through its own direct investment (for example, large-scale civil aviation, and the Interstate Highway System with its attendant rebuilding of cities around car culture). In regard to the regulatory state that emerged around the turn of the twentieth century, New Left historian Gabriel Kolko described the policy objective as "political capitalism."

> *Political capitalism* is the utilization of political outlets to attain conditions of stability, predictability, and security—to attain rationalization—in the economy. *Stability* is the elimination of internecine competition and erratic fluctuations in the economy. *Predictability* is the ability, on the basis of politically stabilized and secured means, to plan future economic action on the basis of fairly calculable expectations. By *security* I mean protection from the political attacks latent in any formally democratic political structure. I do not give to *rationalization* its frequent definition as the improvement of efficiency, output, or internal organization of a company; I mean by the term, rather, the organization of the economy and the larger political and social spheres in a manner that will allow corporations to function in a predictable and secure environment permitting reasonable profits over the long run.[20]

Beyond a certain tipping point, large hierarchical institutions become hegemonic: that is, they become the defining institutional type for society as a whole, and create entire ecology of interlocking and mutually-supporting institutions that choke out competing institutional "species." As Paul Goodman characterized it:

> [T]he genius of our centralized bureaucracies has been, as they interlock, to form a mutually accrediting establishment of decision-makers, with common interests and a common style that nullify the diversity of pluralism.[21]

> A system destroys its competitors by pre-empting the means and channels, and then proves that it is the only conceivable mode of operating.[22]

And because all the "competing" firms in an industry actually exist in an oligopoly environment with cost-plus markup and administered pricing, and all share the same pathological institutional cultures, they suffer little or no real competitive penalty for their bureaucratic irrationality.

Second, even within this protected environment they depend unofficially on the initiative of those who break the rules. Despite every effort of industrial engineers like Andrew Ure and Frederick Taylor to separate labor from skill, reserving the latter to the managerial-technical strata and transform workers into easily replaced appendages of machines, discretion cannot be entirely removed from any process. James Scott writes that it's impossible, by the nature of things, for everything entailed in the production process to be distilled, formalized or codified into a form that's legible to management.

> [T]he formal order encoded in social-engineering designs inevitably leaves out elements that are essential to their actual functioning. If the [East German] factory were forced to operate only within the confines of the roles and functions specified in the simplified design, it would quickly grind to a halt. Collectivized command economies virtually everywhere have limped along thanks to the often desperate improvisation of an informal economy wholly outside its schemata.
>
> Stated somewhat differently, all socially engineered systems of formal order are in fact subsystems of a larger system on which they are ultimately dependent, not to say parasitic. The subsystem relies on a variety of processes—frequently informal or antecedent—which alone it cannot create or maintain. The more schematic, thin, and simplified the formal order, the less resilient and the more vulnerable it is to disturbances outside its narrow parameters. …
>
> It is, I think, a characteristic of large, formal systems of coordination that they are accompanied by what appear to be anomalies but on closer inspection turn out to be integral to that formal order. Much of this might be called 'mētis to the rescue. …' A formal command economy … is contingent on petty trade, bartering, and deals that are typically illegal. … In each case, the nonconforming practice is an indispensable condition for formal order.[23]

> In each case, the necessarily thin, schematic model of social organization and production animating the planning was inadequate as a set of instructions for creating a successful social order. By themselves, the simplified rules can never generate a functioning community, city, or economy. Formal order, to be more explicit, is always and to some considerable degree parasitic on informal processes, which the formal scheme does not recognize, without which it could not exist, and which it alone cannot create or maintain.[24]

David Graeber referred to this as "the communism of everyday life." State bureaucracies and corporations are parasitic on communistic institutions outside the cash nexus:

> Every society in human history has been a foundation built out of this everyday communism of family, household, self-provisioning, gifting and sharing among friends and neighbors, etc., with a scaffolding of market exchange and hierarchies erected on top of it.

But beyond that, the parasitic institutions are internally dependent on the cooperative relationships between actual producers and creators that keeps the world running, despite their irrationality.[25]

Most production jobs involve a fair amount of distributed, job-specific knowledge, and depend on the initiative of workers to improvise, to apply skills in new ways, in the face of events which are either totally unpredictable or cannot be fully anticipated. Although—given the fact that any increase in productivity will be expropriated by management—workers generally do no more than necessary, they nevertheless have an incentive to do the minimum necessary to keep the organization staggering along and performing its ostensible mission at at least the minimal level required to keep their paychecks coming. To do this, they bend or break the rules and exercise initiative in order to get the job done and go home. This is why, despite their bureaucratic irrationality, and despite the enormous unnecessary overhead and waste, American corporations and Soviet state-planned industry were nevertheless able to churn out some non-negligible quantity of consumer goods that worked most of the time. When workers withdraw this initiative, the organization's function comes to a standstill. This is why the traditional labor direct-action tactic of working-to-rule is so devilishly effective.

V. Mene, Mene, Tekel Upharsin

This dependency of the large organization on artificial stability, and on the initiative and active cooperation of its work force, is the basis of its unsustainability.

Barry Stein argued forty years ago, in the context of his remarks above regarding large firms' dependence on suppressing uncertainty for their survival, for the superiority of a lean enterprise integrated into the local community and responding quickly to changing circumstances.

> [I]f firms could respond to local conditions, they would not need to control them. If they must control markets, then it is a reflection of their lack of ability to be adequately responsive.[26]

> Consumer needs, if they are to be supplied efficiently, call increasingly for organizations that are more flexibly arranged and in more direct contact with those customers. The essence of planning, under conditions of increasing uncertainty, is to seek better ways for those who have the needs to influence or control the productive apparatus more effectively, not less.
>
> Under conditions of rapid environmental change, implementing such planning is possible only if the "distance" between those supplied and the locus of decision-making on the part of those producing is reduced …
>
> [The problem of large firms' vulnerability to environmental uncertainty] is to be solved not by the hope of better planning on a large scale … but by the better integration of productive enterprises with the elements of society needing that production.
>
> Under conditions of rapid change in an affluent and complex society, the only means available for meeting differentiated and fluid needs is an array of producing units small enough to be in close contact with their customers, flexible enough to produce for their demands, and able to do so in a relatively short time …
>
> It is a contradiction in terms to speak of the necessity for units large enough to control their environment, but producing products which in fact no one may want![27]

Of course, Galbraith's unstated assumption—in contrast to Stein's—was that the survival of the mass-production corporation was an end in itself, and the surrounding society and people in it were all means to be subordinated to that end. He assumed likewise, on very questionable grounds, that the large, capital-intensive mass-production firm was technologically necessary to produce the kinds of goods and services consumers desired. Stein denied this.

> As to the problem of planning—large firms are said to be needed here because the requirements of sophisticated technology and increasingly specialized knowledge call for long lead times to develop, design, and produce products. Firms must therefore have enough control over the market to assure that the demand needed to justify that time-consuming and costly investment will exist. This argument rests on a foundation of sand; first, because the needs of society should precede, not follow, decisions about what to produce, and second, because the data do not substantiate the need for large production organizations except in rare and unusual instances, like space flight. On the contrary, planning for social needs requires organizations and decision-making capabilities in which the feedback and interplay between productive enterprises and the market in question is accurate and timely—conditions more consistent with smaller organizations than large ones.[28]

Almost ninety years ago, Ralph Borsodi argued (in *The Distribution Age*) that craft production with cheap, electrically powered general-purpose tools near the point of consumption was more efficient than mass production with expensive product-specific machinery, when the added costs of batch-and-queue production, long-distance distribution and marketing were taken into account. In fact, advocates of industrial decentralization (e.g. Pyotr Kropotkin in *Fields, Factories and Workshops*) had been arguing the same thing since the start of the Second Industrial Revolution.

The problem was that the state's subsidies and protections were sufficient to compensate for the inherent inefficiency of large-scale production, so that the potential of decentralized community manufacturing was coopted and enclosed within the preexisting framework of dark satanic mills.

But in any case, continuing technological advances have reduced the necessary capital outlays for manufacturing by additional orders of magnitude since then, and at the same time exacerbated the crisis tendencies of corporate capitalism. The development of a generation of much smaller and cheaper CNC (computer numerical control) tools led to the rise of distributed cooperative micro-manufacturing on the Emilia Romagna/Bologna model in the 1970s, and Chinese job-shop production in the 1980s and 1990s. And the open hardware and maker movements have taken it even further, scaling high-quality production down to tabletop machinery in neighborhood garage factories.

At the same time, the imploding money cost of capital investment for industrial production is exacerbating capitalism's chronic crisis tendencies towards insufficient profitable investment outlets to absorb all the propertied classes' idle capital. It takes greater and greater levels of state intervention to absorb surplus capital and guarantee consumption of industrial output, driving government towards larger chronic deficits, in the process described by James O'Connor in *Fiscal Crisis of the State*. Eventually industry's need for state intervention exceeds the state's resources.

And as technological change destroys the capital-intensiveness of production, it undermines the material basis for large organizational scale and hierarchy. The factory system and wage system originally came about because of the Industrial Revolution's technological shift from affordable craft tools owned by individual workers or small groups to expensive machinery that could only be purchased by groups of rich capitalists who then hired wage laborers to work their machinery. We're now seeing a shift back to a much higher-tech form of craft production, with computer-controlled general-purpose craft tools that small groups of workers can afford. This raises the threat of skilled labor with cheap high-tech tools simply seceding from the economy and undertaking direct production for use.

To counter this threat, capital and other concentrations of power are increasingly shifting away from a model of surplus extraction based on physical control of the means of production, and instead relying on artificial legal barriers controlling the circumstances under which people are allowed to produce even using their own means of production. In the informational and cultural realm this refers, obviously, to the use of copyright to prevent use of the desktop computer as a craft tool for software design, publishing and music production in competition with the old gatekeeping corporations. In the physical realm it means using zoning laws and safety codes to prevent the use of spare capacity in ordinary household goods in home-based micro-breweries or micro-bakeries, cooperative neighborhood childcare and eldercare arrangements, etc. In services it means the use of taxicab medallions or proprietary, walled-garden corporate apps like Uber to suppress cooperative ride-sharing services. And in manufacturing, it means the use of proprietary digital designs and patent law to suppress competition from neighborhood garage factories.

But the same technological advances that are rendering the large organization obsolete for production are also rendering the artificial legal barriers unenforceable. In the information sector, what file-sharing has done to the movie and music industries is common knowledge, even in the face of draconian legislation like the Digital Millennium Copyright Act and questionably legal enforcement efforts shutting down websites wholesale via civil forfeiture.

In manufacturing, patent enforcement in the mass-production age depended on the low transaction costs prevailing when a handful of oligopoly corporations produced a small number of designs for sale in a handful of national retail chains. In an environment of hundreds of thousands of garage factories producing stuff for neighborhood use with pirated CAD/CAM (computer-aided design and manufacturing) files, the costs of enforcement are insurmountable.[29]

And simultaneously with this process of cheapening means of production, "human capital"—the social relationships and skills of the producing classes—has surpassed physical capital as the primary source of value and productivity. This human capital increasingly extends outside the workplace, the basis of what autonomist Marxists like Toni Negri and Nick Dyer-Witheford call the "social factory." So our human relationships are becoming the most important means of production at the same time as even the physical means of production are becoming amenable to ownership and control by small cooperative groups. This sets the stage for what Negri and Michael Hardt, in *Multitude* and *Commonwealth*, call "exodus"—simply taking our productive relationships and tools and seceding from capitalism.[30]

VI. Conclusion: The Superiority of Self-Organization

For every one of the enumerated inefficiencies of hierarchy above, there is a corresponding efficiency of self-organized and self-managed institutions. Where authoritarian institutions render the intelligence of their members less usable, their libertarian counterparts render their members' intelligence *more* so. If conflicts of interest render hierarchical organizations opaque to their leadership despite futile efforts at panoptic surveillance, self-organized and self-managed work within horizontal institutions is fully legible to all who participate in it. To quote Michel Bauwens of the Foundation for Peer-to-Peer Alternatives:

> The capacity to cooperate is verified in the process of cooperation itself. Thus, projects are open to all comers provided they have the necessary skills to contribute to a project. These skills are verified, and communally validated, in the process of production itself.

> This is apparent in open publishing projects such as citizen journalism: anyone can post and anyone can verify the veracity of the articles. Reputation systems are used for communal validation. The filtering is a posteriori, not a priori. Anti-credentialism is therefore to be contrasted to traditional peer review, where credentials are an essential prerequisite to participate.
>
> P2P projects are characterized by holoptism. Holoptism is the implied capacity and design of peer to [peer] processes that allows participants free access to all the information about the other participants; not in terms of privacy, but in terms of their existence and contributions (i.e. horizontal information) and access to the aims, metrics and documentation of the project as a whole (i.e. the vertical dimension). This can be contrasted to the panoptism which is characteristic of hierarchical projects: processes are designed to reserve 'total' knowledge for an elite, while participants only have access on a 'need to know' basis. However, with P2P projects, communication is not top-down and based on strictly defined reporting rules, but feedback is systemic, integrated in the protocol of the cooperative system.[31]

In a prison—governed by panopticism—the warden can see all the prisoners, but the prisoners can't see each other. The reason is so the prisoners can't coordinate their actions independently of the warden. Holopticism is the exact opposite: the members of a group are horizontally legible to one another, and can coordinate their actions. And "everyone has a sense of the emerging whole, and can adjust their actions for the greatest fit."[32]

The unspoken assumption is that a hierarchy exists for the purposes of the management, and a holoptic association exists for the purposes of its members. The people at the top of a hierarchical pyramid can't trust the people doing the job because their interests are diametrically opposed. It's safe to trust one another in a horizontal organization because a common interest in the task can be inferred from participation.

If the authoritarian institution is characterized by one-way communication, the libertarian one is characterized by two-way communication among equals, enabling the kind of constant feedback process necessary to adjust action rationally to its results.

Much of what conservatives frame as negative tendencies of "human nature" is actually the result of coercive intervention to prevent direct communications between human beings, because exploitation depends on keeping the exploited classes divided among themselves. It's telling that the zero-sum results of Prisoner's Dilemma gaming, and the pathological behavior elicited in the Milgram Experiment, both depended on isolating each individual subject under the panoptic supervision of those in authority, and prohibiting any authentic direct communication.

If the exploitative purposes of the authoritarian organization create conflicts of interest between superiors and subordinates, so that those most familiar with the situation cannot be trusted to use their own judgment, the libertarian organization—because it exists only for the purposes of its members—can trust the full use of individual initiative and self-direction. Such organizations are frequently characterized by modular or stigmergic coordination, with a high degree of self-direction and the self-selection of tasks.

Self-managed and user-owned organizations have always had these significant advantages over authoritarian hierarchies. But stigmergically organized activity on the commons-based peer production model, which came about in response to the possibilities offered by networked communications in the Internet era, takes the advantage an order of magnitude further. Stigmergic projects like Wikipedia or free and open-source software design require far less, if any, coordination than more traditional forms of consensus-based management like those in cooperative enterprises.

"Stigmergy" is a term coined by biologist Pierre-Paul Grasse in the 1950s to describe the process by which social insects like termites coordinate their efforts through the independent responses of individuals to environmental triggers like chemical markers, without any recourse to a central coordinating authority.[33] The term was carried over to the social sciences to describe networked forms of organization associated like wikis, group blogs and "leaderless" organizations with networked cell architectures. Yochai Benkler uses software development to illustrate the permissionless nature of stigmergic organization.

> Imagine that one person, or a small group of friends, wants a utility. It could be a text editor, photo-retouching software, or an operating system. The person or small group starts by developing a part of this project, up to a point where the whole utility—if it is simple enough—or some important part of it, is functional, though it might have much room for improvement. At this point, the person makes the program freely available to others, with its source code ... When others begin to use it, they may find bugs, or related utilities that they want to add. ... The person who has found the bug ... may or may not be the best person in the world to actually write the software fix. Nevertheless, he reports the bug ... in an Internet forum of users of the software. That person, or someone else, then thinks that they have a way of tweaking the software to fix the bug or add the new utility. They then do so, just as the first person did, and release a new version of the software with the fix or the added utility. The result is a collaboration between three people—the first author, who wrote the initial software; the second person, who identified a problem or shortcoming; and the third person, who fixed it. This collaboration is not managed by anyone who organizes the three, but is instead the outcome of them all reading the same Internet-based forum and using the same software, which is released under an open, rather than proprietary, license. This enables some of its users to identify problems without asking anyone's permission and without engaging in any transactions.[34]

Because networked or stigmergic organization is permissionless and highly granular, it is capable of aggregating many small contributions without significant transaction costs—unlike projects organized by traditional hierarchical means, which require everyone to be on the same page before anyone can do anything. For example, a traditional encyclopedia like *Britannica* cannot be published until the directors of the project have determined what articles will be included, and contracted out the writing of each article to some scholar or other. It's an all-or-nothing project. In contrast, anyone can note the lack of any Wikipedia article on some topic they consider important, and immediately write a stub for it. Anyone else with knowledge of that topic, or some sub-field of it, who stumbles across the stub can contribute a sentence, a paragraph, or one or more sections. If the hierarchical institution is less than the sum of its parts, the stigmergic organization is more.

Also, because they are permissionless, and can act without submitting proposals for central approval, they are also better at reacting to the surrounding environment than hierarchies. Any innovation developed by a single member or cell in the network immediately becomes part of the available toolkit for the entire network, which any member can apply in circumstances they consider appropriate.

To use a term from military theorist John Boyd, networks go through the OODA process—Observe, Orient, Decide, Act—much faster than hierarchies.[35] They "get inside the OODA loop" of hierarchies—they act faster, and force the hierarchical institutions to react to them. They innovate, act, evaluate the results, and innovate and act again, with much faster iteration cycles than the hierarchies arrayed against them. As a result, networked insurgencies can go through multiple generations of tactical innovation with the speed of replicating yeast while hierarchies like the Transport Security Administration or the music industry are still fighting the last war, ponderously formulating a response to first-generation practices. It's the *speed* with which networks go through generational innovation, enabled by their permissionlessness, that is the key; they may fail much of the time, but they fail faster.

> [T]he primary determinant to winning dogfights was not observing, orienting, planning, or acting better. The primary determinant to winning dogfights was observing, orienting, planning, and acting *faster*. In other words, how quickly one could iterate. *Speed of iteration*, Boyd suggested, beats *quality of iteration*.[36]

OODA loops lengthen or shorten mainly as informational friction increases or decreases between each step in the OODA process. At one end of the spectrum the actor is empowered to directly implement changes in actions based on their own observation of the results of previous action. As barriers are erected between the different sub-processes of the OODA loop—like policy-making procedures within a hierarchy—and feedback is hindered, information-processing and reaction time will slow down.

Since the rise of agriculture and the subsequent development of ruling classes to feed off surplus production, there has been a millennia-long arms race between the productivity created by human initiative and cooperation, and the various methods developed to enclose this productivity for the extraction of rent by temple priesthoods, latifundia owners, feudal landlords, capitalists and state bureaucrats. Sometimes—e.g. fourteenth-century Europe, with the fixing of customary rents and the near-independence of the free towns—the forces of productivity have gained the advantage. At others—like the "long sixteenth century" during which the new absolute states conquered the towns and landed oligarchs abrogated customary peasant land rights, rack-rented and evicted them, and enclosed the open fields for pasturage—the forces of enclosure and extraction came out ahead. With the rise of cheap micro-manufacturing tools, intensive horticulture techniques and networked communications, we are approaching the takeoff point at which the productivity of cooperative labor achieves permanent victory over the forces of enclosure. Post-scarcity technologies are growing in productivity faster than rentiers can enclose them. Post-capitalist transition is the end of humanity's childhood.

Notes

1 R. A. Wilson, "Thirteen Choruses for the Divine Marquis," *Coincidance—A Head Test* (Grand Junction, CO: Hilaritas 2018 [1988]) www.deepleafproductions.com/wilsonlibrary/texts/raw-marquis.html. Original emphasis.
2 Robert Shea and R. A. Wilson, *The Illuminatus! Trilogy* (New York, NY: Dell 1975) 498.
3 Kenneth Boulding, "The Economics of Knowledge and the Knowledge of Economics," *American Economic Review* 56.1–2 (March 1966): 8.
4 James Scott, *Seeing Like a State* (New Haven, CT: Yale UP 1999) 6–7.
5 Martha S. Feldman and James G. March, "Information in Organizations as Signal and Symbol," *Administrative Science Quarterly* 26 (April 1981); it should be noted, in fairness, that Feldman and March were attempting—unsuccessfully in my opinion—to defend corporations *against* the charge of systematic stupidity.
6 Matthew Yglesias, "Two Views of Capitalism," Yglesias, Nov. 22, 2008, http://yglesias.thinkprogress.org/2008/11/two_views_of_capitalism/. Original emphasis.
7 Ivan Illich, *Tools for Conviviality* (New York, NY: Harper 1973) xxii-iii, 84–5.
8 On the other hand, organizational structures like networks, which are based on two-way feedback between equals, result in high rates of "failure." As Clay Shirky puts it, open-source software is a threat because it outfails proprietary systems. It can experiment and fail at less cost. Because failure is more costly to

a hierarchy, hierarchies are biased "in favor of predictable but substandard outcomes." *Here Comes Everybody: The Power of Organizing without Organizations* (New York, NY: Penguin 2008) 245. Failure also reflects the empowerment of workers and customers; most products in the corporate economy are only considered "good enough" because customers are powerless.

9 Edgar Z. Friedenberg, *The Disposal of Liberty and Other Industrial Wastes* (Garden City, NY: Anchor-Doubleday 1976) 1–2. Original emphasis.

10 Friedenberg 18.

11 Ibid. 2.

12 Ibid. 6.

13 Ibid. 16.

14 Paul Goodman, *People or Personnel*, in *People or Personnel* and *Like a Conquered Province* (New York, NY: Vintage 1964, 1966) 52.

15 Goodman 88.

16 John Kenneth Galbraith, *The New Industrial State* (New York, NY: Signet 1967) 16.

17 Galbraith 34-5.

18 Barry Stein, *Size, Efficiency, and Community Enterprise* (Cambridge: Center for Community Economic Development 1974) 43.

19 Goodman 58.

20 Gabriel Kolko, *The Triumph of Conservatism: A Reinterpretation of American History 1900–1916* (New York, NY: Free Press 1963) 3. Original emphasis.

21 Paul Goodman, *Like a Conquered Province*, in *People or Personnel* and *Like a Conquered Province* 357.

22 Goodman, *People or Personnel* 70.

23 Scott, *Seeing Like a State* 351–2.

24 Ibid. 310.

25 David Graeber, *Debt: The First 5,000 Years* (New York, NY: Melville House, 2011) 95.

26 Stein, *Size, Efficiency, and Community Enterprise* 4.

27 Ibid. 44.

28 Ibid. 58.

29 The above material is a brief summary of the argument of my book *The Homebrew Industrial Revolution: A Low-Overhead Manifesto* (np: BookSurge 2010).

30 Antonio Negri and Michael Hardt, *Commonwealth* (Cambridge, MA: Belknap Press of Harvard University Press 2009) 152.

31 Michel Bauwens, "The Political Economy of Peer Production," Ctheory.net, December 1, 2005, www.ctheory.net/articles.aspx?id=499.

32 Alan Rosenblith, "Holopticism," March 5, 2010, www.slideshare.net/AlanRosenblith/holopticism.

33 Mark Elliott, "Stigmergic Collaboration: The Evolution of Group Work," *M/C Journal*, May 2006, http://journal.media-culture.org.au/0605/03-elliott.php.

34 Yochai Benkler, *The Wealth of Networks: How Social Production Transforms Markets and Freedom* (New Haven, CT: Yale UP 2006) 66–7.

35 Col. John R. Boyd, USAF. "Patterns of Conflict," presentation (December 1986), www.ausairpower.net/JRB/poc.pdf, 5–7.

36 Jeff Atwood, "Boyd's Law of Iteration," Coding Horror, February 7, 2007, www.codinghorror.com/blog/2007/02/boyds-law-of-iteration.html. Original emphasis.

27
ANARCHISM FOR AN ECOLOGICAL CRISIS?

Dan C. Shahar

I. Introduction

According to "green" theorists, humanity is on the brink of catastrophe. Our civilization has chased material abundance through the domination of nature, and in so doing we have eroded key planetary systems on which we depend. Moreover, the culture of mass consumption that has grown up around our industrial development has left us spiritually stunted and disconnected from the landscapes we inhabit. Now, looking toward the future, we face serious ecological challenges as well as a deeper struggle to recover richness in our lives.

One influential group of green writers traces these problems to a common source: the *scale* of modern social arrangements. These authors claim our salvation can be found in smaller communities, smaller systems of economic production, and smaller impacts on the natural world. Such views have been advanced under various names—green anarchism,[1] bioregionalism,[2] social ecology[3]—but they are unified by a conviction that our circumstances demand a radical and transformative program of *decentralization*.

The visionary proposals laid out by these authors contrast sharply with the social, political, and economic status quo, and for this reason we must decide how we want to receive them. Most cynically, we can see them as little more than impractical machinations of people who would rather dream of utopias than find workable solutions to our problems. Alternatively, we can regard them as efforts to point the way to self-purification, with greens laying out plans to abandon mainstream society and establish outposts of rectitude while the world crumbles around them.[4] Yet the works of decentralist green authors often seem genuinely interested in describing an approach to social organization that would rescue humanity if only it were embraced.[5] Their earnestness invites us to ask: Have these greens actually identified a compelling and radical alternative to existing arrangements?

The purpose of this chapter will be to investigate this matter with an eye particularly to the practical suitability of decentralization as a tool for addressing an ecological crisis. We will find, ultimately, that in a world where environmental impacts can so often be traced to beliefs and priorities that do not align with green views, greens' decentralist prescriptions would be unlikely to resolve our ecological challenges. We will see that the project of decentralization can be partially rescued by shifting its focus from *mitigating* environmental changes to *adapting* to them. However, even this would require giving up on some of the most distinctive elements of the greens' vision. In the end, then, we will find that avoiding the most serious pathologies of greens' proposals would require adjusting them in ways that would purge them of their radical and transformative character. This might not be such a bad thing, for even moderate greens may have a great deal to teach us about how to live well on our planet. Yet to the extent that green theorists have sought to forge a radical break from the status quo,[6] this chapter will argue their efforts have missed the mark.

II. Why Decentralization?

Greens' calls for decentralization can be traced to serious concerns about modern society. For one thing, greens worry that the unprecedented economic achievements of recent centuries have been made possible only by wreaking havoc on the biosphere. Our ever-growing gross domestic products (GDPs) have come alongside emerging crises of ecological degradation, biodiversity loss, and global climate change. If these trends continue, greens fear we will soon face a reckoning that undoes much of our progress and yields widespread suffering, loss, and dislocation. As Jim Dodge bluntly puts it, "we cannot survive if the natural systems that sustain us are destroyed. That has to be stopped if we want to continue living on this planet. That's not 'environmentalism'; it's ecology with a vengeance."[7]

Making matters worse, greens argue that our economic prosperity has come at a grave spiritual price. Modern societies prioritize economic performance over other values,[8] impelling us to embrace lifestyles inimical to our flourishing[9] and cutting us off from the richness of the natural world.[10] Thus, our attempts to dominate the planet have been largely self-defeating, yielding a world filled with "poverty, frustration, alienation, despair, breakdown, crime, escapism, stress, congestion, ugliness, and spiritual death."[11]

Decentralist greens are skeptical that these problems can be resolved through governmental action. For existing liberal democracies have become "welded to the industrial direction of society"[12] and are thus more likely to perpetuate our dangerous trajectory than to divert it.[13] As Peter Berg sees it, our national leaders

> aren't open to accepting sustainability as a serious goal. They seem barely able to hear outcries against obvious large-scale destruction of the planetary biosphere from merely reform-minded environmentalists now, and aren't likely to take bioregionalists seriously until the District of Columbia itself becomes totally uninhabitable.[14]

Kirkpatrick Sale agrees, and urges greens to look beyond

> the business-as-usual politics of *all* the major parties of *all* the major industrial nations, not one of which has made ecological salvation a significant priority, not one of which is prepared to abandon or even curtail the industrial economy that is imperiling us.[15]

Instead of looking to our "inherently greedy, destabilizing, entropic, disorderly, and illegitimate"[16] governments to solve our problems, these writers seek to empower us to take the future into own hands through a shift toward an ecologically oriented form of anarchism. They insist that they can only go so far in describing how such transformations would play out in practice, since ultimately major decisions would be left to communities to make for themselves.[17] But many of them envision a future in which traditional national boundaries are gradually dissolved in favor of smaller-scale communities delineated along biophysical lines. Objective ecological characteristics like vegetation types, soil characteristics, river basins, and mountain ranges would be used to define distinct "bioregions" to serve as the basis for the civil order.[18] The resulting communities would be intentionally small, never reaching the scales typical of modern metropolitan cities, in order to ensure the possibility of a rich community life built around direct democratic participation.[19] They would also seek to achieve a large degree of self-sufficiency,[20] which would enable them to "not be in vassalage to far-off and uncontrollable bureaucracies or transnational corporations, at the mercy of whims or greeds of politicians and plutocrats."[21]

Leaving communities free to determine their own fates would foster "of necessity a more cohesive, more self-regarding, more self-concerned populace, with a developed sense of community and comradeship as well as the pride and resiliency that come with the knowledge of one's competence, control, stability, and independence."[22] Bioregional publics would also have the opportunity to "reinhabit" the landscapes in which they live, developing deep and intimate connections to their natural environments and cultivating a rich sense of place.[23] These new attitudes in turn would help to drive changes in economic behavior that helped local economies fit more comfortably within ecological limits.[24] Decentralist greens hope that communities reconstructed along these lines could scale back the most ecologically damaging features of modern civilization while restoring richness and meaning to the lives of their members.

III. Obstacles in the Path

The foregoing discussion might seem to suggest that green writers believe embracing a program of decentralization would resolve our ecological predicament as a matter of course. Yet things are not so simple. For one thing, decentralization is not always conducive to increased ecological efficiency. For example, as William Meyer has pointed out, large cities often boast a variety of environmental advantages over their less concentrated counterparts:

> They lessen pressure on ecological systems by confining [environmental impacts] in space, they slow population growth, and they make the consumption of major natural resources more sparing and efficient. Though they concentrate many forms of pollution, they often reduce the total pollution load and can better control emissions.[25]

Likewise, there is evidence that when it comes to corporate enterprises, larger firms produce lower impacts per unit of output relative to smaller firms.[26] This suggests that decentralized societies would not necessarily be more environmentally friendly, and they might even produce *greater* impacts on the natural world.

Another danger is that citizens of smaller, more autonomous communities might not embrace the goals and priorities favored by greens. Although green writers sometimes seem to take for granted that sensible people will share their convictions,[27] in reality they have never decisively won the battle of ideas. Many people—indeed, many communities in their entirety—regard even greens' most foundational claims with suspicion.[28] Greens' priorities have particularly struggled to gain traction in communities facing poverty and other pressing sources of insecurity.[29] There is little reason to expect that decentralization would bring an end to this diversity in perspectives and priorities. Thus, providing communities with additional autonomy could potentially lead some to even starker deviations from greens' preferences than we already see.

One further layer of complications comes from the fact that many ecological challenges are transboundary problems that can be brought under control only through coordination across large scales. It might be easy to envision how a local reorientation of social life could facilitate progress on small-scale threats facing individual communities, but it is harder to see how it could foster solutions to global dangers like climate change. Indeed, insofar as greens' decentralist proposals would have us dismantle the very governmental apparatuses that now enable the enforcement of global political agreements, they might seem like precisely the *opposite* of what is needed to properly address an ecological crisis.

IV. Additional Keys to Success

To their credit, decentralist greens have not failed to appreciate concerns like these. On the contrary, many of their accounts have revolved around overcoming them. For one thing, green writers have emphasized that decentralization cannot be expected to deliver ecological salvation on its own. Rather, its role in resolving the impending crisis is to empower communities to transform themselves in environmentally friendly directions. As Graham Purchase explains:

> The anarchist-environmental r/evolution implies much more than a mere transfer of political power from one group of people to another. It requires, rather, an all-encompassing mini-revolution in every city, suburb, town, and village. Even after the political liberation of all these communities is achieved … the more important task of deconstructing and reconstructing daily life according to communally and environmentally sound principles will remain. This implies that each district must conduct its own r/evolution and apply the ideas of eco-anarchism to itself.[30]

We have already seen that such self-transformations would likely take different forms in different communities. Yet greens hope that groups would be able to converge on certain commonalities that would facilitate favorable environmental outcomes. As Kirkpatrick Sale puts it, "any region true to bioregional principles would necessarily respect the limitations of scale, the virtues of conservation and stability, the importance of self-sufficiency and cooperation, and the desirability of decentralization and diversity."[31] Sale imagines that such foundational commitments could be reinforced by civil and social structures designed to build unity and discourage errant behavior. Thus, he prescribes arrangements where:

> an individual normally feels part of the web of nature and is accorded a particular role and value within it; where bonds of community are strong and social forms supportive and nurturing; where material needs and desires are for the most part fulfilled; where individual or even community actions transgressing bioregional standards are known to everyone and their unfortunate consequences visible to all; and where individual acts of violence or disharmony are perceived as contrary to both communal and ecological principles.[32]

Sale hopes that systems like these could facilitate needed environmental outcomes while allowing people "to be *people*, in all their variousness—and that includes being wrong on occasion, and errant and even evil."[33] In the last resort, he also adds that in virtue of their small size, bioregional communities could ensure that harmful decisions are "channeled and compartmentalized, constricted by scale, so [they] cannot do irreparable damage beyond narrow physical limits."[34]

Of course, not every environmental problem can be contained by shrinking the scale at which harmful decisions are made. Global climate change, for example, is caused by the cumulative impacts of countless decisions whose individual effects are tiny. To resolve problems like these, greens' decentralized communities would need to find some way to coordinate with one another across large geographical scales. To this end, some green writers have emphasized that decentralization must not be construed in isolationist terms:[35] on the contrary, a decentralized society would need to be rich with cooperation, with small-scale communities entering voluntary confederations to tackle common problems.[36] As Purchase explains:

> Social anarchists … do not call for complete self-sufficiency or community isolation; rather, they recommend that society be organized from the bottom up, based upon the natural biogeography of the Earth. Any resulting federations would be voluntary

> associations of local groups formed to address common needs and problems. This principle lies at the heart of anarchist organization: in place of *centralization*, anarchism calls for the *federalization* of all dimensions of human activity—cultural, social, economic, political, recreational, and environmental.[37]

These elaborations help to show how green proponents of decentralization believe the obstacles of the previous section can be overcome. Decentralization would not be expected to ensure favorable outcomes all on its own; rather, its role would be to facilitate a broader program of societal transformation. Greens would not expect every individual to eagerly embrace these changes; rather, they would achieve desired results through social arrangements that promoted social unity, discouraged harmful actions, and confined deviant behaviors to small scales. Nor would greens expect the largest-scale environmental problems to simply disappear; rather, they would achieve cooperation across communities through voluntary forms of confederation.

V. Remaining Difficulties

These responses go some way toward addressing the concerns raised in obstacles we have discussed for greens' vision of decentralization. However, it is doubtful they can fully vindicate the green decentralist program, for none of them takes seriously the likelihood that green views will be resisted not just by scattered individuals but also by dominant majorities in many communities. It is conceivable that in a world where the bulk of citizens embraced green views, an ecological crisis could be forestalled through communal self-transformations and voluntary confederations. But such outcomes are much more difficult to envision in a world where many individuals and communities emphatically reject green views. In this latter kind of world—that is, in the kind of world we actually inhabit—it seems unlikely that following greens' advice would ameliorate our ecological challenges.

To see why, begin by imagining that greens are able to secure sufficient influence around the world to start implementing their decentralist agendas. Thus, greens embark on a program of empowering communities to determine their own futures and urging national leaders to relinquish their grips on public affairs.[38] (This is a far-fetched scenario, to be sure. But it hardly seems worth exploring the practical merits of decentralization as a response to an ecological crisis unless we are willing to grant at least the *possibility* that something like this could be achieved.)

In line with our discussion so far, green leaders around the world work with their neighbors to reshape communities around ideals of self-sufficiency and ecological harmony. Yet even if we grant that greens have secured enough clout to effect decentralization in the first place, we should not expect them to be successful in setting the trajectory of every community. For as we have seen, green perspectives and priorities are controversial among the global population, and there is little reason to expect that this state of affairs will disappear.[39] In some areas, then, we might expect green ideas to win out and become entrenched in foundational political, social, and economic structures. In others, greens will be resisted and pushed aside, leaving other perspectives to shape community arrangements instead. Thus, as the process of decentralization unfolds, we should expect to find some ecologically conscientious green communities living alongside other communities that organize themselves in ways that subordinate the long-term integrity of the biosphere to alternative ends like economic growth and material prosperity.

It would go too far to suppose that if this happened, the non-green communities would simply obliterate the environment in every way they could. Such behaviors often yield direct harm to the communities that engage in them, and this would provide obvious reasons for bringing them under control. Yet it is still plausible that communities of non-greens would be inclined to undertake *many* environmentally impactful activities. In particular, we might expect them to be attracted to actions that were advantageous for their own members and primarily costly to far-off individuals, future generations, and non-human nature (e.g., emitting massive quantities of greenhouse gases to fuel rapid economic growth).

What would stop non-green communities from engaging in such externality-intensive patterns of behavior whenever they found it convenient? The green authors' appeals to a transformation in social conscience and norms cannot provide the answer, since in the relevant communities these transformations will not have occurred. Yet it is unclear that voluntary confederation can provide the answer either. Yes, communities of non-greens *could* form associations with their green neighbors to mitigate large-scale ecological challenges. But why would we expect them to *choose* to enter into such associations, especially on terms that would obstruct them from achieving the goals prioritized by their members?

It is difficult to see how greens could provide a satisfactory answer to this question within the bounds of their theoretical commitments. It might be possible for green communities to control their non-green neighbors by exercising coercion over them, perhaps through the overt use of force, or perhaps through other kinds of political or economic sanctions. Alternatively, greens could try to preserve *some* of the overarching political mechanisms that allow governments to impose needed measures on resistant communities today.[40] Yet these approaches would come with significant theoretical costs. Greens' rhetoric regarding universal self-determination[41] would be rendered hollow by the concession that dissenting communities should be coerced into compliance. And allowing the preservation of centralized mechanisms for political control would raise questions about how and whether green decentralism actually differs from the liberal democratic tradition it claims to abandon. A society that empowers local communities to govern themselves, but only under the umbrella of a central government that handles issues of large-scale concern, would not represent a radical break from the status quo. On the contrary, it is the exact system of government that is described in *The Federalist*[42] and embodied to varying degrees in liberal democracies around the world.

This leaves us with the apparent conclusion that the truly *radical* program of decentralization described by green writers could only be expected to forestall an ecological crisis in a world free from widespread resistance to green views. Only in such a world could it be reasonably thought that global challenges like climate change can be ameliorated entirely in the absence of coercion or centralized political control. For when one grants the likelihood that many communities will reject greens' preferred arrangements in favor of alternative, more ecologically impactful ones, it is difficult to imagine any other outcome than the continued degradation of the biosphere by these non-green communities.[43] Yet, if assuming away disagreement with greens' views is what it takes to make decentralization attractive as a response to an ecological crisis, then this chapter's inquiry will be closed. The literature of green decentralism might still be able to serve as an outlet for green venting or a guide to self-purification, but it would not offer a practical solution to an ecological crisis in an ideologically divided world like our own.

VI. Decentralization as an Adaptation Strategy

So far, this chapter has proceeded on the assumption that greens' rationale for seeking decentralization is to *prevent* an ecological crisis. We have seen that this rationale is dubious: in a world characterized by persistent disagreement over the merits of greens' views and priorities, there is little reason to think decentralization would be effective in forestalling global environmental problems such as climate change. However, there is an alternative possibility for justifying decentralization as a practical response to severe ecological challenges. This is to view decentralization as a means not for *mitigating* these challenges but rather for *adapting* to them.

There are several reasons why decentralization could help facilitate adaptation to an ecological crisis. For example, local decision-makers might be better equipped than distant officials to tailor adaptation strategies to local circumstances, beliefs, and priorities. Especially in areas where citizens possess intimate knowledge of their landscapes and community dynamics, the expansion of local autonomy could promote better decision-making. Smaller and more autonomous communities might also be better able to experiment with a wide range of strategies for navigating environmental difficulties. Misguided experiments would be less damaging in virtue of having been attempted only at small scales. Meanwhile, successful strategies could be replicated by other communities while still leaving room for further experimentation.

For reasons like these, we might expect that when dealing with the *consequences* of an ecological crisis, a decentralized order of autonomous communities would boast important advantages over a society comprised of larger, more centralized units. Decentralization might not be a promising way to prevent ecological challenges from emerging in the first place, but in a world where it is plausible that *nothing* will prevent these challenges, the capacity to alleviate some of their worst impacts would be nothing to scoff at. Refocusing attention away from *mitigating* environmental problems and toward *adapting* to them might therefore help to rescue green decentralism from practical irrelevance.

This recasting is not without its hurdles, however, as some of greens' proposals lie in tension with the goal of facilitating adaptation to ecological challenges. In particular, we have seen that many greens hope decentralization proceeds in the direction of bioregional *self-sufficiency*. In the societies greens envision, goods would be produced "mainly from local materials and mainly for local use"[44] with an eye to fostering arrangements that are intelligible and fulfilling to their participants.[45] Citizens would seek to bring their economies into alignment with the resources available in their bioregions, avoiding economic reliance on other regions as much as possible.[46] Communities would not necessarily seek economic *isolation* from one another, but they would allow relationships to form only "within strict limits—the connections must be nondependent, nonmonetary, and noninjurious."[47]

If greens' primary objective were to facilitate adaptation to an ecological crisis, strictures like these would be counterproductive. Without free economic flows of labor, materials, goods, and services between communities, the task of adapting to rapidly changing ecological conditions would be much more difficult than necessary. For well-functioning market economies are unmatched in their productivity and dynamism, and these qualities would be more essential than ever when facing the challenges greens see on the horizon. Rather than decoupling local economies from broader markets, adaptation-minded greens would be wise to revise their views to insist on maintaining *economic* integration even as they seek decentralization along other dimensions of public life.

There are several reasons why well-integrated economies can be expected to fare better in responding to ecological challenges than bioregionally self-reliant ones. For one thing, it has been widely recognized since Adam Smith's *Inquiry into the Nature and Causes of the Wealth of Nations* that economic performance is importantly connected to the division of labor. Specialization enables individuals to maximize their efficiency as producers, often increasing their outputs by orders of magnitude.[48] Yet the division of labor, Smith observes, is itself related to the extent of the market. If individuals are confined to small networks of trading partners, the limited demand for specific goods and services will not justify highly specialized production strategies. Small, economically separated communities will therefore sustain much more rudimentary divisions of labor than can be achieved in larger, better-connected communities.[49] Hence, they will remain comparatively poor—and comparatively vulnerable to severe ecological hazards.

Integrated economic markets also enable individuals to acquire goods and services that are locally scarce but abundant in other areas—a condition sure to become increasingly common on a rapidly changing planet. In the event of a local crop failure, for example, the citizens of a bioregion that refused to transact with its neighbors would be forced to bear the brunt of the crisis on their own. On the other hand, citizens embedded in an integrated market system could simply turn to more distant producers to meet their needs, offering slightly higher rates to ensure that limited outputs were directed to them instead of other consumers. The resulting increase in market prices would have further effects as well, impelling buyers to consume less of the critical crops while encouraging producers to expand their production. Through these economy-wide adjustments, the regional crop failure could be addressed without the need for anyone to starve.

As F.A. Hayek observes in "The Use of Knowledge in Society,"[50] this kind of mutual adjustment is at the heart of the existing economic order. As prices fluctuate, both consumers and producers are incentivized to respond to changing economic circumstances in socially desirable ways. This occurs even though economic participants inevitably know little about what the relevant circumstances are and why their revised conduct is warranted. In this way, the price system plays a crucial role in helping societies adapt to constantly fluctuating economic conditions.

These observations suggest that if greens hope to use decentralization to facilitate adaptation to an ecological crisis, they must encourage *economic* integration even as they urge communities to proceed along diverging social and political paths. Economically separated communities will be impoverished by a stunted division of labor and cut off from opportunities to use global markets to meet rapidly changing needs. It is by taking advantage of specialization and integrated markets, and not by abandoning them, that communities will position themselves to respond effectively to a planet destabilized by human activities.

None of this is to say that greens must reconceive their decentralist aspirations around unfettered global capitalism. But they *will* have to sharply qualify their visions of bioregional self-sufficiency if their program is to offer a sensible strategy for adapting to ecological changes. There is surely room in a viable green agenda for encouraging economic relationships that are meaningful, intimate, and ecologically conscientious. But communities can hardly expect to overcome a severe ecological crisis by suppressing their primary means for calling others to their aid.

VII. The Dialectical Challenge

We can now see that if greens wish to plausibly defend decentralization as a practical response to an impending ecological crisis, their proposals will need to differ in important ways from the ones that appear in existing green literature. Decentralization must be cast as a tool for *adapting* to ecological challenges rather than for *preventing* them, and it must be pursued with an eye to maintaining *economic* integration even amidst social and political dis-unification.

Reconceived in these ways, we have seen that the program of decentralization could offer interesting possibilities for facilitating adaptation to severe environmental challenges. However, revising green decentralism in the ways I have suggested would invite difficult questions as to whether the project still offers a compelling and radical break from the liberal status quo. Such questions will become especially pointed for those who are not prepared to simply abandon the goal of mitigating global ecological challenges. As we have seen, the most plausible avenues for this mitigation involve the coercive enforcement of environmental norms, perhaps via centralized political authority. If one is tempted to concede that at least *some* coercion might be warranted between communities—and that perhaps this should be coordinated through overarching political bodies—then the vision that results is not very radical at all. Such a view would retain many of the same kinds of collective decision-making mechanisms and globalized market arrangements that already exist, and it would seek to expand communities' autonomy, self-reliance, and ecological sensitivity only within these overarching systems. Is this really something fundamentally distinct from liberal democracy? If so, the key difference is far from clear.

To be sure, it would not be a terrible thing to learn that the most plausible versions of green decentralism offer moderate ways of reforming liberalism rather than radical breaks from the status quo. For reformism along these lines could still have a great deal to teach us. Still, if the purpose of greens' decentralist writings is to offer a practical and radical alternative to the status quo, then we can only say that greens have not given us a compelling case. For those who would hope to vindicate this kind of green decentralism, the dialectical challenge is clear: show how a truly radical and green form of decentralization can be defended in the kinds of circumstances that are relevant for theorizing about an ecological crisis. It is easy to imagine a green program of decentralization achieving felicific results in a world where opposition has evaporated and communities no longer need to rely on markets to protect themselves from harm. But this is not the world we inhabit, and it is unlikely to become so anytime soon. To vindicate their radicalism in *our* world, decentralist greens need to persuade us that their proposals can actually make things better despite the serious obstacles they face.

Notes

1 For example, Graham Purchase, *Anarchism and Environmental Survival* (Tucson, AZ: See Sharp 1994).

2 For example, Kirkpatrick Sale, *Dwellers in the Land: The Bioregional Vision* (Philadelphia, PA: New Society 1985); Van Andruss, Christopher Plant, Judith Plant, and Eleanor Wright (eds.), *Home! A Bioregional Reader* (Philadelphia, PA: New Society 1990).

3 For example, Murray Bookchin, *The Ecology of Freedom: The Emergence and Dissolution of Hierarchy* (Palo Alto, CA: Cheshire 1982).

4 At times, green writers have explicitly embraced this limited aspiration. Jim Dodge, for example, insists that "The chances of bioregionalism succeeding are beside the point. If one person, or a few, or a community of people, live more fulfilling lives from bioregional practice, then it's successful," in "Living by Life: Some Bioregional Theory and Practice," *Home! A Bioregional Reader*, ed. Van Andruss, Christopher Plant, Judith Plant, and Eleanor Wright (Philadelphia, PA: New Society 1990) 5–12, 12.

5 For example, Kirkpatrick Sale writes, "I am certain that in the bioregional paradigm we have a goal, a philosophy, and a process by which to create a world which is not only *necessary* for the continuation of our species, but is also *desirable* and *possible*" (49; original emphasis).

6 Murray Bookchin considers it critical to "challenge the status quo in a far-reaching manner—in the only manner commensurate with the nature of the crisis" (*Ecology* 3). He connects this attitude to the conviction that "Our world … will either undergo revolutionary changes, so far-reaching in character that humanity will totally transform its social relations and its very conception of life, or it will suffer an apocalypse that may well end humanity's tenure on the planet" (*Ecology* 18). Likewise, Edward Goldsmith, Robert Allen, Michael Allaby, John Davoll, and Sam Lawrence write, "We are sufficiently aware of 'political reality' to appreciate that many of the proposals we shall make … will be considered impracticable. However, we believe that if a strategy for survival is to have any chance of success, the solutions must be formulated in the light of the problems and not from a timorous and superficial understanding of what may or may not be immediately feasible. If we plan remedial action with our eyes on political rather than ecological reality, then very reasonably, very practicably, and very surely we shall muddle our way to extinction," in *Blueprint for Survival* (Boston, MA: Houghton Mifflin 1972) 18.

7 Dodge 11.

8 E.F. Schumacher writes, "It is hardly an exaggeration to say that, with increasing affluence, economics has moved into the very centre of public concern, and economic performance, economic growth, economic expansion, and so forth have become the abiding interest, if not the obsession, of all modern societies," in *Small is Beautiful: Economics as if People Mattered, 25 Years Later … with Commentaries* (Vancouver: Hartley & Marks 1999) 27.

9 Schumacher complains, "The modern economy is propelled by a frenzy of greed and indulges in an orgy of envy, and these are not accidental features but the very causes of its expansionist success" (18). He laments "the hollowness and fundamental unsatisfactoriness of a life devoted primarily to the pursuit of material ends, to the neglect of the spiritual" (24). To Bookchin, our society's materialism has grown to the point where the typical individual is inculcated with limitless "needs" unconnected to any authentic interests. In societies like ours, "Needs, in effect, become a force of production, not a subjective force. They become blind in the same sense that the production of commodities becomes blind. Orchestrated by

forces that are external to the subject, they exist beyond its control like the production of the very commodities that are meant to satisfy them. This autonomy of needs … is developed at the expense of the autonomy of the subject. It reveals a fatal flaw in subjectivity itself, in the autonomy and spontaneity of the individual to control the conditions of his or her own life" (*Ecology* 68–69).

10 Kirkpatrick Sale describes a mentality pervading Western civilization whereby nature is "no longer either beautiful or scary but merely *there*, not to be worshipped or celebrated, but more often than not to be *used*, with all the ingenuity and instruments of a scientific culture—gingerly at times, wholeheartedly at others, within limits if need be, heedless of limits if possible, but used—*by* humans, *for* humans" (13). Likewise Schumacher writes, "Modern man does not experience himself as a part of nature but as an outside force destined to dominate and conquer it. He even talks of a battle with nature, forgetting that, if he won the battle, he would find himself on the losing side" (4).

11 Schumacher 56. See along similar lines Goldsmith et al. ch. 4.

12 Peter Berg, "More Than Just Saving What's Left," *Home! A Bioregional Reader*, ed. Van Andruss, Christopher Plant, Judith Plant, and Eleanor Wright (Philadelphia, PA: New Society 1990) 13–16, 13.

13 Goldsmith et al. write, "we can expect our governments to encourage continued increases in GNP regardless of the consequences, which in any case tame 'experts' can be found to play down. It will curb growth only when public opinion demands such a move, in which case it will be politically expedient, and when a method is found for doing so without creating unemployment or excessive pressure on capital" (21).

14 Peter Berg, "Growing a Life-Place Politics," *Home! A Bioregional Reader*, ed. Van Andruss, Christopher Plant, Judith Plant, and Eleanor Wright (Philadelphia, PA: New Society 1990) 137–144, 140.

15 Sale 48. Original emphasis.

16 Gary Snyder, "Bioregional Perspectives," *Home! A Bioregional Reader*, ed. Van Andruss, Christopher Plant, Judith Plant, and Eleanor Wright (Philadelphia, PA: New Society 1990) 19.

17 Bookchin writes, "It is tempting to venture into a utopian description of how an ecological society would look and how it would function, but I have promised to leave such visions to the utopian dialogue that we so direly need today" (*Ecology* 343). Likewise, Sale insists, "Truly autonomous bioregions would inevitably go in separate and not necessarily complementary ways, creating their own political systems according to their own environmental settings and their own ecological needs" (108).

18 For one influential articulation of how these bioregions could be individuated, see Sale, 1985, pp. 56–59.

19 Decentralist green writers give different accounts of exactly *how* small they think communities should be. For example, Bill Mollison imagines communities inhabited by 7,000–40,000 citizens in "Strategies for an Alternative Nation," *Home! A Bioregional Reader*, ed. Van Andruss, Christopher Plant, Judith Plant, and Eleanor Wright (Philadelphia, PA: New Society 1990) 149–154, 149. Meanwhile, E.F. Schumacher places his upper limit for urban populations at 500,000 (49).

20 Peter Berg writes, "Community development in all its aspects from economic activities and housing to social services and transportation should be aimed toward bioregional self-reliance" ("More" 15).

21 Berg, "More" 77.

22 Berg, "More" 78.

23 As Peter Berg and Raymond Dasmann describe it in "Reinhabiting California," *Home! A Bioregional Reader*, ed. Van Andruss, Christopher Plant, Judith Plant, and Eleanor Wright (Philadelphia, PA: New Society 1990) 35–38, "*Reinhabitation* means learning to live-in-place in an area that has been disrupted and injured through past exploitation. It involves becoming native to a place through becoming aware of the particular ecological relationships that operate within and around it. It means understanding activities and evolving social behavior that will enrich the life of that place, restore its life-supporting systems, and establish an ecologically and socially sustainable pattern of existence within it. Simply stated it involves becoming fully alive in and with a place. It involves applying for membership in a biotic community and ceasing to be its exploiter" (35; original emphasis).

24 Sale writes, "People do not, other things being equal, pollute and damage those natural systems on which they depend for life and livelihood if they see directly what is happening; nor voluntarily use up a resource under their feet and before their eyes if they perceive that it is precious, needed, vital; nor kill off species they can see are important for the smooth functioning of the ecosystem" (54).

25 William B. Meyer, *The Environmental Advantages of Cities: Countering Commonsense Antiurbanism* (Cambridge, MA: MIT 2013) 146.

26 See, for example, Matthew A. Cole, Robert J.R. Elliott, and Kenichi Shimamoto, "Industrial Characteristics, Environmental Regulations and Air Pollution: An Analysis of the UK Manufacturing Sector," *Journal of Environmental Economics and Management* 50.1 (2005): 121–43; Bruno Merlevede, Tom Verbeke, and Marc De Clercq, "The EKC for SO_2: Does Firm Size Matter?" *Ecological Economics* 59.4 (2006): 451–61.

27 Kirkpatrick Sale, for example, claims that "The political project of bioregionalism ... has promise precisely because it conforms so well with so many of the underlying trends of the contemporary world" (151), including a deep concern for the environment, affinity with the feminist movement, distrust of centralized and arbitrary authority, and a hostility toward the pathological political and economic systems that dominate the Western world (151–152). In an unguarded moment, Jim Dodge goes even further, portraying modern environmental conflicts as "a struggle between the bioregional forces (who represent intelligence, excellence, and care) and the forces of heartlessness (who represent a greed so lifeless and forsaken it can't even pass as ignorance)" (10).

28 For influential articulations of these competing perspectives, see Wilfred Beckerman, *Through Green-Colored Glasses: Environmentalism Reconsidered* (Washington, DC: Cato 1996); Julian L. Simon, *The Ultimate Resource 2* (Princeton, NJ: PUP) 1996; Bjorn Lomborg, *The Skeptical Environmentalist: Measuring the Real State of the World* (New York, NY: CUP 2001). For discussions of these views as cultural and psychological phenomena, see Dan M. Kahan, "Fixing the Communications Failure," *Nature* 463.7279 (2010): 296–297; Dan M. Kahan, Hank Jenkins-Smith, and Donald Braman, "Cultural Cognition of Scientific Consensus," *Journal of Risk Research* 14.2 (2011): 147–74; Matthew Feinberg and Robb Willer, "The Moral Roots of Environmental Attitudes," *Psychological Science* 24.1 (2013): 56–62; Jacob B. Hirsch, "Environmental Sustainability and National Personality," *Journal of Environmental Psychology* 38 (2014): 233–40.

29 Iddisah Sulemana, Harvey S. James, Jr., and Corinne B. Valdivia find that across a wide range of countries, individuals who perceive themselves as belonging to the "lower class" are significantly less likely to be willing to sacrifice economic growth and job creation for the sake of environmental protection in "Perceived Socioeconomic Status as a Predictor of Environmental Concern in Africa and Developed Countries," *Journal of Environmental Psychology* 46 (2016): 83–95. According to Alex Lo, "National Income and Environmental Concern: Observations from 35 Countries," *Public Understanding of Science* 25.7 (2016): 873–90, the lack of prioritization of environmental concerns in less-developed countries is driven more by a reduced ability to pay for strong protection measures than by a lack of concern for the environment as such. On the other hand, Xueying Yu finds that in China environmental concern is comparatively sparse among rural communities, with individuals commonly pleading ignorance of global problems and attending primarily to issues that visibly affect their communities and livelihoods, in "Is Environment 'A City Thing' in China? Rural-Urban Differences in Environmental Attitudes," *Journal of Environmental Psychology* 38 (2014): 39–48.

30 Purchase 12–13.

31 Sale 108.

32 Sale 109.

33 Ibid.

34 Ibid.

35 Goldsmith et al. write, "Although we believe that the small community should be the basic unit of society and that each community should be as self-sufficient and self-regulating as possible, we would like to stress that we are not proposing that they be inward-looking, self-obsessed, or in any way closed to the rest of the world" (54).

36 According to Murray Bookchin, "Municipal Libertarianism," *Home! A Bioregional Reader*, ed. Van Andruss, Christopher Plant, Judith Plant, and Eleanor Wright (Philadelphia, PA: New Society 1990) 145–46, the formation of a confederal system is "the most important thing" for local communities to achieve (145). On the other hand, some decentralist greens express skepticism about the extent to which this kind of cooperation is likely. Peter Berg, for example, expects that most bioregional communities would primarily seek "to solve problems where they live" ("Life-Place" 144). See similar comments at Sale 96.

37 Purchase 18. Original emphasis.

38 Note that although some green proponents of decentralization have spoken of a desire to implement their visions through *revolutionary* means (e.g., Purchase), others have insisted that such an approach would do more harm than good (e.g., Goldsmith et al. 24). Thus, Sale prescribes a gradual, "evolutionary" process whereby governments slowly step back from their now-pervasive roles and simply *allow* more local autonomy (169–170, 176–177). As he sees it, the bioregional project "asks nothing of the Federal government and needs no national legislation, no governmental regulation, no Presidential dispensation. What commends it especially to its age is that it does not need any Federal presence to promote it, only a Federal obliviousness to permit it" (169).

39 In fact, there is some evidence that levels of environmental concern have been *decreasing* in Axel Franzen and Dominkus Vogl, "Two Decades of Measuring Environmental Attitudes: A Comparative Analysis of 33 Countries," *Global Environmental Change* 23.5 (2013): 1001–08.

40 Decentralist green authors have sometimes written as if they would be open to such suggestions: for example, E.F. Schumacher claims that "We always need both freedom and order. We need the freedom of lots and lots of small, autonomous units, and, at the same time, the orderliness of large-scale, possibly global, unity and coordination" (48). See along similar lines Goldsmith et al. 54, 60; Sale 94.

41 In this connection, Jim Dodge insists that "Anarchy doesn't mean out of control; it means out of *their* control. Anarchy is based upon a sense of interdependent self-reliance, the conviction that we as a community, or a tight, small-scale federation of communities, can mind our own business, and can make decisions regarding our individual and communal lives and gladly accept the responsibilities and consequences of those decisions" (8–9). Graham Purchase likewise insists that green anarchists seek to avoid making impositions on communities: "They hope, rather, that the people, in an attempt to produce a self-managed, directly democratic, and ecologically sustainable social system, will organize themselves from the bottom upwards—at the level of individual communities, interest groups, and workers' organizations" (140). In the world he envisions, communities would be able to see themselves as "independent, self-governing, and answerable to no one" (149).

42 Alexander Hamilton, John Jay, and James Madison, *The Federalist* (Indianapolis, IN: Liberty Fund 2001).

43 Indeed, insofar as some greens would likely abandon their ecological scruples if they did not expect others to engage in reciprocal sacrifices, the actions of dissenting communities might cause non-cooperative behaviors to cascade into green communities as well. For general discussion of these dynamics in the domain of norm-following behavior, see Cristina Bicchieri, *The Grammar of Society: The Nature and Dynamics of Social Norms* (New York, NY: CUP 2006).

44 Schumacher 146.

45 Schumacher hopes that this decentralization of production can promote what he considers the proper objectives of working life: "to give a man a chance to utilize and develop his faculties; to enable him to overcome his ego-centredness by joining with other people in a common task; and to bring forth the goods and services needed for a becoming existence" (39).

46 Sale 46.

47 Sale 79.

48 Adam Smith, *An Inquiry into the Nature and Causes of the Wealth of Nations* (London: Methuen 1904) ch. 1.

49 Smith ch. 3.

50 Friedrich A. Hayek, "The Use of Knowledge in Society," *American Economic Review* 35.4 (1945): 519–30.

28

STATES, INCARCERATION, AND ORGANIZATIONAL STRUCTURE

Towards a General Theory of Imprisonment

Daniel J. D'Amico

I. Introduction

Comparative researchers have converged upon a strong, but under-specified, consensus that "institutions matter" regarding the causes of imprisonment and the rise of mass incarceration. A large and growing body of consistent research reports a robust correlation between socio-political institutional types on the one hand and criminal justice outcomes on the other. Nations with similar economic and political institutional regimes tend to possess similar criminal justice systems and relatively similar punishment outcomes including prison population rates.[1] However, contrasting theoretical perspectives yield different conclusions regarding the ultimate causes of prison growth and mass incarceration. What particular institutional types shape prison population rates, and through what causal processes, remains unresolved. This chapter attempts to make progress towards a generalizable framework designed to foster better understanding imprisonment.

The currently dominant view explains mass incarceration's timing and magnitudes with reference to political efforts intended to effect class- or race-based social control.[2] I will refer to this paradigm as the "social control model." In contrast, a growing body of research accounts for patterns of imprisonment with reference to organizational dynamics and the systemic potentials for error across different degrees of institutional centralization.[3] I will call this latter framework the "government failure model."

Are high incarceration rates primarily the result of political efforts to maintain dominant power and social control? Or is excessive prison growth better understood as an unintended consequence of certain bureaucratic organizational patterns? Are the consequences of supposed "mass incarceration" a failure of societal preferences and political bias, or is mass incarceration a unique form of governmental failure more likely given some organizational arrangements than others? The respective implications and constituent features of these alternative frameworks can be investigated against the empirical record.

Given the well-established economic and social consequences of mass incarceration,[4] proper answers to these questions carry substantial implications for guiding reform efforts. If prison growth is primarily the result of attempts to achieve or maintain social control, then political activism and cultural change are likely needed to reshape outcomes. If mass incarceration instead stems more from incentive arrangements more prevalent within some institutional types than others, then reshaping outcomes may be a more difficult and complex process. If the government failure approach is correct, traditional forms of democratic action may prove ineffective against or even contributory to continual prison growth.

I apply a standard of generalizability to adjudicate between these contrasting frameworks. In an ideal world, fully detailed and accurate measures of imprisonment across times and places would allow for more rigorous causality tests. Given the limitations of currently available data, I argue that prison growth should at least be understood from the vantage point of whichever framework most accords with the best available evidence. At least there now exists a growing body of increasingly more precise and accurate forms of empirics surrounding crime and punishment trends historically and at the cross-national level. The preferred model for comprehending the causes and consequences of imprisonment ought to fit most compatibly with these stylized facts and to require the least degree and quantity of ad hoc adjustments.

To understand which alternative theory is more generally compatible with real imprisonment patterns, I investigate a variety of evidentiary sources, both qualitative and quantitative. I survey the available theory and evidence supporting and challenging each of the two contrasting approaches. I also summarize research surrounding the historical origins of prisons and punishment by incarceration. Where and when were prisons first constructed, and for what purposes? Last, I survey cross-national empirics and related historical research to describe the organizational dynamics of prison development and prison growth.

In summary, these sources stand in substantial contrast to the social control model. Furthermore, the government failure model can be fitted to account for a broader sample of the available evidence. Thus, I propose a spectrum of organizational centralization that better accords with the observed patterns of imprisonment and contemporary trends of mass incarceration. In short, societies appear to commit more material and financial resources towards imprisonment where and when criminal justice institutions are more centralized and hierarchical.

These findings are of particular relevance to anarchist theory and the interested readers of this volume. First, the government failure model broadens the relevant sample of social contexts to include and account for stateless social orders, whereas the social control model tends to focus more exclusively on advanced western democracies. Second, because of this recognition regarding the potentials and limits of statelessness, this framework has the ability to engage normative arguments surrounding prison abolitionism in ways typically unaddressed.[5]

Normative commitments that preclude the role of formal state authorities thus also conveniently avoid the social consequences of and normative concerns raised by mass incarceration. Similarly, as David Boonin has noted, the practical potentials of punitive norms within stateless contexts serve as a unique challenge to the typical justifications for state-based provisions of criminal punishment.[6] Supplanting the social control model of imprisonment with the government failure model establishes a unique standard for the broader justification of state authority. Any punitive paradigm beginning from the presumption of state necessity and or legitimacy must also address and respond to the potential social consequences and normative dilemmas associated with prison growth and excessive imprisonment. I argue that this adjustment in how the causes of imprisonment are best understood would thus reshape much of our normative reflection on criminal punishment. Rather than focusing on debates regarding how to properly justify criminal punishments given state legitimacy, political philosophy must engage the more practical constitutional project of explaining how to justly limit state authority while minimizing systemic errors such as mass incarceration.[7]

The remainder of this chapter is organized as follows. Section II summarizes the social control model as the dominant framework for understanding imprisonment and prison growth historically and across social contexts. Section III summarizes a variety of contemporary research and findings that raise substantial doubts about the generalizability of the social control model. Several of the direct implications within the social control model stand at odds with the available evidence. Section IV provides the outline of an alternative model of government failure for better explaining imprisonment trends. Section V offers some concluding remarks.

II. The Social Control Model

The social control model carries at least three related implications. First, crime rates do not sufficiently explain the patterns of imprisonment. Second, prison growth in the modern era and across developed nations is conspicuously correlated with free market capitalist ideology or public policies. Third, especially in the American experience, mass incarceration was instigated and buttressed by race- and class-based animosities.

One of the most confirmed claims of the dominant social control model is that imprisonment trends are not sufficiently explained as a byproduct of real crime rates. In other words, it does not appear to be the case that prisons were originally designed or constructed or subsequently expanded because of a real societal need for crime control. Instead, it is argued that imprisonment historically provided a unique technological opportunity for the concentration of power. Hence, the subsequent implications of the social control model draw more attention to the particular identities of powerful interest groups: predominant owners of capital and racial majorities. This initial claim about the insufficient explanatory power of real crime trends is not necessarily new, nor is it necessarily unique to the social control perspective. In fact, many alternative models of imprisonment accept that contemporary imprisonment patterns cannot be fully explained with reference to real crime rates.[8]

Michel Foucault popularized the idea that incarceration ought to be understood alongside a fuller awareness of power structures.[9] Drawing on Jeremy Bentham's[10] model of panopticism, Foucault explains: "The whole machinery that has been developing for years around the implementation of sentences, and their adjustment to individuals, creates a proliferation of the authorities of judicial decision-making and extends its powers of decision well beyond the sentence."[11] In short, incarceration not only levies penalties upon criminals but also provides a mechanism for authorities to both deter and encourage entire swaths of human and group behaviors.[12] Furthermore, the disciplinary role of the criminal law provides a technologically unique form of power reserved to governments in the modern era. With such power came a similarly unique and often exploited opportunity for the expression and satisfaction of private and political interests.[13] The social control model implies that the increased usage of incarceration reflects these tendencies towards the achievement and exercise of power rather than alternative explanations framed in light of such factors as real societal needs or supposed moral progress away from brutal penalties and towards humane alternatives. (Foucault famously rejected this latter explanation.)

Foucault drew heavily on the work of Rusche and Kirchheimer, who viewed the growth of imprisonment in conjunction with unemployment trends.[14] Prisons, they argued, helped to ameliorate the social problems associated with surplus labor conditions amidst post-industrial business cycles. Criminal justice via imprisonment was said to provide effective monitoring and deterrence against idleness, criminal opportunism, and organized revolt. Thus, prisons were also thought to assist in the maintenance of a relatively willing and docile industrial labor force.

> [T]he punishment of crime is not the sole element; we must show that punitive measures are not simply 'negative' mechanisms that make it possible to repress, to prevent,

> to exclude, to eliminate; but that they are linked to a whole series of positive and useful effects which it is their task to support.[15]

Thus, on this view the criminal justice system writ large and incarceration in particular ultimately serve to preserve concentrations of wealth and privilege.

Subsequently, more contemporary writings have extended this general theme of prisons as a mechanism for social control with foci on class inequality, mass incarceration, and racial disparity. Wacquant and Garland emphasize the relationship between prison power and economic inequality.[16] Western highlights the strong correlations between economic inequality, criminality, and race in the American experience. And, most notably, Alexander argues that the criminal justice system has supplanted the Jim Crow legal regime as a means of maintaining white dominance over the black community.

This social control model is the more prominent view today, with some or all of the following observations typically seen as supporting it. First, imprisonment supposedly became the standard practice of criminal punishment as and where the Industrial Revolution occurred. In particular, Britain in the late eighteenth and early nineteenth centuries served as the spawning ground for the Industrial Revolution, the Scottish Enlightenment and Bentham's related ideas, and the rise of incarceration as the default form of criminal punishment. Second, the contemporary trend of mass incarceration seems conspicuously related to American practice. It is well established that the net amount and per capita rate of incarceration are greater in the United States than in any other developed nation.[17] Furthermore, as the world's only economic and military superpower, the United States is also perceived as an influencer and disseminator of specifically neoliberal policies and ideology. Presumably, the cross-national patterns of prison growth reflect American influence. In this vein, contemporary expressions of neoliberalism are seen as a consistent extensions of the social control methods used during the Industrial Revolution.[18] Benthamite models of "panoptic" discipline obtained in factories and prisons alike during the eighteenth century; proponents of the social control approach suggest that contemporary neoliberal policies leverage similar incentive systems, featuring monitoring and graduated sanctions, to assure domestic economic performance, international free trade, and the privatization of traditionally public services.[19] Excessive prison population rates result from the policies of neoliberal democratic regimes. Countries with stronger cultural legacies of individualism and more legal and political commitments to free markets tend to host larger prison population rates than do more interventionist and socially redistributive regimes.[20]

Lastly, the social control model suggests that US prison growth resulted in large part from the anxieties of wealthier white voters. Mass incarceration appears to have become a prominent feature of American life in the wake of the civil rights movement, the rise of national political campaigns focused upon law and order, and the war on drugs. Enns demonstrates the strong link between increases in punitive attitudes and public opinion trends.[21] Wasow further shows conspicuous correlations between changes in partisan voter support and their proximity to racially motivated riots.[22] As Clegg and Usmani explain: on the social control model, "American mass incarceration was the means by which white America re-established a system of racial control that had been threatened by the civil rights movement"; they note "more than 150 studies that offer support … and only a handful … that dispute it."[23]

III. What the Social Control Model Cannot Explain

Several of the basic components and implications of the social control model have been in place for decades. But the increased availability of better empirical evidence gives us the opportunity to verify or challenge this dominant paradigm and its constituent claims. In light of this evidence,

I argue that the social control model does not effectively account for the full range of global and historical imprisonment patterns.

First, the early observation that the invention and systemic adoption of incarceration as a standard form of criminal punishment coincided with emergence of Enlightenment ideas and the Industrial Revolution isn't simply inaccurate; but it isn't fully accurate, either. As Spierenburg has demonstrated, imprisonment was first leveraged as a punitive technique within Scandinavian territories prior to the British experience.[24] Scandinavian imprisonment seems to have emerged more as a product of state convenience than as an attempt at full-fledged social control. The first prison facilities were remnant military outposts in which suspected and tried criminals could be housed and monitored at minimal additional social cost or security risk. Similar military spillover effects have shaped the forms and magnitudes of criminal justice techniques and protocols throughout history.[25]

The available evidence doesn't simply contradict the social control model. The milder claim, that the desire to control crime doesn't suffice to explain imprisonment, remains well supported,[26] as does the implication that imprisonment does serve some social control function or functions. Furthermore, it is undisputed that Bentham's designs were highly influential in England and subsequently inspired similar facilities throughout the developed world and especially the United States.[27] However, details regarding the *mechanism* of military resource abundance also complement the recognition that the rise and proliferation of incarceration across primitive contexts coincided with episodes of developed and enhanced state power and capacity.[28] Thus, this evidence alone leaves open the question of the merits of alternative frameworks for understanding incarceration.

Another implication of the social control model potentially reaffirmed or challenged by more recent and detailed evidence is the supposed relationship between the rise and expansion of incarceration and the emergence of global capitalism, neoliberal ideology, and free market public policies. The most obvious confirmatory pieces of evidence compliment the social control model's original narrative linking the rise and proliferation of incarceration to the Enlightenment and developments associated with the early Industrial Revolution. Mass incarceration is most apparently concentrated in the latter-twentieth-century United States. There is strong and detailed evidence of increased punitive preferences amongst voters in this setting.[29]

Recent empirically rooted efforts to establish an institutional framework for understanding cross-country patterns of imprisonment have reported greater prison population rates in nations identified as "neoliberal market democracies." By contrast, more corporatist or socially democratic states apparently host proportionally smaller prison populations.[30] (In this context, "neoliberalism" is defined as "almost the opposite of … the standard meaning of the word 'liberal' when applied to American politics. 'Neo-liberalism' refers to the (politically conservative) late twentieth-century revival of the nineteenth-century approach of economic liberalism, based on free-market capitalism."[31])

Sorting real political regimes into relevant conceptual categories is a difficult task, as objective and quantifiable measures of the salient institutional features and their criminal justice correlates are lacking.[32] When larger data sets are used alongside more sophisticated statistical techniques, a number of findings emerge which don't appear fully consistent with the social control model. First, long-standing claims regarding the contextual influence of unemployment cycles on crime and imprisonment trends cannot be confirmed.[33] Results are mixed, and don't appear strongly consistent *or* inconsistent with the social control model. Some researchers find that unemployment mildly coincides with prison growth,[34] while others find the opposite.[35] Similarly, several studies have reported that it is difficult to verify any consistent or positive relationship between prison population rates and objective measures of free market capitalism. Neither the aggregate size of the economy, growth trends, nor formally measured indexes of capitalism or economic freedom are robustly or significantly correlated with prison population rates.[36] In contrast, the largest and most sophisticated empirical investigations available report that the institutional feature most correlated with contemporary prison largess is years under socialism.[37]

The racial implications of the social control model have also been empirically assessed. While Alexander and others have argued for a causal link between racial anxieties amongst white voters and "tough on crime" political campaigns, the war on drugs, and increases in punitive attitudes and policies, a number of recent studies offer a picture of the development of current criminal justice policies that is more complicated than the one offered by proponents of the social control model and in which racist and right-wing attitudes play less central roles.

It is well established that American voter opinion became more punitive *prior to* as well as in conjunction with the rise of mass incarceration.[38] The usual caveat that correlation does not imply causation correctly applies here.[39] Furthermore, the implication that punitive opinions are foundationally or primarily motivated by racial anxieties is also less certain than proponents of the social control model have assumed. Wasow demonstrates a measurable link between the potency of violent riots amidst the civil rights era and switches from predominant support from Democratic to Republican candidates in proximate counties. Thus, from the impact of racial anxieties on increased imprisonment apart from the influence of real crime and violence is difficult. The link between specifically conservative and white opinions and punitive attitudes is also less clear than proponents of the social control model have supposed. Murakawa shows the pervasive nature of punitive attitudes on the part even of progressive Democratic candidates[40] and Forman Jr (2017) highlights the embrace of such attitudes even by black political leaders.[41] Similarly, Clegg and Usmani, investigating the impact of race on the adoption of punitive policies and incarceration outcomes, conclude that the available "evidence supports a revisionist view which emphasizes that crime [also] shaped black preferences."[42]

The supposed link between specifically American mass incarceration rates and racist intentions is also challenged by comparative cross-national and historical observations. Tonry noted that England, Australia, and Canada all had larger black-to-white inmate ratios than the United States in 1994.[43] Cases drawn from varied histories, cultures, and contexts suggest that, as a general matter, economically disadvantaged ethnic minorities tend to be over-represented in prison populations. Disparate impact may be an inherent component of imprisonment. However, existing rates of racial disparity, though disconcerting, are not prima facie evidence that racism operates as a foundational or predominant cause of prison growth.

IV. The Government Failure Model of Imprisonment

In this section, I develop a preliminary framework for understanding imprisonment as a form of government failure. Furthermore, I argue that this alternative paradigm better accords with the historical and contemporary evidence related to prison population rates. The government failure model posits that prison outcomes are related to the organizational patterns of different criminal justice institutions.

A large and consistent body of theory and research explains the relationships between the dynamics of alternative internal decision-making processes and the effectiveness of these processes across differently organized institutions. First, the concentration of organizational hierarchies within governments helps to explain how effectively decision-making processes promote economic growth.[44] Differently organized systems vary in their respective potentials for error correction and feedback. With discretionary authority concentrated in more centralized decision-making nodes, hierarchies tend to find it more difficult to identify and respond to errors than do polycentric systems.[45] More hierarchical organizations thus tend to err more by suppressing otherwise "good" proposals, whereas polycentric systems err more by permitting a greater number of "bad" proposals.[46] Furthermore, hierarchical bureaucracies tend to suffer from greater inefficiencies resulting from rent-seeking and capture.[47]

Can we extend this general account of institutional dynamics to account for imprisonment outcomes? What are the relevant decision-making processes and how do these processes deal with ineffective or otherwise undesirable policy proposals in the criminal justice context? What alternative responses to criminal behavior might help to avoid and or reduce mass incarceration outcomes?

A credible organizational theory of imprisonment should carry some verifiable implications. We should expect that social environments with more centrally managed criminal justice systems would feature more challenging processes of error correction and greater proneness to bureaucratic inefficiencies and rent-seeking when compared with polycentric alternatives. Polycentric criminal justice systems would err more in so far as they made possible a variety of criminal justice regimes that did not necessarily preempt or alleviate mass incarceration, and some jurisdictions within polycentric systems could also perhaps be expected to punish insufficiently. Furthermore, hierarchically centralized criminal justice systems would err by suppressing punishment strategies that could otherwise successfully avoid or reduce mass incarceration.

Before investigating these specific implications, we must first understand patterns of institutional organization through history and across countries more adequately. Which social environments possess more hierarchical criminal justice systems and which possess more decentralized structures, and how is the existence of such structures correlated with known patterns of imprisonment? Two groups of sources provide relevant details. First, qualitative histories can reveal the institutional breadth and variety of social environments prior to the development and proliferation of incarceration and prior to the recording and accumulation of accurate imprisonment measures. Second, we have reasonably accurate and detailed empirics related to contemporary imprisonment trends across a relatively wide variety of countries.

While the social control model emphasizes the apparent connection between the invention and proliferation of imprisonment on the one hand and industrialization on the other, the government failure model recognizes that governmental institutions were organized in substantially different ways before and after the origins of the prison and the emergence of industrial society. A consistent pattern of decentralized and informal institutional processes is evident in multiple pre-modern and primitive social contexts. The relevant features include consistent legal standards, graduated sanctions against criminal behaviors, sustainable social orders, and restitution-based penalties.[48] As governments became more formalized as city-states, monarchies, and feudal arrangements, so too did the powers of criminal law enforcement become more monopolized by governments.[49] Hence, when we look comparatively at pre-modern stateless societies on the one hand and early feudal and city state environments on the other, we see the initial predictions of the government failure model supported. Stateless environments featuring informal and decentralized governance processes possessed a variety of punitive norms but lacked large-scale incarceration. Punishment by imprisonment does not seem to have been a prominent response to crime in such environments.

As organizational theory predicts, the effectiveness and desirability of punitive norms and outcomes across individual localities within and across polycentric jurisdictions is a mixed bag. On the one hand, pre-modern punitive norms found within such legal rules orders as Hammurabi's code, Draconian law, and the *Ancien Régime* are well recognized as mandating excessive responses to minor violations. Inversely, it is also well understood that such systems essentially underprotected the rights of members of the lower classes.[50] The early dispersed networks of frontier spaces in the new world similarly lacked the enforcement and policing potentials associated with the later rise of centrally coordinated oversight and federal authority.[51] The operations and outcomes of early, formalized state governments are also consistent with the predictions of basic organizational theory. With the emergence of widespread punishment by imprisonment, state authorities were capable of expanding their legislative discretion, taxing powers, and territorial reach.[52]

To further investigate the implications of organizational theory requires broadening the sample of comparative imprisonment contexts. The organizational forms of contemporary nation-states are more varied than those observed in the early modern legal era. The structures of contemporary nation-states exhibit a broad range of varied organizational characteristics, though there are no precise quantitative metrics of the hierarchical or decentralized character of a government. As D'Amico and Williamson demonstrate,[53] legal origin categories, more than any other organizational characteristics, are strongly and robustly correlated with imprisonment outcomes. As is well documented, such categories serve as reliable proxies for significant organizational features across countries.[54] Contemporary nation-states founded on and committed to the common law possess significantly greater incarceration rates than German civil law, French civil law, or Scandinavian civil law societies.[55] Beyond common-law countries, nations with the longest experiences under communism incarcerate people at the highest levels.

At first glance, the correlation between common legal origins and greater prison population rates appears at odds with basic organizational theory. Common-law countries typically embrace more decentralized organizational patterns such as competitive market economies and stronger protections against corruption and rent-seeking.[56] By contrast, as La Porta, Lopez-de-Silanes, and Shleifer indicate, "civil law is associated with a heavier hand of government ownership and regulation."[57] Yet it appears that this typical relationship between the size of centralized governments and legal origins is inverted with regards to imprisonment outcomes.

To account for the common law's decentralized structure and superior economic performance, Glaeser and Shleifer highlight long evolutionary histories in the course of which decentralized institutions were periodically re-affirmed and re-enforced amidst political and cultural revolutions.[58] Hence, D'Amico and Williamson investigated the long historical processes of institutional selection regarding specifically criminal justice policies, practices, and norms across England, France, and the United States.[59] The organizational patterns typically found within market- and civic-oriented legal processes under the respective common- and civil-law traditions are inverted within the criminal justice systems of each. Criminal justice administration under the common law in the British and American experiences has been a long history of continual centralization. By contrast, persistent decentralization is evident in France. The civic and commercial legal sector in civil-law countries fostered more centralized interventions, rent-seeking, and suppressed economic performance, whereas criminal justice institutions were shaped by stronger commitments to local autonomy and decentralization. Similar observations were made by theorists as early as Beaumont and Tocqueville,[60] and have been reaffirmed more recently by Stuntz and by Hinton. Such sources suggest that the effectiveness of the American criminal justice system is largely dependent on the decentralization of enforcement authority across more localized jurisdictions.

In result, the government failure model leverages institutional theory and criminal legal history to outline a rudimentary organizational centralization spectrum that is applicable indifferent national contexts and that consistently illuminates different nations' respective imprisonment patterns. See Figure 28.1 below.

On the far left side of the spectrum are those societies—for instance, primitive and stateless ones—with both the lowest prison population rates and the most decentralized administrative institutions of criminal justice. On the far right end of the spectrum are those societies—totalitarian regimes, say—with the highest rates of imprisonment and the most intensive forms of institutional centralization.

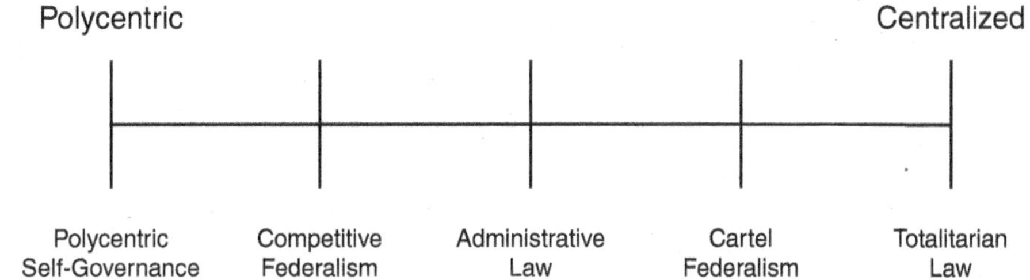

Figure 28.1 Spectrum of legal organization

A consistent arrangement of some intermediate cases within these end points is evident. Polycentric systems that still feature states, such as the overlapping and competing jurisdictions operative in the Anglo-Saxon territories prior to the emergence of the British monarchy, the early American colonies, and the contemporary Swiss cantons are all relatively more centralized than fully stateless orders but still exhibit substantial levels of decentralization. I label this sample of cases "competitive federalism."

Further towards the centralization end of the spectrum are contemporary civil-law jurisdictions such as France, Germany, and the Scandinavian countries. I label these "administrative law" societies. Contemporary common-law countries fit *between* these administrative-law societies and totalitarian societies. These societies were originally decentralized, marked by competitive federalism. However, the criminal justice processes within contemporary common-law jurisdictions, especially the United States, became extremely centralized amidst broader trends of cartel federalism during the latter half of the twentieth century.[61] This framework suggests a consistent relationship between organizational centralization and prison population rates. As criminal justice decision-making becomes more centralized and hierarchical, rent-seeking and bureaucratic growth increase. Simultaneously, discovering, designing, and experimenting with alternative punitive strategies becomes more costly in such cartelized environments than in either the more competitively federalist conditions that preceded them or in civil-law jurisdictions.

The government failure model does not directly contradict to the social control model or its particular implication. Rather, it emphasizes alternative factors as more primarily relevant to the patterns of incarceration and prison growth around the world and throughout history. Whereas the extreme incarceration tendencies of socialist regimes and the potentials of social order observed in stateless environments cannot be consistently accounted for by the social control model, the government failure model does not require ad hoc adjustment in light of these observed features.

V. Conclusion

The governmental failure model is more consistent with the patterns of imprisonment observed around the world and over time relative to the more dominant social control model. These paradigms are not entirely in conflict with one another. However, there are facets of the historical and comparative record that cannot be fully explained from the vantage point of the social control model, but that are well accounted for by the government failure model. In particular, imprisonment was not as tightly linked to the Industrial Revolution or the British experience as many have presumed, nor does any empirical evidence support a consistent relationship between imprisonment and capitalism. Imprisonment emerged across a variety of social settings in consistent conjunction with the rise and formalization of state authority. In addition, most of the contemporary states with the highest imprisonment rates are nations that endured longer socialist experiences. A consistent spectrum demarcating the organizational properties of criminal justice institutions maps neatly onto the broad sample of incarceration patterns. Communities with more centralized criminal justice institutions tend to foster larger prison population rates.

While the available evidence does not allow confident causal or predictive inferences, the alternative frameworks do have substantially different implications for practical reform strategies. The social control model conveniently implies a need for traditional forms of democratic action. In the face of systemic power imbalances and class-based or racial bias, activist efforts to raise awareness, coordinate voting coalitions, and request legislative reforms from elected officials are the most obvious paths towards positive change. Efforts of this sort have taken place in the United States since at least the mid 1980s, yet mass imprisonment has continued to grow. Today, the national trend has essentially plateaued, with the most tangible cases of successful reform happening at the state level.

The government failure model is less sanguine about the effects of traditional political activism, as electoral political action is less capable of reshaping the organizational dynamics of the criminal justice system writ large. Furthermore, if increased centralization is a significant contributing factor to prison growth, we must inquire if any relationship exists between traditional democratic activism and the potentials for institutional centralization. As Murakawa has noted, support in the United States for consistent tendencies towards centralized criminal justice authority at the federal level and the increased professionalization of police have transcended partisan divides. Opportunities for structural change thus tend to be more limited to instances of exogenous shock or crises.[62]

Though it does not yield tangible reform strategies, the government failure model features substantial implications for the more normative political philosophy of punishment. Whereas the vast majority of justificatory frameworks for criminal punishment begin by assuming the legitimacy of formal state authority, the government failure model exhibits predictive power with respect to both traditional states and stateless societies. Formal governance can be recognized as a step towards the centralization of criminal justice administration. Thus, the government failure model offers a substantial challenge that any justificatory paradigm of criminal punishment must address. How can punitive institutions be arranged justly and effectively given the real potentials for errors of excessive imprisonment? If the potential for abuse is an inherent, inevitable feature of more centralized forms of governance, then any justifications for state legitimacy or the role of punitive authority must take account of this potential. Challenging mass incarceration, then, may seem to prompt critical questions about the state itself.

Notes

1 M. Cavadino and J. Dignan, *Penal Systems: A Comparative Approach* (np: Sage, 2005), 3–30; J. Brodeur, "Comparative Penology in Perspective," *Crime and Justice* 36 (2007): 49–91; N. Lacey, *The Prisoners' Dilemma: Political Economy and Punishment in Contemporary Democracies* (Cambridge: Cambridge UP, 2008) 3–55.

2 Clegg and Usmani (2018, 2) identify Alexander (2012), "cited over 6,000 times in just six years," Garland (2002), "cited 9,000 times," and Western (2007), with "2,345 citations," as the sources contributing most substantially to this more popular framework. J. Clegg and A. Usmani, "The Racial Politics of the Punitive Turn" (2018), https://papers.ssrn.com/sol3/papers.cfm?abstract_id=3025670; M. Alexander, *The New Jim Crow: Mass Incarceration in the Age of Colorblindness* (New York, NY: New P, 2012); D. Garland, *The Culture of Control: Crime and Social Order in Contemporary Society* (2002); B. Western, *Punishment and Inequality in America* (New York, NY: Russell Sage Foundation, 2007).

3 See W. Stuntz, *The Collapse of American Criminal Justice* (Cambridge, MA: Harvard UP, 2011); E. Hinton, *From the War on Poverty to the War on Crime: The Making of Mass Incarceration in America* (Cambridge, MA: Harvard UP, 2017); D. D'Amico and C. Williamson, "The Punitive Consequences of Organizational Structures in England, France and the United States," *Journal of Institutional Economics* (forthcoming).

4 It is worth noting that this essay presumes as a starting point of investigation that "mass incarceration" or exceptionally high prison population rates observed in recent decades (especially within the United States) are at least concerning and likely socially inefficient. While writing amidst the peak of American mass incarceration, economic historian Robert Higgs pointedly explained a possible worst-case scenario: "if the total incarcerated population were to continue to grow by 7.3% annually, it would double approximately every ten years .... Hence in the decade of the 2080s, within the lifetime of many people already born, the prison population would overtake the total population." R. Higgs, *Against Leviathan: Government Power and a Free Society* (Oakland, CA: Independent Institute, 2005) 96.

5 Duff (2017) explains that, despite the fact that "insufficient attention is paid [to it] in the philosophical literature," "in principle, the abolitionist challenge is one that must be met, rather than ignored; and it will help to remind us of the ways in which any practice of legal punishment is bound to be morally problematic." A. Duff, "Legal Punishment," *Stanford Encyclopedia of Philosophy* (2017), https://plato.stanford.edu/entries/legal-punishment/#PunCriSta.

6 D. Boonin, *The Problem of Punishment* (Cambridge: Cambridge UP, 2008).

7 M. Pennington, *Robust Political Economy: Classical Liberalism and the Future of Public Policy* (Cheltenham: Edward Elgar, 2011)

8 E. Glaeser, "An Overview of Crime and Punishment" (2000), World Bank, www.worldbank.org.

9 M. Foucault, *Discipline & Punish: The Birth of the Prison* (New York, NY: Vintage Books, 1975).

10 J. Bentham, *Panopticon* (London: T. Payne, 1791).

11 Foucault 21.

12 Defending the panopticon, Bentham writes explicitly: "morals reformed—health preserved—industry invigorated—instruction diffused—public burthens lightened—Economy seated, as it were, upon a rock—the Gordian knot of the Poor—Laws are not cut, but untied—all by a simple idea in Architecture!"

13 B. Benson, "The Development of Criminal Law and its Enforcement: Public Interest or Political Transfers?" *Journal des Economistes et des Etudes Humaines* 3.1 (1992): 79–108.

14 G. Rusche and O. Kirchheimer, *Punishment and Social Structure* (New York, NY: Columbia UP, 1939).

15 Foucault 24.

16 L. Wacquant, *Punishing the Poor: The Neoliberal Government of Social Insecurity* (Durham, NC: Duke UP, 2009); L. Wacquant, *Prisons of Poverty* (Minneapolis, MN: U of Minnesota P, 2010); D. Garland, *Punishment and Modern Society: A Study in Social Theory* (Chicago, IL: U of Chicago P, 1993).

17 R. Walmsley, "Global Incarceration and Prison Trends," *Forum on Crime and Society* 3.1–2 (2003): 65–78.

18 Wacquant, *Punishing*; B. Harcourt, *The Illusion of Free Markets: Punishment and the Myth of Natural Order* (Cambridge, MA: Harvard UP, 2012).

19 P. Mirowski, *Machine Dreams: Economics Becomes a Cyborg Science* (Cambridge: Cambridge UP, 2002).

20 Cavadino and Dignan; Lacey.

21 P. Enns, *Incarceration Nation: How the United States Became the Most Punitive Democracy in the World* (Cambridge: Cambridge UP, 2016).

22 O. Wasow, "Do Protest Tactics Matter? Evidence from the 1960s Black Insurgency" (2017), working manuscript.

23 Clegg and Usmani 1–2.

24 P. Spierenburg, *The Prison Experience: Disciplinary Institutions and Their Inmates in Early Modern Europe* (New Brunswick, NJ: Rutgers UP, 1991).

25 Coyne and Hall explain how contemporary police forces have become technologically enhanced with advanced weaponry and vehicles as a result of increased military expenditures. Similarly, Styles has documented how urban policing strategies in newly industrialized London mimicked colonial tactics used to suppress indigenous uprisings. C. Coyne and A. Hall, "Foreign Intervention, Police Militarization, and the Impact on Minority Groups," *Peace Review* 28 (2016): 165–70; J. Styles, "The Emergence of the Police—Explaining Police Reform in the Eighteenth and Nineteenth Century England," *British Journal of Criminology* 27.1 (1987): 15–22.

26 While texts from diverse perspectives reflect concern regarding crime and social order amidst industrialization, market oriented, enlightenment thinkers were also noted critics of the relevant tough-on-crime politics of their era (see: Mandeville). Contemporary evidence suggests that heightened concerns with crime were largely unwarranted; as Beattie has shown, crime declined more quickly and substantially in newly urbanized industrial centers than in their rural counterparts. B. Mandeville, *An Enquiry into the Causes of the Frequent Executions at Tyburn: And a Proposal for Some Regulations concerning Felons in Prison, and the Good Effects to Be Expected from Them* (Ann Arbor, MI: U of Michigan Library, 1725); J. Beattie, *Crime and the Courts in England 1660–1800* (New York, NY: Oxford UP, 1986).

27 D. Rothman, *The Discovery of the Asylum: Social Order and Disorder in the New Republic* (Boston, MA: Little Brown, 1971).
28 E. Peters, "Prison Before the Prison: The Ancient and Medieval Worlds," *The Oxford History of the Prison: The Practice of Punishment in Western Society*, ed. N. Morris and D. Rothman (New York, NY: Oxford UP, 1998) 3–43; D. Allen, *The World of Prometheus: The Politics of Punishing in Democratic Athens* (Princeton, NJ: Princeton UP, 2002); D. D'Amico, "The Prison in Economics: Private and Public Incarceration in Ancient Greece," *Public Choice* 145.3–4 (2010): 461–82.
29 T. Flanagan and D. Longmire, eds., *Americans View Crime and Justice: A National Public Opinion Survey* (Thousand Oaks, CA: Sage, 1996); Enns.
30 Cavadino and Dignan; Lacey.
31 Cavadino and Dignan 15–16. Reflecting contemporary assumptions about neoliberalism, Wikipedia links neoliberalism "with an increase in human trafficking, the traumatization of the working classes, 'belligerent capitalism,' and high incarceration rates in the U.S. which aim at 'keeping unemployment statistics low, and stimulating economic growth through maintaining a contemporary slave population within the U.S. and promoting prison construction and militarized policing.'" B. Caldwell, "The Chicago School, Hayek, and Neoliberalism" (2000), https://papers.ssrn.com/sol3/papers.cfm?abstract_id=1356899. Thus it is not only the case that neoliberalism is presented as a causal explanation of mass incarceration, but also that, for some, mass incarceration is inherently baked into the meaning of neoliberal ideology.
32 R. Soares, "Crime Reporting as a Measure of Institutional Development," *Economic Development and Cultural Change* 52 (2004): 851–71; R. Soares, "Development, Crime and Punishment: Accounting for the International Differences in Crime Rates," *Journal of Development Economics* 73 (2004): 155–84.
33 Rusche and Kirchheimer.
34 T. Chiricos and M. Delone, "Labor Surplus and Punishment: A Review and Assessment of Theory and Evidence," *Social Problems*, 39 (1992): 421–46; T. Marvel and C. Moody, "Prison Population Growth and Crime Reduction," *Journal of Quantitative Criminology* 10 (1994): 109–40.
35 J. Sutton, "The Political Economy of Imprisonment in Affluent Western Democracies, 1960–1990," *American Sociological Review* 69 (2004): 170–89.
36 J. Neapolitan, "An Examination of Cross-National Variation in Punitiveness," *International Journal of Offender Therapy and Comparative Criminology* 45 (2001): 691–710; J. Sutton, "Imprisonment and Social Classification in Five Common-Law Democracies, 1960–1985," *American Journal of Sociology* 106 (2000): 350–86; Sutton, "Political Economy"; R. Ruddell, "Social Disruption, State Priorities, and Minority Threat," *Punishment and Society* 7 (2005): 7–28.
37 D. D'Amico and C. Williamson, "Do Legal Origins Affect Cross-Country Incarceration Rates?" *Journal of Comparative Economics* 43.3 (2015): 595–612. Furthermore, freer market economies are associated with lower homicide rates (Stringham and Levendis), greater reporting of crimes to police authorities (Soares), and a wide variety of standard proxies for human well being (Gwartney, Lawson, and Hall). E. Stringham and J. Levendis, "The Relationship between Economic Freedom and Homicide," *The Economic Freedom of the World: Annual Report*, ed. J. Gwartney, R. Lawson, and J. Hall (Vancouver: Fraser Institute, 2010): 203–18; Soares, "Crime Reporting"; J. Gwartney, R. Lawson, and J. Hall, *The Economic Freedom of the World: Annual Report.* (Vancouver: Fraser Institute, 2017).
38 Enns.
39 Beckett 1999.
40 N. Murakawa, *The First Civil Right: How Liberals Built Prison America* (New York, NY: Oxford UP, 2014).
41 Forman Jr 2017.
42 Clegg and Usmani 2018.
43 M. Tonry, "Racial Disproportion in U.S. Prisons," *British Journal of Criminology* 34.5 (1994): 97–115.
44 D. North, *Institutions, Institutional Change and Economic Performance* (New York, NY: Cambridge UP, 1990); O. Williamson, *The Economic Institutions of Capitalism* (New York, NY: Free, 1998).
45 J. McGinnis, ed., *Polycentricity and Local Public Economies: Readings from the Workshop in Political Theory and Policy Analysis* (Ann Arbor, MI: U of Michigan P, 1999).
46 R. Sah and J. Stiglitz, "The Architecture of Economic Systems: Hierarchies and Polyarchies," *American Economic Review* 76.4 (1986): 716–27.
47 W. Niskanen, *Bureaucracy and Public Economics* (Edinburgh: Edward Elgar, 1994); G. Tullock, *Bureaucracy* (Indianapolis, IN: Liberty Fund, 2005).
48 D. Friedman, "Private Creation and Enforcement of Law—A Historical Case," *Journal of Legal Studies* 8.2 (1979): 399–415; R. Posner, "A Theory of Primitive Society, with Special Reference to Primitive Law," *Journal of Law and Economics* 23.1 (1980): 1–53; P. Leeson, "Pirates, Prisoners, and Preliterates: Anarchic Context and the Private Enforcement of Law," *European Journal of Law and Economics* 37.3 (2014): 365–79.

49 F. Pollock and F. Maitland, *The History of English Law before the Time of Edward I*, 2 vols. (Indianapolis, IN: Liberty Fund, 1898); T. Plucknett, *A Concise History of the Common Law* (Indianapolis, IN: Liberty Fund, 1929); Benson.

50 Allen.

51 Rothman; L. Friedman, *Crime and Punishment in American History* (New York, NY: Basic Books, 1994).

52 D'Amico, "Prison."

53 D'Amico and Williamson, "Punitive Consequences."

54 R. La Porta, F. Lopez-de-Silanes, and A. Shleifer, "The Economic Consequences of Legal Origins," *Journal of Economic Literature* 46.2 (2008): 285–332.

55 H. Spamann, "Legal Origins, Civil Procedure, and the Quality of Contract Enforcement," *Journal of Institutional and Theoretical Economics* 166.1 (2010): 149–65; M. DeMichele, "Using Weber's Rechtssoziologie to Explain Western Punishment: A Typological Framework," *European Journal of Crime, Criminal Law and Criminal Justice* 21.1 (2013): 85–109; M. DeMichele, "A Panel Analysis of Legal Culture, Political Economics, and Punishment among 15 Western Countries, 1960–2010," *International Criminal Justice Review* (2014).

56 F. Hayek, *The Constitution of Liberty* (Chicago, IL: U of Chicago P 1960).

57 La Porta, Lopez-de-Silanes, and Shleifer 286.

58 E. Glaeser and A. Shleifer, "Legal Origins," *Quarterly Journal of Economics* 107.4 (2002): 1193–1229.

59 D'Amico and Williamson, "Punitive Consequences."

60 G. Beaumont and A. Tocqueville, *On the Penitentiary System in the United States, and Its Application to France: With an Appendix on Penal Colonies* (New York, NY: Augustus M. Kelley, 1833).

61 M. Greve, *The Upside-Down Constitution* (Cambridge, MA: Harvard UP 2012).

62 T. Yeager, *Institutions, Transition Economies, and Economic Development* (New York, NY: Westview, 1999).

29
THE PROBLEMS OF CENTRAL PLANNING IN MILITARY TECHNOLOGY

Abigail R. Hall

I. Introduction

The United States vastly outpaces all other countries on military expenditures. In 2015, global military spending amounted to some $1.6 trillion. U.S. outlays represented 37% of this total.[1] The United States spent nearly $650 billion on military-related expenses in 2018—more than China, Saudi Arabia, India, France, Russia, the United Kingdom, and Germany combined.[2] The Trump administration proposed a military budget of $716 billion for fiscal year (FY) 2019 and the budget for FY 2020 was projected to be some $733 billion.[3]

The influence of the U.S. military extends beyond monetary expenditures. The U.S. armed forces maintain a presence on five continents, with some seventy countries hosting approximately 800 U.S. military bases.[4] The military's real estate portfolio includes some "562,000 facilities ... covering over 24.7 million acres."[5] At the end of FY 2014, U.S. Special Operations Forces operated in more than 130 countries—about 70% of *all* nations on the globe.[6]

The United States also occupies a critical role in the development and dissemination of military technology. For instance, it serves as the world's primary arms dealer. The United States engaged in $55.6 billion in foreign military sales during FY 2018—representing a 33% increase from 2017.[7] The country provides more weapons to developed and developing countries than any other nation. In 2015, for example, the United States agreed to some $40.2 billion in arms agreements with developing nations—50.29% of the market.[8]

The development of military technology is a cornerstone of contemporary policy. Technological innovation is a core component of the Third Offset Strategy of the U.S. military. An offset strategy is a "long-term, competitive strategy ... that aims to generate and sustain strategic advantage."[9] The Third Offset Strategy seeks to leverage the development and integration of technology into the military more than ever before, including the extended use of network-enabled weapons, human-machine collaboration and combat teams, and "deep-learning" systems.[10]

A variety of scholars and policymakers have supported such a strategy and the further development and dissemination of military technologies. The position of the United States as primary global arms supplier, for instance, is viewed by many as a way to secure national security objectives and maintain international stability and regional power balances. It's further argued that by supplying the majority of arms, countries like the United States can push developing nations toward developing other industries as opposed to armaments manufacture.[11] Scholars in economics, political science, and military studies have called for the United States to embrace (what is viewed by some as) its position as an empire and to act as a global hegemon. They posit that doing so would lead to enhanced global financial stability, spark higher exports, promote peace, and allow for the further provision of putative public goods.[12]

My purpose in this chapter is to highlight some of the fundamental problems underlying contemporary scholarship concerned with military provision, paying particular attention to difficulties with the development and implementation of military technology. I highlight the existing literature that questions the dominant frameworks surrounding the provision and execution of military policies as a whole. I seek to advance this discussion by examining issues related to military technology, arguing that military activities as a whole are prone to two distinctive but complementary problems. Issues of the first sort—*planner problems*—result from insufficient knowledge and an inability to perform rational economic calculation outside of the context of markets. Issues of the second sort—*perverse incentives*—stem from issues related to political economy.

I contribute primarily to three strands of literature. First, I contribute to the broader field of defense and peace economics.[13] Within this arena, I seek to expand upon the criticisms related to the dominant models of defense provision. This work most closely relates to Coyne's critiques of the underlying assumptions of defense and peace economics and my work with Coyne related to "non-comprehensive planning."[14] I expand upon this discussion by utilizing the frameworks laid out by Mises, Hayek, and Buchanan regarding incentive and knowledge problems.[15] I apply these ideas to specific examples from U.S. military technology. Second, this work contributes to the overall discussion of the unintended overlooked costs of conflict by highlighting ways in which officials are unlikely to systematically develop "optimal" military technologies.[16] Third, I contribute to the growing literature on the economics of anarchy and national defense.[17] "Defense" is often utilized as the textbook example of a "pure public good." As such, standard economic theory indicates that defense or military services will be underprovided by the market. When discussing the government provision of defense, however, it is often assumed that the centralized provision of military and defense services will be done in an economically optimal sense. This research calls this assumption into question this assumption.

In the rest of the chapter, I proceed as follows. In Section II, I provide a brief overview of the dominant narrative regarding military activity and discuss the existing criticisms of this research. In Section III, I lay out two fundamental problems with the development and implementation of military technology. I discuss the limited knowledge of military planners and analyze the problem of economic calculation in implementing top-down military programs. I investigate the political economy of the military sector, considering the incentives faced by the military and other actors responsible for military activities and ways in which these issues contribute to problems within the military sector. I conclude in Section IV.

II. Military Technology and the Assumed Public Interest

When discussing the construction and execution of military policy, the literature largely assumes that those involved set aside their own goals and instead work to serve some greater "public interest." More specifically, it's assumed that benevolent agents seek to maximize some larger societal welfare function. This welfare function includes, among other things, the provision of national defense. Policymakers, acting as a rational collective body, allocate resources in a way that maximizes the value of national defense (i.e. provides the best possible protection for citizens) as part of overall societal welfare.

Within this framework, public actors are motivated to please the general public—their "employers." Further, the actions of policymakers are reinforced by appropriate feedback mechanisms.[18] If a public official fails to maximize defense or other resources, for example, the theory indicates that the official in question will be appropriately "punished" by the citizenry (e.g. removed from office). It follows from these assumptions that the creation of military policy and the execution of military activities benefit society as a whole rather than a subset of actors. Moreover, this framework implies that resources are always allocated efficiently.

Examining the literature related to defense and peace economics, Coyne highlights this and several other common assumptions.[19] He notes that the vast majority of analyses related to defense assume that (1) defense is a pure public good and will be underprovided by the market, (2) state-provided defense is always "good" and beneficial to society, (3) the state provides the optimal quality and quantity of defense, (4) state defense expenditures are always value-added, and (5) state defense activities are neutral with respect to domestic political institutions. To further clarify and assess these assumptions, Coyne employs Buchanan's discussion of conflicting theories of public finance—the "organismic view" and the "individualistic view."[20] The organismic view, according to Buchanan, models the state as a singular unit that acts as a "fiscal brain" in order to maximize social welfare. The second theory, the "individualistic view," instead focuses analytically on individual decision-makers and their interactions within particular institutional constraints. In stark contrast to the organismic view, this theory treats public finance outcomes as emergent. In contrast to the organismic view, the individualistic view holds that "the state" is not some singular entity seeking to fulfill its own ends. Instead, the state comprises individuals with their own goals and aspirations. It follows from this view that the outcomes of political actions will only benefit society if the incentives facing policymakers align with the goals of the broader public. Building on this individualistic view, Coyne argues that much of the literature in defense and peace economics is fundamentally flawed.

If the dominant assumptions of the literature hold, then the conjectures made regarding optimal provision, institutional neutrality, etc., should in some way be empirically verifiable. Research indicates, however, that there is a profound disconnect between what *should* be seen if a benevolent social welfare maximizer were responsible for defense provision and what is actually observed. In previous work, for example, I have analyzed how policies with respect to the development and use of unmanned aerial vehicles (UAVs) are assumed to serve the public interest. The empirical evidence, however, conflicts with this view.[21] Others have examined similar issues within the area of defense, though academic analyses are uncommon.[22]

III. Further Problems with the Provision of Military Technology

In addition to the problems noted above, two issues—planner problems and perverse incentives—further complicate the provision of military technology. Scholars have noted such issues are present in a number of areas, including economic development.[23] I examine each of these issues in turn.

A. Planner Problems with Military Technology

In order to understand the problems of planning within the context of national defense, it is first necessary to appreciate the problems with state-led (centralized) planning more generally. Simply, such planning runs afoul of the need for effective economic calculation—which is required in order to answer the fundamental economic question of how to allocate finite resources toward their highest-valued use in an arena of infinite possibilities.

Mises examined the problem of economic calculation and planner problems in relation to socialism.[24] He argued that the ability to engage in economic calculation under socialism is impossible. The abolition of private property rights in the means of production inhibits the creation of a functioning market and monetary prices. Absent prices reflecting the relative scarcities of capital goods, decision-makers are unable to engage in rational economic calculation. It follows from this analysis that the market process, within a system of pricing reflective of relative scarcities, along with profit and loss signals that encourage the discovery and correction of errors, is essential for driving scarce resources to their highest-valued uses.

Adding to the critique elaborated by Mises, Hayek argued that the nature of knowledge further disallows economic calculation under socialism.[25] Neither a single individual, nor any group of individuals, can construct a rational economic order through central planning, because doing so requires the knowledge of many people. Individuals possess distinct knowledge of "time and place."[26] It is the interaction of many individuals within the context of market competition that allows for the process of discovery needed to determine how to allocate resources. For Hayek, no group of central planners can engage in rational economic calculation because there is no comparable discovery mechanism outside of the market context.

Mises and Hayek intended their critiques to contribute to a broader discussion in academic, political, and social discourse regarding the capabilities of socialism in general. These critiques are, however, thoroughly applicable to particular instances of central planning—to, for instance, planning related to military technology. Just as those who support central planning argued that various mechanisms would work to allocate resources appropriately in a centrally planned economy, many within the military sector often purport to have developed feedback mechanisms in which those operating at the top of the relevant organizational structures (i.e. those in charge of funding decisions) are appropriately informed of the needs and capabilities of those at lower levels. Through these supposed mechanisms (namely trial and error), top officials are able to develop and implement programs, evaluate them effectively, and reallocate resources in order more effectively to meet the needs of the military and, ultimately, the broader public.

The bureaucratic structure of the military (discussed further below), however, is no substitute for the discovery procedure of the market. Although the government undoubtedly has access to information pertaining to military technologies, officials still lack crucial pieces of knowledge. In order to effectively engage in economic calculation, officials would need to possess knowledge regarding which projects should be implemented to achieve the desired goals, when these projects should be implemented, where the projects would prove most effective, and which projects are most likely to generate the best outcomes. While the answer to these and other questions would be provided in a market setting via competition and profit and loss signals, military planners are at a loss to determine these answers effectively.

These planner problems are further compounded because policymakers are unable to ascertain the secondary effects of the policies they adopt. Those involved in planning and implementing foreign military interventions, for instance, tend to view the world in linear fashion and to exhibit extreme confidence in their ability to solve complex problems.[27] That is, they identify a problem, formulate a solution, and work to implement it. While this kind of approach may be appropriate in some fields (e.g. engineering), it is positively disastrous when it comes to military policy. Policymakers are unable to account for the infinite complexity of the social, political, and economic relationships in the context of which military technologies are introduced and used. Planners simply cannot know how the creation and introduction of military technologies in one arena will impact the broader system of military activity. Their inescapable ignorance leads to serious unintended consequences.

Examples of knowledge failures in the creation and implementation of military technology abound. Consider the use of the Global Hawk Block 30 and other UAVs employed extensively in the "war on terror." The technology was initially touted as (among other things) a means of reducing harm to military personnel. Since UAVs are, by definition, unmanned, policymakers pushed forward with the extended use of UAV technology. What policymakers were unable to foresee, however, was that the use of UAVs would ultimately require *more* "boots on the ground," as their employment necessitated the involvement of "ground pilots," surveillance analysts, maintenance personnel, and other operators.[28] Many of the necessary functions require individuals to be in close proximity to UAVs rather than safely out of harm's way. Policymakers were also unable to anticipate the psychological effects of involvement in UAV combat. The Department of Defense (DOD) has found that drone operators have experienced mental health problems at the same rate as conventional pilots.[29] The Air Force reported that nearly half of UAV operators reported high levels of "operational stress," and some 25% showed signs of "clinical distress," depression, anxiety, or other problems severe enough to impact their family lives and job performances.[30] Former UAV pilot Brandon Bryant reported:

> I felt like a coward because I was halfway across the world … I was haunted by a legion of the dead. My physical health was gone, my mental health was crumbled. I was in so much pain I was ready to eat a bullet myself.[31]

In addition to these problems, policymakers could not predict how UAV technology would come to be used domestically. Coyne and I have highlighted this additional unforeseen consequence of UAV use abroad, documenting at length how UAV technology has come to be employed in a variety of domestic contexts, in ways that have led to serious encroachments on the civil liberties of U.S. citizens.[32]

Some advocates are quick to point out the benefits of military technology as a counter to the sorts of criticisms I've noted, citing inventions like the Internet, microwaves, and Jeeps. But the point of the criticisms is not that the military sector is incapable of creating useful materials, but instead that, absent the mechanisms made possible by private property rights, prices, and profit and loss, the DOD cannot consistently choose successful projects with respect to military technology. Furthermore, the supposed benefits of military technology may be impossible effectively to calculate. Robert Higgs, for example, highlights ways in which the use of standard measures of economic activity proves difficult or impossible when it comes to discussing activities related to the military, particularly those taking place during state-driven wars.[33] He challenges the standard view of "war prosperity" and the idea that World War II "got the economy out of the Depression," noting that prices under a command-and-control economy do not reflect relative scarcities or consumer preferences.

B. Perverse Incentives Related to Military Technology

The inability to engage in rational economic calculation is not the only problem facing key decision-makers with respect to the development and use of military technology. Another difficulty flows from the economics of bureaucracy. A bureaucracy is a "specific form of organization defined by complexity[,] … hierarchical coordination and control, [a] strict chain of command, and legal authority …. In its ideal form, bureaucracy is impersonal … and based on rules."[34] There is perhaps no clearer example of a bureaucratic organization than the DOD. The Secretary of Defense heads the department, subordinate only to the President and (nominally) Congress. Beneath the Secretary, each military branch is headed by its own secretary. Substantial influence is also exerted independently by the Joint Chiefs of Staff. Each of these entities is served by a variety of additional managers—not to mention the entirety of the U.S. fighting force, along with the various specialist agencies (e.g. the Defense Advanced Research Projects Agency) and combatant commands (e.g. CENTCOM, AFRICOM).

Unlike firms operating within the context of the free market, bureaus operating within and at the behest of the government do not compete for profits, but instead compete against other agencies for government resources. Absent the profit and loss mechanisms of the market, bureaucratic institutions must rely on other metrics to gauge their successes. Existing literature on this topic points namely to two primary metrics by means of which a bureaucratic entity's success is characteristically measured—(1) the size of its total or discretionary budget and (2) the number of subordinate personnel it employs.[35] The potential for increased budgets and more personnel creates incentives for bureaus to participate in intensive rent-seeking behavior and mission creep (the expansion of an agency's goals and resultant activities) in attempts to secure more funding.

One need not look far to see the success of the DOD in expanding its budget. While spikes in military spending are expected, especially during times of conflict, the U.S. military budget has increased dramatically over the past several decades. Consider that, in 1950, the United States spent less than $200 billion on the military (in 2018 dollars). During the Reagan Administration spending increased to just under $500 billion. During the "war on terror," spending reached new heights with more than $600 billion in military spending.[36] Spending continues to climb with a proposed budget of $716 billion for FY 2019 and a projected budget for FY 2020 of $733 billion.[37]

Examples of mission creep are likewise plentiful. The U.S. military now engages in a variety of activities apart from war and traditional "defense." Perhaps the most obvious example is the use of military forces in an attempt to spark or sustain economic development and nation-building.[38]

The bureaucratic structure of the military is further relevant to the more specific issue of military technology. When profit and loss signals are unavailable to direct resource allocation, the *political* rules of government dictate the allocation of scarce resources instead.[39] Critically, then, the military faces little or no incentive to minimize costs or please its putative ultimate "customers" (the public). Those who ultimately receive military contracts, for example, may not be those who are best able to provide them at the lowest price—but instead those who are able to effectively engage in rent-seeking. This problem is further compounded as a result of the presence of a number of special interest groups, namely military contractors, who often maintain significant influence over policymakers.[40]

UAVs are again valuably illustrative. When UAVs were introduced as options for combat, their proponents argued that UAV technology would "reduce the dollar cost of using lethal force .... [UAVs] are a bargain compared with the available alternatives."[41] The trumpeted cost savings, however, have yet to materialize. Consider the Global Hawk Block 30 UAV. While the UAV and the U-2 spy plane (considered a Cold War "relic") are estimated to have similar operating costs (approximately $32,000 per hour), the UAV has "twice breached [the] Nunn–McCurdy acquisition cost ceiling," despite initial promises to cut costs.[42] The three Block 30s purchased in FY 2012 cost over $486 million. When questioned regarding the Air Force's desire to halt the further acquisition of the UAVs, Chief of Staff General Norton Schwarz told officials that the "U-2 yielded $2.5 billion in savings" over a five year period compared to the UAV.[43] Though initially proposed because of their purported potential to enhance operational efficiency, the Block 30s have consistently been evaluated by the military as inferior to other, much older technologies UAVs were designed to replace.[44] Instead of using this information to improve existing UAV technology or substitute an alternative, officials continue to fund the Block 30, even requiring its use when the Air Force expressed its desire to retire the UAV. This was a direct result of intensive pressure from the UAV's manufacturer and the subsequent decisions of lawmakers.[45]

Another often-cited example of the perverse incentives plaguing the military sector is the F-35 Lightning II fighter jet (also known as the Joint Strike Fighter), referred to by some as the "great white whale of defense waste."[46] The U.S. Government Accountability Office (GAO) emphasized in a 2015 report that the DOD's "most costly and ambitious program" had "experienced significant cost, schedule, and performance problems."[47] The F-35 was formally unveiled in 2001; the DOD planned to purchase 2,852 of the airplanes at an estimated cost of $233 billion. But substantial cost overruns have plagued the production of the F-35, like that of the Global Hawk. The Pentagon reported that the cost of researching and procuring the fighters was likely to prove some $22 billion more than prior cost assessments. The estimated total cost for operating and supporting the F-35 fleet amounts to some $1.196 *trillion*. In addition to skyrocketing costs, the aircraft have suffered from a number of technical problems, including issues with landing, battery failures in cold weather, and loss of stealth capacity at supersonic speeds. In 2019, the F-35 program reported some sixty-four "category 1" deficiencies, down from 111 the prior year. A category 1 deficiency is one that could "cause death, severe injury or illness, [or] could cause loss or damage to the aircraft or its equipment," among others.[48] Policymakers refuse to jettison the project, however, due in part to the fear that such a move would reduce employment in their districts.[49] Moreover, military contractors continue to apply immense pressure to elected officials; lobbying for the project has come to occupy

> a front row seat on K Street [in Washington, DC], with various actors pouring in big bucks into keeping this expensive program afloat … [A]t least 15 different companies … have filed lobbying disclosures for work on conducted in relation to … the F-35 … Lockheed Martin has spearheaded these lobbying efforts, with 12 in-house [lobbyists] working on the issue.[50]

IV. Conclusion

This chapter has two main implications. First, serious problems complicate traditional studies of military technology. In particular, some of the standard assumptions regarding military policy deserve to be questioned vigorously. The idea of a benevolent, singular entity working to maximize some broader notion of social welfare is likely not an appropriate framework for analyzing policies surrounding the development and implementation of putatively defensive technologies and strategies. This suggests that, when discussing issues of military technology—and military matters more generally—researchers should consider perspectives that appreciate the limitations of knowledge and the incentives facing policymakers.

Second, military technologies may not be created or utilized in a way that promotes the public interest. As the examples of UAVs and the F-35 illustrate, knowledge problems and issues of political economy are likely to present serious problems. Because no one can acquire all relevant information, the development and use of any military technology will likely result in unforeseen consequences affecting a number of intimately interconnected systems. The presence of special interests within the military sector and the structure of the sector itself means that the incentives of policymakers is unlikely to align with the incentives of the general public.

Taken together, these implications call into question the standard narrative that centralized states must necessarily provide defense and military services and open the door for a more critical discussion of how a free (anarchic) society may provide these services. As Mises, Hayek, and others have pointed out, individuals operating within market institutions, beholden to the signals and incentives generated by prices, profit, and loss, are not subjected to the aforementioned knowledge and incentive problems. Undoubtedly, the private provision of defense would carry with it a number of consequences—both positive and negative. The assumption, however, that government provision of these services is categorically superior is far from clear and requires further exploration.

Notes

1 National Priorities Project, "U.S. Military Spending vs. The World," www.nationalpriorities.org/campaigns/us-military-spending-vs-world/ (August 2019; last accessed October 5, 2019).

2 Peter G. Peterson Foundation, "U.S. Defense Spending Compared to Other Countries," www.pgpf.org/chart-archive/0053_defense-comparison (August 2019; last accessed October 5, 2019).

3 Lawrence Korb, "What the FY 2020 Defense Budget Gets Wrong," www.americanprogress.org/issues/security/reports/2019/04/29/469086/fy-2020-defense-budget-gets-wrong/ (April 2019; last accessed October 5, 2019).

4 David Vine, "Where In The World Is the U.S. Military?" www.politico.com/magazine/story/2015/06/us-military-bases-around-the-world-119321 (July/August 2015; last accessed October 5, 2019).

5 United States Department of Defense, "U.S. Department of Defense: Fiscal Year 2015 Budget Request," http://comptroller.defense.gov/budget.aspx (2014; last accessed October 5, 2019).

6 Nick Turse, "The Golden Age of Black Ops: Special Ops Missions Already in 105 Countries in 2015," www.tomdispatch.com/blog/175945/ (January 2015; last accessed October 5, 2019).

7 Eugene Golhz, "Conventional Arms Transfers and US Economic Security." *Strategic Studies Quarterly*, 13.1 (2019): 42–65.

8 Catherine Theohary, "Conventional Arms Transfers to Developing Nations, 2007–2014," www.fas.org/sgp/crs/weapons/R44320.pdf (2015; last accessed October 5, 2019).

9 Katie Lange, "3rd Offset Strategy 101: What It Is, What the Tech Focuses Are," www.dodlive.mil/2016/03/30/3rd-offset-strategy-101-what-it-is-what-the-tech-focuses-are/ (2016; last accessed October 5, 2019).

10 Katie Lange "#3rd Offset Strategy."

11 See Jonathan D. Caverley, "United States Hegemony and the New Economics of Defense," *Security Studies*, 16.4 (2007): 598–614; Jonathan D. Caverley and Ethan B. Kapstein, "Arms Away: How Washington Squandered its Monopoly on Weapons Sales," *Foreign Affairs*, 91.5 (2012): 125–132; and Jonathan D. Caverley and Ethan B. Kapstein, "America and the Arms Trade: From Subsidies to Rent Extraction," (2012) Paper for annual meeting of the American Political Science Association, New Orleans, LA.

12 See Deepak Lal, *In Praise of Empires: Globalization and Order* (New York, NY: Palgrave-Macmillan 2004); Kris James Mitchner and Marc D. Weidenmier, "Empire, Public Goods and the Roosevelt Corollary," National Bureau of Economic Research (2004); Niall Ferguson, *Colossus: The Price of America's Empire* (New York, NY: Penguin 2004); Niall Ferguson and Mortiz Schularick, "The Empire Effect: The Determinants of Country Risk in the First Age of Globalization, 1880–1913," *Journal of Economic History*, 66.2 (2006): 283–312.

13 Charles H. Anderton and John R. Carter, "On Rational Choice Theory and the Study of Terrorism," *Defence and Peace Economics*, 16.4 (2005): 275–282; Kenneth J. Arrow, "Some General Observations on the Economics of Peace and War, Peace Economics," *Peace Economics, Peace Science, and Public Policy*, 2.2 (1995): 1–8; Kenneth E. Boulding, *The Economics of Peace* (New York, NY: Prentice-Hall 1945); Kenneth E. Boulding, *Stable Peace* (Austin, TX: U of Texas P 1978); Jurgen Brauer and Raul Caruso, "Economists and Peacebuilding," *Handbook on Peacebuilding*, ed. Roger MacGintry (London: Routledge 2012); Jurgen Brauer and J. Paul Dunne, *Peace Economics: A Macroeconomic Primer for Violence-Afflicted States* (Washington, D.C.: United States Institute of Peace P 2012); Christopher J. Coyne, "The Institutional Prerequisites for Post-Conflict Reconstruction," *Review of Austrian Economics*, 18.3/4 (2005): 325–342; Christopher J. Coyne, "The Politics of Bureaucracy and the Failure of Post-War Reconstruction," *Public Choice*, 135 (2008): 11–22; Christopher J. Coyne and Tyler Cowen, "Postwar Reconstruction: Some Insights from Public Choice and Institutional Economics," *Constitutional Political Economy*, 16 (2005): 31–48; Christopher J. Coyne and Adam Pellillo, "Economic Reconstruction Amidst Conflict: Insights from Afghanistan and Iraq," *Defence and Peace Economics*, 22.6 (2011): 627–643; Keith Hartley and Todd Sandler, eds., *Handbook of Defense Economics* (Amsterdam: Elsevier 1995); Jack Hirshleifer, *The Dark Side of the Force: Economic Foundations of Conflict Theory* (Cambridge, MA: Cambridge 2001); Walter Isard, *Understanding Conflict and the Science of Peace* (Cambridge, MA: Blackwell 1992); Paul Poast, *The Economics of War* (New York, NY: McGraw-Hill 2006); Todd Sandler and Keith Hartley, *The Economics of Defense* (New York, NY: Cambridge 1995); Ron P. Smith, *Military Economics: The Interaction of Power and Money* (New York, NY: Palgrave 2009).

14 Christopher J. Coyne, "Lobotomizing the Defense Brain," *Review of Austrian Economics*, 28.4 (2015): 371–396; Christopher J. Coyne and Abigail R. Hall, "State-Provided Defense as Non-Comprehensive Planning." *Journal of Private Enterprise*, 34.1 (2019): 75–85.

15 Ludwig von Mises, *Socialism: An Economic and Sociological Analysis* (Indianapolis, IN: Liberty Classics 1981 (1922)); Ludwig von Mises, *Liberalism: The Classical Tradition* (Indianapolis, IN: Liberty Fund 2005 (1927)); Ludwig von Mises, *Bureaucracy* (Grove City, NY: Libertarian P 1983 (1944)); Ludwig von Mises, *Human Action: A Treatise on Economics* (Auburn, AL: Ludwig von Mises Institute 1998 (1949)); James M. Buchanan, "Public Choice: Politics Without Romance," *Policy*, 19.3 (1975): 13–18.

16 Alan T. Peacock and Jack Wiseman, *The Growth of Public Expenditure in the United Kingdom* (Princeton, NJ: Princeton UP 1961); Bruce D. Porter, *War and the Rise of the State: The Military Foundations of Modern Politics* (New York, NY: Free P 1994); John V. Denson, *The Costs of War* (Piscataway, NJ: Transaction 1999); Linda J. Blimes and Joseph E. Stiglitz, *The Three Trillion Dollar War: The True Cost of the Iraq Conflict*

(New York, NY: W.W. Norton & Company 2008); Ivan Eland, "Warfare State to Welfare State: Conflict Causes Government to Expand at Home," *Independent Review: A Journal of Political Economy*, 18.2 (2013): 189–218; Thomas K. Duncan and Christopher J. Coyne, "The Overlooked Costs of the Permanent War Economy," *Review of Austrian Economics* 26.4 (2013): 413–431.

17 Jeffrey Rogers Hummel and Don Lavoie, "National Defense and the Public-Goods Problem," *Anarchy and the Law: The Political Economy of Choice*, ed. Edward P. Stingham (London: Transaction 2007); Roderick Long, "Defending a Free Nation." *Anarchy and the Law: The Political Economy of Choice*, ed. Edward P. Stingham (London: Transaction, 2007).

18 Gordon Tullock, "Public Choice," *The New Pelgrave Dictionary of Economics*, ed. Steven N. Durlauf and Lawrence E. Blume, (New York, NY: Palgrave Macmillan, 2008).

19 Christopher J. Coyne, "Lobotomizing the Defense Brain," *Review of Austrian Economics*, 28.4 (2015): 371–396.

20 James M. Buchanan, "The Pure Theory of Government Finance," *Journal of Political Economy*, 57 (1949): 496–505.

21 Abigail R. Hall, "Drones: Public Interest, Public Choice, and the Expansion of Unmanned Aerial Vehicles," *Peace Economics, Peace Science, and Public Policy*, 21.2 (2015): 2014–2043.

22 Tom Vanden Brook, Ken Dilanian, and Ray Locker, "Retire military officers cash in as well-paid consultants," http://usatoday30.usatoday.com/news/military/2009-11-17-military-mentors_N.htm (November 18, 2009; last visited November 5, 2019); Tom A. Coburn, "Department of Everything: Department of Defense Spending that has Little to Do with National Security," www.coburn.senate.gov/public/index.cfm?a=Files.Serve&File_id=00783b5a-f0fe-4f80-90d6-019695e52d2d (last visited November 5, 2019).

23 Abigail R. Hall, "Drones: Public Interest, Public Choice, and the Expansion of Unmanned Aerial Vehicles," *Peace Economics, Peace Science, and Public Policy*, 21.2 (2015): 2014–2043; Rachel L. Mathers, "The Failure of State-Led Economic Development on American Indian Reservations," *Independent Review*, 17.1 (2012): 65–80; Christopher J. Coyne and Peter T. Leeson, "The Plight of Underdeveloped Countries," *CATO Journal*, 24.3 (2004): 235–249.

24 Ludwig von Mises, *Socialism: An Economic and Sociological Analysis* (Indianapolis, IN: Liberty Classics 1981 (1922)); Ludwig von Mises, *Liberalism: The Classical Tradition* (Indianapolis, IN: Liberty Fund 2005 (1927)); Ludwig von Mises, *Bureaucracy* (Grove City, NY: Libertarian P 1983 (1944)); Ludwig von Mises, *Human Action: A Treatise on Economics* (Auburn, AL: Ludwig von Mises Institute 1998 (1949)).

25 F.A. Hayek, "Competition as a Discovery Procedure," *Quarterly Journal of Austrian Economics*, 5.3 (1968 (2002)): 9–23; F.A. Hayek, "*The Present State of the Debate*," in *Collectivist Economic Planning*, ed. F.A Hayek (New York, NY: Augustus M. Kelley 1935); F.A. Hayek, "The Use of Knowledge in Society," in *Individualism and Economic Order* (Chicago, IL: U of Chicago P, 1945); F.A. Hayek, *The Fatal Conceit: The Errors of Socialism* (Chicago, IL: U of Chicago P 1988); F.A. Hayek, *The Road to Serfdom* (Paris: Collection Quadrige, Presses Universitaire de France 1946–1993); F.A. Hayek, "The Competitive 'Solution'," *Individualism and Economic Order*, ed. F.A. von Hayek (Chicago, IL: U of Chicago P 1940).

26 F.A. Hayek, "The Use of Knowledge in Society." In *Individualism and Economic Order* (Chicago, IL: U of Chicago P 1945).

27 Christopher J. Coyne and Abigail R. Hall, *Tyranny Comes Home: The Domestic Fate of US Militarism* (Stanford, CA: Stanford UP 2018).

28 Micah Zenko, "10 Things You Didn't Know About Drones," www.foreignpolicy.com/articles/2012/02/27/10_things_you_didnt_know_a bout_drones (February 27, 2012; last visited November 5, 2019).

29 Dao, James, "Drone Pilots are Found to Get Stress Disorders Much as Those in Combat Do," www.nytimes.com/2013/02/23/us/drone-pilots-found-to-get-stress-disorders-much-as-those-in-combat-do.html (February 23, 2013; last visited August 18, 2020).

30 Elisabeth Bumiller, "Air Force Operators Report High Levels of Stress," www.nytimes.com/2011/12/19/world/asia/air-force-drone-operators-show-high-levels-of-stress.html (December 18, 2011; last visited November 5, 2019).

31 Quoted in Pratap Chaterjee, "A Chilling New Post-Traumatic Stress Disorder: Why Drone Pilots Are Quitting In Record Numbers," www.salon.com/2015/03/06/a_chilling_new_post_traumatic_stress_disorder_why_drone_pilots_are_quitting_in_record_numbers_partner/ (March 7, 2015; last visited November 5, 2019).

32 See Christopher J. Coyne and Abigail R. Hall, *Tyranny Comes Home: The Domestic Fate of US Militarism* (Stanford, CA: Stanford UP 2018); Abigail R. Hall, "Drones: Public Interest, Public Choice, and the Expansion of Unmanned Aerial Vehicles," *Peace Economics, Peace Science, and Public Policy*, 21.2 (2015): 2014–2043.

33 Robert Higgs, "Wartime Prosperity? A Reassessment of the U.S. Economy in The 1940s," *Journal of Economic History*, 52.1 (1992): 41–60.

34 Bert Rockman, "Bureaucracy," www.britannica.com/topic/bureaucracy (2019; last visited November 5, 2019).

35 See Gordon Tullock, *The Politics of Bureaucracy* (Washington, D.C.: Public Affairs P 1965); William N. Niskanen, "Bureaucrats and Politicians," *Journal of Law and Economics*, 18.3 (1995): 617–43; William N. Niskanen, "The Peculiar Economics of Bureaucracy," *American Economic Review*, 58.2 (1968): 293–305; William N. Niskanen, *Bureaucracy and Representative Government* (Chicago, IL: Aldine, Atherton 1971).

36 Stockholm International Peace Research Institute, "SIPRI Military Expenditure Database," www.sipri.org/databases/milex (2018; last visited August 18, 2020).

37 Lawrence J. Korb, "What the FY 2020 Defense Budget Gets Wrong," www.americanprogress.org/issues/security/reports/2019/04/29/469086/fy-2020-defense-budget-gets-wrong/ (April 29, 2019; last visited November 5, 2019).

38 Christopher J. Coyne, "The Politics of Bureaucracy and the Failure of Post-War Reconstruction," *Public Choice*, 135 (2008): 11–22; Christopher J. Coyne and Tyler Cowen, "Postwar Reconstruction: Some Insights from Public Choice and Institutional Economics," *Constitutional Political Economy*, 16 (2005): 31–48; Christopher J. Coyne and Adam Pellillo, "Economic Reconstruction Amidst Conflict: Insights from Afghanistan and Iraq," *Defence and Peace Economics* 22.6 (2011): 627–643.

39 Ludwig von Mises, *Bureaucracy* (Grove City, PA: Libertarian P (1944 (1983))).

40 See Abigail R. Hall and Christopher J. Coyne,"The Political Economy of Drones," *Defence and Peace Economics*, 25.5 (2013): 445–460; Abigail R. Hall, "Drones: Public Interest, Public Choice, and the Expansion of Unmanned Aerial Vehicles," *Peace Economics, Peace Science, and Public Policy*, 21.2 (2015): 2014–2043; Thomas K. Duncan and Christopher J. Coyne, "The Overlooked Costs of the Permanent War Economy," *Review of Austrian Economics*, 26.4 (2013): 413–431.

41 Rosa Brooks, "Take Two Drones and Call Me in the Morning: The Perils of Our Addiction to Remote-Controlled War," www.foreignpolicy.com/articles/2012/09/12/take_two_drones_and_call _me_in_the_morning (September 12, 2012; last visited November 5, 2019).

42 Chris Pocock, "U.S. Air Force Defends Global Hawk Grounding Decision," www.ainonline.com/aviation-news/2012-03-16/us-air-force-defends-global-hawk-grounding-decision (March, 16, 2012; last visited November 5, 2019). The Nunn–McCurdy Act (10 U.S.C. §2433) requires the U.S. Department of Defense to notify Congress whenever a major program experiences cost overruns that exceeed particular threshholds. Breeches are categorized as Significant or Critical. The latter occurs when the cost increases by 25% or more of the current baseline cost estimate or 50% of the original estimate.

43 Ibid.

44 See H.P. Sia and Alexander Cohen, "The Drone that Wouldn't Die: How a Defesw Contractor Bested the Pentagon," www.theatlantic.com/politics/archive/2013/07/the-drone-that-wouldnt-die-how-a-defense-contractor-bested-the-pentagon/277807/ (July 16, 2013; last visited November 5, 2019); Loren Thompson, "U-2 vs. Global Hawk: Why Drones Aren't Always the Answer to Every Military Need," www.forbes.com/sites/lorenthompson/2014/02/20/u-2-vs-global-hawk-why-drones-arent-the-answer-to-every-military-need/ (February 20, 2014; last visited November 5, 2019).

45 Abigail R. Hall, "Drones: Public Interest, Public Choice, and the Expansion of Unmanned Aerial Vehicles," *Peace Economics, Peace Science, and Public Policy*, 21.2 (2015): 2014–2043.

46 Ross Marchland, "The F-35, The Great White Whale of Defense Waste," www.washingtonexaminer.com/opinion/op-eds/the-f-35-the-great-white-whale-of-defense-waste (November 14, 2018; last visited November 5, 2019).

47 United Sates Government Accountability Office, "F-35 Joint Strike Fighter: Assessment Needed to Address Affordability Challenges," www.gao.gov/assets/670/669619.pdf (2015; last visited November 5, 2019).

48 Valerie Insinna, "FAQ: Your Guide to Understanding How The Military Rates F-35 Technical Shortfalls," www.defensenews.com/smr/hidden-troubles-f35/2019/06/12/faq-your-guide-to-understanding-how-the-military-rates-f-35-technical-shortfalls/ (June 12, 2019; last visited November 5, 2019).

49 William D. Hartung, "The Military Is the Ultimate Special Interest Group," www.thenation.com/article/the-military-is-the-ultimate-special-interest-group/ (November 1, 2018; last visited November 5, 2019).

50 Tess VandenDolder, "Why Everyone Is Lobbying on the F-35 Fighter Jet," www.americaninno.com/dc/why-everyone-is-lobbying-on-the-f-35-fighter-jet/(October 9, 2014; last visited November 5, 2019).

30
ANARCHY AND TRANSHUMANISM

William Gillis

I. Introduction

The term "anarcho-transhumanism" is a relatively recently one, barely mentioned in the 1980s, publicly adopted in the early 2000s and only really popularized in the last decade. But it represents a current of thought that has been present in anarchist circles and theory since William Godwin tied the drive to perpetually improve and perfect our social relations with the drive to perpetually improve and perfect ourselves, our material conditions, and our bodies.

The idea behind anarcho-transhumanism is a simple one:

We should seek to expand our physical freedom just as we seek to expand our social freedom.

Anarcho-transhumanists see their position as the logical extension or deepening of anarchism's existing commitment to maximizing freedom. And the term "morphological freedom" is widely used by transhumanists of many varieties as a label for the positive freedom to alter one's body or material conditions.

Transhumanism is often shallowly characterized in the media in terms of the desire to live forever, the desire to upload one's mind to a computer, or a fantasy in which a self-improving artificial intelligence (AI) suddenly arrives and transforms the world into a paradise. And, of course, some people are attracted to these goals. But the only defining precept of transhumanism is that we should have more freedom to change ourselves and our environment.

Transhumanism thus challenges essentialist definitions of the "human" and is sometimes framed as part of a wider discourse in feminist and queer theory concerned with cyborg identities and "inhumanisms." Transhumanism can be seen as either an aggressive critique of humanism, or alternatively as an extension of specific humanist values beyond the arbitrary species category of "human." Transhumanism demands that we interrogate our desires and values beyond the happenstance of What Is, accepting neither the authority of arbitrary social constructs like gender nor a blind fealty to how our bodies presently function.

As one would expect, transgender issues have been at the core of transhumanism from the start. But transhumanism radically expands on trans liberation to situate it as part of a much wider array of struggles for freedom in the construction and operation of our bodies and the surrounding world. A number of anarcho-transhumanists work on immediately practical projects that give people more control over their bodies—the operation of abortion clinics, the distribution of naloxone, or the 3D printing of open-source prosthetics for children. But transhumanists also ask radical questions like: *Why is it not only the case that our society is okay with the involuntary decay and death of the elderly but also that it moralizes in support of their perpetual extermination?*

The struggle for life extension is certainly not the entirety of transhumanism, but it is an important example of the kind of campaign transhumanists initiated and continue, shockingly, to fight largely alone. The notion that an objectively "good life" extends to seventy or a hundred years but no further is clearly arbitrary, and yet the opinion that it does is both nearly universally held and violently defended. Many early transhumanists were shocked by this response, but it illustrates how people can easily become staunch defenders of existing catastrophes for fear of otherwise having to reconsider standing assumptions in their own lives. In the same way that people will defend mandatory military service or murdering animals for food, the arguments for death are clearly defensive rationalizations—and rational responses are easy to formulate:

- "Death gives life its meaning."Yet how is death at seventy years old more meaningful than death at five years old or at two hundred years old? If an eighty-year-old woman gets to live and work on her poetry for another five decades, does that really undermine your capacity to find meaning so badly that you'd prefer to see her murdered?
- "We would get bored."This seems nothing more than a call to build a world that isn't boring! Never mind the wild possibilities embedded in both anarchism and transhumanism; it would take almost three hundred thousand years to read every book in existence today. There are already 100 million recorded songs in the world. There are thousands of languages with their own conceptual ecosystems and their own poetry. There are hundreds of fields of inquiry, rich and fascinating, in which to immerse yourself. There are vast arrays of experiences and novel kinds of relationships to explore. Surely we can do with a few more centuries at least.
- "Old, static perspectives would clog up the world."It's a pretty absurd and horrifying to instinctively appeal to genocide as the best means to solve the problem of the rigidity of people' perspectives or identities. Over a hundred billion humans have died since the arrival of *Homo sapiens* on the scene. At best they were only able to convey the tiniest sliver of their subjective experiences, their insights and dreams, before everything else inside them was abruptly snuffed out. People say that every time an elder dies it's like a library's being burned to the ground. *We've already lost 100 billion libraries!* There are no doubt infinite myriad ways we might live and change, but it would be strange indeed if the sharp binary of sudden, massive, and irreversible loss that is currently standard were universally ideal.

Life extension is an illustrative example that gets to the heart of what transhumanism offers as a continuation of anarchism's radicalism: the capacity to demand that unexamined norms or conventions justify themselves, to challenge things otherwise accepted.

Anarcho-transhumanism breaks down many other common operating assumptions about the world, just as it seeks to expand and explore the scope of what is possible. Radicalism is all about pressing assumptions and models into alien contexts and seeing what breaks down in order to better clarify what dynamics are more fundamentally rooted. Anarcho-transhumanism seeks to advance anarchism through this kind of clarification—to get it into better fighting shape so it can deal more effectively with the future, to make it capable of fighting in all situations, not just those specific to particular contexts.

It's easy to say "*all this talk of distant science fiction possibilities is an irrelevant distraction.*" Anarcho-transhumanists certainly don't advocate abandoning the day-to-day of anarchist struggles and infrastructure-building. But it is forward thinking that has often won anarchism its biggest advances. Indeed, it's arguable that a great deal of anarchism's potency has historically derived from its correct predictions. And this is a widespread pattern. While the Internet is obviously the site of major conflicts today, many of the freedoms still provided by it were won decades ago by radicals who were tracing out the ramifications and importance of social phenomena and institutions long before the state and capitalism caught up or grasped the ramifications of certain battles.

On the other hand, if there's one takeaway from the last two centuries of struggle, it should be that it often takes radicals a really long time to field responses to new developments. Anarchists have adapted very slowly to changing conditions. It's frequently taken a decade or more for anarchists to try out various approaches, settle on the good ones, and proceed to popularize them. Today, radical leftists have an increasing tendency to dismiss futurism and instead just shrug and say, "We'll solve that problem through praxis." But what that dismissal often boils down to is: "We'll figure it out through trial and error when the shit hits the fan and we don't really have time for years of error and stumbling."

Theorists and activists are finally coming around in large numbers to the realization that the simplicity of radicals' responses and their slow adaptation times have often left them predictable to those in power, their instinctual responses already integrated into rulers' and bosses' plans, with the result that their struggles effectively serve as pressure valves for society—inadvertently helping to sustain existing institutions and practices rather than undermining or transforming them.

It might seem bizarre and disconnected to try to determine exactly what anarchists really means by "freedom" in a technological context in which "selves" and "individuals" are not clearly defined and conventional appeals to autonomy fall short. One might seek to dismiss the relevance of various contemporary phenomena to the project of rethinking the nature of humanness and human connection—of twins conjoined at the brain who use pronouns unconventionally. It might seem easy to treat multicameral minds as "irrelevant" or "marginal" or to treat the possibility of brain-to-brain empathic technologies as too remote to be worth even considering (never mind the couples who've already utilized limited prototypes). But dismissing anything beyond one's present, particular experience serves to confine anarchism to a parochial context, leaving it a superficial and soon-to-be-antiquated historical tendency—incapable of speaking more broadly or claiming any depth or rootedness in our ethical positions.

It's important to be clear, however: Proactive consideration of the possible is not the same thing as small-minded prefiguration. Anarcho-transhumanists are not making the mistake of demanding a single specific future—of laying out a blueprint and demanding that the world comply. Rather, they advocate the enabling of a multiplicity of futures.

II. Historical Antecedents

William Godwin is frequently identified as the first prominent anarchist in modern times, although Pierre-Joseph Proudhon would later be the first person to use the term "anarchist." Godwin was a prominent utilitarian philosopher and novelist, but was eclipsed by his partner Mary Wollstonecraft (often identified as the first modern feminist), and their daughter Mary Shelley (often identified as the first science fiction novelist). Godwin called for the abolition of the state, capitalism, and many other forms of oppression, but also linked his emancipatory agenda with farseeing calls for the radical extension of technological capacity, considering possibilities including life extension and the defeat of death.

Godwin was just one of many historical anarchists who spoke in sharply transhumanist terms. Voltairine de Cleyre, for instance, praised the development of greater technological freedoms and saw the end goal as "an ideal life, in which men and women will be as gods, with a god's power to enjoy and to suffer."[1] And talk of the gradual transformation of both humanity and our environment has been common throughout anarchist ranks historically. One of the most prominent popularizers of anarchism, Errico Malatesta, framed anarchism as a never-ending march towards greater freedom: What matters, he declared, "is not whether we accomplish Anarchism today, tomorrow, or within ten centuries, but that we walk towards Anarchism today, tomorrow, and always."[2]

Anarchists as early as Joseph Déjacque dabbled in wild science fiction, describing future worlds with machines that automated doing the laundry, washing the dishes, etc., and many pressed further still. In particular, Russian anarchists and socialists just prior to the Bolshevik revolution embraced a wide variety of avant-garde movements with extreme technoscientific aspirations. Most striking among these was the Cosmist movement. Cosmist thinkers advocated radical life extension, the merging of human and machine, and the spread of consciousness beyond Earth. While many Cosmists were socialists rather than anarchists and were eventually consumed by the USSR, influencing both the space race and Soviet culture, their slogans like "Storm the Heavens and Conquer Death" have been widely adopted by anarcho-transhumanists today.

Though the sweeping term "cybernetics" is less used today by scientists, a self-conscious "cybernetics" movement attracted considerable attention and intellectual energy from the 1950s through to the 1970s. This movement was often seen as split between the military-industrial complex camp and the radical socialist or anti-authoritarian camp. But the political divide was in practice more messy. For instance, the anarchist Walter Pitts, a homeless runaway who raised money for the fight against Franco, became one of the founders of cognitive science. Many of the themes of cybernetics, like feedback and self-organizing complex systems, were obviously directly in line with anarchist thinking and have been cited and referenced by anarchists within the more mainstream activist milieu.

Those in the open-source and free-software movements have often derived transhumanist implications from their ideals. What if the kind of freedom exemplified by free software were applied to everything? What if our bodies and environmental conditions were made as open-source and reconfigurable as we'd like our computers to be? Many anarcho-transhumanists today see their transhumanism as simply an extension of the values of openness and user agency that drive the free-software (and free-hardware) movement.

There are of course a number of broad transhumanist themes in the broader society that have influenced different lineages of anarcho-transhumanists. They range from common notions of "Prometheanism" to interpretations of Nietzsche to Afrofuturism to countless sub-currents of feminist and queer thought.

III. Practicality

The majority of anarchists around the world are activists who work in immediate struggles from feeding the homeless to resisting immigration-restriction regimes. It is unsurprising, then, that their foci are primarily practical. The most common objection made by many anarchist activists to anarcho-transhumanism is that focusing on the future takes away from transformative practice in the present. This is often bundled with critiques common on the modern left of the "abstract" and calls to center political practice and theory on "everyday life."

Yet it's worth considering the ultimate conclusion of such an orientation. If we lived directly in the present with no reflection, we wouldn't be self-aware. Mental recursion—modeling ourselves, others, and our world—is central to consciousness itself. What defines a mind *as a mind* is its capacity proactively to think a few steps ahead—to avoid rolling immediately down the steepest slope like a rock, but instead to grasp our context, the landscape of our choices and possible paths, and sometimes to choose ones that don't immediately satiate.

There is always the danger of becoming ungrounded; but futurism in no way obliges a disconnect with the struggles of the present. It does, however, have implications for what we prioritize in the present; for example, refusing to accept a reform that might improve our lot in the short term but seriously impede our capacity to struggle in the future. Liberals are famous for their dismissal of the future, an attitude which they use to justify short-sighted actions like ecological devastation and granting the state ever more power over our lives. There's a sense in which we sometimes need to improve our lot in the short term just to keep fighting, but we must always be aware of what we're trading away.

A democratic socialist utopia might immediately improve most people's lives. And perhaps we might be able to realize such a utopia if we all really worked hard to achieve it. But there's a limit on the improvements a state-based solution could achieve. And, once such a putative utopia was in place, its authoritarian tendencies might deepen, with the result that it becomes even harder for future generations to overthrow.

In addition to illuminating challenges on the road ahead, anarcho-transhumanism offers direct insights into our daily struggles and our continuing resistance against the state.

If fascism is so powerful, why hasn't it totally triumphed? Our world could be so much worse than it is. Despite all the sources of contemporary elites' power—all the vast wealth and coercive force they've accumulated, all the ideological and infrastructural control, all the systemic planning and surveillance, all the ways humans are by default inclined to cognitive fallacies, cruelty, and tribalism—they have clearly been massively impeded on every front. And those societies or movements that have sought to embrace the strengths of authoritarianism more directly have failed. Anti-authoritarians—despite myriad shortcomings and imperfections—have won time and time again. The host of those in fealty to absolute power, to mindless surrender and violent simplicity, are legion. And yet grassroots activists have crippled their ambitions, outflanked their worldviews, bogged down their campaigns, sabotaged their projects, creatively struck back, preempted them—and changed the landscape out from under their feet.

Free people are better inventors, better strategists, better hackers, and better scientists, exhibiting the very tendencies transhumanism embraces—tendencies of abstraction, reflection, and churn. The ideology of power fails because of its necessary weakness at leveraging complexity. Philosophies of control innately seek to constrain the possible; freedom is about unleashing it.

Having more tools means having more ways to approach a problem. The "choices" some tools provide can be superficial and can exert limited impact. Choosing certain tools can shrink the range of available choices in other ways. But, at the end of the day, it's not possible to maximize freedom without also continuously expanding one's toolset.

Expanded degrees of freedom in technics typically empower attackers over defenders. When there are more avenues by which to attack and defend, the attackers only need to choose one, while the defenders need to defend all, with the result that the defense of rigid, extended institutions and infrastructure proves harder and harder.

Thus, in the broadest lens, technological development ultimately bends towards empowering minorities to resist domination and makes cultural habits of consensus and autonomy increasingly necessary—because in some sense everyone gets a veto.

Similarly, information technologies unleash positive feedback loops and increase sociocultural complexity. While early, crude information technologies, like radio and television, were seized and controlled by the state and capital to form a monopolistic infrastructure promoting monolithic culture, the wild array of technologies we've blurred together as "the Internet" has empowered people to resist this tendency and promoted an increasing complexity of fluid discourses and subcultures.

This provides an amazing source of resistance because it makes mass-control harder and harder. What is hip moves so fast and is so diverse and contingent that politicians and businesses stumble more and more when trying to exploit it.

Anarcho-transhumanists have argued that this feedbacking sociocultural complexity constitutes a Social Singularity, a reflection of the Technological Singularity—a process in virtue of which collaboratively feedbacking technological insights and inventions grow too fast to be predicted or controlled.

Silicon Valley is desperately trying to avoid the reality that the net profitability of the entire advertising industry is in decline. Since the advent of the Internet, people have begun wising up and, on the whole, advertisers are exerting less and less impact. All that remains marginally effective with the younger generations are more individually-targeted outreach campaigns—think businesses trying to get in the meme game or paying popular Instagram teens to reference their products. But these approaches are clearly yielding diminishing returns. When a hypercomplex teen fashion subculture comprises thirty people it's no longer worth the energy for corporations to try to target them.

Those anarchists skeptical of prediction and strategy, who instead focus on "everyday life" and the immediate, often frame their hostility to abstractions as part of a wider rejection of "mediation." Yet it's worth emphasizing that all causal interactions are "mediated." The air mediates the sounds of our voices. The electromagnetic field and any intervening material mediate our capacity to see. Culture and language mediate the concepts we seek to express. This may seem like a trivial point, but it's a deep one. It's hard to provide an objective metric of just what counts as "more" or "less" mediation, and it's harder still to try and claim that such a metric *means* something.

There is no such thing as "direct experience." To see anything requires an immense amount of processing as raw signals are transformed by neural columns in our visual cortices into ever more abstract signals. Artifacts from this processing can be found in optical illusions and patterned hallucinations. And in turn our experiences shape what pattern recognition circuits form with what strengths. To experience "directly" without mediation would be to not experience or think at all.

One can certainly try to distinguish between "human created" mediation and other varieties, but such a distinction has no fundamental correlation with how viscerally or accurately we experience things. While there's a different flavor of danger to someone tapping or censoring your community mesh Wi-Fi network, such interference or sabotage applies in various ways to *all* our means of communication, including cultural and linguistic constructs.

It's nonsensical to talk of "more" mediation rather than different flavors with different contextual benefits and drawbacks. Even an anarcho-primitivist like John Zerzan wears eye glasses to improve his overall capacity to visually experience and engage with the world around him. In this respect he's a transhumanist. In many ways modern technologies can be used to expand the depth and richness of our engagement with nature and each other.

IV. *Contra* Primitivism

For the most part, anarcho-transhumanism emerged as an explicit response to anarcho-primitivism; many anarcho-transhumanists in the early aughts were former primitivists. As a result, unlike the broader transhumanist movement, which tends to engage minimally or not at all with primitivist critiques, anarcho-transhumanism was *founded* in many ways as a response to primitivist concerns.

Anarcho-transhumanism emphasizes that transhumanism isn't a claim that all tools and applications of them are—in all contexts—totally wonderful and without problematic aspects to be considered, navigated, rejected, challenged, or changed. Nor is transhumanism an embrace of all the infrastructure or norms of tool use that currently exist. Transhumanists hardly imagine that all technologies are positive in every specific situation, that tools never have biases or inclinations, or that some arbitrary, specific set of "higher" technologies should be imposed on everyone. Rather, transhumanists merely argue that people should have more agency and choices with regard to the ways in which they engage with the world.

Being more informed and having a wider array of tools to choose from is critical. In the broadest sense, "technology" is just any means of doing things, and freedom is the availability of more options or means.

While they recognize there will inevitably be a lot of contextual complications in practice, at the end of the day transhumanists want more options in life and in the universe, In much the same way that anarchists have argued for the availability of as many different tactics as possible. Sometimes one tactic or tool will be better for a job, sometimes not. But expanding freedom ultimately necessitates expanding technological options.

What's deplorable about our current condition is the way in which technologies are suppressed until all we are allowed is a single technological monoculture, often with some very sharp biases. On the one hand, more simple or primitive technologies are suppressed or erased. On the other, technological development is viciously slowed or curtailed thanks to intellectual property laws and myriad other injustices. Similarly, the conditions of capitalism and imperialism distort what technologies are more profitable and thus what lines of research are pursued.

That does not mean that technological inventions under capitalism are innately corrupted or useless. And it certainly doesn't mean that we should start entirely from fresh cloth, ignoring all discoveries and knowledge accumulated along our trajectory.

But many of the industries and commodity forms that are standardized in our existing society would be unsustainable and undesirable in a liberated world.

For instance: There are many ways to make photovoltaic solar panels, but when the People's Republic of China reportedly uses slave labor and eminent domain to seize, strip, and poison vast swathes of land, such actions could lower the cost of certain rare earth minerals—and thus steer more money more towards research focused on photovoltaic approaches that use these artificially cheap minerals rather than towards alternative viable research branches that use more common materials. Military forces in the Congo allegedly allow for the replacement of Canadian coltan miners with slaves working in horrific conditions. Or consider another example: two centuries ago, employing not much more than simple mirrors, Augustin Mouchot demonstrated a fully functional and (at the time) cost-efficient solar steam engine at the world's fair. It would have gone into mass production had the British not won battles in India enabling them to effectively enslave large populations and put them to work in coal extraction, thus dramatically driving down coal prices.

It is a simple fact that institutional violence frequently alters the immediate profitability of certain lines of research.

Primitivism oversimplifies the situation, saying that what exists must necessarily be the only way to enable certain technologies. It also frequently implies a single linear arc of development such that everything is dependent upon everything else, ignoring the often enormous latitude and diversity of options along the way and failing to investigate the vast potential for reconfiguration.

Any discussion of "civilization," for example, is necessarily going to involve sweeping and over-simplistic narratives. Our actual history is far more rich and complicated than any tale of simple historical forces can account for. Systems of power have been with us for a long time and are deeply enmeshed in almost every aspect of our society, our culture, our interpersonal relations, and our material infrastructures. But if in using the term "civilization" we mean to speak of some kind of characteristic or fundamental "culture of cities," it's begging the question to write domination in from the start.

There have always been constraining power dynamics in every human society from hunter-gatherers on up. While larger-scale societies have naturally made possible more showy expressions of domination, domination is not inherent in the structures of such societies.

Throughout the historical record, cities have been quite diverse in their degrees of internal hierarchy and relations with surrounding societies and environments. A number of city cultures left no traces of hierarchy or violence. More egalitarian and anarchistic urban societies didn't waste energy building giant monuments or waging wars, and thus are thus less prominent in the historical records available to us. Further, because we currently live under an oppressive global regime, it goes without saying that at some point any more libertarian societies had to be conquered—and victors often intentionally destroy the records of those they subjugate. Similarly, non-anarchist historians have leapt to assume that the presence of any social coordination or technological invention in egalitarian and peaceful city cultures like Harappa proves the presence of some state-like authority—even when there's zero sign of any such authority and there are, indeed, strong indications to the contrary.

Urban concentrations arose in a number of places prior to agriculture. Indeed, in many places around the globe where the land could not support permanent cities, people nevertheless struggled to come together in greater numbers whenever and for however long they could manage to do so. Frequently, the members of early societies would be both temporary hunter-gatherers and temporary city dwellers, transitioning back and forth with the seasons.

This does not remotely fit an account of cities as solely runaway concentrations of wealth and power—of urban life as a cancerous mistake. If the establishment of cities were such a bad idea, why do people with other options keep voluntarily choosing them?

The answer, of course, is that living in large numbers increases the social options available to individuals, opening up a much greater diversity of possible relationships to choose from.

Instead of being confined to tribes of one hundred or two hundred people, while perhaps enjoying opportunities to interact with the members of limited numbers of nearby tribes, people living in cities can form affinities not limited by the happenstance of birth, to organically form their own distinct networks *by choice*. Better than tribes, they can shed the limiting insularity of closed social clusters entirely. There's no good reason your friends should all be forced to be friends with each other as well. Cities enable individuals to form vast panoplies of relationships linking them with far larger and richer networks.

Such cosmopolitanism enables and encourages the empathy necessary to transcend tribal or national othering. It expands our horizons, enabling mutual aid on incredible scales, and helping far richer cultural and cognitive ecosystems than would otherwise be possible to flourish. If there is any single defining characteristic "culture of cities" (otherwise known as "civilization"), it is thus one of wild anarchy, of unleashed complexity and possibility.

And, of course, large-scale cooperation enables technological developments that expand the possible scope of our material conditions.

What we want is a world with the teeming connectedness of cosmopolitanism, but without the centralization and sedentary characteristics of many "civilizations." We want to fulfill the promise and radical potential of cities that have led humans to form them voluntarily again and again throughout history. This may not be in keeping with our biology as Stone Age creatures, whose physical evolution has been incapable of keeping up with our cultural evolution, but so what?

Of course, many primitivists may well enjoy and acknowledge the benefits offered by the fruits of civilization. They may even feel an affinity for the aspirations of anarcho-transhumanism, but nevertheless believe that transhumanist aspirations are pointless because a permanent civilizational collapse is inevitable.

It's true that our present infrastructure and economy are incredibly brittle, destructive, and unsustainable—in many ways serving and intertwined with oppressive social systems. But so many other forms remain possible. Our global civilization is not some magical whole, but a vast and complex battlefield of competing forces and tendencies.

The "inevitability" of the supposedly coming collapse is in fact *itself* quite brittle. Any number of single developments could massively derail it. An abundance of cheap, clean energy, for example, or an abundance of cheap, rare metals. Each would lead to the other, because cheap energy means more cost-effective metals recycling, and the availability of cheap metals means cheaper batteries and expanded access to energy sources like wind. The Earth is not a closed system, and, for example, several major corporations are now racing to seize nearby asteroids so rich in rare metals that successful asteroid mining could crash the metals markets and shutter nearly every mine on Earth.

And let's note that it is highly unlikely that a civilizational collapse would return us to an idyllic Eden. Many centers of power would likely survive, almost no society would fall below Iron Age technology, billions would die horrifically, and the sudden burst of ecological destruction would be incredible. It even turns out that the spread of forests in northern latitudes would perversely end up making global warming worse because trees are ultimately poor carbon sinks and changes to the Earth's albedo (from darker forests) cause it to absorb *more* energy from the sun.

No matter the odds, we must fight against the unfathomable holocaust of a collapse. We have an ethical obligation to struggle, to have some agency with respect to our future and our environment, and to take some responsibility for our destiny. Only with science and technology will we be able to repair ancient disasters like the desertification of the Sahara, manage the decommissioning of horrors, and rewild most of the Earth.

V. Pessimism about Technological Possibilities

One of the most common concerns with transhumanism derives from a misunderstanding of the distinction between "physically doable but not yet engineered" and "who knows."

Much of this stems from ignorance of the relevant fields. Most people wouldn't have to argue over whether or not an "upside down treehouse" would be possible to build; it would just require a bit of work.

While some ideas are highly speculative, many of the things transhumanists talk about fall very far to the doable side of the spectrum—there's no chance they're ruled out by physics, mathematics, chemistry, or the like; they don't require the existence or use of wormholes, for example. The problems that stand in the way of our reaching these transhumanist goals are merely *engineering* problems, albeit challenging ones—problems on which plenty of experts are working, problems that the established consensus is confident we can solve. Asteroid mining, for example, is no more unimaginable or impossible today than placing satellites in Earth orbit was in the 1940s. We know we can do it; we know it will pay off; we just have to complete the mounds of fucking busywork in our way first. CRISPR (clustered regularly interspaced short palindromic repeats) was an amazing advance in gene therapy but it was amazing only in virtue of the suddenness of the breakthrough; gene editing had never seemed strictly infeasible.

Estimates of how long it will be until a given technological development occurs are naturally subjective. But it requires conspiratorial science-denialism to pretend that creating and using mining robots to mine will somehow prove impossibly hard—or require so much human labor that their arrival on the scene won't represent any sort of efficiency gain.

It's very common in radical leftist circles to hear that green technologies are mythical. This is deeply inaccurate, but it's understandable given all the corporate greenwashing and media misrepresentation of technologies. It's thus easy to do a little critical research and assume that scientists have systemically overlooked things like life-cycle analyses. In fact, however, reductions in footprint by a factor of one hundred times or one thousand times would constitute a monumental difference, not some trivial reform—and such reductions are in some cases highly probable.

Humans have always had an effect on their environment, and the Earth's ecosystems have never been static. Our goal should not be some unchanging and sharply constrained lifestyle with literally zero footprint; instead, we should seek to enable our ingenuity and exploration in ways that don't bulldoze the Earth.

If we put a small fraction of the energy unlocked by hydrocarbons into solar energy technologies, we'll have enough power to render hydrocarbon energy obsolete. While hydrocarbons were unquestionably a world-changing source of dense energy, it's possible to get incredibly high power returns from solar technologies using even 1800s technology of mirrors and steam pipes. There are a great many condensed battery options, and more are being developed—for instance, in high-density biochemical storage. Meanwhile, photovoltaic cell technology has leapt past every supposed barrier; and the materials needed to make effective use of this technology have been dramatically diversified. Options now on the table include quite simple approaches featuring tiny ecological footprints. The energy return on solar is close to 12 times and is rocketing upward. The efficiency of solar technology has reached the point at which governments like Spain have required solar power users to pay steep taxes to keep fossil fuels and centralized grids competitive.

While nuclear energy still carries many extremely negative associations among the 1980s eco-punk set, many of these concerns are only valid in the context of Cold War-style reactors—ones built to be highly centralized, to be state-run, and to work only with material capable of producing weaponizable byproducts. On the other hand, many liquid fluoride thorium reactor designs have literally no capacity to melt down, run on a radioactive material already naturally in poisonous abundance on the Earth's surface, and leave remains with relatively low half-lives.

Similarly, while some specious reporting about "cold fusion" and overenthusiastic claims about normal fusion in the 1980s turned fusion into a laughing stock on late-night television, it remains a reasonable and known source of incredible clean energy only limited by engineering challenges rather than any issues of basic science. And recent history has been littered with a chain of incremental successes achieved and benchmarks transcended.

While all these may provide cheap energy, the only safe way to reverse global warming at this point is with carbon-negative technologies that leave behind solid carbon as a byproduct. Proven technologies that do just this—from ancient gassification technologies to an array of algae-farming approaches—are already available.

That none of these have been widely adopted is a matter of politics, not science. State violence subsidizes our incredibly inefficient infrastructure because the maintenance of this infrastructure is beneficial to centralized, large-scale economic entities. Similarly, much of our energy consumption presently goes towards war and frivolities, supply and demand are aggressively distorted, and the environmental costs have been systematically shifted away from certain companies and industries.

It doesn't have to be this way. Technological development innately expands options, so it should come as no surprise that technological innovation isn't underwriting massive, centralized, ham-fisted structures but is instead encouraging organic, decentralized, and reconfigurable approaches along the lines of 3D-printing and open-source technologies.

VI. Other Transhumanist and Promethean Political Traditions

Transhumanism is a quite simple position, and so there's a wide array of people who've been attracted to it and a variety of ways people have spun off from it. Inevitably some of them are short-sighted or reactionary, and in many people's minds "transhumanism" conjures up images of far-right ideologues in Silicon Valley.

Fortunately, many reactionaries abandoned transhumanism when they recognized its liberatory implications regarding gender, race, and class, instead embracing a fascism-for-nerds movement called "neoreaction"—an early predecessor and eventual component of the alt-right. In an amusing reversal, a number now hope for and advocate the collapse of civilization. They expect that this will lead to a post-apocalyptic landscape in which their notions of biological essentialism reign supreme—in which "Real Alpha Men" rule as warlords and the rest of us are used for raping, slaving, or hunting. Or in which we are forced back to tribal-scale relations, better enabling (small-scale) nationalistic identity, social hierarchy, and traditionalism. Others envision small corporate fiefdoms and some kind of AI god that will help them maintain their desired authority structures by stopping oppressed groups from gaining, understanding, or developing technology.

Anarcho-transhumanists are glad such currents have departed the broader transhumanist movement. At the same time, it must be admitted that a majority of transhumanists still presently identify with liberalism, state socialism, social democracy, and similar technocratic cults of power.

Non-anarchist transhumanists are politically naive at best and dangerous at worst; transhumanism without anarchism is totally untenable.

A world in which everyone has increased physical agency is a world in which individuals are super-empowered and are thus obliged to solve disagreements through consensus as though everyone has a veto rather than through the coercion of majoritarian democracy.

To provide people with tools but also to try somehow to restrict from the top down what they can do with those tools or what they can invent is impossible absent an extreme authoritarian system that suppresses almost all the functions of those tools. Consider the struggle to impose and enforce "intellectual property" on the Internet, or the war against general-purpose computing. In this sense, all statist transhumanists fall short of transhumanist ideals because of their lingering fear of liberty and super-empowered proletarians.

On a philosophical level, it's impossible to reconcile transhumanism's embrace of greater agency in our bodies and environment with simultaneous advocacy of oppressive social institutions that broadly *constrain* our agency.

This difference of values is manifested in a number of ways. Anarcho-transhumanists are obviously a lot less sanguine than statist transhumanists about letting states and capitalists monopolize the control or development of new technologies. They support serious resistance efforts—efforts intended both to attack oppressors' centralized infrastructure and to liberate their research and tools for everyone.

Further to the left, the legacy of Cosmism has continued in state socialist and state communist circles. There is a distinct tradition of Left Accelerationism and more diffuse but widely popular political positions often referred to collectively as Fully Automated Luxury Communism. These traditions are broadly Marxist rather than anarchist, and don't always identify as transhumanist, but they have been in close dialogue with anarcho-transhumanists. And traditions like Xenofeminism are in many ways situated at the intersection of pro-technology Marxist and anarchist currents.

It's certainly true that there's much overlap between the political and economic aspirations of anarcho-transhumanists and those Marxist traditions likewise set on radically expanding the wealth available to everyone. Many have commented on the convergence of anarchism and Marxism when the "means of production" shrink from large-scale mechanisms necessarily operated and overseen by large groups to techniques and devices controllable by individuals (as when factories are replaced by 3D printers). Yet significant differences remain.

The divide between Marxism and anarchism has been often referred to as a divide between political philosophy and ethical philosophy. Anarchists focus on tackling domination and constraint on every level, not just the macroscopic or institutional. And anarchists want more than a merely classless society: they want a world without power relations, and thus their ethical analysis necessarily extends to challenging interpersonal dynamics of power, including more complex, subtle, informal, or even mutual relationships of domination and constraint.

While anarchists share their aspirations for a world in which the efficiencies of technologies lead to a world of abundance and liberate people from the drudgery of work it's impossible as anarchists to accept the Left Accelerationists' prescription of "verticalism"—their embrace of organizational hierarchies. Left accelerationists like Nick Srnicek and Alex Williams have critiqued the mainstream left for an embrace of short-sighted immediatism,[3] but anarchists still find in the details of their "strategy" many of the same old Marxist penchants for the establishment of an elite whose members will run the revolution/society. This allegiance leads them to sympathize with and misidentify aspects of our world, suggesting that certain corporate and state structures reflect necessary hierarchies rather than wasteful cancers propped up by systemic violence and actively suppressing scientific and technological development.

More broadly, Marxism shares a troubling tendency with its ideological offshoot primitivism to speak in highly abstract and macroscopic terms like "capitalism" or "civilization." In Marxist analyses, these entities are imbued with a kind of agency or purposefulness and all their elements are seen as constituent dynamics serving a greater whole, rather than as conflicting and capable of being rearranged. Marxists and primitivists are thus both frequently blinded to the aspects of better world now growing within the shell of the old, as well as opportunities for meaningful resistance and positive change that aren't necessarily cataclysmic total breaks.

VII. Other Topics

Vegans have been among the strongest partisans of anarcho-transhumanism, knowing very well that what is "natural" may not be ethical. Biohackers have worked on projects like getting yeast to produce the critical milk enzymes in normal cheese.[4] (To do this, just put yeast in a warm vat with sugar and let it fall out!) Others have, for example, worked on custom algae production that yields useful protein and carbs from sunlight much more efficiently than conventional agriculture—while raising the possibility of dramatically reducing or even entirely eliminating the death toll from tractor operation.

A small fraction of environmentalists have played with ideas of a more ethically engaged stewardship, positing a future in which, after rewilding the majority of the planet and restoring its ecology, we might make tweaks that reduce net suffering among non-human species. Animal liberationists have long criticized the slavery of animal "ownership" and the injustice of breeding certain animals to serve us. But what would assisting animals in their own self-improvement look like? This is a so-far speculative field called "uplifting," and the anarchist take on it is as always to center the subject's perspectives, to try to find ways of communicating and bridging the cultural and phenomenological gap with conscious persons (e.g. cetaceans, elephants, octopi, primates).

The animal-liberationist tendencies at the heart of modern anarchism also come to expression in our responses to the possibility of artificial general intelligence. There's a noteworthy current in non-anarchist transhumanist circles that focuses on the development of AI, with the goal of solving the problem of how to control a mind smarter than your own. Many transhumanists are convinced that AI will unleash an explosion of feedbacking intelligence that can remake the world.[5] To anarchists, this focus is silly given the billions of minds already on this planet and criminally underutilized. If we want an explosion of intelligence then the surer and quicker path would be to liberate and empower all the potential Einsteins currently trapped in slums, *favelas*, open mines, and fields around our planet.

Transhumanism has historically distinguished itself from other celebratory approaches to high technology precisely in its focus on self-alteration. If you want something done, you should do it yourself. If you're worried about what values an alien mind ripped into existence from scratch might develop, you should instead start with humans interested in expanding their own capacities. And while we might reasonably anticipate rapid improvements in our individual cognitive speed and memory, it is how we communicate and collaborate with one another that has served as a real bottleneck on advancement. Instead of a race to create an artificial generalized intelligence, many anarcho-transhumanists have argued that we should instead focus on the benefits of technologies that improve or deepen our connection with one another, so that collectively we can race ahead of any AI.

It's rather terrifying that the default question about AI has largely been: "How can we most effectively control/enslave it?" As anarchists our position is obvious: If we are to develop such minds, they deserve compassion and liberty. All too often, those in AI-focused communities that have spun off from transhumanist circles abandon the ethical dimension of their research. This paradigm is profoundly un-transhumanist because it privileges some kind of static humanity with static values and desires, and then enslaves non-human minds to serve those ends. The entire point of transhumanism is to *embrace* the fluidity and transitory nature of the "human," not to cling to humanness in its current form.

As you would expect when it comes to non-neurotypicals and differently abled people already alive, the transhumanist and anarcho-transhumanist position is to let a billion physical and cognitive architectures bloom! It's important to radically attack and remove stigmas and constraining social norms so that a great diversity of experiences can be lived without oppression. At the same time, it's also important to provide people with the tools to exercise control over their bodies, minds, and life conditions. It should be up to all people *individually* to determine what factors might constitute oppressive impairments in their own lives, and which factors are elements of their identities and unique life experiences.

Ultimately transhumanism is a queering of the distinction between "impairment" and "augmentation" as well as between "want" and "need." No "baseline" should be oppressively normalized. Instead, individuals should be free to grow in whatever directions they see fit.

Notes

1 Interview with Voltairine de Cleyre. 1894. *The Sun* (March 4). Center for a Stateless Society. https://c4ss.org/content/45277.

2 Malatesta, E. n.d. "Towards Anarchism." Anarchy Archives. http://dwardmac.pitzer.edu/Anarchist_Archives/malatesta/towardsanarchy.html.

3 Srnicek, N., and Williams, A. 2015. *Inventing the Future: Postcapitalism and a World Without Work*. New York: Verso.

4 Real Vegan Cheese. n.d. What's vegan cheese? https://realvegancheese.org/.

5 Bostrom, N. 2014. *Superintelligence: Paths, Dangers, Strategies*. Oxford: Oxford University Press.

ANNOTATED BIBLIOGRAPHY

Anarchism in America. Dir. Steven Fischler and Joel Sucher. Perf. Murray Bookchin, Paul Avrich, Jello Biafra, Mollie Steimer, Mildred Loomis, Karl Hess, et al. Pacific Street 1983. DVD. AK 2005.

An evocative documentary that provides an overview of American anarchist thinkers and activists representing multiple schools and backgrounds from the nineteenth century to the present.

An Anarchist-Transhumanist Manifesto. N.p., June 4, 2019. https://docs.google.com/document/d/1wJrXYBXAmNH9zwyfgg1-yAYN_Cda-26pFCk0u_QhyBc/edit.

A lengthy and highly annotated document with many authors, this essay provides extensive commentary on precursors and a bibliography of texts.

Anderson, Terry L., and Hill, P. J. *The Not so Wild, Wild West: Property Rights on the Frontier.* Stanford, CA: Stanford UP 2004.

Anderson and Hall show how property rights emerged informally in the American West prior to their formal codification by the US government. Their work highlights the role that institutional entrepreneurship plays in devising ways of creating wealth by restructuring existing property rights and creating new property rights arrangements.

Aristotle. *Politics.* Trans. Ernest Barker. Ed. Richard Stalley. Oxford: OUP 1995.

The seminal study of theories about how best to organize collectivities, and of the actual collective systems known to Aristotle.

Avrich, Paul. *Anarchist Voices: An Oral History of Anarchism in America.* Oakland, CA: AK 2005.

Invaluable resources related to the anarchist tradition in the United States.

Bader, Ralf M. "Counterfactual Justifications of the State." *Oxford Studies in Political Philosophy* 3 (2017): 101–131.

Bader provides an interpretation of Nozick's justification of the state in *Anarchy, State, and Utopia.* He identifies a form of counterfactual justification of the state that is distinct from traditional hypothetical, teleological, and historical justifications.

Bakunin, Mikhail Aleksandrovich. *Bakunin on Anarchism.* Ed. Sam Dolgoff. Montreal: Black Rose 1980.

———. *God and the State.* Mineola, NY: Dover 1970.

———. *Statism and Anarchy.* Ed. Marshall Shatz. Cambridge: CUP 1990.

Anarchist writings of a passionate Russian sparring-partner of Karl Marx who saw religion and statism as equally illusory and believed that Marx's ideas could be used to justify dictatorship.

Barnett, Randy E. *The Structure of Liberty: Justice and the Rule of Law.* 2d ed. Oxford: OUP 2014.

Offers a framework for understanding the relationship between law and governance, leading to a description of a stateless legal system.

Beito, David T. *From Mutual Aid to the Welfare State: Fraternal Societies and Social Services, 1890–1967.* 2d ed. Chapel Hill, NC: U of North Carolina P 2000.

Before the rise of the welfare state, a massive number of Americans belonged to fraternal societies. They pooled their resources as a means of collective self-reliance, creating a social safety net free from dependence on either the state or wealthy benefactors.

Bell, Tom W. "Special International Zones in Practice and Theory." *Chapman Law Review* 21 (2018): 273–302, www.chapman.edu/law/_files/publications/clr-22-1-Bell.pdf (last visited Aug. 16, 2020).

Documents the splintering of uniform political territories.

———. *Your Next Government? from the Nation State to Stateless Nations*. Cambridge: CUP 2018.

Documents and explains how special jurisdictions are transforming governments across the globe from the bottom up and inside out.

Benkler, Yochai. *The Wealth of Networks: How Social Production Transforms Markets and Freedom*. New Haven: Yale UP 2006.

An examination of the promise of stigmergic organization.

Benson, Bruce L. *The Enterprise of Law: Justice without the State*. 2d ed. Oakland, CA: Independent 2013.

Viewing history and politics through the lens of economic theory, Benson applies the logic of the market process to the task of understanding the private enforcement of law and the private adjudication of legal disputes. Critiquing the notion that law is a public good, Benson demonstrates that private-sector institutions are capable of establishing strong incentives that lead to effective law-making and law enforcement. He shows how the resulting legal constraints facilitate interaction and support social order by inducing cooperation and reducing violent confrontation.

Berkman, Alexander. *What Is Anarchism?* Oakland, CA: AK 2003 [1937].

A simple, clear exposition of what the author labeled "communist anarchism," by a life-long friend and sometime lover of Emma Goldman.

Bicchieri, Cristina. *The Grammar of Society*. New York: CUP 2006.

This was a groundbreaking book, which developed a theoretically compelling account of social norms that could be tested in the lab and in field studies. It has exerted significant influence on academic and policy work concerned with social norms.

——— *Norms in the Wild*. New York: OUP 2016.

This book takes a much deeper look at the mechanics of norm measurement and norm change, informed by work undertaken in the development context. It examines rules and collective behavior in communities that have reasonably minimal exposure to the state, and offers an informative look at the benefits and liabilities of social norms.

Block, Walter. *The Privatization of Roads and Highways: Human and Economic Factors*. Auburn, AL: Mises 2010.

While roads are not public goods in the economist's sense, a stereotypical challenge to anarchists is the question: "Who will build the roads?" Economist Block examines the dynamics of the non-state provision of roads, considering not only its viability but also the societal benefits he believes it likely to yield.

Boétie, Etienne de la. *Discourse on Voluntary Servitude*. Trans. James B. Atkinson and David Sices. Indianapolis, IN: Hackett 2012 [1576].

In this 1576 classic, Etienne de la Boétie argues that power is ultimately distributed, and that domination thus always rests on the assent of the governed. As a result, toppling tyrants is less dependent on positive attacks and more a function of coordinating refusals to comply. The book's arguments provide a foundation both for many anarchist theories of power and strategies of tactical non-violence.

Bookchin, Murray. *The Ecology of Freedom: The Emergence and Dissolution of Hierarchy*. San Francisco: AK 2005 [1982].

———. *Post-Scarcity Anarchism*. 3d ed. Stirling: AK 2004.

Bookchin was the leading advocate of a school of green anarchist thought known as Social Ecology. He traces a multitude of social and ecological ills to the hierarchical relationships that characterize modern political society, and identifies anarchism as a potential approach to tackling all of these problems.

Boonin, David. *The Problem of Punishment*. New York: CUP 2008.

Criminal law lies near the core of state power. Boonin surveys and challenges a wide range of proposed justifications for the practice of punishment. He suggests that the law's focus be changed from harming offenders to securing restitution for victims.

Borders, Max. *The Social Singularity*. Austin, TX: Social Evolution 2018.

A manifesto for the "underthrow" of traditional, political forms of governance—leading to their replacement by new, decentralized ones.

Brennan, Geoffrey, et al. *Explaining Norms*. New York: OUP 2013.

This book offers an account of social norms alternative to Cristina Bicchieri's influential position and explores the role that norms play in creating social meaning.

Brennan, Jason. *When All Else Fails: The Ethics of Resistance to State Injustice*. Princeton, NJ: Princeton UP 2018.

A sustained defense of the thesis that civilians possess the same right to defend themselves and others against government agents that they possess against civilians. Brennan argues that government agents who voluntarily accept government jobs nevertheless retain the right to resist state injustice, sabotage government wrongdoing from within, and violate or ignore wrongful orders.

Buchanan, James M. *The Limits of Liberty: Between Anarchy and Leviathan.* Chicago: U of Chicago P 1975.
A major work by the founder, with Gordon Tullock, of the Public Choice school (or Virginia School) of economics, exploring the emergence of state institutions from anarchy or a state of nature. Buchanan's notion of a "natural equilibrium" is an important development of earlier concepts of "the state of nature."

Bull, Hedley. *The Anarchical Society: A Study of Order in World Politics.* 4th ed. London: Red Globe 2012.
A profoundly important analysis of the international system as an instance of anarchy. Though this isn't Bull's concern, the global persistence of ordered anarchy has served as crucial inspiration for proponents of stateless social arrangements.

Byrd, B. Sharon, and Hruschka, Joachim. *Kant's Doctrine of Right: A Commentary.* Cambridge: CUP 2010.
A very thorough historical commentary on Kant's legal and political philosophy.

Caplan, Bryan. *Anarchist Theory FAQ: Or, Instead of a FAQ, by a Man Too Busy to Write One.* Version 5.2. N.p. n.d. http://econfaculty.gmu.edu/bcaplan/anarfaq.htm (Aug. 16, 2020).
A readable and wide-ranging overview of issues related to anarchism by an academic economist who also writes about philosophy and politics.

Carson, Kevin A. *The Desktop Regulatory State.* Charleston, SC: BookSurge 2016.
Carson creatively reinterprets, synthesizes, and advances ideas from a range of anarchist tendencies, drawing on both nineteenth-century classics like the work of Proudhon and Tucker and more recent work in history, economics, and political theory. In this book, he explains how voluntary institutions could perform regulatory and related functions.

———. "Health Care and Radical Monopoly." *The Freeman: Ideas on Liberty* 60.2 (March 2010): 8–11. https://fee.org/articles/health-care-and-radical-monopoly/ (Aug. 16, 2020).
Carson highlights the role of state intervention in raising the costs of and limiting access to medical care, arguing for the merits of alternative arrangements crafted in the absence of cartelizing regulation.

———. *Organization Theory: A Libertarian Perspective.* Charleston, SC: BookSurge 2009.
Carson explains why organizational hierarchies are inherently inefficient and why state intervention is needed to sustain them, arguing that small, flat organizations interacting by contract on a fluid basis are appealing alternatives to conventional corporations.

Carson, Kevin A. *Studies in Mutualist Political Economy.* Charleston, SC: BookSurge 2007. Mutualist.org, 2007. www.mutualist.org/id47.html (Aug. 16, 2020).
Drawing on both history and economic theory, Carson argues that the mutualism of Tucker and others can be effectively integrated with insights from later economic thinkers. This book is especially provocative in virtue of Carson's arguments for the rehabilitation of a version of the labor theory of value.

Carson, Stephen W. "Biblical Anarchism." LewRockwell.com. June 7, 2011. www.lewrockwell.com/2001/06/stephen-w-carson/no-government-but-god/ (Aug. 20, 2019).
A contemporary Christian market anarchist grapples with Romans 13 and other passages suggesting the legitimacy of the state.

Casey, Gerard. *Libertarian Anarchy.* New York: Continuum 2012.
Casey argues that Lockean self-ownership implies a strong enough conception of individual rights that the state necessarily infringes on them. And, since law can evolve spontaneously, the state is not required as a source of social order.

Chartier, Gary. *Anarchy and Legal Order: Law and Politics for a Stateless Society.* Cambridge: CUP 2012.
Develops a normative account of law rooted in the New Classical Natural Law theory and uses this model both to help (in tandem with a range of other normative and social-scientific considerations) establish the appropriateness of anarchy and to elaborate anarchic legal norms. Argues that natural-law theory is compatible with spontaneous-order theory and that this confluence provides support for a voluntary, polycentric legal order. Defends anarchism via rejection of monopolistic legal power and appreciation for organic cooperation. Argues for an understanding of market anarchism as leftist and anti-capitalist.

Chartier, Gary, and Johnson, Charles W., eds. *Markets Not Capitalism: Individualist Anarchism against Bosses, Inequality, Corporate Power, and Structural Poverty.* New York: Minor Compositions-Autonomedia 2011. http://radgeek.com/gt/2011/10/Markets-Not-Capitalism-2011-Chartier-and-Johnson.pdf (Aug. 16, 2020).
A collection of historical and contemporary essays highlighting the radical orientation and potential of the individualist anarchist tradition.

Chomsky, Noam. *Chomsky on Anarchism.* Oakland, CA: AK 2006.
Not only a premier theoretical linguist and a long-time, articulate critic of the US government's foreign policy, Chomsky is also among the leading social-anarchist thinkers writing today.

Christoyannopoulos, Alexandre. *Christian Anarchism: A Political Commentary on the Gospel.* Abridged ed. Exeter: Imprint Academic 2011.

Christoyannopoulos' work is the first comprehensive study of Christian anarchism. Christoyannopoulos skillfully synthesizes the claims of figures such as Tolstoy, Day, and Ellul in order to provide readers with an overview of Christian anarchist arguments, thinkers, and history.

Churchill, Ward. *Pacifism as Pathology.* Oakland, CA: AK 2003.

Churchill argues that the pacifist victories of the twentieth century only occurred because of background threats of violence and that pacifism mostly helps keep the violent state and social order in place.

Clark, Samuel J. A. *Living without Domination: The Possibility of an Anarchist Utopia.* Farnham: Ashgate 2007.

A corrective analysis of misconceptions about anarchism, utopianism, and human sociability, followed by an analysis of the natural human social activity which shows the possibility of anarchist sociability.

Clark, Stephen R. L. *Civil Peace and Sacred Order.* Oxford: Clarendon-OUP 1989.

Offers both a subdued argument for anarchism and a critique of the idolatrous pretensions of states.

———. *The Political Animal: Biology, Ethics, and Politics.* London: Routledge 1999.

Includes two provocatively anarchic essays: "Slaves and Citizens" and "Anarchists against the Revolution".

Conrad, Ryan, ed. *Against Equality: Queer Revolution, Not Mere Inclusion.* Chico, CA: AK 2014.

This anthology covers a wide range of LGBTQ+ issues, consistently favoring greater autonomy and less state power. Its provocative essays offer critiques of hate crime laws, HIV criminalization, institutionalized marriage, participation in the military, and more.

Crow, Scott. *Black Flags and Windmills: Hope, Anarchy and the Common Ground Collective.* 2d ed. Oakland, CA: PM 2014.

Crow offers a personal account of disaster recovery in post-Katrina New Orleans based on anarchist principles of mutual aid. From the provision of defense against roaming predators to the distribution of aid and the establishment of medical clinics, the Common Ground Collective operated on the basis of an ethic of "solidarity, not charity."

Coyne, Christopher J. "Lobotomizing the Defense Brain." *Review of Austrian Economics* 28. 4 (2015): 371–396.

Coyne examines the dominant narrative and underlying assumptions within the defense and peace economics literature. He identifies and critically analyzes five of these assumptions and argues that an alternative framework is necessary for understanding and providing realistic analyses of defense provision.

Coyne, Christopher J., and Hall, Abigail R. "State-Provided Defense as Non-Comprehensive Planning." *Journal of Private Enterprise* 34.1 (2019): 75–85.

Argues that state-provided defense is a form of non-comprehensive planning and that instances of this kind of planning are subject to two distinct problems—"knowledge problems" and "power problems." These problems are discussed and analyzed within the context of the US defense sector.

Cuboniks, Laboria. "Xenofeminism: A Politics for Alienation." Laboriacuboniks.net, n.d. https://laboriacuboniks.net/manifesto/xenofeminism-a-politics-for-alienation/ (Aug. 16, 2020).

The Xenofeminist manifesto—albeit written primarily for a feminist audience steeped in continental philosophy and deeply suspicious of rationality and humanism—was almost immediately republished by anarcho-transhumanists, and much cross-fertilization has occurred as a result.

Day, Dorothy. *Selected Writings: By Little and by Little.* Ed. and intro. Robert Ellsberg. Maryknoll, NY: Orbis 2005.

This collection introduces readers to the life, work, and thought of the Christian anarchist Dorothy Day. Day was co-founder of the Catholic Worker Movement, which continues to serve as a source of inspiration for many Christian anarchists.

De Cleyre, Voltairine. *The Voltairine de Cleyre Reader.* Ed. A. J. Brigati. Oakland, CA: AK 2004.

A leading American anarchist at the end of the nineteenth century and the beginning of the twentieth, de Cleyre coined the phrase "anarchism without adjectives."

De Jasay, Anthony. *Social Contract, Free Ride: A Study of the Public Goods Problem.* Oxford: Clarendon-OUP 1991.

An economist and philosopher argues on rational-choice grounds that social order is possible without the state but that the emergence of the state is a persistent danger.

DeLeon, David. *The American as Anarchist: Reflections on Indigenous Radicalism.* Baltimore, MD: Johns Hopkins UP 1978.

An historical analysis of anarchism as reflective of a persistent anti-authoritarian strand in American thought.

Dyer-Witheford, Nick. *Cyber-Marx: Cycles and Circuits of Struggle in High-Technology Capitalism.* Urbana, IL: U of Illinois P 1999.

An autonomist classic on the Exodus model of postcapitalist transition.

Edmundson, William E., ed. *The Duty to Obey the Law: Selected Philosophical Readings.* Lanham, MD: Rowman 1999.

A good introduction to contemporary debates about political authority, duties to obey, and the position dubbed "philosophical anarchism." See especially the selections from Robert Paul Wolff, M. B. E. Smith, A. John Simmons, and Joseph Raz.

Egoumenides, Magda. *Philosophical Anarchism and Political Obligation.* London: Bloomsbury Academic 2014.

Demonstrates the value of taking an anarchist approach to the problem of political authority.

Eller, Vernard. *Christian Anarchy: Jesus' Primacy over the Powers.* Grand Rapids, MI: Eerdmans 1987.

Eller's work is a classic of Christian anarchist literature. Eller defends a vision of Christian anarchism as anti-political and anti-revolutionary. In Eller's view, Christian anarchists do not put their faith in any human "arkys," including whatever new "arky" might be established through revolution.

Ellickson, Robert C. *Order without Law: How Neighbors Settle Disputes.* Cambridge, MA: Harvard UP 1991.

Ellickson examines the ways in which the residents of Shasta County, California, often succeed, without the involvement of the state, in coordinating with one another in a mutually advantageous way, by assigning property rights over land despite formal legal rules.

Ellul, Jacques. *Anarchy and Christianity.* Trans. Geoffrey W. Bromiley. Eugene, OR: Wipf & 2011.

Ellul's influential work, first published in 1991, explores the possibility of reconciling Christianity and anarchism. According to Ellul, anarchism—which he understands as the rejection of all violence—is biblically well-founded. Additionally, he argues that anarchists' rejection of Christianity rests on a misunderstanding of biblical faith, which is often betrayed by the religion of the church.

———. *The New Demons.* New York: Seabury 1975.

Ellul argues that the state and revolution are modern sacreds that command respect and fear much like religious gods and totems.

Fedako, James. "Romans 13 and Anarcho-Capitalism." LewRockwell.com. Feb. 25, 2010. www.lewrockwell.com/2010/02/jim-fedako/romans-13-and-anarcho-capitalism/ (Aug. 20, 2019).

Examines attempted Christian justifications for state authority proffered on biblical grounds.

Friedman, David D. *The Machinery of Freedom.* 3d ed. Charleston, SC: CreateSpace 2015.

This book is a modern classic in the theoretical literature concerned with anarchy. In it, Friedman articulates a broadly (but not exclusively) utilitarian case for market anarchism rooted in the law-and-economics tradition, one that might be thought of as a market-anarchist alternative to Rothbard's anarcho-capitalism. Friedman advances an economic analysis of statism and, finding much of it inefficient, suggests alternatives more attuned to maximizing social gains and aligning institutions with individual incentives. Beginning within the context of existing institutions, Friedman suggests a series of specific reforms in the direction of increasing privatization that would produce desirable movements in the direction of a market-anarchist society.

Gandhi, Mohandas K. "Enlightened Anarchy." *The Penguin Gandhi Reader.* Ed. Rudrangshu Mukherjee. New York: Penguin 1996.

Gandhi lays out a case for a pacifist anarchist vision of the world.

Gibbard, Alan. "Natural Property Rights." *Noûs* 10.1 (1976): 77–86.

While this paper does not bill itself as a social-anarchist argument, it contends that core libertarian commitments actually militate against the appropriation of unowned natural resources. Specifically, it notes that there is a "hard libertarian" position that holds that people can lose their natural rights only through voluntary agreement. However, given that people have a natural right to use all unowned resources, it would then follow that others can only strip them of this right via initial appropriation if those others consent to such appropriation.

Gillis, William. "The Incoherence and Unsurvivability of Non-Anarchist Transhumanism." Institute for Ethics and Emerging Technologies. Institute for Ethics and Emerging Technologies, Oct. 29, 2015. https://ieet.org/index.php/IEET2/more/gillis20151029 (Aug. 16, 2020).

Transcript of a talk at a 2015 conference, The Future of Politics, organized by the Institute for Ethics and Emerging Technologies, a transhumanist think tank with social-democratic leanings. It is the most linked and discussed treatment of anarchism within the transhumanist milieu.

Goodway, David, ed. *For Anarchism: History, Theory, and Practice.* London: Routledge 1989.

A collection of essays examining the early stages of twentieth-century anarchism and offering varied perspectives on anarchist theory.

Goldman, Emma. *Anarchism and Other Essays.* New York: Mother Earth 1910.

———. *Living My Life.* New York: Knopf 1931.

Anarchist and feminist who bridged the anarchist movements in the United States and Europe, Goldman famously declared, "I want freedom, the right to self-expression, everybody's right to beautiful, radiant things."

Goldsmith, Edward, et al. *Blueprint for Survival.* New York: Houghton 1972.

This book was first published as a special edition of the British environmental journal *The Ecologist*, and had a major role in stimulating the emergence of the UK's green movement. Although its main purpose was to sound the alarm about the social and ecological dangers facing modern civilization, the book's recommendations for addressing these problems had a radical and anarchistic tenor. The decentralist agenda laid out in this book had an important hand in linking environmentalism with anarchism in the decades that followed.

Goodman, Paul. *Like a Conquered Province*. New York: Vintage 1966.

———. *People or Personnel*. New York: Vintage 1964.

Two books exploring the ways in which the organizational culture of bureaucratic hierarchy has become hegemonic throughout our society.

Graeber, David. *Fragments of an Anarchist Anthropology*. Chicago: Prickly Paradigm 2004. http://prickly-paradigm.com/sites/default/files/Graeber_PPP_14_0.pdf (Aug. 16, 2020).

A compact program for the development of a full-blown anarchist social theory, laying the groundwork for discussions of the state, voluntary associations, and resistance, by a scholar described by a distinguished peer as "the best anthropological theorist of his generation from anywhere in the world."

Graham, Robert, ed. *Anarchism: A Documentary History of Libertarian Ideas 1: From Anarchy to Anarchism (300CE to 1939)*. Montreal: Black Rose 2005.

———. *Anarchism: A Documentary History of Libertarian Ideas 2: The Emergence of the New Anarchism (1939–1977)*. Montreal: Black Rose 2007.

——— *Anarchism: A Documentary History of Libertarian Ideas 3: The New Anarchism (1974 to 2012)*. Montreal: Black Rose 2012.

A vast collection of anarchist source materials from before the Middle Ages to the present. The selections are drawn from multiple intellectual and cultural traditions, many non-Western.

Green, Leslie. *The Authority of the State*. Oxford: Clarendon-OUP 1988.

A comprehensive account of theories defending state authority.

Guérin, Daniel. *Anarchism: From Theory to Practice*. Trans. Mary Klopper. New York: Monthly Review 1970. Anarchist Library 2009. http://theanarchistlibrary.org/HTML/Daniel_Guerin__Anarchism__From_Theory_to_Practice.html (Aug. 16, 2020).

An influential overview of anarchist history and theory which also features historical information about twentieth-century anarchist experiments.

Hasnas, John, "The Obviousness of Anarchy." Long and Machan. 111–132.

Hasnas argues that a stable, successful society without government can exist by reviewing past and current examples of non-governmental order-producing mechanisms. Since a coercive monopoly is not essential for the provision of any good or service, including law, the state is unnecessary and so unwarranted.

Hayek, Friedrich. "Competition as a Discovery Procedure." *Quarterly Journal of Austrian Economics* 5. 3 (2002): 9–23.

Originally published in 1968, this article discusses the meaning and nature of the competitive process, highlighting that many discussions of "competition" do not provide a clear understanding of the concept. It argues that competition is a discovery procedure in which individuals come to find new knowledge regarding costs, potential innovations, and preferences.

Higgs, Robert. *Crisis and Leviathan: Critical Episodes in the Growth of American Government*. Oxford: OUP 1982.

An anarchist economic historian carefully analyzes the link between economic, political, and military crises and the cancerous development of the American state.

———. *Delusions of Power: New Explorations of the State, War, and the Economy*. Oakland, CA: Independent 2012.

Higgs offers both economic and moral arguments against the state. He directs his ire, in particular, at militarism and war, effectively debunking numerous pro-war fallacies.

Hess, Karl. *Dear America*. New York: Morrow 1975.

A Goldwater-speechwriter-turned-New-Leftist explains his conviction that anarchism best expresses American ideals.

Hobbes, Thomas. *Leviathan or the Matter, Forme and Power of a Common-Wealth Ecclesiasticall and Civil*. London: Crooke 1651.

The classic discussion of anarchy and the "state of nature." Perhaps the most important work of modern political philosophy, *Leviathan* is also an important contribution to moral philosophy and to important early-modern ideas about science and knowledge.

Hodgskin, Thomas. *The Natural and Artificial Right of Property Contrasted*. London: Steil 1832.

Hodgskin argues forcefully against Benthamite reformers that moral rights to property are prior to state recognition, and that states are not free to engineer new property rights not grounded in justice. Natural property rights, he contends, are manifestations of individual freedom, while artificial property rights are constructs reflective of unjust privilege.

Holterman, Thom, and van Maarseveen, Henk, eds. *Law and Anarchism*. Montreal: Black Rose 1984.
Essays on the legal problems of a stateless society from diverse perspectives.

Horn, Norman. "New Testament Theology of the State." LewRockwell.com. Sep. 29, 2007, www.lewrockwell.com/2007/09/norman-horn/new-testament-theology-of-the-state/ (Aug. 20, 2019).
A contemporary Christian market anarchist addresses ways in which the New Testament might be relevant to questions of political theology and the authority of the state.

Huemer, Michael. *The Problem of Political Authority*. New York: Palgrave 2013.
Governments purportedly have the power to create in us an obligation to obey some of their commands and laws, and also possess the moral permission to enforce these edicts through violence and threats of violence. Huemer argues that common-sense moral principles are sufficient to rebut any claim that the state can have justification for acts an individual would not. He examines and refutes dozens of putative reasons to attribute these special powers to government. He also provides a psychological diagnosis of why the apparently mistaken belief in government might be so widespread. In the second half of the book, he describes how an anarchist society might effectively function. He concludes that there is no duty on persons to obey the law and no right of the state to coerce.

Illich, Ivan. *Tools for Conviviality*. New York: Harper 1973.
An analysis of ways in which totalizing professional bureaucracies transform society and individuals into means to their own ends.

Karl Hess: Toward Liberty. Dir. Roland Hallé and Peter W. Ladue. Direct Cinema 1980. An Oscar-winning portrait of the gentle, decent anarchist thinker and activist and advocate of local empowerment.

Kauffman, Bill. *Bye Bye Miss American Empire: Neighborhood Patriots, Backcountry Rebels, and Their Underdog Crusades to Redraw America's Political Map*. White River Junction, VT: Chelsea Green 2010.
A literate, contrarian proponent of "front-porch anarchism" pens a love poem to decent secessionist movements, past and present.

Keyt, David. "Aristotle and Anarchism." *Reason Papers* 18 (Fall 1993): 133–152. Rptd. *Aristotle's Politics: Critical Essays*. Ed. Richard Kraut and Steven Skultety. Oxford: Rowman 2005. 203–22).

———. "Aristotle, and the Ancient Roots of Anarchism." *Topoi* 15 (1996): 129–142.
These two papers identify the anarchistical implications of Aristotle's study of properly political organization (that is, of the self-governing and largely self-supporting cities and associated land known as *poleis*—which are not quite the same as "states").

Kinsella, N. Stephan. *Against "Intellectual Property*." Auburn, AL: Mises 2009. www.mises.org/books/against.pdf (Aug. 16, 2020).
An anarchist lawyer and legal theorist offers a sustained case that patents, copyrights, and other forms of intellectual property are unjust creations of the state.

Kolko, Gabriel. *The Triumph of Conservatism: A Reinterpretation of American History, 1900–1916*. New York: Free 1963.
Though not an anarchist himself, Kolko provides ammunition for anarchist critiques of the state in this study of how Progressive-era regulations were shaped to serve the interests of big business.

Konkin, Samuel, III. *New Libertarian Manifesto*. Los Angeles, CA: Koman 1983.
Samuel Konkin III's *New Libertarian Manifesto* is the *locus classicus* for the author's version of anarchism, "agorism." It outlines Konkin's model of libertarian praxis through black-market participation, an important departure in libertarian theory.

Kropotkin, Peter. *The Conquest of Bread*. London: Penguin 2015.
Originally published in 1892, *The Conquest of Bread* outlines Kropotkin's argument for a stateless society. One of the earliest and most masterful expositions of the anarcho-communist position, it features a sweeping description of anarchist normative principles, analyses of existing political and economic organizational arrangements, and prescriptions for what form an anarchist society should take. It profoundly influenced the course of anarchist thought and activism in the twentieth century.

———. *Mutual Aid. A Factor of Evolution*. London: Freedom 1998 [1914]. Project Gutenberg n.d. www.Gutenberg.Org/etext/4341 (Aug. 16, 2020).
Biologist, geographer, and social theorist Kropotkin articulates a vision of anarchy emphasizing cooperation and rootedness in the natural world.

———. *Peter Kropotkin's Revolutionary Pamphlets*. Ed. Petr Alekseevich. Whitefish, MT: Kessinger 2010 [1927].
Not only an anarchist but also a distinguished biologist and natural historian, Kropotkin emphasized the importance of symbiotic and cooperative endeavors in human society and the natural world.

Landauer, Gustav. *Revolution and Other Writings: A Political Reader*. Oakland: PM 2010.

Many essays in this book deal with the issue of violence and war-making. Landauer argues for an anarchist, pacifist practice.

Lavoie, Don. *National Economic Planning: What Is Left?* Arlington, VA: Mercatus 2016.

Lavoie presents the social science behind two systemic problems with central planning: the knowledge problem and the power problem. He also argues that planning represents the militarization of the economy, and that therefore the left's radical goals of abolishing war and injustice are best served by rejecting economic planning.

Leeson, Peter. *Anarchy Unbound*. New York: CUP 2014.

Leeson provides careful empirical evidence that "anarchy works better than you think." He explains why certain kinds of non-government enforcement mechanisms are successful, stable, and efficient. He challenges the conventional wisdom according to which self-governance always performs worse than government. Utilizing rational-choice theory, he analyzes historical examples of the endogenous formation of governance mechanisms and social rules, demonstrating that anarchy has functioned more effectively than economists might otherwise predict.

———. "Governments, Clubs, and Constitutions." *Journal of Economic Behavior and Organization* 80.2 (2011): 301–308.

Many propose constitutions as a means to constrain government, but the mere presence of a constitution does not guarantee it will be enforced. In this paper Peter Leeson argues that clubs formed through voluntary association provide the best enforced constitutions, largely because they are owned by residual claimants and are subject to competition.

———. *The Invisible Hook: The Hidden Economics of Pirates*. Princeton, NJ: Princeton UP 2009.

Defying the conventional presumption of lawlessness among criminals, Leeson's work illustrates the creative capacity of pirates to craft institutions of governance, including constitutions mandating the separation of powers, outside the shadow of the state.

Levy, Jacob T. *Rationalism, Pluralism, and Freedom*. New York: OUP 2014.

Levy explores two strands of thought in the history of liberalism. Rationalism advocates the power of the centralizing, rationalizing state to liberate the individual from the domination of family, religious, feudal, and associational life. Pluralism stresses the value of associations as bulwarks against the predation and domination of modern states. Levy cautions us not to embrace either side of this dichotomy at the total expense of the other.

Linnell, Lexi. "This Machine Kills Ableism." *Anarchotranshuman: A Journal of Radical Possibility and Striving* 3 (2016): 12–15. http://infoshop.io/media/Anarcho-Transhuman%20-%20Issue%203.pdf (Aug. 16, 2020).

While everything in this issue of *Anarchotranshuman* is good, Linnell's piece frames the ethical and philosophical context of anarcho-transhumanism well.

Lipscomb, David. *Civil Government: Its Origin, Mission, and Destiny, and the Christian's Relation to It*. Nashville, TN: McQuiddy 1996.

An important nineteenth-century Christian anarchist work, offering one of the first cases for explicitly Christian anarchism.

Long, Roderick T., and Machan, Tibor. *Anarchism/Minarchism: Is a Government Part of a Free Country?* Farnham: Ashgate 2008.

Up-to-date arguments from people who believe there should no states, and people who believe there should be very limited states.

Martin, James J. *Men against the State*. Colorado Springs, CO: Myles 1970. www.mises.org/books/Men_Against_the_State_Martin.pdf (Aug. 16, 2020).

Martin's masterful, groundbreaking history of the American individualist anarchist movement remains the best available overview of key figures in the movement and of the content and development of their ideas. Martin explores the origins of the uniquely American strains of anarchist thought, distinguishing them carefully from their European cousins and providing important biographical information on the key figures of American individualism.

Marshall, Peter. *Demanding the Impossible: A History of Anarchism*. Oakland, CA: PM 2010.

An extensive global narrative focused on the growth and significance of anarchist ideas and multiple anarchist movements and figures.

Marvin, Carolyn, and Ingle, David. *Blood Sacrifice and Nation: Totem Rituals and the American Flag*. New York: CUP 1999.

Marvin and Ingle argue that American nationalism is a religious that revolves around a religious totem, the American flag, and that state wars are blood sacrifice rituals that periodically purge disunity and help sustain nationalist identity and religious practice.

McElroy, Wendy. *The Debates of Liberty*. New York: Lexington 2003.

This is an extremely helpful study of the contentions advanced and the debates conducted in *Liberty*, the chief organ of the American individualist anarchist movement in the last decades of the nineteenth century.

McKay, Iain et al. *An Anarchist FAQ*. Vol. 2. Chico: AK 2008–12.

An influential exposition of anarchism, featuring contributions from anarchists with a range of viewpoints, discussions of arguments for and against anarchism, and analyses of multiple schools of anarchist thought.

McLaughlin, Paul. *Anarchism and Authority: A Philosophical Introduction to Classical Anarchism*. London: Routledge 2016.

A conceptual and historical analysis of anarchism, of authority, and of the historical, theoretical, and practical relations between the two. Describes, develops, and defends anarchism's philosophy of authority.

Meikle, Scott. *Aristotle's Economic Theory*. 2d ed. New York: OUP 1997.

A serious study of Aristotle's often puzzling discussion of economic justice, and the effects of money in a cooperative society.

Meltzer, Albert. *Anarchism: Arguments for and Against*. Oakland, CA: AK 2001.

A brief primer on anarchist ideas designed to respond to Marxist critiques. Dismisses anarchist thinkers including Tolstoy, Tucker, and Proudhon.

Mises, Ludwig von *Socialism: An Economic and Sociological Analysis*. New Haven: Yale UP 1951.

This classic work highlights the problem of economic calculation for varieties of socialism committed to collective ownership, but also contains some commentary on Christian theological issues.

More, Max, and Vita-More, Natasha, eds. *The Transhumanist Reader: Classical and Contemporary Essays on the Science, Technology, and Philosophy of the Human Future*. New York: Wiley-Blackwell 2013.

A compilation of important texts in the mainstream transhumanist tradition. Of particular note are "Morphological Freedom—Why We Not Just Want It but Need It," by Anders Sandberg, and Natasha Vita-More's original 1982 Manifesto. Radical politics and anarchist derivations are for the most part studiously ignored in this compilation and the contributions of serious philosophers like Nick Bostrom are positioned side-by-side with less impressive selections, but it's the best survey out there.

Mulgan, Richard. "Lycophron and Greek Theories of Social Contract." *Journal of the History of Ideas* 40.1 (1979): 121–128.

Lycophron the Sophist seems to have emphasized the notion of "free contract" as the only proper basis for a just civil society.

Murphy, Robert P. *Chaos Theory: Two Essays on Market Anarchy*. New York: RJ 2002. Mises Institute n.d. www.mises.org/books/chaostheory.pdf (Aug. 16, 2020).

A helpful discussion of the management of the potentially violent in a stateless society.

National Intelligence Council. *Global Trends 2030: Alternative Worlds*. Washington, DC: Office of the Director of National Intelligence 2012. www.dni.gov/files/documents/GlobalTrends_2030.pdf (Aug. 16, 2020).

Recognizing some shockingly radical possibilities, for a government publication, while describing them in soothingly smooth prose.

Negri, Antonio, and Hardt, Michael. *Commonwealth*. Cambridge: Harvard UP 2009.

———. *Multitude: War and Democracy in the Age of Empire*. New York: Penguin 2004.

Two more autonomist classics on the Exodus model of postcapitalist transition.

Newman, Saul. *Postanarchism*. Cambridge: Polity 2015.

Newman charts a course from anarchism to *anarchy*, a new "ontological anti-authoritarianism," freed from the authority of first principles. Newman endeavors here to present a new and different radical politics focused on "self-government and free and spontaneous organization, rather than organization by and through the state."

———. *The Politics of Postanarchism*. Edinburgh: Edinburgh UP 2010.

A contemporary account of anarchist ideas, relations, and practices rooted in a version of poststructuralist philosophy.

———. *Power and Politics in Poststructuralist Thought: New Theories of the Political*. London: Routledge 2007.

Newman examines the influence of poststructuralist thought on contemporary political theory, drawing on figures such as Foucault and Derrida to help him reconsider Stirner and to demonstrate the continued relevance of Stirner's radical critique of essentialism.

———, ed. *Max Stirner*. New York: Palgrave 2011.

This collection brings together some of the most interesting and insightful contemporary scholars working on anarchism to consider how Stirner's work can lead to "a radical rethinking of key political categories." It "is the first ever edited book on Max Stirner published in the English language," an excellent introduction to Stirner's key ideas and the debates that have raged around his often puzzling work.

Niskanen, William N. *Bureaucracy and Representative Government*. London: Routledge 2007 [1971].

Niskanen analyzes output within the context of a public-sector bureaucracy. He argues that, facing incentives to maximize their budgets, bureaux supply up to twice as much output as competitive industries facing identical cost and demand conditions.

Nock, Albert Jay. *Our Enemy, the State*. New York: Morrow 1935.

Highlights the role of the state as an enabler of mercantile interests and as an adversary of society.

North, Douglas C., Wallis, John J., and Weingast, Barry. *Violence and Social Order: A Conceptual Framework for Interpreting Recorded Human History*. New York: CUP 2009.

Empirically explores the development of societies from "natural states," in which order is maintained by fragile coalitions held in place by means of personal relationships, to "open access orders" in which stability, dispute resolution, and political power are maintained using impersonal legal artefacts. Whilst modern liberal democratic states are much "bigger" than medieval monarchies, their power is also more robustly limited. To protect freedom, then, North et al. might be seen as suggesting, we might need a strong state after all.

Nozick, Robert. *Anarchy, State, and Utopia*. New York: Basic 1974.

Assesses the justification of the state and argues with great philosophical sophistication that a minimal state could arise without violating natural rights. The first 40 percent of the book is devoted to a complex critical analysis of and the articulation of a serious challenge to a certain kind of anarchism. The last chapter, "A Framework for Utopia," is pretty anarchic.

O'Neill, Onora. "Reason and Politics in the Kantian Enterprise." *Constructions of Reason: Explorations of Kant's Practical Philosophy*. Cambridge: CUP 1989. 3–27.

Demonstrates how Kant tries to overcome anarchy in different parts of his philosophy.

Oppenheimer, Franz. *The State*. 2d American ed. Charleston, SC: CreateSpace 2017.

Sociologist Oppenheimer defends the idea that the state is product not of social evolution or social contract but rather of conquest. Emphasizes the role of the state in fostering and propping up inequality.

Ostrom, Elinor. *Governing the Commons: The Evolution of Institutions for Collective Action*. New York: CUP 2015 [1990].

This book offers a fascinating account of how informal institutions can solve challenging collective action problems. Ostrom argues for the possibility of successful common property arrangements by appealing to a wide range of stable practices. These cases do not fit neatly into the categories of "market" or "state" institutions, but are instead instances of bottom-up collective self-governance.

Otsuka, Michael. *Libertarianism without Inequality*. New York: OUP 2003.

This book defends a variety of left-libertarianism that is conceptually adjacent to the social-anarchist position. It argues that people can have robust rights of self-ownership where these rights are compatible with an egalitarian distribution of material resources. It also argues for a voluntarist account of state legitimacy.

Pateman, Carole. *The Problem of Political Obligation: A Critique of Liberal Theory*. Berkeley: U of California P 1985.

Pateman disposes effectively of conventional defenses of consensual state authority. While her concern is with grounding political obligation in democracy, her criticisms of conventional theories can easily be read as conveying anarchist implications.

Pogge, Thomas. "Is Kant's *Rechtslehre* a 'Comprehensive Liberalism?'" *Kant's Metaphysics of Morals*. Ed. Mark Timmons. New York: OUP 2002. 133–158.

An influential article that argues forcefully for the "independence thesis"—that Kant's legal philosophy has a foundation independent of his ethics.

Perry, Stephen. "Political Authority and Political Obligation." *Oxford Studies in Philosophy of Law* 2 (2013): 1–74.

Distinguishes political *authority*—the moral power of the state to change the normative situation of its citizens—from political *obligation*.

Proudhon, Pierre-Joseph. *General Idea of the Revolution in the Nineteenth Century*. Trans. John Beverly Robinson. Mineola, NY: Dover 2004 [1923].

———. *System of Economical Contradictions; Or, the Philosophy of Misery*. Trans. Benjamin R. Tucker. New York: Arno 1973 [1888].

———. *What Is Property?* Ed. and trans. David R. Kelley and Bonnie G. Smith. Cambridge: CUP 1994.

Arguably the first person to use the word "anarchist" for himself, Proudhon jousted with Marx and developed a distinctive approach to anarchism he labeled "mutualism."

Purchase, Graham. *Anarchism and Environmental Survival*. Edmonton, AB: Black Cat 2011 [1994].

Alarmed by the prospect of an ecological crisis, Graham Purchase argues that humanity's survival depends on replacing existing states with radically decentralized political communities. Following in a rich tradition of green anarchism, Purchase seeks to grapple with some of the big challenges facing other similar views—especially those having to do with large-scale challenges that transcend local contexts.

Raimondo, Justin. *An Enemy of the State: The Life of Murray N. Rothbard*. Amherst, NY: Prometheus 2000.

This biography follows the father of modern anarcho-capitalism from his early years as a student and devotee of the Old Right through his flirtations with the New Left and his founding of the Libertarian Party to his later return to the right-wing fold as a paleo-libertarian. The work is crucial for scholars of American libertarianism.

Raymond, Eric S. *The Cathedral and the Bazaar: Musings on Linux and Open Source by an Accidental Revolutionary*. Sebastopol, CA: O'Reilly 1999.

The original classic contrast of stigmergic to bureaucratic coordination. Just don't read anything else by him.

Raz, Joseph. *The Authority of Law: Essays on Law and Morality*. 2d ed. New York: OUP 2009.

Raises critical questions regarding the capacity of states to create obligations.

———. *The Morality of Freedom*. Oxford: Clarendon-OUP 1986.

An exemplary philosophical exposition of a moral and political theory of freedom.

Redford, James. *Jesus Is an Anarchist: A Free-Market, Libertarian Anarchist, That Is—Otherwise What Is Called an Anarcho-Capitalist*. Amsterdam: SSRN-Elsevier 2011. https://papers.ssrn.com/sol3/papers.cfm?abstract_id=1337761.

Redford defends the position that Jesus's life and teachings imply anarcho-capitalism. He examines a number of biblical passages and addresses various potential objections to support his argument.

Richman, Barak. *Stateless Commerce: The Diamond Network and the Persistence of Relational Exchange*. Cambridge, MA: Harvard UP 2017.

Richman provides a case of study focused on ways in which ethnic trading networks centered on Manhattan's 47th Street have provided contractual enforcement for participants in the diamond trade outside the scope of the state. Whereas conventional wisdom supposes that technological progress should lead to the displacement of "primitive" commercial networks, Richman reveals the adaptiveness of the commercial practices prevailing in the diamond district, making clear that they represent institutional responses to the transaction costs of state enforcement of property rights in diamonds.

Richman, Sheldon. "Libertarian Left: Free-Market Anti-Capitalism, the Unknown Ideal." *American Conservative* 10.3 (March 2011): 28–32. www.theamericanconservative.com/articles/libertarian-left/ (Aug. 16, 2020).

Provides an overview of a developing intellectual and political movement on the political left, populated largely by anarchists, that interestingly bridges some traditional ideological and strategic divides.

Ripstein, Arthur. *Force and Freedom*. Cambridge, MA: Harvard UP 2009.

A contemporary defense of Kant's legal and political philosophy.

Robb, John. *Brave New War: The Next Stage of Terrorism and the End of Globalization*. Hoboken: Wiley 2007.

An examination of the rise of networked insurgencies and their superiority to the bureaucracies attempting to fight them.

Rocker, Rudolph. *Anarcho-Syndicalism: Theory and Practice*. Oakland, CA: AK 2004.

———. *Pioneers of American Freedom: Origins of Liberal and Radical Thought in America*. Trans. Arthur E. Briggs. Los Angeles, CA: Rocker 1949.

Anarcho-Syndicalism is a classic of anarchist strategy, theory, and history which emphasizes the commitment to freedom shared by proponents of different anarchist tendencies. *Pioneers* is an appreciation of indigenous American radical traditions from the perspective of a titan of European anarchism.

Rosler, Andres. *Political Authority and Obligation in Aristotle*. Oxford: Clarendon-OUP 2005.

A discussion of Aristotle's suggestions for the origin of felt obligations to governing bodies or persons.

Rothbard, Murray N. *The Ethics of Liberty*. 2d ed. New York: New York UP 2003. Mises Institute n.d. http://mises.org/rothbard/ethics/ethics.asp. (Aug. 16, 2020).

Rothbard defends a secular version of natural-law theory that he believes can be wholly understood by reference to two simple principles: self-ownership and homesteading. In quasi- Lockean fashion, he argues for the view that we all come into with an exclusive claim to control our own bodies and lives, and to acquire unowned natural resources through use. And he defends the appropriateness of political and economic institutions he judges to be consistent with this: *yes* to voluntary exchange and contract, *no* to monopoly and the state.

———. *For a New Liberty*. 2nd ed. San Francisco: Fox 1978.

Rothbard's anarchist manifesto, *For a New Liberty* is an important statement of an individualistic anarchist position. It features three important chapters on alternatives to state provision of various services.

———. *Man, Economy, and State*. Scholars ed. Intro. Joseph Stromberg. Auburn, AL: Mises 2004.

The final portion of this general account of economics, "Power and Market," offers economic analyses of issues related to the performance in the state's absence of functions often thought to require state action.

———. "Society without a State." *Nomos* 19 (1978): 191–207.

A frequently cited article in which Rothbard lays out the core distinction between society and state, and outlines how a non-monopolistic legal order might function.

Rousseau, Jean Jacques. *A Discourse on Inequality*. Trans. Maurice Cranston. New York: Penguin 1985 [1754].

One of Rousseau's major political works, developing a conception of the state of nature different from those of his predecessors, Hobbes and Locke.

Ruwart, Mary. *Healing Our World in an Age of Aggression*. 3d ed. Kalamazoo, MI: Sunstar 2003.

A lively and insightful discussion of institutional and personal methods for problem-solving apart from state action.

Sale, Kirkpatrick. *Dwellers in the Land: The Bioregional Vision*. Gabriola Island, BC: New Society 1985.

This book lays out the case for reconstructing our political orders to reflect the ecological contours of the natural world. To Kirkpatrick Sale and other "bioregionalists," our serious ecological challenges can be traced to the fact we live in gargantuan societies that have little connection to the landscapes in which they are imbedded. Sale's proposed alternative would reorganize communities into smaller, more ecologically determined units, pushing us to come to terms with the distinctive possibilities and limits of the places where we live.

Salter, Alexander. "Christian Anarchism: Communitarian or Capitalist?" *Libertarian Papers* 4.1 (2012): 151–162. http://libertarianpapers.org/wp-content/uploads/article/2012/lp-4-1-8.pdf (Aug. 16, 2020).

Offers an extensive literature review of various strands of Christian anarchist thought and discusses ways in which they might bear on socialist and capitalist forms of anarchism.

Sanders, John T. *The Ethical Argument against Government*. Washington, DC: UP of America 1980.

Uses the framework of a Rawlsian "constitutional convention" to argue that rational parties confronted successively with Aristotelean, Hobbesian, Lockean, and Marxian arguments in behalf of the state would remain unconvinced of its reasonableness.

———. "The Free Market Model versus Government: A Reply to Nozick." *Journal of Libertarian Studies* 1.1 (1977): 35–44.

Argues that Nozick's "dominant protection agency" neither meets his monopoly condition for statehood nor need run afoul of his redistributive requirement. This being the case, his argument against market anarchism fails.

——— "Justice and the Initial Acquisition of Property." *Harvard Journal of Law and Public Policy* 10.2 (1987): 367–399.

Argues that the defensibility of some initial claim to property is required by any theory which holds that certain present distributions may be justified, that certain transfers of property are justified, or that restitution ought to be made for previous injustice in transfer or acquisition. Also defends the view that a "Lockean proviso" to principles of just initial acquisition may be self-defeating.

———. "Political Authority." *Monist* 66.4 (1983): 545–556.

Starting with a notion of "authority" that makes a sharp distinction between authority and power, and granting the legitimacy and possible necessity of such authority, this essay traces the devaluation of the idea through varying degrees of institutionalization, culminating in its political cooptation. Argues that what goes by the name of political authority is the very antithesis of the legitimate and necessary element with which the exercise began.

———. "Projects and Property." *Robert Nozick*. Ed. David Schmidtz. Cambridge: CUP 2002. 34–58.

Offers a clarification of the ethical foundations of private property rights that avoids pitfalls common to more strictly Lockean theories, and is thus better prepared to address arguments posed by critics of standard private property arrangements. Also argues against Proudhonian/Waldronian contentions that society has an obligation to ensure that every citizen possesses private property.

———. "The State of Statelessness." Sanders and Narveson. 255–288.

Addresses a handful of issues often raised in discussions of anarchism, whether by anarchists or their critics, from the point of view of a particular version of philosophical anarchism.

Sanders, John T., and Narveson, Jan, eds. *For and against the State: New Philosophical Readings*. MD: Rowman 1996.

A collection of essays on the legitimacy and propriety of the state. All but two were written originally for this book.

Sartwell, Crispin. *Against the State: An Introduction to Anarchist Political Theory*. Buffalo, NY: SUNY 2008.

Demonstrates the inadequacy of traditional arguments for state authority.

Schmidtz, David. *The Limits of Government: An Essay on the Public Goods Argument*. Boulder, CO: Westview 1990.

A critical examination of the view that we need the state because important public goods will not be produced at optimal levels in its absence.

Schumacher, E. F. *Small Is Beautiful: Economics as if People Mattered, Twenty-Five Years Later. With Commentaries*. Vancouver, BC: Hartley 1999.

After spending two decades as Chief Economic Advisor to the British National Coal Board, E. F. Schumacher memorably broke from the mainstream of his profession with this classic 1973 manifesto. Schumacher accused economists of neglecting humanity's spiritual and ecological needs in the service of mindless, soul-crushing, and ecologically devastating growth. In Schumacher's view, a truly humane economy would be reoriented to embrace smallness: small scales of production, small communities, and small impacts on the natural world.

Scott, James C. *Against the Grain: A Deep History of the Earliest States.* New Haven: Yale UP 2018.

Argues that states advanced in conjunction with the cultivation of grain and an entire domestic ecosystem.

———. *The Art of Not Being Governed: An Anarchist History of Upland Southeast Asia.* New Haven: Yale UP 2010.

Describes the role of stateless regions in attacking and supporting states and suffering under their rule.

———. *Seeing like a State: How Certain Schemes to Improve the Human Condition Have Failed.* New Haven: Yale UP 1998.

Scott shows that the imposition of abstract rules that necessarily simplify and re-order spontaneous social relations are necessary to state-building. He examines a range of cases in which programs of top-down societal planning and management have proven unsuccessful. Though he does not argue for anarchism here, he emphasizes the liabilities to which states can be subject and offers multiple examples of state failure.

———. *Two Cheers for Anarchism: Six Easy Pieces on Autonomy, Dignity, and Meaningful Work and Play.* Princeton, NJ: Princeton UP 2012.

A personal, often droll look at the defects of hierarchy and the potential of peaceful, voluntary cooperation to address societal challenges. Scott celebrates human creativity and experimentation in the face of authoritarianism and bureaucratic rigidity. While not completely endorsing political anarchism, Scott asks us to look at the world through an "anarchist squint." From that perspective, he defends open politics over rationalized manipulation, principled law-breaking over unreflective obedience, and fluid complexity over stale homogeneity.

Seel, Gerhard. "How Does Kant Justify the Universal Objective Validity of the Law of Right?" *International Journal of Philosophical Studies* 17 (2009): 71–94.

Argues with extensive textual support against the claim that Kant's positions on legal and moral philosophy rest on independent foundations (the "independence thesis"). Provides an excellent overview over the literature on the topic.

Shaffer, Butler. *In Restraint of Trade: The Business Campaign against Competition, 1918–1938.* Lewisburg, PA: Bucknell UP 1997.

An anarchist legal theorist explains how big business used the regulatory state to its advantage at a crucial period in American history.

Simmons, A. John. "Justification and Legitimacy." *Ethics* 109.4 (1999): 739–771.

Distinguishes legitimacy from justification. The former is understood in terms of a right to impose binding duties and is based on transactional relationships between citizens and the state. The latter is a function of the extent to which the state solves the problems of social interaction. The extent to which a state is justified determines whether and to what extent the state merits our support.

———. *Moral Principles and Political Obligations.* Princeton, NJ: Princeton UP 1979.

A thorough account of the most popular moral defenses of political obligation and of their failure as indicated by philosophical anarchism.

———. "Philosophical Anarchism" *For and against the State: New Philosophical Readings.* Eds. John T. Sanders and Jan Narveson. Lanham, MD: Rowman 1996. 19–39.

A clarifying account of the position of philosophical anarchism within the anarchist tradition and with regard to the problem of authority.

Skarbek, David. *The Social Order of the Underworld: How Prison Gangs Govern the American Penal System.* New York: OUP 2014.

Skarbeck illustrates the creative capacity of prison gangs to foster social order.

Skoble, Aeon J. *Deleting the State: An Argument about Government.* Chicago: Open Court 2008.

Expertly dissects arguments for the necessity and legitimacy of the state. Skoble argues that minimal-state libertarian arguments all involve a tacit assumption about social cooperation that is undercut by research in economics and game theory. Bringing this work to bear on political philosophy, he argues that the basic premises of classical liberalism are sufficient to justify anarchism.

Sorel, Georges. *Reflections on Violence.* New York: CUP 1999.

Sorel argues that an anarcho-syndicalist society can only come about through organized violence and strikes, which he views as creative and life-giving actions.

Spooner, Lysander. *The Collected Works of Lysander Spooner.* Vol 6. Ed. Charles Shively. Weston, MA: M&S 1971.

This collection features almost all of Spooner's works, including his attacks on slavery and the fugitive slave laws, his incendiary "A Letter to Grover Cleveland," his essay in support of revolution in Ireland, and his defense of private property—including intellectual property.

———. *The Lysander Spooner Reader.* Ed. George Smith. San Francisco: Fox 1992.

This collection includes Smith's fine introduction and many of Spooner's writings, including "Vices and not Crimes," Spooner's three "No Treason" essays, and his "Trial by Jury."

———. *Reasonable Religion: Lysander Spooner on Christianity.* Apple Valley, CA: Cobden 2012.

Mikhail Bakunin was not alone in seeing opposition to the authority of traditional religion as an important aspect of the quest for human liberation. Spooner's religious essays make clear his passionate commitment to freedom of thought.

Stephenson, Neal. *The Diamond Age: Or, A Young Lady's Illustrated Primer.* New York: Bantam 1995.

A young woman's life illustrates the conflicts and wonders of a near-future world shaped by remarkable advances in nanotechnology.

———. "The Great Simoleon Caper." *Time*, March 1, 1995. http://content.time.com/time/magazine/article/0,9171,982610,00.html. June 7, 2020.

A short story about a state attempt to thwart public acceptance of a private crypto-currency, and the response of group of hacker-revolutionaries.

———. *Snow Crash.* New York: Del Rey 1992.

A wild ride through a post-state landscape and virtual-scape of viral code and franchised city-states.

Stirner, Max. *The Ego and Its Own.* Trans. David Leopold. Cambridge: CUP 1995.

Stirner's masterwork offers a groundbreaking critique of modernity and its most salient ideas, both employing and parodying Hegel's dialectical approach to deconstruct Christianity, humanism, liberalism, and, indeed, morality itself. Stirner's rejection of universals and essentials anticipates existentialism, poststructuralism, and postmodernist thought generally, positioning the unique individual as the source of all value, unable to brace herself against anything more fundamental than her own arbitrary feelings and desires. Hostile to all fixed systems and ideologies, Stirner attacks capitalism, socialism, and every other political or economic vision, pointing the way to an anarchism that underscores the individual's self-conscious attempts to create meaning for herself.

Stringham, Edward Peter. *Private Governance: Creating Order in Economic and Social Life.* New York: OUP 2015.

This book offers a critique of legal centralism, which postulates that social order requires the provision of law as a public good by government. Many people implicitly believe that rules, governance, and social order can only be provided by the state; Stringham provides both theoretical and empirical evidence against this assumption, documenting private governance in diverse settings including internet commerce, early stock markets, and private policing in San Francisco. He argues that, as a matter of fact, most social rules and economic transactions are enforced through non-governmental means, in part because the transaction costs of enforcement greatly exceed the possible benefits of government enforcement. He suggests that this shows that order and stability cannot be attributed entirely or even mostly to government enforcement.

———, ed. *Anarchy and the Law: The Political Economy of Choice.* Oakland, CA: Independent 2007.

This anthology compiles some of the best available essays on market anarchism, featuring many classic and contemporary arguments for anarchism in philosophy, economics, and history. It features explorations of anarchist theory, debates between anarchists and their classical liberal critics, essays on the history of anarchist thought, and empirical case studies of law enforcement without the state.

———, ed. *Anarchy, State, and Public Choice.* Cheltenham: Elgar 2005.

Offers a range of responses to economic arguments for the necessity or inevitability of the state. Reprints earlier essays by, among others, James Buchanan and Gordon Tullock, generally pairing later defenses with earlier critiques of anarchy.

Tannehill, Morris, and Tannehill, Linda. *The Market for Liberty.* 3d ed. San Francisco: Fox 1993.

A detailed explanation of how the authors believe social cooperation could be managed without the state. Even if some of their observations are problematic, the Tannehills also sometimes exhibit a humane, often charming, hippie sensibility.

Taylor, Michael. *Community, Anarchy and Liberty.* Cambridge: CUP 1982.

A rational-choice defense of a kind of communitarian anarchism. Argues that community plays a vital role in shaping the relations between people required for a stateless social order to be possible.

——— *The Possibility of Cooperation.* Cambridge: CUP 1987.

Argues that traditional game-theoretic defenses of the state, notably those offered by Hume and Hobbes, are unsuccessful.

Tolstoy, Leo. *Government Is Violence: Essays on Anarchism and Pacifism*. New Haven: Phoenix 1990.

———. *The Kingdom of God Is within You*. Trans. Constance Garnett. Charleston, SC: CreateSpace 2014.

Tolstoy argues that Jesus taught radical pacifism, and that the institutional church has betrayed this message. A return to the teachings of Jesus, Tolstoy argues, requires a rejection of violence in all its forms, especially including the violence of the state, which is, indeed, founded on violence. True Christianity thus leads, for Tolstoy, to anarchy.

Tucker, Benjamin R. *Individual Liberty*. New York: Vanguard 1926.

In a moral, political, and economic treatise that represents anarchism without adjectives, Tucker outlines a vision of anarchism as total liberty for the individual—both from the state, and from predatory private actors that the state empowers.

———. *Instead of a Book, by a Man Too Busy to Write One*. 2d ed. New York: Tucker 1897. http://fair-use.org/benjamin-tucker/instead-of-a-book (Aug. 16, 2020).

A collection of key essays published by Tucker in *Liberty*, this book highlights Tucker's radicalism and the range of his interests.

———, ed. *Liberty: Not the Daughter but the Mother of Order (1881–1908)*. Westport, CT: Greenwood 1970.

The journal Tucker edited contains a wide range of lively debates regarding the shape of human freedom.

Tullock, Gordon. *The Politics of Bureaucracy*. Washington, DC: Public Affairs 1965.

Tullock uses the economic way of thinking to explain the behaviors of political officials and regulatory actors. He applies the concepts of incentives, opportunity cost, and knowledge problems to questions regarding the actions of political officials within relevant institutional structures.

Vallentyne, Peter, and Steiner, Hillel, eds. *Left-Libertarianism and Its Critics: The Contemporary Debate*. New York: Palgrave 2000.

———. *The Origins of Left-Libertarianism: An Anthology of Historical Writings*. New York: Palgrave 2001.

"Left-libertarianism" can refer to anarcho-communism, to the style of individualist anarchism associated with a range of leftist political positions, or to a position that endorses individual self-ownership but common originary ownership of property in land. Vallentyne and Steiner collect a range of important historical and contemporary sources related to the last, broadly Georgist (or "Geoist"), position. Debates between left- and right-libertarians have implications for different conceptions of anarchy.

Van der Vossen, Bas. "Imposing Duties and Original Appropriation." *Journal of Political Philosophy* 23.1 (2015): 64–85.

Distinguishes duty-creation from duty-activation and argues that the unilateral original acquisition of property does not amount to an objectionable imposition of duties on others, since it involves the activation rather than the creation of duties.

Van der Walt, Lucien, and Schmidt, Michael. *Black Flame: The Revolutionary Class Politics of Anarchism and Syndicalism*. Edinburgh: AK 2009.

Van der Walt and Schmidt argue forcefully against the "big tent" model of historical anarchism. Instead, they insist that the ideology has always been rooted in the union-based model of activism that was pioneered by Mikhail Bakunin and that bore fruit in anarcho-syndicalism.

Vrousalis, Nicholas. "Libertarian Socialism: A Better Reconciliation between Equality and Self-Ownership." *Social Theory and Practice* 37.2 (Apr 2011): 211–226.

Social anarchism is characterized by its synthesis of libertarian and socialist commitments. Vrousalis offers an understanding of ways in which these commitments might be reconciled by prescribing common ownership of the means of production coupled with each person's being afforded a protective "shell" of private property. The suggestion is that this shell protects a person's effective self-ownership while the joint ownership of the means of production promotes the socialist values of democracy and community.

Ward, Colin. *Anarchism: A Very Short Introduction*. New York: OUP 2004.

———. *Anarchy in Action*. London: Freedom 1982.

Anarchist history, theory, and practice from the perspective of the doyen of post-World War II English anarchism—good-natured, humane, and always thoroughly practical.

Ward, Colin, and Goodway, David. *Talking Anarchy*. Nottingham: Five Leaves 2004.

An extended conversation between anarchist icon Ward and historian Goodway that focuses on a broad range of anarchist activists, ideas, and prospects.

Weber, Max. *The Theory of Social and Economic Organization*. Ed. Talcott Parsons. Trans. A. M. Henderson and Parsons. Oxford: OUP 1947 [1922].

Offers the standard definition of "state."

Wellman, Christopher Heath, and Simmons, A. John. *Is There a Duty to Obey the Law?* New York: CUP 2005.

A debate between Wellman and Simmons on the question of whether there is a duty to obey the law, or at least certain laws issued by certain states. Wellman defends a Good Samaritan theory of obedience, which holds that we owe obedience as a way of helping our fellow citizens. Simmons argues that Wellman's theory fails, and, in particular, that most theories of authority cannot explain why anyone owes obedience specifically to the government that happens to rule the geographic area in which that person resides as opposed to governments elsewhere.

Welsh, John F. *Max Stirner's Dialectical Egoism: A New Interpretation.* Lanham, MD: Lexington-Rowman 2010.

Welsh carefully distinguishes Stirner from the existentialists and postmodernists to whom he is frequently compared, regarding him as offering a truly one-of-a-kind attack on modernism and humanism. Welsh's book provides interesting comparisons of Stirner's thought to, among others, Hegel, Nietzsche, and Marx, as well as a survey of some of the applications of Stirner's thought by prominent egoists such as Benjamin Tucker and Dora Marsden.

Widerquist, Karl, and McCall, Grant S. *Prehistoric Myths in Modern Political Philosophy.* Edinburgh: Edinburgh UP 2017.

A systematic attack on philosophers' conceptions of the state of nature.

Wilbur, Shawn P. *The Libertarian Labyrinth: Mutualist Anarchism and Its Context.* N.p. n.d. http://libertarian-labyrinth.org (Aug. 16, 2020).

Wilbur offers insightful, literate anarchist social theory and commentary, in addition to a broad range of historical texts—the obscure as well as the relatively well known—by American and European anarchists (the latter sometimes available in translation for the first time).

Wolff, Robert Paul. *Defense of Anarchism.* Berkeley: U of California P 1998.

This book defends the view that if we take personal autonomy seriously, we not only have a right to defy the state, but also a duty to reject its claim to authority. The authority of the state to make and enforce laws is inconsistent with our right to be autonomous and to act according to conscience. Wolff begins with the Kantian premise that people are autonomously self-legislating in the sense that they can and must independently determine how they should act in accordance with moral law. However, he maintains that this fact about persons is incompatible with their being obligated to comply with state-made laws in virtue of the fact that those laws are state-made. He also offers a brief statement of his preferred anarchist approach to managing the economy.

INDEX

Page numbers in *italics* refer to information in figures and those followed by 'n' refer to chapter notes with the note number indicated by the number following the 'n'.